New Advances in Distribution Theory and Its Applications

New Advances in Distribution Theory and Its Applications

Guest Editors

Filippo Domma
Francesca Condino

MDPI

Basel • Beijing • Wuhan • Barcelona • Belgrade • Novi Sad • Cluj • Manchester

Guest Editors

Filippo Domma
Department of Economics
Statistics and Finance
"Giovanni Anania"
University of Calabria
Arcavacata di Rende
Italy

Francesca Condino
Department of Economics
Statistics and Finance
"Giovanni Anania"
University of Calabria
Arcavacata di Rende
Italy

Editorial Office
MDPI AG
Grosspeteranlage 5
4052 Basel, Switzerland

This is a reprint of the Special Issue, published open access by the journal *Mathematics* (ISSN 2227-7390), freely accessible at: https://www.mdpi.com/si/mathematics/Distribution_Theory_with_Application.

For citation purposes, cite each article independently as indicated on the article page online and as indicated below:

Lastname, A.A.; Lastname, B.B. Article Title. *Journal Name* **Year**, *Volume Number*, Page Range.

ISBN 978-3-7258-4983-3 (Hbk)
ISBN 978-3-7258-4984-0 (PDF)
https://doi.org/10.3390/books978-3-7258-4984-0

Contents

About the Editors

Filippo Domma

Filippo Domma is a Full Professor of Statistics at the Department of Economics, Statistics and Finance "Giovanni Anania" of the University of Calabria. He obtained his Ph.D in Methodological Statistics at the University of Trento. He was a Coordinator of the Board of Studies in Statistics at the University of Calabria, Head of the Department of Economics, Statistics and Finance and elected Member of the Academic Senate of the University of Calabria. His current research activity mainly pertains to the correct specification of statistical models for economic and social phenomena, with particular reference to economic, territorial, gender and generational inequality. He is the author of over 70 papers published in international and national journals and conference proceedings and has served as a reviewer for many international scientific journals on statistical methodological and applied mathematics.

Francesca Condino

Francesca Condino is an Associate Professor of Statistics at the Department of Economics, Statistics, and Finance "Giovanni Anania" of the University of Calabria. She obtained a degree in Statistics and Actuarial Sciences and later pursued a master's in Economics and Statistics of the Territory, followed by a PhD in Statistics from the University of Naples "Federico II." Prof. Condino has worked with various research institutions, including the National Research Council (CNR) in Italy, and has contributed to advancing statistical theory through both theoretical and applied work. Her publications span a range of topics, from methodological advancements to their practical applications, and her approach to statistics combines methodological considerations with a focus on applying models to complex, real-world problems. Her research interests lie in areas such as dynamic classification, copula functions for modeling dependencies, income distributions and inequality, and the development of new probability distributions. In addition to her research, she has been involved in teaching, having held positions in various degree programs at different universities. She regularly participates in national and international conferences, where she shares her work with the broader academic community.

mathematics

MDPI

Editorial

New Advances in Distribution Theory and Its Applications

Filippo Domma and Francesca Condino *

Department of Economics, Statistics and Finance, University of Calabria, 87036 Arcavacata, Italy; filippo.domma@unical.it
* Correspondence: francesca.condino@unical.it

In recent years, the prolific development of new statistical distributions via various techniques has often led to increased complexity without necessarily enhancing model flexibility or parameter interpretability, a trend that has sometimes diminished the practical relevance of distribution theory. This Special Issue therefore features contributions on meaningful advancements in statistical distribution theory, with a focus on models that are both flexible and interpretable. By emphasizing these priorities, the Special Issue aims to connect theoretical developments with practical applications, so that new models are not only mathematically robust but also accessible and useful for applied work across diverse fields. This collection presents different contributions reflecting the evolving land-scape of distribution theory. Balancing theoretical development with real-world rele-vance, the articles propose models designed to address the challenges of contemporary data analysis, where applicability emerges as a fundamental aspect.

The Study by Contribution 1 introduces a novel discrete analog of the Hjorth distribution. By transforming this continuous distribution into the discrete domain, the authors maintain important theoretical properties such as flexibility and tractability, while increasing its applicability to count data commonly encountered in practice, also in the pres-ence of censored data. The paper thoroughly derives key statistical properties and com-pares the new distribution with existing discrete models. Moreover, the authors demon-strate the model's practical utility through applications to real datasets, highlighting its ability to provide a better fit and deeper insight into discrete phenomena.

Contribution 2 proposes two bivariate extensions of the weighted discretized Fréchet–Weibull distribution. The two proposed models are generated by using minimum and maximum operators to capture complex dependence structures between two discrete random variables. The paper rigorously derives the mathematical foundations of the proposed models, exploring their distributional and dependence properties. A comprehen-sive statistical analysis based on real datasets underscores the practical relevance and flex-ibility of these models in representing bivariate discrete data.

Contribution 3 introduces a new quantile regression model based on the unit ratio-Weibull (URW) distribution, aimed at identifying the factors influencing the COVID-19 mortality rate in Latin America. By examining socio-economic, health system, and demographic variables, the authors identify key factors driving the mortality rate differences. Their findings provide crucial insights for policymakers aiming to improve public health preparedness and responses during pandemics, making a significant contribution to the intersection of statistical modeling and public health analysis.

Contribution 4 develops a novel class of models designed to address the common problem of count data exhibiting an excess of zeros and ones. The proposed models inte-grate a continuous–discrete mixture distribution with covariates, allowing them to accurately represent the complex dynamics of data. The authors formalize the properties, derive estimation procedures, and validate the models through applications to empirical datasets.

Contribution 5 develops surveys a wide range of wrapped distributions for modeling circular data, such as angles or time-of-day measurements. Covering 45 continuous and 10 discrete wrapped distributions, the paper systematically presents their probability functions, cumulative distributions, trigonometric moments, and key descriptive statistics including mean direction and resultant length. The review also proposes some applications obtained by using an R package (version 4.4.1) that facilitates fitting these models, thus serving as a foundational resource for researchers and practitioners working with circular data.

Various stochastic representations for the zero–one-inflated Poisson Lindley distribution have been studied by Contribution 6. The authors describe four different stochastic representations, provide explicit formulas for moments and conditional distributions, and propose some hypothesis tests to investigate the presence of one-inflation in addition to a fixed-rate parameter.

A simulation study is used to investigate the hypotheses and its corresponding likelihood ratio tests, suggesting that all tests are powerful and able to properly handle type I error rates, under a reasonable sample size.

A flexible two-parameter distribution to model data bounded within the unit interval is proposed by Contribution 7. Derived from the exponential distribution, the unit expo-nential distribution can capture both positive and negative skewness. The paper discusses the mathematical properties, including moments and hazard functions, and develops maximum likelihood estimation methods. Applications to environmental and engineer-ing datasets highlight the model's superior fitting capabilities compared to existing alter-natives.

Contribution 8 introduces the NODAL G-classes, new flexible families of distribu-tions useful for modeling a wide variety of hazard shapes—including increasing, decreas-ing, bathtub, and J-shaped hazards—in both continuous and discrete contexts. The au-thors provide the theoretical foundation, propose maximum likelihood estimation tech-niques, and validate their models on diverse real datasets, showing improved fit if com-pared with well-established competitive models.

Contribution 9 develops a general framework for unit distributions and introduce the Unit-Dagum models, a class of distributions for data defined on the unit interval. Two new distributions within this class are obtained by applying different transformations to Dagum random variable. Moreover, by considering the possibility of reparametrizing the distributions to express them in terms of indicators of interest, a regression approach for response variables defined on the unit interval is explored. The resulting models appear to be highly competitive when compared with the most commonly used regression mod-els for this type of data, such as Beta regression.

Contribution 10 proposes a novel bivariate Poisson model derived from the bivariate Bernoulli distribution that facilitates both positive and negative correlations, an advancement over some traditional bivariate Poisson models which typically only capture positive dependence. The authors explore the statistical properties of this model, develop maximum likelihood and moment-based estimation methods, and explore its applicabil-ity on healthcare utilization data. Their results highlight the model's improved flexibility and accuracy in capturing dependence structures in correlated count data.

Finally, Contribution 11 introduces the ExpKum-G class, a finite mixture of exponentiated Kumaraswamy-G distributions. Focusing on the exponentiated Kumaraswamy–Weibull sub-model, the authors derive several statistical properties and propose both maximum likelihood and Bayesian estimation methods under progressive Type II censoring.

Simulation studies demonstrate the effectiveness of these estimation strategies, showing good performance in terms of bias and mean squared error. The application to bladder cancer survival data confirms the usefulness of the proposed model under differ-ent censoring schemes.

We would like to express our sincere gratitude to all the authors who have contributed original works in line with the objectives of this Special Issue. Advancing methodological developments in the field of distribution theory, while pursuing goals such as model flexibility and parameter interpretability, is by no means a simple task. For this reason, we deeply appreciate the studies and proposals presented in this Special Issue.

We would also like to extend our thanks to those authors whose manuscripts, though not accepted through the review process, demonstrated genuine interest in the topics addressed and showed commendable commitment and active participation.

Conflicts of Interest: The authors declare no conflicts of interest.

List of Contributions:

1. Haj Ahmad, H.; Elshahhat, A.A. New Hjorth Distribution in Its Discrete Version. *Mathematics* **2025**, *13*, 875. https://doi.org/10.3390/math13050875.
2. Obeidat, S.T.; Das, D.; Eliwa, M.S.; Das, B.; Hazarika, P.J.; Mohammed, W.W. Two-Dimensional Probability Models for the Weighted Discretized Fréchet–Weibull Random Variable with Min–Max Operators: Mathematical Theory and Statistical Goodness-of-Fit Analysis. *Mathematics* **2025**, *13*, 625. https://doi.org/10.3390/math13040625.
3. de Araújo, F.J.M.; Guerra, R.R.; Peña-Ramírez, F.A. The COVID-19 Mortality Rate in Latin America: A Cross-Country Analysis. *Mathematics* **2024**, *12*, 3934. https://doi.org/10.3390/math12243934.
4. Martínez-Flórez, G.; Tovar-Falón, R.; Gómez, H.W. Mathematical Formalization and Applications to Data with Excess of Zeros and Ones of the Unit-Proportional Hazard Inflated Models. *Mathematics* **2024**, *12*, 3566. https://doi.org/10.3390/math12223566.
5. Bell, W.; Nadarajah, S.A. Review of Wrapped Distributions for Circular Data. *Mathematics* **2024**, *12*, 2440. https://doi.org/10.3390/math12162440.
6. Tajuddin, R.R.M.; Ismail, N. On Stochastic Representations of the Zero–One-Inflated Poisson Lindley Distribution. *Mathematics* **2024**, *12*, 778. https://doi.org/10.3390/math12050778.
7. Bakouch, H.S.; Hussain, T.; Tošić, M.; Stojanović, V.S.; Qarmalah, N. Unit Exponential Probability Distribution: Characterization and Applications in Environmental and Engineering Data Modeling. *Mathematics* **2023**, *11*, 4207. https://doi.org/10.3390/math11194207.
8. Eliwa, M.S.; Tahir, M.H.; Hussain, M.A.; Almohaimeed, B.; Al-Bossly, A.; El-Morshedy, M. Univariate Probability-G Classes for Scattered Samples under Different Forms of Hazard: Continuous and Discrete Version with Their Inferences Tests. *Mathematics* **2023**, *11*, 2929. https://doi.org/10.3390/math11132929.
9. Condino, F.; Domma, F. Unit Distributions: A General Framework, Some Special Cases, and the Regression Unit-Dagum Models. *Mathematics* **2023**, *11*, 2888. https://doi.org/10.3390/math11132888.
10. Qarmalah, N.; Alzaid, A.A. Zero-Dependent Bivariate Poisson Distribution with Applications. *Mathematics* **2023**, *11*, 1194. https://doi.org/10.3390/math11051194.
11. Alotaibi, R.; Baharith, L.A.; Almetwally, E.M.; Khalifa, M.; Ghosh, I.; Rezk, H. Statistical Inference on a Finite Mixture of Exponentiated Kumaraswamy-G Distributions with Progressive Type II Censoring Using Bladder Cancer Data. *Mathematics* **2022**, *10*, 2800. https://doi.org/10.3390/math10152800.

mathematics

MDPI

Article

A New Hjorth Distribution in Its Discrete Version

Hanan Haj Ahmad [1,2,*] **and Ahmed Elshahhat** [3]

1 Department of Basic Science, The General Administration of Preparatory Year, King Faisal University, Hofuf 31982, Al-Ahsa, Saudi Arabia
2 Department of Mathematics and Statistics, College of Science, King Faisal University, Hofuf 31982, Al-Ahsa, Saudi Arabia
3 Faculty of Technology and Development, Zagazig University, Zagazig 44519, Egypt; aelshahhat@ftd.zu.edu.eg
* Correspondence: hhajahmed@kfu.edu.sa

Abstract: The Hjorth distribution is more flexible in modeling various hazard rate shapes, including increasing, decreasing, and bathtub shapes. This makes it highly useful in reliability analysis and survival studies, where different failure rate behaviors must be captured effectively. In some practical experiments, the observed data may appear to be continuous, but their intrinsic discreteness requires the development of specialized techniques for constructing discrete counterparts to continuous distributions. This study extends this methodology by discretizing the Hjorth distribution using the survival function approach. The proposed discrete Hjorth distribution preserves the essential statistical characteristics of its continuous counterpart, such as percentiles and quantiles, making it a valuable tool for modeling lifetime data. The complexity of the transformation requires numerical techniques to ensure accurate estimations and analysis. A key feature of this study is the incorporation of Type-II censored samples. We also derive key statistical properties, including the quantile function and order statistics, and then employ maximum likelihood and Bayesian inference methods. A comparative analysis of these estimation techniques is conducted through simulation studies. Furthermore, the proposed model is validated using two real-world datasets, including electronic device failure times and ball-bearing failure analysis, by applying goodness-of-fit tests against alternative discrete models. The findings emphasize the versatility and applicability of the discrete Hjorth distribution in reliability studies, engineering, and survival analysis, offering a robust framework for modeling discrete data in practical scenarios. To our knowledge, no prior research has explored the use of censored data in analyzing discrete Hjorth-distributed data. This study fills this gap, providing new insights into discrete reliability modeling and broadening the application of the Hjorth distribution in real-world scenarios.

Keywords: discrete Hjorth; likelihood and Bayesian; survival analysis; censoring; order statistics; simulation; real-world applications

MSC: 62F10; 62F15; 62N01; 62N02; 62N05

1. Introduction

In many lifetime experiments, data often seem continuous; however, they are actually discrete observations. This discrepancy drives the development of techniques that transform continuous distributions into discrete versions, offering a suitable match to the observed data. Discrete distributions in statistical modeling are widely encouraged for various compelling reasons. They address limitations in data collection methods, measurement intervals, or the inherent characteristics of observed phenomena, such as electronic device failures or maintenance cycles. Discrete distributions represent data with countable or finite values, such as the number of items tested, people in a queue, coin toss outcomes, or defective products in manufacturing. These distributions are intuitive and easy to interpret, corresponding to datasets with a defined range of possible values.

Moreover, many discrete distributions provide explicit expressions for their probability generating function and/or probability mass function (PMF), simplifying analytical operations and permitting effective moment and probability calculations without requiring integration. They are highly adaptable, making them suitable for modeling diverse real-world phenomena, including ecosystem species distribution, genetic diversity, and network traffic patterns. Their computational efficiency and versatility make them invaluable tools in statistical modeling.

Recently, a variety of discrete models have been developed, with applications in certain fields such as medicine, engineering, reliability studies, and survival analysis. For a deeper understanding and practical applications of discrete distributions, one can explore references Roy and Gupta [1] and Roy and Ghosh [2], among others. However, while these studies have advanced discrete reliability theory and other application areas, they primarily focus on continuous formulations or general discretization techniques that do not specifically address the nuances of the Hjorth distribution.

As a result, many scholars have significantly advanced discrete reliability theory, offering innovative approaches and perspectives. Transforming continuous models into their discrete counterparts involves various discretization techniques, which are extensively discussed and documented in academic research. These methods are designed to create discrete distributions that closely reflect their continuous origins. A range of approaches to discretization have been explored in the literature; one may refer to Bracquemond and Gaudoin [3], Lai [4], and Chakraborty [5].

A prominent approach in the development of discrete distributions involves the application of the survival function as a discretization technique. Notable contributions in this area include the derivation of discrete analogs for normal and Rayleigh distributions, presented by Roy [6,7], respectively, both employing the survival function methodology. Extending this framework, the discrete formulation of the Burr-II distribution was systematically examined by Al-Huniti and AL Dayian [8]. Additionally, Bebbington et al. [9] provided a comprehensive study on the discrete additive counterpart of the Weibull distribution. Further advancements and examples of discrete transformations across various distributions are detailed by Haj Ahmad and Almetwally [10] and Chesneau et al. [11], among others.

This study employs the survival discretization method to transform the continuous Hjorth distribution into its discrete counterpart. Although the Hjorth distribution is highly flexible in modeling various hazard rate shapes in a continuous framework, practical scenarios often involve data recorded in discrete intervals or subject to censoring. Discretizing the Hjorth distribution using the survival function approach not only preserves key statistical features—like percentiles and quantiles—but also facilitates the analysis of data that are subject to constraints such as Type-II censoring. This discrete formulation directly addresses the practical challenges in reliability and survival analysis, where capturing the precise timing of failure events in a discrete manner is crucial for accurate modeling and inference. Unlike other discretization techniques, this method retains the intrinsic properties of the continuous model while providing a framework that is more robust to data irregularities.

Admittedly, the DH model's computational intensity and reliance on numerical techniques are limitations that we address through rigorous simulation studies and methodological refinements. While the DH model has demonstrated superior performance in our comparative analysis, it may exhibit sensitivity to certain types of data distributions, particularly when the failure rate does not follow the bathtub or monotonic hazard rate structures that the model is designed to accommodate.

Consider a scenario where n items undergo a life-testing experiment, and only the first r failure times, denoted by $x_1 < x_2 < \cdots < x_r$, are observed. The set $\mathbf{x} = (x_1, x_2, \ldots, x_r)$ is called a Type-II censored sample. The remaining $n - r$ items are censored and known only to have more than x_r failure times.

Various statistical characteristics, including the quantile function and order statistics, are derived, and statistical inference methods are explored. These methods utilize the maximum likelihood estimation approach and the Bayes framework. To assess the estimators, the two estimation techniques for the newly developed discrete distribution are compared. Simulation studies are conducted using numerical methodologies. To the best of our knowledge, the existing literature does not address the use of censored data to analyze discrete data following the Hjorth distribution. Therefore, this study aims to bridge this gap in distribution theory. Two real-world datasets are analyzed using goodness-of-fit tests to evaluate the effectiveness of the proposed model compared to other discrete alternatives. The first example discusses the failure times of some electronic devices, and the second considers ball-bearing failure analysis.

The rest of this paper is organized as follows: Section 2 introduces the discrete Hjorth distribution, while Section 3 presents some statistical functions. Sections 4 and 5 calculate statistical inference, including maximum likelihood and Bayesian estimation, respectively. Monte Carlo results are presented and commented on in Section 6. Section 7 studies real-world data illustration examples. Section 8 explores the findings and concluding remarks.

2. Discrete Hjorth Distribution

The Hjorth distribution (by Hjorth [12]) is a continuous distribution that extends the Rayleigh, exponential, and linear failure rate distributions. Later, this distribution received some attention in reliability analysis and lifetime experiments. Hence, its statistical properties, inferential statistics, and reliability analysis have been studied by Guess et al. [13]. Yadav et al. [14] used progressive censoring and estimated the parameters of the Hjorth model in addition to the hazard rate and the reliability functions. Pushkarna et al. [15] studied some recurrence relations for the Hjorth moment model under progressive censoring. Pandey et al. [16] used Bayesian inference to estimate Hjorth parameters under a generalized Type-I progressive censoring sample. Korkmaz et al. [17] presented a new regression model using the Hjorth model. It is noted for its effectiveness in modeling datasets with smaller values rather than larger ones. Elshahhat and Nassar [18] examined survival analysis of the Hjorth model by adaptive Type-II progressive hybrid censoring.

We are motivated to use the Hjorth model because it has increasing, decreasing, constant, upside-down, unimodal, and bathtub hazard rates. It can also be considered a suitable model for fitting the bimodal, unimodal, U-shaped, and other-shaped data. Hence, it was observed in the literature that the Hjorth model outperforms several well-known lifetime distributions. Its continuous form, however, limits its use for datasets that are inherently discrete. By converting the Hjorth model into a discrete form, a new distribution is derived that accommodates count data while preserving Hjorth's ability to model tail behavior.

The probability density function of the continuous Hjorth model is expressed as

$$f(x;\boldsymbol{\theta}) = [\alpha x(1+\beta x) + \gamma](1+\beta x)^{-\left(\frac{\gamma}{\beta}+1\right)} e^{-\alpha \frac{x^2}{2}}, \; x \geq 0, \tag{1}$$

where $\boldsymbol{\theta} = (\alpha, \beta, \gamma)^\top$.

The survival function is written as

$$S(x;\boldsymbol{\theta}) = (1+\beta x)^{-\left(\frac{\gamma}{\beta}\right)} e^{-\alpha\frac{x^2}{2}}, \tag{2}$$

in which β and γ are positive shape parameters, and $\alpha > 0$ is a scale parameter.

Here, α controls the rate of decay in the exponential component. Hence, higher values of α result in a faster decay of the density. The parameter β influences the shape of the distribution through the polynomial term $(1+\beta x)$. It affects the tail behavior and the curvature of the density function. A larger β tends to increase the weight in the tail, which affects how quickly the probability mass of the distribution decreases as x increases. γ adjusts the baseline level of the polynomial component. It plays a crucial role in determining the heaviness of the tail and the overall curvature near the origin, thereby influencing the skewness and the rate at which the distribution transitions from its peak to the tail. The hazard rate function for the Hjorth model is

$$h(x;\alpha,\beta,\gamma) = [\alpha x(1+\beta x)+\gamma]. \tag{3}$$

This study aims to develop a novel discrete form of the Hjorth model and perform the statistical analysis under Type-II censored data for time and cost constraints. This counterpart, termed the discrete Hjorth (DH) model, is constructed using the survival discretization approach. In this section, the PMF, cumulative distribution function (CDF), and associated properties of DH model are outlined.

Roy [6,7] used the survival function to define the PMF for the new discrete distribution, which is presented in the following form:

$$P(X{=}k){=}S(k){-}S(k{+}1),\ k{=}\ 0,1,2,\ldots \tag{4}$$

where $S(x)$ is provided in Equation (2); hence, the DH PMF is provided by

$$P(X{=}k) = \Delta(\beta,\gamma,k)e^{-\alpha k_0} - \Delta(\beta,\gamma,k+1)e^{-\alpha k_1}, \tag{5}$$

where $k_0 = \frac{k^2}{2}$, $k_1 = \frac{(k+1)^2}{2}$, and $\Delta(\beta,\gamma,i) = (1+\beta i)^{-\left(\frac{\gamma}{\beta}\right)}$.

The DH using the survival discretization method has the next CDF:

$$P(X{<}k){=}1-\Delta(\beta,\gamma,k+1)e^{-\alpha k_1}. \tag{6}$$

The hazard rate function for the DH model is written as

$$h_{DH}(k) = \frac{\Delta(\beta,\gamma,k)}{\Delta(\beta,\gamma,k+1)} e^{\frac{\alpha(2k+1)}{2}} - 1. \tag{7}$$

Figure 1 illustrates various shapes of the PMF and HRF for the DH distribution, generated using different parameter selections. The PMF of the DH model is shown to exhibit right-skewed or symmetric patterns, while the HRF displays diverse forms, including decreasing, increasing, and bathtub-shaped patterns. Additionally, the shapes presented in the figure highlight that the DH model can naturally represent forward or backward recurrence time patterns within renewal processes.

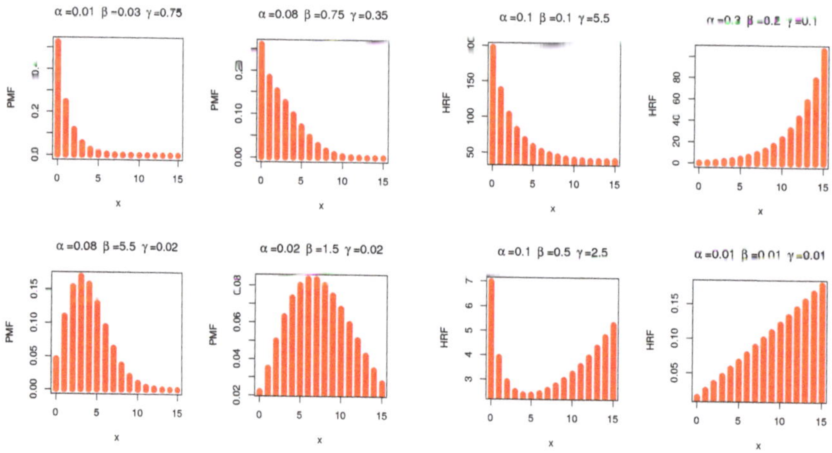

(**a**) PMF (**b**) HRF

Figure 1. The PMF and HRF shapes of the DH distribution.

In the next section, some statistical properties, functions, and characteristics of the DH model are derived, including quantiles, moments, and ordered statistics.

3. Statistical Functions

This section discusses statistical functions for the DH distribution, including the quantile function, moments, skewness, kurtosis, and order statistics.

3.1. Quantile Function and Moments

The quantile function (say, $Q(p)$) for a discrete distribution is the inverse of its CDF. It is used basically to generate random samples for simulation purposes. To determine the quantile function, we solve for k in terms of p:

$$p = 1 - \Delta(\beta, \gamma, k+1)e^{-\alpha \frac{(k+1)^2}{2}}. \tag{8}$$

Rearranging Equation (8), we obtain

$$\Delta(\beta, \gamma, k+1)e^{-\alpha \frac{(k+1)^2}{2}} = 1 - p. \tag{9}$$

Substituting $\Delta(\beta, \gamma, k+1)$ into (9), we have

$$(1 + \beta(k+1))^{-\left(\frac{\gamma}{\beta}\right)} e^{-\alpha \frac{(k+1)^2}{2}} = 1 - p, \tag{10}$$

and its natural logarithm becomes

$$-\frac{\gamma}{\beta} \ln(1 + \beta(k+1)) - \alpha \frac{(k+1)^2}{2} = \ln(1-p). \tag{11}$$

This equation must be solved numerically for k as an analytical closed-form expression is generally not feasible due to the combination of logarithmic and exponential terms. The complexity of the DH's CDF makes direct algebraic inversion infeasible for deriving the quantile function, particularly due to the presence of exponential and power terms. Extracting k from the expression for $\Delta(\boldsymbol{\theta}, k)$ poses significant analytical difficulties and is unlikely to yield an exact solution because of the intricate structure and exponential decay term. As an alternative to an exact analytical form, approximations or numerical techniques can be employed for practical applications. Moments are a crucial statistical tool, offering detailed insights into the shape and properties of a probability distribution. They are widely applied in fields such as quality control, risk assessment, and environmental analysis.

To compute the moments for the DH model, consider a non-negative random variable $l \sim DH(\boldsymbol{\theta})$. The sth moment, say μ_s', can be expressed as follows:

$$\mu_s' = \sum_{l=0}^{\infty} l^s \left[\Delta(\beta,\gamma,l) e^{-\alpha \frac{l^2}{2}} - \Delta(\beta,\gamma,l+1) e^{-\alpha \frac{(l+1)^2}{2}} \right]. \tag{12}$$

An exact expression for the sth moment is not obtainable; thus, numerical methods are necessary to evaluate the moment. Specifically, take $\alpha = (0.25, 0.75, 1.5)$ and several choices from β and γ.

Table 1 illustrates the behavior with respect to the mean ($\mathcal{M}$), variance ($\mathcal{V}$), index of dispersion ($\mathcal{ID}$), coefficient of variation ($\mathcal{CV}$), skewness ($\mathcal{S}$), and kurtosis ($\mathcal{K}$) for the DH model. As a result, we summarize the following points:

- As α grows (for fixed β and γ), the values of $\mathcal{M}$, $\mathcal{V}$, $\mathcal{ID}$, and $\mathcal{K}$ decrease while those for $\mathcal{CV}$ and $\mathcal{S}$ increase.
- As β grows (for fixed α and γ), the values of $\mathcal{M}$ and $\mathcal{V}$ increase while those for $\mathcal{ID}$, $\mathcal{CV}$, $\mathcal{S}$, and $\mathcal{K}$ decrease.
- As γ grows (for fixed α and β), the values of $\mathcal{M}$ and $\mathcal{V}$ decrease while those for $\mathcal{ID}$, $\mathcal{CV}$, $\mathcal{S}$, and $\mathcal{K}$ increase.
- The DH model is well suited for modeling both under- and over-dispersed data as its variance can be smaller than the mean for certain parameter values, while the variance is greater than the mean in other choices regarding parameter values.
- The DH model exhibits flexible dispersion characteristics depending on parameter choices.
- For reliability modeling, higher dispersion ($\mathcal{ID} > 1$) suggests suitability for lifetime data with higher variability.
- The positive skewness values indicate that this distribution is right-skewed. Additionally, a skewness value approaching zero suggests the possibility of a symmetric curve for the PMF.
- Elevated kurtosis signifies greater tail risk and the likelihood of outliers relative to a normal distribution. Changes in the distribution can be observed by adjusting α, β, and γ.

Table 1. Measurements of DH model using several choices regarding its parameter values.

α	β	γ	$\mathcal{M}$	$\mathcal{V}$	$\mathcal{ID}$	$\mathcal{CV}$	$\mathcal{S}$	$\mathcal{K}$
0.25	0.5	0.1	1.765	1.819	1.031	0.764	0.667	3.199
		0.5	1.082	1.442	1.333	1.110	1.075	4.093
		1.0	0.615	0.875	1.522	1.521	1.601	6.421
		1.5	0.364	0.507	1.652	1.954	2.153	9.699
		2.5	0.139	0.175	1.729	3.008	3.445	19.13
	2.5	0.1	1.877	1.858	0.990	0.726	0.616	3.147
		0.5	1.440	1.853	1.259	0.945	0.850	3.311
		1.0	1.041	1.584	1.287	1.209	1.226	4.164
		1.5	0.757	1.250	1.391	1.477	1.579	5.585
		2.5	0.408	0.705	1.422	2.059	2.337	10.21

Table 1. *Cont.*

α	β	γ	$\mathcal{M}$	$\mathcal{V}$	$\mathcal{ID}$	$\mathcal{CV}$	$\mathcal{S}$	$\mathcal{K}$
0.75	0.5	0.1	0.859	0.636	0.741	0.929	0.671	3.074
		0.5	0.584	0.526	0.900	1.241	1.148	3.699
		1.0	0.367	0.367	1.001	1.652	1.768	5.261
		1.5	0.234	0.244	1.062	2.114	2.363	7.871
		2.5	0.098	0.104	1.149	3.291	3.590	17.51
	2.5	0.1	0.895	0.649	0.725	0.900	0.636	3.043
		0.5	0.715	0.615	0.860	1.097	0.887	3.297
		1.0	0.541	0.530	0.981	1.346	1.236	4.073
		1.5	0.410	0.436	1.045	1.609	1.645	5.276
		2.5	0.238	0.273	1.060	2.198	2.518	8.919
1.5	0.5	0.1	0.480	0.340	0.709	1.215	0.793	2.806
		0.5	0.340	0.276	0.812	1.544	1.218	3.582
		1.0	0.223	0.199	0.893	2.003	1.772	5.260
		1.5	0.146	0.138	0.941	2.536	2.379	7.626
		2.5	0.064	0.063	0.986	3.932	3.872	15.69
	2.5	0.1	0.497	0.347	0.699	1.186	0.757	2.769
		0.5	0.403	0.313	0.777	1.388	1.034	3.212
		1.0	0.311	0.265	0.852	1.655	1.384	4.026
		1.5	0.240	0.218	0.907	1.944	1.745	5.145
		2.5	0.143	0.140	0.976	2.609	2.530	8.638

3.2. Ordered Statistics

Consider $W_1, W_2, \ldots, W_n$ as a random sample following the DH model, and assume that $W_{1:n}, W_{2:n}, \ldots, W_{n:n}$ represent the related order statistics; hence, the ith order statistics have a CDF at w, which is

$$F_{i:n}(w;\boldsymbol{\theta}) = \sum_{i=1}^{n} \binom{n}{m} [F_i(w;\boldsymbol{\theta})]^m [1 - F_i(w;\boldsymbol{\theta})]^{n-m}. \tag{13}$$

The negative Binomial theorem can be used as a series representation for the CDF, which can be written as

$$F_{i:n}(w;\boldsymbol{\theta}) = \sum_{i=1}^{n} \sum_{j=1}^{n-m} \binom{n}{m} \binom{n-m}{j} (-1)^{j} [F_i(w;\boldsymbol{\theta})]^{m+j}. \tag{14}$$

Therefore,

$$F_{i:n}(w;\boldsymbol{\theta}) = \sum_{i=1}^{n} \sum_{j=1}^{n-m} \binom{n}{m} \binom{n-m}{j} (-1)^{j} \left[1 - \Delta(\beta,\gamma,w+1) e^{-\alpha\frac{(w+1)^2}{2}}\right]. \tag{15}$$

The ith order statistic under the DH model has PMF that can be expressed as follows

$$f_{i:n}(w;\boldsymbol{\theta}) = \sum_{i=1}^{n} \sum_{j=1}^{n-m} \binom{n}{m} \binom{n-m}{j} (-1)^{j} [\Delta(\beta,\gamma,w) e^{-\alpha\frac{w^2}{2}} - \Delta(\beta,\gamma,w+1) e^{-\alpha\frac{(w+1)^2}{2}}]^{m+j}.$$

Hence, the rth moments of $w_{i:n}$ can be written as follows:

$$E(w_{i:n}^r) = \sum_{w=0}^{\infty} \sum_{i=1}^{n} \sum_{j=1}^{n-m} \binom{n}{m} \binom{n-m}{j} (-1)^{j} w^r \left[\Delta(\beta,\gamma,w) e^{-\alpha\frac{w^2}{2}} - \Delta(\beta,\gamma,w+1) e^{-\alpha\frac{(w+1)^2}{2}}\right]^{m+j}.$$

4. Maximum Likelihood Estimation

In this section, we estimate the undetermined parameters α, β, and γ for the DH model by applying the maximum likelihood estimation (MLE) approach. The MLE estimates are obtained based on the Type-II censoring scheme, and, by using the missing information principle, the variance–covariance matrix (VCM) of α, β, and γ is obtained. This matrix is then utilized to construct asymptotic confidence intervals for α, β, and γ. Let $x_1, \ldots, x_r$ represent a Type-II censored sampling from DH model.

Referring to the PMF in Equation (5) and the CDF in Equation (7), the likelihood and the log-likelihood functions are explored, respectively, as

$$L(\boldsymbol{\theta} \mid \mathbf{x}) = \left[\prod_{i=1}^{r}\left(\Delta(\beta,\gamma,x_i)e^{-\alpha\frac{x_i^2}{2}} - \Delta(\beta,\gamma,x_i+1)e^{-\alpha\frac{(x_i+1)^2}{2}}\right)\right] \times \left[\Delta(\beta,\gamma,x_r)e^{-\alpha\frac{x_r^2}{2}}\right]^{n-r},$$

and

$$\ell(\boldsymbol{\theta} \mid \mathbf{x}) = \sum_{i=1}^{r}\log\left(\Delta(\beta,\gamma,x_i)e^{-\alpha\frac{x_i^2}{2}} - \Delta(\beta,\gamma,x_i+1)e^{-\alpha\frac{(x_i+1)^2}{2}}\right) + (n-r)\log\left(\Delta(\beta,\gamma,x_r)e^{-\alpha\frac{x_r^2}{2}}\right). \tag{16}$$

The parameters' MLEs are obtained by deriving the likelihood function (16) partially for each parameter such as

$$\frac{\partial \ell}{\partial \alpha} = \sum_{i=1}^{r}\frac{A_{i,\alpha}}{A_i(\alpha,\beta,\gamma)} - \frac{(n-r)x_r^2}{2}, \tag{17}$$

$$\frac{\partial \ell}{\partial \beta} = \sum_{i=1}^{r}\frac{A_{i,\beta}}{A_i(\alpha,\beta,\gamma)} + (n-r)\,\psi(\beta,x_r), \tag{18}$$

and

$$\frac{\partial \ell}{\partial \gamma} = \sum_{i=1}^{r}\frac{A_{i,\gamma}}{A_i(\alpha,\beta,\gamma)} - \frac{(n-r)}{\beta}\ln(1+\beta x_r), \tag{19}$$

where

$A_i(\alpha,\beta,\gamma) = \Delta(\beta,\gamma,x_i)e^{-\frac{\alpha x_i^2}{2}} - \Delta(\beta,\gamma,x_i+1)e^{-\frac{\alpha(x_i+1)^2}{2}}$,

$A_{i,\alpha} \equiv \frac{\partial A_i}{\partial \alpha} = -\frac{x_i^2}{2}\Delta(\beta,\gamma,x_i)e^{-\frac{\alpha x_i^2}{2}} + \frac{(x_i+1)^2}{2}\Delta(\beta,\gamma,x_i+1)e^{-\frac{\alpha(x_i+1)^2}{2}}$,

$A_{i,\beta} \equiv \frac{\partial A_i}{\partial \beta} = e^{-\frac{\alpha x_i^2}{2}}\Delta(\beta,\gamma,x_i)\,\psi(\beta,x_i) - e^{-\frac{\alpha(x_i+1)^2}{2}}\Delta(\beta,\gamma,x_i+1)\,\psi(\beta,x_i+1)$,

$A_{i,\gamma} \equiv \frac{\partial A_i}{\partial \gamma} = -\frac{1}{\beta}\ln(1+\beta x_i)\,\Delta(\beta,\gamma,x_i)e^{-\frac{\alpha x_i^2}{2}} + \frac{1}{\beta}\ln(1+\beta(x_i+1))\,\Delta(\beta,\gamma,x_i+1)e^{-\frac{\alpha(x_i+1)^2}{2}}$,

and

$\psi(\beta,x) = \frac{\gamma}{\beta^2}\ln(1+\beta x) - \frac{\gamma x}{\beta(1+\beta x)}$.

The obtained system of nonlinear Equations (17)–(19) is solved by using numerical techniques to determine the parameter estimates. These calculations can be complex and computationally intensive, especially when dealing with sums and exponentials. For actual applications, numerical methods or software packages capable of symbolic differentiation may be beneficial for accurately computing these derivatives, especially when optimizing parameters in practical scenarios. Various numerical techniques have been explored in the literature; in this study, the Newton–Raphson method is employed. This method was selected primarily due to its quadratic convergence rate that enables rapid refinement of estimates when the initial guess is reasonably close to the true solution. The results of the analysis are discussed in Section 6.

To construct the VCM of the DH model parameters $\boldsymbol{\theta}$, we need to use the Fisher Information Matrix (FIM), which is derived from the second-order partial derivatives of the log-likelihood function $\ell(\boldsymbol{\theta})$. The FIM (say, $\mathcal{I}(\cdot)$) is a 3×3 symmetric matrix where each entry corresponds to a second-order partial derivative. The inverse of the FIM provides the VCM (denoted by $\Sigma(\cdot) \cong \mathcal{I}^{-1}(\cdot)$), which is then used to build asymptotic confidence intervals for the parameters.

The FIM and VCM (at $\boldsymbol{\theta} = \hat{\boldsymbol{\theta}}$) are expressed, respectively, as

$$\mathcal{I}(\boldsymbol{\theta}) = \begin{pmatrix} \mathcal{I}_{\alpha\alpha} & \mathcal{I}_{\alpha\beta} & \mathcal{I}_{\alpha\gamma} \\ \mathcal{I}_{\beta\alpha} & \mathcal{I}_{\beta\beta} & \mathcal{I}_{\beta\gamma} \\ \mathcal{I}_{\gamma\alpha} & \mathcal{I}_{\gamma\beta} & \mathcal{I}_{\gamma\gamma} \end{pmatrix}$$

and

$$\Sigma(\boldsymbol{\theta}) = \begin{pmatrix} \mathrm{Var}(\alpha) & \mathrm{Cov}(\alpha,\beta) & \mathrm{Cov}(\alpha,\gamma) \\ \mathrm{Cov}(\beta,\alpha) & \mathrm{Var}(\beta) & \mathrm{Cov}(\beta,\gamma) \\ \mathrm{Cov}(\gamma,\alpha) & \mathrm{Cov}(\gamma,\beta) & \mathrm{Var}(\gamma) \end{pmatrix}.$$

The second-order partial derivatives of the log-likelihood function ℓ are developed as follows:

$$\frac{\partial^2 \ell}{\partial \alpha^2} = \sum_{i=1}^{r} \left[\frac{A_{i,\alpha\alpha}}{A_i} - \left(\frac{A_{i,\alpha}}{A_i} \right)^2 \right], \tag{20}$$

$$\frac{\partial^2 \ell}{\partial \beta^2} = \sum_{i=1}^{r} \left[\frac{A_{i,\beta\beta}}{A_i} - \left(\frac{A_{i,\beta}}{A_i} \right)^2 \right] + (n-r)\, \psi'(\beta, x_r), \tag{21}$$

$$\frac{\partial^2 \ell}{\partial \gamma^2} = \sum_{i=1}^{r} \left[\frac{A_{i,\gamma\gamma}}{A_i} - \left(\frac{A_{i,\gamma}}{A_i} \right)^2 \right], \tag{22}$$

$$\frac{\partial^2 \ell}{\partial \alpha \partial \beta} = \sum_{i=1}^{r} \left[\frac{A_{i,\alpha\beta}}{A_i} - \frac{A_{i,\alpha}\, A_{i,\beta}}{A_i^2} \right], \tag{23}$$

$$\frac{\partial^2 \ell}{\partial \alpha \partial \gamma} = \sum_{i=1}^{r} \left[\frac{A_{i,\alpha\gamma}}{A_i} - \frac{A_{i,\alpha}\, A_{i,\gamma}}{A_i^2} \right], \tag{24}$$

and

$$\frac{\partial^2 \ell}{\partial \beta \partial \gamma} = \sum_{i=1}^{r} \left[\frac{A_{i,\beta\gamma}}{A_i} - \frac{A_{i,\beta}\, A_{i,\gamma}}{A_i^2} \right] + (n-r) \left[\frac{1}{\beta^2} \ln(1+\beta x_r) - \frac{x_r}{\beta(1+\beta x_r)} \right], \tag{25}$$

where $\Delta^\circ = \Delta(\beta,\gamma,x_i)$ and $\Delta^\bullet = \Delta(\beta,\gamma,x_i+1)$

$A_{i,\alpha\alpha} = \frac{x_i^4}{4} \Delta^\circ e^{-\frac{\alpha x_i^2}{2}} - \frac{(x_i+1)^4}{4} \Delta^\bullet e^{-\frac{\alpha (x_i+1)^2}{2}}$,

$A_{i,\beta\beta} = e^{-\frac{\alpha x_i^2}{2}} \Delta^\circ \left[\psi(\beta,x_i)^2 + \psi'(\beta,x_i) \right] - e^{-\frac{\alpha (x_i+1)^2}{2}} \Delta^\bullet \left[\psi(\beta,x_i+1)^2 + \psi'(\beta,x_i+1) \right]$,

$A_{i,\gamma\gamma} = \frac{1}{\beta^2} \ln(1+\beta x_i)^2 \Delta^\circ e^{-\frac{\alpha x_i^2}{2}} - \frac{1}{\beta^2} \ln(1+\beta(x_i+1))^2 \Delta^\bullet e^{-\frac{\alpha (x_i+1)^2}{2}}$,

$\psi'(\beta,x) = -\frac{2\gamma}{\beta^3} \ln(1+\beta x) + \frac{\gamma x}{\beta^2(1+\beta x)} + \frac{\gamma x(1+2\beta x)}{[\beta(1+\beta x)]^2}$,

$A_{i,\alpha\beta} = -\frac{x_i^2}{2} e^{-\frac{\alpha x_i^2}{2}} \Delta^\circ \psi(\beta,x_i) + \frac{(x_i+1)^2}{2} e^{-\frac{\alpha (x_i+1)^2}{2}} \Delta^\bullet \psi(\beta,x_i+1)$,

$A_{i,\alpha\gamma} = \frac{x_i^2}{2\beta} \ln(1+\beta x_i)\, e^{-\frac{\alpha x_i^2}{2}} \Delta^\circ - \frac{(x_i+1)^2}{2\beta} \ln(1+\beta(x_i+1)) e^{-\frac{\alpha (x_i+1)^2}{2}} \Delta^\bullet$

and

$A_{i,\beta\gamma} = -\frac{1}{\beta} e^{-\frac{\alpha x_i^2}{2}} \Delta^\circ \psi(\beta,x_i) \ln(1+\beta x_i) + \frac{1}{\beta} e^{-\frac{\alpha (x_i+1)^2}{2}} \Delta^\bullet \psi(\beta,x_i+1) \ln(1+\beta(x_i+1))$.

Hence, the asymptotic confidence interval for $\theta = (\theta')$ is provided by $\hat{\theta} \pm z_{\frac{\lambda}{2}}\sqrt{Var(\hat{\theta})}$, where $z_{\frac{\lambda}{2}}$ is the critical value from the standard normal distribution for a given λth confidence level.

5. Bayesian Inference

This section deals with the Bayesian estimation, which is applied to estimate the unknown parameters of the DH model. This method treats the parameters as random variables following a certain model, referred to as the prior distribution. Since prior information is often unavailable, it becomes necessary to choose a suitable prior.

A joint conjugate prior distribution is selected for parameters α, β, and γ, with each parameter assumed to follow a gamma distribution. Consequently, $\alpha \sim Gamma(a_1, b_1)$, $\beta \sim Gamma(a_2, b_2)$, and $\gamma \sim Gamma(a_3, b_3)$, where a_i and b_i (for $i = 1, 2, 3$) represent non-negative hyper-parameters of the specified distributions. Therefore, the prior distributions for α, β, and γ are defined as

$$\pi_1(\alpha) = \frac{{b_1}^{a_1}}{\Gamma(a_1)}\alpha^{a_1-1}e^{-b_1\alpha}, \tag{26}$$

$$\pi_2(\beta) = \frac{{b_2}^{a_2}}{\Gamma(a_2)}\beta^{a_2-1}e^{-b_2\beta}, \tag{27}$$

and

$$\pi_3(\gamma) = \frac{{b_3}^{a_3}}{\Gamma(a_3)}\gamma^{a_3-1}e^{-b_3\gamma}. \tag{28}$$

Therefore, the joint prior function for α, β, and γ is

$$\pi(\boldsymbol{\theta}) \propto \alpha^{a_1-1}\beta^{a_2-1}\gamma^{a_3-1}e^{-b_1\alpha-b_2\beta-b_3\gamma}. \tag{29}$$

The joint posterior (say, $P(\cdot)$) of α, β, and γ with data availability is

$$P(\boldsymbol{\theta} \mid \mathbf{x}) = \frac{1}{K}L(\boldsymbol{\theta} \mid \mathbf{x})\pi(\boldsymbol{\theta}), \tag{30}$$

where $K = \int\int\int L(\boldsymbol{\theta} \mid \mathbf{x})\pi(\boldsymbol{\theta})d\alpha d\beta d\gamma$ is the normalizing factor.

The parameter estimation for the DH model has been analyzed using the squared error (SE) loss function. Later, to evaluate the efficiency of the estimation methods and to examine the impact of parameter values on these techniques, a simulation analysis is conducted to assess the efficiency of the estimators based on several metrics, namely average point estimate, mean absolute bias, mean square error, average interval length, and coverage probability.

Under the SE loss function, Bayesian estimation of a parameter θ (for example) is defined as the expected value for the joint posterior distribution as

$$\widehat{\theta}_{SE} = \frac{1}{K}\int \theta L(\theta \mid \mathbf{x})\pi(\theta)d\theta. \tag{31}$$

It is necessary to employ numerical approaches for calculating the triple integration mentioned in Equation (31). To achieve this, we adopted the Markov Chain Monte Carlo (MCMC) approach. A suitable R code was developed to execute this process.

Applying the survival discretization method leads to the development of the DH model, whose PMF is defined in Equation (5). The joint posterior density under a Type-II censored sample is expressed as follows:

$$P(\theta \mid \mathbf{x}) = \frac{1}{K}\left[\prod_{i=1}^{r}\left(\Delta(\beta,\gamma,x_i)e^{-\alpha\frac{x_i^2}{2}} - \Delta(\beta,\gamma,x_i+1)e^{-\alpha\frac{(x_i+1)^2}{2}}\right)\right]\left[\Delta(\beta,\gamma,x_r)e^{-\alpha\frac{x_r^2}{2}}\right]^{n-r} \times \alpha^{a_1-1}\beta^{a_2-1}\gamma^{a_3-1}e^{-b_1\alpha-b_2\beta-b_3\gamma}. \tag{32}$$

Bayesian analysis for the parameters α, β, and γ under the SE loss function is beyond developing their conditional posterior functions, respectively, as

$$P_1(\alpha \mid \beta,\gamma,\mathbf{x}) = L(\boldsymbol{\theta} \mid \mathbf{x})\alpha^{a_1}e^{-b_1\alpha}, \tag{33}$$

$$P_2(\beta \mid \alpha,\gamma,\mathbf{x}) = L(\boldsymbol{\theta} \mid \mathbf{x})\beta^{a_2}e^{-b_2\beta}, \tag{34}$$

and

$$P_3(\gamma \mid \alpha,\beta\mathbf{x}) = L(\boldsymbol{\theta} \mid \mathbf{x})\gamma^{a_3}e^{-b_3\gamma}. \tag{35}$$

The Bayes estimators of α, β, and γ, based on Equations (33)–(35), respectively, cannot follow any known statistical distribution. To handle this problem, the Metropolis–Hastings (M–H) sampler, the most important term of the MCMC family of Bayes calculation techniques, is recommended to evaluate the Bayes point estimates and their Bayesian credible intervals (BCIs). It is useful to remember that the BCI represents a range of values where an unknown parameter is likely to reside with a specified probability based on the obtained data and prior beliefs regarding the parameters.

Now, the implementation of the MCMC approach through the M–H sampler is outlined as listed below:

Step 1: Start by assuming a basic value $(\alpha^{(0)},\beta^{(0)},\gamma^{(0)}) = (\hat{\alpha},\hat{\beta},\hat{\gamma})$.

Step 2: Set $m = 1$.

Step 3: From (33), create $\alpha^\star$ from $N(\alpha^{(m-1)},\mathrm{Var}(\alpha))$, and then follow the next steps (a)–(d):

- (a) Find $C_1 = \frac{P_1(\alpha^\star|\beta^{(m-1)},\gamma^{(m-1)},\mathbf{x})}{P1(\alpha^{(m-1)}|\beta^{(m-1)},\gamma^{(m-1)},\mathbf{x})}$.
- (b) Obtain $\mathcal{Q}_1 = \min\{1, C_1\}$.
- (c) Generate u_1 from $\mathcal{U}(0,1)$.
- (d) If $u_1 < \mathcal{Q}_1$, adopt the proposal and set $\alpha^{(m)} = \alpha^\star$; otherwise, set $\alpha^{(m)} = \alpha^{(m-1)}$.

Step 4: Redo Step 3 for β and γ.

Step 5: Set $m = m + 1$.

Step 6: Obtain $(\alpha^{(l)},\beta^{(l)},\gamma^{(l)})$ for $l = 1,2,\ldots N$ by redoing Steps 2 to 4 N times.

Step 7: Discard the first iterations (say, N^*) as burn-in, and obtain the Bayes estimates of α, β, and γ (say, ψ_j, $j = 1,2,3$) as

$$\tilde{\psi}_j = \frac{1}{N-N^*}\sum_{m=N^*+1}^{N}\psi^{(m)},$$

where $(\psi_1,\psi_2,\psi_3) = (\alpha,\beta,\gamma)$.

Step 8: Sort $\psi_j^{(m)}$, $j = 1,2,3$, $m = N^*+1, N^*+2,\ldots,N$, in ascending order and obtain the 100 $(1-\lambda)\%$ BCIs for ψ_j as

$$\left(\psi_{j((N-N^*)\,\frac{\lambda}{2})},\psi_{j((N-N^*)\,(1-\frac{\lambda}{2}))}\right).$$

6. Numerical Comparisons

In this part, to test the efficiency of the acquired estimators of DH's parameters α, β, and γ, different comparisons via Monte Carlo experiments are performed. After that, some comments on the outcomes of the simulation are provided. The numerical part was performed using the R (64) software package.

6.1. Simulation Scenarios

We now suggest the following steps to gather a Type-II censored dataset from the proposed model:

Step 1: Fix the number of replications as 2000.

Step 2: Fix the values of DH(α,β,γ); that is, (a) Set-1:DH(0.5,0.8,1) and (b) Set-2:DH(1,1.5,2).

Step 3: Set sample size n as $(30,60,100,150,200)$.

Step 4: Obtain u_i for $i=1,2,\ldots,n$ as an independent observation from a uniform distribution $U(0,1)$.

Step 5: Obtain pseudo-random values of size n from the DH distribution as

$$x_i = F^{-1}(u_i;\alpha,\beta,\gamma),\ i=1,2,\ldots,n.$$

Step 6: Sort the outputs in Step 5; then, for a failure percentage (FP%), determine the value of r such as $\frac{r}{n}\times 100 = 40$, 80, and 100%. It is important to note that, when FP%$\rightarrow$ 100%, censored (incomplete) sampling reverts to completed sampling.

Step 7: Fix the informative prior sets of a_i and b_i for $i=1,2,3$ to develop the Bayes point and interval estimations, such as

(i) For Set-1:

- Prior-A:$(a_1,a_2,a_3)=(2.5,0.16,5)$ and $b_i=5$ for $i=1,2,3$;
- Prior-B:$(a_1,a_2,a_3)=(5,0.08,10)$ and $b_i=10$ for $i=1,2,3$.

(ii) For Set-2:

- Prior-A:$(a_1,a_2,a_3)=(5,0.3,10)$ and $b_i=5$ for $i=1,2,3$;
- Prior-B:$(a_1,a_2,a_3)=(10,0.15,20)$ and $b_i=10$ for $i=1,2,3$.

Step 8. Compute the average point estimate (APE) of α (as an example):

$$\text{APE}(\breve{\alpha}) = \frac{1}{2000}\sum\nolimits_{i=1}^{2000}\breve{\alpha}^{[i]},$$

where $\breve{\alpha}$ is the offered estimate of α at ith sample.

Step 9: Compute the mean squared error (MSE) and mean absolute bias (MAB) of α:

$$\text{MSE}(\breve{\alpha}) = \frac{1}{2000}\sum\nolimits_{i=1}^{2000}\left(\breve{\alpha}^{[i]}-\alpha\right)^2,$$

and

$$\text{MAB}(\breve{\alpha}) = \frac{1}{2000}\sum\nolimits_{i=1}^{2000}\left|\breve{\alpha}^{[i]}-\alpha\right|.$$

Step 10: Compute the average interval length (AIL) and coverage provability (CP) of α:

$$\text{ACL}_{95\%}(\alpha) = \frac{1}{2000}\sum\nolimits_{i=1}^{2000}\left(\mathcal{U}_{\breve{\alpha}^{[i]}}(\alpha)-\mathcal{L}_{\breve{\alpha}^{[i]}}(\alpha)\right),$$

and

$$\mathrm{CP}_{95\%}(\alpha) = \frac{1}{2000}\sum_{i=1}^{2000} \mathbb{I}_{\left(\mathcal{L}_{\alpha[i]}\mathcal{U}_{\alpha[i]}\right)}(\alpha),$$

where $(\mathcal{L}(\cdot)\mathcal{U}(\cdot))$ refers to the estimated interval limits and $\mathbb{I}(\cdot)$ denotes the indicator operator.

The chosen prior distributions reflect reasonable assumptions about parameters α, β, and γ based on prior research and empirical observations in reliability and survival studies. Prior-A represents a more informative prior with moderate variance, assuming prior knowledge about the expected parameter range, whereas Prior-B has greater uncertainty by enabling higher variance, making it suitable for scenarios where less prior knowledge is available.

6.2. Simulation Results and Discussion

In Tables 2 and 3, the APEs, MSEs, and MABs of α, β, and γ can be found in the first, second, and third columns, respectively. Additionally, in Tables 4 and 5, the AILs and CPs of α, β, and γ can be found in the first and second columns, respectively.

From the facts presented in Tables 2 and 5 and the plots in Figure 2, the statistical behavior of the proposed estimators for parameters α, β, and γ under various experimental conditions is summarized as follows:

- As the sample size n increases, the performance of all the estimators improves significantly. Specifically, lower MSE, MAB, and AIL values are observed, along with higher CP values. These results demonstrate the asymptotic consistency of the proposed estimation methods, reinforcing their reliability for larger datasets.
- Increasing r (or, equivalently, increasing FP%) enhances the precision of the calculated estimators. This improvement is reflected in reduced MSE, MAB, and AIL values, while CP values exhibit an increasing trend, indicating stronger inferential accuracy.
- As we anticipate, when FP%$\to$ 100%, the precision of all simulation results of α, β, or γ behaves better under a complete sampling situation than others.
- When comparing point estimates of α, β, and γ, the Bayesian estimation approach consistently outperforms the likelihood approach in terms of lower simulated MSE and MAB values. This suggests that the Bayesian framework provides more stable and efficient estimators in finite samples.
- Regarding interval estimation, the BCI method demonstrates superior performance over the ACI method. Specifically, BCI-derived intervals exhibit shorter AIL values while maintaining higher CP values, emphasizing their greater informativeness and accuracy.
- The choice regarding the prior distribution significantly influences the Bayesian estimation results. For all three parameters, α, β, and γ, estimates obtained using Prior-B outperform those derived from Prior-A. This can be attributed to the smaller variance of Prior-B, which leads to more precise and concentrated posterior distributions.
- The overall estimation accuracy varies depending on the data structure. The results from Set-1 yield more precise estimates of α, β, and γ compared to Set-2. Moreover, as the values of these parameters increase, a deterioration in estimation precision is observed, characterized by higher MSE, MAB, and AIL values and a corresponding decline in CP values.
- Finally, for analyzing discrete Hjorth data in the presence of censored observations, the Bayesian framework is strongly recommended due to its robust inferential properties, particularly in handling incomplete data efficiently.

Using the simulated values of MSEs and AILs (for example) corresponding to DH parameters α, β, and γ, Figure 2 provides clearer insights into the simulation results and confirms all the data presented in Tables 2–5.

Table 2. The point results of α, β, and γ from Set-1.

n	FP%	Par.	MLE			Bayes					
Prior →						A			B		
30	40%	α	0.4595	0.3357	0.5327	0.4399	0.0892	0.2437	0.6927	0.0691	0.2125
		β	1.2955	1.1791	1.0403	0.7193	0.6275	0.4825	1.0522	0.1867	0.3960
		γ	1.1438	0.5379	0.6113	0.9556	0.3334	0.5583	0.8510	0.1499	0.3706
	80%	α	0.4691	0.3085	0.4952	0.4802	0.0714	0.2283	0.4713	0.0629	0.2090
		β	0.9478	0.9663	0.8685	0.7054	0.5176	0.4365	1.1733	0.1691	0.3778
		γ	1.0751	0.5133	0.5963	1.0021	0.2452	0.4660	1.0803	0.1170	0.2934
	100%	α	0.9581	0.2854	0.4581	0.4886	0.0661	0.2112	0.6242	0.0582	0.1933
		β	0.9965	0.8939	0.8033	0.7267	0.4788	0.4038	1.1701	0.1516	0.3495
		γ	1.0180	0.4748	0.5452	1.0763	0.2168	0.4311	1.1086	0.1024	0.2714
60	40%	α	0.4219	0.2749	0.4831	0.4904	0.0680	0.1995	0.4689	0.0576	0.1895
		β	1.2951	0.6072	0.6936	1.8196	0.4526	0.4048	1.4113	0.1578	0.3384
		γ	0.9944	0.4727	0.5763	0.8103	0.2444	0.4587	0.9580	0.0931	0.2838
	80%	α	0.5119	0.2613	0.4792	0.5481	0.0660	0.1952	0.5068	0.0520	0.1827
		β	0.9122	0.6063	0.5426	1.6449	0.1853	0.3708	1.2936	0.1378	0.2825
		γ	1.2847	0.4236	0.5363	1.2421	0.2334	0.4364	1.2864	0.0900	0.2750
	100%	α	0.8758	0.2417	0.4433	0.5070	0.0611	0.1805	0.4688	0.0481	0.1690
		β	0.8925	0.5609	0.5019	1.5815	0.1714	0.3430	1.1966	0.1275	0.2613
		γ	1.2541	0.3918	0.4961	1.1489	0.2159	0.4037	0.8994	0.0833	0.2544
100	40%	α	0.4891	0.2569	0.4455	0.4676	0.0628	0.1914	0.4523	0.0517	0.1678
		β	1.2951	0.1612	0.4051	1.4877	0.1383	0.3322	0.7992	0.1179	0.2665
		γ	1.1676	0.3724	0.5123	0.8201	0.1300	0.2919	0.9716	0.0620	0.2213
	80%	α	0.5378	0.2450	0.2192	0.5405	0.0611	0.1885	0.6602	0.0503	0.1603
		β	0.9293	0.1407	0.3679	1.4782	0.0978	0.2756	0.8528	0.0907	0.1902
		γ	1.1275	0.3165	0.4853	1.2888	0.1222	0.2854	1.2627	0.0517	0.1909
	100%	α	0.8758	0.2267	0.2028	0.4999	0.0565	0.1743	0.6507	0.0465	0.1482
		β	0.8925	0.1265	0.3240	1.3674	0.0910	0.2489	0.8881	0.0839	0.1759
		γ	1.2541	0.2793	0.4249	1.1921	0.1160	0.2395	1.2680	0.0448	0.1707
150	40%	α	0.4803	0.2251	0.1942	0.6836	0.0501	0.1817	0.5732	0.0383	0.1525
		β	1.2951	0.1385	0.3390	0.8417	0.0822	0.1833	1.0697	0.0337	0.1548
		γ	0.9868	0.2757	0.4275	0.9444	0.1205	0.2725	0.7920	0.0417	0.1708
	80%	α	0.5174	0.1751	0.1879	0.5085	0.0495	0.1710	0.5407	0.0353	0.1436
		β	0.9403	0.1307	0.3130	1.0509	0.0741	0.1741	0.9142	0.0292	0.1484
		γ	1.3767	0.2259	0.3968	1.0379	0.1003	0.2597	1.0862	0.0277	0.1462
	100%	α	0.5174	0.1593	0.1704	0.4704	0.0458	0.1581	0.5002	0.0326	0.1328
		β	0.9403	0.1169	0.2896	0.9721	0.0685	0.1561	0.8457	0.0271	0.1354
		γ	1.3767	0.2050	0.3567	0.9600	0.0918	0.2402	1.0047	0.0226	0.1305
200	40%	α	0.5254	0.1451	0.1778	0.4864	0.0454	0.1390	0.4949	0.0229	0.1241
		β	1.2951	0.1249	0.2758	1.0504	0.0617	0.1646	0.8633	0.0185	0.1299
		γ	1.0568	0.1973	0.3713	0.9843	0.0905	0.1636	0.9404	0.0201	0.1256
	80%	α	0.5208	0.1351	0.1668	0.5389	0.0397	0.1217	0.4800	0.0214	0.1099
		β	0.9369	0.1187	0.2494	1.0374	0.0565	0.1319	1.0322	0.0139	0.1182
		γ	1.3792	0.1822	0.3581	1.0428	0.0775	0.1405	1.1908	0.0179	0.1148
	100%	α	0.4965	0.1269	0.1543	0.4984	0.0368	0.1125	0.4440	0.0192	0.1016
		β	0.8965	0.1076	0.2307	0.9562	0.0522	0.1172	0.9548	0.0128	0.1120
		γ	1.1125	0.1569	0.3237	0.9646	0.0716	0.1259	1.1015	0.0165	0.1082

Table 3. The point results of α, β, and γ from Set-2.

n	FP%	Par.	MLE			Bayes					
Prior →						A			B		
30	40%	α	1.1737	1.0966	0.9495	0.9770	0.6260	0.7776	1.0820	0.5066	0.6748
		β	2.1669	1.4447	1.2663	1.8700	0.7929	0.7170	1.3988	0.4136	0.5917
		γ	1.8538	0.9218	1.2516	1.8769	0.8264	0.9441	1.8726	0.4612	0.7424
	80%	α	0.9265	0.8285	0.9006	0.9564	0.6096	0.7260	0.9832	0.4650	0.6317
		β	1.8313	1.2496	1.1377	1.5113	0.6358	0.5897	1.8926	0.3733	0.5402
		γ	2.1315	0.8859	1.1467	1.9839	0.7323	0.7222	2.1495	0.4286	0.6854
	100%	α	0.9087	0.7567	0.8244	0.8966	0.5271	0.6806	0.9176	0.4326	0.5923
		β	1.6717	1.1671	1.0566	1.4168	0.5796	0.5653	1.5774	0.3450	0.5065
		γ	1.8317	0.8231	1.0450	1.8599	0.6965	0.6877	1.9870	0.3984	0.6343
60	40%	α	0.9654	0.7529	0.8538	0.9551	0.4540	0.5908	0.8934	0.3848	0.5543
		β	1.6969	1.0875	0.9139	1.6998	0.5755	0.5570	2.1598	0.3604	0.4984
		γ	1.7585	0.8333	1.0948	1.9571	0.6826	0.6194	1.8390	0.3676	0.5637
	80%	α	1.0674	0.4009	0.5696	1.0545	0.3752	0.5317	0.9412	0.3502	0.4902
		β	2.1337	0.9372	0.8490	1.8577	0.4576	0.5197	1.9307	0.3154	0.4759
		γ	2.1798	0.7992	0.8250	2.1503	0.6112	0.5445	2.5056	0.3228	0.5062
	100%	α	1.1265	0.3758	0.5234	0.9886	0.3518	0.4985	0.8982	0.3308	0.4596
		β	1.7550	0.8679	0.7796	1.7416	0.4290	0.4872	1.9781	0.3030	0.4462
		γ	1.9808	0.7349	0.7673	1.8665	0.5730	0.5105	2.1490	0.2964	0.4675
100	40%	α	1.1365	0.3637	0.5191	1.1271	0.3403	0.4763	1.0304	0.3155	0.4386
		β	1.5970	0.8156	0.8346	1.7846	0.4136	0.4969	1.7985	0.2996	0.4597
		γ	2.1245	0.7064	0.7892	1.9665	0.5843	0.4941	1.9662	0.2271	0.4634
	80%	α	0.9541	0.3366	0.4964	1.0945	0.3168	0.4542	1.1486	0.2911	0.4155
		β	1.8494	0.7897	0.7556	1.3489	0.3485	0.4526	1.4606	0.1999	0.3945
		γ	2.2307	0.5262	0.5429	2.1190	0.3600	0.4599	2.3979	0.2115	0.4166
	100%	α	1.0448	0.3155	0.4654	1.0261	0.2970	0.4358	1.0769	0.2729	0.3895
		β	1.9734	0.7540	0.7084	1.2646	0.3287	0.4143	1.3693	0.1874	0.3698
		γ	2.0913	0.4933	0.5134	1.9866	0.3175	0.4231	2.2480	0.1983	0.3905
150	40%	α	1.1643	0.2987	0.4520	1.1920	0.2493	0.3800	1.1528	0.1394	0.3367
		β	1.7970	0.6886	0.7264	1.6941	0.2998	0.4167	2.0060	0.1849	0.3676
		γ	1.9938	0.4749	0.5035	1.7605	0.3181	0.4152	1.9308	0.1753	0.3690
	80%	α	0.8833	0.2784	0.4221	1.1387	0.2424	0.3674	1.1861	0.1243	0.3116
		β	1.8238	0.3184	0.4862	1.4928	0.2754	0.3709	1.5934	0.1658	0.3313
		γ	2.1682	0.4368	0.4095	2.5074	0.1682	0.3576	2.1656	0.1541	0.3284
	100%	α	0.8281	0.2610	0.3957	1.0675	0.2273	0.3445	1.1119	0.1165	0.2922
		β	1.7099	0.2985	0.4558	1.3995	0.2582	0.3477	1.6813	0.1595	0.3155
		γ	2.0327	0.4095	0.3839	2.3507	0.1577	0.3352	2.0655	0.1445	0.3108
200	40%	α	1.1909	0.2637	0.3785	1.0137	0.2002	0.3081	0.9611	0.1173	0.2631
		β	1.5970	0.3024	0.4747	1.5268	0.2465	0.3314	1.8722	0.1473	0.3138
		γ	2.1364	0.4039	0.3760	1.7792	0.1450	0.3124	1.9750	0.1259	0.2689
	80%	α	1.0551	0.2451	0.2793	1.1547	0.1754	0.2645	1.1641	0.1063	0.2259
		β	1.8140	0.2531	0.3711	1.7848	0.2150	0.3140	1.8269	0.1287	0.2724
		γ	2.1482	0.3846	0.3571	2.1201	0.1265	0.2719	2.2701	0.1138	0.2158
	100%	α	0.9892	0.2298	0.2562	1.0825	0.1645	0.2379	1.0914	0.0987	0.1976
		β	1.7807	0.2373	0.3408	1.6732	0.2016	0.2944	1.7127	0.1169	0.2355
		γ	1.9045	0.3605	0.3280	1.9876	0.1186	0.2549	2.1283	0.0986	0.1961

Table 4. The interval results of α, β, and γ from Set-1.

n	FP%	Par	95% ACI		95% BCI			
Prior →					A		B	
30	40%	α	2.583	0.845	1.117	0.902	0.750	0.918
		β	1.691	0.899	1.407	0.904	0.336	0.921
		γ	1.987	0.876	1.275	0.894	0.616	0.911
	80%	α	2.302	0.852	0.909	0.907	0.676	0.922
		β	1.454	0.902	1.313	0.907	0.310	0.922
		γ	1.695	0.882	1.029	0.900	0.577	0.913
	100%	α	2.190	0.858	0.879	0.909	0.644	0.926
		β	1.274	0.908	1.274	0.908	0.288	0.927
		γ	1.565	0.900	0.979	0.901	0.524	0.915
60	40%	α	2.237	0.857	0.897	0.909	0.637	0.924
		β	1.339	0.905	1.237	0.910	0.283	0.924
		γ	1.412	0.885	0.981	0.902	0.551	0.914
	80%	α	2.200	0.860	0.814	0.912	0.536	0.928
		β	1.272	0.908	0.893	0.914	0.256	0.928
		γ	1.297	0.889	0.977	0.904	0.530	0.915
	100%	α	1.960	0.873	0.787	0.915	0.516	0.930
		β	1.140	0.912	0.818	0.916	0.226	0.931
		γ	1.140	0.902	0.876	0.911	0.469	0.920
100	40%	α	2.080	0.865	0.768	0.915	0.491	0.931
		β	1.233	0.910	0.754	0.918	0.219	0.931
		γ	1.094	0.902	0.927	0.905	0.486	0.917
	80%	α	1.946	0.870	0.720	0.917	0.471	0.933
		β	1.201	0.912	0.686	0.923	0.190	0.932
		γ	0.933	0.904	0.764	0.910	0.456	0.918
	100%	α	1.839	0.874	0.680	0.919	0.445	0.937
		β	1.135	0.914	0.619	0.926	0.168	0.934
		γ	0.882	0.909	0.702	0.913	0.431	0.920
150	40%	α	1.688	0.878	0.685	0.919	0.440	0.936
		β	1.150	0.914	0.628	0.925	0.168	0.934
		γ	0.788	0.907	0.591	0.914	0.447	0.918
	80%	α	1.467	0.883	0.609	0.922	0.417	0.937
		β	1.068	0.915	0.585	0.929	0.147	0.935
		γ	0.610	0.909	0.558	0.915	0.427	0.919
	100%	α	1.372	0.887	0.569	0.925	0.390	0.939
		β	0.930	0.918	0.547	0.931	0.124	0.938
		γ	0.527	0.912	0.522	0.918	0.359	0.922
200	40%	α	1.275	0.887	0.525	0.925	0.371	0.940
		β	1.003	0.916	0.548	0.932	0.122	0.936
		γ	0.583	0.912	0.517	0.916	0.412	0.919
	80%	α	1.064	0.893	0.483	0.928	0.318	0.942
		β	0.904	0.919	0.518	0.934	0.101	0.938
		γ	0.543	0.913	0.467	0.919	0.387	0.920
	100%	α	0.995	0.896	0.452	0.930	0.297	0.943
		β	0.845	0.923	0.484	0.937	0.094	0.940
		γ	0.479	0.915	0.436	0.922	0.362	0.921

Table 5. The interval results of α, β, and γ from Set-2.

n	FP%	Par.	95% ACI		95% BCI			
Prior →					A		B	
30	40%	α	3.315	0.832	1.775	0.893	1.167	0.912
		β	2.382	0.883	1.348	0.902	0.711	0.916
		γ	2.221	0.867	1.487	0.886	0.969	0.893
	80%	α	3.157	0.837	1.473	0.897	1.018	0.915
		β	2.154	0.886	1.279	0.905	0.661	0.919
		γ	1.882	0.874	1.433	0.887	0.930	0.895
	100%	α	2.876	0.842	1.367	0.901	0.982	0.917
		β	1.994	0.889	1.212	0.907	0.581	0.921
		γ	1.764	0.876	1.317	0.889	0.894	0.893
60	40%	α	2.967	0.841	1.341	0.899	0.850	0.918
		β	1.818	0.890	1.149	0.908	0.587	0.921
		γ	1.643	0.877	1.388	0.890	0.814	0.900
	80%	α	2.559	0.846	1.190	0.903	0.828	0.920
		β	1.756	0.892	1.082	0.910	0.527	0.922
		γ	1.533	0.880	1.278	0.892	0.790	0.902
	100%	α	2.230	0.851	0.895	0.892	0.739	0.923
		β	1.365	0.899	0.930	0.893	0.457	0.925
		γ	1.297	0.901	0.997	0.888	0.653	0.907
100	40%	α	2.233	0.852	0.934	0.906	0.760	0.923
		β	1.642	0.895	0.918	0.912	0.467	0.924
		γ	1.496	0.882	1.204	0.893	0.762	0.906
	80%	α	1.993	0.857	0.884	0.909	0.715	0.926
		β	1.548	0.897	0.791	0.915	0.425	0.925
		γ	1.233	0.885	1.022	0.896	0.735	0.907
	100%	α	1.883	0.860	0.815	0.912	0.676	0.930
		β	1.463	0.901	0.708	0.917	0.401	0.928
		γ	1.165	0.888	0.927	0.901	0.664	0.910
150	40%	α	1.781	0.863	0.850	0.911	0.690	0.928
		β	1.493	0.900	0.769	0.917	0.386	0.928
		γ	1.006	0.888	0.859	0.901	0.691	0.909
	80%	α	1.559	0.868	0.812	0.913	0.628	0.930
		β	1.451	0.901	0.732	0.918	0.344	0.929
		γ	0.986	0.890	0.814	0.903	0.667	0.910
	100%	α	1.457	0.872	0.759	0.916	0.587	0.933
		β	1.246	0.904	0.685	0.920	0.322	0.931
		γ	0.922	0.893	0.761	0.905	0.624	0.913
200	40%	α	1.498	0.871	0.796	0.915	0.590	0.932
		β	1.390	0.903	0.672	0.920	0.317	0.931
		γ	0.925	0.892	0.780	0.907	0.631	0.912
	80%	α	1.262	0.875	0.755	0.917	0.495	0.935
		β	1.323	0.904	0.620	0.921	0.298	0.932
		γ	0.887	0.895	0.674	0.910	0.604	0.914
	100%	α	1.180	0.877	0.706	0.919	0.463	0.937
		β	1.237	0.906	0.579	0.923	0.278	0.935
		γ	0.829	0.898	0.622	0.912	0.565	0.916

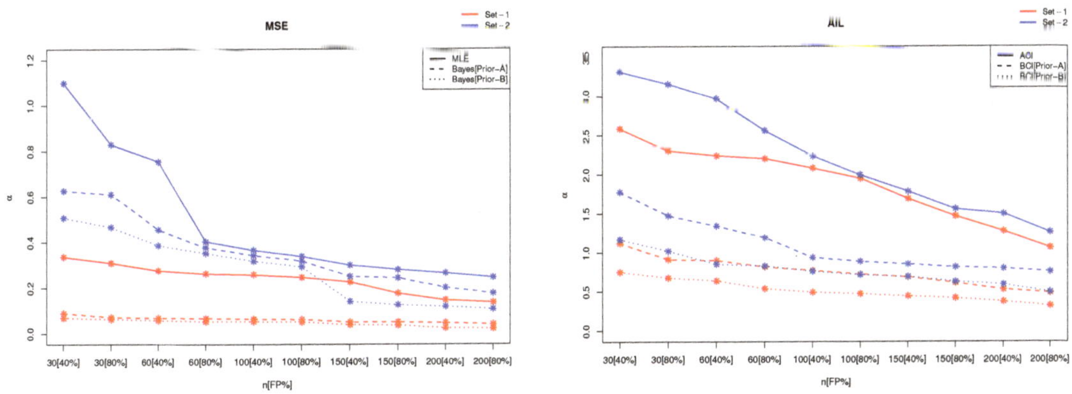

(a) α

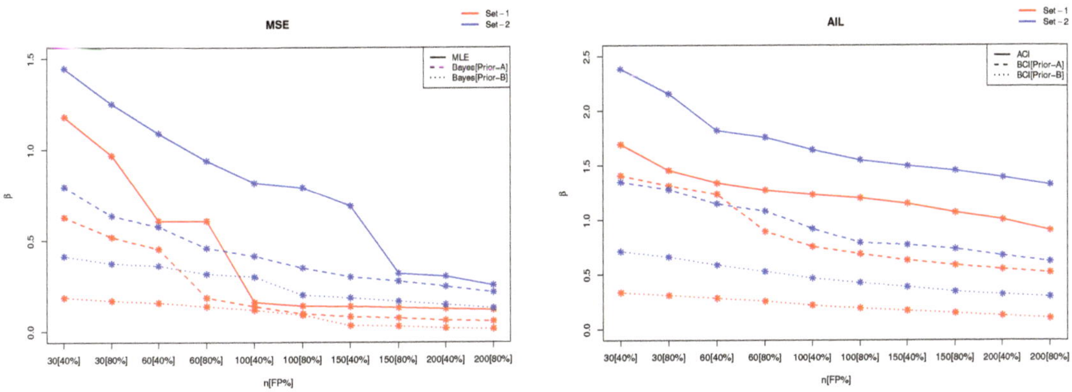

(b) β

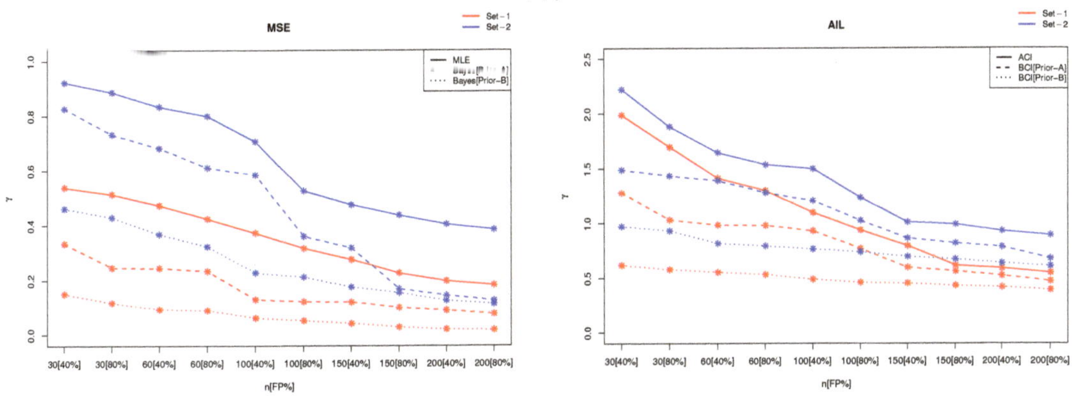

(c) γ

Figure 2. The simulated MSE (**left**) and AIL (**right**) results of α, β, and γ.

7. Real-World Data Analysis

This section analyzes two applications using two separate actual datasets to (i) assess the offered model's adaptation and effectiveness to real problems; (ii) show how the inferential outcomes can be applied to a real-world scenario; and (iii) assess if the suggested model is more appropriate than eight other discrete models in the literature. Now, we consider the following applications:

- The first application (say, App [A]) examines the failure times of eighteen electronic devices. These data were first introduced by Wang [19]; see Table 6.
- The second application (say, App [B]) analyzes how many millions of revolutions each of 22 ball bearings will make before they fail; see Caroni [20]. For computational purposes, we divide each revolution by ten and list the newly transformed ball-bearing data in Table 6.

Table 6. Failure time points in the two applications.

Application	Time									
[A]	0.5	1.1	2.1	3.1	4.6	7.5	9.8	12.2	14.5	16.5	19.6
	22.4	24.5	29.3	32.1	33.0	35.0	42.0				
[B]	1.788	2.892	3.300	4.152	4.212	4.560	4.880	5.184	5.196	5.412	5.556
	6.780	6.864	6.864	6.888	8.412	9.312	9.864	10.512	12.792	12.804	17.340

Briefly, in Table 7, several statistics for applications [A] and [B], namely minimum, maximum, quartiles (1st, 2nd, and 3rd), mean, mode, standard deviation (St.D.), skewness, and kurtosis, are evaluated.

Table 7. Failure time statistics in the two applications.

Application	Minimum	Maximum	Quartiles			Mode	Mean	St.D.	Skewness	Kurtosis
			1st	2nd	3rd					
[A]	0.500	42.00	5.325	15.50	28.10	0.500	17.21	13.15	0.314	1.850
[B]	1.788	17.34	4.640	6.168	9.087	6.864	7.071	3.762	1.066	3.742

Aside from three well-known discrete models, namely negative binomial (NB), geometric (Geom), and Poisson (Pois), based on the above two applications, the DH model will be compared with eight other comparable models from the literature to demonstrate the reliability and advantage of the newly developed model. The competitive distributions include the following:

- Discrete exponentiated-Chen (DEC(α,β,γ)) by Alotaibi et al. [21];
- Exponentiated discrete Weibull (EDW(α,β,γ)) by Nekoukhou and Bidram [22];
- Discrete modified Weibull (DMW(α,β,γ)) by Almalki and Nadarajah [23];
- Discrete Burr Type-XII (DB(α,β)) by Krishna and Pundir [24];
- Discrete Perks (DP(α,β)) by Tyagi et al. [25];
- Discrete generalized-exponential (DGE(α,β)) by Nekoukhou et al. [26];
- Discrete gamma (DG(α,β)) by Chakraborty and Chakravarty [27];
- Discrete Burr–Hatke (DBH(α)) by El-Morshedy et al. [28].

To judge the best model, several metrics are utilized, namely negative log-likelihood (N-LogL), Akaike (Ak.), consistent-Akaike (C-Ak.), Bayesian (Bayes), Hannan–Quinn (H–Q), and Kolmogorov–Smirnov (K–S) statistic (with its p-value). From both applications [A] and [B], the fitted values corresponding to these criteria as well as the MLEs (along with their standard errors (Std.Ers)) of α, β, and γ are obtained; see Table 8. It is clear from Table 8 for both analyzed applications that the fitted DH distribution produces the lowest values for all fitted metrics except the highest p-value among all other fitted competing models. As a result, the DH probability model is better than others.

Several goodness-of-fit visualization tools are employed, including (i) histogram of data with fitted probability lines, (ii) fitted reliability lines, (iii) probability–probability (PP), and (iv) total-time-test (TTT) plots for the DH and its competing distributions, as displayed in Figure 3. Clearly, in Figure 3, we only compared the DH with models with p-values greater than 5%. It exhibits that the newly proposed DH distribution provides the best fit for both applications in terms of estimated PMF, RF, and PP curves.

Table 8. Goodness of fit for the DH and its competitive distributions from the two applications.

App.	Model	MLE (Std.Er)			N-LogL	Ak.	Bayes	C-Ak.	H–Q	K–S (p-Value)
		α	β	γ						
[A]	DH	0.0028(0.0009)	0.3521(0.6590)	0.0683(0.0648)	68.138	142.275	143.990	144.947	142.644	0.106(0.975)
	DEC	0.0241(0.0486)	0.4237(0.1062)	0.8808(0.7033)	68.582	143.164	144.878	145.835	143.532	0.113(0.956)
	EDW	0.9968(0.0019)	1.7621(0.1801)	0.5609(0.1580)	68.648	143.296	145.010	145.967	143.664	0.113(0.957)
	DMW	1.0186(0.0497)	5.0673(11.339)	1.0427(0.0165)	68.407	142.814	144.529	145.485	143.183	0.109(0.973)
	DW	1.2421(0.2470)	18.880(3.7583)	-	69.186	142.372	144.172	145.153	142.677	0.122(0.924)
	DB	13.730(32.516)	0.0298(0.0708)	-	78.846	161.693	162.493	163.473	161.938	0.284(0.089)
	DP	0.0869(0.0286)	0.5727(0.6924)	-	69.025	142.492	144.085	144.983	142.695	0.109(0.971)
	DG	0.0723(0.0265)	1.2811(0.3875)	-	69.419	142.838	143.999	144.969	143.083	0.109(0.966)
	NB	1.2227(0.4391)	17.113(3.7763)	-	69.478	142.955	144.736	145.755	143.078	0.136(0.849)
	DBH	0.9979(0.0111)	-	-	92.832	187.664	187.914	188.555	187.787	0.647(0.002)
	Geom	0.0552(0.0126)	-	-	69.631	143.262	144.152	144.951	143.385	0.141(0.819)
	Pois	17.111(0.9750)	-	-	135.56	273.129	274.015	273.380	273.250	0.342(0.022)
[B]	DH	0.0609(0.0167)	0.0454(0.0068)	0.1119(0.0407)	55.819	117.639	118.972	120.912	118.410	0.147(0.728)
	DEC	0.8106(0.7237)	0.2929(0.1010)	32.879(60.685)	56.971	119.941	121.275	123.214	120.712	0.171(0.541)
	EDW	0.5577(0.6397)	0.8308(0.6029)	11.825(27.309)	56.982	119.964	121.297	123.237	120.735	0.149(0.726)
	DMW	0.9917(0.0086)	7.9939(9.0815)	1.1866(0.0416)	62.367	130.734	132.067	134.007	131.505	0.237(0.167)
	DW	2.1995(0.3484)	8.5805(0.8846)	-	58.258	120.516	121.148	122.698	121.030	0.222(0.231)
	DB	8.8347(32.276)	0.0594(0.2172)	-	78.218	160.436	161.067	162.618	160.950	0.390(0.003)
	DP	0.4233(0.1557)	0.0627(0.0906)	-	58.861	121.723	122.354	123.905	122.237	0.180(0.473)
	DG	0.6151(0.1913)	4.6565(1.3750)	-	57.253	118.506	119.137	120.988	119.020	0.199(0.345)
	NB	8.8040(5.8286)	7.0904(0.7627)	-	57.741	119.483	121.665	120.914	119.997	0.150(0.722)
	DBH	0.9868(0.0261)	-	-	90.521	183.042	183.242	184.133	183.299	0.760(0.004)
	Geom	0.1236(0.0247)	-	-	66.577	135.154	136.245	135.354	135.411	0.366(0.006)
	Pois	7.0909(0.5677)	-	-	60.298	122.596	123.687	122.796	122.853	0.165(0.585)

The estimated TTT lines shown in Figure 3 indicate that the given datasets employed in applications [A] and [B] provide bathtub and increasing failure rates, respectively. These failure rate shapes support the same shapes of the DH model represented in Figure 1. Additionally, all facts shown in Figure 3 support the same numerical findings reported in Table 8. We can therefore infer from the results presented in Figure 3 (or Table 8) that, compared to other traditional (or modern) statistical models, the new DH distribution provides a significantly superior fit.

Type-II censoring is a powerful tool in engineering reliability studies. It enables cost-effective, efficient, and statistically robust failure data analysis, ensuring better product design, maintenance, and quality control. As a result, it provides reliable failure estimates faster and cheaper than complete sampling.

To assess the obtained frequentist and Bayes estimators of α, β, and γ, three artificial Type-II censored samples are obtained for each dataset based on varying the values of r; refer to Table 9. In every sample, the MLEs (along with the 95% ACIs) as well as the Bayes estimation (along with the 95% BCIs) are obtained. All Bayes evaluations are conducted by running the MCMC sampler 50,000 times and discarding the first 10,000 iterations as burn-in. Due to the lack of prior information about the DH's parameters, we set $a_i = b_i = 0.001$ for $i = 1, 2, 3$. In Table 10, the maximum likelihood and Bayes estimates (with their Std.Ers) as well as 95% ACI/BCI bounds (with their interval widths (ILs)) of α, β, and γ are listed. It indicates that the point and interval estimation results developed from the Bayes method outperformed those developed from the likelihood method. When r is increased, all estimates of α, β, or γ behave well because their Std.Er and IL values decreased.

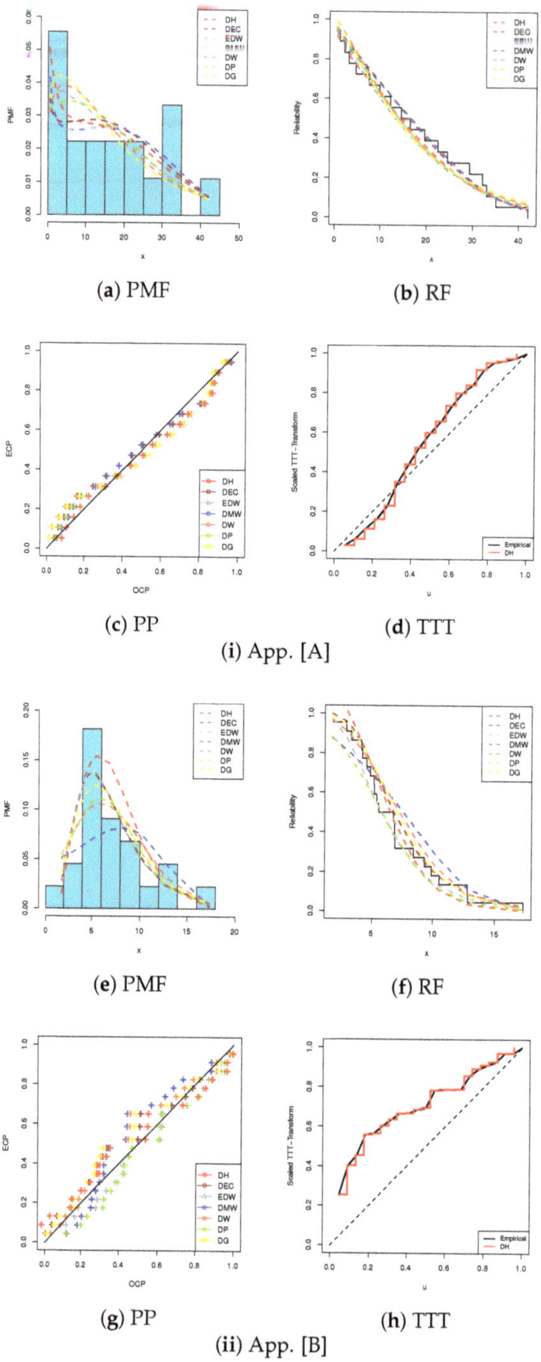

(**a**) PMF (**b**) RF

(**c**) PP (**d**) TTT

(**i**) App. [A]

(**e**) PMF (**f**) RF

(**g**) PP (**h**) TTT

(**ii**) App. [B]

Figure 3. Data visualizations of the DH and its competitors from the two applications.

Table 9. Artificial Type-II censored samples from the two applications.

App.	r	Data											
[A]	8	0.5	1.1	2.1	3.1	4.6	7.5	9.8	12.2				
	12	0.5	1.1	2.1	3.1	4.6	7.5	9.8	12.2	14.5	16.5	19.6	22.4
	18	0.5	1.1	2.1	3.1	4.6	7.5	9.8	12.2	14.5	16.5	19.6	22.4
		24.5	29.3	32.1	33	35	42						
[B]	10	1.788	2.892	3.300	4.152	4.212	4.560	4.880	5.184	5.196	5.412		
	15	1.788	2.892	3.300	4.152	4.212	4.560	4.880	5.184	5.196	5.412	5.556	
		6.780	6.864	6.864	6.888								
	22	1.788	2.892	3.300	4.152	4.212	4.560	4.880	5.184	5.196	5.412	5.556	
		6.780	6.864	6.864	6.888	8.412	9.312	9.864	10.512	12.792	12.804	17.340	

Table 10. Estimates of α, β, and γ from the two applications.

Data	r	Par.	MLE		Bayes		95% ACI			95% BCI		
			Est.	Std.Er	Est.	Std.Er	Low.	Upp.	IL	Low.	Upp.	IL
[A]	8	α	0.00135	0.00475	0.00130	0.00026	0.00000	0.01065	0.01065	0.00081	0.00180	0.00099
		β	0.12382	0.47007	0.12382	0.00025	0.00000	1.04515	1.04515	0.12333	0.12431	0.00098
		γ	0.05994	0.05176	0.05993	0.00025	0.00000	0.16138	0.16138	0.05944	0.06043	0.00099
	12	α	0.00187	0.00178	0.00184	0.00025	0.00000	0.00536	0.00536	0.00136	0.00233	0.00097
		β	0.18077	0.44236	0.18077	0.00025	0.00000	1.04778	1.04778	0.18028	0.18127	0.00099
		γ	0.06241	0.05428	0.06241	0.00025	0.00000	0.16880	0.16880	0.06192	0.06291	0.00099
	18	α	0.00274	0.00103	0.00272	0.00024	0.00072	0.00475	0.00403	0.00225	0.00320	0.00095
		β	0.31689	0.57888	0.31689	0.00025	0.00000	1.45147	1.45147	0.31641	0.31739	0.00098
		γ	0.06686	0.06152	0.06686	0.00025	0.00000	0.18744	0.18744	0.06637	0.06734	0.00098
[B]	10	α	0.50352	0.14345	0.50317	0.00106	0.22236	0.78467	0.56231	0.50118	0.50514	0.00396
		β	0.14670	0.00005	0.14669	0.00101	0.14660	0.14679	0.00019	0.14474	0.14868	0.00394
		γ	0.12099	0.04284	0.12088	0.00101	0.03702	0.20496	0.16794	0.11891	0.12284	0.00394
	15	α	0.28233	0.10461	0.28189	0.00109	0.07729	0.48737	0.41008	0.27993	0.28388	0.00395
		β	0.09847	0.00389	0.09855	0.00101	0.09085	0.10608	0.01524	0.09659	0.10053	0.00394
		γ	0.49199	0.18261	0.49189	0.00101	0.13409	0.84990	0.71582	0.48991	0.49387	0.00397
	22	α	0.06090	0.01667	0.06038	0.00114	0.02823	0.09357	0.06534	0.05833	0.06235	0.00402
		β	0.04554	0.00729	0.04554	0.00101	0.03124	0.05983	0.02859	0.04358	0.04749	0.00391
		γ	0.11187	0.03987	0.11175	0.00102	0.03373	0.19002	0.15629	0.10979	0.11373	0.00394

Based on the last 40,000 outputs for α, β, and γ obtained from the two applications when $r = 8$ and 10 (for example), respectively, Figure 4 shows the trace and density plots along with their sample averages (in solid lines) and 95% two-bound BCIs (in dashed lines). It shows that the MCMC sampler converges highly effectively and that the calculated posteriors for all DH parameters are reasonably symmetric.

Additionally, to explore the convergence and blending of Markovian chains, the acceptance rates of the M–H proposals are calculated, such as

- For App. [A]: The acceptance rates from $r(= 8, 10, 12)$ are 90.12, 93.40, and 95.38%;
- For App. [B]: The acceptance rates from $r(= 10, 15, 22)$ are 89.63, 92.78, and 97.47%.

As a consequence, the estimated acceptance rates in App. [A] (or App. [B]) confirm the same facts revealed in Figure 4; that is, the percentage of iterations in which proposals were approved is significantly higher.

The numerical findings from the two applications employed, among other things, demonstrate that the suggested model outperformed the other models. As a result, the methods for applying the newly discrete Hjorth probability model to electrical devices or ball-bearing datasets provide an adequate explanation.

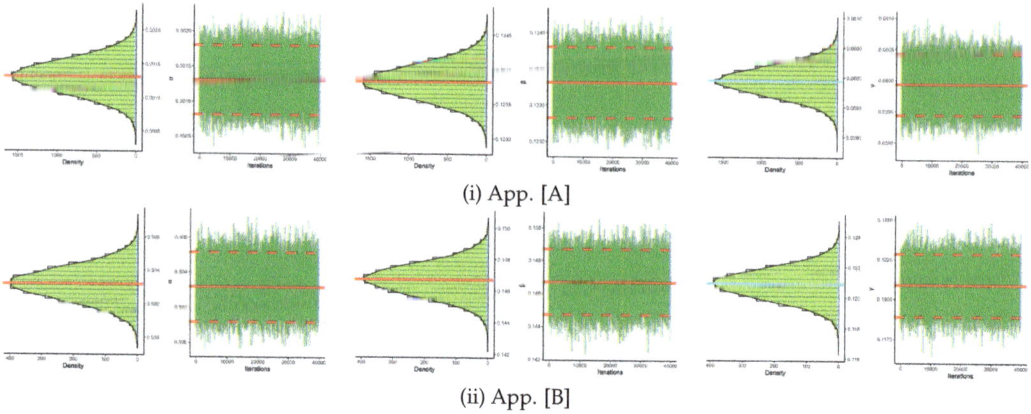

(i) App. [A]

(ii) App. [B]

Figure 4. Trace and density plots of α (**left**), β (**middle**), and γ (**right**) from the two applications.

8. Conclusions

Discrete distributions are well suited for representing data confined to a finite or countably infinite set of data. The straightforward structure, availability of closed-form expressions, and capacity to capture real-world scenarios make them an ideal option. Additionally, they are computationally efficient and effectively handle categorical data modeling. This paper introduced a discrete version of the Hjorth distribution using the survival discretization method, addressing the gap in the literature regarding the use of censored data for analyzing discrete models. The proposed distribution preserved the essential statistical features of the original Hjorth distribution, such as its median, percentiles, and general structure, while providing a flexible framework for modeling real-world discrete data. The statistical properties of the DH model, including the quantile function and order statistics, were thoroughly derived. Maximum likelihood inference and Bayesian methods were employed for parameter estimation, and their performance was evaluated through simulation studies. Type-II censored samples were utilized to demonstrate the practical applicability of the model, with variance–covariance matrices enabling the construction of asymptotic confidence intervals for the parameters. The effectiveness of the DH model was further validated using two real-world datasets: one concerning failure times of electronic devices and another focusing on ball-bearing failures. The goodness-of-fit measures highlighted the superior performance of the proposed model compared to the existing discrete alternatives. Overall, the DH model proved to be a versatile and robust tool for statistical modeling, particularly in reliability and survival analysis. Its ability to adapt to different data patterns, such as decreasing, increasing, and bathtub-shaped hazard rates, underscores its potential for broader applications in various fields, including engineering, medicine, and beyond.

While the proposed DH model demonstrated strong flexibility and effectiveness in capturing various hazard rate shapes, certain limitations can be acknowledged. The model's performance may be less reliable with very small sample sizes due to increased variability in parameter estimates, necessitating techniques such as Bayesian estimation with informative priors. Additionally, while the DH model demonstrated flexibility across various hazard rate trends, its fit may be affected when dealing with datasets exhibiting extreme variance or strong skewness.

Future research could explore refined model selection criteria to guide practitioners in choosing between the DH model and alternative approaches based on dataset characteristics. Future work may explore extending this framework to other distributions, different censoring schemes, and refining the computational methods for enhanced efficiency.

Author Contributions: Methodology, H.H.A. and A.E.; Funding acquisition, H.H.A.; Software, A.E.; Supervision, A.E.; Writing—original draft, H.H.A. and A.E.; Writing—review and editing, H.H.A. and A.E. All authors have read and agreed to the published version of the manuscript.

Funding: This work was supported by the Deanship of Scientific Research, Vice Presidency for Graduate Studies and Scientific Research, King Faisal University, Saudi Arabia [GRANT No. KFU250871].

Data Availability Statement: The authors confirm that the data supporting the findings of this study are available within the article.

Conflicts of Interest: The authors declare no conflicts of interest.

References

1. Roy, D.; Gupta, R.P. Characterizations and Model Selections through Reliability Measures in the Discrete Case. *Stat. Probab. Lett.* **1999**, *43*, 197–206. [CrossRef]
2. Roy, D.; Ghosh, T. A New Discretization Approach with Application in Reliability Estimation. *IEEE Trans. Reliab.* **2009**, *58*, 456–461. [CrossRef]
3. Bracquemond, C.; Gaudoin, O. A Survey on Discrete Lifetime Distributions. *Int. J. Reliab. Qual. Saf. Eng.* **2003**, *10*, 69–98. [CrossRef]
4. Lai, C.D. Issues Concerning Constructions of Discrete Lifetime Models. *Qual. Technol. Quant. Manag.* **2013**, *10*, 251–262. [CrossRef]
5. Chakraborty, S. Generating Discrete Analogues of Continuous Probability Distributions: A Survey of Methods and Constructions. *J. Stat. Distrib. Appl.* **2015**, *2*, 6. [CrossRef]
6. Roy, D. The Discrete Normal Distribution. *Commun. Stat. Theory Methods* **2003**, *32*, 1871–1883. [CrossRef]
7. Roy, D. Discrete Rayleigh Distribution. *IEEE Trans. Reliab.* **2004**, *53*, 255–260. [CrossRef]
8. Al-Huniti, A.A.; AL-Dayian, G.R. Discrete Burr Type III Distribution. *Am. J. Math. Stat.* **2012**, *2*, 145–152. [CrossRef]
9. Bebbington, M.; Lai, C.D.; Wellington, M.; Zitikis, R. The Discrete Additive Weibull Distribution: A Bathtub-Shaped Hazard for Discontinuous Failure Data. *Reliab. Eng. Syst. Saf.* **2012**, *106*, 37–44. [CrossRef]
10. Haj Ahmad, H.; Almetwally, E.M. Generating Optimal Discrete Analogue of the Generalized Pareto Distribution under Bayesian Inference with Applications. *Symmetry* **2022**, *14*, 1457. [CrossRef]
11. Chesneau, C.; Gillariose, J.; Joseph, J.; Tyagi, A. New Discrete Trigonometric Distributions: Estimation with Application to Count Data. *Int. J. Model. Simul.* **2024**, 1–16. [CrossRef]
12. Hjorth, U. A Reliability Distribution with Increasing, Decreasing, Constant, and Bathtub-Shaped Failure Rates. *Technometrics* **1980**, *22*, 99–107. [CrossRef]
13. Guess, F.; Nam, K.H.; Park, D.H. Failure Rate and Mean Residual Life with Trend Changes. *Asia-Pac. J. Oper. Res.* **1998**, *15*, 239–244.
14. Yadav, A.S.; Bakouch, H.S.; Chesneau, C. Bayesian Estimation of the Survival Characteristics for Hjorth Distribution under Progressive Type-II Censoring. *Commun. Stat. Simul. Comput.* **2020**, *51*, 882–900. [CrossRef]
15. Pushkarna, N.; Saran, J.; Verma, K. Progressively Type-II Right Censored Order Statistics from Hjorth Distribution and Related Inference. *Stat. Optim. Inf. Comput.* **2020**, *8*, 481–498. [CrossRef]
16. Pandey, R.; Danish, A. Bayesian Analysis of Hjorth Distribution under Generalised Type I Progressive Hybrid Censoring Scheme. *J. Sci. Res.* **2021**, *65*, 191–201. [CrossRef]
17. Korkmaz, M.C.; Altun, E.; Yousof, H.M.; Hamedani, G.G. The Hjorth's IDB Generator of Distributions: Properties, Characterizations, Regression Modeling and Applications. *J. Stat. Theory Appl.* **2020**, *19*, 59–74. [CrossRef]
18. Elshahhat, A.; Nassar, M. Bayesian Survival Analysis for Adaptive Type-II Progressive Hybrid Censored Hjorth Data. *Comput. Stat.* **2021**, *36*, 1965–1990. [CrossRef]
19. Wang, F.K. A New Model with Bathtub-Shaped Failure Rate Using an Additive Burr XII Distribution. *Reliab. Eng. Syst. Saf.* **2000**, *70*, 305–312. [CrossRef]
20. Caroni, C. The Correct "Ball Bearings" Data. *Lifetime Data Anal.* **2002**, *8*, 395–399. [CrossRef]
21. Alotaibi, R.; Rezk, H.; Park, C.; Elshahhat, A. The Discrete Exponentiated-Chen Model and Its Applications. *Symmetry* **2023**, *15*, 1278. [CrossRef]
22. Nekoukhou, V.; Bidram, H. The Exponentiated Discrete Weibull Distribution. *Sort* **2015**, *39*, 127–146.
23. Almalki, S.J.; Nadarajah, S. A New Discrete Modified Weibull Distribution. *IEEE Trans. Reliab.* **2014**, *63*, 68–80. [CrossRef]
24. Krishna, H.; Pundir, P.S. Discrete Burr and Discrete Pareto Distributions. *Stat. Methodol.* **2009**, *6*, 177–188. [CrossRef]
25. Tyagi, A.; Choudhary, N.; Singh, B. A New Discrete Distribution: Theory and Applications to Discrete Failure Lifetime and Count Data. *J. Appl. Probab. Statist.* **2020**, *15*, 117–143.

26. Nekoukhou, V.; Alamatsaz, M.H.; Bidram, H. Discrete Generalized Exponential Distribution of a Second Type. *Statistics* **2013**, *47*, 876–887. [CrossRef]
27. Chakraborty, S.; Chakravarty, D. Discrete Gamma Distributions: Properties and Parameter Estimations. *Commun. Stat. Theory Methods* **2012**, *41*, 3301–3324. [CrossRef]
28. El-Morshedy, M.; Eliwa, M.S.; Altun, E. Discrete Burr-Hatke Distribution with Properties, Estimation Methods and Regression Model. *IEEE Access* **2020**, *8*, 74359–74370. [CrossRef]

mathematics

MDPI

Article

Two-Dimensional Probability Models for the Weighted Discretized Fréchet–Weibull Random Variable with Min–Max Operators: Mathematical Theory and Statistical Goodness-of-Fit Analysis

Sofian T. Obeidat [1], Diksha Das [2], Mohamed S. Eliwa [3,*], Bhanita Das [2], Partha Jyoti Hazarika [4] and Wael W. Mohammed [1,5]

1 Department of Mathematics, College of Science, University of Ha'il, Ha'il 2440, Saudi Arabia
2 Department of Statistics, North-Eastern Hill University, Meghalaya 793022, India
3 Department of Statistics and Operations Research, College of Science, Qassim University, Saudi Arabia
4 Department of Statistics, Dibrugarh University, Assam 786004, India
5 Department of Mathematics, Faculty of Science, Mansoura University, Mansoura 35516, Egypt
* Correspondence: m.eliwa@qu.edu.sa

Abstract: This study introduces two bivariate extensions of the recently proposed weighted discretized Fréchet–Weibull distribution, termed as bivariate weighted discretized Fréchet–Weibull (BWDFW) distributions. These models are specifically designed for analyzing two-dimensional discrete datasets and are developed using two distinct structural approaches: the minimum operator (BWDFW-I) and the maximum operator (BWDFW-II). A rigorous mathematical formulation is presented, encompassing the joint cumulative distribution function, joint probability mass function, and joint (reversed) hazard rate function. The dependence structure of the models is investigated, demonstrating their capability to capture positive quadrant dependence. Additionally, key statistical measures, including covariance, Pearson's correlation coefficient, Spearman's rho, and Kendall's tau, are derived using the joint probability-generating function. For robust statistical inferences, the parameters of the proposed models are estimated via the maximum likelihood estimation method, with extensive simulation studies conducted to assess the efficiency and accuracy of the estimators. The practical applicability of the BWDFW distributions is demonstrated through their implementation in two real-world datasets: one from the aviation sector and the other from the security and safety domain. Comparative analyses against four existing discrete bivariate Weibull extensions reveal the superior performance of the BWDFW models, with BWDFW-I (minimum operator based) exhibiting greater flexibility and predictive accuracy than BWDFW-II (maximum operator based). These findings underscore the potential of the BWDFW models as effective tools for modeling and analyzing bivariate discrete data in diverse applied contexts.

Keywords: statistical model; bivariate discrete probability distributions; min–max operator methodology; failure analysis; positive quadrant dependence; simulation; data analysis

MSC: 60E05; 60E10; 62H10; 62H15; 62H20

1. Introduction

The Fréchet and Weibull distributions hold a prominent place in research because of their versatility and wide-ranging applications. These continuous probability models are renowned for their ability to encapsulate the characteristics of various other continuous distributions, making them highly adaptable to diverse scenarios. Both distributions are extensively studied as extreme value models, particularly in reliability and survival analysis, where they effectively model critical phenomena. Their applicability spans a broad spectrum of disciplines, including physical sciences, chemistry, environmental studies, medicine, and engineering, where experimental data often exhibit behaviors that align with their properties. This widespread utility underscores their importance as foundational tools in statistical modeling and analysis.

In recent years, numerous generalized distributions have been developed and employed to model a wide range of phenomena. A key characteristic of these generalized distributions is their inclusion of additional parameters, enhancing their flexibility and applicability. Teamah et al. [1] introduced the relatively new Fréchet–Weibull (FW) distribution, which is derived using the T-X method for generating distribution families, as proposed by Alzaatreh et al. [2]. The authors explored the statistical properties of the FW distribution and demonstrated its practical utility by applying it to earthquake datasets. This distribution offers a more adaptable framework for modeling experimental data, with applications consistently demonstrating its superiority in fitting data compared to other extensions of the Weibull distribution.

Although continuous probability distributions play significant roles in various fields, there are numerous practical scenarios where discrete probability distributions are indispensable. In certain cases, measuring the life length of a machine on a continuous scale is either impractical or impossible. Examples include the on–off switching cycles of machines or the lifespan of photocopier bulbs. To address such needs, Das and Das [3] introduced a four-parameter discrete distribution, known as the discretized Fréchet–Weibull (DFW) distribution, derived as a discrete counterpart of the continuous Fréchet–Weibull distribution. This novel discrete distribution was constructed using the survival function approach to discretization, endowing it with a range of flexible properties. The DFW distribution is capable of modeling data with both positive and negative skewness. Additionally, its hazard rate function (HRF) exhibits diverse shapes, including increasing, decreasing, and upside-down bathtub forms, behaviors not commonly observed in many count data distributions. The probability mass function (PMF) of a random variable (Y), following the DFW distribution with shape parameters α and k, and scale parameters β and m, is expressed as follows:

$$P_{DFW}[Y = y] = \exp\left\{-\beta^{\alpha}\left(\frac{m}{y+1}\right)^{\alpha k}\right\} - \exp\left\{-\beta^{\alpha}\left(\frac{m}{y}\right)^{\alpha k}\right\}, \tag{1}$$

where $y \in \mathbf{Z}_{+}$, and the parameters $(\alpha, \beta, m, k) > 0$. Let ξ denote the parameter vector of the DFW distribution, defined as $\xi = (\alpha, \beta, m, k)$, where $\xi \in \mathbb{R}_{+} \times \mathbb{R}_{+} \times \mathbb{R}_{+} \times \mathbb{R}_{+}$. This construction highlights the versatility of the DFW distribution in modeling discrete data arising from real-world applications.

In a subsequent development, Das and Das [4] introduced a novel discrete distribution termed as the weighted discretized Fréchet–Weibull (WDFW) distribution. This distribution builds upon the CDF of the discrete Weibull (DW) distribution to define the weight function as follows:

$$w(y) = 1 - \exp\left\{-\left(\frac{y+1}{m}\right)^{k}\right\}, \quad y \in \mathbf{Z}_{+},$$

where $(m, k) > 0$. The choice of this CDF as the weight function is motivated by its non-negativity and its asymptotic behavior, $w(y) \to 1$ as $k \to \infty$. This weight function plays a crucial role in constructing the WDFW model by modifying the probabilities of the parent distribution to capture complex data behaviors. The PMF of $Y \sim \text{WDFWD}(\alpha, \beta, m, k)$ is given as follows:

$$P_{WDFW}[Y = y; \xi] = \frac{q(y;\xi)}{\sum_{s=0}^{\infty} q(s;\xi)} = \frac{q(y;\xi)}{Q(y;\xi)}. \tag{2}$$

The corresponding CDF and survival function (SF) are expressed as follows:

$$\begin{aligned} F_{WDFW}(y;\xi) &= \frac{\sum_{s=0}^{y} q(s;\xi)}{Q(y;\xi)} = \frac{V(y;\xi)}{Q(y;\xi)}, && (3)\\ S_{WDFW}(y;\xi) &= 1 - F_{WDFW}(y;\xi) + P_{WDFW}[Y = y;\xi]. && (4) \end{aligned}$$

where $q(y;\xi)$ and $Q(y;\xi)$ are defined as follows:

$$\begin{aligned} q(y;\xi) &= w(y) \cdot P[Y = y], \\ Q(y;\xi) &= \sum_{s=0}^{\infty} q(s;\xi), \end{aligned}$$

where $q(y;\xi)$ is computed using the weight function ($w(y)$) and the PMF of the discretized Fréchet–Weibull distribution. Although $Q(y;\xi)$ lacks a closed-form expression, it is finite and can be evaluated numerically. The theory of weighted distributions provides a cohesive framework for addressing model specification and interpreting diverse datasets. Weighted distributions are commonly encountered in fields such as survival analysis, intervention studies, ecology, and biomedicine. A notable aspect of the proposed WDFW distribution is that the introduction of the weight function does not increase the number of parameters relative to the parent distribution, maintaining parsimony. Furthermore, this distribution exhibits diverse hazard rate functions, including increasing, decreasing, and bathtub-shaped behaviors, which are rarely observed in count data models. With support on the set of positive integers, the WDFW distribution proves to be a versatile tool for modeling overdispersed count data, offering a promising alternative for real-world applications requiring such flexibility.

Research on bivariate distributions has been a focal point for statisticians for decades because of their relevance in modeling real-life phenomena involving two dimensions In statistics, bivariate probability distributions are essential for describing scenarios where two interdependent variables are present. Univariate distributions are insufficient for such data, emphasizing the necessity of bivariate models. These models find applications in diverse fields, such as engineering, reliability, meteorology, drought analysis, sports (e.g., goals scored by two competing teams), insurance claims for different causes, symptom types in patients with the same disease, academic performance in two subjects, and many other areas.

Bivariate data naturally occur in many practical settings, driving the development of specialized models to analyze such datasets. These models play a critical role in understanding two-dimensional data structures that arise in a variety of disciplines. The literature contains numerous bivariate extensions of both continuous and discrete univariate distributions. Comprehensive overviews on bivariate distributions are available in the works of Johnson et al. [5] and Balakrishnan and Lai [6], which focus on discrete and continuous distributions, respectively. For continuous bivariate distributions, significant contributions include studies by Kundu and Gupta [7], Sarhan et al. [8], El-Sherpieny [9], Wagner and Artur [10], Balakrishnan and Shiji [11], and El-Gohary et al. [12]. Recent advancements include the bivariate Weibull distribution by Hiba [13], the bivariate exponentiated extended Weibull distribution by Rasool and Akbar [14], the bivariate Gumbel-G family of distributions, and the bivariate odd Weibull-G family of distributions introduced by Eliwa and El-Morshedy [15].

Detailed surveys on discrete bivariate distributions are provided by Kocherlakota and Kocherlakota [16] and Johnson et al. [5]. Further contributions can be found in the works of Basu and Dhar [17], Kumar [18], Kemp [19], Lee and Cha [20], and Nekoukhou and Kundu [21]. Recent developments in discrete bivariate distributions encompass a range of innovative models: the bivariate discrete exponentiated Weibull distribution by El-Morshedy et al. [22] and the bivariate discrete Nadarajah and Haghighi distribution discussed by Ali et al. [23]. Other notable advancements include the bivariate discrete Weibull distribution proposed by Kundu and Nekoukhou [24] and the bivariate discrete modified Weibull distribution developed by Shibu and Beegum [25].

This paper introduces a new flexible discrete bivariate distribution called the BWDFW distribution, designed for application in various data fields. The proposed discrete bivariate model is constructed using three independent random variables that follow the WDFW distribution. The development of the BWDFW distribution is based on two techniques: the minimum operator and the maximum operator, as outlined by Lee and Cha [20]. The model derived using the minimum operator is denoted as BWDFW-I, while the one based on the maximum operator is referred to as BWDFW-II. The motivation for introducing the BWDFW distribution stems from multiple considerations:

1. The proposed distribution is a bivariate extension of the WDFW distribution, offering a robust framework for modeling dispersion phenomena and addressing complex real-life discrete datasets.
2. The joint PMF of the proposed model exhibits remarkable flexibility, allowing for diverse shapes influenced by parameter values. This adaptability makes it suitable for evaluating asymmetric data under various kurtosis structures.
3. The joint HRF and its marginals of the proposed distribution are WDFW distributions, enabling the analysis of various hazard rate functions, such as increasing, decreasing, and bathtub-shaped rates, in discrete settings. This capability supports the comprehensive modeling of diverse data types.
4. The BWDFW distribution possesses positive quadrant dependence, a critical property for modeling interdependencies in bivariate data. This characteristic enhances its relevance in applications requiring the joint modeling of correlated phenomena.
5. The straightforward generation mechanism of the BWDFW distribution facilitates simulation studies, while its versatility makes it applicable to a wide range of fields, including engineering, reliability, and social sciences.

This paper is structured as follows: Section 2 explores the two primary methods for generating discrete bivariate distributions: the minimum operator and the maximum operator. Section 3 introduces the BWDFW distributions, derived using both operators, leading to the BWDFW-I and BWDFW-II models. The examination of positive quadrant dependence is presented in Section 4. Section 5 derives various moments, using the joint probability-generating function. The maximum likelihood estimation method for the model's unknown parameters is discussed in Section 6, with simulation results presented in Section 7. In Section 8, the application of the BWDFW-I and BWDFW-II models to two bivariate count datasets illustrates their superiority over four alternative bivariate distributions. Finally, Section 9 summarizes the key findings, and Section 10 outlines potential future research directions.

2. Construction of a Bivariate Distribution

Consider three independent discrete random variables, U_1, U_2, and U_3, with probability mass functions $f_1(y), f_2(y)$, and $f_3(y)$, respectively. Their corresponding cumulative distribution functions and survival functions are denoted by $F_1(y), F_2(y), F_3(y)$ and $S_1(y), S_2(y), S_3(y)$, respectively. The construction of a bivariate distribution can be achieved using the minimum and maximum operators. Specifically, the minimum operator utilizes the SF of the baseline distribution, while the maximum operator employs the CDF.

2.1. The Minimum Operator

Now consider the following six mutually exclusive cases that encompass all the possible outcomes regarding U_1, U_2, and U_3:

Case 1: $\{U_2 < U_1 \leq U_3\}$, Case 2: $\{U_2 < U_3 < U_1\}$, Case 3: $\{U_1 < U_2 \leq U_3\}$,
Case 4: $\{U_1 < U_3 < U_2\}$, Case 5: $\{U_3 \leq U_1, U_2\}$, Case 6: $\{U_2 = U_1 < U_3\}$.

Theorem 1. *Let U_1, U_2, U_3 be three independent baseline random variables. If $Y_1 = \min\{U_1, U_3\}$ and $Y_2 = \min\{U_2, U_3\}$ then the joint probability mass function is given by*

$$f(y_1, y_2) = \begin{cases} f_2(y_2)\{f_1(y_1)\, S_3(y_1 - 1) + f_3(y_1)\, S_1(y_1)\} & ; y_1 > y_2, \\ f_1(y_1)\{f_2(y_2)\, S_3(y_2 - 1) + f_3(y_2)\, S_2(y_2)\} & ; y_1 < y_2, \\ f_3(y)\, S_2(y-1)\, S_1(y-1) + f_1(y)\, f_2(y)\, S_3(y) & ; y_1 = y_2 = y, \end{cases} \tag{5}$$

where $f_i(.)$ and $S_i(.)$ are the PMF and SF of the baseline random variable.

Proof. To obtain the joint PMF of (Y_1, Y_2), we need to consider the six mutually exclusive subcases, as mentioned in Section 2.1.

Case 1: $y_1 > y_2$

Here, we focus on the relation $Y_1 = min\{U_1, U_3\}$. The value of Y_1 can be determined by U_1 or solely by U_3. Thus, we follow subcases 1 and 2. Also, these two cases are mutually exclusive. First, when the value of Y_1 is determined by U_1, we have subcase 1, therefore

$$\begin{aligned} P[Y_1 = y_1, Y_2 = y_2] &= P(U_1 = y_1, U_2 = y_2, U_3 \geq y_1) \\ &= f_1(y_1)\, f_2(y_2)\, S_3(y_1 - 1). \end{aligned} \tag{6}$$

Second, when the value of Y_1 is determined by U_3, we have subcase 2, therefore

$$\begin{aligned} P[Y_1 = y_1, Y_2 = y_2] &= P(U_3 = y_1, U_2 = y_2, U_1 \geq y_1) \\ &= f_3(y_1)\, f_2(y_2)\, S_1(y_1). \end{aligned} \tag{7}$$

Because subcases 1 and 2 are mutually exclusive, we obtain the desirable result by combining Equations (6) and (7).

Case 2: $y_2 > y_1$

In this case, we focus on the relation $Y_2 = min\{U_2, U_3\}$. The value of Y_2 can be determined by U_2 or solely by U_3. Here, we follow subcases 3 and 4. Proceeding similarly as in case 1, we obtain

$$\begin{aligned} P[Y_1 = y_1, Y_2 = y_2] &= P(U_2 = y_2, U_1 = y_1, U_3 \geq y_2) + P(U_3 = y_2, U_1 = y_1, U_2 > y_2) \\ &= f_2(y_2)\, f_1(y_1)\, S_3(y_2 - 1) + f_3(y_2)\, f_1(y_1)\, S_2(y_2). \end{aligned} \tag{8}$$

Case 3: $y_1 = y_2 = y$

In this case, the values of Y_1 and Y_2 can be determined by U_3 or solely by (U_1, U_2). Here, we follow subcases 5 and 6, such that

$$\begin{aligned} P[Y_1 = y_1, Y_2 = y_2] &= P(U_3 = y, U_2 \geq y, U_1 \geq y) + P(U_1 = y, U_2 = y, U_3 > y) \\ &= f_3(y)\, S_2(y-1)\, S_1(y-1) + f_1(y)\, f_2(y)\, S_3(y). \end{aligned} \tag{9}$$

Hence, the result. □

The concept of the minimum operator has several applications in statistics. For example, in lifetime modeling, an organism may die because of one of two distinct causes: Cause I or Cause II. Denote the times to death of Organisms 1 and 2 from Cause I by U_1 and U_2, respectively. Assume that Cause II represents a shared fatal environmental factor, causing both organisms to die simultaneously while exposed to the same environment. In such a scenario, the random variable U_3 is typically employed to represent the time to death resulting from Cause II. The competing risk models ($Y_1 = \min\{U_1, U_3\}$ and $Y_2 = \min\{U_2, U_3\}$) then define the lifespans of the organisms.

2.2. The Maximum Operator

The following six mutually exclusive cases encompass all the possible outcomes regarding U_1, U_2, and U_3:

Subcase 1: $\{U_3 \leq U_2 < U_1\}$, Subcase 2: $\{U_2 < U_3 < U_1\}$, Subcase 3: $\{U_1 < U_3 < U_2\}$,
Subcase 4: $\{U_3 \leq U_1 < U_2\}$, Subcase 5: $\{U_1, U_2 \leq U_3\}$, Subcase 6: $\{U_3 < U_1 = U_2\}$.

Theorem 2. *For U_1, U_2, U_3 as three independent baseline random variables, if $Y_1 = \max\{U_1, U_3\}$ and $Y_2 = \max\{U_2, U_3\}$ then the joint probability mass function is given by*

$$f(y_1, y_2) = \begin{cases} f_1(y_1)\{f_2(y_2)\, F_3(y_2) + f_3(y_2)\, F_2(y_2 - 1)\}, & y_1 > y_2, \\ f_2(y_2)\{f_1(y_1)\, F_3(y_1) + f_3(y_1)\, F_1(y_1 - 1)\}, & y_1 < y_2, \\ f_3(y)\, F_2(y)\, F_1(y) + f_1(y)\, f_2(y)\, F_3(y-1), & y_1 = y_2 = y, \end{cases} \tag{10}$$

where $f_i(.)$ and $F_i(.)$ represent the PMF and CDF of the baseline random variable, respectively.

Proof. The joint probability mass function of (Y_1, Y_2) is obtained by analyzing the six mutually exclusive subcases outlined in Section 2.2.

Case 1: $y_1 > y_2$

The relationship $Y_1 = \max\{U_1, U_3\}$ is considered. The probability $P[Y_1 = y_1, Y_2 = y_2]$ depends on subcases 1 and 2:

$$\begin{aligned} P[Y_1 = y_1, Y_2 = y_2] &= P(U_1 = y_1, U_2 = y_2, U_3 \leq y_2) + P(U_1 = y_1, U_3 = y_2, U_2 \leq y_2) \\ &= f_1(y_1)\, f_2(y_2)\, F_3(y_2) + f_1(y_1)\, f_3(y_2)\, F_2(y_2 - 1). \end{aligned} \tag{11}$$

Case 2: $y_2 > y_1$

This case follows subcases 3 and 4. Using a similar approach as that in Case 1:

$$\begin{aligned} P[Y_1 = y_1, Y_2 = y_2] &= P(U_1 = y_1, U_2 = y_2, U_3 \leq y_1) + P(U_3 = y_1, U_2 = y_2, U_1 < y_1) \\ &= f_1(y_1)\, f_2(y_2)\, F_3(y_1) + f_3(y_1)\, f_2(y_2)\, F_1(y_1 - 1). \end{aligned} \tag{12}$$

Case 3: $y_1 = y_2 = y$

Subcases 5 and 6 are relevant here, leading to

$$\begin{aligned} P[Y_1 = y_1, Y_2 = y_2] &= P(U_3 = y, U_1 \leq y, U_2 \leq y) + P(U_1 = y, U_2 = y, U_3 < y) \\ &= f_3(y)\, F_1(y)\, F_2(y) + f_1(y)\, f_2(y)\, F_3(y-1). \end{aligned} \tag{13}$$

This completes the proof. □

The maximal-operator-based construct can have meaningful statistical applications. For example, consider a scenario where an organism dies if its stress level exceeds a certain threshold. The stress levels U_1 and U_2 represent the separate, independent stresses experienced by Organisms 1 and 2. Additionally, both organisms are subjected to a common stress level (U_3). Then, $Y_1 = \max\{U_1, U_3\}$ and $Y_2 = \max\{U_2, U_3\}$ describe the dependent stress levels of the two organisms. The joint distribution of (Y_1, Y_2) models the dependent joint life distribution of these organisms.

3. The Bivariate Weighted Discretized Fréchet–Weibull Distribution

3.1. The BWDFW Model Constructed Using the Minimum Operator

Suppose $U_1 \sim$ WDFW (α, β_1, m, k), $U_2 \sim$ WDFW(α, β_2, m, k), and $U_3 \sim$ WDFW (α, β_3, m, k), and these random variables are independently distributed. Define $Y_1 = \min\{U_1, U_3\}$ and $Y_2 = \min\{U_2, U_3\}$. Then, the bivariate vector $\mathbf{Y} = (Y_1, Y_2)$ follows a BWDFW distribution with the parameter vector $\Omega = (\alpha, \beta_1, \beta_2, \beta_3, m, k)^\top$. This bivariate discrete distribution is denoted by BWDFW$(\alpha, \beta_1, \beta_2, \beta_3, m, k)$. The distribution BWDFW constructed using the minimum operator is referred to as the BWDFW-I model. The joint PMF of (Y_1, Y_2) is expressed as

$$\begin{aligned} f_{Y_1,Y_2}(y_1, y_2; \Omega) &= P[Y_1 = y_1, Y_2 = y_2; \Omega] \\ &= \begin{cases} f_1(y_1, y_2; \Omega), & y_1 > y_2, \\ f_2(y_1, y_2; \Omega), & y_1 < y_2, \\ f_3(y; \Omega), & y_1 = y_2 = y, \end{cases} \end{aligned} \tag{14}$$

where the terms are defined as

$$\begin{aligned} f_1(y_1, y_2; \Omega) &= f_2(y_2)\{f_1(y_1)\, S_3(y_1 - 1) + f_3(y_1)\, S_1(y_1)\}, \\ f_2(y_1, y_2; \Omega) &= f_1(y_1)\{f_2(y_2)\, S_3(y_2 - 1) + f_3(y_2)\, S_2(y_2)\}, \\ f_3(y; \Omega) &= f_3(y)\, S_2(y-1)\, S_1(y-1) + f_1(y)\, f_2(y)\, S_3(y), \end{aligned}$$

where $f_i(\cdot)$ and $S_i(\cdot)$ represent the PMF and SF of $U_i \sim$ WDFW(α, β_i, m, k).

3.1.1. The Joint SF of the BWDFW-I Model

The joint SF of (Y_1, Y_2) is given by

$$\begin{aligned} S_{Y_1,Y_2}(y_1, y_2; \Omega) &= P[Y_1 > y_1, Y_2 > y_2; \Omega] \\ &= \begin{cases} S_1(y_1, y_2; \Omega), & y_1 > y_2, \\ S_2(y_1, y_2; \Omega), & y_2 > y_1, \\ S_3(y; \Omega), & y_1 = y_2 = y, \end{cases} \end{aligned} \tag{15}$$

where the terms are defined as follows:

$$\begin{aligned} S_1(y_1, y_2; \Omega) &= S_1(y_1)\, S_2(y_2)\, S_3(y_1), \\ S_2(y_1, y_2; \Omega) &= S_1(y_1)\, S_2(y_2)\, S_3(y_2), \\ S_3(y; \Omega) &= S_1(y)\, S_2(y)\, S_3(y). \end{aligned}$$

$S_i(\cdot)$ denotes the SF of $U_i \sim \text{WDFW}(\alpha, \beta_i, m, k)$. From the joint SF, the marginal SF is derived as

$$S_{Y_i}(y_i) = S_i(y_i)\, S_3(y_i), \quad i = 1, 2. \tag{16}$$

The corresponding marginal PMF is specified as

$$\begin{aligned} f_{Y_i}(y_i) &= S_{Y_i}(y_i) - S_{Y_i}(y_i + 1) \\ &= f_i(y_i)\, S_3(y_i + 1) + f_3(y_i)\, S_i(y_i), \quad y_i \geq 0,\, i = 1, 2, \end{aligned} \tag{17}$$

where $f_i(\cdot)$ and $S_i(\cdot)$ denote the PMF and SF of $U_i \sim \text{WDFW}(\alpha, \beta_i, m, k)$. Figures 1 and 2 present scatter plots of the joint PMF and joint SF of the BWDFW-I model for various parameter values $(\alpha, \beta_1, \beta_2, \beta_3, m, k)$.

The PMF of the BWDFW-I model exhibits versatility in addressing and analyzing a broad range of data types. This model is particularly effective in representing data with varying distributional characteristics, including unimodal and multimodal structures, while accommodating asymmetry in the shape of the distribution. Such flexibility is critical in applications where data do not conform to standard symmetric patterns or exhibit multiple peaks, which are commonly observed in real-world scenarios across diverse fields.

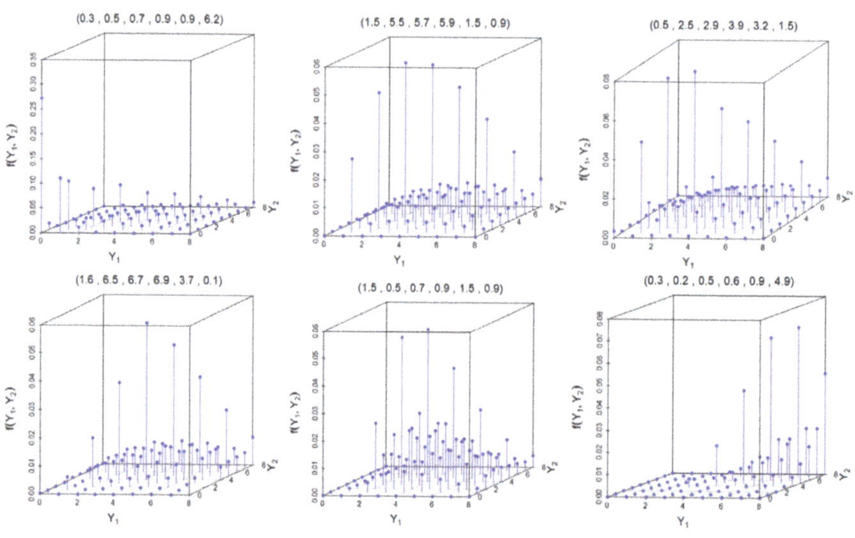

Figure 1. The scatter plots of the joint PMF of the BWDFW-I model for different parameter values $(\alpha, \beta_1, \beta_2, \beta_3, m, k)$.

Moreover, the BWDFW-I model provides a robust framework for handling specialized data scenarios, such as zero-inflated datasets with an excess of zero observations. This feature is crucial in many practical settings, including medical studies, ecological data, or quality-control processes, where zero inflation arises naturally because of underlying phenomena. Additionally, the model is equally adept at analyzing non-inflated datasets, thereby covering the entire spectrum of possible data structures. Another significant advantage of this model is its ability to perform reliably in the presence of outliers or extreme values. Such outliers often distort traditional analyses, leading to biased or misleading conclusions. The BWDFW-I model, with its inherent flexibility and well-defined mathematical structure, offers robust tools for mitigating the impacts of these anomalies. Consequently, it serves as an ideal choice for applications requiring robust statistical modeling under complex conditions, ensuring reliable insights, even in challenging datasets.

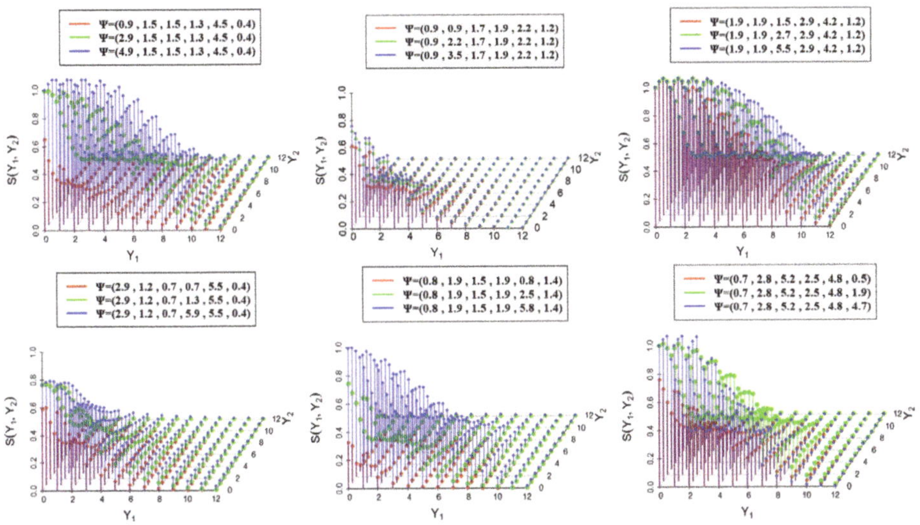

Figure 2. The scatter plots of the joint SF of the BWDFW-I model for different parameter values $(\alpha, \beta_1, \beta_2, \beta_3, m, k)$.

3.1.2. The Joint CDF of the BWDFW-I Model

The joint CDF, (Y_1, Y_2), of the BWDFW-I model can be expressed using the relation

$$F_{Y_1,Y_2}(y_1, y_2) = F_{Y_1}(y_1) + F_{Y_2}(y_2) + S_{Y_1,Y_2}(y_1, y_2) - 1, \tag{18}$$

where $F_{Y_1}(y_1)$ and $F_{Y_2}(y_2)$ represent the marginal CDFs Y_1 and Y_2, respectively, and $S_{Y_1,Y_2}(y_1, y_2)$ denotes the joint SF (Y_1, Y_2) of the BWDFW-I model. The explicit form of the joint CDF, $F_{Y_1,Y_2}(y_1, y_2)$, of the BWDFW-I model is given by

$$F_{Y_1,Y_2}(y_1, y_2; \Omega) \quad = \quad \begin{cases} F_1(y_1, y_2; \Omega), & y_1 > y_2, \\ F_2(y_1, y_2; \Omega), & y_2 > y_1, \\ F_3(y; \Omega), & y_1 = y_2 = y, \end{cases}$$

where F_1, F_2, and F_3 represent different components of the joint CDF, depending on the relative magnitudes of y_1 and y_2. The first and second terms in Equation (18), corresponding to the marginal CDFs Y_1 and Y_2, are expressed as

$$F_{Y_i}(y_i) = 1 - S_{Y_i}(y_i) = 1 - \{S_i(y_i)\, S_3(y_i)\}, \quad i = 1, 2,$$

where $S_i(\cdot)$ is the SF of $U_i \sim \text{WDFW}(\alpha, \beta_i, m, k)$.

3.1.3. The Joint HRF of the BWDFW-I Model

The joint HRF (Y_1, Y_2), denoted by $h(y_1, y_2)$, can be expressed in terms of the joint PMF, $f(y_1, y_2)$, and the joint survival function (SF), $S(y_1, y_2)$, as follows:

$$h(y_1, y_2) = \frac{f(y_1, y_2)}{S(y_1, y_2)}.$$

For the BWDFW-I model, the joint HRF, $h_{Y_1,Y_2}(y_1, y_2; \Omega)$, is defined piecewise based on the relationship between y_1 and y_2:

$$h_{Y_1,Y_2}(y_1, y_2; \Omega) = \begin{cases} h_1(y_1, y_2; \Omega), & y_1 > y_2, \\ h_2(y_1, y_2; \Omega), & y_2 > y_1, \\ h_3(y; \Omega), & y_1 = y_2 = y. \end{cases} \tag{19}$$

The terms $h_1(y_1, y_2; \Omega)$, $h_2(y_1, y_2; \Omega)$, and $h_3(y; \Omega)$ are further specified as follows:

$$h_i(y_1, y_2; \Omega) = \frac{f_i(y_1, y_2; \Omega)}{S_i(y_1, y_2; \Omega)}, \quad (i = 1, 2),$$

and

$$h_3(y; \Omega) = \frac{f_3(y; \Omega)}{S_3(y; \Omega)},$$

where $f_i(y_1, y_2; \Omega)$ and $S_i(y_1, y_2; \Omega)$ represent the PMF and SF for the corresponding components, as defined in Equation (14) and Equation (15), respectively. The various shapes of the joint HRF of the BWDFW-I model for various selections of model parameters are visually illustrated as scatter plots in Figure 3. This demonstrates the adaptability of the BWDFW-I distribution.

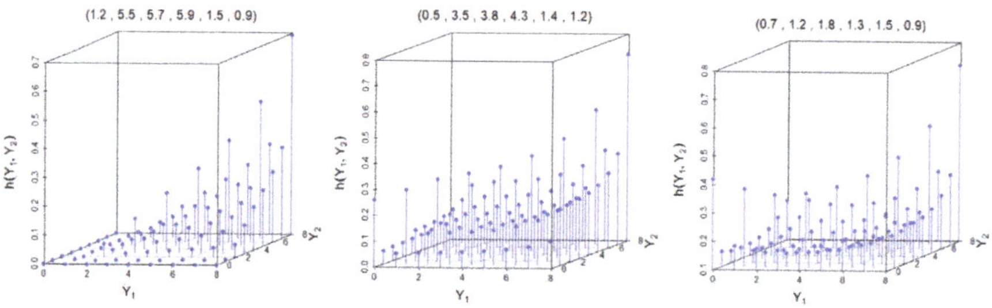

Figure 3. The scatter plots of the joint HRF of the BWDFW-I model for different parameter values $(\alpha, \beta_1, \beta_2, \beta_3, m, k)$.

3.1.4. The Joint Reversed HRF of the BWDFW-I Model

The joint reversed hazard rate function (RHRF), (Y_1, Y_2), of the BWDFW-I model is defined as follows:

$$h^*_{Y_1,Y_2}(y_1, y_2; \Omega) = \begin{cases} h^*_1(y_1, y_2; \Omega), & y_1 > y_2, \\ h^*_2(y_1, y_2; \Omega), & y_2 > y_1, \\ h^*_3(y; \Omega), & y_1 = y_2 = y. \end{cases} \tag{20}$$

The components of the RHRF, $h^*_1(y_1, y_2; \Omega)$, $h^*_2(y_1, y_2; \Omega)$, and $h^*_3(y; \Omega)$, are given by

$$h^*_1(y_1, y_2; \Omega) = \frac{f_1(y_1, y_2; \Omega)}{F_1(y_1, y_2; \Omega)}, \quad h^*_2(y_1, y_2; \Omega) = \frac{f_2(y_1, y_2; \Omega)}{F_2(y_1, y_2; \Omega)}, \quad \text{and} \quad h^*_3(y; \Omega) = \frac{f_3(y; \Omega)}{F_3(y; \Omega)},$$

where $f_i(y_1, y_2; \Omega)$ and $F_i(y_1, y_2; \Omega)$ are the joint PMF and joint CDF of the BWDFW-I model, as defined in Equation (14) and Equation (18), respectively. The joint HRF and the joint RHRF of a bivariate model differ in their conditional interpretations and applications. The joint HRF measures the likelihood of the event pair (Y_1, Y_2) occurring at specific values, given that no event has occurred up to those values, focusing on the "future" conditional risk. In contrast, the joint RHRF assesses the likelihood of the event pair (Y_1, Y_2) occurring at specific values, given that the event has already occurred at or before those values, emphasizing the "past" conditional risk. The joint HRF is commonly used in survival analysis and reliability studies to predict future events, while the joint RHRF is relevant in reversed reliability analysis or retrospective studies to understand the likelihood of past events. These measures provide complementary perspectives, with the joint HRF focusing on the forward-looking risk and the joint RHRF on the retrospective likelihood.

3.2. The BWDFW Model Constructed Using the Maximum Operator

This section involves constructing and discussing the BWDFW distribution, using the maximum operator. Let us define $Y_1 = max\{U_1, U_3\}$ and $Y_2 = max\{U_2, U_3\}$, where $U_i \sim WDFW(\alpha, \beta_i, m, k)\ ;(i = 1,2,3)$, are independently distributed. By definition, the bivariate vector $\mathbf{Y} = (Y_1, Y_2)$ has a BWDFW distribution with the parameter vector $\Omega = (\alpha, \beta_1, \beta_2, \beta_3, m, k)^T$. We denote the BWDFW distribution constructed using the maximum operator as BWDFW-II. Then, the joint PMF of $(Y_1, Y_2) \sim$ BWDFW-II is given by

$$f_{Y_1,Y_2}(y_1, y_2; \Omega) = P[Y_1 = y_1, Y_2 = y_2; \Omega] = \begin{cases} f_1(y_1, y_2; \Omega) & ; y_1 > y_2, \\ f_2(y_1, y_2; \Omega) & ; y_1 < y_2, \\ f_3(y; \Omega) & ; y_1 = y_2 = y, \end{cases} \tag{21}$$

where

$$\begin{aligned} f_1(y_1, y_2; \Omega) &= f_1(y_1)\{f_2(y_2)\, F_3(y_2) + f_3(y_2)\, F_2(y_2 - 1)\}\ ;\ y_1 > y_2, \\ f_2(y_1, y_2; \Omega) &= f_2(y_2)\{f_1(y_1)\, F_3(y_1) + f_3(y_1)\, F_1(y_1 - 1)\}\ ;\ y_1 < y_2, \\ f_3(y; \Omega) &= f_3(y)\, F_2(y)\, F_1(y) + f_1(y)\, f_2(y)\, F_3(y - 1)\ ,\ y_1 = y_2 = y, \end{aligned}$$

where $f_i(.)$ and $F_i(.)$ are the PMF and CDF of $U_i \sim$ WDFW(α, β_i, m, k).

3.2.1. The Joint CDF of the BWDFW-II Model

The joint CDF of the $(Y_1, Y_2) \sim$ BWDFW-II model is given by

$$\begin{aligned} F_{Y_1,Y_2}(y_1, y_2; \Omega) &= P[Y_1 \leq y_1, Y_2 \leq y_2; \Omega] \\ &= P[max\{U_1, U_3\} \leq y_1, max\{U_2, U_3\} \leq y_2; \Omega] \\ &= \begin{cases} F_1(y_1, y_2) & ; y_1 > y_2, \\ F_2(y_1, y_2) & ; y_2 > y_1, \\ F_3(y) & ; y_1 = y_2 = y. \end{cases} \end{aligned} \tag{22}$$

$F_1(y_1, y_2), F_1(y_1, y_2)$, and $F_3(y)$ are defined as follows:

$$\begin{aligned} F_1(y_1, y_2) &= F_1(y_1)\, F_2(y_2)\, F_3(y_2), \\ F_2(y_1, y_2) &= F_1(y_1)\, F_2(y_2)\, F_3(y_1), \\ F_3(y) &= F_1(y)\, F_2(y)\, F_3(y), \end{aligned}$$

where $F_i(.)$ is the cumulative distribution function of $U_i \sim \text{WDFWD}(\alpha, \beta_i, m, k)$, as defined in Equation (3). It is evident that the marginal CDF can be derived from the joint CDF as follows:

$$F_{Y_i}(y_i) = F_i(y_i)\, F_3(y_i) \quad ; \; i = 1, 2. \tag{23}$$

The corresponding marginal PMF can be specified as

$$\begin{aligned} f_{Y_i}(y_i) &= F_{Y_i}(y_i + 1) - F_{Y_i}(y_i) \\ &= F_i(y_i + 1)\, F_3(y_i + 1) + F_i(y_i)\, F_3(y_i) \\ &= f_i(y_i)\, F_3(y_i) + f_3(y_i)\, F_i(y_i + 1) \quad ; \; y_i \geq 0 \; (i = 1, 2), \end{aligned} \tag{24}$$

where $f_i(.)$ and $F_i(.)$ are the PMF and CDF of $U_i \sim \text{WDFW}(\alpha, \beta_i, m, k)$. Figures 4 and 5 represent the scatter plots of the joint PMF and joint CDF of the BWDFW-II model for different parameter values $(\alpha, \beta_1, \beta_2, \beta_3, m, k)$. These plots reveal that the joint PMF of the BWDFW-II model exhibits considerable flexibility, assuming diverse shapes based on the parameter values $(\alpha, \beta_1, \beta_2, \beta_3, m, k)$. Notably, the joint mass can display both long left and long right tails, highlighting its adaptability in capturing various distributional behaviors. This flexibility extends to scenarios involving zero-inflated and non-zero-inflated structures, accommodating excess zeros or the absence thereof in the data. The plots of the CDF illustrate the adaptability of the joint CDF through its wide range of possible shapes, further emphasizing the model's robustness in handling different data patterns, including those with and without zero-inflation.

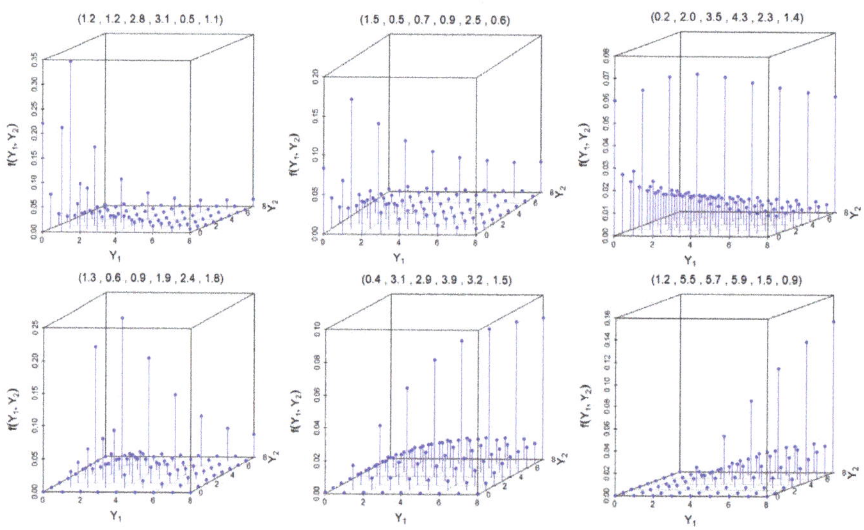

Figure 4. The scatter plots of the joint PMF of the BWDFW-II model for different parameter values $(\alpha, \beta_1, \beta_2, \beta_3, m, k)$.

3.2.2. The Joint SF of the BWDFW-II Model

The joint SF, (Y_1, Y_2), of the BWDFW-II model can be derived using the following relation:

$$S_{Y_1,Y_2}(y_1, y_2) = 1 - F_{Y_1}(y_1) - F_{Y_2}(y_2) + F_{Y_1,Y_2}(y_1, y_2). \tag{25}$$

Thus, the joint SF of the BWDFW-II model can be formulated as

$$S_{Y_1,Y_2}(y_1,y_2;\Omega) = \begin{cases} S_1(y_1,y_2;\Omega) & ;y_1 > y_2, \\ S_2(y_1,y_2;\Omega) & ;y_2 > y_1, \\ S_3(y;\Omega) & ;y_1 = y_2 = y. \end{cases}$$

The second and third terms of Equation (25) represent the marginal cumulative distribution functions (CDFs) Y_1 and Y_2, respectively, as defined in Equation (23). The fourth term, $F_{Y_1,Y_2}(y_1,y_2)$, corresponds to the joint CDF of the BWDFW-II model. Other reliability characteristics, such as the joint hazard rate function and the joint reversed hazard rate function of the BWDFW-II model, can be expressed analogously to those of the BWDFW-I model but are formulated based on Equations (21), (22), and (25), respectively.

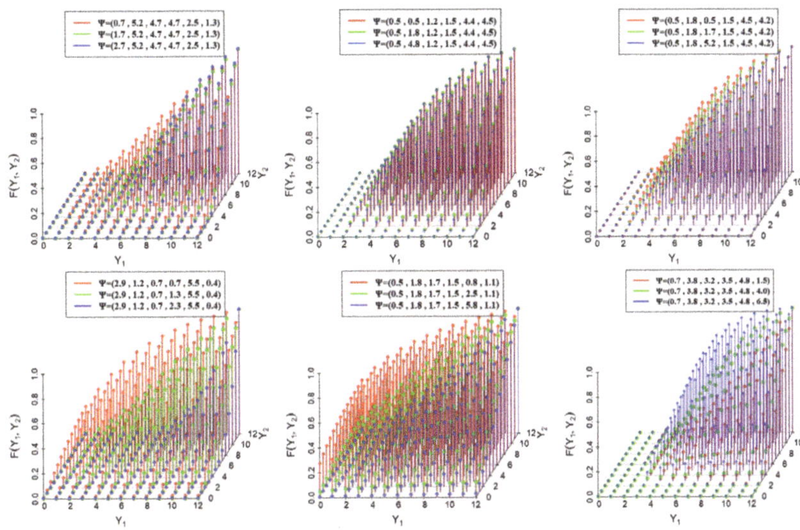

Figure 5. The scatter plots of the joint CDF of the BWDFW-II model for different parameter values $(\alpha, \beta_1, \beta_2, \beta_3, m, k)$.

Figure 6 presents scatter plots that illustrate the joint HRF of the BWDFW-II model in various parameter configurations. The different shapes of these joint HRF information graphics highlight the flexibility of the model.

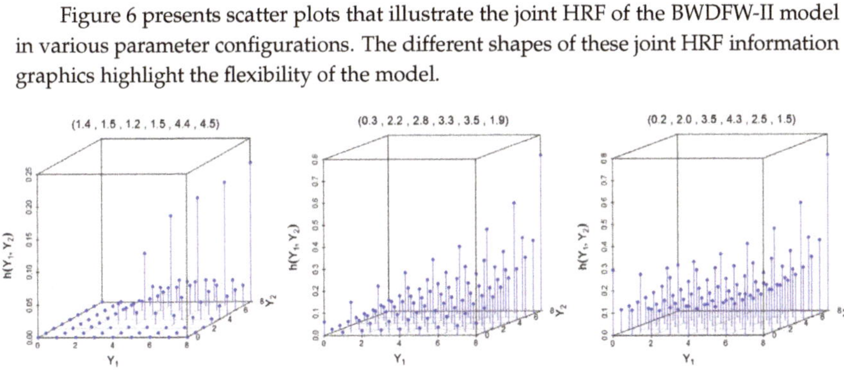

Figure 6. The scatter plots of the joint HRF of the BWDFW-II model for different parameter values $(\alpha, \beta_1, \beta_2, \beta_3, m, k)$.

4. Positive Quadrant Dependence

Positive quadrant dependence (PQD) is a concept that characterizes the relationship between two random variables when they tend to be simultaneously small or large. It represents a form of dependence where the probability of both random variables being small or large together is at least as high as it would be if they were independent. PQD implies that when one variable takes on a higher value, the likelihood of the other variable also being higher increases. Although PQD indicates positive dependence between the bivariate random variables Y_1 and Y_2, it does not necessarily imply that their correlation is always positive. PQD is particularly important in areas such as finance and reliability analysis, as it helps in understanding the dependencies between variables, which is crucial for effective modeling and prediction. In this section, we demonstrate that both the BWDFW-I and BWDFW-II models exhibit PQD. As a result, a bivariate random pair $((Y_1, Y_2))$ from either the BWDFW-I or BWDFW-II model shows positive dependence.

Theorem 3. *If the $(Y_1, Y_2) \sim$ BWDFW-I model, with parameters $(\alpha, \beta_1, \beta_2, \beta_3, m, k)$, such that $Y_1 = min\{U_1, U_3\}$ and $Y_1 = min\{U_1, U_3\}$, where U_1, U_2, and U_3 are the baseline random variables, then Y_1 and Y_2 are PQD.*

Proof. Let $U_i \sim$ WDFW (α, β_i, m, k) be the baseline distribution for Y_1 and Y_2, such that $Y_1 = min\{U_1, U_3\}$ and $Y_1 = min\{U_1, U_3\}$. Then, by definition, $(Y_1, Y_2) \sim$ the BWDFW-I model, with the parameter set $(\alpha, \beta_1, \beta_2, \beta_3, m, k)$. And to prove that Y_1 and Y_2 are PQD, it is sufficient to prove the inequality

$$P(Y_1 > y_1,\ Y_2 > y_2) \ \geq\ P(Y_1 > y_1)\ P(Y_2 > y_2)\ ;\ \forall\ y_1, y_2. \tag{26}$$

Considering the right-hand side of Equation (26),

$$\begin{aligned} P(Y_1 > y_1)\ P(Y_2 > y_2) &= S_1(y_1)\ S_2(y_2) \\ &= S_1(y_1)\ S_3(y_1)\ S_2(y_2)\ S_3(y_2). \end{aligned} \tag{27}$$

Now, for the left-hand side of Equation (26), we need to consider two cases as follows:

Case 1: $y_1 \geq y_2$

$$\begin{aligned} P(Y_1 > y_1,\ Y_2 > y_2) &= S_{Y_1,Y_2}(y_1, y_2)\Big|_{y_1 \geq y_2} \\ &= S_1(y_1)\ S_2(y_2)\ S_3(y_1). \end{aligned} \tag{28}$$

Case 2: $y_1 < y_2$

$$\begin{aligned} P(Y_1 > y_1,\ Y_2 > y_2) &= S_{Y_1,Y_2}(y_1, y_2)\Big|_{y_2 > y_1} \\ &= S_1(y_1)\ S_2(y_2)\ S_3(y_2). \end{aligned} \tag{29}$$

It is clearly seen that Equation (28) $\geq$ Equation (27), and Equation (29) $\geq$ Equation (27). Thus, the result. □

Theorem 4. *If $(Y_1, Y_2) \sim$ the BWDFW-II model, such that $Y_1 = max\{U_1, U_3\}$ and $Y_1 = max\{U_1, U_3\}$, where U_1, U_2, and U_3 are the baseline random variables, then Y_1 and Y_2 are PQD.*

Proof. If $(Y_1, Y_2) \sim$ the BWDFW-II model, with parameters $(\alpha, \beta_1, \beta_2, \beta_3, m, k)$, then, to prove that Y_1 and Y_2 are PQD, it is sufficient to prove the inequality

$$P(Y_1 \leq y_1,\ Y_2 \leq y_2)\ \geq\ P(Y_1 \leq y_1)\ P(Y_2 \leq y_2)\ ;\ \forall\ y_1, y_2. \tag{30}$$

Considering the right-hand side of Equation (30),

$$P(Y_1 \leq y_1)\ P(Y_2 \leq y_2) = F_1(y_1)\ F_3(y_1)\ F_2(y_2)\ F_3(y_2). \tag{31}$$

Now, for the left-hand side of Equation (30), we need to consider two cases as follows:

Case 1: $y_1 \leq y_2$

$$P(Y_1 \leq y_1,\ Y_2 \leq y_2) = F_1(y_1)\ F_2(y_2)\ F_3(y_2). \tag{32}$$

Case 2: $y_1 < y_2$

$$P(Y_1 \leq y_1,\ Y_2 \leq y_2) = F_1(y_1)\ F_2(y_2)\ F_3(y_1). \tag{33}$$

It is clearly seen that Equation (32) $\geq$ Equation (31), and Equation (33) $\geq$ Equation (31). Thus, the result. □

5. The Joint Probability-Generating Function Along with Associated Measures

If the bivariate vector, $(Y_1, Y_2), \sim$ the BWDFW-I model with parameter set $(\alpha, \beta_1, \beta_2, \beta_3, m, k)$, then the joint probability-generating function (PGF) of Y_1 and Y_2 for $|t_1| < 1$ and $|t_2| < 1$ can be written as

$$\begin{aligned} G_{Y_1,Y_2}(t_1, t_2) &= E(t_1^{Y_1} t_2^{Y_2}) \\ &= \sum_{j,i=0}^{\infty} P[Y_1 = i, Y_2 = j]\ t_1^i\ t_2^j \\ &= \sum_{j=0}^{\infty} \sum_{i=0}^{j-1} f_1(y_1, y_2; \Omega)\ t_1^i\ t_2^j + \sum_{i=0}^{\infty} \sum_{j=i+1}^{\infty} f_1(y_1, y_2; \Omega)\ t_1^i\ t_2^j \\ &\quad + \sum_{i=0}^{\infty} f_3(y; \Omega)\ t_1^i\ t_2^i \qquad ; \quad |t_1|, |t_2| < 1, \end{aligned} \tag{34}$$

where $f_1(y_1, y_2; \Omega)$, $f_2(y_1, y_2; \Omega)$, and $f_3(y; \Omega)$ are the joint PMF of the BWDFW-I model, as defined in Equation (14).

Similarly, the joint PGF of the BWDFW-II model can also be expressed, where $f_1(y_1, y_2; \Omega)$, $f_2(y_1, y_2; \Omega)$, and $f_3(y; \Omega)$ represent the joint PMF of the BWDFW-II model, as defined in Equation (21). It is widely recognized that the joint PGF serves as a valuable tool for deriving various moments and product moments. Utilizing this joint PGF in the BWDFW-I and BWDFW-II models, different factorial moments, raw moments, and product moments can be represented as infinite series. For a bivariate vector, (Y_1, Y_2), taking the partial derivative of the joint PGF $G_{Y_1,Y_2}(t_1, t_2)$ with respect to t_i for r times gives the rth factorial moment of Y_i (where $i = 1, 2$). This can be expressed as follows:

$$\mu'_{Y_i(r)} = \frac{\partial^r}{\partial t_i^r} G_{Y_1,Y_2}(t_1, t_2)\big|_{t_1=1, t_2=1} \qquad ; i = 1, 2, \tag{35}$$

where $\mu'_{Y_i(r)}$ is the rth factorial moment of Y_i ; $(i = 1, 2)$. Taking the first and second partial derivatives of Equation (35) with respect to "t_i" and substituting in $t_1 = 1$ and $t_2 = 1$, respectively, yields the following relations:

$$\begin{aligned} \mu'_{Y_i(1)} &= \frac{\partial}{\partial t_i} G_{Y_1,Y_2}(t_1,t_2)\big|_{t_1=1,t_2=1} = E(Y_i), \\ \mu'_{Y_i(2)} &= \frac{\partial^2}{\partial t_i^2} G_{Y_1,Y_2}(t_1,t_2)\big|_{t_1=1,t_2=1}. \end{aligned} \tag{36}$$

Similarly, from Equation (35), we can have

$$E(Y_1Y_2) = \frac{\partial^2}{\partial t_1 \partial t_2} G_{Y_1,Y_2}(t_1,t_2)\big|_{t_1=1,t_2=1}.$$

Thus, the variances Y_i $(i = 1, 2)$ and the covariance (Y_1, Y_2) can be obtained using the relations

$$Var(Y_i) = \mu'_{Y_i(2)} + \mu'_{Y_i(1)} - \{\mu'_{Y_i(1)}\}^2, \tag{37}$$

$$Cov(Y_1, Y_2) = E(Y_1Y_2) - \mu'_{Y_1(1)}\, \mu'_{Y_2(1)}. \tag{38}$$

Table 1 presents the descriptive statistics for a randomly selected pair (Y_1, Y_2) generated from the BWDFW-I model, including an analysis of covariance, Pearson's correlation coefficient, Spearman's rho (ρ), and Kendall's tau (τ). Likewise, Table 2 provides the corresponding values for the BWDFW-II model.

From Tables 1 and 2, it is evident that for both the BWDFW-I and BWDFW-II models, the values of covariance, correlation, Spearman's rho, and Kendall's tau are greater than zero. This observation directly reflects the property of the PQD.

Table 1. Some descriptive statistics for the BWDFW-I model.

α	β_1	β_2	β_3	m	k	Cov(Y_1,Y_2)	Cor(Y_1,Y_2)	$\rho(Y_1,Y_2)$	$\tau(Y_1,Y_2)$
0.5						2.39225	0.96608	0.90881	0.87911
0.9	4.5	2.5	6.4	2.5	7.5	0.46123	0.85967	0.82312	0.80758
1.7						0.13837	0.53373	0.50025	0.49463
	1.7					1.07347	0.92541	0.85927	0.83332
0.7	4.5	2.3	6.0	2.7	7.2	1.14286	0.90563	0.81902	0.78072
	6.0					1.18204	0.90642	0.78258	0.74836
		2.5				0.17551	0.61911	0.58162	0.55979
1.8	4.0	4.5	5.2	3.5	6.5	0.12939	0.79906	0.69577	0.68757
		6.0				0.28939	0.82651	0.87992	0.86742
			3.8			0.11673	0.54648	0.53101	0.51852
1.5	5.2	2.4	4.8	2.6	5.1	0.12490	0.51522	0.48029	0.46688
			5.2			0.17551	0.59312	0.52037	0.50695
				2.4		0.29918	0.73049	0.66068	0.64165
1.3	5.4	2.5	3.5	3.5	5.5	0.44898	0.80526	0.74152	0.70841
				4.5		0.78928	0.87736	0.82274	0.78307
					2.5	1.71511	0.96606	0.95796	0.92875
1.7	4.5	3.2	4.2	2.7	4.0	0.33347	0.72678	0.66341	0.63503
					7.2	0.01633	0.14744	0.14744	0.14744

Table 2. Some descriptive statistics for the BWDFW-II model.

α	β_1	β_2	β_3	m	k	$\mathrm{Cov}(Y_1, Y_2)$	$\mathrm{Cor}(Y_1, Y_2)$	$\rho(Y_1, Y_2)$	$\tau(Y_1, Y_2)$
0.6						3.04980	0.98617	0.97905	0.96399
1.3	3.8	5.5	4.2	1.9	5.6	1.56408	0.89377	0.90127	0.89458
1.8						0.53061	0.93037	0.92779	0.92758
	1.5					0.30082	0.82114	0.80861	0.79306
0.8	2.4	4.5	3.4	1.5	6.2	0.37755	0.95183	0.96047	0.95197
	3.2					0.40735	0.97604	0.96826	0.96753
		1.5				0.35918	0.75211	0.69959	0.66731
1.5	0.9	2.7	3.0	2.7	4.1	0.48980	0.88828	0.89514	0.85235
		3.2				0.46939	0.90915	0.93774	0.90086
			1.3			0.18491	0.67127	0.59604	0.58744
1.2	0.9	2.7	2.2	2.5	4.5	0.22908	0.73535	0.63395	0.61371
			2.9			0.23306	0.75522	0.67167	0.65002
				1.5		0.29918	0.73049	0.66068	0.64165
2.2	1.8	1.9	2.8	2.4	3.4	0.44898	0.80526	0.74152	0.70841
				3.3		0.78928	0.87736	0.82274	0.78307
					2.7	0.85878	0.88365	0.84753	0.79743
1.9	1.7	2.3	2.4	2.3	3.5	0.51265	0.82018	0.79669	0.78712
					4.4	0.22082	0.75264	0.76424	0.74579

6. The Maximum Likelihood Estimation

Let us consider a bivariate sample of size n of the form $\{(y_{11}, y_{21}), (y_{12}, y_{22}), \dots, (y_{1n}, y_{2n})\}$ from the BWDFW-I model. Now, to estimate the values of the unknown parameters $(\alpha, \beta_1, \beta_2, \beta_3, m, k)$ of the BWDFW-I model, using the maximum likelihood estimation (MLE) method, let us assume $I_1 = \{y_{1j} < y_{2j}\}$, $I_2 = \{y_{1j} > y_{2j}\}$, and $I_3 = \{y_{1j} = y_{2j} = y_j\}$, such that $I = I_1 \cup I_2 \cup I_3$. Also, let the numbers of elements in I_1, I_2, and I_3 be n_1, n_2, and n_3, respectively, such that $n = n_1 + n_2 + n_3$. Using these notations, for the parameter vector $\Omega = (\alpha, \beta_1, \beta_2, \beta_3, m, k)^T$, the likelihood function of the BWDFW-I model is given by

$$L(\Omega) = \prod_{j=1}^{n_1} f_1(y_{1j}, y_{2j}; \Omega) \prod_{j=1}^{n_2} f_2(y_{1j}, y_{2j}; \Omega) \prod_{j=1}^{n_3} f_3(y_j; \Omega).$$

Then, the log-likelihood function can be formulated as

$$l(\Omega) = \sum_{j=1}^{n_1} \ln f_1(y_{1j}, y_{2j}; \Omega) + \sum_{j=1}^{n_2} \ln f_2(y_{1j}, y_{2j}; \Omega) + \sum_{j=1}^{n_3} \ln f_3(y_j; \Omega), \tag{39}$$

where $f_1(y_{1j}, y_{2j}; \Omega)$, $f_2(y_{1j}, y_{2j}; \Omega)$, and $f_3(y_j; \Omega)$ are the joint PMF cases of the BWDFW-I model, as defined in Equation (14). The MLE of parameters $\alpha, \beta_1, \beta_2, \beta_3, m$, and k can be obtained by solving the partial derivatives of Equation (39) with respect to $\alpha, \beta_1, \beta_2, \beta_3, m$, and k and then equating the results to zero. The partial derivatives are expressed as follows:

$$
\begin{aligned}
\frac{\partial l}{\partial \alpha} &= \frac{\partial l_1}{\partial \alpha}+\frac{\partial l_2}{\partial \alpha}+\frac{\partial l_3}{\partial \alpha},\\
\frac{\partial l_1}{\partial \alpha} &= \sum_{j=1}^{n_1} \psi_1(y_{2j};\alpha,\beta_2,m,k)\Big[\{\psi_1(y_{1j};\alpha,\beta_1,m,k)\times\psi_2(y_{1j}-1;\alpha,\beta_3,m,k)\}\\
&\quad+\{\psi_1(y_{1j};\alpha,\beta_3,m,k)\times\psi_2(y_{1j};\alpha,\beta_1,m,k)\}\Big],\\
\frac{\partial l_2}{\partial \alpha} &= \sum_{j=1}^{n_2} \psi_1(y_{1j};\alpha,\beta_1,m,k)\Big[\{\psi_1(y_{2j};\alpha,\beta_2,m,k)\times\psi_2(y_{2j}-1;\alpha,\beta_3,m,k)\}\\
&\quad+\{\psi_1(y_{2j};\alpha,\beta_3,m,k)\times\psi_2(y_{2j};\alpha,\beta_2,m,k)\}\Big],\\
\frac{\partial l_3}{\partial \alpha} &= \sum_{j=1}^{n_3} \Big[\{\psi_1(y_j;\alpha,\beta_3,m,k)\times\psi_2(y_j-1;\alpha,\beta_2,m,k)\times\psi_2(y_j-1;\alpha,\beta_1,m,k)\}\\
&\quad+\{\psi_1(y_j;\alpha,\beta_1,m,k)\times\psi_1(y_j;\alpha,\beta_2,m,k)\times\psi_2(y_j;\alpha,\beta_3,m,k)\}\Big].
\end{aligned}
$$

$$
\begin{aligned}
\frac{\partial l}{\partial m} &= \frac{\partial l_1}{\partial m}+\frac{\partial l_2}{\partial m}+\frac{\partial l_3}{\partial m},\\
\frac{\partial l_1}{\partial m} &= \sum_{j=1}^{n_1} \Psi_1(y_{2j};\alpha,\beta_2,m,k)\Big[\{\Psi_1(y_{1j};\alpha,\beta_1,m,k)\times\Psi_2(y_{1j}-1;\alpha,\beta_3,m,k)\}\\
&\quad+\{\Psi_1(y_{1j};\alpha,\beta_3,m,k)\times\Psi_2(y_{1j};\alpha,\beta_1,m,k)\}\Big],\\
\frac{\partial l_2}{\partial m} &= \sum_{j=1}^{n_2} \Psi_1(y_{1j};\alpha,\beta_1,m,k)\Big[\{\Psi_1(y_{2j};\alpha,\beta_2,m,k)\times\Psi_2(y_{2j}-1;\alpha,\beta_3,m,k)\}\\
&\quad+\{\Psi_1(y_{2j};\alpha,\beta_3,m,k)\times\Psi_2(y_{2j};\alpha,\beta_2,m,k)\}\Big],\\
\frac{\partial l_3}{\partial m} &= \sum_{j=1}^{n_3} \Big[\{\Psi_1(y_j;\alpha,\beta_3,m,k)\times\Psi_2(y_j-1;\alpha,\beta_2,m,k)\times\Psi_2(y_j-1;\alpha,\beta_1,m,k)\}\\
&\quad+\{\Psi_1(y_j;\alpha,\beta_1,m,k)\times\Psi_1(y_j;\alpha,\beta_2,m,k)\times\Psi_2(y_j;\alpha,\beta_3,m,k)\}\Big].
\end{aligned}
$$

$$
\begin{aligned}
\frac{\partial l}{\partial k} &= \frac{\partial l_1}{\partial k}+\frac{\partial l_2}{\partial k}+\frac{\partial l_3}{\partial k},\\
\frac{\partial l_1}{\partial k} &= \sum_{j=1}^{n_1} \Phi_1(y_{2j};\alpha,\beta_2,m,k)\Big[\{\Phi_1(y_{1j};\alpha,\beta_1,m,k)\times\Phi_2(y_{1j}-1;\alpha,\beta_3,m,k)\}\\
&\quad+\{\Phi_1(y_{1j};\alpha,\beta_3,m,k)\times\Phi_2(y_{1j};\alpha,\beta_1,m,k)\}\Big],\\
\frac{\partial l_2}{\partial k} &= \sum_{j=1}^{n_2} \Phi_1(y_{1j};\alpha,\beta_1,m,k)\Big[\{\Phi_1(y_{2j};\alpha,\beta_2,m,k)\times\Phi_2(y_{2j}-1;\alpha,\beta_3,m,k)\}\\
&\quad+\{\Phi_1(y_{2j};\alpha,\beta_3,m,k)\times\Phi_2(y_{2j};\alpha,\beta_2,m,k)\}\Big],\\
\frac{\partial l_3}{\partial k} &= \sum_{j=1}^{n_3} \Big[\{\Phi_1(y_j;\alpha,\beta_3,m,k)\times\Phi_2(y_j-1;\alpha,\beta_2,m,k)\times\Phi_2(y_j-1;\alpha,\beta_1,m,k)\}\\
&\quad+\{\Phi_1(y_j;\alpha,\beta_1,m,k)\times\Phi_1(y_j;\alpha,\beta_2,m,k)\times\Phi_2(y_j;\alpha,\beta_3,m,k)\}\Big].
\end{aligned}
$$

$\psi_1(y), \psi_2(y), \Psi_1(y), \Psi_2(y), \Phi_1(y)$, and $\Phi_2(y)$ are defined as follows:

$$\begin{aligned}
\psi_1(y;\alpha,\beta_i,m,k) &= \frac{E_i(y_j+1)\,F_i(y_j+1)-E_i(y_j)\,F_i(y_j)}{[G_i(y_j)]^2},\\
\psi_2(y;\alpha,\beta_i,m,k) &= -\,\psi_1(y;\alpha,\beta_i,m,k),\\
\Psi_1(y;\alpha,\beta_i,m,k) &= m^{-1}\frac{A_i(y_j)\,B_i(y_j)}{D_i(y_j)}+\frac{E_i(y_j+1)\,H_i(y_j+1)-E_i(y_j)\,H_i(y_j)}{[G_i(y_j)]^2},\\
\Psi_2(y;\alpha,\beta_i,m,k) &= -\,\Psi_1(y;\alpha,\beta_i,m,k),\\
\Phi_1(y;\alpha,\beta_i,m,k) &= \frac{A_i(y_j)\,B_i(y_j)\,C_i(y_j)}{D_i(y_j)}+\frac{E_i(y_j+1)\,I_i(y_j+1)-E_i(y_j)\,I_i(y_j)}{[G_i(y_j)]^2},\\
\Phi_2(y;\alpha,\beta_i,m,k) &= -\,\Phi_1(y;\alpha,\beta_i,m,k),
\end{aligned}$$

whereas $A_i(y), B_i(y), C_i(y), D_i(y), E_i(y), F_i(y), G_i(y), H_i(y)$, and $I_i(y)$ are defined as follows:

$$\begin{aligned}
A(y_i) &= exp\left\{-(\frac{y_i+1}{m})^k\right\}, & B(y_i) &= (\frac{y_i+1}{m})^k,\\
C(y_i) &= log_e(\frac{y_i+1}{m}), & D(y_i) &= 1-exp\left\{-\left(\frac{y_i+1}{m}\right)^k\right\},\\
E(y_i) &= exp\left\{-\beta^\alpha\left(\frac{m}{y_i}\right)^{\alpha k}\right\}, & F(y_i) &= \left\{-\alpha\beta\left(\frac{m}{y_i}\right)^k\right\}^{\alpha-1},\\
H(y_i) &= -\,\alpha k\beta^\alpha m^{\alpha k-1}y^{-\alpha k}, & I(y_i) &= -\alpha^2\beta^\alpha k\left(\frac{m}{y_i}\right)^{\alpha k-1},
\end{aligned}$$

and

$$G(y_i) = P[Y=y_i] = exp\left\{-\beta^\alpha\left(\frac{m}{y+1}\right)^{\alpha k}\right\} - exp\left\{-\beta^\alpha\left(\frac{m}{y}\right)^{\alpha k}\right\}.$$

These equations are not easy to solve. We need a numerical technique for the maximum likelihood estimators, like the Newton–Raphson method. The log-likelihood function can similarly be expressed for the BWDFW-II model by considering the cases in the joint PMF, as given by Equation (21). For both models, we used the statistical package *"MLE"* in R-programming software Version 5 to obtain the maximum likelihood estimates.

7. Simulation: Behaviors of Estimators

Bivariate discrete data generation is crucial in statistical modeling, particularly for real-world applications in medical, engineering, and reliability studies. The BWDFW-I and BWDFW-II models offer enhanced flexibility in capturing overdispersion, skewness, and dependency structures in discrete count data. To assess the performances of their MLEs, a simulation study was conducted using the *stats4* package version 5 in R. This section describes the data generation process for these models, considering various sample sizes ($n = 50, 80, 120, 150$, and 200). Parameter values ($\alpha, \beta_1, \beta_2, \beta_3, m$, and k) were generated with 1000 replications, demonstrating the models' practical significance.

7.1. Generation Process of Bivariate Discrete Data

The generation of bivariate discrete data from BWDFW-I and BWDFW-II follows a structured methodology:

Step 1: Define the marginal distributions. Both BWDFW-I and BWDFW-II versions define marginal probability mass functions (PMFs) for each variable.

Step 2: Construct the bivariate joint distribution. To introduce dependency, a copula-based or conditional sampling approach is applied. The joint probability function can be modeled as follows:

$$P(X = x, Y = y) = C(F_X(x), F_Y(y); \rho),$$

where $C(\cdot, \cdot; \rho)$ represents a suitable copula function incorporating correlation ρ into the model dependency.

Step 3: Generate random samples. For various sample sizes ($n = 50, 80, 120, 150$, and 200), the following steps are executed:

1. Generate uniform random variables U_1, U_2 from $U(0, 1)$.
2. Transform these uniform variables using the inverse CDF method:

$$X = F_X^{-1}(U_1), \quad Y = F_Y^{-1}(U_2),$$

   where F_X^{-1} and F_Y^{-1} are the inverse CDFs of BWDFW-I and BWDFW-II.
3. Apply a copula-based transformation if a dependency structure is required.
4. Repeat this process until the desired sample size is achieved.

7.2. Sample Size Considerations and Importance

The choice of the sample size significantly impacts the accuracy and reliability of the statistical inference:

- Small samples ($n = 50, n = 80$) are suitable for preliminary analysis, small samples' property testing, and exploratory data assessment;
- Medium samples ($n = 120, n = 150$) provide more stability in parameter estimation and model validation;
- Large samples ($n = 200$) allow for robust inferential procedures, including hypothesis testing and model selection.

7.3. The Accuracy and Precision of the Estimation Method

The accuracy and precision of the estimation method are evaluated using two key criteria:

- Bias:

$$Bias(\delta) = \frac{1}{1000} \sum_{i=1}^{1000} (\hat{\delta}_i - \delta),$$

- Mean-squared error (MSE):

$$MSE(\delta) = \frac{1}{1000} \sum_{i=1}^{1000} (\hat{\delta}_i - \delta)^2,$$

where $\hat{\delta}$ represents the estimated value of the parameter δ obtained using the MLE method. Choosing parameters for a bivariate model simulation involves selecting the appropriate model type, defining marginal distributions, establishing the dependence structure, determining the sample size and covariance, testing different parameter combinations, and validating the results against theoretical or real-world data. Based on the simulation results presented in Tables 3 and 4, it is observed that as the sample size (n) increases, the bias approaches zero, and the mean-squared errors (MSEs) decrease to zero as well. These findings demonstrate the consistency and unbiasedness of the MLE estimates. Furthermore, for large values of n, the average estimate and the initial values are approximately equal. From these observations, it can be concluded that the MLE method provides reliable and effective estimates for parameter analysis in data analysis.

Table 3. The average estimates, biases, and MSEs for the BWDFW-I model.

Case I	$\alpha = 1.5\,,\ \beta_1 = 4.5\,,\ \beta_2 = 2.5\,,\ \beta_3 = 6.4\,,\ m = 2.5\,,\ k = 7.5$						
	Size "n"	$\hat{\alpha}$	$\hat{\beta_1}$	$\hat{\beta_2}$	$\hat{\beta_3}$	$\hat{m}$	$\hat{k}$
Avg. Est.	50	1.0788	3.3717	1.8259	7.2105	3.4408	6.8215
	80	1.3655	3.3952	1.8259	7.2105	3.4408	6.8215
	120	1.7361	4.1145	2.2081	6.7314	2.8126	7.2314
	150	1.6221	4.3336	2.4002	6.5121	2.7003	7.4008
	200	1.5113	4.5112	2.5013	6.3908	2.5022	7.5040
Bias	50	−0.4212	−0.1283	−0.6741	0.8105	0.9408	−0.6785
	80	−0.1345	−0.6048	−0.4774	0.5042	0.7511	−0.5379
	120	0.2361	−0.3855	−0.2919	0.3314	0.3126	−0.2686
	150	0.1221	−0.1664	−0.0998	0.1121	0.2003	−0.0992
	200	0.0113	0.0111	0.0103	−0.0092	0.0022	0.0040
MSE	50	1.0159	1.0047	0.8543	0.9373	1.0049	1.0008
	80	0.8241	0.7341	0.5225	0.7714	0.6674	0.4673
	120	0.4304	0.5201	0.4927	0.4218	0.5005	0.2155
	150	0.2005	0.1404	0.1881	0.1994	0.3117	0.1074
	200	0.0541	0.0715	0.0335	0.0392	0.1022	0.0093

Table 4. The average estimates, biases and MSEs for the BWDFW-II model.

Case II	$\alpha = 1.3\,,\ \beta_1 = 0.6\,,\ \beta_2 = 0.9\,,\ \beta_3 = 1.9\,,\ m = 2.4\,,\ k = 1.8$						
	Size "n"	$\hat{\alpha}$	$\hat{\beta_1}$	$\hat{\beta_2}$	$\hat{\beta_3}$	$\hat{m}$	$\hat{k}$
Avg. Est.	50	1.6323	0.8942	1.1347	1.5252	2.1056	2.1104
	80	1.5005	0.8095	1.1058	1.6866	2.2217	2.0026
	120	1.4702	0.7522	1.0448	1.8014	2.2993	1.9413
	150	1.3908	0.6995	1.9213	1.8657	2.3541	1.8522
	200	1.3152	0.6092	0.9047	1.8878	2.3982	1.8041
Bias	50	0.3323	0.2942	0.3347	−0.3748	−0.2944	0.3104
	80	0.2005	0.2095	0.2058	−0.2134	−0.1783	0.2026
	120	0.1702	0.1522	0.1448	−0.0986	−0.1007	0.1413
	150	0.0908	0.0995	0.0213	−0.0343	−0.0459	0.0522
	200	0.0152	0.0092	0.0217	0.0122	0.0018	0.0041
MSE	50	0.8542	1.0243	09747	1.0051	0.9827	0.8073
	80	0.5313	0.7204	0.6053	0.8252	0.7224	0.4517
	120	0.2252	0.2415	0.1838	0.4107	0.4318	0.1038
	150	0.0827	0.1008	0.0172	0.1228	0.1427	0.0574
	200	0.0414	0.0342	0.0094	0.0415	0.0219	0.0033

8. Goodness of Fit and Decision Making in Real Data Analysis

This section investigates the practical applicability of the proposed BWDFW-I and BWDFW-II models using two real-world bivariate datasets. To assess the performances of these models, comparisons are made with four other competitive distributions: the bivariate discretized Fréchet–Weibull (BDFW), bivariate discrete generalized inverse Weibull (BDGIW), bivariate discrete inverse Weibull (BDIW), and bivariate discrete Weibull (BDW) distributions. The MLEs of the parameters were computed, and the goodness of fit for each distribution was evaluated using the Akaike information criterion (AIC), Bayesian information criterion (BIC), and consistent Akaike information criterion (CAIC). The distribution that yields the lowest AIC, BIC, and CAIC values is considered as the best fit. These criteria provide a tradeoff between the model's fit and complexity, helping to mitigate the risk of overfitting. For a graphical comparison, the observed and estimated bivariate frequency plots for BWDFW-I, BWDFW-II, BDFW, BDGIW, BDIW, and BDW are provided for each dataset.

8.1. Aviation Field: Dataset I

The first dataset considered herein consists of the number of flight aborts by 109 flights in two consecutive periods of 6 months each. The two successive periods considered for this dataset are Y_1 and Y_2 (where Y_1 = the first six-month period, and Y_2 = the second six-month period). This dataset is extracted from Barbiero [26] and earlier discussed in the work of Mitchell and Paulson [27]. The original data consist of 109 pairs of observations (Y_{1_i}, Y_{2_i}), where Y_{1_i} represents the number of aborts by flight "i" in the first 6 months, and Y_{2_i} the number of aborts by flight "i" in the second 6 months of one year. The frequency distribution of bivariate dataset I is presented in Table 5, and the summary statistics for this dataset are presented in Table 6.

Table 5. Bivariate frequency distribution of dataset I.

Y_1 \ Y_2	0	1	2	3	$\geq$4	Total
0	34	20	4	6	4	68
1	17	7	0	0	0	24
2	6	4	1	0	0	11
3	0	4	0	0	0	4
4	0	0	0	0	0	0
$\geq$5	2	0	0	0	0	2
Total	59	35	5	6	4	109

Based on the summary values in Table 6, it is evident that both Y_1 and Y_2 exhibit right skewness. Additionally, for dataset I, the Pearson's correlation coefficient, Spearman's rho (ρ), and Kendall's tau (τ) values for Y_1 and Y_2 are 0.9214558, 0.888931, and 0.8735868, respectively. These observations indicate a strong positive relationship between Y_1 and Y_2. Therefore, these data can be utilized for modeling with the BWDFW-I and BWDFW-II models.

Table 6. Descriptive statistics for dataset I.

Median		**Mean**		**Covariance**	**Pearson's Correlation**	**Spearman's Rho**	**Kendall's Tau**
Y_1	Y_2	Y_1	Y_2	$Cov(Y_1,Y_2)$	$Cor(Y_1,Y_2)$	$\rho(Y_1,Y_2)$	$\tau(Y_1,Y_2)$
0.00	0.00	0.6239	0.7248	0.96959	0.92146	0.88893	0.87359

In Table 7, the MLEs (SEs in parentheses), 95% confidence intervals, -log l, AIC, BIC, and CAIC obtained using dataset I are presented for the BWDFW-I, BWDFW-II, BDFW, BDGIW, BDIW, and BDW distributions.

From Table 7, it can be observed that for dataset I, the values of the -log likelihood, AIC, BIC, and CAIC are comparatively the lowest for both the BWDFW-I and BWDFW-II models. However, the lowest values for the BWDFW-I model suggest that it provides the best fit for dataset I. Figure 7 shows the profiles of the L functions for BWDFW-I, which indicate that the estimators are unique. In Figure 8, the estimated joint frequency distributions for the BWDFW-I and BWDFW-II models, along with the BDFW, BDGIW, BDIW, and BDW distributions, are shown. The graphical representation clearly indicates that the BWDFW-I model fits dataset I the best.

Table 7. The MLEs (SEs in parentheses), 95% confidence intervals, −log l, AIC, BIC, and CAIC for dataset I.

Model	Estimate (SE)	95% CI	$-\log l$	AIC	BIC	CAIC
BWDFW-I	$\hat{\alpha} = 0.34295$ (0.07636)	(0.1933, 0.4926)	75.0703	162.1406	170.5477	166.3442
	$\hat{\beta}_1 = 2.23410$ (0.32125)	(1.6045, 2.8638)				
	$\hat{\beta}_2 = 0.50341$ (0.14022)	(0.2286, 0.7782)				
	$\hat{\beta}_3 = 0.85167$ (0.29515)	(0.2732, 1.4302)				
	$\hat{m} = 0.12472$ (0.02116)	(0.0832, 0.1662)				
	$\hat{k} = 0.02679$ (0.00587)	(0.0153, 0.0383)				
BWDFW-II	$\hat{\alpha} = 0.53243$ (0.14004)	(0.2580, 0.8069)	103.9928	219.9856	228.3928	224.1892
	$\hat{\beta}_1 = 1.03863$ (0.50223)	(0.0543, 2.0230)				
	$\hat{\beta}_2 = 1.12495$ (0.53445)	(0.0774, 2.1725)				
	$\hat{\beta}_3 = 0.65389$ (0.29125)	(0.0830, 1.2247)				
	$\hat{m} = 0.19232$ (0.01557)	(0.1618, 0.2228)				
	$\hat{k} = 0.04263$ (0.00116)	(0.0404, 0.0449)				
BDFW	$\hat{\theta}_1 = 0.93438$ (0.03144)	(0.8728, 0.9960)	202.6919	413.3838	418.9889	416.1862
	$\hat{\theta}_2 = 0.79851$ (0.04603)	(0.7083, 0.8887)				
	$\hat{\theta}_3 = 0.64339$ (0.04776)	(0.5498, 0.7370)				
	$\hat{\lambda} = 1.77364$ (0.21815)	(1.3461, 2.2012)				
BDGIW	$\hat{q}_1 = 0.95428$ (0.03247)	(0.8906, 1.0179)	202.9543	413.9086	419.5133	416.7109
	$\hat{q}_2 = 0.80018$ (0.04271)	(0.7165, 0.8839)				
	$\hat{q}_3 = 0.64235$ (0.04590)	(0.5524, 0.7323)				
	$\hat{\alpha} = 1.80019$ (0.21268)	(1.3833, 2.2170)				
BDIW	$\hat{\alpha}_1 = 0.91438$ (0.04139)	(0.8333, 0.9955)	207.2054	422.4107	428.9611	425.6859
	$\hat{\alpha}_2 = 0.75121$ (0.02448)	(0.7032, 0.7992)				
	$\hat{\alpha}_3 = 0.54523$ (0.06228)	(0.4232, 0.6673)				
	$\hat{\beta} = 1.47366$ (0.30729)	(0.8714, 2.0759)				
BDW	$\hat{p}_1 = 0.39143$ (0.04539)	(0.3025, 0.4804)	249.5335	507.067	512.6718	509.8694
	$\hat{p}_2 = 0.44779$ (0.08535)	(0.2805, 0.6151)				
	$\hat{p}_3 = 0.96749$ (0.20109)	(0.5734, 1.3616)				
	$\hat{\alpha} = 1.12852$ (0.10729)	(0.9182, 1.3388)				

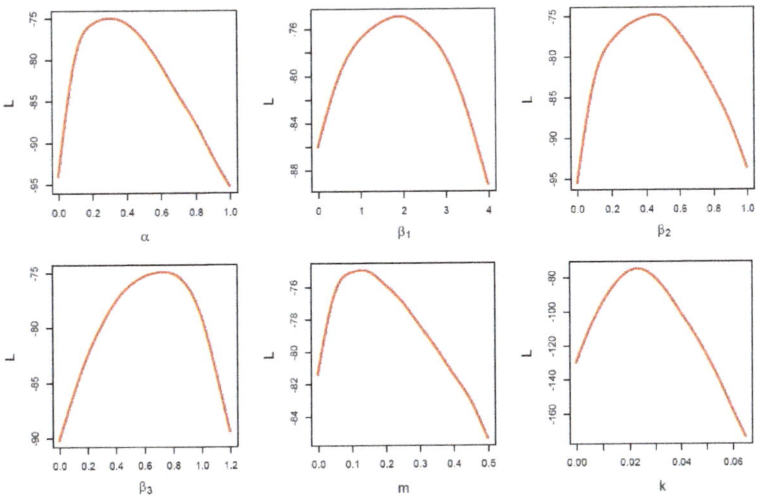

Figure 7. The profiles of the L functions obtained using dataset I.

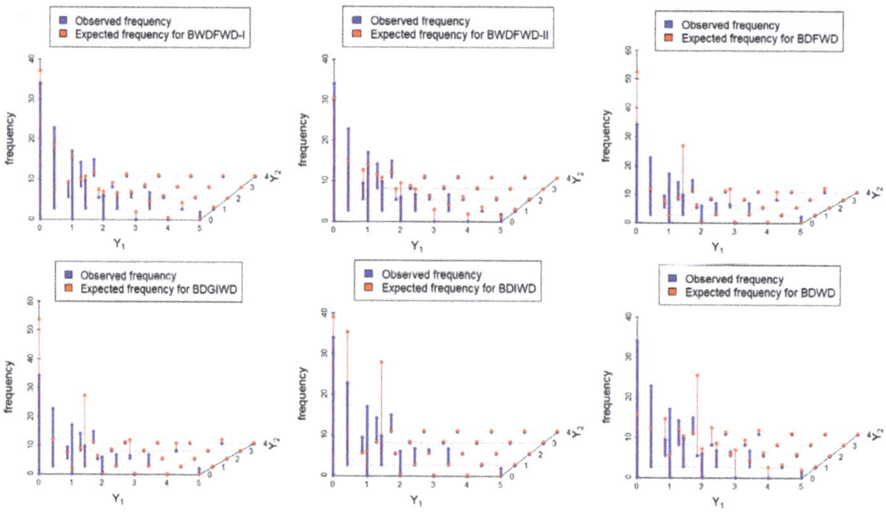

Figure 8. The observed and estimated joint frequency distribution plots of dataset I.

8.2. Security and Safety Field: Dataset II

The second dataset is accident data from 122 experienced shunters, where random variables Y_1 and Y_2 respectively represent the numbers of accidents in 1937–1942 and 1943–1947 (see Zamani et al. [28]). The frequency distribution of bivariate dataset II is presented in Table 8, and the summary statistics for this dataset are presented in Table 9.

Table 8. Bivariate frequency distribution of dataset II.

Y_1 \ Y_2	0	1	2	3	4	≥5	Total
0	21	13	4	2	0	0	40
1	18	14	5	1	0	1	39
2	8	10	4	3	1	0	26
3	2	1	2	2	1	0	8
4	1	4	1	0	0	0	6
5	0	1	0	1	0	0	2
6	0	0	1	0	0	0	1
Total	50	43	17	9	2	1	122

From the summary values presented in Table 9, it is clear that Y_1 exhibits a left tail, while Y_2 shows a right tail. Moreover, for dataset II, the values of the Pearson's correlation coefficient, Spearman's rho (ρ), and Kendall's tau (τ) indicate a strong positive correlation between Y_1 and Y_2. Therefore, these data are appropriate for modeling using the BWDFW-I and BWDFW-II models.

Table 9. Descriptive statistics for dataset II.

Median		**Mean**		**Covariance**	**Pearson's Correlation**	**Spearman's Rho**	**Kendall's Tau**
Y_1	Y_2	Y_1	Y_2	Cov(Y_1,Y_2)	Cor(Y_1,Y_2)	$\rho(Y_1, Y_2)$	$\tau(Y_1, Y_2)$
1.00	1.00	1.2700	0.9754	1.36208	0.93013	0.91082	0.87229

In Table 10, the MLEs (SEs in parentheses), 95% confidence intervals, $-\log l$, AIC, BIC, and CAIC obtained using dataset II are presented for the BWDFW-I, BWDFW-II, BDFW, BDGIW, BDIW, and BDW distributions.

Table 10. The MLEs (SEs in parentheses), 95% confidence intervals, $-\log l$, AIC, BIC, and CAIC for dataset II.

Model	Estimate (SE)	95% CI	$-\log l$	AIC	BIC	CAIC
BWDFW-I	$\hat{\alpha} = 1.45323$ (0.19872)	(1.0637, 1.8427)	118.0931	248.1862	258.6122	253.3992
	$\hat{\beta}_1 = 2.08623$ (0.32629)	(1.4467, 2.7258)				
	$\hat{\beta}_2 = 2.22495$ (0.38345)	(1.4734, 2.9765)				
	$\hat{\beta}_3 = 0.64388$ (0.08354)	(0.4801, 0.8076)				
	$\hat{m} = 1.19231$ (0.12209)	(0.9530, 1.4316)				
	$\hat{k} = 0.03662$ (0.00561)	(0.0256, 0.0476)				
BWDFW-II	$\hat{\alpha} = 0.21199$ (0.03842)	(0.1367, 0.2873)	123.6967	259.3934	269.8194	264.6064
	$\hat{\beta}_1 = 1.61515$ (0.38433)	(0.8619, 2.3684)				
	$\hat{\beta}_2 = 1.25150$ (0.29413)	(0.6750, 1.8280)				
	$\hat{\beta}_3 = 1.23137$ (0.18540)	(0.8680, 1.5948)				
	$\hat{m} = 1.04923$ (0.22088)	(0.6163, 1.4822)				
	$\hat{k} = 0.11366$ (0.04613)	(0.0232, 0.2041)				
BDFW	$\hat{\theta}_1 = 0.53722$ (0.05599)	(0.4275, 0.6470)	304.4232	616.8464	623.7971	620.3218
	$\hat{\theta}_2 = 0.96836$ (0.03091)	(0.9078, 1.0289)				
	$\hat{\theta}_3 = 0.42012$ (0.04545)	(0.3310, 0.5092)				
	$\hat{\lambda} = 1.78756$ (0.15202)	(1.4896, 2.0855)				
BDGIW	$\hat{q}_1 = 0.73722$ (0.08495)	(0.5707, 0.9037)	324.4139	656.8277	663.7784	660.3031
	$\hat{q}_2 = 0.68359$ (0.01927)	(0.6458, 0.7214)				
	$\hat{q}_3 = 0.44223$ (0.03147)	(0.3805, 0.5039)				
	$\hat{\alpha} = 1.55918$ (0.12410)	(1.3159, 1.8024)				
BDIW	$\hat{\alpha}_1 = 0.61985$ (0.07761)	(0.4677, 0.7720)	335.704	679.408	686.3587	682.8833
	$\hat{\alpha}_2 = 0.80355$ (0.09387)	(0.6196, 0.9875)				
	$\hat{\alpha}_3 = 0.17942$ (0.02531)	(0.1298, 0.2290)				
	$\hat{\beta} = 1.61707$ (0.10622)	(1.2529, 1.9029)				
BDW	$\hat{p}_1 = 0.68978$ (0.03364)	(0.6238, 0.7557)	367.2133	742.4266	749.3772	745.9019
	$\hat{p}_2 = 0.57694$ (0.04008)	(0.4984, 0.6555)				
	$\hat{p}_3 = 0.43879$ (0.07138)	(0.2989, 0.5787)				
	$\hat{\alpha} = 1.47306$ (0.09988)	(1.2773, 1.6688)				

Dataset II best fits the suggested BWDFW-I model, as shown in Table 10, where the values of the -log likelihood, AIC, BIC, and CAIC are the lowest for BWDFWD Model 1. Figure 9 shows the profiles of the L functions for BWDFW-I. Furthermore, Figure 10 presents the estimated joint frequency distributions for the BWDFW-I, BWDFW-II, BDFW, BDGIW, BDIW, and BDW distributions. The graphical representation also clearly shows that dataset II is best fitted by the BWDFW-I model.

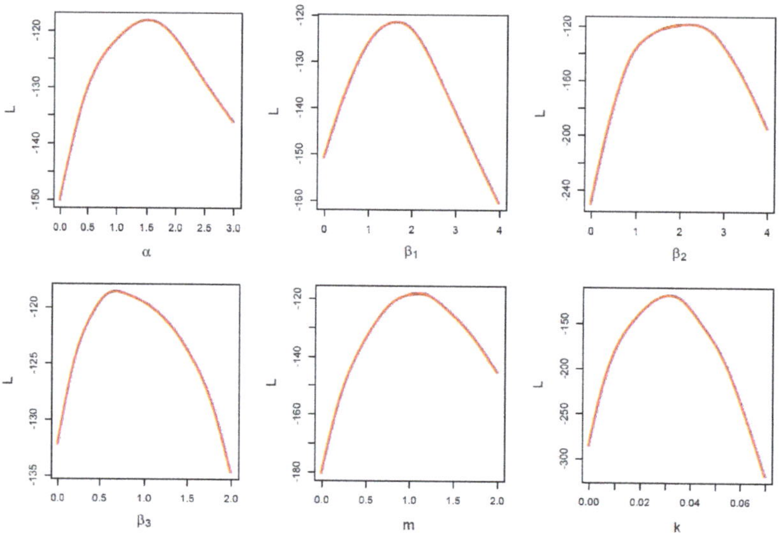

Figure 9. The profiles of the L functions obtained using dataset II.

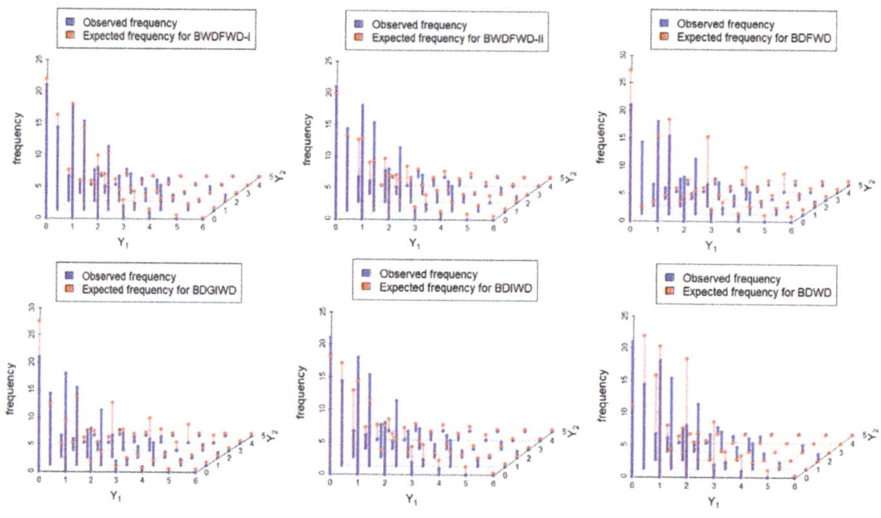

Figure 10. The observed and estimated joint frequency distribution plots of dataset II.

9. Summary of the Key Findings

In this article, we proposed a bivariate extension of the weighted discretized Fréchet–Weibull distribution (WDFWD) using two different methods of operators. The first method involved taking the minimum of the two baseline random variables, resulting in what we called the BWDFW-I model. The second method, on the other hand, considered the maximum of the two baseline random variables and was referred to as the BWDFW-II model. Statistical properties, including the joint probability mass function, joint hazard rate, and joint reversed hazard rate functions, were presented for both distributions. The graphs illustrated that both the BWDFW-I and BWDFW-II models exhibited long right and left tails. Additionally, the various shapes of the joint hazard rate functions demonstrated their flexibility. The proposed models could also be applied to discuss dispersion data under various shapes of kurtosis. The joint probability-generating function was derived to obtain different moments and product moments. Positive quadrant dependence was proven. The simulation indicated that the MLE could be effectively used in the estimation process. To demonstrate the practical applicability of the two proposed models, we analyzed two real-life bivariate datasets (from the security and safety field and the aviation field) and compared them to four other discrete bivariate versions of the Weibull and extended Weibull distributions, namely, BDW, BDIW, BDGIW, and BDFW. It is widely acknowledged that augmenting the number of parameters enhances the distribution's flexibility. Moreover, weighted distribution theory offers a valuable framework for comprehending distributions and contributes to their increased adaptability. The newly introduced bivariate weighted discretized Fréchet–Weibull distribution, which extends the weighted DFWD in a bivariate manner and incorporates six parameters, clearly exhibits greater flexibility than the four other distributions under consideration. Both BWDFW-I and BWDFW-II showed superior performances, yielding the lowest values for AIC, BIC, and CAIC. Furthermore, it was noted that the BWDFW-I model outperformed the BWDFW-II model, as the former exhibited lower values compared to the latter.

10. Future Directions

Bivariate distributions play a crucial role in modeling complex relationships between paired data across various disciplines, offering extensive practical applications. In this context, the BWDFW-I and BWDFW-II models provide a novel framework that can be effectively applied to real-world bivariate datasets. These models have the potential to yield a better fit compared to existing discrete bivariate distributions, making them valuable tools for analyzing dependent data structures in diverse fields.

To enhance the utility and robustness of these models, future research will focus on developing and implementing various parameter estimation techniques. Specifically, different algorithms, including the Expectation–Maximization (EM) algorithm, will be explored to optimize parameter estimation for datasets exhibiting complex dependency structures. Additionally, alternative estimation approaches tailored to different data types and distributions will be investigated to improve the accuracy and efficiency of statistical inferences.

Several existing studies have demonstrated the effectiveness of such algorithms in similar contexts. For instance, the EM algorithm has been successfully applied in a multivariate Student-t process model to analyze dependent tail-weighted degradation data (see Xu et al. [29]). This study highlights the advantages of the EM algorithm in handling complex multivariate structures with heavy tails, making it a promising method for extending the BWDFW models.

Furthermore, stress–strength reliability models have been widely used in reliability analysis, particularly in evaluating system performance under stress conditions. A notable example is the bivariate iterated Farlie–Gumbel–Morgenstern stress–strength reliability model developed for Rayleigh-distributed margins (see Chandra et al. [30]). This model provides valuable insights into the reliability properties of dependent systems, reinforcing the importance of adopting advanced estimation techniques for bivariate models.

Building on these advancements, future research will not only refine the estimation techniques for BWDFW models but also extend their applicability to a broader range of real-life bivariate datasets. This will include exploring hybrid approaches that integrate Bayesian and frequentist methods, leveraging computational techniques, such as Markov Chain Monte Carlo simulations, and assessing the performances of these models under different censoring schemes. By addressing these research directions, the proposed models will contribute significantly to the advancement of discrete bivariate modeling, offering practical solutions for real-world data analysis and decision making.

Author Contributions: Conceptualization, M.S.E., D.D. and B.D.; methodology, D.D. and S.T.O.; software, B.D., D.D. and M.S.E.; validation, S.T.O., W.W.M. and B.D.; formal analysis, S.T.O., P.J.H. and M.S.E.; investigation, S.T.O., D.D. and W.W.M.; resources, W.W.M. and P.J.H.; data curation, D.D., M.S.E. and B.D.; writing—original draft, D.D. and P.J.H.; writing—review and editing, B.D. and M.S.E.; visualization, D.D. and M.S.E. All authors have read and agreed to the published version of the manuscript.

Funding: This research was funded by the Deanship of Graduate Studies and Scientific Research at Qassim University.

Data Availability Statement: The original contributions presented in this study are included in this article; further inquiries can be directed to the corresponding author.

Acknowledgments: The researchers would like to thank the Deanship of Graduate Studies and Scientific Research at Qassim University for financial support (QU-APC-2025).

Conflicts of Interest: The authors declare no conflicts of interest.

References

1. Teamah, A.-E.A.M.; Elbanna, A.; Ahmed, M. Fréchet-Weibull distribution with application to earthquakes data sets. *Pak. J. Stat.* **2020**, *36*, 135–147.
2. Alzaatreh, A.; Lee, C.; Famoye, F. A new method for generating families of continuous distributions. *Metron* **2013**, *71*, 63–79. [CrossRef]
3. Das, D.; Das, B. Discretized Fréchet–Weibull distribution: Properties and application. *J. Indian Soc. Probab. Stat.* **2023**, *24*, 243–282. [CrossRef]
4. Das, D.; Das, B. On weighted discretized Fréchet–Weibull distribution with application to real life data. *Appl. Math. Inf. Sci. Int. J.* **2023**, *7*, 791–806.
5. Johnson, N.L.; Kotz, S.; Balakrishnan, N. *Discrete Multivariate Distributions*; Wiley: Hoboken, NJ, USA, 1997.
6. Balakrishnan, N.; Lai, C. *Continuous Bivariate Distributions*, 2nd ed.; Springer: Berlin/Heidelberg, Germany, 2009.
7. Kundu, D.; Gupta, R.D. Bivariate generalized exponential distribution. *J. Multivar. Anal.* **2009**, *100*, 581–593. [CrossRef]
8. Sarhan, A.; Hamilton, D.C.; Smith, B.; Kundu, D. The bivariate generalized linear failure rate distribution and its multivariate extension. *Comput. Stat. Data Anal.* **2011**, *55*, 644–654. [CrossRef]
9. El-Sherpieny, E.A.; Ibrahim, S.A.; Bedar, R.E. A new bivariate distribution with generalized Gompertz marginals. *Asian J. Appl. Sci.* **2013**, *1*, 141–150.
10. Wagner, B.S.; Artur, J.L. Bivariate Kumaraswamy distribution: Properties and a new method to generate bivariate classes. *Statistics* **2013**, *47*, 1321–1342.
11. Balakrishnan, N.; Shiji, K. On a class of bivariate exponential distributions. *Stat. Probab. Lett.* **2014**, *85*, 153–160. [CrossRef]
12. El-Gohary, A.; El-Bassiouny, A.H.; El-Morshedy, M. Bivariate exponentiated modified Weibull extension distribution. *J. Appl. Probab. Stat.* **2016**, *5*, 67–78. [CrossRef]
13. Hiba, Z.M. Bivariate inverse Weibull distribution. *J. Stat. Comput. Simul.* **2016**, *86*, 2335–2345.
14. Rasool, R.; Akbar, A.J. On bivariate exponentiated extended Weibull family of distributions. *Ciência Nat.* **2016**, *38*, 564–576.
15. Eliwa, M.; El-Morshedy, M. Bivariate odd Weibull-G family of distributions: Properties, Bayesian and non-Bayesian estimation with bootstrap confidence intervals and application. *J. Taibah Univ. Sci.* **2020**, *14*, 331–345. [CrossRef]
16. Kocherlakota, S.; Kocherlakota, K. *Bivariate Discrete Distributions*; Marcel Dekker: New York, NY, USA, 1992.
17. Basu, A.P.; Dhar, S.K. Bivariate geometric distribution. *J. Appl. Stat. Sci.* **1995**, *2*, 33–44.
18. Kumar, C.S. A unified approach to bivariate discrete distributions. *Metrika* **2008**, *67*, 113–123. [CrossRef]
19. Kemp, A.W. New discrete Appell and Humbert distributions with relevance to bivariate accident data. *J. Multivar. Anal.* **2013**, *113*, 2–6. [CrossRef]
20. Lee, H.; Cha, J.H. On two general classes of discrete bivariate distributions. *Am. Stat.* **2015**, *69*, 221–230. [CrossRef]
21. Nekoukhou, V.; Kundu, D. Bivariate discrete generalized exponential distribution. *Statistics* **2017**, *51*, 1143–1158. [CrossRef]
22. El-Morshedy, M.; Eliwa, M.S.; Gohary, A.E.; Khalil, A.A. Bivariate exponentiated discrete Weibull distribution: Statistical properties, estimation, simulation and applications. *Math. Sci.* **2020**, *14*, 29–42. [CrossRef]
23. Ali, S.; Shafqat, M.; Shah, I.; Dey, S. Bivariate discrete Nadarajah and Haghighi distribution: Properties and different methods of estimation. *Filomat* **2019**, *33*, 5589–5610. [CrossRef]
24. Kundu, D.; Nekoukhou, V. On bivariate discrete Weibull distribution. *Commun. Stat.—Theory Methods* **2019**, *48*, 3464–3481. [CrossRef]

25. Shibu, D.S.; Beegum, N. Bivariate Discrete Modified Weibull (BDMW) Distribution. *Statistica* **2021**, *81*, 231–264.
26. Barbiero, A. Discrete analogues of continuous bivariate probability distributions. *Ann. Oper. Res.* **2022**, *312*, 23–43. [CrossRef]
27. Mitchell, C.R.; Paulson, A.S. A new bivariate negative binomial distribution. *Nav. Res. Logist. Q.* **1981**, *28*, 359–374. [CrossRef]
28. Zamani, H.; Faroughi, P.; Ismail, N. Bivariate Poisson-weighted exponential distribution with applications. *AIP Conf. Proc.* **2014**, *1602*, 964–968.
29. Xu, A.; Fang, G.; Zhuang, L.; Gu, C. A multivariate student-t process model for dependent tail-weighted degradation data. *IISE Trans.* **2024**, 1–17. [CrossRef]
30. Chandra, N.; James, A.; Domma, F.; Rehman, H. Bivariate iterated Farlie–Gumbel–Morgenstern stress–strength reliability model for Rayleigh margins: Properties and estimation. *Stat. Theory Relat. Field* **2024**, *8*, 315–334. [CrossRef]

mathematics

MDPI

Article

The COVID-19 Mortality Rate in Latin America: A Cross-Country Analysis

Fernando José Monteiro de Araújo [1,*], Renata Rojas Guerra [1,2] and Fernando Arturo Peña-Ramírez [2]

1 Graduate Program of Statistics, Universidade Federal do Rio Grande do Sul, Porto Alegre 90010-150, Brazil
2 Departament of Statistics, Universidade Federal de Santa Maria, Santa Maria 97105-900, Brazil; renata.r.guerra@ufsm.br (R.R.G.); fernando.p.ramirez@ufsm.br (F.A.P.-R.)
* Correspondence: fernando.monteiro@ufrgs.br

Abstract: Latin America was one of the hotspots of COVID-19 during the pandemic. Therefore, understanding the COVID-19 mortality rate in Latin America is crucial, as it can help identify at-risk populations and evaluate the quality of healthcare. In an effort to find a more flexible and suitable model, this work formulates a new quantile regression model based on the unit ratio-Weibull (URW) distribution, aiming to identify the factors that explain the COVID-19 mortality rate in Latin America. We define a systematic structure for the two parameters of the distribution: one represents a quantile of the distribution, while the other is a shape parameter. Additionally, some mathematical properties of the new regression model are presented. Point and interval estimates of maximum likelihood in finite samples are evaluated through Monte Carlo simulations. Diagnostic analysis and model selection are also discussed. Finally, an empirical application is presented to understand and quantify the effects of economic, social, demographic, public health, and climatic variables on the COVID-19 mortality rate quantiles in Latin America. The utility of the proposed model is illustrated by comparing it with other widely explored quantile models in the literature, such as Kumaraswamy and unit Weibull regressions.

Keywords: epidemiology; quantiles; unit extended Weibull families; unit regression

MSC: 62J20; 62E10

1. Introduction

The severe acute respiratory syndrome coronavirus 2 (SARS-CoV-2) is the etiological agent of coronavirus disease 2019 (COVID-19). On 11 March 2020, the WHO declared COVID-19 a global pandemic [1]. Approximately a year and two months after the WHO declared the COVID-19 epidemic a global public health emergency, on 23 March 2021, Brazil reported 3158 deaths in just 24 h. This figure was the highest number of deaths reported worldwide since the beginning of the pandemic. That same day, Argentina appeared in the top 10 countries with the highest number of daily infections (9405), and Colombia occupied the 11th position in total deaths (62,274) since the beginning of the emergency. Peru was also cataloged as the country in the Latin American region with more deaths per 1000 inhabitants (0.516).

In May 2020, the World Health Organization (WHO) declared that South America had become the new epicenter of the COVID-19 pandemic, with countries like Brazil, Argentina, and Peru reporting some of the highest per capita mortality rates worldwide [2]. As the pandemic progressed, Latin America became again an epicenter in September 2020. Although the United States continued to lead globally in total cases and deaths, Brazil ranked second, followed by other heavily affected countries in the region, such as Peru, Chile, Mexico, Colombia, Ecuador, Argentina, and Bolivia [3]. Between March and June 2021, the epicenter shifted back to Latin America, driven by the spread of the Delta variant, which quickly became the dominant strain globally [4]. The prevalence of comorbidities such as diarrhea and diabetes leaves the region in a complex and delicate clinical and epidemiological environment. The situation worsens with the coexistence of other epidemics, such as dengue and yellow fever, in addition to the long-term consequences of chikungunya and Zika [5].

In the context of epidemic modeling, predicting infections and mortality rates at a regional or national level is essential. [6] discusses the use of compartmental models such as susceptible-infected-recovered (SIR) and its variants, including susceptible-exposed-infected-recovered (SEIR) and susceptible-infected-susceptible (SIS), among others. The SIS model, initially proposed by [7], is a mathematical model developed to describe the dynamics of epidemics, such as infection rate and population immunity, and quantifies how an infectious disease spreads over time. These models remain widely used, as demonstrated by [8], who applied the SIR model to predict the number of cases of COVID-19 in Malaysia during different pandemic phases.

Considering probabilistic modeling, several authors, such as [9,10], have investigated how climatic and cultural factors influence the death rate from COVID-19. In such cases, classic linear regression models have been fitted to explore these associations, accounting for factors like temperature, humidity, and cultural dimensions. It is common to apply this methodology to explain mortality rates based on other variables. Additionally, recent works by [11,12] have utilized regression models to analyze the impacts of factors such as government effectiveness, testing rates, and public health measures on COVID-19 mortality. However, this methodology brings some limitations, particularly the assumption of normal distribution in the response variable. This assumption does not capture the character of the response variable since the rates are bounded random variables and, most of the time, asymmetric. The normal distribution cannot represent this characteristic, and we note that the specialized literature has paid little attention to this fact.

A modeling alternative is to assume a distribution in the exponential family for the response variable. These are the well-known generalized linear models (GLMs) pioneered by [13]. However, this assumption remains restrictive. Another class of more general and flexible models assumes that the response distribution is deliberately left general with no explicit distribution specified, and its parameters vary as a function of explanatory variables. They are the Generalized Additive Models for Location, Scale, and Shape (GAMLSS) framework [14]. Recently, applications and proposals for models based on the GAMLSS approach have gained prominence. For example, in the study by [15], a variety of models were used, including beta, simplex, unit gamma (UG), and unit Lindley (UL) regressions, to identify covariates associated with the proportion of votes in municipal elections.

In this paper, we directly utilize the GAMLSS framework to formulate a new regression model based on the Weibull distribution, aimed at explaining the COVID-19 mortality rate in Latin America. We define a structure of systematic components on the two parameters of the distribution: one of which represents a quantile of the distribution and the other its dispersion. Modeling on the median is preferable over the mean when the variable of interest is not symmetric (i.e., skewed), especially in the presence of outliers [16], in addition to being a more robust measure of central tendency [17].

The main contribution of this paper is to propose a new regression model that facilitates understanding and quantifying the impact of economic variables, social and demographic indicators, and public health measures on the quantiles of the COVID-19 mortality rate. Unlike commonly used models for these purposes, this model accommodates the typical asymmetry and bounded nature of mortality rate data. We hope that our approach can serve as a valuable tool for policymakers in decision-making. We focus on the initial mortality rates of the pandemic, as other variables, such as government responses through public policies promoting mask-wearing, widespread testing, and social isolation, began to influence these rates as the pandemic advanced. Such initiatives underscore the importance of government interventions in public health to mitigate the pandemic's impacts.

The model can be effectively applied to analyze mortality rates of diseases with low fatality rates, such as measles, or other epidemic diseases, such as dengue and yellow fever. This model can be extended to analyze various economic and engineering applications. In economics, it can model data like the Gini index and poverty rates, which are proportions between 0 and 1 and often exhibit positive skewness. In engineering, the model can be used to analyze failure rates of systems or efficiency metrics, which may also be expressed as percentages (ranging from 0 to 100%) and are typically skewed. These applications highlight the importance of using more flexible models to interpret complex, asymmetrical data.

The remainder of the paper is outlined as follows. Section 2 introduces the new regression model, the unit ratio-Weibull distribution for the COVID-19 mortality rates in Latin American countries. Further estimation and goodness-of-fit aspects are also presented. In Section 3, a Monte Carlo simulation study is conducted to evaluate the performance of the maximum likelihood estimators of the proposed regression model. Section 4 describes the data preparation and carries out the regression analysis by comparing the novel model with other quantile regressions in the unit interval. The concluding remarks are addressed in Section 5.

2. The Unit Ratio-Weibull Regression

This section introduces a new quantile regression for modeling double-bounded epidemiological data. By focusing on COVID-19 applications, our approach arises as an alternative to analyze the impact of demographic and epidemiological indicators on the mortality rate of this disease. The proposed regression is based on the unit ratio-Weibull (URW) distribution, which belongs to the unit ratio-extended Weibull family and was pioneered by [18].

A random variable Y has a URW distribution, denoted by $Y\sim URW(\sigma,\mu)$, if its cumulative distribution function (cdf) and probability density function (pdf) are

$$F(y|\sigma,\mu) = 1-(1-\tau)^{y^{\sigma}(1-\mu)^{\sigma}/[\mu^{\sigma}(1-y)^{\sigma}]}, \quad y\in(0,1) \tag{1}$$

and

$$f(y|\sigma,\mu) = \frac{\sigma\, y^{\sigma-1}\,(1-\mu)^{\sigma}}{\mu^{\sigma}\,(1-y)^{\sigma+1}}\log\left[(1-\tau)^{-1}\right]\,(1-\tau)^{y^{\sigma}\,(1-\mu)^{\sigma}/[\mu^{\sigma}\,(1-y)^{\sigma}]}, \tag{2}$$

respectively, where $\sigma>0$ is a shape parameter, and $\mu\in(0,1)$ is the τth quantile of the distribution. For $\sigma=2$, the unit ratio-Rayleigh (URR) distribution yields a special case. The corresponding quantile function (qf) is

$$Q(u|\sigma,\mu) = \frac{\left[\frac{\mu^{\sigma}\,\log(1-u)}{(1-\mu)^{\sigma}\log(1-\tau)}\right]^{1/\sigma}}{1+\left[\frac{\mu^{\sigma}\,\log(1-u)}{(1-\mu)^{\sigma}\log(1-\tau)}\right]^{1/\sigma}}. \tag{3}$$

Since $Q(\tau|\sigma,\mu)=\mu$, it follows that μ is a location parameter corresponding to the URW τth quantile.

The flexibility and advantages of the URW distribution and its special case are illustrated by numerical experiments in real and simulated data sets [18]. However, the URW does not accommodate explanatory variables in the modeling. The current paper overcomes this limitation by introducing the URW regression in which the quantile and the shape parameters can be related to a linear predictor. The useful parameterization of the URW allows us to formulate a quantile regression model that consists of two components, namely:

(i) a random component in which $Y_1,\ldots,Y_n$ is a sample of n independent random variables, where each Y_t, $t=1,\ldots,n$, follows a URW distribution with quantile μ_t and shape parameter σ_t, that is, $Y_t\sim URW(\sigma_t,\mu_t)$;

(ii) systematic components through the linear predictors

$$\eta_{1t} = g_1(\mu_t) = \boldsymbol{x}_t^\top \boldsymbol{\beta}, \tag{4}$$

and

$$\eta_{2t} = g_2(\sigma_t) = \boldsymbol{z}_t^\top \boldsymbol{\gamma}, \tag{5}$$

where $\boldsymbol{x}_t = (1, x_{t2}, \ldots, x_{tk})^\top$ and $\boldsymbol{z}_t = (1, z_{t2}, \ldots, z_{tl})^\top$ are $k \times 1$ and $l \times 1$ vectors that contain observations of k and l known covariates $(k + l < n)$, respectively. The vectors of unknown regression parameters are $\boldsymbol{\beta} = (\beta_1, \ldots, \beta_k)^\top \in \mathbb{R}^k$ and $\boldsymbol{\gamma} = (\gamma_1, \ldots, \gamma_l)^\top \in \mathbb{R}^l$. Finally, $g_1 : (0,1) \to \mathbb{R}$ and $g_2 : \mathbb{R}^+ \to \mathbb{R}$ are strictly monotonic and twice differentiable link functions that differ on the mapping required. Ref. [13] provides an overview of some classical link functions under the generalized linear models approach.

2.1. Parameter Estimation

Several approaches to parameter estimation are explored in the literature. However, given its desirable and known asymptotic properties, the maximum likelihood method is the most widely used. In this section, we determine the maximum likelihood estimators (MLEs) of the parameters of the URW regression. Let $\boldsymbol{\theta}^\top = (\boldsymbol{\beta}^\top, \boldsymbol{\gamma}^\top)$ be the URW regression parameter vector, and $\boldsymbol{y}^\top = (y_1, \ldots, y_n)$ the corresponding sample of n independent observations. The log-likelihood function for this sample is

$$\begin{aligned}\ell_t(\sigma_t, \mu_t) = &\sum_{t=1}^{n} \log\left(\frac{\sigma_t}{y_t}\right) + \sum_{t=1}^{n} \log\left[\frac{\log(1-\tau)}{y_t - 1}\right] + \sum_{t=1}^{n} \log\left[\frac{y_t(1-\mu_t)}{\mu_t(1-y_t)}\right]^{\sigma_t} \\ &+ \log(1-\tau) \sum_{t=1}^{n} \left[\frac{y_t(1-\mu_t)}{\mu_t(1-y_t)}\right]^{\sigma_t},\end{aligned} \tag{6}$$

where $\mu_t = g_1^{-1}(\eta_{1t})$, and $\sigma_t = g_2^{-1}(\eta_{2t})$, with η_{1t} and η_{2t} given in (4) and (5), respectively.

The score function is obtained by $\boldsymbol{U} = (\boldsymbol{U}_\beta(\beta, \gamma)^\top, \boldsymbol{U}_\gamma(\beta, \gamma)^\top)^\top$, where

$$\boldsymbol{U}_\beta(\boldsymbol{\theta}) = \partial\ell(\boldsymbol{\theta})/\partial\boldsymbol{\beta}^\top = \mathbf{X}^\top \boldsymbol{T}\boldsymbol{w},$$

with $\boldsymbol{X}$ is a $n \times k$ matrix whose tth row is $x_t^\top$, $\boldsymbol{T} = \text{diag}\{1/g_1'(\mu_1), \ldots, 1/g_1'(\mu_n)\}$, $\boldsymbol{w} = (w_1, \ldots, w_n)$ wherein

$$w_t = \frac{\sigma_t}{\mu_t(\mu_t - 1)}\left[1 + \log(1-\tau)k_t^{\sigma_t}\right],$$

$k_t = y_t(\mu_t - 1)/\mu_t(y_t - 1)$, and $g_1'(\mu_t)$ is the differentiating of $g_1(\mu_t)$ with respect to μ_t, and

$$\boldsymbol{U}_\gamma(\boldsymbol{\theta}) = \partial\ell(\boldsymbol{\theta})/\partial\boldsymbol{\gamma}^\top = \mathbf{Z}^\top \boldsymbol{S}\boldsymbol{u},$$

wherein $\mathbf{Z}$ is a $n \times l$ matrix whose tth row is $z_t^\top$, $\boldsymbol{S} = \text{diag}\{1/g_2'(\sigma_1), \ldots, 1/g_2'(\sigma_n)\}$, $\boldsymbol{u} = (u_1, \ldots, u_n)$ with

$$u_t = \frac{1}{\sigma_t} + \log(k_t)\left[1 + \log(1-\tau)k_t^{\sigma_t}\right],$$

and $g_2'(\sigma_t)$ is the differentiating of $g_2(\sigma_t)$ with respect to σ_t.

The Hessian matrix is given by

$$K(\boldsymbol{\theta}) = \frac{\partial^2 \ell(\boldsymbol{\theta})}{\partial \boldsymbol{\theta} \partial \boldsymbol{\theta}^\top} = \begin{pmatrix} \frac{\partial^2 \ell(\boldsymbol{\theta})}{\partial \beta^2} & \frac{\partial^2 \ell(\boldsymbol{\theta})}{\partial \beta \partial \gamma^\top} \\ \frac{\partial^2 \ell(\boldsymbol{\theta})}{\partial \gamma \partial \beta^\top} & \frac{\partial^2 \ell(\boldsymbol{\theta})}{\partial \gamma^2} \end{pmatrix},$$

where

$$\frac{\partial^2 \ell(\boldsymbol{\theta})}{\partial \beta^2} = \mathbf{X}^\top \boldsymbol{M} \mathbf{X},$$

$$\frac{\partial^2 \ell(\boldsymbol{\theta})}{\partial \gamma^2} = \mathbf{Z}^\top \boldsymbol{B} \mathbf{Z},$$

$$\frac{\partial^2 \ell(\boldsymbol{\theta})}{\partial \beta \partial \gamma^\top} = \frac{\partial^2 \ell(\boldsymbol{\theta})}{\partial \gamma \partial \beta^\top} = \mathbf{Z}^\top \boldsymbol{D} \mathbf{X},$$

and $\boldsymbol{M} = \text{diag}\{m_1, \ldots, m_n\}$, $\boldsymbol{B} = \text{diag}\{b_1, \ldots, b_n\}$, $\boldsymbol{D} = \text{diag}\{d_1, \ldots, d_n\}$, wherein

$$m_t = \frac{\sigma_t}{\mu_t^2(\mu_t - 1)^2}\left[1 - 2\mu_t + k_t^{\sigma_t} \log(1-\tau)(1 - 2\mu_t + \sigma_t)\right]\left[\frac{1}{g_1'(\mu_t)}\right]^2,$$

$$b_t = \left[k_t^{\sigma_t} \log^2(k_t) \log(1-\tau) - \frac{1}{\sigma_t^2}\right]\left[\frac{1}{g_2'(\sigma_t)}\right]^2$$

and

$$d_t = \frac{1}{\mu_t(\mu_t - 1)}\left\{1 + k_t^{\sigma_t} \log(1-\tau)[1 + \sigma_t \log(k_t)]\right\}\left[\frac{1}{g_1'(\mu_t)}\right]\left[\frac{1}{g_2'(\sigma_t)}\right].$$

Under regularity conditions, the asymptotic normality property of EMVs ensures that when the sample size is large,

$$\begin{pmatrix} \hat{\beta} \\ \hat{\gamma} \end{pmatrix} \sim N_{k+l}\left(\begin{pmatrix} \beta \\ \gamma \end{pmatrix}, [-\boldsymbol{K}(\boldsymbol{\theta})]^{-1}\right),$$

approximately. Moreover, $[-\boldsymbol{K}(\boldsymbol{\theta})]^{-1}$ is the asymptotic variance–covariance matrix of $\hat{\boldsymbol{\theta}}$, and $-\boldsymbol{K}(\boldsymbol{\theta})$ is the observed information matrix.

To determine the MLEs of $\boldsymbol{\theta}$, denoted as $\hat{\boldsymbol{\theta}} = (\hat{\beta}, \hat{\gamma})^\top$, is necessary to maximize (6) by setting the score vector components at zero and solving the system of equations simultaneously. However, that is a non-linear system, and numerical methods must be used. Since the proposed model resembles the Generalized Additive Models for Location, Scale, and Shape (GAMLSS) approach [14,19], we implement the URW regression as a gamlss class object in R programming language, which is available in the gamlss package [20,21] and uses the RS algorithm for maximizing the log-likelihood given in (6). The computational codes for the URW model and the simulation and application studies can be downloaded from https://github.com/Fernando-code8/URW-Unit-Ratio-Weibull-Regression- (accessed on 18 October 2024). The cdf (1), pdf (2), and qf (3) can be computed using the dURW, pURW, and qURW functions, respectively. Samples of the URW model can be generated using the rURW function.

2.2. Diagnostic Measures and Model Selection

Diagnostic measures are customarily adopted to check if a fitted regression model adequately represents the data dynamics. To that end, we perform residual analysis using the quantile residuals introduced by [22]. For the URW regression, such a residual is given by $r_t = \Phi^{-1}[F(y_t|\hat{\sigma}_t, \hat{\mu}_t)]$, where $F(\cdot|\hat{\sigma}_t, \hat{\mu}_t)$ is obtained from the URW cdf (1) evaluated at $\hat{\mu}_t = g_1^{-1}\left(x_t^\top \hat{\beta}\right)$ and $\hat{\sigma}_t = g_2^{-1}(z_t^\top \hat{\gamma})$. In the literature, several authors have been considering the quantile residuals since they are standard normally distributed when the model is correctly specified [22]. See [17,23,24] for instance.

We also consider the worm plot of the residuals to verify whether the assumed distribution fits properly for the dependent variable [25]. We expect that $100(1-\alpha)\%$ of the points to be inside the two elliptic curves in the middle of the figure. A large proportion of points outside this region and the occurrence of any specific shape in the points indicate that the fitted model is inadequate.

The generalized coefficient of determination (R_G^2) is considered to measure the predictive capacity of URW-fitted regressions. Defined by [26], the R_G^2 is given by $R_G^2 = 1 - \exp\{-2/n[\ell(\hat{\theta}) - \ell(\hat{\theta}_0)]\}$, where $\ell(\hat{\theta})$ is the log-likelihood of the fitted model, and $\ell(\hat{\theta}_0)$ is the log-likelihood of the model without covariates, i.e., the null model. The higher the R_G^2, the better the fitted model to explain the variability of the response variable.

Finally, Akaike information criteria (AIC) are suggested for model selection. The AIC is widely used to select the more suitable model among a class of candidate models and is defined by [27] as $\text{AIC} = 2[m - \ell(\hat{\theta})]$, where $m = k + l$ is the number of estimated parameters. The better model is the one with a smaller AIC.

The model performance was assessed using leave-one-out cross-validation (LOOCV); see [28] for details. This methodology involves sequentially partitioning the dataset into two parts. Consider a dataset $\{(y_1, \boldsymbol{x}_1), \ldots, (y_n, \boldsymbol{x}_n)\}$ consisting of responses Y and their associated vectors of k covariates, $\boldsymbol{x}_i = (x_{i1}, \ldots, x_{ik})$, where $i = 1, \ldots, n$. Let $\hat{y}_i^*$ be the estimate of the value y_i, obtained by excluding the i–th observation from the fit. Specifically, this involves fitting a regression model to the dataset $\{(y_1, \boldsymbol{x}_1), \ldots, (y_{i-1}, \boldsymbol{x}_{i-1}), (y_{i+1}, \boldsymbol{x}_{i+1}), \ldots, (y_n, \boldsymbol{x}_n)\}$ and then substituting $\boldsymbol{x}_i$ into the fitted regression structure to compute the estimate of y_i, denoted by $\hat{y}_i^*$. This procedure is repeated for all observations in the dataset to obtain $y_1^*, \ldots y_n^*$.

To compare the predicted values of the fitted models, we use the mean absolute error (MAE), defined as $\text{MAE} = \frac{1}{n}\sum_{i=1}^n |y_i - \hat{y}_i^*|$. MAE quantifies the absolute difference between observed and predicted values. Therefore, a lower MAE indicates better model performance.

3. Numerical Evidence

In what follows, we report Monte Carlo experiments to explore the performance of the maximum likelihood method and the assumptions on the empirical distribution of r_t for the proposed methodology. We generate 10,000 replications of a URW regression with the systematic components given by (4) and (5) for the quantile and shape parameters, respectively. The logit link function is used for μ, $\text{logit}(\mu) = \log[\mu/(1-\mu)]$, and the log link function is used for σ. The sample sizes are set at $n \in \{10, 15, 30, 70, 150, 300\}$ and the values of the covariates are generated from the standard uniform distribution. For the parameter values, two different scenarios are considered, namely:

- Scenario 1: $\beta_1 = -3.75$, $\beta_2 = 0.25$, $\gamma_1 = 1.5$, and $\gamma_2 = 1.5$;
- Scenario 2 :$\beta_1 = -5$, $\beta_2 = 1.75$, $\gamma_1 = 2$, and $\gamma_2 = 1.25$.

For brevity, we will present the results with $\tau = 0.5$, which represents the median of the response variable. The numerical evidence for other quantiles was quite similar and is reported in the Appendix A.

The measurements calculated to evaluate the point estimators are the percentage relative bias (RB%), mean square error (MSE), coefficient of skewness (CS), and kurtosis (K). We also compute the coverage rate (CR%) for the interval estimators with a nominal level at 0.95. The results are summarized in Table 1. Notice the point estimators become more accurate and precise as the sample size increases; for example, when $n = 300$, the MSE is less than 0.15 for all parameter estimates and scenarios. The CS and K coefficients are in line with the expected since they get closer to 0 and 3, respectively, as n increases. When analyzing the CR%, we verify values close to the nominal level. The largest difference, of only 0.1248, occurs for $\hat{\beta}_1$ with the smallest sample size of $n = 10$ in Scenario 1. This still represents a minor discrepancy, particularly given the small sample size.

We evaluate the mean, variance, CS, and K measures to study the empirical distribution of the quantile residuals. We expect those statistics to be close to 0, 1, 0, and 3, respectively, since the quantile residual distribution is expected to be approximately standard normal. In this sense, we also compute the null rejection rates for the Shapiro–Wilk normality test at the 10%, 5%, and 1% significance levels, which are referred to as NRR10%, NRR5%, and NRR1%, respectively. Table 2 reports the results for the residual simulations. The calculated statistics show that the distribution of r_t is approximated by its reference distribution. The normality test corroborates this result since the null rejection rates are close to the test nominal level for all scenarios.

Table 1. Results of simulation of URW regression with $\tau = 0.5$.

Measures	n	**Scenario 1**				**Scenario 2**			
		$\hat{\beta}_1$	$\hat{\beta}_2$	$\hat{\gamma}_1$	$\hat{\gamma}_2$	$\hat{\beta}_1$	$\hat{\beta}_2$	$\hat{\gamma}_1$	$\hat{\gamma}_2$
RB%	10	0.4321	−9.4939	66.3225	−13.6220	0.1536	−2.2519	55.3137	−17.9652
	15	0.0532	−5.1174	27.2422	17.6428	0.6361	1.9085	28.6735	7.1978
	30	0.0342	−1.0949	13.7665	4.5770	0.0308	−0.0859	13.5165	2.1807
	70	0.0036	−0.1549	3.9841	5.0650	0.0000	−0.0153	3.9081	5.8399
	150	−0.0048	−0.3322	1.7043	2.5107	−0.0033	−0.0404	1.7326	2.7387
	300	−0.0055	−0.5761	1.0077	0.8726	−0.0044	−0.0708	0.9927	0.8967
MSE	10	0.0858	0.4924	9.8697	22.0775	0.0644	0.3705	13.0225	28.6075
	15	0.0691	0.2481	1.2178	5.1895	0.1011	0.1814	2.2252	5.8772
	30	0.0429	0.1130	0.4112	1.3282	0.0306	0.0827	0.6725	1.8748
	70	0.0130	0.0326	0.1368	0.5958	0.0097	0.0246	0.2164	0.8274
	150	0.0055	0.0181	0.0391	0.1932	0.0041	0.0134	0.0637	0.2644
	300	0.0027	0.0072	0.0232	0.1047	0.0020	0.0054	0.0370	0.1441
CS	10	−0.4821	0.0163	1.3254	−0.0668	−0.4807	0.0217	1.3911	−0.0769
	15	−0.3653	−0.0450	1.6770	0.1168	−0.4961	0.2488	1.8602	−0.2006
	30	−0.2080	0.0287	1.4250	−0.0677	−0.2165	0.0293	1.2909	−0.1013
	70	−0.1485	0.0161	0.6854	0.0520	−0.1490	0.0167	0.6490	0.0402
	150	−0.1197	0.0100	0.4637	0.0724	−0.1187	0.0134	0.4418	0.0514
	300	−0.1205	0.0032	0.3357	0.0099	−0.1185	0.0037	0.3177	−0.0048
K	10	3.7022	3.4739	6.1684	4.0920	3.6177	3.4202	6.9478	4.2937
	15	3.4778	3.3128	7.2405	4.4532	3.6312	3.4633	8.6702	4.8173
	30	3.1766	3.2517	6.8859	4.0104	3.1935	3.2596	6.0387	3.9389
	70	3.1527	3.1266	3.9511	3.4472	3.1691	3.1243	3.8532	3.4277
	150	3.0272	2.9784	3.3380	3.2861	3.0159	2.9739	3.2966	3.2884
	300	3.0321	3.0402	3.1597	3.0193	3.0371	3.0379	3.1356	3.0045
CR%	10	0.8371	0.8252	0.9327	0.9308	0.8420	0.8303	0.9334	0.9324
	15	0.8709	0.8659	0.9365	0.9261	0.8661	0.8647	0.9404	0.9378
	30	0.9101	0.9128	0.9433	0.9374	0.9077	0.9131	0.9443	0.9375
	70	0.9360	0.9404	0.9487	0.9475	0.9378	0.9396	0.9474	0.9467
	150	0.9446	0.9408	0.9537	0.9505	0.9443	0.9409	0.9531	0.9497
	300	0.9479	0.9488	0.9476	0.9467	0.9474	0.9471	0.9482	0.9479

Table 2. Simulation results for the quantile residuals of the URW regression with $\tau = 0.5$.

Scenario	n	Mean	Variance	CS	K	NRR10%	NRR5%	NRR1%
1	10	0.0086	1.1376	−0.0801	2.2805	0.0747	0.0316	0.0059
	15	0.0022	1.0920	−0.0668	2.3691	0.0877	0.0379	0.0036
	30	−0.0011	1.0464	−0.0298	2.6328	0.0874	0.0391	0.0050
	70	−0.0005	1.0203	−0.0146	2.8228	0.0902	0.0436	0.0073
	150	−0.0003	1.0097	−0.0090	2.9047	0.0848	0.0405	0.0075
	300	0.0004	1.0050	−0.0054	2.9518	0.0909	0.0420	0.0077
2	10	0.0068	1.1398	−0.0871	2.2747	0.0745	0.0296	0.0047
	15	0.0032	1.0946	−0.0764	2.3614	0.0816	0.0340	0.0036
	30	−0.0015	1.0471	−0.0304	2.6306	0.0869	0.0389	0.0051
	70	−0.0008	1.0206	−0.0148	2.8220	0.0900	0.0428	0.0075
	150	−0.0003	1.0099	−0.0091	2.9042	0.0842	0.0410	0.0072
	300	0.0003	1.0051	−0.0054	2.9518	0.0904	0.0418	0.0079

4. An Analysis of COVID-19 Mortality Rate

The current section outlines the data preparation employed to investigate the COVID-19 mortality rate. We consider data from 19 Latin American countries: Argentina, Belize, Bolivia, Brazil, Chile, Colombia, Costa Rica, Ecuador, El Salvador, Guatemala, Honduras, Mexico, Nicaragua, Panama, Paraguay, Peru, Suriname, Uruguay, and Venezuela. For comparative purposes, the response variable is defined as the initial mortality rate (MR) per thousand people 90 days after the 20th detected case. We fit the URW regression concurrently with the Kumaraswamy [29] (KW) and unit Weibull [17] (UW) quantile regressions. Those are well-known unit regressions that may be alternatives when the interest lies in modeling the impact of explanatory variables in a quantile of the mortality rate.

We analyze the impact of pre-existing country characteristics such as social, demographic, and health indicators in the MR. To this aim, we consider the data from the most recent year available, which were collected from [30]. The selected explanatory variables are presented in Table 3. The rest of the section presents a descriptive summary and correlation analysis for the considered variables and the regression models' results. This information can be helpful to reveal epidemiological differences across Latin American countries, identify the covariates with larger influence in the response variable, and understand their impact on the initial COVID-19 mortality rate. Finally, the results may contribute to shaping a direction for predicting regional or national infections and mortality in future research.

Table 3. Definition of the variables.

Variable	Description
CHE	Current health expenditure: Level of current health expenditure expressed as a percentage of the gross domestic product in the year. It includes healthcare goods and services consumed during each year 2017. This indicator does not include capital health expenditures such as buildings, machinery, and stocks of vaccines for emergencies or outbreaks.
DGGHE	Domestic general government health expenditure: Public expenditure on health from domestic sources as a share of the economy as measured by the percentage of the gross domestic product in 2017.
DP	Diabetes prevalence: percentage of people ages 20–79 who have type 1 or type 2 diabetes in the year 2019.
GDP	Gross domestic product per capita: gross domestic product divided by midyear population in 2019. The exceptions are Cuba and Venezuela, which the more recent information was for 2018 and 2014, respectively.
HDI	Human development index in 2018.
UP	Urban population: percentage of the total population of people living in urban areas in 2019.

4.1. Descriptive Summary and Correlation Analysis

The COVID-19 mortality rate had an asymmetrical and dispersed behavior among the Latin American countries; see its skewness and percentage coefficient of variation (CV%) in Table 4. From Figure 1, notice the MR is mostly concentrated on the left tail, indicating a right-skewed and decreasing shape on the histogram. Thus, the MR is heterogeneous among the Latin American countries, which is a typical feature for these kind of data. For example, [12] reported that the COVID-19 mortality rate varies greatly and has a right-skewed distribution across countries, and [3] verified that this disease manifests differently among the various regions of Latin America.

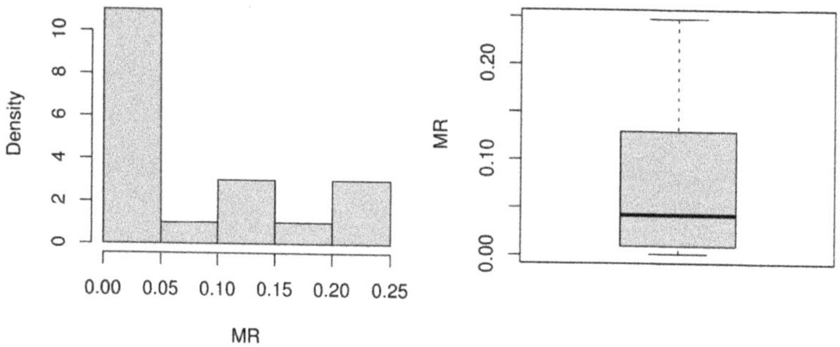

(a) Histogram (b) Box plot

Figure 1. Histogram and box plot of the MR.

Table 4 also shows a descriptive summary for the explanatory variables. The highest variability is observed for the GDP, which has CV% around 240 and also presents the highest positive value of skewness. [31] highlights, through the Gini Index, how inequality among Latin American countries in relation to GDP has persisted over time. The HDI presents the lower CV% and most of the countries are classified with high, between 0.7–0.799 [32], or very high, between 0.8–1 [32]. Variables CHE, DGGHE, HDI, and UP have negative skewness. The variables MR, UP, and HDI, given their negative kurtosis, have light-tailed distributions. The variables with the heaviest-tailed distributions are PD and GDP.

Table 4. Descriptive summary for the response variable and covariates.

Variable	Mean	Median	Skewness	Kurtosis	Min.	Max.	CV (%)
CHE	7.0112	7.2276	−1.1365	1.5606	1.1812	9.4675	28.0252
DGGHE	4.0354	4.3616	−0.4765	0.4420	0.1883	6.6089	37.1126
DP	9.0789	8.6000	1.1076	0.6581	5.5000	17.1000	32.1934
GDP	3.2553	0.0226	2.3576	4.6840	0.0039	29.7482	239.1504
HDI	0.7405	0.7580	−0.2021	−0.9595	0.6230	0.8470	8.4062
MR	0.0793	0.0422	0.7314	−1.0656	0.0014	0.2473	109.1801
UP	72.9568	72.7460	−0.1786	−1.1724	45.8660	95.4260	19.4462

Table 5 presents the correlation matrix for the studied variables. The correlations presented are those corresponding to the Spearman method. We can observe negative correlations between the response variable (MR) and the GDP and DP variables. On the other hand, the highest positive correlation is that associated with the HB variable. Figure 2 displays scatterplots of the MR versus other covariates and provides a visual inspection of the correlation measure.

Table 5. Spearman's correlation coefficient between all variables.

Variables	DGGHE	DP	GDP	HDI	MR	UP
CHE	0.6895	−0.1676	0.8939	0.3549	0.0947	0.2930
DGGHE		−0.2255	0.7924	0.4207	−0.1351	0.3842
DP			0.4178	−0.2241	−0.2159	−0.3668
GDP				0.2143	0.3130	0.2143
HDI					0.1880	0.7668
MR						0.0211

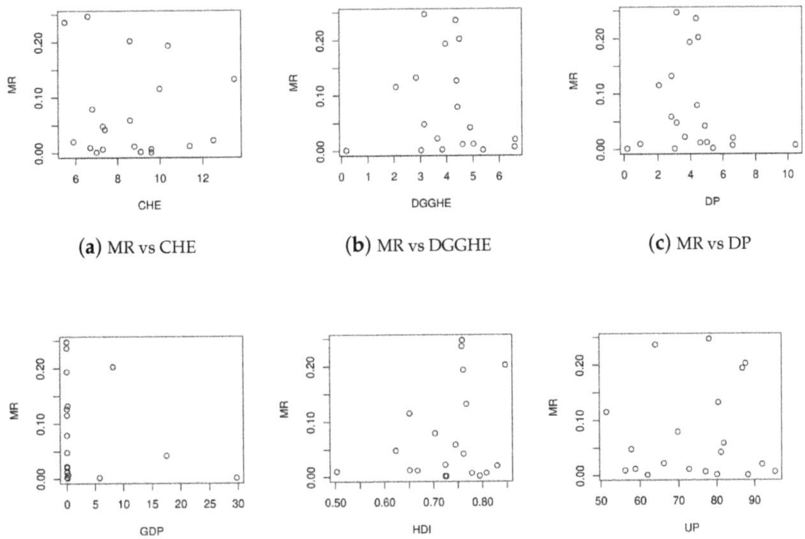

(**a**) MR vs CHE (**b**) MR vs DGGHE (**c**) MR vs DP

(**d**) MR vs GDP (**e**) MR vs HDI (**f**) MR vs UP

Figure 2. Dispersion plots of MR as a function of CHE, DGGHE, DP, GDP, HDI and UP.

4.2. Regression Results and Discussion

The COVID-19 mortality rate analysis is performed by taking the MR as the response variable in the proposed regression. Two competitor unit models are considered and compared to the URW regression. The Kumaraswamy and UW quantile regressions have their random components given by the pdfs

$$f(y|\sigma,\mu) = \frac{\log(1-\tau)}{\sigma\log(1-\mu^{1/\sigma})} y^{1/\sigma-1}(1-y^{1/\sigma})^{\log(1-\tau)/\log(1-\mu^{1/\sigma})-1},$$

and

$$f(y|\sigma,\mu) = \frac{\sigma}{y}\left(\frac{\log\tau}{\log\mu}\right)\left(\frac{\log y}{\log\mu}\right)^{\sigma-1}\tau^{(\log y/\log\mu)^{\sigma}},$$

respectively, where $\mu \in (0,1)$ is the τth quantile, $\tau \in (0,1)$ is assumed known, and $\sigma > 0$ is a shape parameter. For both competitor models, we define systematic components analogous to those in Equations (4) and (5) and set $\tau = 0.5$ to model the median of the response variable.

After evaluating all possible subsets of regressions through the significance of the predictors, AIC, and residual analysis, the systematic components for all classes of regressions are defined by

$$\text{logit}(\mu_t) = \beta_1 + \beta_2\text{GDP}_t + \beta_3\text{HDI}_t + \beta_4\text{DP}_t + \beta_5\text{DGGHE}_t,$$

and

$$\log(\sigma_t) = \gamma_1 + \gamma_2\text{GDP}_t + \gamma_3\text{UP}_t,$$

where $\text{logit}(\mu_t) = \log[\mu_t/(1-\mu_t)]$ is the logit link function.

The final fitted regressions and their goodness-of-fit measures are reported in Tables 6 and 7, respectively. Table 6 presents the parameter estimates and corresponding p-values for the KW, URW, and UW models. In the case of the UW regression, many p-values were not statistically significant at the 5% level, capturing only the effects of UP on the response variable MR. The adjusted KW and URW models proved competitive, with all estimates significant at the 5% level, except for the GDP predictor, which was significant at the 10% level. Table 7 shows the results of the Anderson-Darling (AD) test, which we performed to verify the null hypothesis that the quantile residuals are normally distributed. For the UW regression, the AD test rejects the normality hypothesis at the 1% significance level, suggesting that this model is not adequate to the current data. The URW and KW remain as competitive regressions. However, it is noteworthy that our model outperforms the KW for all goodness-of-fit measures. The AIC of the URW regression is the lowest, and the R^2_G is also in favor of the proposed model, indicating that the URW-fitted model is able to explain about 72.78% of the total variability in the MR. The URW regression model produced the lowest MAE; however, this difference is minimal when considering the scale of MR. To address this limitation and derive a unit-independent metric, the MAE-$\bar{MR}$ ratio was employed, calculated as the quotient of the MAE and the mean MR. The results of this ratio more distinctly demonstrate the advantage of the URW model over the others, underscoring its superiority in terms of predictive accuracy.

Figures 3 and 4 present the diagnostic plots based on the quantile residuals for the fitted URW and KW regressions, respectively. Both fitted regression models, URW and KW, demonstrate suitable results in the graphical analysis of residuals. In the residual plot, the quantile residuals are randomly distributed around zero. In the worm plot, all points lie within the confidence bands and remain close to the central line, with no visible trend. The QQ plot indicates that the sample quantiles are within the limits of the confidence envelopes, suggesting an adequate fit to the data.

Overall, these analyses indicate that the URW regression provides superior fit quality, as evidenced by the lower MAE and MAE-$\bar{MR}$ statistics shown in Table 7, based on the LOOCV approach. These results suggest that the URW regression yields more accurate predictions compared to the KW regression. Therefore, we confirm that the URW model is appropriate and provides better fit quality.

Table 6. Summary of the final fitted regressions for the MR.

	KW		URW		UW	
Coefficients	**Estimate**	***p*-Value**	**Estimate**	***p*-Value**	**Estimate**	***p*-Value**
Intercept (for μ)	−5.9618	0.0421	−6.0836	0.0332	−5.9614	0.6237
GDP	−0.1539	0.0004	−0.1515	0.0006	−0.1520	0.6028
HDI	10.2217	0.0069	10.4728	0.0042	10.4197	0.4536
CHE	0.4216	0.0462	0.4023	0.0468	0.3899	0.6049
DP	−0.3115	0.0000	−0.3082	0.0001	−0.3097	0.1822
DGGHE	−1.0982	0.0004	−1.0861	0.0003	−1.0808	0.3560
Intercept (for σ)	7.0900	0.0000	6.4348	0.0000	6.4599	0.0013
GDP	−0.0431	0.0680	−0.0379	0.0875	−0.0388	0.3108
UP	−0.0718	0.0000	−0.0643	0.0001	−0.0641	0.0014

Table 7. Goodness-of-fit measures for the final fitted regressions.

Regression	AIC	R_G^2	p-Value (AD)	MAE	MAE-$\overline{MR}$
KW	−69.4907	0.7258	0.7321	0.0556	0.7013
URW	−69.9176	0.7286	0.8473	0.0480	0.6054
UW	−41.4766	−0.1750	0.0002	0.0401	0.5058

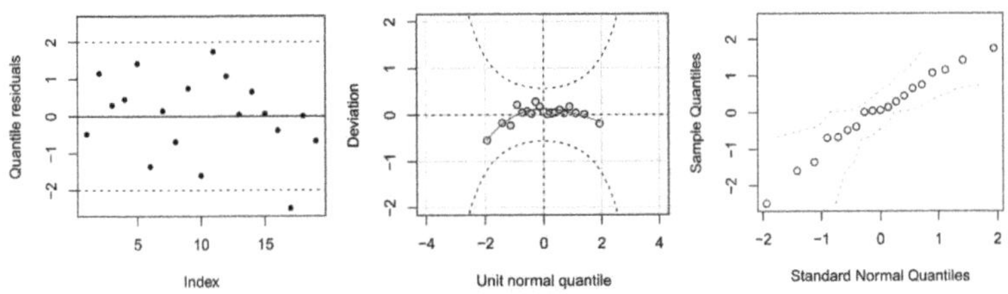

(**a**) Residual plot (**b**) Worm plot (**c**) QQ-plot

Figure 3. Residuals plots for the fitted URW regression.

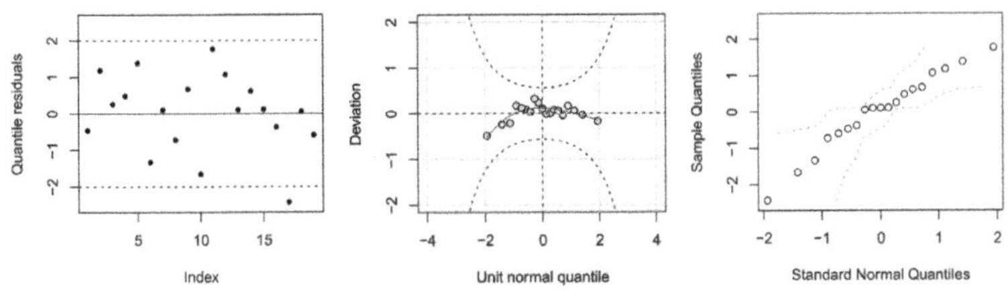

(**a**) Residual plot (**b**) Worm plot (**c**) QQ-plot

Figure 4. Residuals plots for the fitted KW regression.

The URW model for the median mortality rate due to COVID-19 revealed positive estimated coefficients for HDI (10.4728) and CHE (0.4023) and negative coefficients for GDP (−0.1515), DP (−0.3082), and DGGHE (−1.0861). In terms of variation, a one-unit increase in GDP per capita reduces the median mortality rate by 14.26, while an increase in DGGHE reduces this rate by 66.2%. The DP variable reduces the median rate by 26.5%. On the other hand, an increase in HDI is associated with a significant increase in the median mortality rate, suggesting complex relationships with other factors, while a one-unit increase in the CHE index is associated with a 49.5% increase in the median mortality rate. For the submodel, negative estimated coefficients were found for GDP (−0.0379) and UP (−0.0643). This means that a one-unit increase in GDP per capita and in UP is associated with a reduction of approximately 3.7% and 6.2% in the value of the parameter σ, respectively.

Based on the fitted URW regression, relevant observations were identified regarding the modeling of the median mortality rate due to COVID-19 in Latin American countries. The variables GDP and DGGHE showed negative coefficients, suggesting that increases in GDP and government spending on health infrastructure are associated with a significant reduction in the median mortality rate due to COVID-19. That is, a more robust economy and higher public spending on health seem to enhance resilience against mortality from the disease.

On the other hand, the variable DP showed unexpected results, indicating a negative effect on the response variable. The variables HDI and CHE, also yielding unexpected results, presented positive coefficients, suggesting that increases in the HDI and DGGHE indicators of countries are associated with a higher median mortality rate due to COVID-19. This counterintuitive interpretation suggests more complex interactions, possibly influenced by other variables such as GDP and DGGHE, which also tend to correlate with economic development, health investment, and diabetes prevalence across countries.

In interpreting the coefficients of the submodel for the parameter σ, both GDP and UP exhibited negative signs, suggesting that increases in GDP and urbanization are associated with a reduction in σ. This indicates that in regions with higher GDP and urbanization, the mortality rate due to COVID-19 tends to accelerate less and stabilize more quickly over time. These results indicate that in areas of higher urban density, the probability of transmission is naturally greater. However, more developed regions with structured economies quickly require the implementation of strict measures, such as social distancing, mask use, and interventions to control the spread of the virus.

5. Concluding Remarks

This article presents a new regression model that explores the relationship between demographic indicators, economic variables, and public health measures with the COVID-19 mortality rate among Latin American countries, a region heavily impacted and regarded as one of the pandemic's epicenters. It is introduced based on the unit ratio-Weibull distribution, which is a helpful tool for modeling random variables in the interval (0, 1), such as rates, proportions, and indices. A general and useful quantile parameterization is introduced to define the new regression model for double-bounded epidemiological data modeling. We defined a systematic structure for the two parameters of the distribution: one represents the quantile of the distribution, and the other, the shape parameter. The parameters were estimated by maximum likelihood, and the performance of the estimators was evaluated through Monte Carlo simulations under different scenarios, considering varying quantile values and finite sample sizes. The URW model was compared with the Kumaraswamy and unit Weibull regressions, proving to be competitive and providing the best fit across various selection criteria and predictive accuracy measures. From the adjusted regression, it was identified that factors such as economic development, Human Development Index, percentage of the urban population, and government investment in health infrastructure are associated with lower COVID-19 mortality rates in Latin American countries. The results indicate that investments in public health and economic infrastructure are essential to reducing the impact of future pandemics and improving public health response policies. The URW regression offers a more robust alternative for capturing the asymmetric and bounded characteristics of mortality rates. This approach provides valuable insights for more effective public policies, helping to understand the impacts of economic and demographic variables on mortality. The ability to apply this methodology to a wide range of fields underscores its versatility, with potential applications in areas such as health, economics, and engineering. Future research could explore its use in analyzing mortality rates from diseases like measles in health, inequality indices like the Gini index and poverty rates in economics, and failure rates or equipment efficiency in engineering. Furthermore, comparing the performance of the proposed model with other approaches across these diverse fields would provide valuable insights into its effectiveness and adaptability.

Author Contributions: Conceptualization, F.A.P.-R. and R.R.G.; methodology, F.A.P.-R., F.J.M.d.A. and R.R.G.; software, F.A.P.-R., F.J.M.d.A. and R.R.G.; validation, F.J.M.d.A., F.A.P.-R. and R.R.G.; formal analysis, F.A.P.-R. and R.R.G.; investigation, F.J.M.d.A., F.A.P.-R. and R.R.G.; resources, F.A.P.-R. and R.R.G.; data curation, F.J.M.d.A.; writing—original draft preparation, F.J.M.d.A.; writing—review and editing, F.A.P.-R. and R.R.G.; visualization, F.J.M.d.A.; supervision, F.A.P.-R. and R.R.G.; project administration, F.A.P.-R. and R.R.G.; funding acquisition, F.A.P.-R. and R.R.G. All authors have read and agreed to the published version of the manuscript.

Funding: This research was funded by FAPERGS/23/2551-0001595-1, CNPq/306274/2022-1, and Instituto Serrapilheira - 2211-41692, Brazil.

Data Availability Statement: In the article, a set of real data are used, which can be found through the link (https://github.com/Fernando-code8/URW-Unit-Ratio-Weibull-Regression- (accessed on 18 October 2024)).

Acknowledgments: We gratefully acknowledge partial financial support from Serrapilheira Institute - Serra - 2211-41692; Fundação de Amparo à pesquisa do Estado do RS - FAPERGS/23/2551-0001595-1. The autor Renata Rojas Guerra acknowledges the Conselho Nacional de Desenvolvimento Científico e Tecnológico - CNPq/306274/2022-1.

Conflicts of Interest: The funders had no role in the design of the study, the collection, analyses, or interpretation of data, the writing of the manuscript, or in the decision to publish the results.

Abbreviations

The following abbreviations are used in this manuscript:

COVID-19	Coronavirus Disease 2019
URW	Unit Ratio-Weibull
SARS-CoV-2	Severe Acute Respiratory Syndrome Coronavirus 2
GLM	Generalized Linear Models
GAMLSS	Generalized additive Models for Locarion, Scale, and Shape
MLE	Maximum Likelihood Estimators
AIC	Akaike information criteria
LOOCV	Leave-One-Out Cross-Validation
MAE	Mean Absolute Error
RB%	Relative Bias
MSE	Mean Square Error
CS	Coefficient of Skewness
K	Kurtosis
CR%	Coverage Rate
NRR	Null Rejection Rates
MR	Mortality Rate
KW	Kumaraswamy
UW	unit Weibull
CHE	Current Health Expenditure
DGGHE	Domestic General Government Health Expenditure
DP	Diabetes Prevalence
GDP	Gross Domestic Product per capita
HDI	Human Development Index
UP	Urban Population
CV%	Coefficient of Variation
AD	Anderson-Darling

Appendix A

In the appendix, we provide supplementary results to Section 3. The numerical results of the Monte Carlo simulations for other quantiles of the proposed URW regression are explored below.

Table A1. Results of simulation of URW regression with $\tau = 0.25$.

Measures	n	Scenario 1				Scenario 2			
		$\hat{\beta}_1$	$\hat{\beta}_2$	$\hat{\gamma}_1$	$\hat{\gamma}_2$	$\hat{\beta}_1$	$\hat{\beta}_2$	$\hat{\gamma}_1$	$\hat{\gamma}_2$
RB%	10	0.8955	−12.3577	26.1715	−3.9051	0.9435	−0.9402	17.1284	−3.2589
	15	0.7920	13.0612	19.6379	−2.8108	0.2532	−0.9762	8.6795	17.4380
	30	−0.1949	−2.4211	10.1151	2.8109	0.0268	−0.2949	8.6986	−2.0248
	70	−0.1938	−0.6672	3.1095	4.9114	−0.0034	0.1235	2.9153	3.1665
	150	−0.0813	−0.2715	1.5041	2.1208	−0.0151	−0.0103	1.6613	0.6487
	300	−0.0333	−0.2937	0.6905	1.1025	−0.0036	−0.0082	0.6089	1.0906

Table A1. *Cont.*

Measures	n	Scenario 1				Scenario 2			
		$\hat{\beta}_1$	$\hat{\beta}_2$	$\hat{\gamma}_1$	$\hat{\gamma}_2$	$\hat{\beta}_1$	$\hat{\beta}_2$	$\hat{\gamma}_1$	$\hat{\gamma}_2$
MSE	10	0.1127	0.5730	3.4659	9.2046	0.0905	0.4523	4.1580	10.6474
	15	0.0980	0.2119	0.6815	2.0895	0.0738	0.1989	0.5999	2.7986
	30	0.0515	0.1199	0.2082	0.6609	0.0371	0.0894	0.3144	0.8253
	70	0.0140	0.0333	0.0522	0.2487	0.0145	0.0271	0.1081	0.3871
	150	0.0069	0.0151	0.0228	0.1185	0.0057	0.0118	0.0399	0.1478
	300	0.0038	0.0085	0.0103	0.0524	0.0027	0.0057	0.0195	0.0765
CS	10	−0.4748	−0.0204	1.1914	0.0696	−0.4858	−0.0093	1.1418	0.1661
	15	−0.4204	0.1240	1.5304	−0.0829	−0.3588	0.0110	1.2062	0.4756
	30	−0.2306	0.0049	1.1835	0.0575	−0.2294	0.0056	0.9943	0.0051
	70	−0.1365	−0.0526	0.6925	0.2627	−0.1321	0.0130	0.6636	0.0908
	150	−0.0336	−0.0321	0.4305	0.2132	−0.1298	−0.0123	0.3829	0.1229
	300	−0.0537	−0.0328	0.2891	0.1429	−0.0664	0.0068	0.3245	0.0706
K	10	3.6347	3.8061	6.3411	4.5570	3.7019	3.8261	6.2545	4.8212
	15	3.4237	3.3723	7.6680	4.4074	3.3342	3.2400	6.0103	4.6433
	30	3.2373	3.3288	5.4315	3.7133	3.2729	3.3480	4.6430	3.4521
	70	3.0450	3.0384	4.0062	3.3648	3.0745	3.1062	3.8198	3.3480
	150	2.9745	2.9595	3.3899	3.1429	3.1177	3.1842	3.3017	3.1480
	300	2.9697	2.9734	3.1233	3.0300	3.0000	3.0280	3.2266	3.1211
CR%	10	0.9000	0.8699	0.9627	0.9622	0.9031	0.8740	0.9597	0.9668
	15	0.9081	0.9019	0.9715	0.9597	0.9229	0.9130	0.9575	0.9632
	30	0.9262	0.9216	0.9552	0.9562	0.9329	0.9272	0.9629	0.9601
	70	0.9363	0.9358	0.9507	0.9505	0.9400	0.9384	0.9558	0.9524
	150	0.9436	0.9446	0.9518	0.9493	0.9499	0.9487	0.9547	0.9525
	300	0.9482	0.9480	0.9505	0.9521	0.9484	0.9499	0.9511	0.9500

Table A2. Simulation results for the quantile residuals of the URW regression with $\tau = 0.25$.

Scenario	n	Mean	Variance	CS	K	NRR10%	NRR5%	NRR1%
1	10	0.0044	1.1585	−0.2039	2.1817	0.0984	0.0390	0.0046
	15	0.0071	1.1059	−0.1692	2.3633	0.1034	0.0451	0.0058
	30	0.0059	1.0488	−0.0759	2.6334	0.0953	0.0435	0.0059
	70	0.0028	1.0210	−0.0354	2.8241	0.0920	0.0442	0.0066
	150	0.0018	1.0092	−0.0158	2.9108	0.0824	0.0407	0.0072
	300	0.0017	1.0043	−0.0098	2.9532	0.0892	0.0427	0.0078
2	10	0.0020	1.1650	−0.2231	2.1788	0.1058	0.0407	0.0048
	15	0.0082	1.1011	−0.1475	2.3926	0.1024	0.0446	0.0061
	30	0.0043	1.0514	−0.0816	2.6208	0.0956	0.0447	0.0065
	70	0.0029	1.0217	−0.0379	2.8211	0.0950	0.0467	0.0060
	150	0.0022	1.0096	−0.0189	2.9110	0.0875	0.0416	0.0081
	300	0.0021	1.0038	−0.0095	2.9534	0.0921	0.0440	0.0087

Table A3. Results of simulation of URW regression with $\tau = 0.75$.

Measures	n	Scenario 1				Scenario 2			
		$\hat{\beta}_1$	$\hat{\beta}_2$	$\hat{\gamma}_1$	$\hat{\gamma}_2$	$\hat{\beta}_1$	$\hat{\beta}_2$	$\hat{\gamma}_1$	$\hat{\gamma}_2$
RB%	10	1.5139	7.0198	59.4137	−15.7750	1.0066	1.0272	50.3627	−15.8088
	15	0.9394	−5.5294	10.4376	58.9365	0.5469	−0.4434	20.8548	19.1723
	30	0.5489	2.1688	12.8607	3.8494	0.3910	0.4465	11.7262	0.5419
	70	0.1713	−0.8342	4.3563	3.9296	0.1220	−0.0153	2.9261	8.5480
	150	0.0951	0.1653	2.2395	1.1441	0.0606	−0.0033	1.8062	2.2326
	300	0.0569	0.2216	0.9944	0.7903	0.0251	−0.0434	0.8836	1.1722

Table A3. *Cont.*

Measures	n	Scenario 1				Scenario 2			
		$\hat{\beta}_1$	$\hat{\beta}_2$	$\hat{\gamma}_1$	$\hat{\gamma}_2$	$\hat{\beta}_1$	$\hat{\beta}_2$	$\hat{\gamma}_1$	$\hat{\gamma}_2$
MSE	10	0.0762	0.4276	8.8373	19.6653	0.0576	0.3214	12.0601	26.4214
	15	0.0596	0.2170	0.9523	8.5802	0.0470	0.1831	1.9961	8.4663
	30	0.0388	0.1069	0.4495	1.4973	0.0277	0.0780	0.7014	2.0920
	70	0.0097	0.0389	0.1595	0.6060	0.0099	0.0255	0.2353	0.9759
	150	0.0048	0.0139	0.0708	0.2595	0.0040	0.0125	0.0886	0.3329
	300	0.0027	0.0082	0.0250	0.1098	0.0020	0.0062	0.0406	0.1717
CS	10	−0.5182	0.1293	1.3932	−0.1506	−0.4724	0.0761	1.3552	−0.0990
	15	−0.3864	−0.0399	1.1578	0.8260	−0.3172	−0.0624	1.5891	0.0852
	30	−0.1942	0.0519	1.2827	−0.1398	−0.2190	0.0562	1.1600	−0.1521
	70	−0.1104	−0.0524	0.6154	0.0133	−0.1763	0.0369	0.4554	0.1434
	150	−0.1260	0.0217	0.5416	−0.0837	−0.0893	−0.0071	0.4727	0.0027
	300	−0.0580	0.0006	0.2772	0.0145	−0.0400	0.0247	0.3023	0.0043
K	10	3.7395	3.5907	6.7588	4.1142	3.6278	3.5253	6.5626	4.1212
	15	3.5437	3.3600	5.6210	4.9085	3.3445	3.2608	7.9806	4.1577
	30	3.1248	3.1764	6.1000	3.6655	3.2356	3.2399	5.5435	3.6156
	70	3.1267	3.1935	3.6814	3.2058	3.1825	3.1104	3.2776	3.2182
	150	2.9852	2.9519	3.5492	3.1539	3.0646	2.9997	3.3876	3.1305
	300	2.9573	2.9404	3.0739	3.0106	2.9913	3.0221	3.1717	3.0464
CR%	10	0.8427	0.8475	0.9389	0.9402	0.8391	0.8450	0.9386	0.9413
	15	0.8503	0.8496	0.9033	0.9073	0.8815	0.8780	0.9191	0.9157
	30	0.9100	0.9174	0.9410	0.9389	0.9104	0.9190	0.9408	0.9375
	70	0.9372	0.9387	0.9429	0.9465	0.9357	0.9361	0.9443	0.9458
	150	0.9393	0.9389	0.9495	0.9474	0.9417	0.9393	0.9462	0.9450
	300	0.9494	0.9498	0.9523	0.9526	0.9479	0.9495	0.9504	0.9489

Table A4. Simulation results for the quantile residuals of the URW regression with $\tau = 0.75$.

Scenario	n	Mean	Variance	CS	K	NRR10%	NRR5%	NRR1%
1	10	−0.0089	1.1467	−0.1145	2.2479	0.0909	0.0422	0.0058
	15	−0.0023	1.0776	0.0049	2.4589	0.0862	0.0372	0.0037
	30	−0.0034	1.0388	0.0060	2.6568	0.0846	0.0385	0.0053
	70	−0.0007	1.0166	0.0052	2.8431	0.0878	0.0398	0.0066
	150	−0.0005	1.0080	0.0016	2.9171	0.0863	0.0400	0.0061
	300	−0.0003	1.0042	−0.0001	2.9565	0.0921	0.0450	0.0078
2	10	−0.0078	1.1472	−0.1131	2.2581	0.0886	0.0411	0.0061
	15	−0.0055	1.0830	−0.0146	2.4164	0.0852	0.0372	0.0043
	30	−0.0035	1.0399	0.0018	2.6503	0.0854	0.0374	0.0050
	70	−0.0009	1.0173	0.0022	2.8406	0.0879	0.0388	0.0075
	150	−0.0004	1.0079	0.0026	2.9179	0.0873	0.0402	0.0071
	300	−0.0002	1.0043	−0.0005	2.9567	0.0899	0.0402	0.0071

References

1. World Health Organization (WHO). Indicators. 2024. Available online: https://www.who.int/emergencies/diseases/novel-coronavirus-2019 (accessed on 13 October 2024).
2. Ashmore, P.; Sherwood, E. An overview of COVID-19 global epidemiology and discussion of potential drivers of variable global pandemic impacts. *J. Antimicrob. Chemother.* **2023**, *78*, ii2–ii11. [CrossRef]
3. Ashktorab, H.; Pizuorno, A.; Oskroch, G.; Fierro, N.A.; Sherif, Z.A.; Brim, H. COVID-19 in Latin America: Symptoms, Morbidities, and Gastrointestinal Manifestations. *Gastroenterology* **2021**, *160*, 938–940. [CrossRef] [PubMed]
4. Li, J.; Lai, S.; Gao, G.F.; Shi, W. The emergence, genomic diversity and global spread of SARS-CoV-2. *Nature* **2021**, *600*, 408–418. [CrossRef] [PubMed]
5. Cimerman, S.; Chebabo, A.; Cunha, C.A.D.; Rodríguez-Morales, A.J. Deep impact of COVID-19 in the healthcare of Latin America: The case of Brazil. *Braz. J. Infect. Dis.* **2020**, *24*, 93–95. [CrossRef] [PubMed]
6. Anderson, R.M.; May, R.M. *Infectious Diseases of Humans: Dynamics and Control*; Oxford University Press: Oxford, UK, 1991.

7. Kermack, W.O.; McKendrick, A.G. A contribution to the mathematical theory of epidemics. *Proc. R. Soc. Lond. Ser. A Contain. Pap. Math. Phys. Character* **1927**, *115*, 700–721.
8. Fauzi, N.F.; Bakhtiar, N.S.A.; Khairudin, N.I.; Halim, H.Z.A.; Shafii, N.H. A Performance of SIR Model in Predicting the Number of COVID-19 Cases in Malaysia based on Different Phase of COVID-19 Outbreak. *J. Comput. Res. Innov.* **2023**, *8*, 75–83. [CrossRef]
9. Kodera, S.; Rashed, E.A.; Hirata, A. Correlation between COVID-19 morbidity and mortality rates in Japan and local population density, temperature, and absolute humidity. *Int. J. Environ. Res. Public Health* **2020**, *17*, 5477. [CrossRef] [PubMed]
10. Ozkan, A.; Ozkan, G.; Yalaman, A.; Yildiz, Y. Climate risk, culture and the Covid-19 mortality: A cross-country analysis. *World Dev.* **2021**, *141*, 105412. [CrossRef] [PubMed]
11. Leffler, C.T.; Ing, E.; Lykins, J.D.; Hogan, M.C.; McKeown, C.A.; Grzybowski, A. Association of country-wide coronavirus mortality with demographics, testing, lockdowns, and public wearing of masks. *Am. J. Trop. Med. Hyg.* **2020**, *103*, 2400–2411. [CrossRef] [PubMed]
12. Liang, L.L.; Tseng, C.H.; Ho, H.J.; Wu, C.Y. COVID-19 mortality is negatively associated with test number and government effectiveness. *Sci. Rep.* **2020**, *10*, 12567. [CrossRef] [PubMed]
13. McCullagh, P.; Nelder, J.A. *Generalized Linear Models*, 2nd ed.; Chapman and Hall: London, UK, 1989.
14. Rigby, R.A.; Stasinopoulos, D.M. Generalized additive models for location, scale and shape. *J. R. Stat. Soc. Ser. C Appl. Stat.* **2005**, *54*, 507–554. [CrossRef]
15. Guerra, R.R.; Peña-Ramírez, F.A.; Ribeiro, T.F.; Cordeiro, G.M.; Mafalda, C.P. Unit Regression Models to Explain Vote Proportions in the Brazilian Presidential Elections in 2018. *Rev. Colomb. Estadística* **2024**, *47*, 283–300.
16. Lemonte, A.J.; Bazán, J.L. New class of Johnson distributions and its associated regression model for rates and proportions. *Biom. J.* **2016**, *58*, 727–746. [CrossRef] [PubMed]
17. Mazucheli, J.; Menezes, A.F.B.; Fernandes, L.B.; de Oliveira, R.P.; Ghitany, M.E. The unit-Weibull distribution as an alternative to the Kumaraswamy distribution for the modeling of quantiles conditional on covariates. *J. Appl. Stat.* **2020**, *47*, 954–974. [CrossRef] [PubMed]
18. Peña-Ramírez, F.A.; Guerra, R.R.; Mafalda, C.P. The unit ratio-extended Weibull family and the dropout rate in Brazilian undergraduate courses. *PLoS ONE* **2023**, *18*, e0290885. [CrossRef] [PubMed]
19. Rigby, R.; Stasinopoulos, D. The GAMLSS project: A flexible approach to statistical modelling. In *New Trends in Statistical Modelling, Proceedings of the 16th International Workshop on Statistical Modelling, Odense, Denmark, 2–6 July 2001*; Statistical Modelling Society: Amsterdam, The Netherlands, 2001; Volume 337.
20. Stasinopoulos, D.M.; Rigby, R.A. Generalized additive models for location scale and shape (GAMLSS) in R. *J. Stat. Softw.* **2007**, *23*, 1–46. [CrossRef]
21. Stasinopoulos, M.D.; Rigby, R.A.; Heller, G.Z.; Voudouris, V.; De Bastiani, F. *Flexible Regression and Smoothing: Using GAMLSS in R*; CRC Press: Boca Raton, FL, USA, 2017.
22. Dunn, P.K.; Smyth, G.K. Randomized quantile residuals. *J. Comput. Graph. Stat.* **1996**, *5*, 236–244. [CrossRef]
23. Pereira, G.H. On quantile residuals in beta regression. *Commun. Stat.-Simul. Comput.* **2019**, *48*, 302–316. [CrossRef]
24. Queiroz, F.F.; Lemonte, A.J. A broad class of zero-or-one inflated regression models for rates and proportions. *Can. J. Stat.* **2020**, *49*, 566–590. [CrossRef]
25. Buuren, S.V.; Fredriks, M. Worm plot: A simple diagnostic device for modelling growth reference curves. *Stat. Med.* **2001**, *20*, 1259–1277. [CrossRef] [PubMed]
26. Nagelkerke, N.J. A note on a general definition of the coefficient of determination. *Biometrika* **1991**, *78*, 691–692. [CrossRef]
27. Akaike, H. A new look at the statistical model identification. *IEEE Trans. Autom. Control* **1974**, *19*, 716–723. [CrossRef]
28. James, G.; Witten, D.; Hastie, T.; Tibshirani, R.; Taylor, J. *An Introduction to Statistical Learning*; Springer: Berlin/Heidelberg, Germany, 2013; Volume 112.
29. Bayes, C.L.; Bazán, J.L.; De Castro, M. A quantile parametric mixed regression model for bounded response variables. *Stat. Its Interface* **2017**, *10*, 483–493. [CrossRef]
30. The World Bank. Indicators. 2021. Available online: https://data.worldbank.org/indicator (accessed on 19 December 2020).
31. Adeleye, B.N.; Gershon, O.; Ogundipe, A.; Owolabi, O.; Ogunrinola, I.; Adediran, O. Comparative investigation of the growth-poverty-inequality trilemma in Sub-Saharan Africa and Latin American and Caribbean Countries. *Heliyon* **2020**, *6*, e05631. [CrossRef]
32. Conceição, P. *Human Development Report 2020—The Next Frontier: Human Development and the Anthropocene*; Human Development Report Series; United Nations Development Programme: New York, NY, USA, 2020.

mathematics

MDPI

Article

Mathematical Formalization and Applications to Data with Excess of Zeros and Ones of the Unit-Proportional Hazard Inflated Models

Guillermo Martínez-Flórez [1], Roger Tovar-Falón [1,*] and Héctor W. Gómez [2]

[1] Departamento de Matemáticas y Estadística, Universidad de Córdoba, Montería 230002, Colombia; guillermomartinez@correo.unicordoba.edu.co

[2] Departamento de Estadística y Ciencia de Datos, Facultad de Ciencias Básicas, Universidad de Antofagasta, Antofagasta 1240000, Chile; hector.gomez@uantof.cl

* Correspondence: rjtovar@correo.unicordoba.edu.co

Abstract: In this study, we model the rate or proportion of a specific phenomenon using a set of known covariates. To fit the regression model, which explains the phenomenon within the intervals $(0,1)$, $[0,1)$, $(0,1]$, or $[0,1]$, we employ a logit link function. This approach ensures that the model's predictions remain within the appropriate range of zero to one. In cases of inflation at zero, one, or both, the logit link function is similarly applied to model the dichotomous Bernoulli-type variable with a multinomial response. The findings demonstrate that the model yields a non-singular information matrix, ensuring valid statistical inference. This ensures the invertibility of the information matrix, allowing for hypothesis testing based on likelihood statistics regarding the parameters in the model. This is not possible with other asymmetric models, such as those derived from the skew-normal distribution, which has a singular information matrix at the boundary of the skewness parameter. Finally, empirical results show the model's effectiveness in analyzing proportion data with inflation at zero and one, proving its robustness and practicality for analyzing bounded data in various fields of research.

Keywords: unit proportional hazard distribution; censoring; proportion data; truncation; zero-one inflation

MSC: 62J05; 62E15

1. Introduction

In recent years, probability distributions have seen significant advancements, particularly through the creation of new families derived from extensions or generalizations of classical distributions. These innovations aim to overcome the limitations of traditional models and provide greater flexibility to better fit the complex phenomena observed in various fields of knowledge. Examples of these distributions include those based on transformations such as the generalized beta distribution by Eugene et al. [1], the family of generalized distributions based on the Kumaraswamy distribution, referred to as Kw-distributions and introduced by Cordeiro and De Castro [2] (Kw-normal, Kw-Weibull, Kw-gamma, Kw-Gumbel, and Kw-inverse Gaussian distribution); and the beta modified Weibull distribution of Silva et al. [3]. These new distributions not only better capture data characteristics like skewness and kurtosis but also improve accuracy in modeling extreme events or phenomena with heavy tails. Furthermore, their implementation has proven useful in fields such as biomedicine, economics, and engineering, where classical models fail to adequately describe the reality of the data.

In parallel, truncated distributions have emerged as another essential tool, particularly when the data are bounded within a specific range. These distributions are modifications of classical ones, where values outside a certain interval are truncated, improving the model's fit for data restricted by natural or experimental constraints [4]. For example, the truncated normal distribution is widely used in reliability analysis and survival studies where negative values are not possible [5,6]. Similarly, the truncated Weibull distribution has been applied in actuarial sciences to model the time to event data [7], offering greater flexibility when standard distributions fail to capture the behavior of the tail.

A method for creating new families of distributions involves using a generating distribution as a base. This method has been widely employed by various authors, including Cordeiro et al. [8,9], Zografos and Balakrishnan [10], Ristić and Balakrishnan [11], Castellares et al. [12], and Cordeiro et al. [13]. In the same context, Mahdavi and Silva [4] introduced a method for generating families of truncated distributions, producing a two-parameter extension of the base distribution. This method has been used to derive distributions such as the truncated exponential-exponential and the truncated Lomax-Exponential. These innovations in probability distributions have proven to be valuable tools in statistical analysis, providing more robust and adaptable models for complex data.

The method introduced by Mahdavi and Silva [4] can be summarized as follows:

- Definition of the Truncated Distribution: A random variable U with support in the interval (a, b), where $a \leq 0$ and $b \geq 1$, and cumulative distribution function (CDF) F is considered. The CDF of the truncated random variable U in the interval $(0, 1)$ is defined as:

$$F_{U_t}(u) = \frac{F(u) - F(0)}{F(1) - F(0)}. \tag{1}$$

- Generation of the New Family of Distributions: Using the truncated CDF, the new truncated F–G family of distributions is introduced. For each absolutely continuous G distribution (denoted as the baseline distribution), the TF–G distribution is associated. The CDF of the TF–G class of distributions is defined as:

$$G_X(x) = \frac{F(G(x)) - F(0)}{F(1) - F(0)}, \tag{2}$$

where G is the CDF of the random variable V used to generate a new distribution.

The probability density function (PDF), $f_X(x)$, survival function, and hazard rate function are given, respectively, by:

$$f_X(x) = \frac{g(x) f(G(x))}{F(1) - F(0)}, \tag{3}$$

$$S_X(x) = \frac{F(1) - F(G(x))}{F(1) - F(0)}. \tag{4}$$

and

$$h_X(x) = \frac{g(x) f(G(x))}{F(1) - F(G(x))}, \tag{5}$$

where f and g are the PDF of the random variables U and V, respectively. The extension to the location-scale case of the model (3) is obtained from the transformation $Y = \mu + \sigma X$, where $X \sim$ TF-G, for $\mu \in \mathbb{R}$ y $\sigma \in \mathbb{R}^+$; it has PDF given by:

$$f_Y(y) = \frac{1}{\sigma} \frac{g(x) f(G(x))}{F(x_1) - F(x_0)}, \tag{6}$$

where

$$x = \frac{y - \mu}{\sigma}, \quad x_0 = \frac{a - \mu}{\sigma}, \quad x_1 = \frac{b - \mu}{\sigma}.$$

Some distributions that have been derived using the generator proposed by [4] are the truncated exponential-exponential (TEE), the truncated Lomax-Exponential by Enami [14], the truncated exponential Marshall Olkin Lomax distribution of Hadi and Al-Noor [15] and the truncated Nadarajah-Haghighi Exponential by Al-Habib et al. [16]. The generator proposed by [4] can also be used to derive distributions useful for modeling data in the interval $(0,1)$, such as proportions, rates, or indices.

The analysis of phenomena represented by proportion data, confined to values between zero and one, is essential across various scientific disciplines. These data elucidate part-to-whole relationships and are prevalent in numerous applications, including the prevalence of diseases, the distribution of resources in economics, the survival rates of species, and the utilization of habitats in ecology [17]. Modeling such data can be highly challenging when there is high zero-to-one inflation in proportion data. Traditional statistical models, such as the censored normal or censored log-normal models, may not be the best solution, as they often struggle to accurately characterize the underlying distribution of proportion data with inflated extremes.

Numerous authors have collaborated to develop more robust models than the censored normal and censored log-normal models for this type of data. By incorporating distributions such as the Birnbaum–Saunders [18,19], Student-t [20,21], skew-normal (SN) [22–25], and power-normal (PN) [26,27] distributions, among others, they offer a framework for analyzing data with high degrees of skewness and kurtosis compared with traditional models.

Perhaps the beta distribution is the most well-known in the statistical literature and is commonly used for fitting unit interval data. However, it has limitations when modeling unit data with zero-one inflation. Recent proposals, such as the zero-one inflated beta models, have been made to overcome this limitation and have proven to be viable alternatives for handling data with certain degrees of asymmetry [28–33]. Despite advancements in modeling data with inflation and asymmetry, there remains a gap in adequately addressing zero-one inflation in proportion data. Existing models fail to fully capture the unique distributional characteristics and complexities introduced by these inflations, leading to biased estimators and imprecise inferences [34,35].

The primary aim of this study is to introduce and develop unit-proportional hazard zero-one inflated (UPHZOI) models, a novel class of regression models specifically designed to address the challenges posed by zero-one inflation in proportional data confined to the unit interval. UPHZOI models combine a continuous-discrete mixture distribution with covariates, enabling them to effectively capture the complex dynamics of such data.

The remainder of this article is structured as follows: Section 2 provides background on the asymmetric proportional hazard model and introduces the truncated proportional hazard model. It also presents the process of parameter estimation, considering a classical approach using the maximum likelihood method. In Section 3, we introduce new regression models for unit interval data with inflation, including the model formulation, parameter estimation, and elements of the Hessian matrix. Section 4 demonstrates the application of these models through empirical case studies on doubly censored data and zero-inflated data. Section 5 presents an analysis of the major results, limitations, and future research directions. The article concludes with Section 6.

2. An Asymmetric Distribution for Skew Data

This section provides background on the proportional hazard (PH) distribution introduced by Martínez-Flórez et al. [36] for modeling data with high or low kurtosis and a wide range of skewness. Additionally, the unit-proportional hazard distribution is introduced, derived using the truncated method of [4]. The latter serves as the foundation for formulating the UPHZOI models, from which regression models for proportion data are developed.

2.1. Proportional Hazard Distribution and Its Modeling

The PDF of the PH distribution is given by

$$\phi_{\mathrm{PH}}(y;\boldsymbol{\theta}) = \alpha f\left(\frac{y-\xi}{\sigma}\right)\left\{1-F\left(\frac{y-\xi}{\sigma}\right)\right\}^{\alpha-1}, \; y \in \mathbb{R}, \tag{7}$$

where $\boldsymbol{\theta} = (\xi, \sigma, \alpha)$, with $\xi \in \mathbb{R}$ is a location parameter, $\sigma \in \mathbb{R}^+$ is a scale parameter, α is a positive real number and, F is an absolutely continuous distribution function with continuous density function $f = dF$. The notation $Y \sim \text{PH}(\xi, \sigma, \alpha)$ indicates that Y follows an PH distribution with parameters ξ, σ, and α.

Under the PH model, the hazard function is presented as

$$h_{\text{PH}}(y, \alpha) = \alpha h_f(y),$$

where $h_f(\cdot) = f(\cdot)/(1 - F(\cdot))$ is the hazard function regarding the density f. When the CDF F in the (7) model corresponds to the CDF of the standard normal distribution, that is, $F = \Phi$ and therefore $f = \phi$, we obtain the model denominated proportional hazard normal (PHN), whose PDF is given by

$$\phi_{\text{PHN}}(y; \boldsymbol{\theta}) = \alpha\phi\left(\frac{y-\xi}{\sigma}\right)\left\{S\left(\frac{y-\xi}{\sigma}\right)\right\}^{\alpha-1}, \ y \in \mathbb{R}, \tag{8}$$

where $S(\cdot)$ is the survival function of the standard normal PDF. This model also serves as an alternative for fitting data with much wider ranges of skewness and kurtosis than those of the normal distribution, which the latter cannot adequately capture. The CDF of the $\text{PHN}(\mu, \sigma, \alpha)$ is given by:

$$\Phi_{\text{PHN}}(y; \boldsymbol{\theta}) = 1 - \left\{S\left(\frac{y-\xi}{\sigma}\right)\right\}^{\alpha}, \ y \in \mathbb{R}. \tag{9}$$

By considering various values of α, Martínez-Flórez et al. [36] found that the range of the asymmetry and kurtosis coefficients, $\sqrt{\beta_1}$ and β_2, for the variable $Y \sim \text{PHN}(0, 1, \alpha)$ are the intervals $(-1.1578, 0.9918)$ and $(1.1513, 4.3023)$, respectively. This indicates that the PHN model is superior to both the SN and PN models in terms of asymmetry and kurtosis. Furthermore, ref. [36] demonstrate that the information matrix of the PHN distribution is non-singular. This is advantageous for statistical inference, as it allows for hypothesis testing based on likelihood ratio statistics.

2.2. Truncated Proportional Hazard Normal Distribution

Based on the TF-G distribution, we define the truncated proportional hazard normal (TPHN) distribution in the unit interval $[0, 1]$. Let $F(\cdot)$ be the CDF of the PHN distribution and $G(\cdot)$ the CDF of a continuous uniform distribution on $[0, 1]$; then, we have that the PDF of the TPHN model is

$$\phi_{\text{TPHN}}(y; \xi, \sigma, \alpha) = \frac{\frac{\alpha}{\sigma}\phi_{\text{PHN}}\left(\frac{y-\xi}{\sigma}\right)}{\left\{S\left(\frac{-\xi}{\sigma}\right)\right\}^{\alpha} - \left\{S\left(\frac{1-\xi}{\sigma}\right)\right\}^{\alpha}}, \quad 0 < y < 1, \tag{10}$$

where ϕ_{PHN} and S are defined in (8). The standardization terms, which facilitate the normalization of the data within the specified limits, are defined as

$$z = \frac{y-\xi}{\sigma}, \quad z_0 = -\frac{\xi}{\sigma}, \quad z_1 = \frac{1-\xi}{\sigma}.$$

This is denoted by $\text{TPHN}(\xi, \sigma, \alpha)$. It can be seen from (10) that the CDF, survival function, and hazard function for the TPHN distribution are given by:

$$\Phi_{\text{TPHN}}(y; \xi, \sigma, \alpha) = \frac{\{S(z_0)\}^{\alpha} - \{S(z)\}^{\alpha}}{\{S(z_0)\}^{\alpha} - \{S(z_1)\}^{\alpha}}, \tag{11}$$

$$S_{\text{TPHN}}(y; \xi, \sigma, \alpha) = \frac{\{S(z)\}^{\alpha} - \{S(z_1)\}^{\alpha}}{\{S(z_0)\}^{\alpha} - \{S(z_1)\}^{\alpha}}, \tag{12}$$

and

$$h_{\mathrm{TPHN}}(y;\xi,\sigma,\alpha)=\frac{\alpha}{\sigma}\frac{\phi(z)\{S(z)\}^{\alpha-1}}{\{S(z)\}^{\alpha}-\{S(z_1)\}^{\alpha}}=\alpha\frac{\{S(z)\}^{\alpha}}{\{S(z)\}^{\alpha}-\{S(z_1)\}^{\alpha}}h(y), \tag{13}$$

respectively, where $h(y)$ is the hazard function of the normal distribution.

The moments of a random variable with TPHN distribution can be obtained using the expression

$$\mathbb{E}(Y^r)=\frac{\alpha\sum_{j=1}^{r}\xi^{r-j}\sigma^j\lambda^j}{\{S(z_0)\}^{\alpha}-\{S(z_1)\}^{\alpha}},\quad r=1,2,\ldots \tag{14}$$

where

$$\lambda=\int_{S(z_1)}^{S(z_0)}\Phi^{-1}(1-u)u^{\alpha-1}du$$

being $\Phi^{-1}(\cdot)$ the inverse of the function $\Phi(\cdot)$.

2.3. Parameter Estimation in the TPHN Model

The TPHN parameters can be estimated using the maximum likelihood (ML) method by maximizing the log-likelihood function. We consider a random sample of n observations, $Y_1,Y_2,\ldots,Y_n$ from the TPHN(ξ,σ,α) distribution; the log-likelihood function of $\boldsymbol{\theta}=(\xi,\sigma,\alpha)^\top$ is obtained by taking the natural logarithm of the joint likelihood function defined as $L(\boldsymbol{\theta},\boldsymbol{y})=\prod_{i=1}^{n}\phi_{TPHN}(y_i;\boldsymbol{\theta})$, where now $\boldsymbol{\theta}=(\xi,\sigma,\alpha)$. Taking the natural logarithm in the above expression, we obtain the log-likelihood function established as

$$\begin{aligned}\ell(\boldsymbol{\theta}) &= n\log(\alpha)-n\log(\sigma)+\sum_{i=1}^{n}\log(\phi(z_i))\\ &\quad+(\alpha-1)\sum_{i=1}^{n}\log(S(z_i))-n\log(W(\xi,\sigma,\alpha)),\end{aligned} \tag{15}$$

where $z_i=\frac{y_i-\xi}{\sigma}$ and $W=W(\xi,\sigma,\alpha)=\log(\{S(z_0)\}^{\alpha}-\{S(z_1)\}^{\alpha})$. By taking the first derivatives of the function presented in (15) with respect to the parameters, $\dot{\ell}(\boldsymbol{\theta})=\partial\ell(\boldsymbol{\theta})/\partial\boldsymbol{\theta}$, we obtain the score elements. For the location parameter ξ, the score function is formulated as

$$\dot{\ell}(\alpha)=\frac{n}{\alpha}+\sum_{i-1}^{n}\log(S(z_i))-n\frac{\{S(z_0)\}^{\alpha}\log(S(z_0))-\{S(z_1)\}^{\alpha}\log(S(z_1))}{W}. \tag{16}$$

For the scale parameter σ, the score function is defined as

$$\dot{\ell}(\mu)=\frac{1}{\sigma}\sum_{i=1}^{n}z_i+\frac{\alpha-1}{\sigma}\sum_{i=1}^{n}\frac{\phi(z_i)}{S(z_i)}-n\frac{\alpha}{\sigma}\frac{h(z_0)\{S(z_0)\}^{\alpha}-h(z_1)\{S(z_1)\}^{\alpha}}{W}. \tag{17}$$

For the shape parameter α, the score is formulated as

$$\dot{\ell}(\sigma)=-\frac{n}{\sigma}+\frac{1}{\sigma}\sum_{i=1}^{n}z_i^2+\frac{\alpha-1}{\sigma}\sum_{i=1}^{n}z_i\frac{\phi(z_i)}{S(z_i)}-n\frac{\alpha}{\sigma}\frac{z_0h(z_0)\{S(z_0)\}^{\alpha}-z_1h(z_1)\{S(z_1)\}^{\alpha}}{W}. \tag{18}$$

The maximum likelihood estimate (MLE) of the parameters is obtained by solving the system of equations formed by setting (16)–(18) equal to zero. This system is generally solved using iterative numerical methods, such as the Newton–Raphson or quasi-Newton algorithms, which iteratively refine the parameter estimates to maximize the likelihood function.

2.4. Information Matrix in TPHN Model

The observed information matrix can be approximated by the negative of the Hessian matrix, which is obtained from the second derivatives of the log-likelihood function. The second derivatives of the log-likelihood function for $\xi\xi,\xi\sigma,\sigma\sigma,\xi\alpha,\sigma\alpha$ an $\alpha\alpha$ are given in the Appendix A.1. To derive the information matrix, it suffices to find the expected value of the elements of the observed information matrix. According to [36], the family of proportional hazard distributions is regular; thus, the information matrix of the PHN model is non-singular, as demonstrated in Martínez-Flórez et al. [36]. Consequently, the information matrix of the truncated distribution on $[0,1]$ is non-singular, and its covariance matrix is given by

$$\boldsymbol{\Sigma} = \boldsymbol{\Sigma}(\xi, \sigma, \alpha) = I^{-1}(\xi, \sigma, \alpha) = (\mathbb{E}(J(\xi, \sigma, \alpha)))^{-1}.$$

It follows that, for large n, $\widehat{\boldsymbol{\theta}}$ is consistent and, furthermore, by the central limit theorem, $\widehat{\boldsymbol{\theta}}$ is asymptotically normally distributed with mean vector $\boldsymbol{\theta}$ and covariance matrix $\boldsymbol{\Sigma}$, i.e.,

$$\widehat{\boldsymbol{\theta}} \xrightarrow{D} N_3(\boldsymbol{\theta}, \boldsymbol{\Sigma}),$$

Details of this result can be found in [37].

In practice, since the matrix $J(\boldsymbol{\theta})$ is consistent for $I(\boldsymbol{\theta})$, we can take $\boldsymbol{\Sigma} = J^{-1}(\boldsymbol{\theta})$ as the covariance matrix of the estimator vector for the TPHN model.

2.5. *Unit-Proportional Hazard Regression Model*

We now introduce the unit-proportional hazard normal (UPHN) regression model to fit proportion data from the TPHN distribution by changing the location parameter ξ in (10) to the linear predictor $\xi_i = \boldsymbol{x}_i^\top \boldsymbol{\beta}$, where $\boldsymbol{x}_i = (1, x_{1i}, \ldots, x_{pi})^\top$ is an observed covariate vector for the observation i, and $\boldsymbol{\beta} = (\beta_0, \beta_1, \ldots, \beta_p)^\top$ is the regression coefficient vector. The response (dependent) variable Y_i can be modeled by

$$Y_i = \beta_0 + \beta_1 x_{1i} + \cdots + \beta_p x_{pi} + \varepsilon_i, \quad i = 1, \ldots, n, \tag{19}$$

where $\varepsilon_i \sim \text{TPHN}(0, \sigma, \alpha)$. It follows from the natural form that

$$Y_i \sim \text{TPHN}(\boldsymbol{x}_i^\top \boldsymbol{\beta}, \sigma, \alpha), \quad i = 1, 2, \ldots, n.$$

Since our focus is on cases where the variable of interest lies within the unit interval $(0,1)$, issues may arise with the expected response or predicted value, which could fall outside this standard unit interval $(0,1)$, potentially resulting in negative estimates that lack interpretation and/or meaning. To avoid these issues, we change the assumption that the response variable Y is a linear function of the vector of explanatory variables $\boldsymbol{x}_i^\top = (x_1, x_2, \ldots, x_p)$ to a nonlinear transformation of this set of variables. This model will be obtained by assuming that the location parameter of y_i can be written as

$$g(\mu_i) = \xi_i = \boldsymbol{x}_i^\top \boldsymbol{\beta}, \quad i = 1, \ldots, n, \tag{20}$$

where $g(\cdot)$ is a strictly monotonic and twice differentiable link function that maps $(0,1)$ to $\mathbb{R}$. There are several options for choosing the link function $g(\cdot)$; two commonly used for this particular case are the logit function $g(\mu_i) = \log(\mu_i/(1-\mu_i))$, and the probit function $g(\mu_i) = \Phi(\mu_i)$. These two options yield very similar results in predicted values, with some exceptions for extreme values. Because the logit and probit functions provide very similar results in terms of model fit, and unlike the probit function, the logit link function allows for simpler algebraic manipulations and obtaining expressions for the score function, elements of the information matrix and expectation calculations among others, we opt for the logit function. Thus, in this case, we write

$$\mu_i = \frac{\exp(\boldsymbol{x}_i^\top \boldsymbol{\beta})}{1 + \exp(\boldsymbol{x}_i^\top \boldsymbol{\beta})}, \quad i = 1, 2, \ldots, n. \tag{21}$$

For this model, the parameters are interpreted based on the odds ratio between the odds of the prediction or mean when one of the variables is increased by m units (while keeping the other explanatory variables constant) and the odds without this increase. It has been demonstrated that this odds ratio is given by $\exp(m\beta_k)$, where β_k is the parameter associated with the explanatory variable increased by m units. It follows that the distribution of the variable under study is

$$y_i \sim \text{TPHN}(\mu_i, \sigma, \alpha), \quad i = 1, 2, \ldots, n.$$

The estimates of the parameters of the UPHN regression model with a logit link function can be obtained using the ML method. The log-likelihood function for the parameter vector $\boldsymbol{\theta} = (\boldsymbol{\beta}, \sigma, \alpha)$ given a sample of n observations is given by

$$\begin{aligned}\ell(\boldsymbol{\theta}) &= n\log(\alpha) - n\log(\sigma) + \sum_{i=1}^{n}\log(\phi(z_i)) \\ &+ (\alpha-1)\sum_{i=1}^{n}\log(S(z_i)) - \sum_{i=1}^{n}\log(W_i(\mu_i,\sigma,\alpha)),\end{aligned} \tag{22}$$

where $W_i = W_i(\mu_i, \sigma, \alpha) = \log(\{S(z_{0i})\}^{\alpha} - \{S(z_{1i})\}^{\alpha})$ with

$$z_i = \frac{y_i - \mu_i}{\sigma}, \quad z_{0i} = -\frac{\mu_i}{\sigma}, \quad z_{1i} = \frac{1-\mu_i}{\sigma}.$$

Thus, the score function, defined as the derivative of the log-likelihood function with respect to each of the parameters, is given for the vector whose components are given by:

$$\begin{aligned}\dot{\ell}(\alpha) &= \frac{n}{\alpha} + \sum_{i=1}^{n}\log(S(z_i)) - \sum_{i=1}^{n}\frac{\{S(z_{0i})\}^{\alpha}\log(S(z_{0i})) - \{S(z_{1i})\}^{\alpha}\log(S(z_{1i}))}{W_i}, \\ \dot{\ell}(\beta_j) &= \frac{1}{\sigma}\sum_{i=1}^{n}x_{ij}z_i\mu_i(1-\mu_i) + \frac{\alpha-1}{\sigma}\sum_{i=1}^{n}\frac{x_{ij}\mu_i(1-\mu_i)\phi(z_i)}{S(z_i)} \\ &\quad -\frac{\alpha}{\sigma}\sum_{i=1}^{n}\frac{x_{ij}\mu_i(1-\mu_i)\left(h(z_{0i})\{S(z_{0i})\}^{\alpha} - h(z_{1i})\{S(z_{1i})\}^{\alpha}\right)}{W_i}, \\ \dot{\ell}(\sigma) &= -\frac{n}{\sigma} + \frac{1}{\sigma}\sum_{i=1}^{n}z_i^2 + \frac{\alpha-1}{\sigma}\sum_{i=1}^{n}z_i\frac{\phi(z_i)}{S(z_i)} - \frac{\alpha}{\sigma}\sum_{i=1}^{n}\frac{z_{0i}h(z_{0i})\{S(z_{0i})\}^{\alpha} - z_{1i}h(z_{1i})\{S(z_{1i})\}^{\alpha}}{W_i}.\end{aligned}$$

Setting these expressions to zero, we get the corresponding score equations whose numerical solution leads to the MLE. The elements of the information matrix are obtained using the chain rule and are presented in Appendix A.2.

It can be seen that, for large sample sizes, we have

$$\hat{\boldsymbol{\theta}} \xrightarrow{D} N_{p+3}(\boldsymbol{\theta}, I_F(\boldsymbol{\theta})^{-1}).$$

where, "D" indicates convergence in distribution. In this way, inferences can be made about the parameters using likelihood ratio statistics.

2.6. MCMC Methods for the PHN Model

Bayesian methods can also be implemented to perform statistical inference within the PHN distribution family. Although there is limited statistical literature addressing this issue in power-normal distributions, Sarabia and Castillo [38] provides some initial ideas on how to approach it. In this section, we do not aim to propose specific Bayesian methods but rather open the door to exploring these methods within the PHN model class.

We consider the standard case of the $\text{PHN}(0, 1, \alpha) \equiv \text{PHN}(\alpha)$ model, and, similar to [38], we assume a gamma distribution for the shape parameter α. The model we consider is

$$Y \mid \alpha \sim \text{PHN}(\alpha) \tag{23}$$

$$\alpha \sim Gamma(\delta_0, \lambda_0), \tag{24}$$

where $Gamma(\delta_0, \lambda_0)$ denotes a gamma random variable with PDF proportional to $s^{\delta_0 - 1}e^{-\lambda_0 s}$ with δ_0 and λ_0 known. If we denote by $m(y)$ the marginal distribution of Y and by $\pi(\alpha \mid Y)$ the posterior distribution of the shape parameter α, we have that:

$$\begin{aligned} m(y) &= \int_0^\infty \alpha\phi(y)[1-\Phi(y)]^{\alpha-1}\frac{\lambda_0^{\delta_0}}{\Gamma(\delta_0)}\alpha^{\delta_0-1}e^{-\lambda_0\alpha}d\alpha \\ &= \frac{\lambda_0^{\delta_0}}{\Gamma(\delta_0)}\frac{\phi(y)}{1-\Phi(y)}\frac{\Gamma(\delta_0+1)}{\{\lambda_0-\log[1-\Phi(y)]\}^{\delta_0-1}}, \end{aligned} \tag{25}$$

from which it follows that:

$$\pi(\alpha \mid Y) = \frac{\{\lambda_0 - \log[1-\Phi(y)]\}^{\delta_0+1}}{\Gamma(\delta_0+1)}\alpha^{\delta_0}e^{-(\lambda_0-\log[1-\Phi(y)])\alpha}, \tag{26}$$

which is the PDF of a random variable Gamma(δ_1, λ_1), where δ_1 and λ_1 are given by

$$\delta_1 = \delta_0 + 1, \quad \lambda_1 = \lambda_0 - \log[1-\Phi(y)]$$

Inference about the parameter α is carried out based on the posterior distribution given in (26). For the location-scale case, PHN(ξ, σ, α), prior distributions for the parameters ξ and σ that can be considered are the normal and inverse-gamma distributions, respectively.

3. UPHN Zero-One Inflated Regression Model

In this section, we present some regression models for unit interval (proportion) data that account for inflation at values zero and one or any value between zero and one.

3.1. Models for Censored Data

Cragg proposed a two-part model [39], which is a framework for fitting the mixture of a discrete and a continuous random variable. This model is represented by:

$$g(y_i) = p_i I_i + (1-p_i)f(y_i)(1-I_i),$$

where p_i is the probability that determines the relative contribution of the point mass distribution made by the discrete variable, $f(\cdot)$ is a PDF, and I_i is an indicator variable that takes values of 0 or 1. This model is optimal in cases where the model is inflated at the point mass value (for example, $y_i = a$), whose probability at $y = a$ cannot be explained by the CDF associated with the PDF $f(\cdot)$. Cragg's model can be extended to the case of a variable with double censoring or two-point mass values, for example, 0 and 1, in which case it is given by:

$$g(y_i) = p_{0i}I_{0i} + (1-p_{0i}-p_{1i})f(y_i)(1-I_{0i}-I_{1i}) + p_{1i}I_{1i},$$

where $p_{0i} = \Pr(y_i = 0)$, $p_{1i} = \Pr(y_i = 1)$, I_{0i} is the indicator variable that takes the value 1 if $y_i = 0$ and zero otherwise. Similarly, I_{1i} is the indicator variable for $y_i = 1$. In this model, the three components are determined by different stochastic processes, thus necessarily leading to a positive response from f. On the other hand, a zero or a one comes from the distribution of a point mass.

3.2. Zero-One Inflated PHN Distribution

Based on Cragg's model, we proposed the zero-one inflated PHN model as a means of

$$g(y) = \begin{cases} \rho_0, & \text{if } y = 0, \\ \frac{\alpha}{\sigma}(1-\rho_0-\rho_1)\phi(z)\{S(z)\}^{\alpha-1}, & \text{if } 0 < y < 1, \\ \rho_1, & \text{if } y = 1, \end{cases}$$

where

$$z = \frac{y-\mu}{\sigma}, \quad \rho_0 = \Pr(y=0), \quad \rho_1 = \Pr(y=1).$$

From this model, cases of inflation only at zero follow by taking $\rho_1 = 0$ or inflation only at one by taking $\rho_0 = 0$.

The CDF is represented by:

$$G(y) = \begin{cases} \rho_0, & \text{if } y \leq 0, \\ \rho_0 + (1-\rho_0-\rho_1)\left[\{S(z_0)\}^{\alpha} - \{S(z)\}^{\alpha}\right], & \text{if } 0 < y < 1, \\ 1, & \text{if } y \geq 1. \end{cases}$$

The most interesting case in this new model is when covariates are used to explain the response both in the censored part (0 and 1) and in the uncensored part (the continuous part in $(0,1)$). Thus, for the discrete part, it is assumed that the responses at zero and one can be explained by the covariate vectors $\boldsymbol{x}_{(0)i} = (1, x_{0i1}, \ldots, x_{0iq})^\top$ and $\boldsymbol{x}_{(1)i} = (1, x_{1i1}, \ldots, x_{1ir})^\top$ respectively. Then, to determine the probabilities ρ_0 and ρ_1, a logistic model with a polytomous response can be constructed such that:

$$\rho_{0i} = \Pr(y_i = 0) = \frac{\exp(\boldsymbol{x}_{(0)i}^\top \boldsymbol{\beta}_{(0)})}{1 + \exp(\boldsymbol{x}_{(0)i}^\top \boldsymbol{\beta}_{(0)}) + \exp(\boldsymbol{x}_{(1)i}^\top \boldsymbol{\beta}_{(1)})}, \tag{27}$$

$$\rho_{1i} = \Pr(y_i = 1) = \frac{\exp(\boldsymbol{x}_{(1)i}^\top \boldsymbol{\beta}_{(1)})}{1 + \exp(\boldsymbol{x}_{(0)i}^\top \boldsymbol{\beta}_{(0)}) + \exp(\boldsymbol{x}_{(1)i}^\top \boldsymbol{\beta}_{(1)})}, \tag{28}$$

$$\rho_{01i} = 1 - \rho_{0i} - \rho_{1i} = \Pr(y_i \in (0,1)) = \frac{1}{1 + \exp(\boldsymbol{x}_{(0)i}^\top \boldsymbol{\beta}_{(0)}) + \exp(\boldsymbol{x}_{(1)i}^\top \boldsymbol{\beta}_{(1)})}, \tag{29}$$

where $\boldsymbol{\beta}_{(0)} = (\beta_{00}, \beta_{01}, \ldots, \beta_{0q})^\top$ y $\boldsymbol{\beta}_{(1)} = (\beta_{10}, \beta_{11}, \ldots, \beta_{1r})^\top$ are vectors of unknown parameters associated respectively with the covariate vectors $\boldsymbol{x}_{(0)}$ and $\boldsymbol{x}_{(1)}$.

Similarly, for the continuous component of the model, a unit model $\mathrm{PHN}(\mu_i, \sigma, \alpha)$ is still assumed with a logit link function in the mean response, i.e., $\log(\mu_i/(1-\mu_i)) = x_i^\top \boldsymbol{\beta}$, where $x_i = (x_{i1}, x_{i2}, \ldots, x_{ip})$ is a vector of covariates with associated coefficient vector $\boldsymbol{\beta} = (\beta_0, \beta_1, \beta_2, \ldots, \beta_p)^\top$. For this model, it is easy to verify that the log-likelihood function for the parameter vector $\boldsymbol{\theta} = (\boldsymbol{\beta}_{(0)}^\top, \boldsymbol{\beta}_{(1)}^\top, \boldsymbol{\beta}^\top, \sigma, \alpha)^\top$ given $\boldsymbol{X}_{(0)}, \boldsymbol{X}, \boldsymbol{X}_{(1)}$ and $\boldsymbol{Y}$ can be written in the form:

$$\ell(\boldsymbol{\theta}) = \ell(\boldsymbol{\beta}_{(0)}, \boldsymbol{\beta}_{(1)}) + \ell(\boldsymbol{\beta}, \sigma, \alpha),$$

where

$$\ell(\boldsymbol{\beta}_{(0)}, \boldsymbol{\beta}_{(1)}) = \sum_{0} \boldsymbol{x}_{(0)i} \boldsymbol{\beta}_{(0)} + \sum_{1} \boldsymbol{x}_{(1)i} \boldsymbol{\beta}_{(1)} - \sum_{i=1}^{n} \log\left[1 + \exp(\boldsymbol{x}_{(0)i}^\top \boldsymbol{\beta}_{(0)}) + \exp(\boldsymbol{x}_{(1)i}^\top \boldsymbol{\beta}_{(1)})\right].$$

and

$$\ell(\boldsymbol{\beta}, \sigma, \alpha) = \sum_{y_i \in (0,1)} (\log(\alpha) - \log(\sigma) + \log(\phi(z_i)) + (\alpha - 1)\log(S(z_i))).$$

Given these characteristics, the MLEs of the model parameters can be obtained separately for each component of the log-likelihood function. The score function is derived by differentiating each component of the log-likelihood function. It can be shown that the Fisher information matrix can be written as a block diagonal matrix in the form:

$$I(\boldsymbol{\theta}) = \mathrm{Diag}\left\{ I(\boldsymbol{\beta}_{(0)}, \boldsymbol{\beta}_{(1)}), I(\boldsymbol{\beta}, \sigma, \alpha), \right\}$$

where $I(\boldsymbol{\beta}_{(0)}, \boldsymbol{\beta}_{(1)})$ corresponds to the information matrix of the discrete part. The elements of the observed information matrix for the discrete part are given in the Appendix A.3.

The respective Fisher information matrix is obtained by calculating the expectation of the elements of the observed information matrix. Furthermore, since the inverse of a block diagonal matrix is the block diagonal matrix of the respective inverses, it follows that the variance-covariance matrix is given by:

$$\boldsymbol{\Sigma} = \text{Diag}\{I^{-1}_{(\boldsymbol{\beta}_{(0)},\boldsymbol{\beta}_{(1)})}, I^{-1}_{(\boldsymbol{\beta},\sigma,\alpha)}\}.$$

Here, for large sample sizes it follows that for $\boldsymbol{\theta} = (\boldsymbol{\beta}, \boldsymbol{\beta}_{(0)}, \boldsymbol{\beta}_{(1)}, \sigma, \alpha)^\top$

$$\hat{\boldsymbol{\theta}} \xrightarrow{D} N_{p+q+r+3}(\boldsymbol{\theta}, I_F(\boldsymbol{\theta})^{-1}).$$

Confidence intervals for θ_r with of confidence coefficient $\omega = 100(1-\psi)\%$ can be obtained as $\hat{\theta}_r \mp z_{1-\omega/2}\sqrt{\hat{\sigma}(\hat{\theta}_r)}$. By talking $\rho_{1i} = 0$, the zero-inflated model is followed and, making $\rho_{0i} = 0$, the zero-inflated model is obtained.

3.3. The Zero-One Inflated UPHN Model

Similarly to how the zero-one inflated PHN model was constructed, a zero and/or one-inflated UPHN distribution can be proposed, which is given by:

$$f(y_i) = \begin{cases} \rho_0, & \text{if } y = 0, \\ \frac{\alpha}{\sigma}(1-\rho_0-\rho_1)\dfrac{\phi(z)\{S(z)\}^{\alpha-1}}{\{S(z_0)\}^\alpha - \{S(z_1)\}^\alpha}, & \text{if } 0 < y < 1, \\ \rho_1, & \text{if } y = 1. \end{cases}$$

where z, $\rho_0 = \Pr(y=0)$ and $\rho_1 = \Pr(y=1)$ are defined as in the zero-one inflated PHN model.

The CDF of this distribution is represented by

$$F(y) = \begin{cases} \rho_0, & \text{if } y \leq 0, \\ \rho_0 + (1-\rho_0-\rho_1)\dfrac{\{S(z_0)\}^\alpha - \{S(z)\}^\alpha}{\{S(z_0)\}^\alpha - \{S(z_1)\}^\alpha}, & \text{if } 0 < y < 1, \\ 1, & \text{if } y \geq 1. \end{cases}$$

For the case of covariates in the model, $\boldsymbol{x}_{(0)i} = (1, x_{0i1}, \ldots, x_{0iq})^\top$ and $\boldsymbol{x}_{(1)i} = (1, x_{1i1}, \ldots, x_{1ir})^\top$ for the zero- and one-inflated part, with associated coefficient vector $\boldsymbol{\beta}_{(0)} = (\beta_{00}, \beta_{01}, \ldots, \beta_{0q})^\top$ and $\boldsymbol{\beta}_{(1)} = (\beta_{10}, \beta_{11}, \ldots, \beta_{1r})^\top$. For the continuous component of the model, we connect the response variable with the linear predictor using the logit link function. As before, we choose this link function because, in addition to ensuring that the predictions model is within the $(0,1)$ interval, the logit function allows for more explicit expressions of the score function elements and the information matrix compared to the probit function, which depends on the integral of the cumulative distribution function of the standard normal distribution. In this way, we assume relationship $\log(\mu_i/(1-\mu_i)) = \boldsymbol{x}_i^\top\boldsymbol{\beta}$, where $\boldsymbol{x}_i = (1, x_{i1}, x_{i2}, \ldots, x_{ip})^\top$ is a vector of covariates with vector of coefficients $\boldsymbol{\beta} = (\beta_0, \beta_1, \beta_2, \ldots, \beta_p)^\top$.

The proposal again is to use a polytomous logistic model to explain the probabilities ρ_{0i} and ρ_{1i}. As in the case of the inflated PHN model, we have that the log-likelihood function is given by

$$\ell(\boldsymbol{\theta}) = \ell(\boldsymbol{\beta}_{(0)}, \boldsymbol{\beta}_{(1)}) + \ell(\boldsymbol{\beta}, \sigma, \alpha),$$

where $\ell(\boldsymbol{\beta}_{(0)}, \boldsymbol{\beta}_{(1)})$ is the same as the inflated PHN model, while

$$\ell(\theta;\mathbf{y}) = n_{01}\log(\alpha) - n_{01}\log(\sigma) + \sum_{y_i\in(0,1)} \log(\phi(z_i)) + (\alpha-1)\sum_{y_i\in(0,1)} \log(S(z_i)) - \sum_{y_i\in(0,1)} \log(W_i(\mu_i,\sigma,\alpha)),$$

where z_i, $W_i = W_i(\mu_i,\sigma,\alpha)$, z_{0i} and z_{1i} are as defined in (22).

The score function is obtained by differentiating each component of the log-likelihood function and the Fisher information matrix can be written as a diagonal block matrix in the form:

$$I(\boldsymbol{\theta}) = \text{Diag}\Big\{I(\boldsymbol{\beta}_{(0)},\boldsymbol{\beta}_{(1)}), I(\boldsymbol{\beta},\sigma,\alpha)\Big\}.$$

The elements of the matrix $I(\boldsymbol{\beta}_{(0)},\boldsymbol{\beta}_{(1)})$ are like those given in the inflated PHN model, while the elements of the matrix $I(\boldsymbol{\beta},\sigma,\alpha)$ are like those given in the information matrix of the UPHN regression model.

3.4. Generalized Two-Part PHN Model

Cragg's two-part model [39] encounters the issue that some censored points may be values at the boundary of the censoring limit. This is particularly problematic for a distribution $f(\cdot)$ within the unit interval $[0,1]$, where a zero or one could either be a realization from the point mass distribution or a partial observation of $f(\cdot)$ having a critical value that is not precisely known but is close to $(0,T_1)$ or $(T_2,1)$ for small values of the pre-specified constants T_1 and T_2. In practice, the values T_1 and T_2 are, in some cases, defined as those for which the instruments cannot record measurements below or above, respectively, and, consequently, are treated as censoring values. In other cases, these observational limits are defined for ethical or practical reasons. For example, in clinical studies, it may be unethical to continue observing a patient under certain conditions, or the costs of prolonged observation may become prohibitive.

To address this issue in the two-part model, Moulton and Halsey [40] propose a new approach to adjust the mixture of continuous and discrete random variables. This approach allows for the possibility that some limiting responses result from an interval censoring of $f(\cdot)$. The model proposed by Moulton and Halsey (1995) for left censoring at point a is given by: $g(y_i) = [p_i + (1-p_i)F(T)]I_i + (1-p_i)f(y_i)(1-I_i)$, where F is the CDF associated to f and, T It is a pre-established constant within the interval (a,T) where some limiting responses are considered censored. Similarly to how we generalized Cragg's model, Moulton and Halsey's model can also be generalized for left and right censoring or two boundary inflation points within the definition interval of the pdf $f(\cdot)$. In our case, for the unit PHN distribution within the interval $[0,1]$, this generalization of Moulton and Halsey's model is given by:

$$g(y_i) = (p_{0i} + (1-p_{0i}-p_{1i})(1-\{S(z_{0i})\}^{\alpha}))I_{0i} + \frac{\alpha(1-p_{0i}-p_{1i})}{\sigma}\phi(z_i)\{S(z_i)\}^{\alpha-1}I_{(0,1)i} + (p_{1i} + (1-p_{0i}-p_{1i})\{S(z_{1i})\}^{\alpha})I_{1i}.$$

It can be observed that this distribution is a model with double censoring (at zero and one) and, therefore, allows for the fit of datasets with inflation at zero and one. This represents an alternative to the double-censored Tobit model, where the CDF of the normal distribution does not efficiently fit the probability of the point mass where double censoring occurs, i.e., the probability of the inflation points.

Extending this model to the case of covariates in each part of the model, we again assume that $\boldsymbol{x}_{(0)i} = (1, x_{0i1},\ldots,x_{0iq})^\top$ and $\boldsymbol{x}_{(1)i} = (1, x_{1i1},\ldots,x_{1ir})^\top$ are sets of auxiliary covariates for the discrete part at zero and one, respectively; and a set of covariates $x_i = (1, x_{i1},\ldots,x_{ip})'$ for the continuous part in the interval $(0,1)$. Then, denoting by ρ_0 the proportion of observations below zero, $y_i = 0$ (lower detection limit), and by ρ_1 the proportion of observations above one, $y_i = 1$ (upper detection limit), the extension of the Moulton and Halsey model to the double-censored PHN case can be expressed through the PDF given by

$$g(y_i) = \begin{cases} \rho_{0i} + (1-\rho_{0i}-\rho_{1i})(1-\{S(z_{0i})\}^{\alpha}), & \text{if } y_i \leq 0, \\ \frac{\alpha}{\sigma}(1-\rho_{0i}-\rho_{1i})\phi(z_i)\{S(z_i)\}^{\alpha-1}, & \text{if } 0 < y_i < 1, \\ \rho_{1i} + (1-\rho_{0i}-\rho_{1i})\{S(z_{1i})\}^{\alpha}, & \text{if } y_i \geq 1, \end{cases}$$

where ρ_{0i} and ρ_{1i} are the probability masses at points zero and one, while z_{0i}, z_{1i}, z_i are as defined above; $\log(\mu_i/(1-\mu_i)) = \boldsymbol{x}_i^\top \boldsymbol{\beta}$, where $\boldsymbol{\beta}$ is the set of coefficients associated with the covariate vector $\boldsymbol{x}_i = (1, x_{i1}, \ldots, x_{ip})^\top$.

The CDF of this model is represented by

$$G(y_i) = \begin{cases} \rho_{0i} + (1-\rho_{0i}-\rho_{1i})(1-\{S(z_{0i})\}^{\alpha}), & \text{if } y_i \leq 0, \\ \rho_{0i} + (1-\rho_{0i}-\rho_{1i})\left[1-\{S(z_i)\}^{\alpha}\right], & \text{if } 0 < y_i < 1, \\ 1, & \text{if } y_i \geq 1. \end{cases}$$

To model the responses at the point masses $y_i = 0$ and $y_i = 1$, a multinomial logistic model with a logit link function is used again, where $\boldsymbol{\beta}_{(0)}^\top, \boldsymbol{\beta}_{(1)}^\top$ are the vectors of coefficients associated with the sets of covariates $\boldsymbol{x}_{(0)i} = (1, x_{0i1}, \ldots, x_{0iq})^\top$ and $\boldsymbol{x}_{(1)i} = (1, x_{1i1}, \ldots, x_{1ir})^\top$.

The log-likelihood function for parameter vector estimation $\boldsymbol{\theta} = (\boldsymbol{\beta}_{(0)}^\top, \boldsymbol{\beta}_{(1)}^\top, \boldsymbol{\beta}^\top, \sigma, \alpha)^\top$ conditionally on $\boldsymbol{X}_{(0)}, \boldsymbol{X}, \boldsymbol{X}_{(1)}$, is given by:

$$\begin{aligned} \ell(\boldsymbol{\theta}) &= \sum_0 \log\left[\exp(\boldsymbol{x}_{(0)i}^\top \boldsymbol{\beta}_{(0)}) + 1 - \{S(z_{0i})\}^{\alpha}\right] + \sum_1 \log\left[\exp(\boldsymbol{x}_{(1)i}^\top \boldsymbol{\beta}_{(1)}) + \{S(z_{1i})\}^{\alpha}\right] \\ &\quad + \sum_{i \in (0,1)} (\log(\alpha) - \log(\sigma) + \log(\phi(z_i)) + (\alpha-1)\log(S(z_i))) \\ &\quad - \sum_{i=1}^{n} \log\left[1 + \exp(\boldsymbol{x}_{(0)i}^\top \boldsymbol{\beta}_{(0)}) + \exp(\boldsymbol{x}_{(1)i}^\top \boldsymbol{\beta}_{(1)})\right]. \end{aligned} \tag{30}$$

The score equations are obtained by performing the first derivatives with respect to the model parameters $\boldsymbol{\theta} = (\boldsymbol{\beta}_{(0)}^\top, \boldsymbol{\beta}_{(1)}^\top, \boldsymbol{\beta}^\top, \sigma, \alpha)^\top$ while the information matrix is obtained by proceeding as in the models studied previously. Models with inflation only at zero or only at one can be studied by taking $\rho_0 = 0$ or $\rho_1 = 0$, respectively.

4. Empirical Applications

In this section, we illustrate the application of the proposed models and compare it with other models using real data. We show that the proposed model can be a valid alternative to some existing regression models in the statistical literature.

4.1. Application 1: Case Study on Students' Dropout Data

Student dropout is a major problem many Latin American countries face. In some universities in Colombia, this phenomenon can lead to more than 50% of students who enroll in a university program abandoning their higher education studies. This phenomenon has its greatest impact in the first four semesters of undergraduate studies, which is why it is important to determine the main causes leading to this abandonment of higher education.

This application refers to student dropout in the Faculty of Veterinary Medicine and Zootechnics (MVZ, by its acronym in Spanish) at the University of Córdoba, Colombia. The analyzed information corresponds to a sample of students who dropped out during one of the first four semesters (early dropout) of the programs in the MVZ Faculty at the University of Córdoba. The data correspond to variables from the SPADIES System of the Ministry of National Education (MEN by its acronym in Spanish) and the university itself.

The response variable y corresponds to the proportion of subjects passed up to the point of dropout. The explanatory variables considered were: x_1 = Saber 11 test score (exams taken at the end of secondary education); x_2 = age at the time of taking the Saber 11 test; x_3 = variable indicating whether the student received financial support (taking values 1 = yes, 0 = no); x_4 = mother's educational level (categorized as 1 if professional and, 0 otherwise); x_5 = number of siblings; x_6 = socioeconomic status of the student (categorized as 1 if from strata 1, 2, or 3, referred to as low and 0, otherwise); and x_7 = student's gender (categorized as 1 if male and 0 otherwise).

The zero-one inflated model, PHN, UPHN, and Doubly-Censored PHN (DCPHN) were fitted since some students drop out in the first semester without passing any subjects, and others drop out in the first four semesters even after passing all enrolled subjects.

The results obtained with the models studied in this article show that in all models, the significant variables for $0 < y < 1$ were the Saber 11 test score (x_1), age at the time of taking the Saber 11 test (x_2), and number of siblings (x_5). Similarly, the censored part at zero ($y = 0$) is not explained by any variable in any of the three models, while the censored part at one ($y = 1$) showed significance in variables such as age at the time of taking the Saber 11 test (directly related to the age of university entry) and number of siblings.

Table 1 shows the results of the best-fitted model for each of the considered models. To determine which model presents better performance, we used the AIC criteria [41] and the corrected AIC (AICc) [42]. These criteria are defined as:

$$AIC = -2\ell(\theta) + 2p \quad \text{and} \quad AICc = -2\ell(\theta) + \frac{2n(p+1)}{n-p-2},$$

where p is the number of parameters of the model in question.

The MLEs, with standard errors in parentheses, are given in Table 1. According to the AIC and AICc criteria, the model that best fits the student dropout data is the UPHN, followed by the DCPHN model.

Table 1. ML estimates of the indicated parameter and model for the dropout data and their AIC and AICc.

Estimador	PHN	UPHN	DCPHN
$\hat{\beta}_{00}$	−2.1624	−2.1624	−2.4371
	(0.2071)	(0.2071)	(0.3025)
$\hat{\beta}_{10}$	2.9392	0.9771	1.3859
	(0.0144)	(0.0223)	(0.6003)
$\hat{\beta}_{11}$	0.0142	0.0273	0.0208
	(0.0092)	(0.0041)	(0.0096)
$\hat{\beta}_{12}$	−0.3281	−0.2844	−0.2687
	(0.0125)	(0.0175)	(0.0905)
$\hat{\beta}_{15}$	0.1295	0.2129	0.1847
	(0.0146)	(0.0205)	(0.0910)
$\hat{\beta}_{20}$	14.5124	14.5124	16.0286
	(7.9470)	(7.9470)	(13.6058)
$\hat{\beta}_{21}$	0.0208	0.0208	
	(0.0127)	(0.0127)	
$\hat{\beta}_{22}$	−1.2230	−1.2230	−1.2024
	(0.5150)	(0.5150)	(0.8650)
$\hat{\beta}_{25}$	0.4998	0.4998	
	(0.2509)	(0.2509)	
$\hat{\sigma}$	0.1064	0.1160	0.1238
	(0.0104)	(0.0057)	(0.0598)
$\hat{\alpha}$	0.1538	0.1427	0.1721
	(0.0364)	(0.0197)	(0.1933)
AIC	195.0036	182.4216	183.6414
AICc	198.4687	185.6696	186.6646

Where PHN is proportional hazard normal, UPHN is truncated proportional hazard normal, DCPHN is doubly censored proportional hazard normal, AIC is Akaike information criterion, and AICc is corrected Akaike information criterion.

To identify outliers and/or model misspecification, we examined the transformation of the martingale residual, rMT_i, as proposed by Barros et al. [43]. These residuals are defined by

$$rMT_i = \text{sgn}(rM_i)\sqrt{-2[rM_i + \delta_i \log(\delta_i - rM_i)]}; \quad i = 1,2,3,\cdots,n,$$

where $rM_i = \delta_i + \log(S(e_i,\hat{\theta}))$ is the martingal residual proposed by Ortega et al. [44], where $\delta_i = 0,1$ indicates whether the ith observation is censored or not, respectively, $\text{sgn}(rM_i)$ denotes the sign of rM_i and $S(e_i;\hat{\theta})$ represents the survival function evaluated at e_i, where $\hat{\theta}$ are the MLE for θ.

The plots of rMT_i with confidence envelope graphs generated for the PHN, UPHN, and DCPHN models, shown in Figures 1 and 2, indicate that the fitted regression models PHN, UPHN, and DCPHN, with a logit link function, exhibit a good fit.

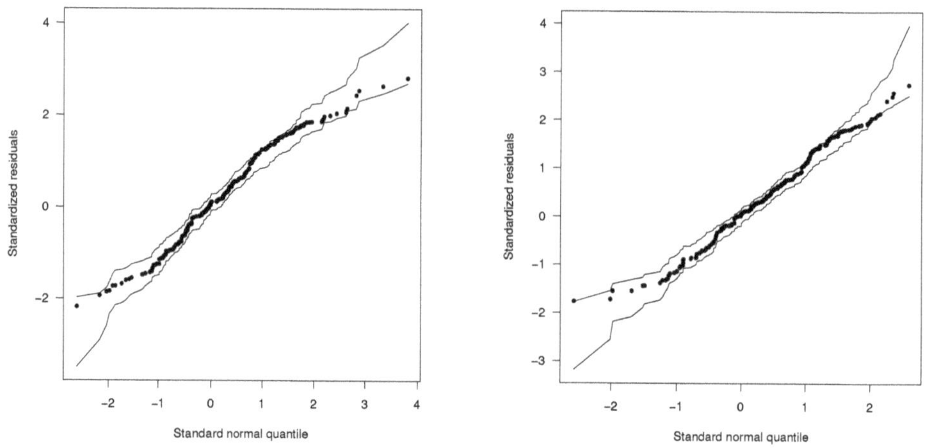

Figure 1. Plots of envelopes for rMT_i using: (**Left**) PHN and (**Right**) UPHN models and dropout data.

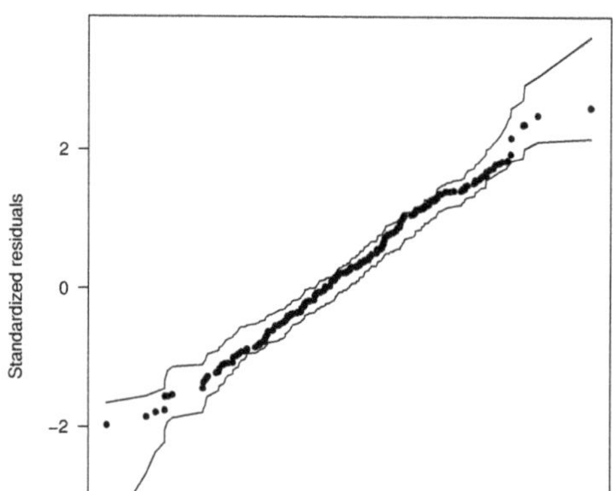

Figure 2. Plots of envelopes for rMT_i using DCPHN model and dropout data.

4.2. Application 2: Case Study on Periodontal Disease Data

The data motivating this second application come from a clinical study in which the clinical attachment level (CAL), a key marker of periodontal disease (PD), was measured at six sites on each tooth of a subject. The primary statistical question is to estimate functions that model the relationship between the "proportion of diseased sites associated with a specific tooth type (incisors, canines, premolars, and first molars)" and the covariates described below. The full dataset was previously analyzed by Galvis et al. [45] and includes information from 290 individuals. The response variable in this study is the proportion of diseased sites for the premolars (denoted as Y), with auxiliary covariates being gender (X_1), age (X_2), glycosylated hemoglobin (X_3), and smoking status (X_4).

The dataset exhibits significant inflation at $Y = 0$, but for certain subjects, we also observe $Y = 1$. To account for this, we applied the beta zero-one inflated (BIZU), truncated log-normal zero-one inflated (LNIZU), doubly censored proportional hazard normal (DCPHN), and the UPHN inflated zero-one (UPHNIZU) regression models. Our analysis revealed that only the covariates X_1 and X_2 were statistically significant. For the DCPHN model, only X_2 was significant for both the discrete outcomes.

We used several information criteria to compare the various models, including AIC and the AIC$_C$. We also used the Bayesian Information Criterion (BIC) and the Hannan–Quinn Information Criterion, defined as follows:

$$BIC = -2\ell(\theta) + p\log(n), \quad HQC = -2\ell(\theta) + 2p\log(\log(n)),$$

where p is the number of parameters of the model in question.

The MLEs, with standard errors in parentheses, are given in Table 2.

Table 2. ML estimates of the indicated parameter and model for the tooth data and their AIC, AICc, BIC, and HQC.

Estimador	BIZU	LNIZU	DCPHN	UPHNIZU
β_{00}	0.6337 (0.7408)	0.6337 (0.7408)	−7.2205 (0.8854)	0.6337 (0.7408)
β_{02}	−0.0376 (0.0135)	−0.0376 (0.0135)	−0.0935 (0.0161)	−0.0376 (0.0135)
β_{10}	−1.3885 (0.3957)	−2.8949 (1.1453)	−2.4039 (0.6809)	−5.2246 (3.1908)
β_{11}	−0.5366 (0.1613)	−1.3134 (0.4387)	−0.5517 (0.2420)	−2.9349 (1.4567)
β_{12}	0.0217 (0.0068)	0.0393 (0.0194)	0.0363 (0.0123)	0.1325 (0.0735)
β_{20}	−8.0316 (2.3153)	−8.0316 (2.3145)	−12.7261 (1.4938)	−8.0316 (2.3153)
β_{22}	0.0788 (0.0358)	0.0788 (0.0358)	−0.0487 (0.0236)	0.0788 (0.0358)
σ	0.0903 (0.0652)	0.3096 (0.0796)	0.3060 (0.0305)	0.6011 (0.1354)
α			1.5871 (0.0974)	2.8429 (0.7634)
AIC	311.7097	316.0700	325.2363	308.0793
AICC	314.3525	318.7128	328.3095	310.8678
BIC	341.0687	345.4290	358.2652	341.1082
HQC	323.4723	327.8326	338.4693	321.3123

In Figures 3–6, it can be observed that the best fits correspond to the BIZU and UPHNIZU models. Additionally, note that in three of the criteria, the UPHNIZU model performs better than the BIZU model, while for the fourth criterion (BIC), no significant differences are found between the two models. It is important to consider that the BIZU model has one less parameter, which further supports the superior fit of the UPHNIZU model. This allows us to conclude that the UPHNIZU model is a promising new alternative for modeling responses within the unit interval $[0, 1]$ with zero-one inflation.

We also generated standardized residual plots to identify the presence of outliers when fitting the UPHNIZU model. Additionally, we present the cumulative distribution function (CDF) plot of the UPHN model (Figure 5). From these, the model shows a good fit, and no outliers are detected. In addition, envelope plots were obtained for the fitted models BIZU, LNIZU, and DCLPHN, which are presented in Figures 3 and 4. These plots demonstrate that the BIZU and LNIZU models exhibit a better fit than the DCPHN model.

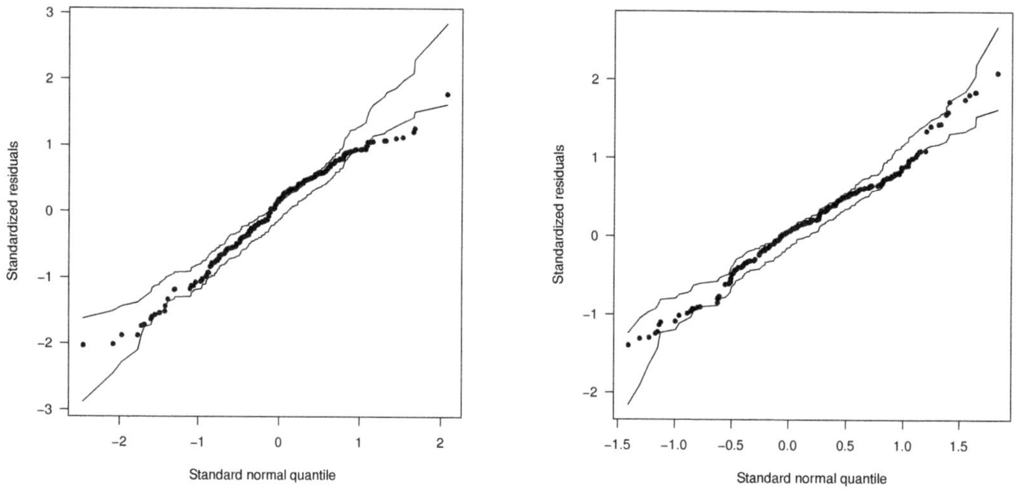

Figure 3. Plots of envelopes for rMT_i using: (**Left**) BIZU and (**Right**) LNIZU models and periodontal data.

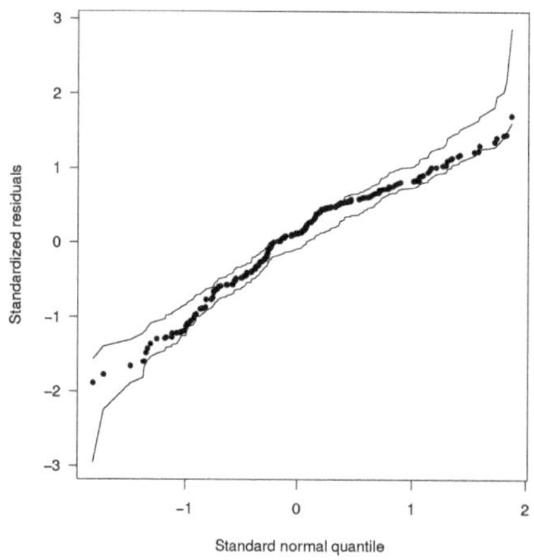

Figure 4. Plots of envelopes for rMT_i using DCPHN model and periodontal data.

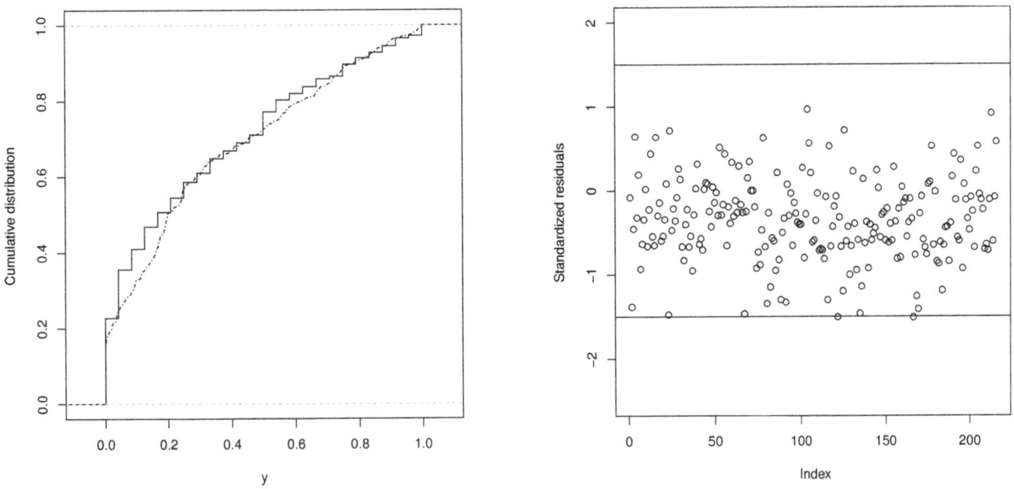

Figure 5. (**Left**) Empirical CDF of the residuals of the UPHNIZU model (solid line) and fitted CDF (dashed line). (**Right**) Plots of the standardized residuals of the UPHNIZU model, periodontal data.

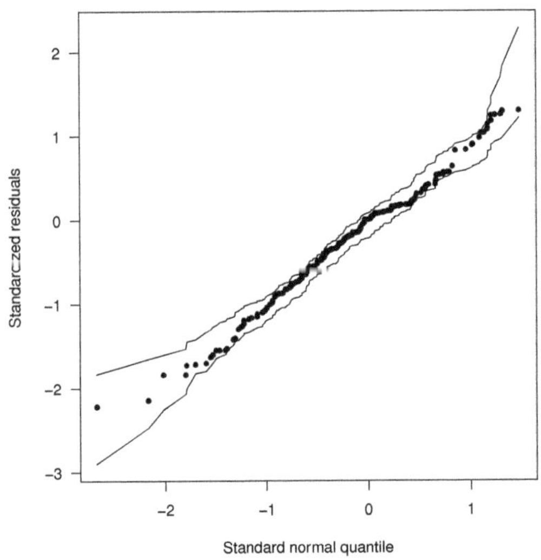

Figure 6. Plots of envelopes for rMT_i using UPHNIZU model and periodontal data.

5. Discussion

In this article, we introduced a broad class of skew regression models designed for response variables that lie within the unit interval, which may exhibit an excess of zeros or ones. These models were derived from a continuous-discrete mixture distribution that incorporates covariates in both its discrete and continuous components. As evidenced by applications using real data, the models we propose serve as a viable alternative for modeling rates and proportions that are inflated at either zero or one.

5.1. Major Results and Implications

Our findings demonstrate that the UPHNIZU model consistently surpassed other models in terms of AIC, AICc, BIC, and HQC values. These models delivered a superior fit for the data obtained from the case study on students' dropout data and the clinical study on periodontal disease, where the response variable was the proportion of diseased tooth sites.

Our findings also demonstrate that UPHNIZU models generate a non-singular information matrix, allowing valid statistical inferences and outperforming other asymmetric models like those derived from the skew-normal distribution or the beta distribution. Empirical results show the models' effectiveness in analyzing proportional data with zero and one inflation, highlighting their robustness and practicality in various research fields such as biomedicine, economics, and engineering. Additionally, they present parameter estimation methods using maximum likelihood and discuss applications in student dropout studies and periodontal disease. UPHNIZU models are a promising alternative for analyzing bounded data with extreme inflation, providing a robust and flexible tool to capture the complex characteristics of such data. The research also emphasizes the importance of innovations in probability distributions and their application in modeling complex phenomena, offering an advanced solution for the challenges of modeling proportional data with zero and one inflation.

5.2. Model Limitations

Although the results are encouraging, our study has several limitations. First, the models' complexity and reliance on iterative numerical methods for parameter estimation can lead to high computational demands. Second, while the models showed strong performance with the datasets utilized in this research, additional validation on different types of data is required to ensure their applicability in broader contexts.

5.3. Prospects for Further Investigation

Future research may explore several avenues, including the creation of more efficient algorithms to lessen the computational demands of fitting these models. Furthermore, applying these models in fields like economics or environmental studies could offer additional validation and reveal new applications.

Given the importance of model performance in our analysis, while the methods employed—such as AIC, AICc, BIC, HQC, and martingale residuals—are effective for evaluating model adequacy, there is room for improvement. Future research could investigate additional goodness-of-fit tests specifically designed for bounded and inflated data, which could offer a more thorough evaluation of model performance and robustness. Additionally, exploring Bayesian inference methods for unit interval data with inflation could provide valuable insights and enhance the analytical framework.

An intriguing avenue for future research involves adapting these models to accommodate longitudinal or hierarchical data structures. This would require methods to manage correlations within subjects or groups, often present in practical datasets. Additionally, examining the robustness of these models in various misspecification scenarios could lead to more resilient modeling strategies.

6. Conclusions

Analyzing proportion data, particularly when values are inflated at zero and one, presents significant challenges across various scientific disciplines. Conventional models, such as beta and Tobit regression models, frequently fail to accurately capture the complexities associated with such data. This underscores the need for more sophisticated modeling techniques capable of addressing the unique distributional characteristics of zero-one inflation.

This work tackled these challenges by introducing the proportional hazard normal zero-one inflated models. These models incorporate a continuous-discrete mixture distribution with covariates in both components, offering an advanced framework for analyzing proportion data with specific inflation points. Consequently, the proportional hazard normal zero-one inflated models provide a robust and flexible method for capturing asymmetrically distributed data and mixed discrete-continuous characteristics, prevalent in fields such as medicine, sociology, humanities, and economics.

Our applications, which pertain to two case studies on student dropout and periodontal data, demonstrated that the proportional hazard normal zero-one inflated models with the logit link function are an excellent alternative to traditional models. The transformation of martingale residuals and the generation of simulated envelopes further validated the robustness of our models, underscoring their effectiveness in identifying model misfits and outliers. The proposed models address a critical gap in statistical modeling, providing valuable insights and reliable estimators for handling bounded and inflated data. The flexibility and robustness of the proportional hazard normal zero-one inflated models make them a viable alternative for describing proportion data that are inflated at zero or one.

In conclusion, the proportional hazard-normal zero-one inflated models signify a significant advancement in statistical modeling techniques for proportion data exhibiting zero-one inflation. These models provide a robust and adaptable framework for analyzing such data, yielding deeper insights and more reliable estimators.

Author Contributions: Conceptualization: G.M.-F., R.T.-F. and H.W.G.; data curation: G.M.-F. and R.T.-F.; formal analysis: G.M.-F., R.T.-F. and H.W.G.; investigation: G.M.-F., R.T.-F. and H.W.G.; methodology: G.M.-F., R.T.-F. and H.W.G.; writing—original draft: G.M.-F.; writing—review and editing: R.T-F. All authors have read and agreed to the published version of the manuscript.

Funding: This research was supported by Vice-rectorate for Research of the Universidad de Córdoba, Colombia, project grant FCB-06-22: "Estudio de la deserción en los programas de pregrado de la Universidad de Córdoba usando diferentes metodologías estadísticas" (G.M.-F. and R.T.-F).

Data Availability Statement: The data and codes used in this study are available upon request to the authors.

Conflicts of Interest: The authors declare that they have no known competing financial interests or personal relationships that could have appeared to influence the work reported in this article.

Appendix A. Elements of the Observed Information Matrix

Appendix A.1. Truncated Proportional Hazard Normal Model

$$
\begin{aligned}
\ddot{\ell}(\xi\xi) \;=\;& \frac{n}{\sigma^2} + n\frac{\alpha-1}{\sigma^2}\left[\overline{h^2} - \overline{zh}\right] + n\frac{\alpha}{\sigma^2}\frac{\left(h(z_0)\{S(z_0)\}^\alpha - h(z_1)\{S(z_1)\}^\alpha\right)^2}{W^2} \\
& -n\frac{\alpha}{\sigma^2}\frac{z_0 h(z_0)\{S(z_0)\}^\alpha - z_1 h(z_1)\{S(z_1)\}^\alpha + (\alpha-1)\left(h^2(z_0)\{S(z_0)\}^\alpha - h^2(z_1)\{S(z_1)\}^\alpha\right)}{W}, \\
\ddot{\ell}(\xi\sigma) \;=\;& \frac{2n}{\sigma^2}\overline{z} + n\frac{\alpha-1}{\sigma^2}\left[-\overline{zh^2} - \overline{z^2h} + \overline{h}\right] + n\frac{\alpha}{\sigma^2}\frac{h(z_0)\{S(z_0)\}^\alpha - h(z_1)\{S(z_1)\}^\alpha}{W} \\
& +n\frac{\alpha}{\sigma^2}\frac{\left(h(z_0)\{S(z_0)\}^\alpha - h(z_1)\{S(z_1)\}^\alpha\right)\left(z_0 h(z_0)\{S(z_0)\}^\alpha - z_1 h(z_1)\{S(z_1)\}^\alpha\right)}{W^2} \\
& -n\frac{\alpha}{\sigma^2}\frac{z_0^2 h(z_0)\{S(z_0)\}^\alpha - z_1^2 h(z_1)\{S(z_1)\}^\alpha + (\alpha-1)\left(z_0 h^2(z_0)\{S(z_0)\}^\alpha - z_1 h^2(z_1)\{S(z_1)\}^\alpha\right)}{W}, \\
\ddot{\ell}(\sigma\sigma) \;=\;& -\frac{n}{\sigma^2} + \frac{3n}{\sigma^2}\overline{z^2} + n\frac{\alpha-1}{\sigma^2}\left[2\overline{zh} + \overline{z^2h^2} - \overline{z^3h}\right] + n\frac{\alpha}{\sigma^2}\frac{\left(z_0 h(z_0)\{S(z_0)\}^\alpha - z_1 h(z_1)\{S(z_1)\}^\alpha\right)^2}{W^2} \\
& +n\frac{\alpha}{\sigma^2}\frac{-z_0 h(z_0)\{S(z_0)\}^\alpha\left(-2 + z_0^2 + (\alpha-1)z_0 h(z_0)\right) + z_1 h(z_1)\{S(z_1)\}^\alpha\left(-2 + z_1^2 + (\alpha-1)z_1 h(z_1)\right)}{W},
\end{aligned}
$$

$$\ddot{\ell}(\xi\alpha) = -\frac{n}{\sigma}\overline{h} + n\frac{\alpha}{\sigma}\frac{\left(h(z_0)\{S(z_0)\}^{\alpha} - h(z_1)\{S(z_1)\}^{\alpha}\right)\left(\{S(z_0)\}^{\alpha}\log(S(z_0)) - \{S(z_1)\}^{\alpha}\log(S(z_1))\right)}{W^2}$$
$$-\frac{n}{\sigma}\frac{\left(h(z_0)\{S(z_0)\}^{\alpha} - h(z_1)\{S(z_1)\}^{\alpha}\right) + \alpha\left(h(z_0)\{S(z_0)\}^{\alpha}\log(S(z_0)) - h(z_1)\{S(z_1)\}^{\alpha}\log(S(z_1))\right)}{W},$$

$$\ddot{\ell}(\sigma\alpha) = -\frac{n}{\sigma}\overline{zh} + n\frac{\alpha}{\sigma}\frac{\left(z_0h(z_0)\{S(z_0)\}^{\alpha} - z_1h(z_1)\{S(z_1)\}^{\alpha}\right)\left(\{S(z_0)\}^{\alpha}\log(S(z_0)) - \{S(z_1)\}^{\alpha}\log(S(z_1))\right)}{W^2}$$
$$-\frac{n}{\sigma}\frac{\left(z_0h(z_0)\{S(z_0)\}^{\alpha} - z_1h(z_1)\{S(z_1)\}^{\alpha}\right) + \alpha\left(z_0h(z_0)\{S(z_0)\}^{\alpha}\log(S(z_0)) - z_1h(z_1)\{S(z_1)\}^{\alpha}\log(S(z_1))\right)}{W},$$

$$\ddot{\ell}(\alpha\alpha) = \frac{n}{\alpha} - n\frac{\left(\{S(z_0)\}^{\alpha}\log^2(S(z_0)) - \{S(z_1)\}^{\alpha}\log^2(S(z_1))\right)}{W}$$
$$+n\frac{\left(\{S(z_0)\}^{\alpha}\log(S(z_0)) - \{S(z_1)\}^{\alpha}\log(S(z_1))\right)^2}{W^2},$$

where $h(z_i) = \frac{\phi(z_i)}{S(z_i)}$, $\overline{h} = \frac{1}{n}\sum_{i=1}^{n} h(z_i)$, $\overline{h^2} = \frac{1}{n}\sum_{i=1}^{n} h^2(z_i)$, $\overline{zh} = \frac{1}{n}\sum_{i=1}^{n} z_i h(z_i), \ldots, \overline{z^2h^2} = \frac{1}{n}\sum_{i=1}^{n} z_i^2 h^2(z_i)$, $\overline{z^3h} = \frac{1}{n}\sum_{i=1}^{n} z_i^3 h(z_i)$,

Appendix A.2. Unit-Proportional Hazard Normal Regression Model

$$\ddot{\ell}(\beta_j\beta_k) = \frac{n}{\sigma^2} + \frac{\alpha-1}{\sigma^2}\sum_{i=1}^{n} x_{ij}x_{ik}\mu_i^2(1-\mu_i)^2\left[h^2(z_i) - z_ih(z_i)\right]$$
$$+\frac{\alpha}{\sigma^2}\sum_{i=1}^{n} x_{ij}x_{ik}\mu_i^2(1-\mu_i)^2\frac{\left(h(z_{0i})\{S(z_{0i})\}^{\alpha} - h(z_{1i})\{S(z_{1i})\}^{\alpha}\right)^2}{W_i^2}$$
$$-\frac{\alpha}{\sigma^2}\sum_{i=1}^{n} x_{ij}x_{ik}\mu_i^2(1-\mu_i)^2\frac{z_{0i}h(z_{0i})\{S(z_{0i})\}^{\alpha} - z_{1i}h(z_{1i})\{S(z_{1i})\}^{\alpha}}{W_i}$$
$$-\frac{\alpha(\alpha-1)}{\sigma^2}\sum_{i=1}^{n} x_{ij}x_{ik}\mu_i^2(1-\mu_i)^2\frac{\left(h^2(z_{0i})\{S(z_{0i})\}^{\alpha} - h^2(z_{1i})\{S(z_{1i})\}^{\alpha}\right)}{W_i}$$
$$-\frac{1}{\sigma}\sum_{i=1}^{n} x_{ij}x_{ik}\mu_i(1-\mu_i)(1-2\mu_i)z_i - \frac{\alpha-1}{\sigma}\sum_{i=1}^{n} x_{ij}x_{ik}\mu_i(1-\mu_i)(1-2\mu_i)h(z_i)$$
$$+\frac{\alpha}{\sigma}\sum_{i=1}^{n} x_{ij}x_{ik}\mu_i(1-\mu_i)(1-2\mu_i)\frac{h(z_{0i})\{S(z_{0i})\}^{\alpha} - h(z_{1i})\{S(z_{1i})\}^{\alpha}}{W_i},$$

$$\ddot{\ell}(\beta_j\sigma) = \frac{2}{\sigma^2}\sum_{i=1}^{n} x_{ij}\mu_i(1-\mu_i)z_i + \frac{\alpha-1}{\sigma^2}\sum_{i=1}^{n} x_{ij}\mu_i(1-\mu_i)\left[-z_ih^2(z_i) - z_i^2h(z_i) + h(z_i)\right]$$
$$+\frac{\alpha}{\sigma^2}\sum_{i=1}^{n} x_{ij}\mu_i(1-\mu_i)\frac{h(z_{0i})\{S(z_{0i})\}^{\alpha} - h(z_{1i})\{S(z_{1i})\}^{\alpha}}{W_i}$$
$$+\frac{\alpha}{\sigma^2}\sum_{i=1}^{n} x_{ij}\mu_i(1-\mu_i)\frac{\left(h(z_{0i})\{S(z_{0i})\}^{\alpha} - h(z_{1i})\{S(z_{1i})\}^{\alpha}\right)\left(z_{0i}h(z_{0i})\{S(z_{0i})\}^{\alpha} - z_{1i}h(z_{1i})\{S(z_{1i})\}^{\alpha}\right)}{W_i^2}$$
$$-\frac{\alpha}{\sigma^2}\sum_{i=1}^{n} x_{ij}\mu_i(1-\mu_i)\frac{z_{0i}^2h(z_{0i})\{S(z_{0i})\}^{\alpha} - z_{1i}^2h(z_{1i})\{S(z_{1i})\}^{\alpha}}{W_i}$$
$$-\frac{\alpha(\alpha-1)}{\sigma^2}\sum_{i=1}^{n} x_{ij}\mu_i(1-\mu_i)\frac{\left(z_{0i}h^2(z_{0i})\{S(z_{0i})\}^{\alpha} - z_{1i}h^2(z_{1i})\{S(z_{1i})\}^{\alpha}\right)}{W_i},$$

$$\begin{aligned}
\ddot{\ell}(\sigma\sigma) &= -\frac{n}{\sigma^2}+\frac{3}{\sigma^2}\sum_{i=1}^{n} z_i^2+\frac{\alpha-1}{\sigma^2}\sum_{i=1}^{n}\Big[2z_ih(z_i)+z_i^2h^2(z_i)-z_i^3h(z_i)\Big] \\
&+\frac{\alpha}{\sigma^2}\sum_{i=1}^{n}\frac{(z_{0i}h(z_{0i})\{S(z_{0i})\}^{\alpha}-z_{1i}h(z_{1i})\{S(z_{1i})\}^{\alpha})^2}{W_i^2} \\
&-\frac{\alpha}{\sigma^2}\sum_{i=1}^{n}\frac{z_{0i}h(z_{0i})\{S(z_{0i})\}^{\alpha}(-2+z_{0i}^2+(\alpha-1)z_{0i}h(z_{0i}))}{W_i} \\
&+\frac{\alpha}{\sigma^2}\sum_{i=1}^{n}\frac{+z_{1i}h(z_{1i})\{S(z_{1i})\}^{\alpha}(-2+z_{1i}^2+(\alpha-1)z_{1i}h(z_{1i}))}{W_i}, \\
\ddot{\ell}(\beta_j\alpha) &= -\frac{n}{\sigma}\sum_{i=1}^{n}x_{ij}\mu_i(1-\mu_i)h(z_i)-\frac{1}{\sigma}\sum_{i=1}^{n}x_{ij}\mu_i(1-\mu_i)\frac{h(z_{0i})\{S(z_{0i})\}^{\alpha}-h(z_{1i})\{S(z_{1i})\}^{\alpha}}{W_i} \\
&+\frac{\alpha}{\sigma}\sum_{i=1}^{n}x_{ij}\mu_i(1-\mu_i)\frac{h(z_{0i})\{S(z_{0i})\}^{\alpha}(\{S(z_{0i})\}^{\alpha}\log(S(z_{0i}))-\{S(z_{1i})\}^{\alpha}\log(S(z_{1i})))}{W_i^2} \\
&-\frac{\alpha}{\sigma}\sum_{i=1}^{n}x_{ij}\mu_i(1-\mu_i)\frac{h(z_{1i})\{S(z_{1i})\}^{\alpha}(\{S(z_{0i})\}^{\alpha}\log(S(z_{0i}))-\{S(z_{1i})\}^{\alpha}\log(S(z_{1i})))}{W_i^2} \\
&-\frac{\alpha}{\sigma}\sum_{i=1}^{n}x_{ij}\mu_i(1-\mu_i)\frac{h(z_{0i})\{S(z_{0i})\}^{\alpha}\log(S(z_{0i}))-h(z_{1i})\{S(z_{1i})\}^{\alpha}\log(S(z_{1i}))}{W_i}, \\
\ddot{\ell}(\sigma\alpha) &= -\frac{1}{\sigma}\sum_{i=1}^{n}z_ih(z_i)+\frac{\alpha}{\sigma}\sum_{i=1}^{n}\frac{z_{0i}h(z_{0i})\{S(z_{0i})\}^{\alpha}(\{S(z_{0i})\}^{\alpha}\log(S(z_{0i}))-\{S(z_{1i})\}^{\alpha}\log(S(z_{1i})))}{W_i^2} \\
&-\frac{\alpha}{\sigma}\sum_{i=1}^{n}\frac{z_{1i}h(z_{1i})\{S(z_{1i})\}(\{S(z_{0i})\}^{\alpha}\log(S(z_{0i}))-\{S(z_{1i})\}^{\alpha}\log(S(z_{1i})))}{W_i^2} \\
&-\frac{1}{\sigma}\sum_{i=1}^{n}\frac{z_{0i}h(z_{0i})\{S(z_{0i})\}^{\alpha}-z_{1i}h(z_{1i})\{S(z_{1i})\}^{\alpha}}{W_i} \\
&-\frac{\alpha}{\sigma}\sum_{i=1}^{n}\frac{z_{0i}h(z_{0i})\{S(z_{0i})\}^{\alpha}\log(S(z_{0i}))-z_{1i}h(z_{1i})\{S(z_{1i})\}^{\alpha}\log(S(z_{1i}))}{W_i}, \\
\ddot{\ell}(\alpha\alpha) &= \frac{n}{\alpha}-\sum_{i=1}^{n}\frac{\{S(z_{0i})\}^{\alpha}\log^2(S(z_{0i}))-\{S(z_{1i})\}^{\alpha}\log^2(S(z_{1i}))}{W_i} \\
&+\sum_{i=1}^{n}\frac{(\{S(z_{0i})\}^{\alpha}\log(S(z_{0i}))-\{S(z_{1i})\}^{\alpha}\log(S(z_{1i})))^2}{W_i^2},
\end{aligned}$$

where $z_i=\frac{y_i-\mu_i}{\sigma}$, $z_{0i}=-\frac{\mu_i}{\sigma}$, $z_{1i}=\frac{1-\mu_i}{\sigma}$ and $W_i=W_i(\mu_i,\sigma,\alpha)=\log(\{S(z_{0i})\}^{\alpha}-\{S(z_{1i})\}^{\alpha})$.

Appendix A.3. UPHN Regression Model Inflated at Zero and/or One

For the discrete part, the elements of the observed information matrix are given by:

$$\ddot{\ell}(\beta_{(0)r}\beta_{(0)r'})=\sum_{i=1}^{n}\frac{x_{(0)ip}x_{(0)ip'}\exp(\boldsymbol{x}_{(0)i}^{\top}\boldsymbol{\beta}_{(0)})\left[1+\exp(\boldsymbol{x}_{(1)i}^{\top}\boldsymbol{\beta}_{(1)})\right]}{\left(1+\exp(\boldsymbol{x}_{(0)i}^{\top}\boldsymbol{\beta}_{(0)})+\exp(\boldsymbol{x}_{(1)i}^{\top}\boldsymbol{\beta}_{(1)})\right)^2},$$

$$\ddot{\ell}(\beta_{(1)q}\beta_{(0)r})=-\sum_{i=1}^{n}\frac{x_{(0)ip}x_{(1)iq}\exp(\boldsymbol{x}_{(0)i}^{\top}\boldsymbol{\beta}_{(0)})\exp(\boldsymbol{x}_{(1)i}^{\top}\boldsymbol{\beta}_{(1)})}{\left(1+\exp(\boldsymbol{x}_{(0)i}^{\top}\boldsymbol{\beta}_{(0)})+\exp(\boldsymbol{x}_{(1)i}^{\top}\boldsymbol{\beta}_{(1)})\right)^2},$$

$$\ddot{\ell}(\beta_{(1)q}\beta_{(1)q'})=\sum_{i=1}^{n}\frac{x_{(1)iq}x_{(1)iq'}\exp(\boldsymbol{x}_{(1)i}^{\top}\boldsymbol{\beta}_{(1)})\left[1+\exp(\boldsymbol{x}_{(0)i}^{\top}\boldsymbol{\beta}_{(0)})\right]}{\left(1+\exp(\boldsymbol{x}_{(0)i}^{\top}\boldsymbol{\beta}_{(0)})+\exp(\boldsymbol{x}_{(1)i}^{\top}\boldsymbol{\beta}_{(1)})\right)^2},$$

while the elements for the continuous part are given by:

$$\begin{aligned}
\ddot{\ell}(\beta_j\beta_k) &= \frac{n_{01}}{\sigma^2} + \frac{\alpha-1}{\sigma^2}\sum_{y_i\in(0,1)} x_{ij}x_{ik}\mu_i^2(1-\mu_i)^2\left[h^2(z_i) - z_i h(z_i)\right] \\
&\quad -\frac{1}{\sigma}\sum_{y_i\in(0,1)} x_{ij}x_{ik}\mu_i(1-\mu_i)(1-2\mu_i)z_i - \frac{\alpha-1}{\sigma}\sum_{y_i\in(0,1)} x_{ij}x_{ik}\mu_i(1-\mu_i)(1-2\mu_i)h(z_i), \\
\ddot{\ell}(\beta_j\sigma) &= \frac{2}{\sigma^2}\sum_{y_i\in(0,1)} x_{ij}\mu_i(1-\mu_i)z_i + \frac{\alpha-1}{\sigma^2}\sum_{y_i\in(0,1)} x_{ij}\mu_i(1-\mu_i)\left[-z_i h^2(z_i) - z_i^2 h(z_i) + h(z_i)\right], \\
\ddot{\ell}(\sigma\sigma) &= -\frac{n_{01}}{\sigma^2} + \frac{3}{\sigma^2}\sum_{y_i\in(0,1)} z_i^2 + \frac{\alpha-1}{\sigma^2}\sum_{y_i\in(0,1)}\left[2z_i h(z_i) + z_i^2 h^2(z_i) - z_i^3 h(z_i)\right], \\
\ddot{\ell}(\beta_j\alpha) &= -\frac{n}{\sigma}\sum_{y_i\in(0,1)} x_{ij}\mu_i(1-\mu_i)h(z_i), \\
\ddot{\ell}(\sigma\alpha) &= -\frac{1}{\sigma}\sum_{y_i\in(0,1)} z_i h(z_i), \\
\ddot{\ell}(\alpha\alpha) &= \frac{n_{01}}{\alpha},
\end{aligned}$$

where $z_i = \frac{y_i-\mu_i}{\sigma}$ and n_{01} is the number of sample elements that belong to the interval $(0,1)$.

References

1. Eugene, N.; Lee, C.; Famoye, F. Beta-normal Distribution and Its Applications. *Commun.-Stat.-Theory Methods* **2002**, *31*, 497–512. [CrossRef]
2. Cordeiro, G.M.; de Castro, M. A New Family of Generalized Distributions. *J. Stat. Comput. Simul.* **2011**, *81*, 883–898. [CrossRef]
3. Silva, G.O.; Ortega, E.M.M.; Cordeiro, G.M. The Beta Modified Weibull Distribution. *Lifetime Data Anal.* **2010**, *16*, 409–430. [CrossRef] [PubMed]
4. Mahdavi, M.; Silva, G.O. A method to expand family of continuous distributions based on truncated distributions. *J. Statist. Res.* **2016**, *13*, 231–247. [CrossRef]
5. Chen, S.; Gui, W. Estimation of unknown parameters of Truncated Normal Distribution under Adaptive Progressive Type II Censoring Scheme. *Mathematics* **2021**, *9*, 49. [CrossRef]
6. Taketomi, N.; Yamamoto, K.; Chesneau, C.; Emura, T. Parametric Distributions for Survival and Reliability Analyses, a Review and Historical Sketch. *Mathematics* **2022**, *10*, 3907. [CrossRef]
7. Kreer, M.; Kızılersü, A.; Thomas, A.W.; Egídio dos Reis, A.D. Goodness-of-fit tests and applications for left-truncated Weibull distributions to non-life insurance. *Eur. Actuar. J.* **2015**, *5*, 139–163. [CrossRef]
8. Cordeiro, G.M.; Silva, G.O.; Ortega, E.M.M. The Beta-Weibull Geometric Distribution. *Statistics* **2013**, *47*, 817–834. [CrossRef]
9. Cordeiro, G.M.; Ortega, E.M.M.; Silva, G.O. The Kumaraswamy Modified Weibull Distribution: Theory and Applications. *J. Stat. Comput. Simul.* **2014**, *84*, 1387–1411. [CrossRef]
10. Zografos, K.; Balakrishnan, N. On Families of Beta-and Generalized Gamma generated Distributions and Associated Inference. *Stat. Methodol.* **2009**, *6*, 344–362. [CrossRef]
11. Ristić, M.M.; Balakrishnan, N. The Gamma-exponentiated Exponential Distribution. *J. Stat. Comput. Simul.* **2012**, *82*, 1191–1206. [CrossRef]
12. Castellares, F.; Santos, M.A.C.; Montenegro, L.C.; Cordeiro, G.M. A Gamma-Generated Logistic Distribution: Properties and Inference. *Am. J. Math. Manag. Sci.* **2015**, *34*, 14–39.
13. Cordeiro, G.M.; Lima, M.C.S.; Cysneiros, A.H.M.A.; Pascoa, M.A.R.; Pescim, R.R.; Ortega, E.M.M. An Extended Birnbaum–Saunders Distribution: Theory, Estimation, and Applications. *Commun. Stat.-Theory Methods* **2016**, *45*, 2268–2297. [CrossRef]
14. Enami, S.H. Truncated Lomax-exponential distribution ans its fitting to financial data. *J. Mahani Math. Res.* **2023**, *12*, 201–216.
15. Hadi, H.H.; Al-Noor, N.H. Truncated exponential Marshall Olkin Lomax distribution: Properties, entropies, and applications. *AIP Conf. Proc.* **2023**, *2414*, 201–216.
16. Al-Habib, K.H.; Khaleel, M.H.; Al-Mofleh, H. Statistical Properties and Application for [0,1] Truncated Nadarajah-Haghighi Exponential Distribution. *Ibn-Haitham J. Pure Appl. Sci.* **2024**, *37*, 363–377.
17. Schaminée, J.H.; Hennekens, S.M.; Chytry, M.; Rodwell, J.S. Vegetation-plot data and databases in Europe: An overview. *Preslia* **2009**, *81*, 173–185.
18. Desousa, M.; Saulo, H.; Leiva, V.; Scalco, P. On a tobit-Birnbaum–Saunders model with an application to medical data. *J. Appl. Stat.* **2018**, *45*, 932–955. [CrossRef]
19. Sanchez, L.; Leiva, V.; Galea, M.; Saulo, H. Birnbaum–Saunders quantile regression and its diagnostics with application to economic data. *Appl. Stoch. Model. Bus. Ind.* **2021**, *37*, 53–73. [CrossRef]

20. Arellano-Valle, R.B.; Gómez, H.W.; Quintana, F. Statistical inference for a general class of asymmetric distributions. *J. Stat. Plan. Inference* **2005**, *128*, 427–443. [CrossRef]
21. Barros, M.; Galea, M.; Leiva, V.; Santos-Neto, M. Generalized tobit models: Diagnostics and application in econometrics. *J. Appl. Stat.* **2018**, *45*, 145–167. [CrossRef]
22. Azzalini, A. A class of distributions which includes the normal ones. *Scand. J. Stat.* **1985**, *12*, 171–178.
23. Azzalini, A. Further results on a class of distributions which includes the normal ones. *Statistica* **1986**, *46*, 199–208.
24. Henze, N. A probabilistic representation of the skew-normal distribution. *Scand. J. Stat.* **1986**, *13*, 271–275.
25. Castillo, N.O.; Gómez, H.W.; Leiva, V.; Sanhueza, A. On the Fernández-Steel distribution: Inference and application. *Comput. Stat. Data Anal.* **2011**, *55*, 2951–2961. [CrossRef]
26. Gupta, R.D.; Gupta, R.C. Analyzing skewed data by power normal model. *Test* **2008**, *17*, 197–210. [CrossRef]
27. Pewsey, A.; Gómez, H.W.; Bolfarine, H. Likelihood-based inference for power distributions. *Test* **2012**, *21*, 775–789. [CrossRef]
28. Mohammadi, Z.; Sajjadnia, Z.; Bakouch, H.S.; Sharafi, M. Zero-and-one inflated Poisson-Lindley INAR (1) process for modelling count time series with extra zeros and ones. *J. Stat. Comput. Simul.* **2022**, *92*, 2018–2040. [CrossRef]
29. Lee, B.S.; Haran, M. A class of models for large zero-inflated spatial data. *J. Agric. Biol. Environ. Stat.* **2024**. [CrossRef]
30. Figueroa-Zúñiga, J.; Niklitschek, S.; Leiva, V.; Liu, S. Modeling heavy-tailed bounded data by the trapezoidal beta distribution with applications. *REVSTAT—Stat. J.* **2022**, *20*, 387–404.
31. Jornsatian, C.; Bodhisuwan, W. Zero-one inflated negative binomial-beta exponential distribution for count data with many zeros and ones. *Commun. Stat.-Theory Methods* **2022**, *51*, 8517–8531. [CrossRef]
32. Keim, J.L.; DeWitt, P.D.; Fitzpatrick, J.J.; Jenni, N.S. Estimating plant abundance using inflated beta distributions: Applied learnings from a Lichen-Caribou ecosystem. *Ecol. Evol.* **2017**, *7*, 486–493. [CrossRef] [PubMed]
33. Benites, L.; Maehara, R.; Lachos, V.H.; Bolfarine, H. Linear regression models using finite mixtures of skew heavy-tailed distributions. *Chil. J. Stat.* **2019**, *10*, 21–41.
34. Desousa, M.; Saulo, H.; Santos-Neto, M.; Leiva, V. On a new mixture-based regression model: Simulation and application to data with high censoring. *J. Stat. Comput. Simul.* **2020**, *90*, 2861–2877. [CrossRef]
35. Arellano-Valle, R.B.; Gómez, H.W.; Quintana, F. A new class of skew-normal distributions. *Commun. Stat.-Theory Methods* **2004**, *33*, 1465–1480. [CrossRef]
36. Martínez-Flórez, G.; Moreno-Arenas, G.; Vergara-Cardozo, S. Properties and inference for proportional hazard Models. *Rev. Colomb. Estadística* **2013**, *36*, 95–114.
37. Lehmann, E.L.; Casella, G. *Theory of Point Estimation*, 2nd ed.; Springer: New York, NY, USA, 1998.
38. Sarabia, J.M.; Castillo, E. About a class of max-stable families with applications to income distributions. *Int. J. Stat.* **2005**, *LXIII*, 505–527.
39. Cragg, J. Some statistical models for limited dependent variables with application to the demand for durable goods. *Econometrica* **1971**, *39*, 829–844. [CrossRef]
40. Moulton, L.; Halsey, N.A. A mixture model with detection limits for regression analysses of antibody response to vaccine. *Biometrics* **1995**, *51*, 1570–1578. [CrossRef]
41. Akaike, H. A new look at statistical model identification. *IEEE Trans. Autom. Control.* **1974**, *AU-19*, 716–722. [CrossRef]
42. Cavanaugh, J.E. Unifying the derivations for the Akaike and corrected Akaike information criteria. *Stat. Probab. Lett.* **1997**, *33*, 201–208. [CrossRef]
43. Barros, M.; Paula, G.A.; Leiva, V. A new class of survival regression models with heavy-tailed errors: Robustness and diagnostics. *Lifetime Data Anal.* **2010**, *14*, 316–332. [CrossRef] [PubMed]
44. Ortega, E.M.; Bolfarine, H.; Paula, G.A. Influence diagnostics in generalized log-gamma regression models. *Comput. Stat. Data Anal.* **2003**, *42*, 165–186. [CrossRef]
45. Galvis, D.M.; Bandyopadhyay, D.; Lachos, V.H. Augmented mixed beta regression models for periodontal proportion data. *Stat. Med.* **2014**, *33*, 3759–3771. [CrossRef]

mathematics

MDPI

Article

A Review of Wrapped Distributions for Circular Data

William Bell and Saralees Nadarajah *

Department of Mathematics, University of Manchester, Manchester M13 9PL, UK; william.bell-4@postgrad.manchester.ac.uk
* Correspondence: mbbsssn2@manchester.ac.uk

Abstract: The wrapped method is the most widely used method for constructing distributions for circular data. In this paper, we provide a review of all known wrapped distributions, including 45 distributions for continuous circular data and 10 distributions for discrete circular data. For each wrapped distribution, we state its nth trigonometric moment, mean direction, mean resultant length, skewness, and kurtosis. We also discuss data applications and limitations of each wrapped distribution. This review could be a useful reference and encourage the development of more wrapped distributions. We also mention an R package available for fitting all of the reviewed distributions and illustrate its applications.

Keywords: kurtosis; mean direction; mean resultant length; skewness; trigonometric moment

MSC: 62E99

1. Introduction

Circular data, also known as directional data, refer to measurements where the values are cyclical and repeat over a defined interval. This kind of data arises naturally in situations where the end of the scale reconnects with the beginning, such as angles, time, and compass directions. For example, angles measured in degrees or radians are circular because 0 is the same as 360, and similarly, 0 radians equates to 2π radians. This cyclical nature poses unique challenges for statistical analysis because traditional linear methods are not suitable for data that wrap around.

Practical examples of circular data abound in various fields. In meteorology, wind directions recorded over time create circular datasets, as the direction can be anywhere between 0 and 360. In biology, the study of animal movement, such as the migratory patterns of birds or the rotational behavior of certain animals, often involves circular data. Time-related data are another common example; for instance, the times of day at which certain events occur (like sleep cycles or peak traffic hours) are inherently circular because they repeat every 24 h. Analyzing such data requires careful consideration of its circular nature to avoid misinterpretation and to uncover meaningful patterns and insights.

There have been many distributions proposed for circular data. Refs. [1–6] provide excellent reviews. Most of the distributions for circular data are based on the method of wrapping. Hence, we feel it is appropriate to provide a review of all known wrapped distributions to date, which is the aim of this paper. No such review is known to date. Such a review could be a useful reference for those interested in both the theory and applications of wrapped distributions. It could also enhance the development of more wrapped distributions.

The method of wrapping can be described as follows. Suppose g is a valid probability density function (PDF). If g is defined on the positive real line, then the PDF of the wrapped distribution is

$$f(\theta) = \sum_{k=0}^{\infty} g(\theta + 2k\pi) \tag{1}$$

for $0 \leq \theta < 2\pi$. If g is defined on the entire real line, then the PDF of the wrapped distribution is

$$f(\theta) = \sum_{k=-\infty}^{\infty} g(\theta + 2k\pi) \tag{2}$$

for $0 \leq \theta < 2\pi$.

On the other hand, now suppose g is a valid probability mass function (PMF). If g is defined on the positive real line, then the PMF of the wrapped distribution is

$$\Pr\left(\Theta = \frac{2\pi r}{m}\right) = \sum_{k=0}^{\infty} g(r + km) \tag{3}$$

for $r = 0, 1, \ldots, m-1$, and $m \geq 1$. If g is defined on the entire real line, then the PMF of the wrapped distribution is

$$\Pr\left(\Theta = \frac{2\pi r}{m}\right) = \sum_{k=-\infty}^{\infty} g(r + km) \tag{4}$$

for $r = 0, 1, \ldots, m-1$, and $m \geq 1$.

The most important properties of a circular random variable, say Θ, are its nth trigonometric moment denoted by m_n, mean direction denoted by μ, mean resultant length denoted by ρ, skewness denoted by γ_1, and kurtosis denoted by γ_2, defined by

$$m_n = E[\cos(n\Theta)] + \mathrm{i}E[\sin(n\Theta)], \tag{5}$$

$$\mu = \arcsin \frac{E[\sin(\Theta)]}{\sqrt{\{E[\cos(\Theta)]\}^2 + \{E[\sin(\Theta)]\}^2}}, \tag{6}$$

$$\rho = \sqrt{\{E[\cos(\Theta)]\}^2 + \{E[\sin(\Theta)]\}^2}, \tag{7}$$

$$\gamma_1 = \frac{\exp(-2\mu)}{(1-\rho)^{\frac{3}{2}}} E[\sin(2\Theta)], \tag{8}$$

and

$$\gamma_1 = \frac{\exp(-2\mu)}{1-\rho^2} E[\cos(2\Theta)] - \frac{\rho^4}{1-\rho^2}, \tag{9}$$

respectively. For each reviewed distribution, we list expressions for (5)–(9) as well as expressions for the cumulative distribution function (CDF) corresponding to (1)–(4), if they are available. We also discuss data applications as well as the limitations of each reviewed distribution. Section 2 lists all known expressions corresponding to (1)–(2). Section 3 lists all known expressions corresponding to (3)–(4). The properties (5)–(9) not listed in Sections 2 and 3 could provide readers with avenues for future work.

The expressions listed in Sections 2 and 3 involve several special functions, including the Lerch function defined by

$$\Phi(z;s,a) = \sum_{k=0}^{\infty} \frac{z^k}{(a+k)^s};$$

the gamma function defined by

$$\Gamma(a) = \int_0^{\infty} t^{a-1} e^{-t} dt;$$

the lower incomplete gamma function defined by

$$\gamma(a,x) = \int_0^{x} t^{a-1} e^{-t} dt;$$

the upper incomplete gamma function defined by

$$\Gamma(a,x) = \int_x^{\infty} t^{a-1} e^{-t} dt;$$

the standard normal probability density function defined by

$$\phi(x) = \frac{1}{\sqrt{2\pi}} e^{-\frac{x^2}{2}};$$

the standard normal cumulative distribution function defined by

$$\Phi(x) = \int_{-\infty}^{x} \frac{1}{\sqrt{2\pi}} e^{-\frac{t^2}{2}} dt;$$

and the modified Bessel function of the second kind defined by

$$K_\nu(x) = \begin{cases} \dfrac{\pi \csc(\pi\nu)}{2} [I_{-\nu}(x) - I_\nu(x)], & \text{if } \nu \notin \mathbb{Z}, \\ \lim\limits_{\mu \to \nu} K_\mu(x), & \text{if } \nu \in \mathbb{Z}; \end{cases}$$

the modified Bessel function of the first kind of order ν defined by

$$I_\nu(x) = \sum_{k=0}^{\infty} \frac{1}{\Gamma(k+\nu+1)k!} \left(\frac{x}{2}\right)^{2k+\nu}.$$

The properties of these special functions can be found in [7,8]. We also set $\mathrm{i} = \sqrt{-1}$ throughout.

An R software package (version 4.4.1) for fitting of all of the reviewed distributions has been created by the second author [9]. Three data applications illustrating the R package are given in Section 4.

2. A Review of Continuous Wrapped Distributions

In this section, we review wrapped Akash, wrapped Aradhana, wrapped binormal, wrapped Birnbaum–Saunders, wrapped Cauchy, wrapped chi-square, wrapped exponential, wrapped exponentiated inverted Weibull, wrapped gamma, wrapped generalized geometric stable, wrapped generalized Gompertz, wrapped generalized normal Laplace, wrapped generalized skew normal [10], wrapped generalized skew normal [11], wrapped half-logistic, wrapped half-normal, wrapped [12]'s skew Laplace, wrapped hypoexponential, wrapped Ishita, wrapped Laplace, wrapped length-biased weighted exponential, wrapped Levy, wrapped Lindley, wrapped Linnik, wrapped Lomax, wrapped modified

Lindley, wrapped new Weibull–Pareto, wrapped normal, wrapped Pareto, wrapped quasi-Lindley, wrapped Rama, wrapped Richard, wrapped Shanker, wrapped skew Laplace, wrapped skew normal, wrapped stable, wrapped Student's t, wrapped transmuted exponential, wrapped two-parameter Lindley, wrapped two-sided Lindley, wrapped variance gamma, wrapped weighted exponential, wrapped Weibull, wrapped XGamma and wrapped XLindley distributions.

2.1. Wrapped Akash Distribution

Ref. [13] took g to be the PDF of the Akash distribution to obtain the wrapped Akash distribution. Its PDF and CDF are

$$f(\theta) = \frac{\lambda^3 e^{-\lambda\theta}\left[\left(1+\theta^2\right)\left(1-e^{-2\pi\lambda}\right)^2 + 4\pi e^{-2\pi\lambda}\left(\theta+\pi+\pi e^{-2\pi\lambda}-\theta e^{-2\pi\lambda}\right)\right]}{\left(\lambda^2+2\right)\left(1-e^{-2\pi\lambda}\right)^3}$$

and

$$F(\theta) = \frac{4\pi\lambda e^{-2\pi\lambda}\left\{\left[1-(1+\lambda\theta)e^{-\lambda\theta}\right]\left(1-e^{-2\pi\lambda}\right)+\pi\lambda\left(1-e^{-\lambda\theta}\right)\left(1+e^{-2\pi\lambda}\right)\right\}}{\left(\lambda^2+2\right)\left(1-e^{-2\pi\lambda}\right)^3} + \frac{\left(1-e^{-\lambda\theta}\right)\left(\lambda^2+2\right)-\lambda\theta(2+\lambda\theta)e^{-\lambda\theta}}{\left(\lambda^2+2\right)\left(1-e^{-2\pi\lambda}\right)},$$

respectively, for $0 \leq \theta < 2\pi$ and $\lambda > 0$. The nth trigonometric moment is

$$m_n = \frac{\lambda^3}{\lambda^2+2}\frac{\lambda^2-2in\lambda-n^2+2}{(\lambda-in)^3}$$

for $n = 1, 2, \ldots$. The mean direction, mean resultant length, skewness, and kurtosis are

$$\mu = 3\arctan\left(\frac{1}{\lambda}\right) - \arctan\left(\frac{2\lambda}{\lambda^2+1}\right),$$

$$\rho = \frac{\lambda^3}{\lambda^2+2}\sqrt{\frac{\left(\lambda^2+1\right)^2+4\lambda^2}{\left(\lambda^2+1\right)^2}},$$

$$\gamma_1 = \frac{\frac{\lambda^3}{\lambda^2+2}\sqrt{\frac{\left(\lambda^2-2\right)^2+16\lambda^2}{\left(\lambda^2+4\right)^3}}\sin\left(\kappa_{\lambda,2}\right)}{\left[1-\frac{\lambda^3}{\lambda^2+2}\sqrt{\frac{\left(\lambda^2+1\right)^2+4\lambda^2}{\left(\lambda^2+1\right)^3}}\right]^{\frac{3}{2}}},$$

and

$$\gamma_2 = \frac{\frac{\lambda^3}{\lambda^2+2}\sqrt{\frac{\left(\lambda^2-2\right)^2+16\lambda^2}{\left(\lambda^2+4\right)^3}}\cos\left(\kappa_{\lambda,2}\right) - \left[\frac{\lambda^3}{\lambda^2+2}\sqrt{\frac{\left(\lambda^2+1\right)^2+4\lambda^2}{\left(\lambda^2+1\right)^3}}\right]^4}{\left[1-\frac{\lambda^3}{\lambda^2+2}\sqrt{\frac{\left(\lambda^2+1\right)^2+4\lambda^2}{\left(\lambda^2+1\right)^3}}\right]^2},$$

respectively, where $\kappa_{\lambda,2} = 3\arctan\left(\frac{2}{\lambda}\right) - \arctan\left(\frac{4\lambda}{\lambda^2-2}\right) - 6\arctan\left(\frac{1}{\lambda}\right) + 2\arctan\left(\frac{2\lambda}{\lambda^2+1}\right)$. The wrapped Akash distribution was used on a dataset from [1] regarding the long-axis orientations of 60 feldspar laths in basalt rock. It demonstrated a better fit to the data compared to the wrapped exponential distribution and the wrapped Lindley distribution.

Despite having only one parameter, the wrapped Akash distribution proved to be a flexible model. Additionally, it allows for closed form expressions for both its PDF and its CDF.

2.2. Wrapped Aradhana Distribution

Ref. [14] took g to be the PDF of the Aradhana distribution to obtain the wrapped Aradhana distribution. Its PDF and CDF are

$$f(\theta) = \frac{\lambda^3 e^{-\lambda\theta}}{\lambda^2 + 2\lambda + 2}\left[\frac{(1+\theta)^2}{1 - e^{-2\pi\lambda}} + \frac{4(\theta+1)\pi e^{-2\pi\lambda}}{\left(1 - e^{-2\pi\lambda}\right)^2} + \frac{4\pi^2 e^{-2\pi\lambda}\left(1 + e^{-2\pi\lambda}\right)}{\left(1 - e^{-2\pi\lambda}\right)^3}\right]$$

and

$$\begin{aligned} F(\theta) = {} & \frac{1 - e^{-\lambda\theta}}{1 - e^{-2\pi\lambda}} - \frac{\lambda\theta(\lambda\theta + 2\lambda + 2)e^{-\lambda\theta}}{(\lambda^2 + 2\lambda + 2)\left(1 - e^{-2\pi\lambda}\right)} + \frac{4\pi\lambda e^{-2\pi\lambda}\left[(1+\lambda)\left(1 - e^{-\lambda\theta}\right) - \lambda\theta e^{-\lambda\theta}\right]}{(\lambda^2 + 2\lambda + 2)\left(1 - e^{-2\pi\lambda}\right)^2} \\ & + \frac{4\pi^2\lambda^2\left(1 - e^{-\lambda\theta}\right)\left(1 + e^{-2\pi\lambda}\right)e^{-2\pi\lambda}}{(\lambda^2 + 2\lambda + 2)\left(1 - e^{-2\pi\lambda}\right)^3}, \end{aligned}$$

respectively, for $0 \le \theta < 2\pi$ and $\lambda > 0$. The nth trigonometric moment is given by

$$m_n = \frac{\lambda^3\left[\lambda^2 + 2\lambda - n^2 + 2 - 2in(1+\lambda)\right]}{(\lambda^2 + 2)(\lambda - in)^3}$$

for $n = 1, 2, \ldots$. The mean direction, mean resultant length, skewness, and kurtosis are

$$\mu = 3\arctan\left(\frac{1}{\lambda}\right) - \arctan\left[\frac{2(1+\lambda)}{\lambda^2 + 2\lambda + 1}\right],$$

$$\rho = \frac{\lambda^3}{\lambda^2 + 2\lambda + 2}\sqrt{\frac{\left(\lambda^2 + 2\lambda + 1\right)^2 + 4(1+\lambda^2)}{(\lambda^2+1)^3}},$$

$$\gamma_1 = \frac{\frac{\lambda^3}{\lambda^2+2\lambda+2}\sqrt{\frac{\left(\lambda^2+2\lambda-2\right)^2+16(1+\lambda^2)}{(\lambda^2+4)^3}}\sin(\mu_2 - 2\mu)}{\left[1 - \sqrt{\frac{\left(\lambda^2+2\lambda+1\right)^2+4(1+\lambda^2)}{(\lambda^2+1)^3}}\right]^{\frac{3}{2}}},$$

and

$$\gamma_2 = \frac{\frac{\lambda^3}{\lambda^2+2\lambda+2}\sqrt{\frac{\left(\lambda^2+2\lambda-2\right)^2+16(1+\lambda^2)}{(\lambda^2+4)^3}}\cos(\mu_2 - 2\mu) - \left[\frac{\lambda^3}{\lambda^2+2\lambda+2}\sqrt{\frac{\left(\lambda^2+2\lambda-2\right)^2+16(1+\lambda^2)}{(\lambda^2+4)^3}}\right]^4}{\left[1 - \sqrt{\frac{\left(\lambda^2+2\lambda+1\right)^2+4(1+\lambda^2)}{(\lambda^2+1)^3}}\right]^2},$$

respectively, where $\mu_2 = 3\arctan\left(\frac{2}{\lambda}\right) - \arctan\left(\frac{4(1+\lambda)}{\lambda^2+2\lambda-2}\right)$. The wrapped Aradhana distribution has only one parameter, which might restrict its versatility and relevance to real-world datasets. However, it does have closed form expressions for the PDF and CDF.

2.3. Wrapped Binormal Distribution

Ref. [15] took g to be the PDF of the binormal distribution to obtain the wrapped binormal distribution. Its PDF is

$$f(\theta) = \begin{cases} \sum_{k=-\infty}^{\infty} \sqrt{\frac{2}{\pi}} \frac{1}{\sigma_1 + \sigma_2} e^{-\frac{(\theta + 2k\pi - \mu)^2}{2\sigma_1^2}}, & \theta \leq \mu, \\ \sum_{k=-\infty}^{\infty} \sqrt{\frac{2}{\pi}} \frac{1}{\sigma_1 + \sigma_2} e^{-\frac{(\theta + 2k\pi - \mu)^2}{2\sigma_2^2}}, & \theta > \mu \end{cases}$$

for $0 \leq \theta < 2\pi, \theta > \mu$, and $\sigma > 0$. The nth trigonometric moment is

$$m_n = 2[b_n \cos(p\mu) - c_n \sin(p\mu)] + 2\mathrm{i}[b_n \sin(p\mu) + c_n \cos(p\mu)],$$

where

$$b_p = \frac{1}{2}\left(\frac{\sigma_1}{\sigma_1 + \sigma_2} e^{\frac{-p^2\sigma_1^2}{2}} + \frac{\sigma_2}{\sigma_1 + \sigma_2} e^{\frac{-p^2\sigma_2^2}{2}}\right)$$

and

$$c_p = -\frac{1}{\sqrt{\pi}} \frac{\sigma_1}{\sigma_1 + \sigma_2} e^{\frac{-p^2\sigma_1^2}{2}} \sum_{n=1}^{\infty} \frac{\left(\frac{p\sigma_1}{\sqrt{2}}\right)^{2n-1}}{(2n-1)(n-1)!} + \frac{2}{\sqrt{\pi}} \frac{\sigma_2}{\sigma_1 + \sigma_2} e^{\frac{-p^2\sigma_2^2}{2}} \sum_{n=1}^{\infty} \frac{\left(\frac{p\sigma_2}{\sqrt{2}}\right)^{2n-1}}{(2n-1)(n-1)!}.$$

The mean direction, mean resultant length, skewness, and kurtosis are

$$\mu = \arctan\left[\frac{b_1 \sin(\mu) + c_1 \cos(\mu)}{b_1 \cos(\mu) - c_1 \sin(\mu)}\right],$$

$$\rho = 2\sqrt{(b_1 \cos\mu - c_1 \sin\mu)^2 + (b_1 \sin\mu + c_1 \cos\mu)^2},$$

$$\gamma_1 = \frac{\sqrt{[b_2 \cos(2\mu) - c_2 \sin(2\mu)]^2 + [b_2 \sin(2\mu) + c_2 \cos(2\mu)]^2} \sin(\mu_2 - 2\mu)}{\left[1 - 2\sqrt{(b_1 \cos\mu - c_1 \sin\mu)^2 + (b_1 \sin\mu + c_1 \cos\mu)^2}\right]^{\frac{3}{2}}},$$

and

$$\gamma_2 = \frac{2\sqrt{[b_2 \cos(2\mu) - c_2 \sin(2\mu)]^2 + [b_2 \sin(2\mu) + c_2 \cos(2\mu)]^2} \sin(\mu_2 - 2\mu)}{\left[1 - 2\sqrt{(b_1 \cos\mu - c_1 \sin\mu)^2 + (b_1 \sin\mu + c_1 \cos\mu)^2}\right]^2} - \frac{\left[2\sqrt{(b_1 \cos\mu - c_1 \sin\mu)^2 + (b_1 \sin\mu + c_1 \cos\mu)^2}\right]^4}{\left[1 - 2\sqrt{(b_1 \cos\mu - c_1 \sin\mu)^2 + (b_1 \sin\mu + c_1 \cos\mu)^2}\right]^2},$$

respectively, where $\mu_2 = \arctan\left[\frac{b_2 \sin(2\mu) + c_2 \cos(2\mu)}{b_2 \cos(2\mu) - c_2 \sin(2\mu)}\right]$. The wrapped binormal distribution lacks practicality due to its non-closed-form PDF.

2.4. Wrapped Birnbaum–Saunders Distribution

Ref. [16] took g to be the PDF of the Birnbaum-Saunders distribution to obtain the wrapped Birnbaum–Saunders distribution. Its PDF and CDF are

$$f(\theta) = \frac{e^{\frac{\delta}{2}}\sqrt{\delta+1}}{4\sqrt{\pi\mu}} \sum_{k=0}^{\infty} \frac{\theta + 2k\pi + \frac{\delta\mu}{\delta+1}}{(\theta+2k\pi)^{\frac{3}{2}}} e^{-\frac{\delta}{4}\left[\frac{(\theta+2k\pi)(\delta+1)}{\delta\mu} + \frac{\delta\mu}{(\theta+2k\pi)(\delta+1)}\right]}$$

and

$$F(\theta) = \sum_{k=0}^{\infty} \Phi\left(\sqrt{\frac{\delta}{2}}\left[\sqrt{\frac{(\theta+2k\pi)(\delta+1)}{\delta\mu}} - \sqrt{\frac{\delta\mu}{(\theta+2k\pi)(\delta+1)}}\right]\right)$$
$$- \sum_{k=0}^{\infty} \Phi\left(\sqrt{\frac{\delta}{2}}\left[\sqrt{\frac{2k\pi(\delta+1)}{\delta\mu}} - \sqrt{\frac{\delta\mu}{2k\pi(\delta+1)}}\right]\right),$$

respectively, for $0 \le \theta < 2\pi$, $0 \le \mu < 2\pi$, and $\delta > 0$. The nth trigonometric moment is

$$m_n = \frac{1}{2}\left[1 + \frac{\sqrt{\delta+1}}{\sqrt{\delta+1-4ni\mu}}\right] e^{\frac{\delta\left[\sqrt{\delta+1}-\sqrt{\delta+1-4ni\mu}\right]}{2\sqrt{\delta+1}}}$$

for $n = 1, 2, \ldots$. The wrapped Birnbaum–Saunders distribution was used on a dataset examined by [1] and originally gathered by [17]. The dataset includes 100 ant directions in reaction to a uniformly lit black target. The wrapped Birnbaum–Saunders distribution fit the data better than both symmetric and asymmetric von Mises distributions.

2.5. Wrapped Cauchy Distribution

Ref. [18] took g to be the PDF of the Cauchy distribution to obtain the wrapped Cauchy distribution. Its PDF is

$$f(\theta) = \sum_{k=-\infty}^{\infty} \frac{\gamma}{\mu(\gamma^2 + (\theta - \mu + 2\pi n)^2)} = \frac{1}{2\pi} \frac{\sinh\gamma}{\cosh\gamma - \cos(\theta-\mu)}$$

for $0 \le \theta < 2\pi$, $\gamma > 0$, and $-\infty < \mu < \infty$. The nth trigonometric moment is

$$m_n = e^{in\mu - n\gamma}$$

for $n = 1, 2, \ldots$. The mean direction, mean resultant length, skewness, and kurtosis are

$$\mu,$$

$$\rho = e^{-\gamma},$$

$$\gamma_1 = 0,$$

and

$$\gamma_2 = \frac{e^{-2\gamma} - e^{-8\gamma}}{(1-e^{-\gamma})^2},$$

respectively. Notably, the wrapped Cauchy distribution has a closed-form expression for its PDF. However, it is a symmetric distribution and, as such, has limited applicability to skewed datasets.

2.6. Wrapped Chi-Square Distribution

Ref. [19] took g to be the PDF of a chi-square distribution to obtain the wrapped chi-square distribution. Its PDF is

$$f(\theta) = \frac{e^{-\frac{\theta}{2}} \pi^{\frac{k}{2}-1}}{2\Gamma\left(\frac{k}{2}\right)} \Phi\left(e^{-\pi}; 1 - \frac{k}{2}, \frac{\theta}{2\pi}\right)$$

for $0 \leq \theta < 2\pi$ and $k > 0$. The nth trigonometric moment is

$$m_n = (1 - 2in)^{-\frac{k}{2}}$$

for $n = 1, 2, \ldots$. The mean direction, mean resultant length, skewness, and kurtosis are

$$\mu = \frac{k}{2} \arctan(2),$$

$$\rho = 5^{-\frac{k}{4}},$$

$$\gamma_1 = \frac{17^{-\frac{k}{4}} \sin\left[\frac{k}{2} \arctan(4) - k \arctan(2)\right]}{\left(1 - 5^{-\frac{k}{4}}\right)^{\frac{3}{2}}},$$

and

$$\gamma_2 = \frac{17^{-\frac{k}{4}} \cos\left[\frac{k}{2} \arctan(4) - k \arctan(2)\right] - 5^{-k}}{\left(1 - 5^{-\frac{k}{4}}\right)^{2}},$$

respectively. The wrapped chi-square distribution faces limitations due to its non-closed-form PDF, as defined in terms of the Lerch function.

2.7. Wrapped Exponential Distribution

Ref. [20] took g to be the PDF of the exponential distribution to obtain the wrapped exponential distribution. Its PDF and CDF are

$$f(\theta) = \frac{\lambda e^{-\lambda\theta}}{1 - e^{-2\pi\lambda}}$$

and

$$F(\theta) = \frac{1 - e^{-\lambda\theta}}{1 - e^{-2\pi\lambda}},$$

respectively, for $0 \leq \theta < 2\pi$ and $\lambda > 0$. The nth trigonometric moment is

$$m_n = \frac{\lambda}{\lambda - in}$$

for $n = 1, 2, \ldots$. The mean direction, mean resultant length, skewness, and kurtosis are

$$\mu = \arctan\left(\frac{1}{\lambda}\right),$$

$$\rho = \frac{\lambda}{\sqrt{1+\lambda^2}},$$

$$\gamma_1 = \frac{-2\lambda}{(1+\lambda^2)^{\frac{1}{4}}(4+\lambda^2)\left(\sqrt{1+\lambda^2}-\lambda\right)^{\frac{3}{2}}},$$

and

$$\gamma_2 = \frac{3\lambda^2}{(1+\lambda^2)(4+\lambda^2)\left(\sqrt{1+\lambda^2}-\lambda\right)^{2}},$$

respectively. The wrapped exponential distribution adequately fits various real-life distributions, as reported by [1]. It offers straightforward closed-form expressions for the PDF and CDF. Nevertheless, its limitation lies in being a one-parameter distribution, restricting its flexibility.

2.8. Wrapped Exponentiated Inverted Weibull Distribution

Ref. [21] took g to be the PDF of the exponentiated inverted Weibull distribution to obtain the wrapped exponential inverted Weibull distribution. Its PDF is

$$f(\theta) = c\sum_{k=0}^{\infty} \lambda(\theta+2\pi k)^{-(c+1)}\left[e^{-(\theta+2\pi k)^{-c}}\right]^{\lambda}$$

for $0 \leq \theta < 2\pi$, $c > 0$, and $\lambda > 0$. The nth trigonometric moment is

$$m_n = \sum_{k=0}^{\infty} \frac{\left(it\lambda^{\frac{1}{c}}\right)^{k}}{k!}\Gamma\left(1-\frac{k}{c}\right) = b_t + ic_t$$

for $n = 1, 2, \ldots$, where

$$b_n = \sum_{k=0}^{\infty} \frac{(-1)^k\left(n\lambda^{\frac{1}{c}}\right)^{2k}}{(2k)!}\Gamma\left(1-\frac{2k}{c}\right)$$

and

$$c_n = \sum_{k=0}^{\infty} \frac{(-1)^k\left(n\lambda^{\frac{1}{c}}\right)^{2k+1}}{(2k+1)!}\Gamma\left(1-\frac{2k+1}{c}\right).$$

The mean direction, mean resultant length, skewness, and kurtosis are

$$\mu = \arctan\left(\frac{c_1}{b_1}\right),$$

$$\rho = \sqrt{b_1^2+c_1^2},$$

$$\gamma_1 = \frac{\sqrt{b_2^2+c_2^2}\sin(\mu_2-2\mu)}{\left(1-\sqrt{b_1^2+c_1^2}\right)^{\frac{3}{2}}},$$

and

$$\gamma_2 = \frac{\sqrt{b_2^2 + c_2^2}\cos(\mu_2 - 2\mu) - \left(\sqrt{b_1^2 + c_1^2}\right)^4}{\left(1 - \sqrt{b_1^2 + c_1^2}\right)^{\frac{3}{2}}},$$

respectively, where $\mu_2 = \arctan\left(\frac{c_2}{b_2}\right)$. The wrapped exponential inverted Weibull distribution was used to analyze the orientation data of 76 turtles post egg-laying, as documented by [1]. This distribution exhibited a superior fit compared to the wrapped new Weibull–Pareto distribution. Nonetheless, a limitation is noted due to the absence of a closed-form PDF.

2.9. Wrapped Gamma Distribution

Ref. [22] took g to be the PDF of the gamma distribution to obtain the wrapped gamma distribution. Its PDF is

$$f(\theta) = \frac{\lambda^r}{\Gamma(r)} e^{-\lambda\theta} (2\pi)^{r-1} \Phi\left(e^{-2\lambda\pi}; 1 - r, \frac{\theta}{2\pi}\right)$$

for $0 \le \theta < 2\pi, r > 0$, and $\lambda > 0$. The nth trigonometric moment is

$$m_n = \lambda^r (\lambda - in)^{-r}$$

for $n = 1, 2, \ldots$. The mean direction, mean resultant length, skewness, and kurtosis are

$$\mu = r \arctan\left(\frac{1}{\lambda}\right),$$

$$\rho = \lambda^r \left(\lambda^2 + 1\right)^{-\frac{r}{2}},$$

$$\gamma_1 = \frac{\lambda^r (\lambda^2 + 4)^{-\frac{r}{2}} \sin(\mu_2 - 2\mu)}{\left[1 - \lambda^r (\lambda^2 + 1)^{-\frac{r}{2}}\right]^{\frac{3}{2}}},$$

and

$$\gamma_2 = \frac{\lambda^r (\lambda^2 + 4)^{-\frac{r}{2}} \sin(\mu_2 - 2\mu) - \left[\lambda^r (\lambda^2 + 1)^{-\frac{r}{2}}\right]^4}{\left[1 - \lambda^r (\lambda^2 + 1)^{-\frac{r}{2}}\right]^2},$$

respectively, where $\mu_2 = r \arctan\left(\frac{2}{\lambda}\right)$. The wrapped gamma distribution is constrained by its non-closed-form PDF, expressed in terms of the Lerch function.

2.10. Wrapped Generalized Geometric Stable Distribution

Ref. [23] took g to be the PDF of the generalized geometric stable distribution to obtain the wrapped generalized geometric stable distribution. Its PDF and CDF are

$$f(\theta) = \frac{1}{2\pi} \left\{ 1 + 2 \sum_{k=1}^{\infty} [\alpha_k \cos(k\theta) + \beta_k \sin(k\theta)] \right\}$$

and

$$F(\theta) = \frac{1}{2\pi}\left\{1 + 2\sum_{k=1}^{\infty}\left[\frac{\alpha_k}{k}\sin(k\theta) + \frac{\beta_k}{k} - \frac{\beta_k}{k}\cos(k\theta)\right]\right\},$$

respectively, for $0 \leq \theta < 2\pi$, where

$$\alpha_k = \begin{cases} \left\{(1+\sigma^\alpha k^\alpha)^2 + \left[\sigma^\alpha k^\alpha \beta \tan\left(\frac{\pi\alpha}{2}\right) + \mu^* k\right]^2\right\}^{-\frac{\lambda}{2}} \cos\left\{\lambda \arctan\left[\frac{\sigma^\alpha k^\alpha \beta \tan\left(\frac{\pi\alpha}{2}\right) + \mu^* k}{1+\sigma^\alpha k^\alpha}\right]\right\}, & \text{if } \alpha \neq 1, \\ \left\{(1+\sigma^\alpha k^\alpha)^2 + \left[\mu^* k - \frac{2\sigma^\alpha k^\alpha \beta}{\pi}\log|k|\right]^2\right\}^{-\frac{\lambda}{2}} \cos\left\{\lambda \arctan\left(\frac{\mu^* k - \frac{2\sigma^\alpha k^\alpha \beta}{\pi}\log|k|}{1+\sigma^\alpha k^\alpha}\right)\right\}, & \text{if } \alpha = 1 \end{cases}$$

and

$$\beta_k = \begin{cases} \left\{(1+\sigma^\alpha k^\alpha)^2 + \left[\sigma^\alpha k^\alpha \beta \tan\left(\frac{\pi\alpha}{2}\right) + \mu^* k\right]^2\right\}^{-\frac{\lambda}{2}} \sin\left\{\lambda \arctan\left[\frac{\sigma^\alpha k^\alpha \beta \tan\left(\frac{\pi\alpha}{2}\right) + \mu^* k}{1+\sigma^\alpha k^\alpha}\right]\right\}, & \text{if } \alpha \neq 1, \\ \left\{(1+\sigma^\alpha k^\alpha)^2 + \left[\mu^* k - \frac{2\sigma^\alpha k^\alpha \beta}{\pi}\log|k|\right]^2\right\}^{-\frac{\lambda}{2}} \sin\left\{\lambda \arctan\left(\frac{\mu^* k - \frac{2\sigma^\alpha k^\alpha \beta}{\pi}\log|k|}{1+\sigma^\alpha k^\alpha}\right)\right\}, & \text{if } \alpha = 1 \end{cases}$$

for $0 < \alpha \leq 2$, $\lambda > 0$, $\sigma > 0$, $-1 \leq \beta \leq 1$, $-\infty\mu < \infty$, and $\mu^* = \mu \bmod 2\pi$. The nth trigonometric moment is

$$m_n = \alpha_n + \mathrm{i}\beta_n$$

for $n = 1, 2, \ldots$. The mean direction and mean resultant length are

$$\mu = \begin{cases} \lambda \arctan\left[\frac{\mu^* + \sigma^\alpha \beta \tan\left(\frac{\pi\alpha}{2}\right)}{1+\sigma^\alpha}\right] \text{ and } 2\pi, & \text{if } \alpha \neq 1, \\ \lambda \arctan\left[\frac{\mu^*}{1+\sigma^\alpha}\right] \text{ and } 2\pi, & \text{if } \alpha = 1 \end{cases}$$

and

$$\rho = \begin{cases} \left\{(1+\sigma^\alpha)^2 + \left[\mu^* \sigma^\alpha \beta \tan\left(\frac{\pi\alpha}{2}\right)\right]^2\right\}^{-\frac{\lambda}{2}}, & \text{if } \alpha \neq 1, \\ \left\{(1+\sigma)^2 + (\mu^*)^2\right\}^{-\frac{\lambda}{2}}, & \text{if } \alpha = 1, \end{cases}$$

respectively. The wrapped generalized geometric stable distribution was used to analyze hourly wind direction data collected over three days at a location on Black Mountain, ACT, Australia, as reported by [24] and discussed by [1]. Although the distribution was found to fit the data effectively, its drawback lies in its high number of parameters. Simplified distributions with fewer parameters might prove more practical.

2.11. Wrapped Generalized Gompertz Distribution

Ref. [25] took g to be the PDF of the generalized Gompertz distribution to obtain the wrapped generalized Gompertz distribution. Its PDF and CDF are

$$f(\theta) = \frac{1}{b\Gamma(c)} \sum_{k=-\infty}^{\infty} \exp\left(c\frac{\theta + 2\pi k - a}{b} - e^{\frac{\theta+2\pi k-a}{b}} \right)$$

and

$$F(\theta) = \sum_{k=-\infty}^{\infty} \frac{1}{\Gamma(c)} \left[\Gamma\left(c, e^{\frac{2\pi k-a}{b}}\right) - \Gamma\left(c, e^{\frac{\theta+2\pi k-a}{b}}\right) \right],$$

respectively, for $0 \leq \theta < 2\pi$, $0 \leq a < 2\pi$, $b > 0$, $c > 0$, and $\theta + 2\pi k > a$. The nth trigonometric moment is

$$m_n = e^{ina} \frac{\Gamma(inb + c)}{\Gamma(c)}$$

for $n = 1, 2, \ldots$. The mean direction, mean resultant length, skewness, and kurtosis are

$$\mu = a,$$

$$\rho = \frac{\Gamma(ib + c)}{\Gamma(c)},$$

$$\gamma_1 = 0,$$

and

$$\gamma_2 = \frac{\frac{\Gamma(2ib+c)}{\Gamma(c)} - \left[\frac{\Gamma(ib+c)}{\Gamma(c)}\right]^4}{\left[1 - \frac{\Gamma(ib+c)}{\Gamma(c)}\right]^2},$$

respectively. The wrapped generalized Gompertz distribution was used to analyze the orientations of 50 noisy scrub bird nests along a creek bank, as reported by [1]. While this distribution was found to fit the data effectively, it involves several parameters. Thus, there might be alternative distributions with fewer parameters that offer a better fit to the data.

2.12. Wrapped Generalized Normal Laplace Distribution

Ref. [26] took g to be the PDF of the generalized normal Laplace distribution to obtain the wrapped generalized normal Laplace distribution. Its PDF is

$$f(\theta) = \frac{1}{2\pi} \left\{ 1 + 2\sum_{k=1}^{\infty} \left[\alpha_k \cos(k\theta) + \beta_k \sin(k\theta) \right] \right\}$$

for $0 \leq \theta < 2\pi$, where

$$\alpha_k = \left[\frac{e^{-\tau^2 k^2}}{(1 + a^2 k^2)(1 + b^2 k^2)} \right]^{\frac{\zeta}{2}} \cos\left\{ \arctan\left[\frac{(1 + abk^2)\cos(\eta k) + (b - a)k\sin(\eta k)}{(1 + abk^2)\sin(\eta k) + (b - a)k\cos(\eta k)} \right] \right\}$$

and

$$\beta_k = \left[\frac{e^{-\tau^2 k^2}}{(1 + a^2k^2)(1 + b^2k^2)} \right]^{\frac{\zeta}{2}} \sin\left\{ \arctan\left[\frac{(1 + abk^2)\cos(\eta k) + (b - a)k \sin(\eta k)}{(1 + abk^2)\sin(\eta k) + (b - a)k \cos(\eta k)} \right] \right\}$$

for $-\infty < \eta < \infty$, $-\infty < \tau < \infty$, $a > 0$, $b > 0$, and $\zeta > 0$. The nth trigonometric moment is

$$m_n = \left[\frac{e^{i\eta n - \frac{\tau^2 n^2}{2}}}{(1 - ian)(1 - ibn)} \right]^{\zeta}$$

for $n = 1, 2, \ldots$. The mean direction and mean resultant length are

$$\mu = \zeta \left[\eta + \arctan\left(\frac{a - b}{1 + ab} \right) \right] \bmod 2\pi$$

and

$$\rho = \left[\frac{e^{-\tau^2}}{(1 + a^2)(1 + b^2)} \right]^{\frac{\zeta}{2}},$$

respectively. The wrapped generalized normal Laplace distribution was used to analyze a dataset containing 1827 flight headings of migrating birds, as documented by [27]. It was found that this distribution offers a superior fit compared to a five-parameter mixture of two von Mises distributions but that it is not as effective as a four-parameter mixture incorporating circular uniform and skew normal components.

2.13. Wrapped Generalized Skew Normal Distribution [10]

Ref. [10] took g to be the PDF of the generalized skew normal distribution to obtain the wrapped generalized skew normal distribution. Its PDF is

$$f(\theta) = \frac{2}{\sigma(\alpha + 2)} \sum_{k=-\infty}^{\infty} \phi\left(\frac{\theta + 2\pi k - \mu}{\sigma} \right) \left[1 + \alpha \Phi\left(\frac{\lambda}{\sigma}(\theta + 2\pi k - \mu) \right) \right]$$

for $0 \le \theta < 2\pi$, $-\infty < \mu < \infty$, $\sigma > 0$, $-\infty < \lambda < \infty$, and $\alpha \ge -1$. The nth trigonometric moment is

$$m_n = e^{i\mu n} \left\{ \frac{\gamma}{\left[\alpha^2 - (\beta + in)^2 \right]^{\frac{1}{2}}} \right\}^{2\lambda}$$

for $n = 1, 2, \ldots$. The mean direction, mean resultant length, skewness, and kurtosis are

$$\mu = \arctan \frac{\sin \mu + \frac{\alpha}{\alpha+2} G(\delta\sigma) \cos \mu}{\cos \mu - \frac{\alpha}{\alpha+2} G(\delta\sigma) \sin \mu},$$

$$\rho = \eta e^{-\frac{\sigma^2}{2}},$$

$$\gamma_1 = \frac{e^{-\frac{p^2\sigma^2}{2}} \left\{ \sin[p(2\mu - \omega)] + \frac{\alpha}{\alpha+2} G(p\delta\sigma) \cos[p(2\mu - \omega)] \right\}}{\left(1 - \eta e^{-\frac{\sigma^2}{2}} \right)^{\frac{3}{2}}},$$

and

$$\gamma_2 = \frac{e^{-\frac{p^2\sigma^2}{2}}\left[\cos p\omega - \frac{\alpha}{\alpha+2}G(\delta\sigma p)\sin p\omega\right] - \eta^4 e^{-2\sigma^2}}{\left(1-\eta e^{-\frac{\sigma^2}{2}}\right)^2},$$

respectively, where $\eta = \sqrt{1+\frac{\alpha}{2+\alpha}G(\delta\sigma)}$, $G(d) = \sqrt{\frac{2}{\pi}}\sum_{n=0}^{\infty}\frac{d^{2n+1}}{2^n n!(2n+1)}$ for d real, and $\omega = \mu - \frac{\sin\mu+\frac{\alpha}{\alpha+2}G(p\delta\sigma)\cos\mu}{\cos\mu-\frac{\alpha}{\alpha+2}G(p\delta\sigma)\sin\mu}$. The wrapped generalized skew normal distribution is hindered by its non-closed-form PDF and excessive parameters, potentially outperformed by simpler models.

2.14. Wrapped Generalized Skew Normal Distribution [11]

Ref. [11] took g to be the PDF of the generalized skew normal distribution to obtain the wrapped generalized skew normal distribution. Its PDF is

$$f(\theta) = \frac{2}{w}\sum_{k=-\infty}^{\infty}\phi\left(\frac{\theta+2\pi k-\mu}{w}\right)\Phi\left(\alpha\left(\frac{\theta+2\pi k-\mu}{w}\right)+\beta\left(\frac{\theta+2\pi k-\mu}{w}\right)^3\right)$$

for $0 \le \theta < 2\pi$, $-\infty < \mu < \infty$, $w > 0$, $-\infty < \alpha < \infty$, and $-\infty < \beta < \infty$. No properties were derived for this distribution. The wrapped generalized skew normal distribution was utilized to analyze wind direction data from a meteorological station in Villena, Alicante, Spain. The data, collected in June 2009 using an Oregon Scientific WMR928NX automatic weather station, were split into sea breeze and mountain breeze subsets. The wrapped generalized skew normal distribution appeared to be the most suitable fit for both the entire dataset and the mountain breeze period. However, for the sea breeze period, the Jones and Pewsey sine-skewed distribution demonstrated the best fit.

2.15. Wrapped Half-Logistic Distribution

Ref. [15] took g to be the PDF of the half-logistic distribution to obtain the wrapped half-logistic distribution. Its PDF is

$$f(\theta) = \sum_{k=-\infty}^{\infty}\frac{1}{2\sigma}\operatorname{sech}^2\left(\frac{\theta+2k\pi-\mu}{2\sigma}\right)$$

for $0 \le \theta < 2\pi$, $0 \le \mu < 2\pi$, and $\sigma > 0$. The nth trigonometric moment is

$$m_n = 2[b_n\cos(p\mu) - c_n\sin(p\mu)] + 2\mathrm{i}[b_n\sin(p\mu) + c_n\cos(p\mu)],$$

where

$$b_n = \int_0^a \cos(p\sigma y)\frac{e^{-y}}{(1+e^{-y})^2}dy + \sum_{n=1}^{\infty}(-1)^{n-1}\frac{ne^{-na}}{n^2+p^2\sigma^2}[n\cos(p\sigma a) - p\sigma\sin(p\sigma a)]$$

and

$$c_n = \int_0^a \sin(p\sigma y)\frac{e^{-y}}{(1+e^{-y})^2}dy + \sum_{n=1}^{\infty}(-1)^{n-1}\frac{ne^{-na}}{n^2+p^2\sigma^2}[n\sin(p\sigma a) + p\sigma\cos(p\sigma a)].$$

The mean direction, mean resultant length, skewness, and kurtosis are

$$\mu = \arctan\left[\frac{b_1\sin(\mu) + c_1\cos(\mu)}{b_1\cos(\mu) - c_1\sin(\mu)}\right],$$

$$\rho = 2\sqrt{(b_1\cos\mu - c_1\sin\mu)^2 + (b_1\sin\mu + c_1\cos\mu)^2},$$

$$\gamma_1 = \frac{2\sqrt{[b_2\cos(2\mu) - c_2\sin(2\mu)]^2 + [b_2\sin(2\mu) + c_2\cos(2\mu)]^2}\cos(\mu_2 - 2\mu)}{\left[1 - 2\sqrt{(b_1\cos\mu - c_1\sin\mu)^2 + (b_1\sin\mu + c_1\cos\mu)^2}\right]^{\frac{3}{2}}},$$

and

$$\gamma_2 = \frac{2\sqrt{[b_2\cos(2\mu) - c_2\sin(2\mu)]^2 + [b_2\sin(2\mu) + c_2\cos(2\mu)]^2}\sin(\mu_2 - 2\mu)}{\left[1 - 2\sqrt{(b_1\cos\mu - c_1\sin\mu)^2 + (b_1\sin\mu + c_1\cos\mu)^2}\right]^{2}} - \frac{\left[2\sqrt{(b_1\cos\mu - c_1\sin\mu)^2 + (b_1\sin\mu + c_1\cos\mu)^2}\right]^4}{\left[1 - 2\sqrt{(b_1\cos\mu - c_1\sin\mu)^2 + (b_1\sin\mu + c_1\cos\mu)^2}\right]^{2}},$$

respectively, where $\mu_2 = \arctan\left[\frac{b_2\sin(2\mu)+c_2\cos(2\mu)}{b_2\cos(2\mu)-c_2\sin(2\mu)}\right]$. The utility of the wrapped half-logistic distribution is restricted by its non-closed-form PDF.

2.16. Wrapped Half-Normal Distribution

If g is the pdf of the half-normal distribution we obtain the wrapped half-normal distribution. Its pdf is

$$f(\theta) = \sum_{k=0}^{\infty} \frac{1}{2\sigma}\operatorname{sech}^2\left(\frac{\theta + 2k\pi - \mu}{2\sigma}\right)$$

for $0 \leq \theta < 2\pi$ and $\sigma > 0$. The nth trigonometric moment is

$$m_n = 2[b_n\cos(p\mu) - c_n\sin(p\mu)] + 2\mathrm{i}[b_n\sin(p\mu) + c_n\cos(p\mu)],$$

where

$$b_n = \int_0^a \cos(p\sigma y)\frac{e^{-y}}{(1+e^{-y})^2}dy + \sum_{n=1}^{\infty}(-1)^{n-1}\frac{ne^{-m}}{n^2 + p^2\sigma^2}\begin{pmatrix} n\cos(p\sigma a) \\ -p\sigma\sin p\sigma a\end{pmatrix}$$

and

$$c_n = \int_0^a \cos(p\sigma y)\frac{e^{-y}}{(1+e^{-y})^2}dy + \sum_{n=1}^{\infty}(-1)^{n-1}\frac{ne^{-m}}{n^2 + p^2\sigma^2}\begin{pmatrix} n\sin(p\sigma a) \\ p\sigma\cos p\sigma a\end{pmatrix}.$$

The mean direction, mean resultant length, skewness, and kurtosis are

$$\mu = \arctan\left[\frac{b_1\sin(\mu) + c_1\cos(\mu)}{b_1\cos(\mu) - c_1\sin(\mu)}\right],$$

$$\rho = 2\sqrt{(b_1\cos\mu - c_1\sin\mu)^2 + (b_1\sin\mu + c_1\cos\mu)^2},$$

$$\gamma_1 = \frac{2\sqrt{[b_2\cos(2\mu) - c_2\sin(2\mu)]^2 + [b_2\sin(2\mu) + c_2\cos(2\mu)]^2}\sin(\mu_2 - 2\mu)}{\left[1 - 2\sqrt{(b_1\cos\mu - c_1\sin\mu)^2 + (b_1\sin\mu + c_1\cos\mu)^2}\right]^{\frac{3}{2}}}$$

and

$$\gamma_2 = \frac{2\sqrt{[b_2\cos(2\mu) - c_2\sin(2\mu)]^2 + [b_2\sin(2\mu) + c_2\cos(2\mu)]^2}\sin(\mu_2 - 2\mu)}{\left[1 - 2\sqrt{(b_1\cos\mu - c_1\sin\mu)^2 + (b_1\sin\mu + c_1\cos\mu)^2}\right]^2}$$
$$- \frac{\left[2\sqrt{(b_1\cos\mu - c_1\sin\mu)^2 + (b_1\sin\mu + c_1\cos\mu)^2}\right]^4}{\left[1 - 2\sqrt{(b_1\cos\mu - c_1\sin\mu)^2 + (b_1\sin\mu + c_1\cos\mu)^2}\right]^2},$$

respectively, where $\mu_2 = \arctan\left[\frac{b_2\sin(2\mu)+c_2\cos(2\mu)}{b_2\cos(2\mu)-c_2\sin(2\mu)}\right]$.

2.17. Wrapped [12]'s Skew Laplace Distribution

Ref. [28] took g to be the PDF of [12]'s skew Laplace distribution to obtain the wrapped [12]'s skew Laplace distribution. Its PDF and CDF are

$$f(\theta) = \frac{pce^{c(\beta+2\pi-2\beta\pi-\theta)} + (1-p)e^{c+(2\pi-1)c\beta}}{e^{2\pi c} - 1}$$

and

$$F(\theta) = \frac{pe^{c(\beta+2\pi-2\beta\pi)}\left(1 - e^{-c\theta}\right) + (1-p)e^{(2\pi-1)c\beta}\left(e^{c\theta} - 1\right)}{e^{2\pi c} - 1},$$

respectively, for $0 \leq \theta < 2\pi$, $-\infty < \beta < \infty$, $c > 0$, and $0 < p < 1$. The nth trigonometric moment is

$$m_n = \alpha_n + \mathrm{i}\beta_n$$

for $n = 1, 2, \ldots$, where

$$\alpha_n = \frac{c^2}{n^2 + c^2}\left[ne^{(1-2\pi)\beta c} + (1-n)e^{(2\pi-1)\beta c}\right]$$

and

$$\beta_n = \frac{nc}{n^2 + c^2}\left[(n-1)e^{(2\pi-1)\beta c} - ne^{(1-2\pi)\beta c}\right].$$

The distribution was tested on the Black Mountain wind direction dataset [1]. It showed a superior fit compared to other distributions, specifically the wrapped variance gamma distribution and the generalized von Mises distribution, which have more parameters.

2.18. Wrapped Hypoexponential Distribution

Ref. [29] took g to be the PDF of the hypoexponential distribution to obtain the wrapped hypoexponential distribution. Its PDF is

$$f(\theta) = \frac{\lambda_1\lambda_2}{\lambda_2 - \lambda_1}\left(e^{-\lambda_1\theta}\sum_{k=0}^{\infty} e^{-2k\pi\lambda_1} - e^{-\lambda_2\theta}\sum_{k=0}^{\infty} e^{-2k\pi\lambda_2}\right)$$

for $0 \leq \theta < 2\pi$, $\lambda_1 > 0$, and $\lambda_2 > 0$. The nth trigonometric moment is

$$m_n = \frac{\lambda_1\lambda_2}{(\lambda_1 - \mathrm{i}n)(\lambda_2 - \mathrm{i}n)}$$

for $n = 1, 2, \ldots$. The mean direction, mean resultant length, skewness, and kurtosis are

$$\mu = \arctan\left(\frac{1}{\lambda_1} + \frac{1}{\lambda_2}\right),$$

$$\rho = \frac{\lambda_1 \lambda_2}{\sqrt{\left(1+\lambda_1^2\right)\left(1+\lambda_2^2\right)}},$$

$$\gamma_1 = \frac{\frac{\lambda_1\lambda_2}{\sqrt{\left(4+\lambda_1^2\right)\left(4+\lambda_2^2\right)}} \sin\left[\arctan\left(\frac{2}{\lambda_1} + \frac{2}{\lambda_2}\right) - 2\arctan\left(\frac{1}{\lambda_1} + \frac{1}{\lambda_2}\right)\right]}{\left[1 - \frac{\lambda_1\lambda_2}{\sqrt{\left(1+\lambda_1^2\right)\left(1+\lambda_2^2\right)}}\right]^{\frac{3}{4}}},$$

and

$$\gamma_2 = \frac{\frac{\lambda_1\lambda_2}{\sqrt{\left(4+\lambda_1^2\right)\left(4+\lambda_2^2\right)}} \sin\left[\arctan\left(\frac{2}{\lambda_1} + \frac{2}{\lambda_2}\right) - 2\arctan\left(\frac{1}{\lambda_1} + \frac{1}{\lambda_2}\right)\right] - \frac{\lambda_1^4\lambda_2^4}{\left(1+\lambda_1^2\right)^2\left(1+\lambda_2^2\right)^2}}{\left[1 - \frac{\lambda_1\lambda_2}{\sqrt{\left(1+\lambda_1^2\right)\left(1+\lambda_2^2\right)}}\right]^{2}},$$

respectively, The wrapped hypoexponential distribution has a PDF that can be recast into a closed form. It also offers additional flexibility compared to one-parameter models.

2.19. Wrapped Ishita Distribution

Ref. [30] took g to be the PDF of the Ishita distribution to obtain the wrapped Ishita distribution. Its PDF and CDF are

$$f(\theta) = \frac{\lambda^3 e^{-\lambda\theta}}{\lambda+2}\left[\frac{\lambda+\theta^2}{1-e^{-2\pi\lambda}} + \frac{4\pi\theta e^{-2\pi\lambda}}{\left(1-e^{-2\pi\lambda}\right)^2} + \frac{4\pi^2 e^{-2\pi\lambda}\left(1+e^{-2\pi\lambda}\right)}{\left(1-e^{-2\pi\lambda}\right)^3}\right]$$

and

$$\begin{aligned} F(\theta) = \frac{1}{\lambda^3+2}\Bigg\{ & \frac{\lambda^3+2-\left[\lambda^3+2+\lambda\theta(\lambda\theta+2)\right]e^{-\lambda\theta}}{1-e^{-2\pi\lambda}} \\ & + \frac{4\pi\lambda\left[1-(\lambda\theta+1)e^{-\lambda\theta}\right]e^{-2\lambda\pi}}{\left(1-e^{-2\pi\lambda}\right)^2} \\ & + \frac{4\pi^2\lambda^2\left(1-e^{-\lambda\theta}\right)\left(1+e^{-2\pi\lambda}\right)e^{-2\lambda\pi}}{\left(1-e^{-2\pi\lambda}\right)^3}\Bigg\}, \end{aligned}$$

respectively, for $0 \le \theta < 2\pi$ and $\lambda > 0$. The nth trigonometric moment is

$$m_n = \frac{\lambda^3}{\lambda^3+2}\frac{\lambda^3 - n^2\lambda + 2 - 2in\lambda^2}{(\lambda - in)^3}$$

for $n = 1, 2, \ldots$. The mean direction, mean resultant length, skewness, and kurtosis are

$$\mu = 3\arctan\left(\frac{1}{\lambda}\right) - \arctan\left(\frac{2\lambda^2}{\lambda^3 - \lambda + 2}\right),$$

$$\rho = \frac{\lambda^3}{\lambda^3+2}\sqrt{\frac{(\lambda^3-\lambda+2)^2+4\lambda^4}{(\lambda^2+1)^3}},$$

$$\gamma_1 = \frac{\frac{\lambda^3}{\lambda^3+2}\sqrt{\frac{(\lambda^3-4\lambda+2)^2+16\lambda^4}{(\lambda^2+4)^3}}\sin(\kappa_{\lambda,2})}{\left[1-\frac{\lambda^3}{\lambda^3+2}\sqrt{\frac{(\lambda^3-\lambda+2)^2+4\lambda^4}{(\lambda^2+1)^3}}\right]^{\frac{3}{2}}},$$

and

$$\gamma_2 = \frac{\frac{\lambda^3}{\lambda^3+2}\sqrt{\frac{(\lambda^3-4\lambda+2)^2+16\lambda^4}{(\lambda^2+4)^3}}\cos(\kappa_{\lambda,2}) - \left[\frac{\lambda^3}{\lambda^2+2}\sqrt{\frac{(\lambda^2-\lambda+2)^2+4\lambda^2}{(\lambda^2+1)^3}}\right]^4}{\left[1-\frac{\lambda^3}{\lambda^2+2}\sqrt{\frac{(\lambda^2-\lambda+2)^2+4\lambda^2}{(\lambda^2+1)^3}}\right]^2},$$

respectively, where $\kappa_{\lambda,2} = 3\arctan\left(\frac{2}{\lambda}\right) - \arctan\left(\frac{4\lambda^2}{\lambda^3-4\lambda+2}\right) - 6\arctan\left(\frac{1}{\lambda}\right) + 2\arctan\left(\frac{2\lambda^2}{\lambda^3-\lambda+2}\right)$. The wrapped Ishita distribution, despite having closed-form expressions for PDF and CDF, might be unsuitable for some real-life datasets, as its flexibility is restricted by the fact it only has one parameter.

2.20. Wrapped Laplace Distribution

Ref. [31] took g to be the PDF of the Laplace distribution to obtain the wrapped Laplace distribution. Its PDF and CDF are

$$f(\theta) = \frac{\lambda\kappa}{1+\kappa^2}\left(\frac{e^{-\lambda\kappa\theta}}{1-e^{-2\pi\lambda\kappa}} + \frac{e^{\frac{\lambda\theta}{\kappa}}}{e^{\frac{2\pi\lambda}{\kappa}}-1}\right)$$

and

$$F(\theta) = \frac{1}{1+\kappa^2}\frac{1-e^{-\kappa\lambda\theta}}{1-e^{-2\pi\kappa\lambda}} + \frac{\kappa^2}{1+\kappa^2}\frac{e^{\frac{\lambda\theta}{\kappa}}-1}{1-e^{-\frac{2\pi\lambda}{\kappa}}},$$

respectively, for $0 \leq \theta < 2\pi$, $\kappa > 0$, and $\lambda > 0$. The nth trigonometric moment is

$$m_n = \frac{1}{\left(1-\frac{in}{\lambda\kappa}\right)\left[1+\frac{in}{\left(\frac{\lambda}{\kappa}\right)}\right]}$$

for $n = 1, 2, \ldots$. The mean direction, mean resultant length, skewness, and kurtosis are

$$\mu = \begin{cases} \arctan\left(\frac{1}{\lambda\kappa}\right) - \arctan\left(\frac{\kappa}{\lambda}\right), & \text{for } \kappa \leq 1, \\ 2\pi + \arctan\left(\frac{1}{\lambda\kappa}\right) - \arctan\left(\frac{\kappa}{\lambda}\right), & \text{for } \kappa > 1, \end{cases}$$

$$\rho = \frac{\lambda^2}{\sqrt{1+(\lambda\kappa)^2}\sqrt{\frac{\lambda^2}{\kappa^2}+1}},$$

$$\gamma_1 = \frac{-2\lambda}{(1+\lambda^2)^{\frac{1}{4}}(4+\lambda^2)\left(\sqrt{1+\lambda^2}-\lambda\right)^{\frac{3}{2}}},$$

and

$$\gamma_2 = \frac{3\lambda^2}{(1+\lambda^2)(4+\lambda^2)\left(\sqrt{1+\lambda^2}-|\lambda|\right)^{2}},$$

respectively. The ant orientation data from [17] were analyzed using the wrapped Laplace distribution, which demonstrated a superior fit compared to the von Mises distribution. However, the scope of conclusions is constrained by the limited number of distributions considered. To better evaluate the goodness of fit, it is essential to compare the wrapped Laplace distribution against a broader range of distributions.

2.21. Wrapped Length-Biased Weighted Exponential Distribution

Ref. [32] took g to be the PDF of the length-biased weighted exponential distribution to obtain the wrapped length-biased weighted exponential distribution. Its PDF and CDF are

$$f(\theta) = \frac{[\lambda(\alpha+1)]^2}{\alpha(\alpha+2)} e^{-\lambda\beta}\left\{\frac{1}{1-e^{-2\pi\lambda}}\left(\beta+\frac{2\pi e^{-2\pi\lambda}}{1-e^{-2\pi\lambda}}\right)-\frac{e^{-\alpha\beta\lambda}}{1-e^{-2\pi\lambda(1+\alpha)}}\left[\beta+\frac{2\pi e^{-2\pi\lambda(1+\alpha)}}{1-e^{-2\pi\lambda(1+\alpha)}}\right]\right\}$$

and

$$\begin{aligned} F(\theta) = \frac{1}{\alpha(\alpha+2)}&\left\{\frac{(1+\alpha)^2[1-(1+\beta)e^{-\beta}]}{1-e^{-2\pi}}+\frac{(1+\alpha)^2 2\pi(1-e^{-\beta})e^{-2\pi}}{(1-e^{-2\pi})^2}\right. \\ &\left.+\frac{e^{-\beta(1+\alpha)}[1+\beta(1+\alpha)]-1}{1-e^{-2\pi(1+\alpha)}}+\frac{2\pi(1+\alpha)e^{-2\pi(1+\alpha)}\left[e^{-\beta(1+\alpha)}-1\right]}{\left[1-e^{-2\pi(1+\alpha)}\right]^2}\right\}, \end{aligned}$$

respectively, for $0 \leq \theta < 2\pi$, $\alpha > 0$, $\lambda > 0$, and $0 < \beta \leq 2\pi$. The nth trigonometric moment is

$$m_n = \frac{(1-in)^{-2}\left(1-\frac{in}{1+\alpha}\right)^{-2}}{\left(1-\frac{2in}{2+\alpha}\right)^{-1}}$$

for $n = 1, 2, \ldots$. The mean direction, mean resultant length, skewness, and kurtosis are

$$\mu = \arctan(1) + \arctan\left(\frac{1}{1+\alpha}\right) - \arctan\left(\frac{2}{2+\alpha}\right),$$

$$\rho = \frac{\sqrt{1+(2+\alpha)^{-2}}}{2[1+(1+\alpha)^{-2}]},$$

$$\gamma_1 = \frac{\sin(\mu_2 - 2\mu)}{5\left\{1-\frac{[1+(2+\alpha)^{-2}]^{-\frac{1}{2}}}{2[1+(1+\alpha)^{-2}]}\right\}^{\frac{3}{2}}[1+4(1+\alpha)^{-2}]\sqrt{1+\left(\frac{4}{2+\alpha}\right)^2}},$$

and

$$\gamma_2 = \frac{\cos(\mu_2 - 2\mu)}{5\left\{1 - \frac{[1+(2+\alpha)^{-2}]^{-\frac{1}{2}}}{2[1+(1+\alpha)^{-2}]}\right\}^2 [1+4(1+\alpha)^{-2}]\sqrt{1+\left(\frac{4}{2+\alpha}\right)^2}} - \frac{\left\{\frac{[1+(2+\alpha)^{-2}]^{-\frac{1}{2}}}{2[1+(1+\alpha)^{-2}]}\right\}^4}{\left\{1 - \frac{[1+(2+\alpha)^{-2}]^{-\frac{1}{2}}}{2[1+(1+\alpha)^{-2}]}\right\}^2},$$

respectively, where $\mu_2 = \arctan(2) + \arctan\left(\frac{2}{1+\alpha}\right) - \arctan\left(\frac{4}{2+\alpha}\right)$. The wrapped length-biased weighted exponential distribution was used to analyze the feldspar laths dataset obtained from [33] and published by [1]. Watson's U^2 test indicated a good fit of the distribution to the data. No comparisons with other distributions were performed.

2.22. Wrapped Levy Distribution

Ref. [1] took g to be the PDF of the Levy distribution to obtain the wrapped Levy distribution. Its PDF is

$$f(\theta) = \sum_{k=-\infty}^{\infty} \sqrt{\frac{c}{2\pi}} \frac{e^{-\frac{c}{2}(\theta+2\pi n-\mu)}}{(\theta+2\pi n-\mu)^{\frac{3}{2}}}$$

for $0 \leq \theta < 2\pi$, the summand is zero if $\theta + 2\pi n - \mu \leq 0$, $c > 0$, and $-\infty < \mu < \infty$. The nth trigonometric moment is

$$m_n = e^{\mathrm{i}n\mu - \sqrt{c|n|}[1-\mathrm{i}\,\mathrm{sgn}(n)]} = e^{\mathrm{i}n\mu - \sqrt{cn}(1-\mathrm{i})}$$

for $n = 1, 2, \ldots$. The mean direction, mean resultant length, skewness, and kurtosis are

$$\mu + \sqrt{c},$$

$$\rho = e^{-\sqrt{c}},$$

$$\gamma_1 = \frac{e^{-\sqrt{2c}} \sin\left(\sqrt{2c} - 2\sqrt{c}\right)}{\left(1 - e^{-\sqrt{c}}\right)^{\frac{3}{2}}},$$

and

$$\gamma_2 = \frac{e^{-\sqrt{2c}} \cos\left(\sqrt{2c} - 2\sqrt{c}\right) - e^{-4\sqrt{c}}}{\left(1 - e^{-\sqrt{c}}\right)^2},$$

respectively. The practical utility of the wrapped Levy distribution is hampered by its non-closed-form PDF.

2.23. Wrapped Lindley Distribution

Ref. [34] took g to be the PDF of the Lindley distribution to obtain the wrapped Lindley distribution. Its PDF and CDF are

$$f(\theta) = \frac{\lambda^2}{1+\lambda} e^{-\lambda\theta} \left[\frac{1+\theta}{1-e^{-2\pi\lambda}} + \frac{2\pi e^{-2\pi\lambda}}{(1-e^{-2\pi\lambda})^2}\right]$$

and

$$F(\theta) = \frac{1}{1-e^{-2\pi\lambda}}\left(1 - e^{-\lambda\theta} - \frac{\lambda\theta}{\lambda+1}e^{-\lambda\theta}\right) - \frac{2\pi\lambda}{\lambda+1}\frac{e^{-2\pi\lambda}\left(1-e^{-\lambda\theta}\right)}{\left(1-e^{-2\pi\lambda}\right)^2},$$

respectively, for $0 \leq \theta < 2\pi$ and $\lambda > 0$. The nth trigonometric moment is given by

$$m_n = \frac{\lambda^2}{1+\lambda}\frac{(1+\lambda-in)}{(\lambda-in)^2}$$

for $n = 1, 2, \ldots$. The mean direction, mean resultant length, skewness, and kurtosis are

$$\mu = 2\arctan\left(\frac{1}{\lambda}\right) - \arctan\left(\frac{1}{\lambda+1}\right),$$

$$\rho = \frac{\lambda^2\sqrt{(\lambda+1)^2+1}}{(1+\lambda)(\lambda^2+1)},$$

$$\gamma_1 = \frac{\lambda^2\sqrt{4+(1+\lambda)^2}\sin(\mu_2-2\mu)}{(1+\lambda)(4+\lambda^2)\left\{1-\frac{\lambda^2[1+(1+\lambda)^2]^{\frac{1}{2}}}{(1+\lambda)(1+\lambda^2)}\right\}^{\frac{3}{2}}},$$

and

$$\gamma_2 = \frac{\lambda^2\sqrt{4+(1+\lambda)^2}\cos(\mu_2-2\mu) - \left[\frac{\lambda^2\sqrt{1+(1+\lambda)^2}}{(1+\lambda)(1+\lambda^2)}\right]^4}{(1+\lambda)(4+\lambda^2)\left[1-\frac{\lambda^2\sqrt{1+(1+\lambda)^2}}{(1+\lambda)(1+\lambda^2)}\right]^4},$$

respectively, where $\mu_2 = 2\arctan\left(\frac{2}{\lambda}\right) - \arctan\left(\frac{2}{\lambda+1}\right)$. The wrapped Lindley distribution was used to analyze a dataset concerning the orientations of 76 turtles after laying eggs, as documented by [1]. This distribution seemed to match the data effectively and performed better than the alternative distribution it was contrasted with, the wrapped exponential distribution.

2.24. Wrapped Linnik Distribution

Ref. [35] took g to be the PDF of the Linnik distribution to obtain the wrapped Linnik distribution. Its PDF and CDF are

$$f(\theta) = \frac{1}{2\pi}\left[1 + 2\sum_{k=1}^{\infty}\frac{\cos(k\theta)}{1+\sigma k^{\alpha}}\right]$$

and

$$F(\theta) = \frac{1}{2\pi}\left[\theta + 2\sum_{k=1}^{\infty}\frac{\sin(k\theta)}{k(1+\sigma k^{\alpha})}\right],$$

respectively, for $0 \leq \theta < 2\pi$, $\sigma > 0$, and $0 < \alpha \leq 2$. The nth trigonometric moment is

$$m_n = \frac{1}{1+\sigma \mid n \mid^{\alpha}}$$

for $n = 1, 2, \ldots$. The mean direction, mean resultant length, skewness, and kurtosis are

$$\mu = 0,$$

$$\rho = \frac{1}{1+\sigma},$$

$$\gamma_1 = 0,$$

and

$$\gamma_2 = \frac{(1+\sigma)^4 - (1+2^\alpha\sigma)}{\sigma^{2\alpha}(1+2^\alpha\sigma)(1+\sigma)^2},$$

respectively. The wrapped Linnik distribution was used to analyze the frequency of traffic accidents throughout the day in Srinagar, India, in 2016, sourced from reports from the National Crime Records Bureau, India. This distribution was also applied to ant data collected by [17]. Results indicated that the wrapped Linnik distribution provided a better fit for both datasets compared to the wrapped stable distribution.

2.25. Wrapped Lomax Distribution

Ref. [36] took g to be the PDF of the Lomax distribution to obtain the wrapped Lomax distribution. Its PDF and CDF are

$$f(\theta) = \frac{\alpha}{\sigma}\sum_{k=0}^{\infty}\left(1+\frac{\theta+2k\pi}{\sigma}\right)^{-\alpha-1}$$

and

$$F(\theta) = \sum_{k=0}^{\infty}\left(1+\frac{2k\pi}{\sigma}\right)^{-\alpha} - \sum_{k=0}^{\infty}\left(1+\frac{\theta+2k\pi}{\sigma}\right)^{-\alpha},$$

respectively, for $0 \leq \theta < 2\pi$, $\sigma > 0$, and $\alpha > 0$. The wrapped Lomax distribution faces limitations due to its non-closed-form PDF.

2.26. Wrapped Modified Lindley Distribution

Ref. [37] took g to be the PDF of the modified Lindley distribution to obtain the wrapped modified Lindley distribution. Its PDF and CDF are

$$f(\theta) = \frac{\lambda e^{-\lambda\theta}}{1-e^{-4\lambda\pi}}\left\{1+e^{-2\lambda\pi}+\frac{e^{-\lambda\theta}}{1+\lambda}\left[2\lambda\theta-1+\frac{4\lambda\pi e^{-4\lambda\pi}}{1-e^{-4\lambda\pi}}\right]\right\}$$

and

$$F(\theta) = \frac{1-e^{-\lambda\theta}}{1-e^{-2\lambda\pi}} + \frac{2\lambda\pi e^{-4\lambda\pi}(1-e^{-2\lambda\theta})}{(1+\lambda)(1-e^{-4\lambda\theta})^2} - \frac{\lambda\theta e^{-2\lambda\theta}}{(1+\lambda)(1-e^{-4\lambda\theta})},$$

respectively, for $0 \leq \theta < 2\pi$ and $\lambda > 0$. The nth trigonometric moment is

$$m_n = \frac{\lambda}{\lambda - ni} + \frac{\lambda ni}{(1+\lambda)(2\lambda - ni)^2}$$

for $n = 1, 2, \ldots$. The mean direction, mean resultant length, skewness, and kurtosis are

$$\mu = \begin{cases} \pi + \arctan\left(\frac{\beta_1}{\alpha_1}\right), & \text{if } \alpha_1 < 0, \beta_1 \geq 0, \\ \frac{\pi}{2}, & \text{if } \alpha_1 < 0, \beta_1 > 0, \\ \arctan\left(\frac{\beta_1}{\alpha_1}\right), & \text{if } \alpha_1 > 0, \\ \text{undefined}, & \text{if } \alpha_1 = 0, \beta_1 = 0 \end{cases}$$

and

$$\rho = \lambda^2 \sqrt{\frac{16\lambda^4 + 32\lambda^3 + 24\lambda^2 + 16\lambda + 10}{(1+\lambda)^2(\lambda^2+1)(4\lambda^2+1)^2}},$$

respectively, where

$$\alpha_1 = \frac{\lambda^2}{\lambda^2+1} + \frac{4\lambda^2}{(1+\lambda)(4\lambda^2+1)^2}$$

and

$$\beta_1 = \frac{\lambda}{\lambda^2+1} + \frac{4\lambda^3}{(1+\lambda)(4\lambda^2+1)^2} - \frac{\lambda}{(1+\lambda)(4\lambda^2+1)^2}.$$

The wrapped modified Lindley distribution was used on two real-life datasets from [1]. The first set involves 76 turtles' egg-laying orientations, while the second set has 133 measurements of feldspar lath orientations in basalt. This distribution was compared with the wrapped exponential distribution, transmuted wrapped exponential distribution, and wrapped Lindley distribution for goodness of fit. The wrapped modified Lindley distribution provided a competitive fit for both datasets. It offered the best fit for the turtle dataset but did not outperform the transmuted wrapped exponential distribution for the feldspar lath dataset.

2.27. Wrapped New Weibull–Pareto Distribution

Ref. [38] took g to be the PDF of the new Weibull–Pareto distribution to obtain the wrapped new Weibull–Pareto distribution. Its PDF is

$$f(\theta) = \sum_{k=-\infty}^{\infty} \frac{1}{4\sigma} \operatorname{sech}^2\left(\frac{\theta + 2k\pi - \mu}{2\sigma}\right)$$

for $0 \leq \theta < 2\pi$, $\theta > \mu$, and $\sigma > 0$. The nth trigonometric moment is

$$m_n = \frac{\pi\sigma n}{\sinh \pi\sigma n} e^{in\mu}$$

for $n = 1, 2, \ldots$. The mean direction, mean resultant length, skewness, and kurtosis are

$$\mu,$$

$$\rho = \frac{\pi\sigma p}{\sinh \pi\sigma p},$$

$$\gamma_1 = 0,$$

and

$$\gamma_2 = \frac{\frac{2\pi\sigma}{\sinh(2\pi\sigma)} - \left[\frac{\pi\sigma}{\sinh(\pi\sigma)}\right]^4}{\left[1 - \frac{\pi\sigma}{\sinh(\pi\sigma)}\right]^2},$$

respectively. The wrapped new Weibull–Pareto distribution and the wrapped exponentiated inverted Weibull distribution were tested on the turtle dataset from [1]. Both models fit the data well, but the wrapped exponentiated inverted Weibull distribution slightly outperformed the wrapped new Weibull–Pareto distribution.

2.28. Wrapped Normal Distribution

Ref. [39] took g to be the PDF of the normal distribution to obtain the wrapped normal distribution. Its PDF and CDF are

$$f(\theta) = \frac{1}{\sqrt{2\pi}\sigma} \sum_{k=-\infty}^{\infty} e^{-\frac{(\theta-\mu+2\pi k)^2}{2\sigma^2}}$$

and

$$F(\theta) = \sum_{k=-\infty}^{\infty} \left[\Phi\left(\frac{\theta + 2\pi k - \mu}{\sigma}\right) - \Phi\left(\frac{2\pi k - \mu}{\sigma}\right)\right],$$

respectively, for $0 \leq \theta < 2\pi$, $-\infty < \mu < \infty$, and $\sigma > 0$. The nth trigonometric moment is

$$m_n = e^{in\mu - \frac{n^2\sigma^2}{2}}$$

for $n = 1, 2, \ldots$. The mean direction, mean resultant length, skewness, and kurtosis are

$$\mu,$$

$$\rho = e^{-\frac{\sigma^2}{2}},$$

$$\gamma_1 = 0,$$

and

$$\gamma_2 = 0,$$

respectively. The wrapped normal distribution, commonly used in literature, adequately fits real-life data but is restricted by its non-closed-form PDF.

2.29. Wrapped Pareto Distribution

Ref. [40] took g to be the PDF of a Pareto distribution to obtain the wrapped Pareto distribution. Its PDF is

$$f(\theta) = \frac{\alpha^{-\frac{1}{\alpha}}}{\Gamma\left(\frac{1}{\alpha}\right)} \int_0^{\infty} \frac{\lambda s e^{-\lambda s\theta}}{1 - e^{-2\pi\lambda s}} s^{\frac{1}{\alpha}-1} e^{-\frac{s}{\alpha}} ds$$

for $0 \leq \theta < 2\pi$, $\lambda > 0$, and $\alpha > 0$. The nth trigonometric moment is

$$m_n = \frac{\alpha^{-\frac{1}{\alpha}}}{\Gamma\left(\frac{1}{\alpha}\right)} \int_0^\infty \left(1 - \frac{in}{\lambda s}\right)^{-1} s^{\frac{1}{\alpha}-1} e^{-\frac{s}{\alpha}} ds$$

for $n = 1, 2, \ldots$. The wrapped Pareto distribution is constrained by its non-closed-form PDF.

2.30. Wrapped Quasi-Lindley Distribution

Ref. [41] took g to be the PDF of the quasi-Lindley distribution to obtain the wrapped quasi-Lindley distribution. Its PDF is

$$f(\theta) = \frac{be^{-b\theta}}{a+1}\left[\frac{a+b\theta}{1-e^{-2\pi b}} + \frac{2\pi b e^{-2\pi b}}{\left(1-e^{-2\pi b}\right)^2}\right]$$

for $0 \leq \theta < 2\pi$, $a > 0$, and $b > 0$. The nth trigonometric moment is

$$m_n = \alpha_n + i\beta_n$$

for $n = 1, 2, \ldots$, where

$$\alpha_n = \frac{\sqrt{b^4(a+1)^2 + n^2a^2b^2}}{(a+1)(b^2+n^2)} \cos\left\{2\arctan\left(\frac{n}{b}\right) - \arctan\left[\frac{na}{b(1+a)}\right]\right\}$$

and

$$\beta_n = \frac{\sqrt{b^4(a+1)^2 + n^2a^2b^2}}{(a+1)(b^2+n^2)} \sin\left\{2\arctan\left(\frac{n}{b}\right) - \arctan\left[\frac{na}{b(1+a)}\right]\right\}.$$

The mean direction, mean resultant length, skewness, and kurtosis are

$$\mu = 2\arctan\left(\frac{1}{b}\right) - a\arctan\left[\frac{a}{b(1+a)}\right],$$

$$\rho = \frac{\sqrt{b^4(a+1)^2 + a^2b^2}}{(a+1)(b^2+1)},$$

$$\gamma_1 = \frac{\overline{\beta}_2}{\rho^{\frac{3}{2}}},$$

and

$$\gamma_2 = \frac{\overline{\alpha}_2 - \rho^4}{\rho^2},$$

respectively, where

$$\overline{\alpha}_2 = \frac{\sqrt{b^4(a+1)^2 + 4a^2b^2}}{(a+1)(b^2+4)} \cos\left\{2\arctan\left(\frac{2}{b}\right) - \arctan\left[\frac{2a}{b(1+a)}\right] - 4\arctan\left(\frac{1}{b}\right) + \arctan\left[\frac{a}{b(1+a)}\right]\right\}$$

and

$$\overline{\beta}_2 = \frac{\sqrt{b^4(a+1)^2 + 4a^2b^2}}{(a+1)(b^2+4)} \sin\left\{2\arctan\left(\frac{2}{b}\right) - \arctan\left[\frac{2a}{b(1+a)}\right] - 4\arctan\left(\frac{1}{b}\right) + \arctan\left[\frac{a}{b(1+a)}\right]\right\}.$$

2.31. Wrapped Rama Distribution

Ref. [42] took g to be the PDF of the Rama distribution to obtain the wrapped Rama distribution. Its PDF and CDF are

$$f(\theta) = Ae^{-\lambda\theta}\left(\theta^3 + B\theta^2 + C\theta + D\right)$$

and

$$F(\theta) = \frac{A}{\lambda^4}\left[\gamma(4,\lambda\theta) + B\lambda\gamma(3,\lambda\theta) + C\lambda^2\gamma(2,\lambda\theta) + D\lambda^3\gamma(1,\lambda\theta)\right]$$

for $0 \leq \theta < 2\pi$ and $\lambda > 0$, where

$$A = \frac{\lambda^4}{(\lambda^3+6)\left(1-e^{-2\lambda\pi}\right)},$$

$$B = \frac{6\pi e^{-2\lambda\pi}}{1-e^{-2\lambda\pi}},$$

$$C = \frac{2\pi\left(e^{-2\lambda\pi}+1\right)B}{1-e^{-2\lambda\pi}},$$

and

$$D = 1 + \frac{8\pi^3 e^{-2\lambda\pi}\left(e^{-4\lambda\pi}+4e^{-2\lambda\pi}+1\right)}{\left(1-e^{-2\lambda\pi}\right)^3}.$$

The nth trigonometric moment is

$$m_n = \frac{A}{(\lambda^2+n^2)^4}\left[\left(c_0 + c_2 n^2 + c_4 n^4 + c_6 n^6\right) + \mathrm{i}\left(d_1 n + d_3 n^2 + d_5 n^5 + d_7 n^7\right)\right]$$

for $n = 1, 2, \ldots$, where

$$c_0 = \lambda^7 - 4\frac{\lambda^6 B\pi}{\left(e^{\pi\lambda}\right)^2} - 4\frac{\lambda^7 B\pi^2}{e^{2\pi\lambda}} - 2\frac{\lambda^7 C\pi}{e^{2\pi\lambda}} - 2\frac{\lambda^5 B}{e^{2\pi\lambda}} - \frac{\lambda^6 C}{e^{2\pi\lambda}} - 6\frac{\lambda^4}{e^{2\pi\lambda}} - 12\frac{\pi^2\lambda^6}{e^{2\pi\lambda}}$$
$$- 8\frac{\pi^3\lambda^7}{e^{2\pi\lambda}} - 12\frac{\pi\lambda^5}{e^{2\pi\lambda}} + 6\lambda^4 + \lambda^6 C - \frac{\lambda^7}{e^{2\pi\lambda}} + 2\lambda^5 B,$$

$$c_2 = -\frac{\lambda^4 C}{e^{2\pi\lambda}} + 4\frac{\lambda^3 B}{e^{2\pi\lambda}} + 24\frac{\pi\lambda^3}{e^{2\pi\lambda}} - 12\frac{\pi^2\lambda^4}{e^{2\pi\lambda}} - 24\frac{\pi^3\lambda^5}{e^{2\pi\lambda}} + \lambda^4 C - 3\frac{\lambda^5}{e^{2\pi\lambda}} - 4\lambda^3 B - 36\lambda^2$$
$$+ 36\frac{\lambda^2}{e^{2\pi\lambda}} + 3\lambda^5 - 4\frac{\lambda^4 B\pi}{e^{2\pi\lambda}} - 6\frac{\lambda^5 C\pi}{e^{2\pi\lambda}} - 12\frac{\lambda^5 B\pi^2}{e^{2\pi\lambda}},$$

$$c_4 = \frac{\lambda^2 C}{e^{2\pi\lambda}} + 6\frac{\lambda B}{e^{2\pi\lambda}} + 36\frac{\pi\lambda}{e^{2\pi\lambda}} + 12\frac{\pi^2\lambda^2}{e^{2\pi\lambda}} - 24\frac{\pi^3\lambda^3}{e^{2\pi\lambda}} - 3\frac{\lambda^3}{e^{2\pi\lambda}} - \lambda^2 C - 6\lambda B - \frac{6}{e^{2\pi\lambda}}$$
$$+ 6 + 3\lambda^3 - 6\frac{C\pi\lambda^3}{e^{2\pi\lambda}} - 12\frac{B\pi^2\lambda^3}{e^{2\pi\lambda}} + 4\frac{B\pi\lambda^2}{e^{2\pi\lambda}},$$

$$c_6 = 4\frac{B\pi}{e^{2\pi\lambda}} - 8\frac{\pi^3\lambda}{e^{2\pi\lambda}} - \frac{\lambda}{e^{2\pi\lambda}} + \frac{C}{e^{2\pi\lambda}} + 12\frac{\pi^2}{e^{2\pi\lambda}} + \lambda - C - 2\frac{\lambda C\pi}{e^{2\pi\lambda}} - 4\frac{\lambda B\pi^2}{e^{2\pi\lambda}},$$

$$d_1 = 2\lambda^5 C - \frac{\lambda^6}{e^{2\pi\lambda}} + 6\lambda^4 B - 6\frac{\lambda^4 B}{e^{2\pi\lambda}} - 2\frac{\lambda^5 C}{e^{2\pi\lambda}} - 24\frac{\pi^2\lambda^5}{e^{2\pi\lambda}} - 8\frac{\pi^3\lambda^6}{e^{2\pi\lambda}} - 3\frac{\pi\lambda^4}{e^{2\pi\lambda}} + 24\lambda^3$$
$$- 24\frac{\lambda^3}{e^{2\pi\lambda}} + \lambda^6 - 8\frac{\lambda^5 B\pi}{e^{2\pi\lambda}} - 4\frac{\lambda^6 B\pi^2}{e^{2\pi\lambda}} - 2\frac{\lambda^6 C\pi}{e^{2\pi\lambda}},$$

$$d_3 = -3\frac{\lambda^4}{e^{2\pi\lambda}} + 4\lambda^3 C + 4\lambda^2 B - 4\frac{\lambda^3 C}{e^{2\pi\lambda}} - 4\frac{\lambda^2 B}{e^{2\pi\lambda}} - 24\frac{\pi\lambda^2}{e^{2\pi\lambda}} - 48\frac{\pi^2\lambda^3}{e^{2\pi\lambda}} - 24\frac{\pi^3\lambda^4}{e^{2\pi\lambda}} - 24\lambda$$
$$+ 24\frac{\lambda}{e^{2\pi\lambda}} + 3\lambda^4 - 6\frac{\lambda^4 C\pi}{e^{2\pi\lambda}} - 12\frac{\lambda^4 B\pi^2}{e^{2\pi\lambda}} - 16\frac{\lambda^3 B\pi}{e^{2\pi\lambda}},$$

$$d_5 = 2\lambda C + 2\frac{B}{e^{2\pi\lambda}} - 3\frac{\lambda^2}{e^{2\pi\lambda}} - 2\frac{\lambda C}{e^{2\pi\lambda}} - 24\frac{\pi^2\lambda}{e^{2\pi\lambda}} - 24\frac{\pi^3\lambda^2}{e^{2\pi\lambda}} + 12\frac{\pi}{e^{2\pi\lambda}} + 3\lambda^2 - 2B$$
$$- 6\frac{\lambda^2 C\pi}{e^{2\pi\lambda}} - 12\frac{\lambda^2 B\pi^2}{e^{2\pi\lambda}} - 8\frac{\lambda B\pi}{e^{2\pi\lambda}},$$

and

$$d_7 = 1 - 2\frac{C\pi}{e^{2\pi\lambda}} - 4\frac{B\pi^2}{e^{2\pi\lambda}} - 8\frac{\pi^3}{e^{2\pi\lambda}} - \frac{1}{e^{2\pi\lambda}}.$$

The mean direction, mean resultant length, skewness, and kurtosis are

$$\mu = \arcsin\left[\frac{d_1 + d_3 + d_5 + d_7}{\sqrt{(c_0 + c_2 + c_4 + c_6)^2 + (d_1 + d_3 + d_5 + d_7)^2}}\right],$$

$$\rho = \frac{A}{(\lambda^2 + 1)^4}\sqrt{(c_0 + c_2 + c_4 + c_6)^2 + (d_1 + d_3 + d_5 + d_7)^2},$$

$$\gamma_1 = \frac{Ae^{-2\mu}}{v^{\frac{3}{2}}(\lambda^2 + 4)^4}(2d_1 + 4d_3 + 32d_5 + 128d_7),$$

and

$$\gamma_2 = \frac{Ae^{-2\mu}}{(1 - \rho^2)(\lambda^2 + 4)^4}(c_0 + 4c_2 + 16c_4 + 64c_6) - \frac{\rho^4}{1 - \rho^2},$$

respectively. The wrapped Rama distribution boasts closed-form expressions for its PDF and CDF. This feature, coupled with its good fit to various datasets, makes it a compelling choice for statistical analysis. In fact, it outperformed six other widely used distributions (with up to three parameters) when applied to two specific datasets. The first dataset, initially obtained by [33] and later published by [1], consists of long-axis orientation measurements for 60 feldspar laths in basalt, recorded in degrees. The second dataset, also reported by [1], comprises horizontal axis values for 100 outwash pebbles collected from a late Wisconsin outwash terrace near Cary, Illinois, along the Fox River.

2.32. Wrapped Richard Distribution

Ref. [43] introduced a wrapped distribution based on the Richard link function. Its PDF is

$$f(\theta) = \sum_{k=0}^{\infty} \frac{ke^{-k(\theta+2\pi n)}}{1 - m^{\frac{1}{1-m}}}\left[1 + (m-1)e^{-k(\theta+2\pi n)}\right]^{\frac{m}{1-m}}$$

for $0 \leq \theta < 2\pi$, $m \geq 1$, and $n \geq 1$. The wrapped Richard distribution is limited by its non-closed-form PDF.

2.33. Wrapped Shanker Distribution

Ref. [44] took g to be the PDF of the Shanker distribution to obtain the wrapped Shanker distribution. Its PDF and CDF are

$$f(\theta) = \frac{\lambda^2}{\lambda^2+1} e^{-\lambda\theta} \left[\frac{\lambda+\theta}{1-e^{-2\pi\lambda}} + \frac{2\pi e^{-2\pi\lambda}}{\left(1-e^{-2\pi\lambda}\right)^2} \right]$$

and

$$F(\theta) = \frac{1}{1-e^{-2\pi\lambda}} \left(1 - e^{-\lambda\theta} - \frac{\lambda\theta e^{-\lambda\theta}}{\lambda^2+1} \right) + \frac{2\pi\lambda\left(1-e^{-\lambda\theta}\right)e^{-2\pi\lambda}}{\left(\lambda^2+1\right)\left(1-e^{-2\pi\lambda}\right)^2},$$

respectively, for $0 \leq \theta < 2\pi$ and $\lambda > 0$. The nth trigonometric moment is

$$m_n = \frac{\lambda^2\left(1-e^{-2\pi\lambda}\right)\left(e^{2\pi(in-\lambda)}-1\right)\left[\lambda(in-\lambda)-1\right] + 2\pi\lambda^2(in-\lambda)e^{2\pi(in-\lambda)}}{\left(\lambda^2+1\right)\left(1-e^{-2\pi\lambda}\right)^2(in-\lambda)^2}$$

for $n = 1, 2, \ldots$. The mean direction, mean resultant length, skewness, and kurtosis are

$$\mu = 2\arctan\left(\frac{1}{\lambda}\right) - \arctan\left(\frac{\lambda}{\lambda^2+1}\right),$$

$$\rho = \frac{\lambda^2\sqrt{\left(\lambda^2+1\right)^2+\lambda^2}}{\left(\lambda^2+1\right)^2},$$

$$\gamma_1 = \frac{\frac{\lambda^2\sqrt{\left(\lambda^2+1\right)^2+4\lambda^2}}{\left(\lambda^2+1\right)\left(\lambda^2+4\right)} \sin\kappa_{2,\lambda}}{\left[1 - \frac{\lambda^2\sqrt{\left(\lambda^2+1\right)^2+\lambda^2}}{\left(\lambda^2+1\right)^2}\right]^{\frac{3}{2}}},$$

and

$$\gamma_2 = \frac{\frac{\lambda^2\sqrt{\left(\lambda^2+1\right)^2+4\lambda^2}}{\left(\lambda^2+1\right)\left(\lambda^2+4\right)} \cos\kappa_{2,\lambda} - \left[\frac{\lambda^2\sqrt{\left(\lambda^2+1\right)^2+\lambda^2}}{\left(\lambda^2+1\right)^2}\right]^4}{\left[1 - \frac{\lambda^2\sqrt{\left(\lambda^2+1\right)^2+\lambda^2}}{\left(\lambda^2+1\right)^2}\right]^2},$$

respectively, where $\kappa_{\lambda,2} = 2\arctan\left(\frac{2}{\lambda}\right) - \arctan\left(\frac{2\lambda}{\lambda^2+1}\right) - 4\arctan\left(\frac{1}{\lambda}\right) + 2\arctan\left(\frac{\lambda}{\lambda^2+1}\right)$. The wrapped Shanker distribution has closed-form expressions for the PDF and CDF, but it might have limited utility for real-life data modeling due to the fact it only has one parameter.

2.34. Wrapped Skew Laplace Distribution

Ref. [45] took g to be the PDF of a skew Laplace distribution to obtain a wrapped skew Laplace distribution. Its PDF is

$$f(\theta) = \frac{1}{2\sigma}\left[e^{-\frac{|\theta-\mu|}{\sigma}} + \frac{e^{\frac{\theta-\mu}{\sigma}} + e^{\frac{\mu-\theta}{\sigma}}}{e^{\frac{2\pi}{\sigma}} - 1} + A(\theta; \lambda_1, \lambda_2, \lambda_3)\right]$$

for $0 \leq \theta < 2\pi$, $-\infty < \lambda_1 < \infty$, $\lambda_2 > 0$, $-\infty < \lambda_3 < \infty$, $-\infty < \mu < \infty$, and $\sigma > 0$, where

$$A(\theta) = \sum_{k=-\infty}^{\infty} e^{-\frac{|\theta+2\pi k-\mu|}{\sigma}}\left[1 - e^{-\left|g\left(\frac{\theta+2\pi k-\mu}{\sigma}\right)\right|}\right] \operatorname{sign}\left[g\left(\frac{\theta+2\pi k-\mu}{\sigma}\right)\right]$$

and

$$g(x) = \frac{\lambda_1 x + \lambda_3 x^3}{\sqrt{1+\lambda_2 x^2}}.$$

The nth trigonometric moment is

$$m_n = \alpha_n + i\beta_n$$

for $n = 1, 2, \ldots$, where

$$\alpha_n = \frac{\cos(n\mu) + 2\nabla e^{-\xi}\sin(n\mu)\xi_n}{n^2\sigma^2+1} - \frac{\Delta n\sigma\sin(n\mu)}{n^2\sigma^2+1} - \Delta^2 C_n,$$

$$\beta_n = \frac{\sin(n\mu) - 2\nabla e^{-\xi}\cos(n\mu)\xi_n}{n^2\sigma^2+1} - \frac{\Delta n\sigma\cos(n\mu)}{n^2\sigma^2+1} - \Delta^2 S_n,$$

$$\nabla = \begin{cases} \operatorname{sign}(\lambda_1), & \text{if } \lambda_1\lambda_3 < 0, \\ 0, & \text{if } \lambda_1\lambda_3 \geq 0, \end{cases}$$

$$\Delta = \begin{cases} 0, & \text{if } \lambda_1 = \lambda_3 = 0, \\ \operatorname{sign}(\lambda_3), & \text{if } \lambda_1 = 0, \lambda_3 \neq 0, \\ \operatorname{sign}(\lambda_1), & \text{if } \lambda_1 \geq 0, \end{cases}$$

$$C_n = \frac{1}{2\sigma}\sum_{k=-\infty}^{\infty}\int_0^{2\pi}\cos(n\theta)e^{-\frac{|\theta+2\pi k-\mu|}{\sigma}}e^{-\left|g\left(\frac{\theta+2\pi k-\mu}{\sigma}\right)\right|}\operatorname{sign}\left[g\left(\frac{\theta+2\pi k-\mu}{\sigma}\right)\right]d\theta,$$

$$S_n = \frac{1}{2\sigma}\sum_{k=-\infty}^{\infty}\int_0^{2\pi}\sin(n\theta)e^{-\frac{|\theta+2\pi k-\mu|}{\sigma}}e^{-\left|g\left(\frac{\theta+2\pi k-\mu}{\sigma}\right)\right|}\operatorname{sign}\left[g\left(\frac{\theta+2\pi k-\mu}{\sigma}\right)\right]d\theta,$$

$$\xi_n = \sin(\xi n\sigma) + n\sigma\cos(\xi n\sigma),$$

and

$$\xi = \begin{cases} \sqrt{-\frac{\lambda_1}{\lambda_3}}, & \text{if } \lambda_1\lambda_3 < 0, \\ 0, & \text{if } \lambda_1\lambda_3 \geq 0. \end{cases}$$

The mean direction, mean resultant length, skewness, and kurtosis are

$$\mu = \arctan\left[\frac{1}{\sigma\Delta - \Delta^2 S_1(1+\sigma^2) - 2\nabla e^{-\xi}\xi_1}\right],$$

$$\rho = \left(\frac{\sigma\Delta}{\sigma^2+1} - \Delta^2 S_1 - \frac{2\nabla e^{-\xi}\xi_1}{\sigma^2+1}\right)\sin\mu + \frac{\cos\mu}{\sigma^2+1},$$

$$\gamma_1 = \frac{\left[2\sigma\Delta - \Delta^2 S_2(4\sigma^2+1) - 2\nabla e^{-\xi}\xi_2\right]\cos(2\mu) - \sin(2\mu)}{(4\sigma^2+1)(1-\rho)^{\frac{3}{2}}},$$

and

$$\gamma_2 = \frac{\left[2\sigma\Delta - \Delta^2 S_2(4\sigma^2+1) - 2\nabla e^{-\xi}\xi_2\right]\sin(2\mu) - \cos(2\mu) - (4\sigma^2+1)\rho^4}{(4\sigma^2+1)(1-\rho)^2},$$

respectively. The wrapped skew Laplace distribution was used on the turtle and ant datasets discussed by [1]. It was observed that this distribution provided a better fit for the first dataset compared to the wrapped Lindley, exponential, transmuted wrapped exponential, and non-negative trigonometric sums distributions [46]. Similarly, for the second dataset, the wrapped skew Laplace distribution outperformed the symmetric wrapped Laplace and non-negative trigonometric sums distributions.

2.35. Wrapped Skew Normal Distribution

Ref. [47] took g to be the PDF of the skew normal distribution to obtain the wrapped skew normal distribution. Its PDF is

$$f(\theta) = \frac{2}{\eta}\sum_{k=-\infty}^{\infty}\phi\left(\frac{\theta+2\pi r-\xi}{\eta}\right)\Phi\left(\lambda\left(\frac{\theta+2\pi r-\xi}{\eta}\right)\right)$$

for $0 \leq \theta < 2\pi$, $-\infty < \xi < \infty$, $\eta > 0$, and $-\infty < \lambda < \infty$. The nth trigonometric moment is

$$m_n = e^{in\xi - \frac{1}{2}n^2\eta^2}[1 + i\mathcal{J}(\delta\eta n)]$$

for $n = 1, 2, \ldots$, where

$$\mathcal{J}(x) = \int_0^x be^{\frac{u^2}{2}}du$$

and $\delta = \frac{\lambda}{\sqrt{1+\lambda^2}}$. The mean direction, mean resultant length, skewness, and kurtosis are

$$\mu = \arctan\left[\frac{\sin\xi + \mathcal{J}(\delta\eta)\cos\xi}{\cos\xi - \mathcal{J}(\delta\eta)\sin\xi}\right],$$

$$\rho = e^{-\frac{\eta^2}{2}}\left[1 + \mathcal{J}^2(\delta\eta)\right]^{\frac{1}{2}},$$

$$\gamma_1 = \frac{\frac{\omega^4\{\mathcal{J}(2\delta\eta)[1-\mathcal{J}^2(\delta\eta)]-2\mathcal{J}(\delta\eta)\}}{1+\mathcal{J}^2(\delta\eta)}}{\left\{1-e^{-\frac{\eta^2}{2}}[1+\mathcal{J}^2(\delta\eta)]^{\frac{1}{2}}\right\}^{\frac{3}{2}}},$$

and

$$\gamma_2 = \frac{\frac{\omega^4[1-\mathcal{J}^2(\delta\eta)+2\mathcal{J}(\delta\eta)\mathcal{J}(2\delta\eta)]}{1+\mathcal{J}^2(\delta\eta)} - \left\{e^{-\frac{\eta^2}{2}}[1+\mathcal{J}^2(\delta\eta)]^{\frac{1}{2}}\right\}^4}{\left\{1-e^{-\frac{\eta^2}{2}}[1+\mathcal{J}^2(\delta\eta)]^{\frac{1}{2}}\right\}^2},$$

respectively. The wrapped skew normal distribution was used to analyze bird heading data from the autumn migration of 1987 [27]. Although it fit the data well, its PDF does not have a simple mathematical expression, which might restrict its practical utility.

2.36. Wrapped Stable Distribution

Ref. [48] took g to be the PDF of the stable distribution to obtain the wrapped stable distribution. The nth trigonometric moment is

$$m_n = \begin{cases} e^{-\gamma^\alpha n^\alpha}\left\{1+\mathrm{i}\beta\left[(\gamma n)^{1-\alpha}-1\right]\tan\left(\frac{\pi\alpha}{2}\right)\right\}+\mathrm{i}\delta_0^* n, & \text{if } \alpha \neq 1, \\ e^{-\gamma n}\left[1+\frac{2\beta\mathrm{i}}{\pi}\log(\gamma n)\right]+\mathrm{i}\delta_0^* n, & \text{if } \alpha = 1 \end{cases}$$

for $n = 1, 2, \ldots$, where $0 < \alpha \leq 2$, $-1 \leq \beta \leq 1$, $\gamma > 0$, $-\infty < \delta_0 < \infty$, and $\delta_0^* = \delta_0 \bmod 2\pi$. The mean direction, mean resultant length, skewness, and kurtosis are

$$\mu = \begin{cases} \delta_0^* + \beta(\gamma^\alpha - \gamma)\tan\left(\frac{\pi\alpha}{2}\right) \bmod 2\pi, & \text{if } \alpha \neq 1, \\ \delta_0^* - \frac{2\beta\gamma}{\pi}\log\gamma \bmod 2\pi, & \text{if } \alpha = 1, \end{cases}$$

$$\rho = e^{-\gamma^\alpha},$$

$$\gamma_1 = \frac{\overline{\beta}_2}{(1-\rho)^{\frac{3}{2}}},$$

and

$$\gamma_2 = \frac{\overline{\alpha}_2 - \rho^4}{(1-\rho)^2},$$

respectively, where

$$\overline{\alpha}_2 = \begin{cases} \rho^{2^\alpha}\cos\left[\beta\gamma^\alpha(2^\alpha-2)\tan\left(\frac{\pi\alpha}{2}\right)\right], & \text{if } \alpha \neq 1, \\ \rho^{2^\alpha}\cos\left(-\frac{2\beta\gamma\log 2}{\pi}\right), & \text{if } \alpha = 1 \end{cases}$$

and

$$\overline{\beta}_2 = \begin{cases} \rho^{2^\alpha} \sin\left[\beta\gamma^\alpha (2^\alpha - 2) \tan\left(\frac{\pi\alpha}{2}\right)\right], & \text{if } \alpha \neq 1, \\ \rho^{2^\alpha} \sin\left(-\frac{2\beta\gamma \log 2}{\pi}\right), & \text{if } \alpha = 1. \end{cases}$$

The wrapped stable distribution demonstrated a slightly superior fit compared to a mixture distribution incorporating circular uniform and wrapped skew normal components when analyzing the bird heading data from [27].

2.37. Wrapped Student's t Distribution

Ref. [49] took g to be the PDF of the Student's t distribution to obtain the wrapped Student's t distribution. Its PDF is

$$f(\theta) = \frac{c}{\lambda} \sum_{k=-\infty}^{\infty} \left[1 + \frac{(\theta + 2\pi k - \mu_0)^2}{\lambda^2 \nu}\right]^{-\frac{\nu+1}{2}}$$

for $0 \leq \theta < 2\pi, 0 \leq \mu < 2\pi$, $\lambda > 0$, and $\nu > 0$, where

$$c = \frac{\Gamma\left(\frac{\nu+1}{2}\right)}{\Gamma\left(\frac{\nu}{2}\right)\sqrt{\pi\nu}}.$$

The nth trigonometric moment is

$$m_n = \frac{K_{\frac{\nu}{2}}(n\sqrt{\nu})(n\sqrt{\nu})^{\frac{\nu}{2}}}{\Gamma(\frac{\nu}{2})2^{\frac{\nu}{2}-1}}$$

for $n = 1, 2, \ldots$. The mean direction, mean resultant length, skewness, and kurtosis are

$$\mu,$$

$$\rho = \frac{K_{\frac{\nu}{2}}(\lambda\sqrt{\nu})(\lambda\sqrt{\nu})^{\frac{\nu}{2}}}{\Gamma(\frac{\nu}{2})2^{\frac{\nu}{2}-1}},$$

$$\gamma_1 = \frac{e^{-\sqrt{2c}} \sin(\sqrt{2c} - 2\sqrt{c})}{\left(1 - e^{-\sqrt{c}}\right)^{\frac{3}{2}}},$$

and

$$\gamma_2 = \frac{e^{-\sqrt{2c}} \cos\left(\sqrt{2c} - 2\sqrt{c}\right) - e^{-4\sqrt{c}}}{\left(1 - e^{-\sqrt{c}}\right)^2},$$

respectively. The wrapped Student's t distribution was used on a dataset of 104 cross-bed measurements from Himalayan molasse in Pakistan, as discussed by [1]. The wrapped Student's t distribution yielded a better fit to this dataset compared to the von Mises distribution.

2.38. Wrapped Transmuted Exponential Distribution

Ref. [50] took g to be the PDF of the transmuted exponential distribution to obtain the wrapped transmuted exponential distribution. Its PDF and CDF are

$$f(\theta) = \frac{2\lambda\Lambda e^{-\lambda\theta}\left(e^{-\theta\lambda} - 1\right)}{c^2} - \frac{\lambda e^{-\lambda\theta}(\Lambda + 1)}{c}$$

and

$$F(\theta) = \frac{\left(e^{-\lambda\theta} - 1\right)\left[c + \Lambda\left(1 + c - e^{-\lambda\theta}\right)\right]}{c^2},$$

respectively, for $0 \leq \theta < 2\pi$, $\lambda > 0$, $|\Lambda| \leq 1$, and $c = e^{-2\pi\lambda} - 1$. The nth trigonometric moment is

$$m_n = \frac{\lambda(\lambda + in)(2\Lambda + c + c\Lambda)\left[(c+1)e^{2\pi ni} - 1\right]}{c^2(\lambda^2 + n^2)} - \frac{2\lambda\Lambda(2\lambda + in)\left[(c+1)^2 e^{2i\pi n} - 1\right]}{c^2(4\lambda^2 + n^2)}$$

for $n = 1, 2, \ldots$. The mean direction, mean resultant length, skewness, and kurtosis are

$$\mu = \arctan \frac{c - 2\Lambda + 4\lambda^2\Lambda + 4c\lambda^2 - c\Lambda + 2c\lambda^2\Lambda}{\lambda(4c\lambda^2 - 6\Lambda + c - 3c\Lambda)},$$

$$\rho = \sqrt{\frac{\lambda^2(2\Lambda - c + c\Lambda)^2 + 4c^2\lambda^4}{c^2(4\lambda^2 + 1)(\lambda^2 + 1)}},$$

$$\gamma_1 = -\frac{\frac{\lambda(\lambda \sin 2\mu - 2\cos 2\mu)(2\Lambda + c + c\Lambda))}{c(\lambda^2+4)} - \frac{\lambda\Lambda(c+2)(\cos 2\mu - \lambda \sin 2\mu)}{c(\lambda^2+1)}}{\left[1 - \sqrt{\frac{\lambda^2(2\Lambda - c + c\Lambda)^2 + 4c^2\lambda^4}{c^2(4\lambda^2+1)(\lambda^2+1)}}\right]^{\frac{3}{2}}},$$

and

$$\gamma_2 = \frac{\frac{\lambda^2(2\Lambda + 2c + \Lambda c) + 2c(1 - \Lambda) - 4\Lambda}{c\left(\lambda^4 + 5\lambda^2 + 4\right)}\lambda \sin 2\mu + \frac{c\lambda\left(1 + \lambda^2 - 3\Lambda\right) - 6\lambda\Lambda}{c\left(\lambda^4 + 5\lambda^2 + 4\right)}\lambda \cos 2\mu - \frac{\left[(2\Lambda - c + \Lambda c)^2 + 4\lambda^4 c^2\right]^2}{c^4\left(4\lambda^2+1\right)^2\left(\lambda^2+1\right)^2}}{\left[1 - \sqrt{\frac{\lambda^2(2\Lambda - c + c\Lambda)^2 + 4c^2\lambda^4}{c^2(4\lambda^2+1)(\lambda^2+1)}}\right]^2},$$

respectively. The transmuted wrapped exponential distribution was used on the turtle dataset from [1]. It outperformed the wrapped exponential and wrapped Lindley distributions. It offers closed-form expressions for the PDF and CDF. Additionally, it is more flexible than commonly used one-parameter distributions.

2.39. Wrapped Two-Parameter Lindley Distribution

Ref. [51] took g to be the PDF of the two-parameter Lindley distribution to obtain the wrapped two-parameter Lindley distribution. Its PDF and CDF are

$$f(\theta) = \left(\frac{\xi^2}{\xi + \alpha} e^{-\xi\theta}\right)\left[\frac{1 + \alpha\theta}{1 - e^{-2\pi\xi}} + \frac{2\pi\alpha e^{-2\pi\xi}}{\left(1 - e^{-2\pi\xi}\right)^2}\right]$$

and

$$F(\theta) = \frac{1}{1-e^{-2\pi\xi}}\left(1-e^{-\xi\theta}-\frac{\alpha\xi\theta}{\alpha+\xi}\right)+\frac{2\pi\alpha\xi}{\alpha+\xi}\left(1-e^{-\xi\theta}\right)\frac{e^{-2\pi\xi}}{\left(1-e^{-2\pi\xi}\right)^2},$$

respectively, for $0 \le \theta < 2\pi$, $\xi > 0$, and $\alpha > -\xi$. The nth trigonometric moment is

$$m_n = \frac{\xi^2(\xi+\alpha-in)}{(\xi+\alpha)(\xi-in)}$$

for $n = 1, 2, \ldots$. The mean direction, mean resultant length, skewness, and kurtosis are

$$\mu = 2\arctan\left(\frac{1}{\xi}\right) - \arctan\left(\frac{1}{\xi+\alpha}\right),$$

$$\rho = \frac{\xi^2\left[(\xi+\alpha)^2+1\right]^{\frac{1}{2}}}{(\xi+\alpha)(\xi^2+1)},$$

$$\gamma_1 = \frac{\frac{\xi^2\sqrt{(\alpha+\xi)^2+4}}{(\alpha+\xi)(4+\xi^2)}\sin(\mu_2-2\mu)}{\left[1-\frac{\xi^2\sqrt{(\alpha+\xi)^2+1}}{(\alpha+\xi)(1+\xi^2)}\right]^{\frac{3}{2}}},$$

and

$$\gamma_2 = \frac{\frac{\xi^2\sqrt{(\alpha+\xi)^2+4}}{(\alpha+\xi)(4+\xi^2)}\cos(\mu_2-2\mu)-\left[\frac{\xi^2\sqrt{(\alpha+\xi)^2+1}}{(\alpha+\xi)(1+\xi^2)}\right]^4}{\left(1-\frac{\xi^2\sqrt{(\alpha+\xi)^2+1}}{(\alpha+\xi)(1+\xi^2)}\right]^2},$$

respectively, where$\mu_2 = 2\arctan\left(\frac{2}{\xi}\right) - \arctan\left(\frac{2}{\alpha+\xi}\right)$. The two-parameter wrapped Lindley distribution was used for analyzing two datasets: the feldspar lath dataset from [1], Appendix B5, and a dataset on wind directions observed at Gorleston, England, during summer Sundays in 1968 [52]. It was found that this distribution provided a better fit for the first dataset compared to the wrapped exponential distribution and the wrapped Lindley distribution. Additionally, for the second dataset, it was observed that the wrapped two-parameter Lindley distribution outperformed the wrapped Lindley distribution in terms of fitting.

2.40. Wrapped Two-Sided Lindley Distribution

Ref. [53] took g to be the PDF of the two-sided Lindley distribution to obtain the wrapped two-sided Lindley distribution. Its PDF and CDF are

$$f(\theta) = \frac{e^{-\alpha\theta}}{2\Lambda_\alpha\Lambda_\beta}\left\{\alpha^2e^{2\pi\alpha}\Lambda_\beta\left[(\theta+1)e^{2\pi\alpha}-\theta+2\pi-1\right]+\beta^2e^{\theta(\alpha+\beta)}\Lambda_\alpha\left[(2\pi+1-\theta)e^{2\pi\beta}+\theta-1\right]\right\}$$

and

$$\begin{aligned} F(\theta) = {} & \frac{e^{\alpha(2\pi-\theta)}}{2\Lambda_\alpha}\left\{(\alpha+1)e^{\alpha(\theta+2\pi)}+[(2\pi-1)\alpha-1]e^{\alpha\theta}+\alpha(\theta-2\pi+1)-e^{2\pi\alpha}(\alpha\theta+\alpha+1)+1\right\} \\ & +\frac{1}{2\Lambda_\beta}\left\{e^{\beta\theta}[\beta(\theta-1)-1]+\beta-e^{2\pi\beta}(2\pi\beta+\beta+1)+e^{\beta(\theta+2\pi)}(-\beta\theta+2\pi\beta+\beta+1)+1\right\}, \end{aligned}$$

respectively, for $0 \leq \theta < 2\pi$, $\alpha > 0$, and $\beta > 0$, where $\Lambda_\alpha = \left(e^{2\pi\alpha} - 1\right)^2(\alpha + 1)$ and $\Lambda_\beta = \left(e^{2\pi\beta} - 1\right)^2(\beta + 1)$. The nth trigonometric moment is

$$\begin{aligned} m_n = {} & \frac{\alpha^2 (n + i\alpha)^2}{2\Lambda_\alpha} e^{2i\pi n}\left(e^{2\pi\alpha} - 1\right)\left[2\pi\alpha - e^{2\pi(\alpha - in)} - 2i\pi n + 1\right] \\ & + \frac{\alpha^2}{2(n + i\alpha)\Lambda_\alpha}\left(e^{2\pi\alpha} - e^{2ipn}\right)\left(2\pi + e^{2\pi\alpha} - 1\right) \\ & + \frac{\beta^2}{2\Lambda_\beta(\beta + in)^2}\left(1 - e^{2\pi\beta}\right)\left[1 + e^{2\pi(\beta + in)}(2\pi\beta + 2i\pi n - 1)\right] \\ & + \frac{\beta^2}{2(\beta + in)\Lambda_\beta}\left[1 - e^{2\pi(\beta + in)}\right]\left[1 - (1 + 2\pi)e^{2\pi\beta}\right] \end{aligned}$$

for $n = 1, 2, \ldots$. The wrapped two-sided Lindley distribution has been applied to the ant dataset discussed by [1] and was shown to provide a good fit to this dataset.

2.41. Wrapped Variance Gamma Distribution

Ref. [54] took g to be the PDF of the variance gamma distribution to obtain the wrapped variance gamma distribution. Its PDF is

$$f(\theta) = \frac{\gamma^{2\lambda} e^{\beta(\theta - \mu)}}{\sqrt{\pi}\Gamma(\lambda)(2\alpha)^{\lambda - \frac{1}{2}}} \sum_{m=-\infty}^{\infty} \frac{e^{2\pi m\beta} K_{\lambda - \frac{1}{2}}(\alpha|\theta + 2m\pi - \mu|)}{|\theta + 2m\pi - \mu|^{\lambda - \frac{1}{2}}}$$

for $0 \leq \theta < 2\pi$, $\alpha > 0$, $\beta > 0$, $0 \leq |\beta| < \alpha$, and $\lambda \in \mathbb{R}$. The nth trigonometric moment is

$$m_n = e^{i\mu n}\left(\frac{\gamma}{\sqrt{\alpha^2 - (\beta + in)^2}}\right)^{2\lambda}$$

for $n = 1, 2, \ldots$. The mean direction, mean resultant length, skewness, and kurtosis are

$$\mu,$$

$$\rho = \left[\frac{\gamma}{(\alpha^2 - (\beta + i)^2)^{\frac{1}{2}}}\right]^{2\lambda},$$

$$\gamma_1 = 0,$$

and

$$\gamma_2 = \frac{\left[\frac{\gamma}{(\alpha^2 - (\beta + 2i)^2}\right]^{2\lambda} - \left[\frac{\gamma}{(\alpha^2 - (\beta + i)^2)}\right]^{8\lambda}}{\left[1 - \left\{\frac{\gamma}{[\alpha^2 - (\beta + i)^2]}\right\}^{2\lambda}\right]^2},$$

respectively. The wrapped variance gamma distribution was used to analyze the Black Mountain wind direction dataset from [1]. It fit the data well, but its practical utility is limited because it lacks a closed-form PDF or CDF.

2.42. Wrapped Weighted Exponential Distribution

Ref. [55] took g to be the PDF of the weighted exponential distribution to obtain the wrapped weighted exponential distribution. Its PDF is

$$f(\theta) = \frac{\alpha+1}{\alpha}\lambda e^{-\lambda\theta}\sum_{k=0}^{\infty} e^{-2k\pi\lambda}\left[1-e^{-\alpha\lambda(\theta+2k\pi)}\right]$$

for $0 \leq \theta < 2\pi$, $\alpha > 0$, and $\lambda > 0$. The nth trigonometric moment is

$$m_n = \alpha_n + \mathrm{i}\beta_n,$$

where

$$\alpha_n = \frac{\lambda^2 \cos\left[\arctan\left(\frac{n}{\lambda}\frac{2+\alpha}{1+\alpha}\right)\right]}{\sqrt{\lambda^2+n^2}\sqrt{\lambda^2+\frac{n^2}{(1+\alpha)^2}}}$$

and

$$\beta_n = \frac{\lambda^2 \sin\left[\arctan\left(\frac{n}{\lambda}\frac{2+\alpha}{1+\alpha}\right)\right]}{\sqrt{\lambda^2+n^2}\sqrt{\lambda^2+\frac{n^2}{(1+\alpha)^2}}}.$$

The mean direction, mean resultant length, skewness, and kurtosis are

$$\mu = \arctan\left[\frac{2+\alpha}{\lambda(1+\alpha)}\right],$$

$$\rho = \frac{\lambda^2}{\sqrt{\lambda^2+1}\sqrt{\lambda^2+\frac{1}{(1+\alpha)^2}}},$$

$$\gamma_1 = \frac{\lambda^2 \sin\left[\arctan\left(\frac{2}{\lambda}\frac{2+\alpha}{1+\alpha}\right)-2\arctan\left(\frac{1}{\lambda}\frac{2+\alpha}{1+\alpha}\right)\right]}{\sqrt{\lambda^2+4}\sqrt{\lambda^2+\frac{4}{(1+\alpha)^2}}(1-\rho)^{\frac{3}{2}}},$$

and

$$\gamma_2 = \frac{\lambda^2 \cos\left[\arctan\left(\frac{2}{\lambda}\frac{2+\alpha}{1+\alpha}\right)-2\arctan\left(\frac{1}{\lambda}\frac{2+\alpha}{1+\alpha}\right)\right]-\rho^4}{\sqrt{\lambda^2+4}\sqrt{\lambda^2+\frac{4}{(1+\alpha)^2}}(1-\rho)^2},$$

respectively. The wrapped weighted exponential distribution is a flexible model with a PDF that can be recast into a closed form.

2.43. Wrapped Weibull Distribution

Ref. [40] took g to be the PDF of the Weibull distribution to obtain the wrapped Weibull distribution. Its PDF is

$$f(\theta) = \sum_{k=0}^{\infty}\frac{1}{2\sigma}\mathrm{sech}^2\left(\frac{\theta+2k\pi-\mu}{2\sigma}\right)$$

for $0 \leq \theta < 2\pi$ and $c > 0$. The nth trigonometric moment is

$$m_n = \sum_{k=0}^{\infty}\frac{\mathrm{i}^k n^k}{k!}\Gamma\left(1+\frac{k}{c}\right) = b_n + \mathrm{i}c_n,$$

where

$$b_n = \sum_{k=0}^{\infty} \frac{(-1)^k t^{2k}}{(2k)!} \Gamma\left(1 + \frac{2k}{c}\right)$$

and

$$c_n = \sum_{k=0}^{\infty} \frac{(-1)^k t^{2k+1}}{(2k+1)!} \Gamma\left(1 + \frac{2k+1}{c}\right).$$

The mean direction, mean resultant length, skewness, and kurtosis are

$$\mu = \arctan\left(\frac{c_1}{b_1}\right),$$

$$\rho = 2\sqrt{(b_1 \cos\mu - c_1 \sin\mu)^2 + (b_1 \sin\mu + c_1 \cos\mu)^2},$$

$$\gamma_1 = \frac{\sqrt{b_1^2 + c_1^2} \sin(\mu_2 - 2\mu)}{\left(1 - \sqrt{b_1^2 + c_1^2}\right)^{\frac{3}{2}}},$$

and

$$\gamma_2 = \frac{\sqrt{b_1^2 + c_1^2} \cos(\mu_2 - 2\mu) - \left(\sqrt{b_1^2 + c_1^2}\right)^4}{\left(1 - \sqrt{b_1^2 + c_1^2}\right)^2},$$

respectively, where $\mu_2 = \arctan\left(\frac{c_2}{b_2}\right)$. The wrapped Weibull distribution is limited by the fact that it does not admit a closed-form PDF.

2.44. Wrapped XGamma Distribution

Ref. [56] took g to be the PDF of the XGamma distribution to obtain the wrapped XGamma distribution. Its PDF and CDF are

$$f(\theta) = \frac{\lambda^2 e^{-\theta\lambda}}{(\lambda+1)(1-e^{-2\pi\lambda})} \left\{1 + \frac{\lambda\theta^2}{2} + 2\pi\lambda\left[(\pi-\theta)e^{-2\pi\lambda} + (\theta+\pi)\right] \frac{e^{-2\pi\lambda}}{(1-e^{-2\pi\lambda})^2}\right\}$$

and

$$F(\theta) = \left[1 - \frac{1 + \lambda(1+\theta) + \frac{\theta^2\lambda^2}{2}}{\lambda+1} e^{-\theta\lambda}\right] \frac{1}{1-e^{-2\pi\lambda}} + \frac{2\pi\lambda}{\lambda+1}\left[1 - (1+\theta\lambda)e^{-\theta\lambda}\right] \frac{e^{-2\pi\lambda}}{(1-e^{-2\pi\lambda})^2}$$
$$+ \frac{2\pi^2\lambda^2}{\lambda+1}\left(1 - e^{-\theta\lambda}\right) \frac{e^{-2\pi\lambda}(1+e^{-2\pi\lambda})}{(1-e^{-2\pi\lambda})^3},$$

respectively, for $0 \le \theta < 2\pi$ and $\lambda > 0$. The nth trigonometric moment is

$$m_n = \frac{\lambda^2\left[\lambda^2 + \lambda(1-2in) - n^2\right]}{(\lambda+1)(\lambda-in)^3}$$

for $n = 1, 2, \ldots$. The mean direction, mean resultant length, skewness, and kurtosis are

$$\mu = 3\arctan\left(\frac{1}{\lambda}\right) - \arctan\left(\frac{2\lambda}{\lambda^2+\lambda-1}\right),$$

$$\rho = \frac{\lambda^2}{\lambda+1}\sqrt{\frac{\left(\lambda^2+\lambda-1\right)^2+4\lambda^2}{\left(\lambda^2+1\right)^3}},$$

$$\gamma_1 = \frac{\frac{\lambda^2}{\lambda+1}\sqrt{\frac{\left(\lambda^2+\lambda-4\right)^2+16\lambda^2}{\left(\lambda^2+4\right)^2}}\sin(\kappa_{\lambda,2})}{\left[1-\frac{\lambda^2}{\lambda+1}\sqrt{\frac{\left(\lambda^2+\lambda-1\right)^2+4\lambda^2}{\left(\lambda^2+1\right)^3}}\right]^{\frac{3}{2}}},$$

and

$$\gamma_2 = \frac{\frac{\lambda^2}{\lambda+1}\sqrt{\frac{\left(\lambda^2+\lambda-4\right)^2+16\lambda^2}{\left(\lambda^2+4\right)^2}}\cos(\kappa_{\lambda,2}) - \left[\frac{\lambda^2}{1+\lambda}\sqrt{\frac{\left(\lambda^2+\lambda-1\right)^2+4\lambda^2}{\left(\lambda^2+1\right)^3}}\right]^4}{\left[1-\frac{\lambda^2}{\lambda+1}\sqrt{\frac{\left(\lambda^2+\lambda-1\right)^2+4\lambda^2}{\left(\lambda^2+1\right)^3}}\right]^2},$$

respectively, where $\kappa_{\lambda,2} = \arctan\left(\frac{2}{\lambda}\right) - 6\arctan\left(\frac{1}{\lambda}\right) + 2\arctan\left(\frac{2\lambda}{\lambda^2+\lambda-1}\right) - \arctan\left(\frac{4\lambda}{\lambda^2+\lambda-4}\right)$. The wrapped XGamma distribution was used to analyze the feldspar lath dataset from [1]. It demonstrated superior fit compared to the wrapped exponential and the wrapped Lindley distributions.

2.45. Wrapped XLindley Distribution

Ref. [57] took g to be the PDF of the XLindley distribution to obtain the wrapped XLindley distribution. Its PDF and CDF are

$$f(\theta) = \frac{\lambda^2 e^{-\theta\lambda}}{(\lambda+1)^2\left(1-e^{-2\pi\lambda}\right)^2}\left[\left(1-e^{-2\pi\lambda}\right)(\lambda+\theta+2)+2\pi e^{-2\pi\lambda}\right]$$

and

$$F(\theta) = \frac{1-e^{-\theta\lambda}\left(1+\frac{\lambda\theta}{(\lambda+1)^2}\right)}{1-e^{-2\pi\lambda}} + \frac{2\pi\lambda e^{-2\pi\lambda}\left(1-e^{-\theta\lambda}\right)}{(\lambda+1)^2\left(1-e^{-2\pi\lambda}\right)^2},$$

respectively, for $0 \le \theta < 2\pi$ and $\lambda > 0$. The nth trigonometric moment is

$$m_n = \frac{\lambda^2}{(\lambda+1)(\lambda-in)} + \frac{\lambda^2(1+\lambda-in)}{(\lambda+1)^2(\lambda-in)^2}$$

for $n = 1, 2, \ldots$. The mean direction, mean resultant length, skewness and kurtosis are

$$\mu = 2\arctan\left(\frac{1}{\lambda}\right) - \arctan\left(\frac{\lambda+2}{(\lambda+1)^2}\right),$$

$$\rho = \frac{\lambda^2\sqrt{(\lambda+1)^4+(\lambda+2)^2}}{(\lambda+1)^2\left(\lambda^2+1\right)},$$

$$\gamma_1 = \frac{\lambda^2 \sqrt{4(\lambda^2+2)^2 + (\lambda+1)^4} \sin(\mu_2 - 2\mu)}{(\lambda+1)^2(\lambda^2+4)\left[1 - \frac{\lambda^2\sqrt{(\lambda+1)^4+(\lambda+2)^2}}{(\lambda+1)^2(\lambda^2+1)}\right]^{\frac{3}{2}}},$$

and

$$\gamma_2 = \frac{\frac{\lambda^2\sqrt{4(\lambda^2+2)^2+(\lambda+1)^4}\cos(\mu_2-2\mu)}{(\lambda+1)^2(\lambda^2+4)} - \frac{\lambda^8\left[(\lambda+2)^2+(\lambda+1)^4\right]^2}{(\lambda+1)^8(\lambda^2+1)^4}}{\left[1 - \frac{\lambda^2\sqrt{(\lambda+1)^4+(\lambda+2)^2}}{(\lambda+1)^2(\lambda^2+1)}\right]^2},$$

respectively, where $\mu_2 = 2\arctan\left(\frac{2}{\lambda}\right) - \arctan\left[\frac{2(\lambda+2)}{(\lambda+1)^2}\right]$. The wrapped XLindley distribution was used to analyze two datasets: one consisted of sun directions recorded from 50 starhead topminnows under overcast conditions [1], and the other included 349 transactions occurring between 1 January 2020 and 29 July 2020 [58]. Although the wrapped XLindley distribution outperformed some distributions based on certain goodness-of-fit measures, it was not consistently superior in all cases.

3. A Review of Discrete Wrapped Distributions

In this section, we review wrapped binomial, wrapped discrete Cauchy, wrapped discrete exponential, wrapped discrete Mittag–Leffler, wrapped discrete skew Laplace, wrapped geometric, wrapped negative binomial, wrapped Poisson, wrapped Poisson–Lindley, and wrapped zero-inflated Poisson distributions.

3.1. Wrapped Binomial Distribution

Ref. [59] took g to be the PDF of the binomial distribution to obtain the wrapped binomial distribution. Its PMF is

$$P\left(\Theta = \frac{2\pi r}{m}\right) = \sum_{k=0}^{\left[\frac{n-r}{m}\right]} \binom{n}{r+km} p_1^{r+km} q_1^{n-r-km}$$

for $0 \leq \theta < 2\pi$, $r = 0, 1, \ldots, m-1$, $m \geq 1$, $n \geq m-1$, $0 < p_1 < 1$, and $q_1 = 1 - p_1$. The nth trigonometric moment is

$$m_n = \left[q_1 + p_1 \cos\left(\frac{2n\pi}{m}\right) + i p_1 \sin\left(\frac{2n\pi}{m}\right)\right]^n$$

for $n = 1, 2, \ldots$. The mean direction, mean resultant length, skewness, and kurtosis are

$$\mu = n \arctan\left[\frac{p_1 \sin\left(\frac{2\pi}{m}\right)}{q_1 + p_1 \sin\left(\frac{2\pi}{m}\right)}\right],$$

$$\rho = \left[p_1^2 + q_1^2 + 2p_1 q_1 \sin\left(\frac{2\pi}{m}\right)\right]^{\frac{n}{2}},$$

$$\gamma_1 = \frac{\beta_2 \cos(2\mu) - \alpha_2 \sin(2\mu)}{(1-\rho)^{\frac{3}{2}}},$$

and

$$\gamma_2 = \frac{\alpha_2 \cos(2\mu) + \beta_2 \sin(2\mu) - \rho^4}{(1-\rho)^2},$$

respectively, where

$$\alpha_2 = \left[p_1^2 + q_1^2 + 2p_1q_1 \cos\left(\frac{4\pi}{m}\right)\right]^{\frac{n}{2}} \cos\left\{2 \arctan\left[\frac{p_1 \sin\left(\frac{4\pi}{m}\right)}{q_1 + p_1 \cos\left(\frac{4\pi}{m}\right)}\right]\right\}$$

and

$$\beta_2 = \left[p_1^2 + q_1^2 + 2p_1q_1 \cos\left(\frac{4\pi}{m}\right)\right]^{\frac{n}{2}} \sin\left\{2 \arctan\left[\frac{p_1 \sin\left(\frac{4\pi}{m}\right)}{q_1 + p_1 \cos\left(\frac{4\pi}{m}\right)}\right]\right\}.$$

The wrapped binomial distribution faces practical limitations due to its non-closed-form PMF.

3.2. Wrapped Discrete Cauchy Distribution

Ref. [60] introduced the wrapped discrete Cauchy distribution. Its PMF is

$$P\left(\Theta = \frac{2\pi r}{m}\right) = \frac{(1-a^2)\left[1 + a^{2m} - 2a^m \cos(m\mu)\right]}{m(1-a^{2m})[1 + a^2 - 2a\cos(\theta - \mu)]}$$

for $0 < a < 1$, $0 \leq \theta < 2\pi$, $r = 0, 1, \ldots, m-1$, and m is a positive integer. The nth trigonometric moment is

$$m_n = \frac{(1-a^2)\left[1 + a^{2m} - 2a^m \cos(m\mu)\right]}{m(1-a^{2m})} \sum_{r=0}^{m-1} \frac{e^{n\theta}}{1 + a^2 - 2a\cos(\theta - \mu)}$$

for $n = 1, 2, \ldots$. The wrapped discrete Cauchy distribution has the advantage of having a closed-form PMF.

3.3. Wrapped Discrete Exponential Distribution

Ref. [61] introduced the wrapped discrete exponential distribution. Its PMF and CDF are

$$P\left(\Theta = \frac{2\pi r}{m}\right) = \frac{e^{-\lambda\theta}}{1 - e^{-2\pi\lambda}}\left(1 - e^{-\frac{2\pi\lambda}{m}}\right)$$

and

$$F(\Theta \leq k) = \frac{1 - e^{-\frac{2\pi\lambda(k+1)}{m}}}{1 - e^{-2\pi\lambda}}, \quad k = 0, 1, \ldots, m-1,$$

respectively, for $\lambda > 0$, $r = 0, 1, \ldots, m-1$, and m is a positive integer. The nth trigonometric moment is

$$m_n = \frac{1 - e^{-\frac{2\pi\lambda}{m}}}{1 - e^{-2\pi\lambda}} \left(\frac{1 - e^{-2\pi\lambda + 2\pi i n}}{1 - e^{-\frac{2\pi\lambda}{m} + \frac{2\pi i n}{m}}}\right)$$

for $n = 1, 2, \ldots$. The mean direction, mean resultant length, skewness, and kurtosis are

$$\mu = \arctan\left[\frac{e^{-\frac{2\pi\lambda}{m}} \sin\left(\frac{2\pi}{m}\right) - e^{-\frac{4\pi\lambda}{m}} \sin\left(\frac{2\pi}{m}\right)}{1 - e^{-\frac{2\pi\lambda}{m}} \cos\left(\frac{2\pi}{m}\right) - e^{-\frac{2\pi\lambda}{m}} + e^{-\frac{4\pi\lambda}{m}} \cos\left(\frac{2\pi}{m}\right)}\right],$$

$$\rho=\sqrt{\frac{\left[1-e^{-\frac{2\pi\lambda}{m}}\cos\left(\frac{2\pi}{m}\right)-e^{-\frac{2\pi\lambda}{m}}+e^{-\frac{4\pi\lambda}{m}}\cos\left(\frac{2\pi}{m}\right)\right]^2+\left[e^{-\frac{2\pi\lambda}{m}}\sin\left(\frac{2\pi}{m}\right)-e^{-\frac{4\pi\lambda}{m}}\sin\left(\frac{2\pi}{m}\right)\right]^2}{\left[1+e^{-\frac{4\pi\lambda}{m}}-2e^{-\frac{2\pi\lambda}{m}}\cos\left(\frac{2\pi}{m}\right)\right]^2}},$$

$$\gamma_1=\frac{\sqrt{\frac{\left[1-e^{-\frac{2\pi\lambda}{m}}\cos\left(\frac{4\pi}{m}\right)-e^{-\frac{2\pi\lambda}{m}}+e^{-\frac{4\pi\lambda}{m}}\cos\left(\frac{4\pi}{m}\right)\right]^2+\left[e^{-\frac{2\pi\lambda}{m}}\sin\left(\frac{4\pi}{m}\right)-e^{-\frac{4\pi\lambda}{m}}\sin\left(\frac{4\pi}{m}\right)\right]^2}{\left[1+e^{-\frac{4\pi\lambda}{m}}-2e^{-\frac{2\pi\lambda}{m}}\cos\left(\frac{4\pi}{m}\right)\right]^2}}\sin(\mu_2-2\mu)}{\left\{1-\sqrt{\frac{\left[1-e^{-\frac{2\pi\lambda}{m}}\cos\left(\frac{2\pi}{m}\right)-e^{-\frac{2\pi\lambda}{m}}+e^{-\frac{4\pi\lambda}{m}}\cos\left(\frac{2\pi}{m}\right)\right]^2+\left[e^{-\frac{2\pi\lambda}{m}}\sin\left(\frac{2\pi}{m}\right)-e^{-\frac{4\pi\lambda}{m}}\sin\left(\frac{2\pi}{m}\right)\right]^2}{\left[1+e^{-\frac{4\pi\lambda}{m}}-2e^{-\frac{2\pi\lambda}{m}}\cos\left(\frac{2\pi}{m}\right)\right]^2}}\right\}^{\frac{3}{2}}},$$

and

$$\gamma_2=\frac{\sqrt{\frac{\left[1-e^{-\frac{2\pi\lambda}{m}}\cos\left(\frac{4\pi}{m}\right)-e^{-\frac{2\pi\lambda}{m}}+e^{-\frac{4\pi\lambda}{m}}\cos\left(\frac{4\pi}{m}\right)\right]^2+\left[e^{-\frac{2\pi\lambda}{m}}\sin\left(\frac{4\pi}{m}\right)-e^{-\frac{4\pi\lambda}{m}}\sin\left(\frac{4\pi}{m}\right)\right]^2}{\left[1+e^{-\frac{4\pi\lambda}{m}}-2e^{-\frac{2\pi\lambda}{m}}\cos\left(\frac{4\pi}{m}\right)\right]^2}}\cos(\mu_2-2\mu)}{\left\{1-\sqrt{\frac{\left[1-e^{-\frac{2\pi\lambda}{m}}\cos\left(\frac{2\pi}{m}\right)-e^{-\frac{2\pi\lambda}{m}}+e^{-\frac{4\pi\lambda}{m}}\cos\left(\frac{2\pi}{m}\right)\right]^2+\left[e^{-\frac{2\pi\lambda}{m}}\sin\left(\frac{2\pi}{m}\right)-e^{-\frac{4\pi\lambda}{m}}\sin\left(\frac{2\pi}{m}\right)\right]^2}{\left[1+e^{-\frac{4\pi\lambda}{m}}-2e^{-\frac{2\pi\lambda}{m}}\cos\left(\frac{2\pi}{m}\right)\right]^2}}\right\}^{2}}-\frac{\left\{\frac{\left[1-e^{-\frac{2\pi\lambda}{m}}\cos\left(\frac{2\pi}{m}\right)-e^{-\frac{2\pi\lambda}{m}}+e^{-\frac{4\pi\lambda}{m}}\cos\left(\frac{2\pi}{m}\right)\right]^2+\left[e^{-\frac{2\pi\lambda}{m}}\sin\left(\frac{2\pi}{m}\right)-e^{-\frac{4\pi\lambda}{m}}\sin\left(\frac{2\pi}{m}\right)\right]^2}{\left[1+e^{-\frac{4\pi\lambda}{m}}-2e^{-\frac{2\pi\lambda}{m}}\cos\left(\frac{2\pi}{m}\right)\right]^2}\right\}^{2}}{\left\{1-\sqrt{\frac{\left[1-e^{-\frac{2\pi\lambda}{m}}\cos\left(\frac{2\pi}{m}\right)-e^{-\frac{2\pi\lambda}{m}}+e^{-\frac{4\pi\lambda}{m}}\cos\left(\frac{2\pi}{m}\right)\right]^2+\left[e^{-\frac{2\pi\lambda}{m}}\sin\left(\frac{2\pi}{m}\right)-e^{-\frac{4\pi\lambda}{m}}\sin\left(\frac{2\pi}{m}\right)\right]^2}{\left[1+e^{-\frac{4\pi\lambda}{m}}-2e^{-\frac{2\pi\lambda}{m}}\cos\left(\frac{2\pi}{m}\right)\right]^2}}\right\}^{2}},$$

respectively. The wrapped discrete exponential distribution is a simple model with a closed-form PMF. For this reason, some may consider it more practical than competing distributions.

3.4. Wrapped Discrete Mittag–Leffler Distribution

Ref. [62] introduced the discrete Mittag–Leffler distribution. Its nth trigonometric moment is given by

$$m_n=\left[1+\frac{1-\delta}{\delta}\left(1-e^{\frac{2\pi in}{m}}\right)^{\alpha}\right]^{-1}$$

for $n=1,2,\ldots$, where $0<\delta<1$, $0<\alpha<1$, and $m=1,2,\ldots$. The wrapped discrete Mittag–Leffler distribution has the disadvantage of having a non-closed-form PMF.

3.5. Wrapped Discrete Skew Laplace Distribution

Ref. [63] obtained the wrapped discrete skew Laplace distribution. Its PMF and CDF are

$$P\left(\Theta=\frac{2\pi r}{m}\right)=\frac{(1-p)(1-q)}{1-pq}\left[\frac{q^{m-r}(1-p^m)+p^r(1-q^m)}{(1-p^m)(1-q^m)}\right]$$

and

$$F(\Theta \leq s) = \frac{(1-p)(1-q)}{(1-pq)(1-p^m)(1-q^m)} \left\{ \frac{(1-p^m)(q^m - s^m)q}{q-s} + \frac{[1-(ps)^m](1-q^m)}{1-ps} \right\}, \quad s = 0,1,\ldots,m-1,$$

respectively, for $m \in \mathbb{N}$, $r = 0,1,\ldots,m-1$, and $\lambda > 0$. The nth trigonometric moment is given by

$$m_n = \frac{(1-p)(1-q)}{\left(1 - pe^{\frac{i2\pi n}{m}}\right)\left(1 - qe^{-\frac{2i\pi n}{m}}\right)}$$

for $n = 1,2,\ldots$. The mean direction, mean resultant length, skewness, and kurtosis are

$$\mu = \arctan\left[\frac{(p-q)\sin\left(\frac{2\pi}{m}\right)}{1+pq-(p+q)\cos\left(\frac{2\pi}{m}\right)}\right],$$

$$\rho = \frac{(1-p)(1-q)}{\sqrt{\left[1+pq-(p+q)\cos\left(\frac{2\pi}{m}\right)\right]^2 + \left[(p-q)\sin\left(\frac{2\pi}{m}\right)\right]^2}},$$

$$\gamma_1 = \frac{\frac{(1-p)(1-q)}{\sqrt{\left[1+pq-(p+q)\cos\left(\frac{4\pi}{m}\right)\right]^2+\left[(p-q)\sin\left(\frac{4\pi}{m}\right)\right]^2}}\sin(\mu_2 - 2\mu)}{\left\{1 - \frac{(1-p)(1-q)}{\sqrt{\left[1+pq-(p+q)\cos\left(\frac{2\pi}{m}\right)\right]^2+\left[(p-q)\sin\left(\frac{2\pi}{m}\right)\right]^2}}\right\}^{\frac{3}{2}}},$$

and

$$\gamma_2 = \frac{\frac{(1-p)(1-q)}{\sqrt{\left[1+pq-(p+q)\cos\left(\frac{4\pi}{m}\right)\right]^2+\left[(p-q)\sin\left(\frac{4\pi}{m}\right)\right]^2}}\cos(\mu_2 - 2\mu) - \frac{((1-p)(1-q))^2}{\left[1+pq-(p+q)\cos\left(\frac{2\pi n}{m}\right)\right]^2+\left[(p-q)\sin\left(\frac{2\pi n}{m}\right)\right]^2}}{\left\{1 - \frac{(1-p)(1-q)}{\sqrt{\left[1+pq-(p+q)\cos\left(\frac{2\pi}{m}\right)\right]^2+\left[(p-q)\sin\left(\frac{2\pi}{m}\right)\right]^2}}\right\}^2},$$

respectively, where $\mu_2 = \arctan\left[\frac{(p-q)\sin\left(\frac{4\pi}{m}\right)}{1+pq-(p+q)\cos\left(\frac{4\pi}{m}\right)}\right]$. The wrapped discrete skew Laplace distribution may be considered more practical than certain other models due to it having a closed-form PMF.

3.6. Wrapped Geometric Distribution

Ref. [62] obtained the wrapped geometric distribution. Its PMF and CDF are

$$P\left(\Theta = \frac{2\pi r}{m}\right) = \frac{\delta(1-\delta)^r}{1-(1-\delta)^m}$$

and

$$F(\Theta \leq y) = \sum_{r=0}^{y} \frac{\delta(1-\delta)^r}{1-(1-\delta)^m}, \quad y = 0,1,\ldots,m-1,$$

respectively, for $m \in \mathbb{N}$, $r = 0,1,\ldots,m-1$, and $\delta > 0$. The nth trigonometric moment is

$$m_n = \frac{\delta}{x - iy},$$

where $x = 1 - (1-\delta)\cos\frac{2\pi n}{m}$ and $y = (1-\delta)\sin\frac{2\pi n}{m}$ for $n \neq 0 \pmod m$, $n = 1, 2, \ldots$. The mean direction, mean resultant length, skewness, and kurtosis are

$$\mu = \arctan\left[\frac{(1-\delta)\sin\frac{2\pi}{m}}{1-(1-\delta)\cos\frac{2\pi}{m}}\right],$$

$$\rho = \frac{\delta}{\sqrt{\delta^2 + 2(1-\delta)\left(1-\cos\frac{2\pi}{m}\right)}},$$

$$\gamma_1 = \frac{\delta\sin(\mu_2 - 2\mu)}{\sqrt{\left[1-(1-\delta)\cos\left(\frac{4\pi}{m}\right)\right]^2 + \left[(1-\delta)\sin\left(\frac{4\pi}{m}\right)\right]^2}\left\{1 - \frac{\delta}{\sqrt{\delta^2+2(1-\delta)\left[1-\cos\left(\frac{2\pi}{m}\right)\right]}}\right\}^{\frac{3}{2}}},$$

and

$$\gamma_2 = \frac{\frac{\delta\cos(\mu_2-2\mu)}{\sqrt{\left[1-(1-\delta)\cos\left(\frac{4\pi}{m}\right)\right]^2+\left[(1-\delta)\sin\left(\frac{4\pi}{m}\right)\right]^2}} - \frac{\delta^4}{\left\{\delta^2+2(1-\delta)\left[1-\cos\left(\frac{2\pi}{m}\right)\right]\right\}^2}}{\left\{1 - \frac{\delta}{\sqrt{\delta^2+2(1-\delta)\left[1-\cos\left(\frac{2\pi}{m}\right)\right]}}\right\}^2},$$

respectively, where $\mu_2 = \arctan\left[\frac{(1-\delta)\sin\frac{4\pi}{m}}{1-(1-\delta)\cos\frac{4\pi}{m}}\right]$. The wrapped geometric distribution is a simple discrete circular model with the practical advantage of having a closed-form PMF.

3.7. Wrapped Negative Binomial Distribution

Ref. [64] introduced the wrapped negative binomial distribution. Its PMF and CDF are

$$P\left(\Theta = \frac{2\pi r}{m}\right) = \sum_{k=0}^{\infty}\binom{r+km+n-1}{n-1}p_1^n q_1^{r+km}$$

and

$$F(\Theta \leq y) = \sum_{r=0}^{y}\binom{r+km+n-1}{n-1}p_1^n q_1^{r+km}, \quad y = 0, 1, \ldots, m-1,$$

respectively, for $p_1 \in [0,1]$, $p_1 + q_1 = 1$, and $n \in \mathbb{Z}^+$. The nth trigonometric moment is

$$m_n = \left\{\frac{p_1\left[1 - q_1\cos\left(\frac{2\pi n}{m}\right)\right] + ip_1q_1\sin\left(\frac{2\pi n}{m}\right)}{1 + q_1^2 - 2q_1\cos\left(\frac{2\pi n}{m}\right)}\right\}^n$$

for $n = 1, 2, \ldots$. The mean direction, mean resultant length, skewness, and kurtosis are

$$\mu = n\arctan\left\{\frac{p_1q_1\left(\frac{2\pi}{m}\right)}{p_1\left[1 - q_1\cos\left(\frac{2\pi}{m}\right)\right]}\right\},$$

$$\rho = \left[\frac{p_1}{\sqrt{1 + q_1^2 - 2q_1\cos\left(\frac{2\pi}{m}\right)}}\right]^n,$$

$$\gamma_1 = \frac{\left[\frac{p_1}{\sqrt{1+q_1^2-2q_1\cos\left(\frac{4\pi}{m}\right)}}\right]^n \sin(\mu_2 - 2\mu)}{\left\{1-\left[\frac{p_1}{\sqrt{1+q_1^2-2q_1\cos\left(\frac{2\pi}{m}\right)}}\right]^n\right\}^{\frac{3}{2}}},$$

and

$$\gamma_2 = \frac{\left[\frac{p_1}{\sqrt{1+q_1^2-2q_1\cos\left(\frac{4\pi}{m}\right)}}\right]^n \cos(\mu_2 - 2\mu) - \left[\frac{p_1}{\sqrt{1+q_1^2-2q_1\cos\left(\frac{4\pi}{m}\right)}}\right]^{4n}}{\left\{1-\left[\frac{p_1}{\sqrt{1+q_1^2-2q_1\cos\left(\frac{2\pi}{m}\right)}}\right]^n\right\}^2},$$

respectively, where $\mu_2 = n \arctan\left\{\frac{p_1 q_1 \sin\left(\frac{4\pi}{m}\right)}{p_1\left[1-q_1\cos\left(\frac{4\pi}{m}\right)\right]}\right\}$. The wrapped negative binomial distribution does not have a closed-form PMF.

3.8. Wrapped Poisson Distribution

Ref. [39] obtained the wrapped Poisson distribution. Its PMF and CDF are

$$P\left(\Theta = \frac{2\pi r}{m}\right) = \sum_{k=0}^{\infty} \frac{e^{-\lambda}\lambda^{r+km}}{(r+km)!}$$

and

$$F(\Theta \leq y) = \sum_{r=0}^{y} P\left(\theta = \frac{2\pi r}{m}\right), \quad y = 0, 1, \ldots, m-1,$$

respectively, for $m \in \mathbb{N}$, $r = 0, 1, \ldots, m-1$, and $\lambda > 0$. The nth trigonometric moment is

$$m_n = e^{-\lambda\left[1-\cos\left(\frac{2\pi n}{m}\right)\right] + \mathrm{i}\sin\left(\frac{\lambda 2\pi n}{m}\right)}$$

for $n = 1, 2, \ldots$. The mean direction, mean resultant length, skewness, and kurtosis are

$$\mu = \lambda \sin\left(\frac{2\pi}{m}\right),$$

$$\rho = e^{-\lambda\left[1-\cos\left(\frac{2\pi}{m}\right)\right]},$$

$$\gamma_1 = \frac{e^{-\lambda\left[1-\cos\left(\frac{4\pi}{m}\right)\right]} \sin\left[\lambda \sin\left(\frac{4\pi}{m}\right) - 2\mu\right]}{\left\{1 - e^{-\lambda\left[1-\cos\left(\frac{2\pi}{m}\right)\right]}\right\}^{\frac{3}{2}}},$$

and

$$\gamma_2 = \frac{e^{-\lambda\left[1-\cos\left(\frac{4\pi}{m}\right)\right]} \cos\left[\lambda \sin\left(\frac{4\pi}{m}\right) - 2\mu\right] - e^{-4\lambda\left[1-\cos\left(\frac{2\pi}{m}\right)\right]}}{\left\{1 - e^{-\lambda\left[1-\cos\left(\frac{2\pi}{m}\right)\right]}\right\}^2},$$

respectively. The wrapped Poisson distribution lacks a closed-form PMF, limiting its practical usefulness.

3.9. Wrapped Poisson–Lindley Distribution

Ref. [65] obtained the wrapped Poisson–Lindley distribution. Its PMF and CDF are

$$P\left(\Theta = \frac{2\pi r}{m}\right) = \frac{\theta^2(1+\theta)^m\{(r+\theta+2)[(1+\theta)^m-1]+m\}}{(1+\theta)^{r+3}[(1+\theta)^m-1]^2}$$

and

$$F(\Theta \le y) = \frac{(1+\theta)^{m-y-3}}{[(1+\theta)^m-1]^2}\Bigg[1-(1+\theta)^m-\theta\{m+(3+y+\theta)[(1+\theta)^m-1]\} + (1+\theta)^{1+y}\left[-1-2\theta+m\theta-\theta^2+(1+\theta)^{2+m}\right]\Bigg], \quad y=0,1,\ldots,m-1,$$

respectively, for $m \in \mathbb{N}$ and $r = 0,1,\ldots,m-1$. The wrapped Poisson–Lindley distribution was used to analyze the turtle dataset and the Gorleston wind direction dataset discussed by [1]. Additionally, it was applied to a dataset consisting of arrival directions of low showers of cosmic rays, with declination and right ascension as the coordinate system [66]. The goodness of fit of the wrapped Poisson–Lindley distribution was compared to that of the wrapped geometric distribution. The wrapped Poisson–Lindley distribution showed the best fit for the first and third datasets, but not for the second dataset.

3.10. Wrapped Zero-Inflated Poisson Distribution

Ref. [67] introduced the wrapped zero-inflated Poisson distribution. Its PMF and CDF are

$$P\left(\Theta = \frac{2\pi r}{m}\right) = \sum_{k=-\infty}^{\infty} p(r+km)$$

and

$$F(\Theta \le y) = \sum_{r=0}^{y} P\left(\theta = \frac{2\pi r}{m}\right), \quad y=0,1,\ldots,m-1,$$

respectively, for $m \in \mathbb{N}$, $r = 0,1,\ldots,m-1$, $\lambda > 0$, and $w \in [0,1]$, where

$$p(x) = \begin{cases} w+(1-w)e^{-\lambda}, & \text{if } x=0, \\ \dfrac{(1-w)e^{-\lambda}\lambda^x}{x!}, & \text{if } x=1,2,\ldots. \end{cases}$$

The nth trigonometric moment is

$$m_n = w+(1-w)e^{-\lambda+\lambda e^{in}}$$

for $n = 1,2,\ldots$. The mean direction, mean resultant length, skewness, and kurtosis are

$$\mu = \arctan\left\{\frac{(1-w)e^{-\lambda\left[1-\cos\left(\frac{2\pi}{m}\right)\right]}\sin\left[\lambda\sin\left(\frac{2\pi}{m}\right)\right]}{w+(1-w)e^{-\lambda\left[1-\cos\left(\frac{2\pi}{m}\right)\right]}\cos\left[\lambda\sin\left(\frac{2\pi}{m}\right)\right]}\right\},$$

$$\rho = \sqrt{w^2+(1-w)^2e^{-2\lambda\left[1-\cos\left(\frac{2\pi p}{m}\right)\right]}+2w(1-w)e^{-\lambda\left[1-\cos\left(\frac{2\pi p}{m}\right)\right]}\cos\left[\lambda\sin\left(\frac{2\pi p}{m}\right)\right]},$$

$$\gamma_1 = \frac{w \sin 2\mu + (1-w)e^{-\lambda\left[1-\cos\left(\frac{4\pi}{m}\right)\right]} \sin\left[\lambda \sin\left(\frac{4\pi}{m}\right) - 2\mu\right]}{\left\{1 - \sqrt{a_1^2 + b_1^2 + 2a_1 b_1 \cos\left[\lambda \sin\left(\frac{2\pi}{m}\right)\right]}\right\}^{\frac{3}{2}}},$$

and

$$\gamma_2 = \frac{w \cos 2\mu + (1-w)e^{-\lambda\left[1-\cos\left(\frac{4\pi}{m}\right)\right]} \cos\left[\lambda \sin\left(\frac{4\pi}{m}\right) - 2\mu\right] - \left\{a_1^2 + b_1^2 + 2a_1 b_1 \cos\left[\lambda \sin\left(\frac{2\pi}{m}\right)\right]\right\}^2}{\left\{1 - \sqrt{a_1^2 + b_1^2 + 2a_1 b_1 \cos\left[\lambda \sin\left(\frac{2\pi}{m}\right)\right]}\right\}^2},$$

respectively, where $a_1 = w$ and $b_1 = (1-w)e^{-\lambda\left[1-\cos\left(\frac{2\pi}{m}\right)\right]}$. The wrapped zero-inflated Poisson distribution, a more flexible alternative to the one-parameter wrapped Poisson distribution, is useful for directional data with a high number of zero counts.

4. Data Applications

All of the distributions reviewed in Sections 2 and 3 can be fit by using the package Wrapped due to [9]. The package computes the PDF, CDF, quantile function, random samples, maximum likelihood estimates, standard errors, confidence intervals, and measures of goodness of fit associated with (1)–(2) for any specified g. In this section, we illustrate three data applications by fitting all of the reviewed distributions using Wrapped. In each data application, the following distributions gave the best fits: wrapped exponential, wrapped gamma, wrapped Weibull, wrapped Pareto, wrapped normal, wrapped Cauchy, wrapped Laplace and, wrapped t distributions. Hence, the tables and figures will be limited to these distributions.

4.1. Dataset 1

This data taken from [1] contain arrival times on a 24 h clock of 254 patients at an intensive care unit over a period of about 12 months. The maximized log-likelihood values as well as the corresponding values of AIC and BIC are given in Table 1.

Table 1. Fitted distributions and values of $\log L$, AIC, and BIC for dataset 1.

Distribution	$\log L$	AIC	BIC
Wrapped exponential	−468.6	939.2	942.8
Wrapped gamma	−436.9	877.8	884.9
Wrapped Weibull	−441.0	886.1	893.1
Wrapped Pareto	−446.1	896.2	903.3
Wrapped normal	−438.5	881.1	888.1
Wrapped Cauchy	−443.6	891.2	898.2
Wrapped Laplace	−443.4	890.8	897.9
Wrapped t	−438.5	883.1	893.7

We see that the wrapped gamma distribution gives the best fit in terms of AIC and BIC. The wrapped exponential distribution gives the worst fit in terms of AIC and BIC. These findings are confirmed by the density plots shown in Figure 1.

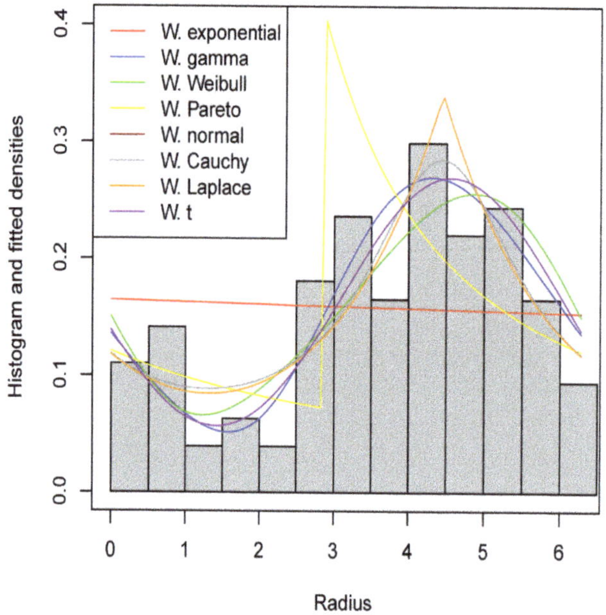

Figure 1. Histogram of the data and fitted densities for dataset 1.

4.2. Dataset 2

These data taken from [1] contain measurements of the directions taken by 76 turtles after treatment. The maximized log-likelihood values as well as the corresponding values of AIC and BIC are given in Table 2.

Table 2. Fitted distributions and values of $\log L$, AIC, and BIC for dataset 2.

Distribution	$\log L$	AIC	BIC
Wrapped exponential	−122.3	246.7	249.0
Wrapped gamma	−119.6	243.2	247.9
Wrapped Weibull	−120.6	245.3	249.9
Wrapped Pareto	−135.9	275.8	280.5
Wrapped normal	−125.1	254.1	258.8
Wrapped Cauchy	−113.9	231.9	236.6
Wrapped Laplace	−116.7	237.3	242.0
Wrapped t	−113.7	233.5	240.5

We see that the wrapped Cauchy distribution gives the best fit in terms of AIC and BIC. The wrapped Pareto distribution gives the worst fit in terms of AIC and BIC. These findings are confirmed by the density plots shown in Figure 2.

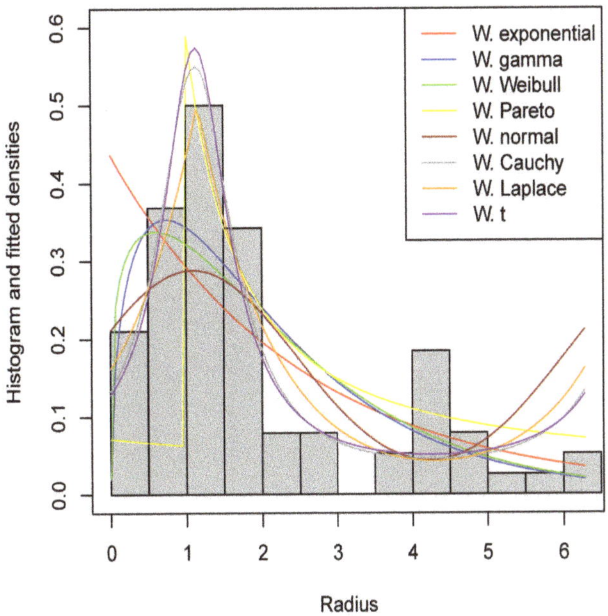

Figure 2. Histogram of the data and fitted densities for dataset 2.

4.3. Dataset 3

These data taken from [1] contain measurements of long-axis orientation of 133 feldspar laths in basalt. The maximized log-likelihood values as well as the corresponding values of AIC and BIC are given in Table 3.

Table 3. Fitted distributions and values of log *L*, AIC, and BIC for dataset 3.

Distribution	log *L*	AIC	BIC
Wrapped exponential	−243.9	489.8	492.6
Wrapped gamma	−243.9	491.8	497.5
Wrapped Weibull	−243.9	491.8	497.5
Wrapped Pareto	−247.6	499.2	505.0
Wrapped normal	−242.4	488.7	494.5
Wrapped Cauchy	−242.7	489.5	495.3
Wrapped Laplace	−243.9	491.9	497.6
Wrapped *t*	−242.4	490.7	499.4

We can see that the wrapped normal distribution gives the best fit in terms of AIC, whereas the wrapped exponential distribution gives the best fit in terms of BIC. The wrapped Pareto distribution gives the worst fit in terms of AIC and BIC. These findings are confirmed by the density plots shown in Figure 3.

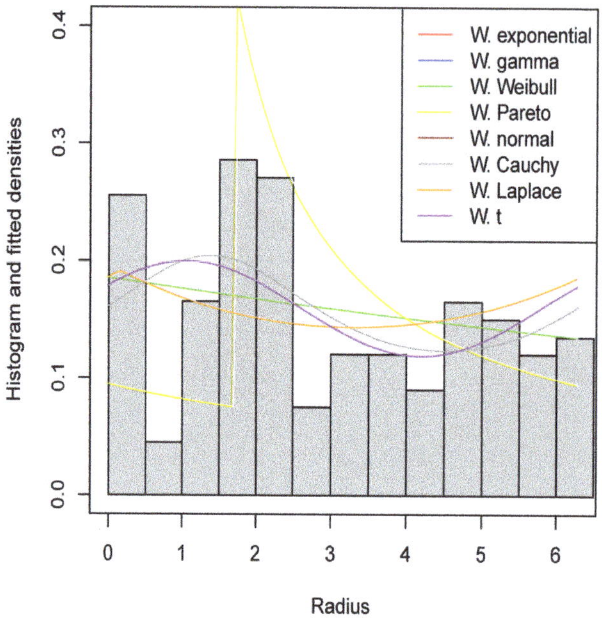

Figure 3. Histogram of the data and fitted densities for dataset 3.

5. Conclusions

In this paper, we have reviewed 45 wrapped distributions for continuous circular data and 10 wrapped distributions for discrete circular data by listing their probability density/mass functions, cumulative distribution functions, trigonometric moments, mean directions, mean resultant lengths, skewness, and kurtosis (whenever they are available). We have also discussed data applications and limitations of the reviewed distributions. This paper could be a source of reference and may encourage further developments in the area of wrapped distributions.

Future work may provide similar reviews for wrapped bivariate distributions, wrapped multivariate distributions, wrapped matrix variate distributions, and wrapped complex variate distributions. Another future possibility is to write R packages for fitting wrapped bivariate distributions, wrapped multivariate distributions, wrapped matrix variate distributions, and wrapped complex variate distributions.

Author Contributions: Investigation, W.B. and S.N.; methodology, W.B. and S.N.; formal analysis, W.B. and S.N.; software, W.B. and S.N.; writing—review and editing, W.B. and S.N. Both authors have read and agreed to the published version of the manuscript.

Funding: This research received no external funding.

Data Availability Statement: The original contributions presented in the study are included in the article, and further inquiries can be directed to the corresponding author.

Acknowledgments: The authors would like to thank the editor and the two referees for careful reading and comments, which greatly improved the paper.

Conflicts of Interest: The authors declare no conflicts of interest.

References

1. Fisher, N.I. *Statistical Analysis of Circular Data;* Cambridge University Press: Cambridge, UK, 1996.
2. Fisher, N.I. *Statistical Analysis of Circular Data;* Cambridge University Press: Cambridge, UK, 2011.
3. Jones, M.C. On families of distributions with shape parameters. *Int. Stat. Rev.* **2015**, *83*, 175–192. [CrossRef]

4. Ley, C.; Verdebout, T. *Modern Directional Statistics*; CRC Press: Boca Raton, FL, USA, 2017.
5. Pewsey, A.; Garcia-Portugues, E. Recent advances in directional statistics. *Test* **2021**, *30*, 1–58. [CrossRef]
6. Ley, C.; Babic, S.; Craens, D. Flexible models for complex data with applications. *Annu. Rev. Stat. Its Appl.* **2021**, *8*, 369–391. [CrossRef]
7. Prudnikov, A.P.; Brychkov, Y.A.; Marichev, O.I. *Integrals and Series*; Gordon and Breach Science Publishers: Amsterdam, The Netherlands, 1986; Volumes 1–3.
8. Gradshteyn, I.S.; Ryzhik, I.M. *Table of Integrals, Series, and Products*, 6th ed.; Academic Press: San Diego, CA, USA, 2000.
9. Nadarajah, S.; Zhang, Y. Wrapped: An R package for circular data. *PLoS ONE* **2017**, *12*, e0188512. [CrossRef] [PubMed]
10. Kumar, C.S.; Alex, R. Wrapped generalized skew normal distribution. *Stoch. Model. Appl.* **2021**, *25*, 1–7.
11. Hernandez-Sanchez, E.; Scarpa, B. A wrapped flexible generalized skew-normal model for a bimodal circular distribution of wind directions. *Chil. J. Stat.* **2012**, *3*, 129–141.
12. Holla, M.S.; Bhattacharya, S.K. On a compound Gaussian distribution. *Ann. Inst. Stat. Math.* **1968**, *20*, 331–336. [CrossRef]
13. Al-Khazaleh, A.; Al-Meanazel, T.R. Wrapped Akash distribution. *Electron. J. Appl. Stat. Anal.* **2021**, *14*, 305–317.
14. Ganaie, R.; Rajagopalan, V.; Rather, A. Weighted Aradhana distribution: Properties and applications. *J. Inf. Technol. Res.* **2019**, *IX*, 392–406.
15. Ramabhadra Sarma, I.; Dattatreya Rao, A.V.; Girija, S.V.S. On characteristic functions of wrapped half logistic and binormal distributions. *Int. J. Stat. Syst.* **2009**, *4*, 33–45.
16. Saraiva, M.A.; de Azevedo Cysneiros, F.J. Wrapped Birnbaum-Saunders distribution: Definition and estimation. *Nexus Math.* **2022**, *5*, 200010. [CrossRef]
17. Jander, R. Die optische Richtungsorientierung derroten Waldameise (*Formica rufa*). *Z. Fur-Vergle-Ichende Physiol.* **1957**, *40*, 162–238. [CrossRef]
18. Levy, P. L'addition des variables aléatoires définies sur une circonférence. *Bull. SociéTé MathéMatique Fr.* **1939**, *67*, 1–41. [CrossRef]
19. Roy, S.; Adnan, M.A.S. Wrapped Chi-Square Distribution. Available online: https://www.researchgate.net/publication/263080292_Wrapped_Chi-square_distribution (accessed on 3 August 2024).
20. Rao, J.S.; Kozubowski, T.J. A wrapped exponential circular model. *Proc. AP Acad. Sci.* **2001**, *5*, 43–56.
21. Subrahmanyam, P.S.; Dattatreya Rao, A.V.; Girija, S.V.S. On wrapping of exponentiated inverted Weibull distribution. *Int. J. Innov. Res. Sci. Technol.* **2017**, *3*, 18–25.
22. Coelho, C.A. The wrapped gamma distribution and wrapped sums and linear combinations of independent gamma and Laplace distributions. *J. Stat. Theory Pract.* **2007**, *1*, 1–29. [CrossRef]
23. Jayakumar, K.; Sajayan, T. Wrapped generalized geometric stable distributions with an application to wind direction. *Far East J. Theor. Stat.* **2022**, *66*, 147–166.
24. Cameron, M.A. The comparison of time series recorders. *Technometrics* **1983**, *25*, 9–22. [CrossRef]
25. Roy, S.; Adnan, M.A.S. Wrapped generalized Gompertz distribution: An application to ornithology. *J. Biom. Biostat.* **2012**, *3*, 153–156. [CrossRef]
26. Reed, W.J.; Pewsey, A. Two nested families of skew-symmetric circular distributions. *Test* **2009**, *18*, 516–528. [CrossRef]
27. Bruderer, B.; Jenni, L. Migration across the alps. In *Bird Migration*; Springer: Berlin/Heidelberg, Germany, 1990; pp. 60–77.
28. Varghese, J.; Jose, K.K. Wrapped hb-skewed laplace distribution and its application in meteorology. *Biom. Biostat. Int. J.* **2018**, *7*, 525–530.
29. Adnan, M.A.S.; Roy, S. Wrapped hypo-exponential distribution. *J. Stat. Manag. Syst.* **2013**, *16*, 1–11. [CrossRef]
30. Al-Meanazel, T.R.; Al-Khazaleh, A. Wrapped Ishita distribution. *J. Stat. Appl. Probab.* **2021**, *10*, 293–299.
31. Jammalamadaka, S.R.; Kozubowski, T. A new family of circular models: The wrapped Laplace distributions. *Adv. Appl. Stat.* **2003**, *3*, 77–103.
32. Bhattacharjee, S.; Borah, D. Wrapped length biased weighted exponential distribution. *Thail. Stat.* **2019**, *17*, 223–234.
33. Smith, N.M. Reconstruction of the Tertiary Drainage Systems of the Inverell Region. Unpublished B.Sc. Ph.D. Thesis, Department of Geography, University of Sydney, Sydney, Australia, 1988.
34. Joshi, S.; Jose, K.K. Wrapped Lindley distribution. *Commun. -Stat.-Theory Methods* **2018**, *47*, 1013–1021. [CrossRef]
35. Jacob, S. Study on Circular Distributions. Ph.D. Thesis, Department of Statistics, University of Calicut, Calicut, India, 2012.
36. Subba Rao, R.; Ravindranath, V.; Dattatreya Rao, A.V.; Prasad, G.; Ravi Kishore, P. Wrapped Lomax distribution: A new circular probability model. *Int. J. Eng. Technol.* **2018**, *7*, 150–152. [CrossRef]
37. Chesneau, C.; Tomy, L.; Jose, M. Wrapped modified Lindley distribution. *J. Stat. Manag. Syst.* **2021**, *24*, 1025–1040. [CrossRef]
38. Subrahmanyam, P.S., Dattatreya Rao, A.V.; Girija, S.V.S. On wrapping of new Weibull Pareto distribution. *Int. J. Adv. Res. Rev.* **2017**, *2*, 10–20.
39. Mardia, K.V. Statistics of Directional Data. In *Probability and Mathematical Statistics*; Academic Press: London, UK, 1972.
40. Jammalamadaka, S.R.; Kozubowski, T.J. A general approach for obtaining wrapped circular distributions via mixtures. *Sankhyā A* **2017**, *79*, 133–157. [CrossRef]
41. Bhattacharjee, S. Exploration of some distributional properties, parameter estimates and applications of the wrapped quasi Lindley distribution. *J. Math. Comput. Sci.* **2020**, *10*, 2390–2407.
42. Bell, W.; Nadarajah, S. The wrapped Rama distribution. *Preprint* **2023**.
43. Demirelli, A.E.; Gürcan, M. New wrapped distribution via Richard link function. *AIP Conf. Proc.* **2017**, *1863*, 350002.

44. Al-Meanazel, T.R.; Al-Khazaleh, A. Wrapped Shanker distribution. *Ital. J. Pure Appl. Math.* **2021**, *46*, 184–194.
45. Yilmaz, A. Wrapped flexible skew Laplace distribution. *J. Turk. Stat. Assoc.* **2018**, *11*, 53–64.
46. Fernandez-Duran, J.J. Circular distributions based on nonnegative trigonometric sums. *Biometrics* **2004**, *60*, 499–503. [CrossRef] [PubMed]
47. Pewsey, A. The wrapped skew-normal distribution on the circle. *Commun. -Stat.—Theory Methods* **2000**, *29*, 2459–2472. [CrossRef]
48. Pewsey, A. The wrapped stable family of distributions as a flexible model for circular data. *Comput. Stat. Data Anal.* **2008**, *52*, 1516–1523. [CrossRef]
49. Pewsey, A.; Lewis, T.; Jones, M. The wrapped *t* family of circular distributions. *Aust. N. Z. J. Stat.* **2007**, *49*, 79–91.
50. Yilmaz, A.; Bicer, C. A new wrapped exponential distribution. *Math. Sci.* **2018**, *12*, 285–293. [CrossRef]
51. Bhattacharjee, S.; Ahmed, I.; Das, K.K. Wrapped two-parameter Lindley distribution for modelling circular data. *Thail. Stat.* **2020**, *19*, 81–94.
52. Mardia, K.V.; Jupp, P.E. *Directional Statistics*; John Wiley and Sons: New York, NY, USA, 2000.
53. Bicer, C.; Yilmaz, A. Wrapped two sided Lindley distribution. In *Research and Reviews in Science and Mathematics*; Iyit, N., Dogan, H.H., Akgul, H., Eds.; Gece Academy Publishing: Ankara, Turkey, 2022; pp. 1–13.
54. Adnan, M.A.S.; Roy, S. Wrapped variance gamma distribution with an application to wind direction. *J. Environ. Stat.* **2014**, *6*, 1–10.
55. Roy, S.; Adnan, M.A.S. Wrapped weighted exponential distributions. *Stat. Probab. Lett.* **2012**, *82*, 77–83. [CrossRef]
56. Al-Mofleh, H.; Sen, S. The wrapped Xgamma distribution for modeling circular data appearing in geological context. *arXiv* **2019**, arXiv:1903.00177.
57. Zinhom, E.; Nassar, M.M.; Radwan, S.S.; Elmasry, A. The wrapped XLindley distribution. *Environ. Ecol. Stat.* **2023**, *30*, 669–686. [CrossRef]
58. Bahnsen, A.C.; Stojanovic, A.; Aouada, D.; Ottersten, B. Improving credit card fraud detection with calibrated probabilities. In Proceedings of the 2014 SIAM International Conference on Data Mining, Philadelphia, PA, USA, 24–26 April 2014 ; pp. 677–685, SIAM.
59. Girija, S.V.S.; Dattatreya Rao, A.V.; Srihari, V.L.N. On wrapped binomial model characteristics. *Math. Stat.* **2014**, *2*, 231–234. [CrossRef]
60. Girija, S.V.S.; Srihari, G.V.L.N.; Srinivas, R. On discrete wrapped Cauchy model. *Math. Theory Model.* **2019**, *9*, 15–23.
61. Srinivas, R.; Srihari, G.V.L.N.; Girija, S.V.S. On construction of discrete wrapped Lindley distribution. *i-Manag. J. Math.* **2008**, *7*, 10–19. [CrossRef]
62. Jacob, S.; Jayakumar, K. Wrapped geometric distribution: A new probability model for circular data. *J. Stat. Theory Appl.* **2013**, *12*, 348–355. [CrossRef]
63. Jayakumar, K.; Jacob, S. Wrapped skew Laplace distribution on integers: A new probability model for circular data. *Open J. Stat.* **2012**, *2*, 106–114. [CrossRef]
64. Srihari, G.V.L.N.; Girija, S.V.S.; Rao, A.V.D. On wrapped negative binomial model. *Int. J. Math. Arch.* **2018**, *9*, 148–153.
65. Chesneau, C.; Bakouch, H.S.; Hussain, T. Modeling and applications to circular data with a wrapped Poisson-Lindley model. *J. Math. Study* **2022**, *55*, 139–157. [CrossRef]
66. Fisher, N.I.; Lewis, T.; Embleton, B.J.J. *Statistical Analysis of Spherical Data*; Cambridge University Press: New York, NY, USA, 1987.
67. Thavaneswaran, A.; Mandal, S.; Pathmanathan, D. Estimation for wrapped zero inflated Poisson and wrapped Poisson distributions. *Int. J. Stat. Probab.* **2016**, *5*, 1–8. [CrossRef]

mathematics

Article

On Stochastic Representations of the Zero–One-Inflated Poisson Lindley Distribution

Razik Ridzuan Mohd Tajuddin * and Noriszura Ismail

Department of Mathematical Sciences, Universiti Kebangsaan Malaysia, Bangi 43600, Malaysia; ni@ukm.edu.my
* Correspondence: rrmt@ukm.edu.my

Abstract: A zero–one-inflated Poisson Lindley distribution has been introduced recently as an alternative to the zero–one-inflated Poisson distribution for describing count data with a substantial number of zeros and ones. Several stochastic representations of the zero–one-inflated Poisson Lindley distribution and their equivalence to some well-known distributions under some conditions are presented. Using these stochastic representations, the distributional properties such as the nth moments, as well as the conditional distributions are discussed. These stochastic representations can be used to explain the relationship between two or more distributions. Several likelihood ratio tests are developed and examined for the presence of one-inflation and fixed rate parameters. The likelihood ratio tests are found to be powerful and have ability to control the error rates as the sample size increases. A sample size of 1000 is acceptable and sufficient for the likelihood ratio tests to be useful.

Keywords: degenerate; multinomial; Poisson Lindley; zero-inflated Poisson Lindley; zero-truncated Poisson Lindley; zero–one-inflated Poisson Lindley

MSC: 62E10; 62F03

1. Introduction

One common phenomenon in statistics is the presence of excess zeroes only. This phenomenon happens when there are more zero-valued observations than explained by the Poisson distribution. There have been numerous studies conducted in analysing count data with zero-inflation such as zero-inflated models [1–4], hurdle models [4], zero-altered models [3] and others. Young et al. [5] has provided a comprehensive review on the use of the zero-inflated models and its associated regression models. The zero-inflated models are commonly used to explain the excess zeroes by introducing an inflation parameter known as zero-inflation parameter.

Recently, the presence of excess zeros and ones in count data have been gaining attraction by researchers as they are also common in statistics. This phenomenon happens when there is an abundance of observed events that are not happening and happening only once. This phenomenon arises quite naturally depending on the questions we would like to answer. Lin and Tsai [6] have provided a list of questions that will ultimately give the observations inflated at zero and non-zero. For inflation at zero and one, asking questions about a memorable event that happened in one's life such as the number of marriages [6] will certainly yield results that have a huge spike at zero and one because it is natural and common across time for mankind to either stay single or get married to one person at a time or in life. The phenomenon of excess zeros and ones can also be found in various fields such as medicine [6] as well as quantitative criminology [7,8].

Introducing two inflation parameters into an existing distribution to describe excess zeros and ones, respectively, is normal and extensively researched [6–10]. Although the zero–one-inflated Poisson distribution (*ZOIP*) was introduced in the late 20th century by Melkersson and Olsson [9], its stochastic representations were not explored until

17 years later by Zhang et al. [10]. The study by Zhang et al. [10] interrelates the $ZOIP$ distribution with other known Poisson distributions such as the zero-inflated Poisson, the zero-truncated Poisson and the one-truncated Poisson distributions. Following the idea of Zhang et al. [10], this paper examines and discusses some notes on the stochastic representations for the zero–one-inflated Poisson Lindley distribution ($ZOIPL$) developed by Tajuddin et al. [8]. Likelihood ratio tests are also developed to investigate whether the presence of one-inflation and fixed parameters is significant.

The probability mass function (pmf) for a random variable Y following the $ZOIPL$ distribution [8] is given as:

$$\Pr(Y=y) = \begin{cases} \omega_0 + (1-\omega_0-\omega_1)\frac{\theta^2(\theta+2)}{(\theta+1)^3}; y=0 \\ \omega_1 + (1-\omega_0-\omega_1)\frac{\theta^2(\theta+3)}{(\theta+1)^4}; y=1 \\ (1-\omega_0-\omega_1)\frac{\theta^2(\theta+y+2)}{(\theta+1)^{y+3}}; y\geq 2 \end{cases}, \quad (1)$$

where ω_0 and ω_1 explain the excess zeroes and ones, respectively, and θ is the parameter of the Poisson Lindley, PL distribution [11]. The PL distribution has been shown to provide a better fit than the Poisson distribution due to its ability to handle overdispersion in the data [11,12]. The parameter θ in the PL distribution plays a crucial role in determining the variation in the distribution. As θ increases, the variance and the mean of the PL distribution approach to an identical value, a phenomenon known as equidispersion (see [12], 2009 for further explanation). Similarly, the $ZOIPL$ distribution has also been shown to provide better model fittings over the $ZOIP$ distribution due to its ability to handle extra dispersion, of which cannot be single-handedly described by the inflation parameters in the $ZOIP$ distribution [8].

Note that, if $\omega_0 = 0$, the $ZOIPL$ distribution reduces to a one-inflated Poisson Lindley, $OIPL$ distribution with parameters ω_1 and θ, which have not been studied yet. Readers are advised to not be confused with a one-inflated-positive Poisson Lindley distribution, which was developed to cater for inflation in one-valued data in positive count data [13]. If $\omega_1 = 0$, the $ZOIPL$ distribution reduces to the zero-inflated Poisson Lindley distribution ($ZIPL$) with parameters ω_0 and θ [14]. If both $\omega_0, \omega_1 = 0$, the $ZOIPL$ distribution reduces to the standard PL distribution with parameter θ. From the special cases, we can already identify the relationship between these distributions. Based on this idea, the stochastic representations of the $ZOIPL$ distribution can be studied.

Before proceeding with the stochastic representations, we first adopt the definition of a degenerate distribution from Zhang et al. [10] to obtain an identical but compact representation for the pmf of the $ZOIPL$ distribution. Let $\xi_c \sim Degen(c)$ be a random variable which follows a degenerate distribution at a single constant point c with $\Pr(\xi_c = c) = 1$. Let $\xi_0 \sim Degen(0)$, $\xi_1 \sim Degen(1)$ and $X \sim PL(\theta)$ be mutually independent. Therefore, the pmf of the $ZOIPL$ can be written as

$$\begin{aligned} \Pr(Y=y) &= \omega_0\Pr(\xi_0=y) + \omega_1\Pr(\xi_1=y) + \omega_2\Pr(X=y) \\ &= \left[\omega_0 + \omega_2\frac{\theta^2(\theta+2)}{(\theta+1)^3}\right]I_{(y=0)} + \left[\omega_1 + \omega_2\frac{\theta^2(\theta+3)}{(\theta+1)^4}\right]I_{(y=1)} + \left[\omega_2\frac{\theta^2(\theta+y+2)}{(\theta+1)^{y+3}}\right]I_{(y\geq 2)}, \end{aligned} \quad (2)$$

where $I_{(.)}$ refers to the indicator function, $0 \leq \omega_0, \omega_1, \omega_2 < 1$, $\omega_2 = 1-\omega_0-\omega_1$ and ω_0, ω_1 refers to the inflation parameters for excess zeroes and ones, respectively.

The paper is organized as follows: Section 2 describes various stochastic representations of the $ZOIPL$ distribution. Section 3 describes the derivations of nth moments based on the different stochastic representations. Section 4 describes the derivations of conditional distributions for selected stochastic representations. Section 5 presents several likelihood ratio tests to assess the presence of inflating parameters as well as fixed θ. Section 6 examines the performance of the likelihood ratio tests through a simulation study. Section 7 concludes the study.

2. Stochastic Representation (SR)

Several stochastic representations are discussed to highlight the relationship between the *ZOIPL* distribution with the zero-inflated Poisson Lindley (*ZIPL*), the zero-truncated Poisson Lindley (*ZTPL*) and the Poisson Lindley, *PL* distributions. Table 1 provides the probability mass functions for the remaining three distributions.

Table 1. The probability mass functions for the *ZIPL*, *PL* and the *ZTPL* distributions.

Distribution	Probability Mass Function
ZIPL	$\Pr(Y^* = y\vert\omega_0, \omega_1, \theta) = \begin{cases} \omega_0 + \omega_1 \frac{\theta^2(\theta+2)}{(\theta+1)^3}; y^* = 0 \\ \omega_1 \frac{\theta^2(\theta+y^*+2)}{(\theta+1)^{y^*+3}}; y^* \geq 1 \end{cases}$ where $\omega_1 = 1 - \omega_0$ and ω_0 refers to the inflation parameter for the excess zeroes.
PL	$\Pr(X = y^*\vert\theta) = \frac{\theta^2(\theta+y^*+2)}{(\theta+1)^{y^*+3}}; y^* \geq 0$
ZTPL	$\Pr(V = v\vert\theta) = \frac{\theta^2(\theta+v+2)}{(\theta^2+3\theta+1)(\theta+1)^v}; v \geq 1$

Before the stochastic representations for the *ZOIPL* distribution is discussed, we adapt some notations from Zhang et al. [10] and present them in Table 2 to facilitate the understanding of the stochastic representations.

Table 2. Notations and their descriptions.

Notation	Description
$A \sim Q(\tau)$	Random variable A follows a Q distribution with parameter τ.
$\boldsymbol{A}$	Vector A.
$\boldsymbol{A}^T$	Transpose of vector A.
$A \perp\!\!\!\perp B \perp\!\!\!\perp C$	Random variables A, B and C are mutually independent.
$A \overset{d}{=} B + C$	Random variables A and $B + C$ have the same distribution.

2.1. *First Stochastic Representation (SR1)*

Let $\mathbf{Z} = (Z_0, Z_1, Z_2)^T \sim Multinomial(1; \omega_0, \omega_1, \omega_2)$ and $X \sim PL(\theta)$, such that $\mathbf{Z} \perp\!\!\!\perp X$. The first SR for random variable $Y \sim ZOIPL(\omega_0, \omega_1, \theta)$ is given as $Y \overset{d}{=} Z_0(0) + Z_1(1) + Z_2 X = Z_1 + Z_2 X$, or equivalently, $Y = \begin{cases} 0; \text{ with probability } \omega_0 \\ 1; \text{ with probability } \omega_1 \\ X; \text{ with probability } \omega_2 \end{cases}$. Since $Z_0 + Z_1 + Z_2 = 1$ with $\Pr(Z_i = 1) = \omega_i$ where $i = 1, 2, 3$, the pmf of Y can be written as:

$$\begin{aligned} \Pr(Y = 0) &= \Pr(Z_0 = 1) + \Pr(Z_2 = 1, X = 0) = \omega_0 + \omega_2 \frac{\theta^2(\theta+2)}{(\theta+1)^3} \\ \Pr(Y = 1) &= \Pr(Z_1 = 1) + \Pr(Z_2 = 1, X = 1) = \omega_1 + \omega_2 \frac{\theta^2(\theta+3)}{(\theta+1)^4} \\ \Pr(Y = y) &= \Pr(Z_2 = 1, X = y) = \omega_2 \frac{\theta^2(\theta+y+2)}{(\theta+1)^{y+3}}, y \geq 2. \end{aligned} \tag{3}$$

From the first SR, the pmf is identical as the pmf of the *ZOIPL* distribution. Therefore, the random variable $Y \sim ZOIPL(\omega_0, \omega_1, \theta)$ can be denoted as the mixture of $\xi_0 \sim Degen(0)$, $\xi_1 \sim Degen(1)$ and $X \sim PL(\theta)$ distributions.

2.2. Second Stochastic Representation (SR2)

Let $Z \sim Bernoulli(1-w)$, $\mathrm{H} \sim Bernoulli(p)$ and $X \sim PL(\theta)$, such that $\mathrm{Z} \perp\!\!\!\perp \mathrm{H} \perp\!\!\!\perp \mathrm{X}$. The second SR for random variable $Y \sim ZOIPL(\omega_0, \omega_1, \theta)$ is given as $Y \stackrel{d}{=} (1-\mathrm{Z})\mathrm{H} + ZX$, or equivalently,

$$Y = \begin{cases} \mathrm{H};\ \text{with probability } w \\ X;\ \text{with probability } 1-w \end{cases}.$$

Thus, the pmf of Y is given as

$$\begin{aligned}
\Pr(Y=0) &= \Pr(Z=0, Y=0) + \Pr(Z=1, Y=0) = \Pr(\mathrm{Z}=0, \mathrm{H}=0) + \Pr(\mathrm{Z}=1, X=0) \\
&= w(1-p) + (1-w)\tfrac{\theta^2(\theta+2)}{(\theta+1)^3} \\
\Pr(Y=1) &= \Pr(Z=0, Y=1) + \Pr(Z=1, Y=1) = \Pr(\mathrm{Z}=0, \mathrm{H}=1) + \Pr(\mathrm{Z}=1, X=1) \\
&= wp + (1-w)\tfrac{\theta^2(\theta+3)}{(\theta+1)^4} \\
\Pr(Y=y) &= \Pr(Z=1, X=y) = (1-w)\tfrac{\theta^2(\theta+y+2)}{(\theta+1)^{y+3}}; y \geq 2
\end{aligned} \tag{4}$$

Using the reparameterizations $\omega_0 = w(1-p)$ and $\omega_1 = wp$, it can be obtained that $w = \omega_0 + \omega_1$ and $p = \omega_1/(\omega_0 + \omega_1)$. In other words, the random variable $Y \sim ZOIPL(\omega_0, \omega_1, \theta)$ can be denoted as the mixture of $Bernoulli(\omega_1/(\omega_0+\omega_1))$ and $PL(\theta)$.

2.3. Third Stochastic Representation (SR3)

Let $Z \sim Bernoulli(1-w)$, $\xi_1 \sim Degen(1)$ and $Y^* \sim ZIPL(w^*, \theta)$, such that $\mathrm{Z} \perp\!\!\!\perp \xi_1 \perp\!\!\!\perp Y^*$. The third SR for random variable $Y \sim ZOIPL(\omega_0, \omega_1, \theta)$ is given as $Y \stackrel{d}{=} (1-\mathrm{Z})\xi_1 + ZY^*$, or equivalently,

$$Y = \begin{cases} 1;\ \text{with probability } w \\ Y^*;\ \text{with probability } 1-w \end{cases}.$$

Thus, the pmf of Y is given as

$$\begin{aligned}
\Pr(Y=0) &= \Pr(Z=1, Y^*=0) \\
&= (1-w)\left[w^* + (1-w^*)\tfrac{\theta^2(\theta+2)}{(\theta+1)^3}\right] \\
&= w^*(1-w) + (1-w)(1-w^*)\tfrac{\theta^2(\theta+2)}{(\theta+1)^3}
\end{aligned} \tag{5}$$

$$\begin{aligned}
\Pr(Y=1) &= \Pr(Z=0) + \Pr(Z=1, Y^*=1) \\
&= w + (1-w)(1-w^*)\tfrac{\theta^2(\theta+3)}{(\theta+1)^4}
\end{aligned} \tag{6}$$

$$\Pr(Y=y) = \Pr(Z=1, Y^*=y) = (1-w)(1-w^*)\frac{\theta^2(\theta+y+2)}{(\theta+1)^{y+3}}; y \geq 2 \tag{7}$$

Using the reparameterizations $\omega_0 = w^*(1-w)$, $\omega_1 = w$ and $\omega_2 = (1-w)(1-w^*)$, one can obtain that $w = \omega_1$ and $w^* = \omega_0/(1-\omega_1)$. In other words, the random variable $Y \sim ZOIPL(\omega_0, \omega_1, \theta)$ can be denoted as the mixture of $Degen(1)$ and $ZIPL(\omega_0/(1-\omega_1), \theta)$.

2.4. Fourth Stochastic Representation (SR4)

Let $V \sim ZTPL(\theta)$, $\mathbf{Z}^* = (Z_0^*, Z_1^*, Z_2^*)^T \sim Multinomial(1; \omega_0^*, \omega_1^*, \omega_2^*)$, such that $V \perp\!\!\!\perp \mathbf{Z}^*$. The fourth SR for random variable $Y \sim ZOIPL(\omega_0, \omega_1, \theta)$ is given as $Y \overset{d}{=} Z_0^*(0) + Z_1^*(1) + Z_2^* V = Z_1^* + Z_2^* V$, or equivalently,

$$Y = \begin{cases} 0; \text{ with probability } \omega_0^* \\ 1; \text{ with probability } \omega_1^* \\ V; \text{ with probability } \omega_2^* \end{cases}.$$

Thus, the pmf of Y is given as

$$\Pr(Y = 0) = \Pr(Z_0^* = 1) = \omega_0^*$$

$$\begin{aligned} \Pr(Y = 1) &= \Pr(Z_1^* = 1) + \Pr(Z_2^* = 1, V = 1) \\ &= \omega_1^* + \omega_2^* \tfrac{\theta^2(\theta+3)}{(\theta^2+3\theta+1)(\theta+1)^4} \end{aligned} \tag{8}$$

$$\Pr(Y = y) = \Pr(Z_2^* = 1, V = y) = \omega_2^* \tfrac{\theta^2(\theta+y+2)}{(\theta^2+3\theta+1)(\theta+1)^{y+3}}; y \geq 2$$

Using the reparameterizations $\omega_0^* = \omega_0 + \omega_2\theta^2(\theta+2)/(\theta+1)^3$, $\omega_1^* = \omega_1$ and $\omega_2^* = \omega_2(\theta^2 + 3\theta + 1)$, one can obtain that $\omega_1 = \omega_1^*$, $\omega_2 = \omega_2^*/(\theta^2 + 3\theta + 1)$ and $\omega_0 = \omega_0^* - \omega_2^*\theta^2(\theta+2)/\left[(\theta^2 + 3\theta + 1)(\theta+1)^3\right]$. Therefore, $Y \sim ZOIPL(\omega_0, \omega_1, \theta)$ can be denoted as the mixture of $Degen(0)$, $Degen(1)$ and $ZTPL(\theta)$.

3. The nth Moments

In this section, the nth moments for the $ZOIPL$ distribution using the four stochastic representations, explained in Section 2, will be utilized. Usually, the nth moments for any zero–one-inflated distributions are obtained directly as

$$E(Y^n) = \sum_{y=0}^{\infty} y^n \Pr(Y = y) = \Pr(Y = 1) + \sum_{y=2}^{\infty} y^n \Pr(Y = y). \tag{9}$$

With the help from the four stochastic representations, new forms of the nth moments will be developed. The nth moments are important in obtaining the mean, variance, skewness, and kurtosis of the distribution. Here, we only show the derivation of the nth moments using different stochastic representations.

3.1. First Stochastic Representation

Referring to SR1, $Y \overset{d}{=} Z_1 + Z_2 X$. Therefore, the nth moment of Y is derived as follows:

$$E(Y^n) = E[(Z_1 + Z_2X)^n] = E\left[\sum_{k=0}^{n} \binom{n}{k} \left({Z_1}^k {Z_2}^{n-k}\right) X^{n-k}\right]. \tag{10}$$

Zhang et al. [10] has mentioned that for any integers i and j, ${Z_i}^k {Z_j}^{n-k} \sim Degen(0)$ for $i \neq j$. Furthermore, it is trivial to show that $E({Z_i}^n) = E(Z_i)$. Therefore, the nth moment of Y can be simplified as

$$\begin{aligned} E(Y^n) &= \sum_{k=0}^{n} \binom{n}{k} E\left({Z_1}^k {Z_2}^{n-k}\right) E\left(X^{n-k}\right) \\ &= E({Z_2}^n)E(X^n) + \sum_{k=1}^{n-1} \binom{n}{k} E\left({Z_1}^k {Z_2}^{n-k}\right) E\left(X^{n-k}\right) + E({Z_1}^n) \\ &= \omega_1 + \omega_2 E(X^n). \end{aligned} \tag{11}$$

3.2. Second Stochastic Representation

Referring to SR2, $Y \overset{d}{=} (1-Z)\mathrm{H} + ZX$. Therefore, the nth moment of Y is derived as follows:

$$E(Y^n) = E\{[(1-Z)\mathrm{H} + ZX]^n\} = E\left\{\sum_{k=0}^{n} \binom{n}{k} \left[(1-Z)^k Z^{n-k}\right] \mathrm{H}^k X^{n-k}\right\}. \tag{12}$$

The nth moment of Y can be simplified as

$$\begin{aligned} E(Y^n) &= \sum_{k=0}^{n} \binom{n}{k} E\left[(1-Z)^k Z^{n-k}\right] E\left(\mathrm{H}^k\right) E\left(X^{n-k}\right) \\ &= E(Z^n)E(X^n) + \sum_{k=1}^{n-1} \binom{n}{k} E\left[(1-Z)^k Z^{n-k}\right] E\left(\mathrm{H}^k\right) E\left(X^{n-k}\right) + E[(1-Z)^n]E(\mathrm{H}^n) \\ &= wp + (1-w)E(X^n). \end{aligned}$$

3.3. Third Stochastic Representation

Referring to SR3, $Y \overset{d}{=} (1-Z)\xi + ZY^*$. Therefore, the nth moment of Y is derived as follows:

$$E(Y^n) = E\{[(1-Z)\xi + ZY^*]^n\} = E\left\{\sum_{k=0}^{n} \binom{n}{k} \left[(1-Z)^k Z^{n-k}\right] \xi^k Y^{*n-k}\right\}. \tag{13}$$

The nth moment of Y can be simplified as

$$\begin{aligned} E(Y^n) &= \sum_{k=0}^{n} \binom{n}{k} E\left[(1-Z)^k Z^{n-k}\right] E\left(\xi^k\right) E\left(Y^{*n-k}\right) \\ &= E(Z^n)E(Y^{*n}) + \sum_{k=1}^{n-1} \binom{n}{k} E\left[(1-Z)^k Z^{n-k}\right] E\left(\xi^k\right) E\left(Y^{*n-k}\right) + E[(1-Z)^n]E(\xi^n) \\ &= w + (1-w)E(Y^{*n}). \end{aligned}$$

3.4. Fourth Stochastic Representation

Referring to SR4, $Y \overset{d}{=} Z_1{}^* + Z_1{}^*V$. Therefore, the nth moment of Y is derived as follows:

$$E(Y^n) = E\left[(Z_1{}^* + Z_2{}^*V)^n\right] = E\left\{\sum_{k=0}^{n} \binom{n}{k} \left[Z_1{}^{*k} Z_2{}^{*n-k}\right] V^{n-k}\right\}. \tag{14}$$

The nth moment of Y can be simplified as

$$\begin{aligned} E(Y^n) &= \sum_{k=0}^{n} \binom{n}{k} E\left[Z_1{}^{*k} Z_2{}^{*n-k}\right] E\left(V^{n-k}\right) \\ &= E(Z_2{}^{*n})E(V^n) + \sum_{k=1}^{n-1} \binom{n}{k} E\left[Z_1{}^{*k} Z_2{}^{*n-k}\right] E\left(V^{n-k}\right) + E(Z_1{}^{*n}) \\ &= \omega_1{}^* + \omega_2{}^* E(V^n). \end{aligned}$$

4. Conditional Distributions

In this section, the conditional distributions based on the first two stochastic representations will be discussed.

4.1. First Stochastic Representation

Recall that in SR1, $Y \overset{d}{=} Z_1 + Z_2X$ where $\mathbf{Z} = (Z_0, Z_1, Z_2)^T \sim Multinomial(1; \omega_0, \omega_1, \omega_2)$ and $X \sim PL(\theta)$, such that $\mathbf{Z} \perp\!\!\!\perp X$. We would like to find the conditional distribution for $\mathbf{Z}|Y$ and $X|Y$. The conditional distributions are given in the following theorems.

Theorem 1. *The joint conditional distribution for* $\mathbf{Z}|Y$ is given as

$$\mathbf{Z}|(Y=y) \sim \begin{cases} \text{Multinomial}(1;\beta_1,0,1-\beta_1) & ;\text{if } y=0, \\ \text{Multinomial}(1;0,\beta_2,1-\beta_2) & ;\text{if } y=1, \\ \text{Multinomial}(1;0,0,1) & ;\text{if } y\geq 2, \end{cases} \quad (15)$$

where

$$\beta_1 = \frac{\omega_0}{\omega_0 + \omega_2 \frac{\theta^2(\theta+2)}{(\theta+1)^3}} \text{ and } \beta_2 = \frac{\omega_1}{\omega_1 + \omega_2 \frac{\theta^2(\theta+3)}{(\theta+1)^4}}.$$

Proof. Recall that $\mathbf{Z}$ can take on $(1,0,0)^T,(0,1,0)^T,(0,0,1)^T$ and $\Pr(\mathbf{Z}=\mathbf{z}|Y=y) = \Pr(Z_0=z_0,Z_1=z_1,Z_2=z_2,Y=y)/\Pr(Y=y)$. For $Y=0$,

$$\begin{aligned} \Pr\left(\mathbf{z}=(1,0,0)^T \middle| Y=0\right) &= \beta_1, \\ \Pr\left(\mathbf{z}=(0,1,0)^T \middle| Y=0\right) &= 0, \\ \Pr\left(\mathbf{z}=(0,0,1)^T \middle| Y=0\right) &= 1-\beta_1. \end{aligned} \quad (16)$$

Therefore, $\mathbf{Z}|(Y=0) \sim \textit{Multinomial}(1;\beta_1,0,1-\beta_1)$. For $Y=1$,

$$\begin{aligned} \Pr\left(\mathbf{z}=(1,0,0)^T \middle| Y=1\right) &= 0, \\ \Pr\left(\mathbf{z}=(0,1,0)^T \middle| Y=1\right) &= \beta_2, \\ \Pr\left(\mathbf{z}=(0,0,1)^T \middle| Y=1\right) &= 1-\beta_2. \end{aligned} \quad (17)$$

Therefore, $\mathbf{Z}|(Y=1) = \textit{Multinomial}(1;0,\beta_2,1-\beta_2)$. Finally, for $Y\geq 2$,

$$\begin{aligned} \Pr\left(\mathbf{z}=(1,0,0)^T \middle| Y=1\right) &= 0, \\ \Pr\left(\mathbf{z}=(0,1,0)^T \middle| Y=1\right) &= 0, \\ \Pr\left(\mathbf{z}=(0,0,1)^T \middle| Y=1\right) &= 1. \end{aligned} \quad (18)$$

Therefore, $\mathbf{Z}|(Y=y) = \textit{Multinomial}(1;0,0,1)$ for $y\geq 2$. □

Corollary 1. *The marginal conditional distribution* $Z_i|Y$ *based on SR1 is*

$$\begin{aligned} Z_0|(Y=y) &\sim \begin{cases} \textit{Bernoulli}(\beta_1) & ;y=0, \\ \textit{Degen}(0) & ;y\neq 0, \end{cases} \\ Z_1|(Y=y) &\sim \begin{cases} \textit{Bernoulli}(\beta_2) & ;y=1, \\ \textit{Degen}(0) & ;y\neq 1, \end{cases} \\ Z_2|(Y=y) &\sim \begin{cases} \textit{Bernoulli}(1-\beta_1) & ;y=0, \\ \textit{Bernoulli}(1-\beta_2) & ;y=1, \\ \textit{Degen}(1) & ;y\geq 2. \end{cases} \end{aligned} \quad (19)$$

Theorem 2. *The conditional distribution for* $X|Y$ *is given as*

$$X|(Y=y) \sim \begin{cases} \textit{ZIPL}(1-\beta_1,\theta) & ;\text{ if } y=0, \\ \textit{OIPL}(1-\beta_2,\theta) & ;\text{ if } y=1, \\ \textit{Degen}(y) & ;\text{ if } y\geq 2. \end{cases} \quad (20)$$

Proof. Recall that $X \sim PL(\theta)$ and $\Pr(X|Y=y) = \Pr(X=x, Y=y)/\Pr(Y=y)$. For $Y=0$,

$$\begin{aligned}\frac{\Pr(X{=}x,Y{=}0)}{\Pr(Y{=}0)} &= \frac{\Pr(X{=}0,Z_1{=}0)}{\Pr(Y{=}0)} I_{(X=0)} + \frac{\Pr(X{=}x,Z_0{=}1)}{\Pr(Y{=}0)} I_{(X\neq 0)} \\ &= \frac{\frac{\theta^2(\theta+2)}{(\theta+1)^3}(1-\omega_1)}{\omega_0+\omega_2\frac{\theta^2(\theta+2)}{(\theta+1)^3}} I_{(X=0)} + \frac{\frac{\theta^2(\theta+x+2)}{(\theta+1)^{x+3}}\omega_0}{\omega_0+\omega_2\frac{\theta^2(\theta+2)}{(\theta+1)^3}} I_{(X\neq 0)} \\ &= \left[1-\beta_1+\beta_1\frac{\theta^2(\theta+2)}{(\theta+1)^3}\right] I_{(X=0)} + \left[\beta_1\frac{\theta^2(\theta+x+2)}{(\theta+1)^{x+3}}\right] I_{(X\neq 0)}.\end{aligned} \tag{21}$$

Therefore, $X|(Y=0) \sim ZIPL(1-\beta_1, \theta)$. For $Y=1$,

$$\begin{aligned}\frac{\Pr(X{=}x,Y{=}1)}{\Pr(Y{=}1)} &= \frac{\Pr(X{=}1,Z_0{=}0)}{\Pr(Y{=}1)} I_{(X=1)} + \frac{\Pr(X{=}x,Z_1{=}1)}{\Pr(Y{=}1)} I_{(X\neq 1)} \\ &= \frac{\frac{\theta^2(\theta+3)}{(\theta+1)^4}(1-\omega_0)}{\omega_1+\omega_2\frac{\theta^2(\theta+3)}{(\theta+1)^4}} I_{(X=1)} + \frac{\frac{\theta^2(\theta+x+2)}{(\theta+1)^{x+3}}\omega_1}{\omega_1+\omega_2\frac{\theta^2(\theta+2)}{(\theta+1)^3}} I_{(X\neq 1)} \\ &= \left[1-\beta_2+\beta_2\frac{\theta^2(\theta+3)}{(\theta+1)^4}\right] I_{(X=1)} + \left[\beta_2\frac{\theta^2(\theta+x+2)}{(\theta+1)^{x+3}}\right] I_{(X\neq 1)}.\end{aligned} \tag{22}$$

Therefore, $X|(Y=1) \sim OIPL(1-\beta_2, \theta)$. Note that the $OIPL$ distribution has not been explored yet. For $Y \geq 2$,

$$\frac{\Pr(X=x, Y=y)}{\Pr(Y=y)} = \frac{\Pr(X=y, Z_2=1)}{\Pr(Y=y)} = 1. \tag{23}$$

Therefore, $X|(Y=y) \sim Degen(y)$ for $y \geq 2$. □

4.2. Second Stochastic Representation

Recall that in SR2, $Y \stackrel{d}{=} (1-Z)\mathrm{H} + ZX$ where $Z \sim Bernoulli(1-w)$, $\mathrm{H} \sim Bernoulli(p)$ and $X \sim PL(\theta)$, such that $Z \perp\!\!\!\perp \mathrm{H} \perp\!\!\!\perp X$.

Theorem 3. *The conditional distribution* $Z|Y$ *is given as*

$$\Pr(Z|Y=y) = \begin{cases} Bernoulli(\lambda_1) & ;\text{if } y=0, \\ Bernoulli(\lambda_2) & ;\text{if } y=1, \\ Degen(1) & ;\text{if } y \geq 2, \end{cases} \tag{24}$$

where

$$\lambda_1 = \frac{(1-w)\frac{\theta^2(\theta+2)}{(\theta+1)^3}}{w(1-p)+(1-w)\frac{\theta^2(\theta+2)}{(\theta+1)^3}} \text{ and } \lambda_2 = \frac{(1-w)\frac{\theta^2(\theta+3)}{(\theta+1)^4}}{wp+(1-w)\frac{\theta^2(\theta+3)}{(\theta+1)^4}},$$

or equivalently, $\lambda_1 = 1-\beta_1$ *and* $\lambda_2 = 1-\beta_2$.

Proof. Recall that $\Pr(Z=z|Y=y) = \Pr(Z=z, Y=y)/\Pr(Y=y)$ and Z can take on the values of either 0 or 1. For $Y=0$,

$$\frac{\Pr(Z=z, Y=0)}{\Pr(Y=0)} = \frac{\Pr(Z=1, X=0)}{\Pr(Y=0)} = \lambda_1. \tag{25}$$

Therefore, $Z|(Y=0) \sim Bernoulli(\lambda_1)$. For $Y=1$,

$$\frac{\Pr(Z=z, Y=1)}{\Pr(Y=1)} = \frac{\Pr(Z=1, X=1)}{\Pr(Y=1)} = \lambda_2.$$

Therefore, $Z|(Y=1) \sim Bernoulli(\lambda_2)$. For $Y \geq 2$,

$$\frac{\Pr(Z=z, Y=y)}{\Pr(Y=y)} = \frac{\Pr(Z=1, X=y)}{\Pr(Y=y)} = 1.$$

Therefore, $Z|(Y=y) \sim Degen(1)$ for $y \geq 2$. Using the reparameterization in SR2, the conditional distribution $Z|Y$ can be written as

$$\Pr(Z|Y=y) = \begin{cases} Bernoulli(1-\beta_1) & ;\text{if } y=0, \\ Bernoulli(1-\beta_2) & ;\text{if } y=1, \\ Degen(1) & ;\text{if } y \geq 2, \end{cases} \quad (26)$$

or equivalently,

$$\Pr(Z|Y=y) = \begin{cases} Bernoulli(\lambda_1) & ;\text{if } y=0, \\ Bernoulli(\lambda_2) & ;\text{if } y=1, \\ Degen(1) & ;\text{if } y \geq 2. \end{cases}$$

□

Theorem 4. *The conditional distribution* $H|Y$ *is given as*

$$\Pr(H|Y=y) = \begin{cases} Bernoulli(\lambda_3) & ;\text{if } y=0, \\ Bernoulli(\lambda_4) & ;\text{if } y=1, \\ Bernoulli(p) & ;\text{if } y \geq 2, \end{cases} \quad (27)$$

where

$$\lambda_3 = \frac{p(1-w)\frac{\theta^2(\theta+2)}{(\theta+1)^3}}{w(1-p)+(1-w)\frac{\theta^2(\theta+2)}{(\theta+1)^3}} \text{ and } \lambda_4 = \frac{p\left[w+(1-w)\frac{\theta^2(\theta+3)}{(\theta+1)^4}\right]}{wp+(1-w)\frac{\theta^2(\theta+3)}{(\theta+1)^4}},$$

or equivalently, $\lambda_3 = p\lambda_1 = p(1-\beta_1)$ *and* $\lambda_4 = 1-(1-p)\lambda_2 = 1-(1-p)(1-\beta_2)$.

Proof. Recall that $\Pr(H=\eta|Y=y) = \Pr(H=\eta, Y=y)/\Pr(Y=y)$ and $H=\eta$ can take on the values of either 0 or 1. For $Y=0$,

$$\frac{\Pr(H=\eta, Y=0)}{\Pr(Y=0)} = \frac{\Pr(H=1, Z=1, X=0)}{\Pr(Y=0)} = \lambda_3. \quad (28)$$

Therefore, $H|(Y=0) \sim Bernoulli(\lambda_3)$. For $Y=1$,

$$\frac{\Pr(H=\eta, Y=1)}{\Pr(Y=1)} = \frac{\Pr(H=1, Z=1, X=1) + \Pr(H=1, Z=0)}{\Pr(Y=1)} = \lambda_4.$$

Therefore, $H|(Y=1) \sim Bernoulli(\lambda_4)$. For $Y \geq 2$,

$$\frac{\Pr(H=\eta, Y=y)}{\Pr(Y=y)} = \frac{\Pr(H=1, Z=1, X=y)}{\Pr(Y=y)} = p.$$

Therefore, $H|(Y=y) \sim Bernoulli(p)$. Using the reparameterization in SR2 and from Theorem 3, the conditional distribution $H|Y$ can be written as

$$\Pr(H|Y=y) = \begin{cases} Bernoulli(p(1-\beta_1)) & ;\text{if } y=0, \\ Bernoulli(1-(1-p)(1-\beta_2)) & ;\text{if } y=1, \\ Bernoulli(p) & ;\text{if } y \geq 2, \end{cases} \quad (29)$$

or equivalently,

$$\Pr(\mathrm{H}|Y=y) = \begin{cases} Bernoulli(p\lambda_1) & ;\text{if } y=0, \\ Bernoulli(1-(1-p)\lambda_2) & ;\text{if } y=1, \\ Bernoulli(p) & ;\text{if } y\geq 2, \end{cases}$$

or equivalently,

$$\Pr(\mathrm{H}|Y=y) = \begin{cases} Bernoulli(\lambda_3) & ;\text{if } y=0, \\ Bernoulli(\lambda_4) & ;\text{if } y=1, \\ Bernoulli(p) & ;\text{if } y\geq 2. \end{cases}$$

□

Theorem 5. *The conditional distribution for X|Y is given as*

$$\mathrm{X}|(Y=y) \sim \begin{cases} ZIPL(1-\beta_1,\theta) & ;\text{if } y=0, \\ OIPL(1-\beta_2,\theta) & ;\text{if } y=1, \\ Degen(y) & ;\text{if } y\geq 2. \end{cases}$$

Proof. Similar to the proof for Theorem 2. □

5. Hypotheses Testing

This section presents two hypotheses involving the presence of one-inflation and a fixed θ. The hypothesis about the presence of one-inflation is examined using a likelihood ratio test, while the hypothesis about a fixed θ involves a two-sided test. The hypothesis about the presence of zero–one-inflation cannot be examined with the likelihood ratio test because the parameter values are situated at the boundary of the confined parameter space [10].

5.1. The Presence of One-Inflation

To investigate the existence of excess ones in the observations, the following null and alternative hypotheses are considered.

$$H_0 : \omega_1 = 0 \text{ vs } H_1 : \omega_1 > 0.$$

The likelihood ratio (LR) test statistics is given as

$$S_1 = -2\{l(\hat{\omega}_{0,H_0}, 0, \hat{\theta}_{H_0}) - l(\hat{\omega}_0, \hat{\omega}_1, \hat{\theta})\},$$

where $l(\cdot)$ refers to the log-likelihood function. This hypothesis tests whether the *ZIPL* distribution is sufficient to describe the data compared to the *ZOIPL* distribution. Zhang et al. [10] investigated a similar test, but their study refers to the zero–one-inflated Poisson distribution. The authors mentioned that H_0 results in ω_0 being on the edge of the parameter space. Moreover, the appropriate null distribution is a mixture of $Degen(0)$ and ${\chi^2}_{(1)}$ with equal proportion [10,15]. The same conclusion can be drawn for this distribution since the nature of Poisson and *ZOIPL* distributions is similar to that of the zero–one-inflated Poisson distribution. Therefore, H_0 is rejected if $\Pr(S_1 > s_1) = \frac{1}{2}\Pr\left({\chi^2}_{(1)} > s_1\right)$ is smaller than the significance level, which is set at $\alpha = 0.05$. For more information on the asymptotic properties of likelihood ratio tests, see [16].

5.2. For Fixed $\theta = \theta_0$

To investigate the existence of excess ones in the observations, the following null and alternative hypotheses are considered.

$$H_0 : \theta = \theta_0 \text{ vs } H_1 : \theta \neq \theta_0.$$

The likelihood ratio (LR) test statistics is given as

$$S_2 = -2\{l(\hat{\omega}_{0,H_0}, \hat{\omega}_{1,H_0}, \theta_0) - l(\hat{\omega}_0, \hat{\omega}_1, \hat{\theta})\}.$$

This hypothesis investigates if a fixed θ_0 but varying ω_0 and ω_1 are adequate in describing the data with comparison to the $ZOIPL$ distribution with three varying parameters. The H_0 is rejected if $\Pr(S_2 > s_2) = \Pr\left(\chi^2{}_{(1)} > s_2\right)$ is less than the significant level, which is set at $\alpha = 0.05$.

6. Simulation Studies

In this section, the hypotheses and its corresponding likelihood ratio tests will be investigated via simulation studies. The simulation studies aim to compare the type I error rates under H_0 and the powers under H_1.

6.1. Data Generation

To generate random data which follow the $ZOIPL$ distribution, first, recall the SR1. We independently draw $z_1^{(m)}, \ldots, z_n^{(m)} \sim Multinomial(1; \omega_0, \omega_1, \omega_2)$ for $m = 1, 2, \ldots, M$, where $z_i^{(m)} = \left(Z_{0i}^{(m)}, Z_{1i}^{(m)}, Z_{2i}^{(m)}\right)^T$ for $i = 1, 2, \ldots, n$. We also draw $X_1^{(m)}, \ldots, X_n^{(m)} \sim PL(\theta)$ independently. Then, we set $Y_i^{(m)} = Z_{1i}^{(m)} + Z_{2i}^{(m)} \times X_i^{(m)}$ for $i = 1, 2, \ldots, n$ and $m = 1, 2, \ldots, M$, where $M = 1000$.

6.2. General Algorithm for Hypothesis Testing

Let r be the number of rejecting the H_0. The type I error rate is obtained by computing r/M when H_0 is true, whereas the power of the test is obtained by computing r/M when we fail to reject H_0. For the type I error and the power of the test, the sample sizes are set to be $n = 200$ (200) 1000. The procedure to determine the type I error rate and the power of the test is repeated 1000 times. The adjusted Wald technique [17] is used to obtain the 95% confidence interval for the type I error rates. Bradley's liberal criterion [18] has outlined that if the type I error rates are in the interval $\alpha \pm 0.05\alpha$, the test is robust. In this case, $\alpha = 0.05$, so the test is considered robust when type I error rates are between 0.025 and 0.075.

6.3. The Presence of One-Inflation

Recall that the $H_0 : \omega_1 = 0$ and $H_1 : \omega_1 > 0$. For this simulation study, the value of θ is fixed at 1.0, while the value of ω_0 varies: $\omega_0 = 0.6,\ 0.7,\ 0.8,\ 0.9$. These different values of ω_0 were selected based on previous studies [8] for the $ZOIPL$ distribution. These ω_0s are used to study the type I error rates. The results of the simulation studies are shown in Figure 1. Figure 1 shows the type I error rate plots for varying ω_0. When $\omega_0 = 0.60$, a sample size of 400 is sufficient to make the type I error rate fall below 0.05. On the other hand, when $\omega_0 = 0.70,\ 0.90$, at least a sample size of 800 is needed to make a type I error rate fall below 0.05. Surprisingly, when $\omega_0 = 0.80$, even 200 samples are sufficient. It can be observed that for each value of ω_0, the type I error rates decrease with increasing sample size n and fall below 0.05. Zhang et al. [10] mentioned that the smaller the type I error rate, the better the performance of the likelihood ratio test in controlling the error rates.

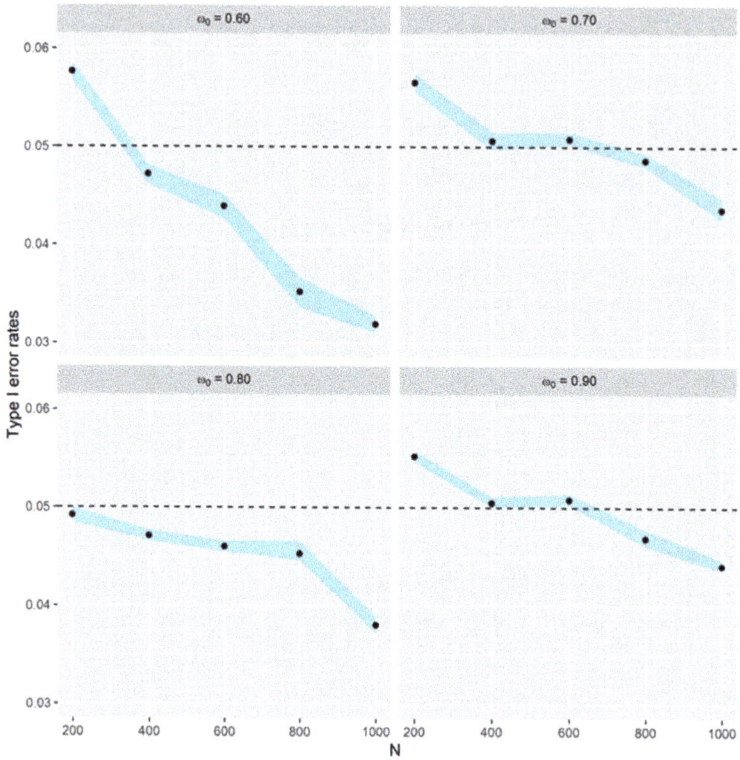

Figure 1. Type I error rates for different values of ω_0 and N.

To assess the power of the test, the values of ω_1 under H_1 are set at 0.02, 0.04, 0.06, 0.08, 0.10, 0.12 with $\theta = 1.0$. Let r be the number of rejections of H_0. The power of the test is obtained by calculating r/M when $\omega_1 > 0$. The results of the simulation studies are shown in Figure 2. Figure 2 shows the plots for the power of the test when ω_1 varies. It can be observed that the power of the test increases when ω_1 and the sample size n increase. Achieving at least 80% power can be carried out for $\omega_1 \geq 0.06$ with at least a sample size of 800. For $\omega_1 < 0.06$, a large sample size is required for the test to obtain 80% power. This means that when ω_1 is small and close to zero, the test cannot accurately identify the existence of excess ones in the data. Generally, the larger the value of ω_1, the quicker the power of the test increases as the sample size increases.

6.4. *Fixed* $\theta = \theta_0$

Recall that the $H_0 : \theta = \theta_0$ and $H_1 : \theta \neq \theta_0$. For this simulation study, the value of θ_0 varies: $\theta_0 = 0.5,\ 1.0,\ 1.5,\ 2.0$ for the study of Type I error rates. The values for $\omega_0 = 0.75$ and $\omega_1 = 0.10$ are fixed. Figure 3 shows the simulation results of the test. From Figure 3, when $\theta = 0.5,\ 1.0$, a sample size of 600 is sufficient to make a type I error rate fall below 0.05. When $\theta = 1.5$, at least a sample size of 800 is needed to make a type I error rate fall below 0.05. Furthermore, a total of 1000 samples are required when $\theta = 2.0$. Generally, the larger the value of θ, the larger the sample size required so that the type I error becomes smaller than 0.05.

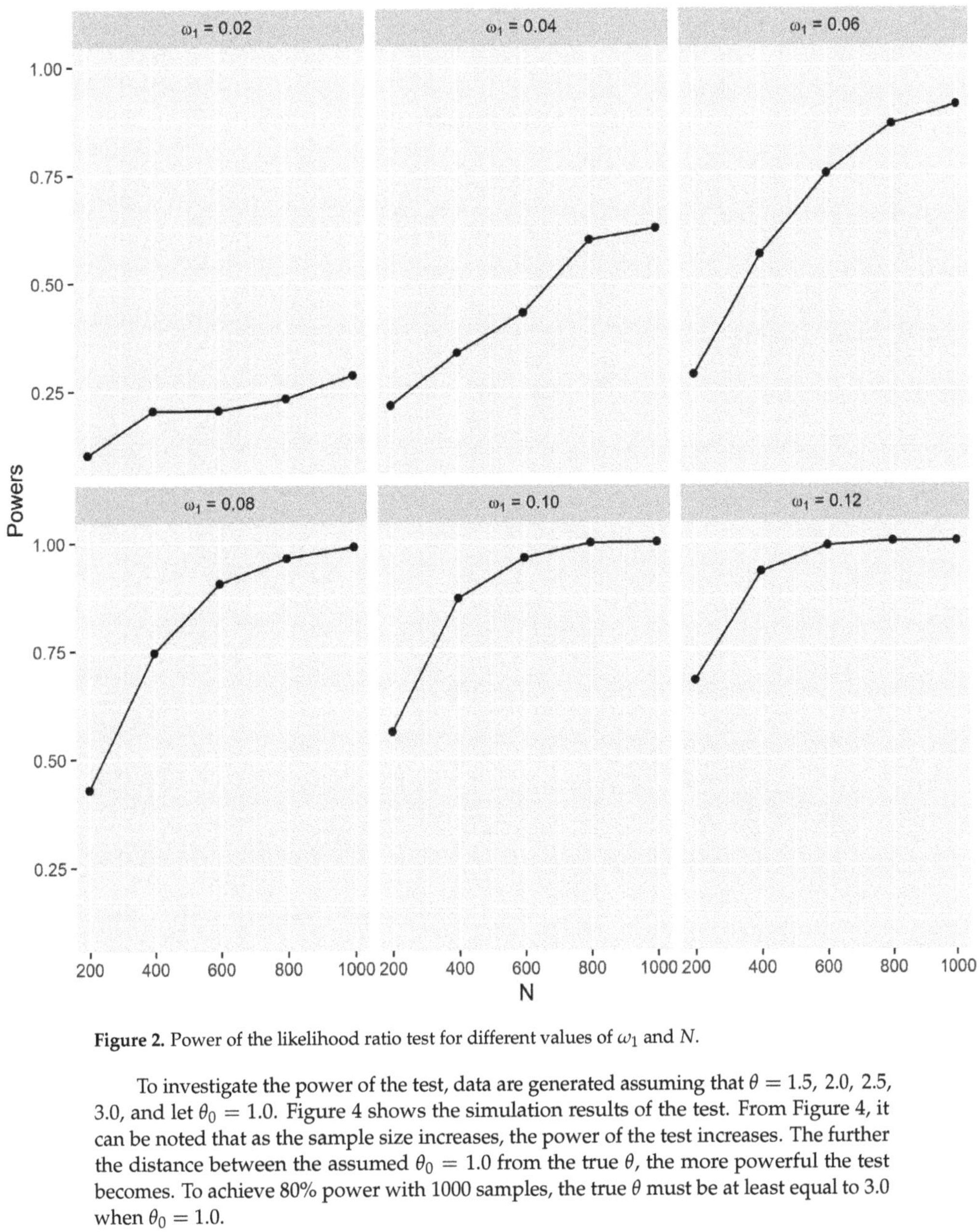

Figure 2. Power of the likelihood ratio test for different values of ω_1 and N.

To investigate the power of the test, data are generated assuming that $\theta = 1.5$, 2.0, 2.5, 3.0, and let $\theta_0 = 1.0$. Figure 4 shows the simulation results of the test. From Figure 4, it can be noted that as the sample size increases, the power of the test increases. The further the distance between the assumed $\theta_0 = 1.0$ from the true θ, the more powerful the test becomes. To achieve 80% power with 1000 samples, the true θ must be at least equal to 3.0 when $\theta_0 = 1.0$.

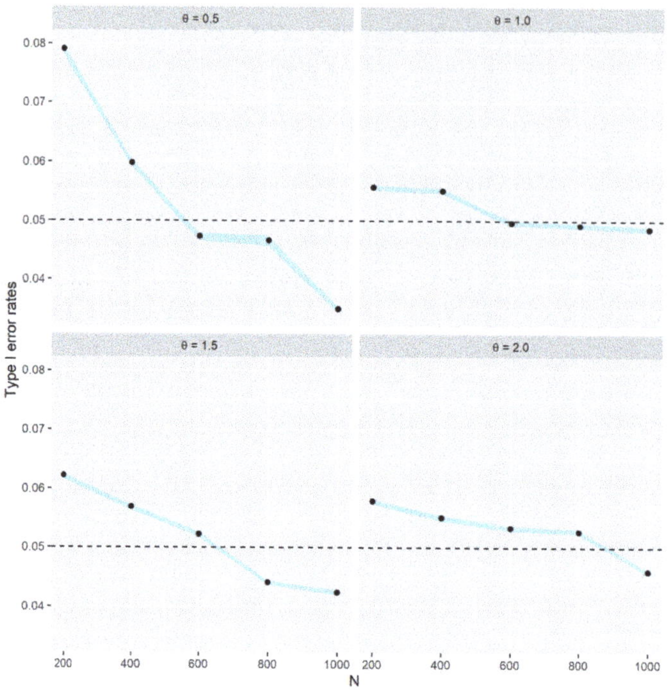

Figure 3. Type I error rates for different values of θ and N.

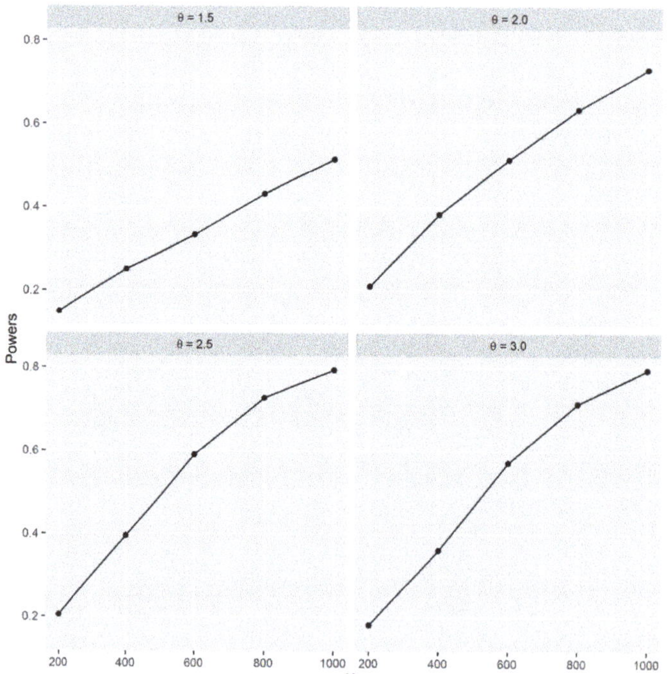

Figure 4. Power of the likelihood ratio test for different values of θ and N.

7. Conclusions

In this paper, various stochastic representations for the zero–one-inflated Poisson Lindley distribution have been studied extensively. The stochastic representations allow for us to view the zero–one-inflated Poisson Lindley distribution in different ways by combining several established distributions such as multinomial, degenerate, Poisson Lindley and other distributions. When handling data with excess zeroes and ones, as well as dispersion, these stochastic representations can be exploited. For example, if we are interested in studying positive count data distributions (observed) but we are presented with a full set of data containing both observed and unobserved values, instead of separating the full set of data into both observed and unobserved values, which may incur unnecessary costs, one may use the full set of data and use the fourth stochastic representation to identify the estimated parameter which describes the distribution of the unobserved data.

Besides that, some hypothesis tests have been conducted to investigate the presence of one-inflation in addition to fixed-rate parameters. The extensive simulation studies conducted investigate the ability of the test to handle both type I error and type II error rates in terms of errors as well as powers. All tests, which involve likelihood ratios, are found to be able to handle type I error rates and are found to be powerful as the sample sizes increases; hence, are found to be useful. It is suggested that a sample size of at least 1000 is sufficient for the tests to be useful.

Author Contributions: Conceptualization, R.R.M.T. and N.I.; methodology, R.R.M.T. and N.I.; software, R.R.M.T.; validation, N.I.; formal analysis, R.R.M.T.; writing—original draft preparation, R.R.M.T.; writing—review and editing, R.R.M.T. and N.I.; visualization, R.R.M.T.; supervision, N.I. All authors have read and agreed to the published version of the manuscript.

Funding: This research received no external funding.

Data Availability Statement: Not applicable.

Conflicts of Interest: The authors declare no conflict of interest.

References

1. Iddi, S.; Doku-Amponsah, K. Statistical Model for Overdispersed Count Outcome with Many Zeros: An Approach for Marginal Inference. *S. Afr. Stat. J.* **2016**, *50*, 313–337. [CrossRef]
2. Lambert, D. Zero-Inflated Poisson Regression, with an Application to Defects in Manufacturing. *Technometrics* **1992**, *34*, 1–14. [CrossRef]
3. Neelon, B.H.; O'Malley, A.J.; Normand, S.-L.T. A Bayesian Model for Repeated Measures Zero-Inflated Count Data with Application to Outpatient Psychiatric Service Use. *Stat. Model.* **2010**, *10*, 421–439. [CrossRef] [PubMed]
4. Ridout, M.; Demétrio, C.G.B.; Hinde, J. Models for Count Data with Many Zeros. In Proceedings of the XIXth International Biometric Conference, Cape Town, South Africa, 14–18 December 1998; International Biometric Society Invited Papers: Cape Town, South Africa, 1998; Volume 19, pp. 179–192.
5. Young, D.S.; Roemmele, E.S.; Yeh, P. Zero-inflated Modeling Part I: Traditional Zero-inflated Count Regression Models, Their Applications, and Computational Tools. *Wiley Interdiscip. Rev. Comput. Stat.* **2020**, *14*, e1541. [CrossRef]
6. Lin, T.H.; Tsai, M. Modeling Health Survey Data with Excessive Zero and K Responses. *Stat. Med.* **2012**, *32*, 1572–1583. [CrossRef] [PubMed]
7. Jornsatian, C.; Bodhisuwan, W. Zero-One Inflated Negative Binomial—Beta Exponential Distribution for Count Data with Many Zeros and Ones. *Commun. Stat.-Theory Methods* **2022**, *51*, 8517–8531. [CrossRef]
8. Tajuddin, R.R.M.; Ismail, N.; Ibrahim, K.; Bakar, S.A.A. A New Zero–One-Inflated Poisson–Lindley Distribution for Modelling Overdispersed Count Data. *Bull. Malays. Math. Sci. Soc.* **2022**, *45*, 21–35. [CrossRef]
9. Melkersson, M.; Olsson, C. *Is Visiting the Dentist a Good Habit?: Analyzing Count Data with Excess Zeros and Excess Ones*; University of Umeå: Umeå, Sweden, 1999.
10. Zhang, C.; Tian, G.L.; Ng, K.W. Properties of the Zero-and-One Inflated Poisson Distribution and Likelihood-Based Inference Methods. *Stat. Interface* **2016**, *9*, 11–32. [CrossRef]
11. Sankaran, M. 275. Note: The Discrete Poisson-Lindley Distribution. *Biometrics* **1970**, *26*, 145–149. [CrossRef]
12. Ghitany, M.E.; Al-Mutairi, D.K. Estimation Methods for the Discrete Poisson–Lindley Distribution. *J. Stat. Comput. Simul.* **2009**, *79*, 1–9. [CrossRef]

13. Tajuddin, R.R.M.; Ismail, N.; Ibrahim, K. Estimating Population Size of Criminals: A New Horvitz–Thompson Estimator under One-Inflated Positive Poisson–Lindley Model. *Crime Delinq.* **2022**, *68*, 1004–1034. [CrossRef]
14. Borah, M.; Nath, A.D. A Study on the Inflated Poisson Lindley Distribution. *J. Indian Soc. Agric. Stat.* **2001**, *54*, 317–323.
15. Joe, H.; Zhu, R. Generalized Poisson Distribution: The Property of Mixture of Poisson and Comparison with Negative Binomial Distribution. *Biom. J.* **2005**, *47*, 219–229. [CrossRef] [PubMed]
16. Self, S.G.; Liang, K.-Y. Asymptotic Properties of Maximum Likelihood Estimators and Likelihood Ratio Tests under Nonstandard Conditions. *J. Am. Stat. Assoc.* **1987**, *82*, 605–610. [CrossRef]
17. Agresti, A.; Coull, B.A. Approximate Is Better than "Exact" for Interval Estimation of Binomial Proportions. *Am. Stat.* **1998**, *52*, 119–126. [CrossRef]
18. Bradley, J.V. Robustness? *Br. J. Math. Stat. Psychol.* **1978**, *31*, 144–152. [CrossRef]

mathematics

MDPI

Article

Unit Exponential Probability Distribution: Characterization and Applications in Environmental and Engineering Data Modeling

Hassan S. Bakouch [1,2], Tassaddaq Hussain [3], Marina Tošić [4], Vladica S. Stojanović [5,*] and Najla Qarmalah [6,*]

1 Department of Mathematics, College of Science, Qassim University, Buraydah 51452, Saudi Arabia; h.bakouch@qu.edu.sa
2 Department of Mathematics, Faculty of Science, Tanta University, Tanta 31111, Egypt; hassan.bakouch@science.tanta.edu.eg
3 Department of Statistics, Mirpur University of Science and Technology, Mirpur 10250, Pakistan; tassaddaq.stat@must.edu.pk
4 Department of Mathematics, Faculty of Sciences & Mathematics, University of Priština in Kosovska Mitrovica, 38220 Kosovska Mitrovica, Serbia; marina.tosic@pr.ac.rs
5 Department of Informatics & Computer Sciences, University of Criminal Investigation and Police Studies, 11060 Belgrade, Serbia
6 Department of Mathematical Sciences, College of Science, Princess Nourah bint Abdulrahman University, Riyadh 11671, Saudi Arabia
* Correspondence: vladica.stojanovic@kpu.edu.rs (V.S.S.); nmbinqurmalah@pnu.edu.sa (N.Q.); Tel.: +381-60-390-0552 (V.S.S.); +966-11-823-6238 (N.Q.)

Abstract: Distributions with bounded support show considerable sparsity over those with unbounded support, despite the fact that there are a number of real-world contexts where observations take values from a bounded range (proportions, percentages, and fractions are typical examples). For proportion modeling, a flexible family of two-parameter distribution functions associated with the exponential distribution is proposed here. The mathematical and statistical properties of the novel distribution are examined, including the quantiles, mode, moments, hazard rate function, and its characterization. The parameter estimation procedure using the maximum likelihood method is carried out, and applications to environmental and engineering data are also considered. To this end, various statistical tests are used, along with some other information criterion indicators to determine how well the model fits the data. The proposed model is found to be the most efficient plan in most cases for the datasets considered.

Keywords: unit distribution; statistical model; hazard function; characterizations; estimation; simulation; application

MSC: 60E05; 62E15; 62F10

1. Introduction

Proportional variables are often encountered in data science, where they are used as stochastic models that describe, for instance, the number of successes divided by the number of attempts, party votes, the proportion of money spent on a cause, or the attendance rate of public events. Therefore, proportion analysis is necessary in various fields such as healthcare, economics, and engineering. Usually, to model the behavior of such random variables (RVs), distributions defined on a unit interval are used, which are highly valuable in modeling proportions and percentages. It is conceivable to model and forecast such variables, but one must look outside the traditional model because the data are limited to the range $(0, 1)$. For further study, readers are referred to [1–3].

In this context, the beta model was proposed by Bayes [4], which in many fields of statistics is a convenient and helpful model widely used for modeling percentages and proportions. However, there are a number of scenarios where it seems to not be a suitable one.

Therefore, alternatively, several distributions have been developed for modeling bounded variables like proportions, indices, and rates, such as the unit distribution studied in [5], the unit Johnson distribution proposed in [6], the four-parameter distribution introduced in [7], the distribution proposed in [8], the Topp–Leone distribution studied in [9], and the unit gamma distribution introduced in [10]. More recently, many other unit interval distribution functions have been introduced, such as the cumulative distribution function (CDF) quantile distribution [11], new unit interval distribution [12], the unit-inverse Gaussian distribution [13], the log-xgamma distribution [14], unit Gompertz, unit Lindley, and unit Weibull distributions [15–17], the log-weighted exponential distribution [18], the unit Johnson SU distribution [19], the unit log–log distribution [20], the new unit distribution [21], the unit–power Burr X distribution [22], and the unit Teissier distribution [23], while in [24], the unit interval distribution via the conditional distribution approach was studied. Notice that all of these distributions are potential candidates for describing proportions. It is worth noting that the approaches mentioned above are mainly based on conventional strategies, namely the following:

(i) Log transformation approaches;
(ii) The CDF and quantile methodology;
(iii) Reciprocal transformation;
(iv) Exponential transformation;
(v) The conditional distribution methodology;
(vi) The T-X family approach.

However, all of the earlier models and others seem to be casual ways of generating unit interval distributions. In the current study, our motivational strategies begin with recalling the epsilon function examined in [25], which is defined as

$$\varepsilon_{\lambda,a}(x) = \begin{cases} \left(\dfrac{a+x}{a-x}\right)^{\frac{\lambda a}{2}}, & -a < x < a \\ 0, & \text{otherwise,} \end{cases} \tag{1}$$

where $\lambda \in \mathbb{R} \setminus \{0\}$ and $a > 0$. For comprehensive details about the above and its bounded version, readers are referred to [25]. The function $y = \varepsilon_{\lambda,a}(x)$ is the solution of an epsilon differential equation of the first order:

$$y' = \frac{\lambda\, a^2 y}{a^2 - x^2},$$

In addition, it satisfies the following property of the exponential limit:

$$\lim_{a \to +\infty} \varepsilon_{\lambda,a}(x) = e^{\lambda x}, \quad \forall x \in (-a, +a).$$

Furthermore, it is also related to the CDF class proposed in [7], which is based on the exponential function. However, the unit interval variants thus proposed differ from the design of our CDF. As will be seen, the distribution proposed here is much more flexible and exhibits both positive and negative skewness. Moreover, as will be seen below, the hazard rate function (HRF) of the proposed model purely yields an increasing failure rate (IFR) behavior, or all values of $\lambda > 0$ thus belong to the decreasing mean residual life (DMRL) class.

The rest of the manuscript is organized as follows. In the next section, the basic stochastic properties of the proposed distribution are presented. The mode, quantiles, HRF, and characterization of the new distribution, among other properties, are examined. Section 3 shows the procedure for estimating the parameters of the proposed distribution using the maximum likelihood (ML) method, along with a Monte Carlo simulation study. Applications to a number of real-world datasets are given in Section 4, while the last section provides some concluding remarks.

2. The Proposed Unit Exponential Distribution

Let X be a bounded RV, and without loss of generality, it is convenient that values of X belong to the unit interval $[0,1]$. Also, suppose that the CDF of the RV X is defined by the following equality:

$$F(x) = \begin{cases} 1 - \exp\left[\alpha\left(1 - \left(\frac{1+x}{1-x}\right)^{\beta}\right)\right], & 0 \le x < 1; \\ 1, & x = 1; \end{cases} \tag{2}$$

where $\alpha, \beta > 0$. The CDF given by Equation (2) is called the unit exponential distribution (UED) (with the parameters α and β) and referred to as the UED (α, β). Note that the UED is related to the epsilon function defined in Equation (1). Indeed, when taking $a = 1$ and $\beta = \lambda/2$, Equation (2) becomes

$$F(x) = 1 - \exp\left[\alpha\left(1 - \varepsilon_{2\beta,1}(x)\right)\right],$$

when $0 \le x < 1$. Note that in this form, the function $F(x)$ represents the composition of the CDF of the so-called one-shifted exponential distribution [26] and the epsilon function mentioned above. At the same time, it is obvious that $F(x)$ approaches 0 and 1 when $x \to 0$ and $x \to 1$, respectively, and thus represents a valid unit CDF. Graphical representations of the CDFs of the UED for different parameters α and β are shown in Figure 1. It portrays that for $\alpha \to 0$ and $\beta \ge 3$, the CDF curve is concave (bent inward), while for $\alpha \to 1$, the CDF curve is convex (bent outward).

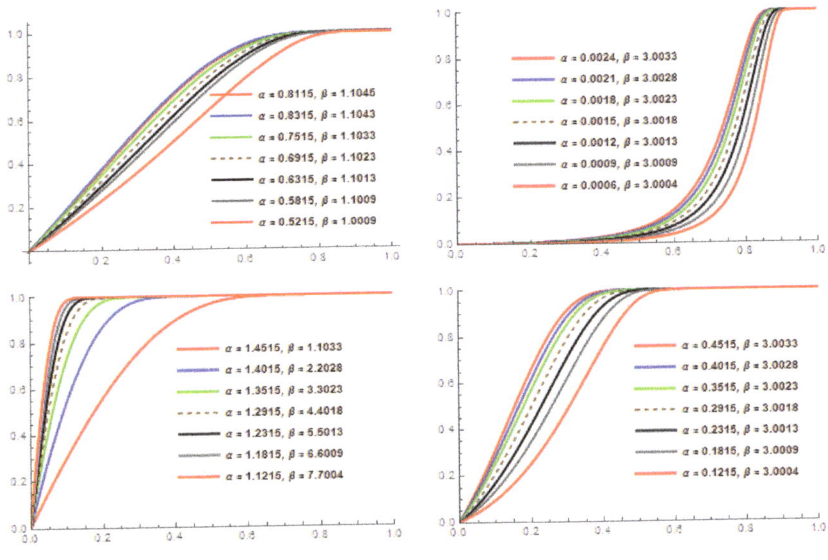

Figure 1. Plots of the CDFs of the UED for varying parameters.

By differentiating the CDF given by Equation (2), the probability density function (PDF) of the UED when $0 \le x < 1$ can be easily obtained as follows:

$$f(x) = \frac{2\alpha\beta}{1-x^2}\left(\frac{1+x}{1-x}\right)^{\beta}\overline{F}(x). \tag{3}$$

Here, $\overline{F}(x) = 1 - F(x)$ is the tail of the CDF $F(x)$. Notice that the UED has two parameters $\alpha, \beta > 0$, where one is like a dispersion and the other is like a shape parameter. Also, this PDF structure is similar to one of the simpler forms of the so-called proper dispersion models introduced in [7], but it does not belong to that class.

2.1. Properties of the Model

In practice, it is required that the proposed UED, whose PDF is defined by Equation (3), presents flexibility to describe the data adequately. In this regard, it exhibits negative and positive skewness for all values of $\alpha > 0$ and $\beta > 0$. The flexibility property of the UED can be visualized as in Figure 2, where the various cases of the appropriate PDF are shown, depending on the parameter values α and $\beta > 0$. These plots show the different skewness possibilities and the existence of modes of the UED that can be used to fit some real-world datasets.

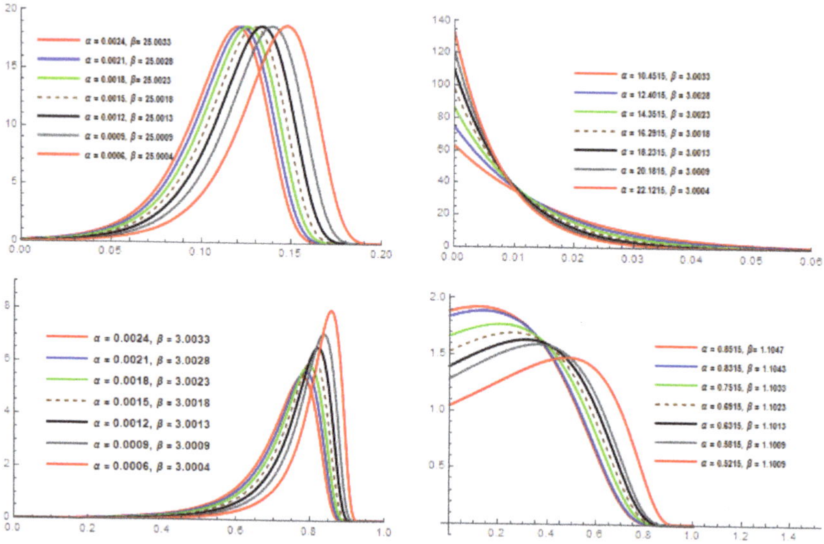

Figure 2. Plots of the PDFs of the UED for varying parameters.

2.1.1. Quantile

As a first property, the quantile function of the UED is quite manageable. By inverting the CDF $F(x)$, given by Equation (2), the quantile function is determined as follows:

$$Q(y) = F^{-1}(y) = \frac{(1 - \ln(1-y)/\alpha)^{1/\beta} - 1}{(1 - \ln(1-y)/\alpha)^{1/\beta} + 1}, \quad y \in (0,1).$$

Thanks to this function, the median of the UED is given by

$$M_e = Q(1/2) = \frac{(1 + \ln 2/\alpha)^{1/\beta} - 1}{(1 + \ln 2/\alpha)^{1/\beta} + 1}.$$

Using $Q(y)$, we are able to define various measures of skewness and kurtosis, as well as important actuarial measures (see, for example, [2,27]).

2.1.2. Mode

Note that Figure 2 shows that the PDF of the proposed model can have (at most) one mode. To identify this property, we should prove the following result, which collects these findings and their implications:

Proposition 1. *The PDF $f(x)$, given by Equation (3), has a unique mode if and only if $0 < \alpha < 1$. Otherwise, the UED does not have any modes.*

Proof. The mode of the PDF $f(x)$ is a solution of the equation $f'(x) = 0$, which after certain calculations and simplification becomes

$$x + \beta - \alpha\beta\left(\frac{1+x}{1-x}\right)^{\beta} = 0. \tag{4}$$

If we denote by $\psi(x)$ the left-hand side of Equation (4), then the following is easily obtained:

$$\lim_{x\to 1^-} \psi(x) < 0 \quad \text{and} \quad \lim_{x\to 0^+} \psi(x) = \beta(1-\alpha).$$

Obviously, the inequalities $0 < \alpha < 1$ and $\beta > 0$ give $\beta(1-\alpha) > 0$. Then, Equation (4) has real solutions, which guarantee that $f(x)$ has at least one mode. Next, the function $\psi(x)$ defined above has the derivative

$$\psi'(x) = 1 - \frac{2\alpha\beta^2}{1-x^2}\left(\frac{1+x}{1-x}\right)^{\beta}.$$

Note that $\psi'(x)$ is strictly decreasing because

$$\psi''(x) = -\frac{4\alpha\beta^2(x+\beta)}{(1-x^2)^2}\left(\frac{1+x}{1-x}\right)^{\beta} < 0.$$

This fact then implies that the previously detected mode is unique. □

2.1.3. Behavior of the PDF at $x \to 0^+$ and $x \to 1^-$

The behavior of the PDF $f(x)$ at the ends of the unit interval (i.e., when $x \to 0^+$ and $x \to 1^-$) indicates how $f(x)$ converges or not in these limits. In terms of data modeling, these facts would reflect the empirical limits on the extremes that the data show. At the limit $x \to 0^+$, according to Equations (2) and (3), the following is easily obtained:

$$\lim_{x\to 0^+} f(x) = 2\alpha\beta.$$

On the other hand, to analyze the limit of $f(x)$ at $x \to 1^-$, we observe the function $\ln f(x)$, which can be written as

$$\begin{aligned}\ln f(x) &= \ln(2\alpha\beta) + (\beta-1)\ln(1+x) - (\beta+1)\ln(1-x) + \alpha\left(1 - \left(\frac{1+x}{1-x}\right)^{\beta}\right) \\ &= \frac{1}{(1-x)^{\beta}}\Big((1-x)^{\beta}(\ln(2\alpha\beta) + (\beta-1)\ln(1+x) - (\beta+1)\ln(1-x) + \alpha) \\ &\qquad -\alpha(1+x)^{\beta}\Big).\end{aligned}$$

Hence, we obtain

$$\lim_{x\to 1^-} (1-x)^{\beta} \ln f(x) = -\alpha\, 2^{\beta},$$

which implies that in a data representation, the data would decay at exponential rates when $x \to 1^-$.

2.1.4. Moments

Let X be an RV with the CDF given by Equation (2). Then, the rth moment of X, using partial integration, can be expressed as follows:

$$\begin{aligned} E(X^r) &= \int_0^1 x^r dF(x) = \int_1^0 x^r d(1-F(x)) = r\int_0^1 x^{r-1}(1-F(x))dx \\ &= r\exp(\alpha)\int_0^1 x^{r-1}\exp\left[-\alpha\left(\frac{1+x}{1-x}\right)^{\beta}\right]dx. \end{aligned}$$

This integral can be determined numerically with the use of many pieces of software, such as R, MATHEMATICA, and MATLAB. The following result proposes a series expansion of $E(X^r)$ that can be used for numerical approximation:

Proposition 2. *The rth moment of X can be expanded as follows:*

$$E(X^r) = \frac{2r\alpha^{1/\beta}\exp(\alpha)}{\beta}\sum_{k=0}^{r-1}\sum_{\ell=0}^{+\infty}\binom{r-1}{k}\binom{-(r+1)}{\ell}(-1)^k\alpha^{(k+\ell+1)/\beta}\Gamma\left(-\frac{k+\ell+1}{\beta},\alpha\right),$$

where $\Gamma(a,x)$ denotes the upper incomplete gamma function (i.e., $\Gamma(a,x)=\int_x^{+\infty}t^{a-1}\exp(-t)dt$).

Proof. By applying the change in the variable $y=(1+x)/(1-x)$, we have

$$E(X^r) = 2r\exp(\alpha)\int_1^{+\infty}\frac{(y-1)^{r-1}}{(y+1)^{r+1}}\exp(-\alpha y^{\beta})dy. \tag{5}$$

Then, using the "generalized version" of the binomial formula two times in a row, since $y>1$, we find

$$\begin{aligned} \frac{(y-1)^{r-1}}{(y+1)^{r+1}} &= y^{-2}\frac{(1-1/y)^{r-1}}{(1+1/y)^{r+1}} \\ &= y^{-2}\left[\sum_{k=0}^{r-1}\binom{r-1}{k}(-1)^k y^{-k}\right]\left[\sum_{\ell=0}^{+\infty}\binom{-(r+1)}{\ell}y^{-\ell}\right] \\ &= \sum_{k=0}^{r-1}\sum_{\ell=0}^{+\infty}\binom{r-1}{k}\binom{-(r+1)}{\ell}(-1)^k y^{-(k+\ell+2)}. \end{aligned} \tag{6}$$

Also, with the change in the variable $z=\alpha y^{\beta}$, the following is obtained:

$$\begin{aligned} \int_1^{+\infty} y^{-(k+\ell+2)}\exp(-\alpha y^{\beta})dy &= \frac{\alpha^{(k+\ell+1)/\beta}}{\beta}\int_{\alpha}^{+\infty} z^{-(k+\ell+1)/\beta-1}\exp(-z)dz \\ &= \frac{\alpha^{(k+\ell+1)/\beta}}{\beta}\Gamma\left(-\frac{k+\ell+1}{\beta},\alpha\right). \end{aligned} \tag{7}$$

Therefore, by substituting Equations (6) and (7) into Equation (5), as well as by inverting the sign of the integral and the sum, the desired result is obtained. □

2.1.5. Failure (Hazard) Rate Function

The HRF of the UED is given by

$$h(x) = \frac{f(x)}{\bar{F}(x)} = \frac{2\alpha\beta}{1-x^2}\left(\frac{1+x}{1-x}\right)^{\beta}. \tag{8}$$

When $x\to 0^+$, the limit of $h(x)$ is $2\alpha\beta>0$, and when $x\to 1^-$, the limit is $+\infty$. Thus, this function is strictly increasing, as can be seen in Figure 3, meaning that when x increases, the frequency at which an engineered system or component fails also increases.

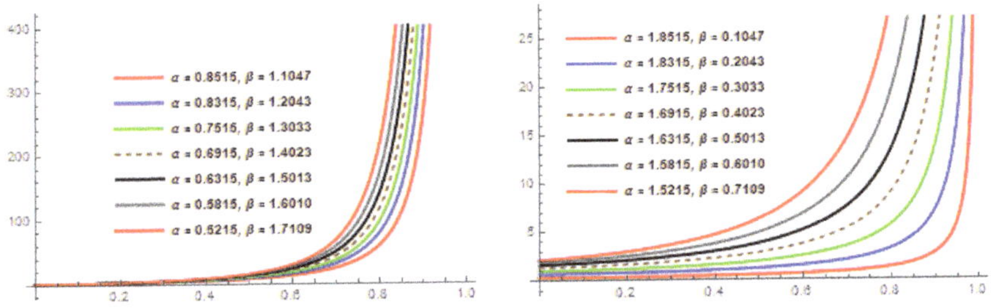

Figure 3. Plots of the HRFs of the UED for varying parameters.

2.2. Characterizations

To interpret the HRF realistically, we shall try to characterize Equation (3) with hazard and mean residual life functions. Characterization in general terms implies that under certain conditions, a family of distributions is the only one possessing a designated property. Researchers can identify the actual probability distribution with the help of characterization. For detailed study, readers are referred to the works of Ahsanullah et al. [28,29] and Hamedani [30]. In this regard, we characterize the proposed model with the HRF and truncated moments, and the characterizing conditions are defined as follows:

Proposition 3. *The RV* $X : \Omega \longrightarrow (0, +\infty)$ *has a continuous PDF* $f(x)$ *if and only if the HRF* $h(x)$ *satisfies the following equation:*

$$\frac{f'(x)}{f(x)} = \frac{h'(x)}{h(x)} - h(x). \tag{9}$$

Proof. According to the definition of the HRF, given by the first equality in Equation (8), it follows that

$$\frac{h'(x)}{h(x)} = \frac{f'(x)\overline{F}(x) + f^2(x)}{\overline{F}^2(x)} \cdot \frac{\overline{F}(x)}{f(x)} = \frac{f'(x)}{f(x)} + h(x).$$

Thus, the statement of proposition immediately follows. □

Proposition 4. *The RV* $X : \Omega \longrightarrow (0, +\infty)$ *has a UED* (α, β) *if and only if the HRF* $h(x)$*, defined by Equation* (8)*, satisfies the following equation:*

$$\frac{h'(x)}{(h(x))^2} = \frac{x+\beta}{\alpha\beta}\left(\frac{1-x}{1+x}\right)^{\beta}. \tag{10}$$

Proof. *Necessity*: Assume that $X \sim \text{UED}(\alpha, \beta)$, with the PDF $f(x)$ defined by Equation (3). Then, the logarithm of this PDF, in the same way as in Section 2.1.3, can be expressed as:

$$\ln(f(x)) = \ln(2\alpha\beta) + (\beta - 1)\ln(1+x) - (\beta+1)\ln(1-x) + \alpha\left(1 - \left(\frac{1+x}{1-x}\right)^{\beta}\right).$$

By differentiating both sides of this equality with respect to x, we obtain

$$\frac{f'(x)}{f(x)} = \frac{\beta-1}{1+x} + \frac{\beta+1}{1-x} - \frac{2\alpha\beta}{(1-x)^2}\left(\frac{1+x}{1-x}\right)^{\beta-1} = \frac{2}{1-x^2}\left(x + \beta - \alpha\beta\left(\frac{1+x}{1-x}\right)^{\beta}\right). \tag{11}$$

Thus, according to Equations (8) and (9), it follows that

$$\frac{h'(x)}{h(x)} = \frac{f'(x)}{f(x)} + h(x) = \frac{2(x+\beta)}{1-x^2},$$

which after certain simplification yields Equation (10).

Sufficiency: Suppose that Equation (10) holds. After integration, it can be rewritten as follows:

$$\int \frac{h'(x)}{(h(x))^2}dx = \int \frac{x+\beta}{\alpha\beta}\left(\frac{1-x}{1+x}\right)^{\beta}dx,$$

That is, we have

$$-\frac{1}{h(x)} = \frac{x^2-1}{2\alpha\beta}\left(\frac{1-x}{1+x}\right)^{\beta}.$$

From the above equation, we obtain the HRF $h(x)$ as shown in Equation (8). Furthermore, by replacing this function in Equation (9), and after integration, we obtain

$$\begin{aligned}\int \frac{f'(x)}{f(x)}dx &= 2\int \left[\frac{x+\beta}{1-x^2} - \frac{\alpha\beta}{1-x^2}\left(\frac{1+x}{1-x}\right)^{\beta}\right]dx + C_1 \\ &= (\beta-1)\ln(1+x) - (\beta+1)\ln(1-x) - \alpha\left(\frac{1+x}{1-x}\right)^{\beta} + C_1,\end{aligned}$$

that is, we have

$$f(x) = \frac{\exp\left[C_1 - \alpha\left(\frac{x+1}{1-x}\right)^{\beta}\right]}{1-x^2}\left(\frac{1+x}{1-x}\right)^{\beta}.$$

Another integration implies that

$$F(x) = \int f(x)dx + C_2 = -\frac{\exp\left[C_1 - \alpha\left(\frac{x+1}{1-x}\right)^{\beta}\right]}{2\alpha\beta} + C_2,$$

whereby from the conditions $F(0) = 0$ and $F(1) = 1$, the constants $C_1 = \alpha + \ln(2\alpha\beta)$ and $C_2 = 1$ are obtained. Thus, the function $F(x)$ is indeed the CDF from $UED(\alpha, \beta)$, which completes the proof. □

The following theorem was used in [31] as well as [28,29] in order to characterize different univariate continuous distributions:

Theorem 1. *Let $(\Omega; F; P)$ be a given probability space, and let $\mathbb{H} = [a, b]$ be an interval for some $a < b$, where $a = -\infty$ and $b = +\infty$ might as well be allowed. Also, let $X : \Omega \to \mathbb{H}$ be a continuous RV with the CDF $F(x)$ and $g(x)$ and $t(x)$ be two real functions defined on $\mathbb{H}$ and such that*

$$\mathbb{E}[g(X)|X \geq x] = \xi(x)\,\mathbb{E}[t(X)|X \geq x], \qquad x \in \mathbb{H}$$

is defined with some real function $\xi(x)$. Assume that $g(x), t(x) \in C^1(\mathbb{H}), \xi(x) \in C^2(\mathbb{H})$, and $F(x)$ is a twice continuously differentiable and strictly monotone function on the set $\mathbb{H}$. Finally, assume that the equation $t(x)\xi(x) = g(x)$ has no real solution in the interior of $\mathbb{H}$. Then, $F(x)$ is uniquely determined by the functions $g(x), t(x)$, and $\xi(x)$ as follows:

$$F(x) = C\int_0^x \left|\frac{\xi'(u)}{\xi(u)t(u) - g(u)}\right| e^{-s(u)}du, \tag{12}$$

where the function $s(x)$ is a solution of the differential equation

$$s'(x) = \frac{\xi'(x)t(x)}{\xi(x)t(x) - g(x)},$$

and C is a constant such that $\int_{\mathbb{H}} dF(x) = 1$.

Now, we discuss the characterization of the UED based on Theorem 1 and some simple relationship between two functions and the RV $X \sim UED(\alpha, \beta)$.

Proposition 5. *Let $X : \Omega \to [0, 1)$ be a continuous RV and*

$$t(x) = 3 \exp\left[2\alpha\left(1 - \left(\frac{1+x}{1-x}\right)^{\beta}\right)\right], \qquad x \in [0, 1)$$

$$g(x) = 2 \exp\left[\alpha\left(1 - \left(\frac{1+x}{1-x}\right)^{\beta}\right)\right], \qquad x \in [0, 1).$$

The RV X has a PDF defined by Equation (3) if and only if there exists a function $\xi(x)$, defined as in Theorem 1, that satisfies the differential equation

$$\frac{\xi'(x)}{\xi(x)t(x) - g(x)} = \frac{2\alpha\beta}{1-x^2}\left(\frac{1+x}{1-x}\right)^{\beta} \exp\left[-2\alpha\left(1 - \left(\frac{1+x}{1-x}\right)^{\beta}\right)\right], \qquad 0 \leq x < 1. \quad (13)$$

Proof. *Necessity:* For the RV $X \sim UED(\alpha, \beta)$, with the CDF and PDF given by Equations (2) and (3), respectively, after a certain computation, we obtain

$$\begin{aligned}(1 - F(x))\mathbb{E}[t(X)|X \geq x] &= 3\,e^{\alpha r(x;\beta)} \int_x^1 \frac{2\alpha\beta}{1-u^2}\left(\frac{1+u}{1-u}\right)^{\beta} e^{3\alpha r(u;\beta)}du \\ &= \exp\left[4\alpha\left(1 - \left(\frac{1+x}{1-x}\right)^{\beta}\right)\right], \\ (1 - F(x))\mathbb{E}[g(X)|X \geq x] &= 2\,e^{\alpha r(x;\beta)} \int_x^1 \frac{2\alpha\beta}{1-u^2}\left(\frac{1+u}{1-u}\right)^{\beta} e^{2\alpha r(u;\beta)}du \\ &= \exp\left[3\alpha\left(1 - \left(\frac{1+x}{1-x}\right)^{\beta}\right)\right],\end{aligned}$$

where $0 < x < 1$ and $r(x) := 1 - \left(\frac{1+x}{1-x}\right)^{\beta}$. This implies that

$$\xi(x) := \frac{\mathbb{E}(g(x)|X \geq x)}{\mathbb{E}(t(x)|X \geq x)} = \exp\left[-\alpha\left(1 - \left(\frac{1+x}{1-x}\right)^{\beta}\right)\right], \qquad 0 < x < 1, \qquad (14)$$

that is, we have

$$\xi(x)t(x) - g(x) = 3\,e^{\alpha r(x;\beta)} - 2\,e^{\alpha r(x;\beta)} = \exp\left[\alpha\left(1 - \left(\frac{1+x}{1-x}\right)^{\beta}\right)\right] > 0, \qquad 0 < x < 1.$$

Hence, Equation (13) clearly holds.

Sufficiency: If the function $\xi(x)$ satisfies the differential Equation (13), then it follows that

$$s'(x) = \frac{\xi'(x)t(x)}{\xi(x)t(x) - g(x)} = \frac{6\alpha\beta}{1-x^2}\left(\frac{1+x}{1-x}\right)^{\beta}, \quad 0 < x < 1,$$

Therefore, one can take

$$s(x) = -3\alpha\left(1 - \left(\frac{1+x}{1-x}\right)^{\beta}\right).$$

Using Equation (12), it is easy to obtain that the RV X has a PDF given by Equation (3). □

According to the previous proposition, one immediately obtains the following:

Corollary 1. *Let $X : \Omega \to [0, +\infty)$ be a continuous RV and functions $t(x)$ and $g(x)$ be given as in Proposition 5. Then, $X \sim UED(\alpha, \beta)$, with the PDF as shown in Equation (3) if and only if the function $\xi(x)$ has the form in Equation (14).*

3. Estimation and Simulation Procedures

Let us assume that $x_1, \ldots, x_n$ are observed values of the sample of size n taken from the $UED(\alpha, \beta)$. We propose the maximum likelihood method for estimating the pair of parameters (α, β). This means that the estimates of those parameters are the ones that maximize the likelihood function

$$L(\alpha, \beta | x_1, \ldots, x_n) = \prod_{i=1}^{n} f(x_i).$$

As is known, this solution also corresponds to the one that maximizes the log-likelihood function; in other words, it maximizes

$$l = l(\alpha, \beta | x_1, \ldots, x_n) = \sum_{i=1}^{n} \ln f(x_i).$$

By differentiating the function l with respect to each parameter, the estimators of α and β can be obtained by solving the coupled equations

$$\begin{aligned}
\frac{\partial l}{\partial \alpha} &= \frac{n}{\alpha} + \sum_{i=1}^{n} \left(1 - \left(\frac{1+x_i}{1-x_i}\right)^{\beta}\right) &= 0 \\
\frac{\partial l}{\partial \beta} &= \frac{n}{\beta} + \sum_{i=1}^{n} \ln\left(\frac{1+x_i}{1-x_i}\right) - \alpha \sum_{i=1}^{n} \left(\frac{1+x_i}{1-x_i}\right)^{\beta} \ln\left(\frac{1+x_i}{1-x_i}\right) &= 0.
\end{aligned}$$

From the first equation, we obtain

$$\alpha = \left[\frac{1}{n} \sum_{i=1}^{n} \left(\frac{1+x_i}{1-x_i}\right)^{\beta} - 1\right]^{-1},$$

and by replacing this output in the second coupled equation, we obtain

$$\frac{n}{\beta} + \sum_{i=1}^{n} \ln\left(\frac{1+x_i}{1-x_i}\right) + \frac{\sum_{i=1}^{n} \left(\frac{1+x_i}{1-x_i}\right)^{\beta} \ln\left(\frac{1+x_i}{1-x_i}\right)}{1 - \frac{1}{n} \sum_{i=1}^{n} \left(\frac{1+x_i}{1-x_i}\right)^{\beta}} = 0.$$

Obviously, the last equation has only β as an unknown parameter. Now, by denoting $z_i = (1+x_i)/(1-x_i) > 1$, $i = 1, \ldots, n$, and

$$\mathcal{L}(\beta) = \frac{n}{\beta} + \sum_{i=1}^{n} \ln z_i + \frac{\sum_{i=1}^{n} z_i^{\beta} \ln z_i}{1 - \frac{1}{n} \sum_{i=1}^{n} z_i^{\beta}},$$

then by applying the L'Hopital's rule, one obtains

$$\begin{aligned}
\lim_{\beta \to 0^+} \mathcal{L}(\beta) &= \sum_{i=1}^{n} \ln z_i + n \lim_{\beta \to 0^+} \frac{\sum_{i=1}^{n} \left(1 - z_i^{\beta} + \beta z_i^{\beta} \ln z_i\right)}{\beta \sum_{i=1}^{n} \left(1 - z_i^{\beta}\right)} \\
&= \sum_{i=1}^{n} \ln z_i + n \lim_{\beta \to 0^+} \frac{\sum_{i=1}^{n} \left(-z_i^{\beta} \ln z_i + \ln z_i\right)}{\sum_{i=1}^{n} \left(1 - z_i^{\beta} - \beta z_i^{\beta} \ln z_i\right)} \\
&= \sum_{i=1}^{n} \ln z_i + n \lim_{\beta \to 0^+} \frac{\sum_{i=1}^{n} \left(-z_i^{\beta} \ln^2 z_i\right)}{\sum_{i=1}^{n} \left(-z_i^{\beta} \ln z_i - \ln z_i\right)} \\
&= \sum_{i=1}^{n} \ln z_i + \frac{n}{2} \cdot \frac{\sum_{i=1}^{n} \ln^2 z_i}{\sum_{i=1}^{n} \ln z_i} > 0.
\end{aligned}$$

On the other hand, assuming that $z_1 > \max\{z_2, \ldots, z_n\}$, it follows that

$$\begin{aligned}\lim_{\beta\to+\infty} \mathcal{L}(\beta) &= \sum_{i=1}^{n} \ln z_i + \lim_{\beta\to+\infty} \frac{\ln z_1 + \sum_{i=2}^{n}\left(\frac{z_i}{z_1}\right)^{\beta} \ln z_i}{z_1^{-\beta} - \frac{1}{n} - \frac{1}{n}\sum_{i=2}^{n}\left(\frac{z_i}{z_1}\right)^{\beta}} \\ &= \sum_{i=1}^{n} \ln z_i - n \ln z_1 < 0.\end{aligned}$$

Hence, equation $\mathcal{L}(\beta) = 0$ has at least one solution, and it can be solved numerically, for instance, by using the Newton–Raphson algorithm. This task may be performed using the function "`uniroot`" available in the statistical programming software "R" (version 4.3.1). Once β is estimated, this output can be used for estimating α.

For computing the interval estimators for $\boldsymbol{\theta} = (\alpha, \beta)'$ and testing hypotheses with these parameters, we find the observed matrix information:

$$\boldsymbol{I}(\boldsymbol{\theta}) = -\begin{pmatrix} \dfrac{\partial^2 l(\boldsymbol{\theta})}{\partial \alpha^2} & \dfrac{\partial^2 l(\boldsymbol{\theta})}{\partial \alpha \partial \beta} \\ \dfrac{\partial^2 l(\boldsymbol{\theta})}{\partial \beta \partial \alpha} & \dfrac{\partial^2 l(\boldsymbol{\theta})}{\partial \beta^2} \end{pmatrix},$$

where

$$\begin{aligned}\frac{\partial^2 l(\boldsymbol{\theta})}{\partial \alpha^2} &= -\frac{n}{\alpha^2} \\ \frac{\partial^2 l(\boldsymbol{\theta})}{\partial \alpha \partial \beta} &= \frac{\partial^2 l(\boldsymbol{\theta})}{\partial \beta \partial \alpha} = -\sum_{i=1}^{n}\left(\frac{1+x_i}{1-x_i}\right)^{\beta} \ln\left(\frac{1+x_i}{1-x_i}\right) \\ \frac{\partial^2 l(\boldsymbol{\theta})}{\partial \beta^2} &= -\frac{n}{\beta^2} - \alpha \sum_{i=1}^{n}\left(\frac{1+x_i}{1-x_i}\right)^{\beta} \ln^2\left(\frac{1+x_i}{1-x_i}\right).\end{aligned}$$

Note that $\boldsymbol{I}(\widehat{\boldsymbol{\theta}})$ is a consistent estimator of the expected Fisher information matrix $\mathrm{E}[\boldsymbol{I}(\boldsymbol{\theta})]$ (see, for example, [32]). Under some suitable conditions, the approximation to a normal distribution $\widehat{\boldsymbol{\theta}} \approx \mathcal{N}(\boldsymbol{\theta}, \boldsymbol{I}(\widehat{\boldsymbol{\theta}})^{-1})$ holds, and more generally, we have

$$\boldsymbol{a}'\widehat{\boldsymbol{\theta}} \approx \mathcal{N}(\boldsymbol{a}'\boldsymbol{\theta}, \boldsymbol{a}'\boldsymbol{I}(\widehat{\boldsymbol{\theta}})^{-1}\boldsymbol{a}),$$

for any vector $\boldsymbol{a} = (a_1, a_2)'$. By choosing $\boldsymbol{a} = (1,1)'$, we find the $100 \times (1-\delta)$ % confidence interval:

$$\theta_i \pm z_{\delta/2}\sqrt{(\boldsymbol{I}(\widehat{\boldsymbol{\theta}})^{-1})_{ii}},$$

where $0 < \delta < 1$ and $z_{\delta/2}$ is the $1 - \delta/2$ quantile of the standard normal distribution.

Simulation Study

In this part, we shall discuss the effectiveness of the proposed MLE procedure, which will be used in application for better predictions of a phenomenon. In this regard, we considered four sets of parameters and conducted a Monte Carlo simulation with 20,000 replications in order to generate samples of various sizes (i.e., $n = 25, 50, 150, 350, 500$) from the UED (α, β). The parameter combinations are listed below:

Set-I: $\alpha = 0.9856$, $\beta = 0.2178$;
Set-II: $\alpha = 1.8986$, $\beta = 0.3218$;
Set-III: $\alpha = 2.4390$, $\beta = 2.5145$;
Set-IV: $\alpha = 0.4390$, $\beta = 1.5145$.

For all of them, the MLE estimates were obtained by using MATHEMATICA 13.0 software. The simulation results are portrayed in Tables 1–4, where they are compiled according to the following definitions:

$$\text{Bias} := \mathbb{E}(\hat{\Theta}) - \Theta;$$
$$\text{Mean square error (MSE)} := \mathbb{E}((\hat{\Theta} - \Theta)^2);$$
$$\text{Lower Confidence Limit} := \text{LCL} = \hat{\Theta} - z_{\frac{\delta}{2}} \frac{\sqrt{Var(\hat{\Theta})}}{n};$$
$$\text{Upper Confidence Limit} := \text{UCL} = \hat{\Theta} + z_{\frac{\delta}{2}} \frac{\sqrt{Var(\hat{\Theta})}}{n},$$

where $\Theta = (\alpha, \beta)$. From these tables, there is evidence that both the bias and MSE of the MLE estimates tended toward zero as the sample sizes increased, whereas the 95% confidence limits became compact as the sample size increased.

Table 1. Mean, bias, MSE, LCL, and UCL for Set-I.

Sample Size	Parameter	Estimate	Bias	MSE	LCL	UCL
$n = 25$	α	0.9417	−0.0439	0.0111	0.9335	0.9499
	β	0.2180	0.0013	0.00008	0.2172	0.2189
$n = 50$	α	0.9511	−0.0344	0.0068	0.9479	0.9544
	β	0.2189	0.0012	0.00007	0.2186	0.2193
$n = 150$	α	0.9655	−0.0200	0.0032	0.9648	0.9663
	β	0.2192	0.0014	0.00004	0.2192	0.2192
$n = 350$	α	0.9685	−0.0171	0.0022	0.9683	0.9688
	β	0.2194	0.0016	0.00003	0.2194	0.2194
$n = 500$	α	0.9729	−0.0126	0.0015	0.9728	0.9732
	β	0.2194	0.0016	0.00002	0.2194	0.2194

Moreover, Table 1 shows a downward bias for $\hat{\alpha}$ and an upward one for $\hat{\beta}$. Similarly, the MSE approached zero as the sample size increased.

Table 2. Mean, bias, MSE, LCL, and UCL for Set-II.

Sample Size	Parameter	Estimate	Bias	MSE	LCL	UCL
$n = 25$	α	1.8547	−0.0438	0.0472	1.8376	1.8717
	β	0.3140	−0.0077	0.0004	0.3125	0.3155
$n = 50$	α	1.8902	−0.0084	0.0230	1.8843	1.8962
	β	0.3149	−0.0068	0.0003	0.3143	0.3156
$n = 150$	α	1.9204	0.0217	0.0117	1.9161	1.9246
	β	0.3167	−0.0050	0.0001	0.3163	0.3172
$n = 350$	α	1.9346	0.0359	0.0071	1.9341	1.9352
	β	0.3171	−0.0046	0.0001	0.3172	0.3172
$n = 500$	α	1.9337	0.0351	0.0063	1.9334	1.9342
	β	0.3171	−0.0047	0.00008	0.3170	0.3171

Also, Table 2 portrays a downward bias for $\hat{\alpha}$ and $\hat{\beta}$ when the sample sizes were less than or equal to 50, while there was an upward bias for $\hat{\alpha}$ when the sample size increased. However, the MSE approached zero as the sample size increased.

Table 3. Mean, bias, MSE, LCL, and UCL for Set-III.

Sample Size	Parameter	Estimate	Bias	MSE	LCL	UCL
$n = 25$	α	2.3256	−0.1133	0.0578	2.307	2.3445
	β	2.4995	−0.0149	0.0126	2.4908	2.5084
$n = 50$	α	2.3539	−0.0850	0.0316	2.3472	2.3620
	β	2.4871	−0.0274	0.0136	2.4826	2.4916
$n = 150$	α	2.3915	−0.0475	0.0123	2.3900	2.3929
	β	2.5121	−0.0023	0.0048	2.5113	2.5132
$n = 350$	α	2.4044	−0.0345	0.0065	2.4040	2.40491
	β	2.5155	0.0010	0.0028	2.5152	2.5158
$n = 500$	α	2.4051	−0.0338	0.0052	2.4048	2.4055
	β	2.5180	0.0035	0.0023	2.5179	2.5183

In the case of Set-III, shown in Table 3, the bias was downward for $\hat{\alpha}$ for all sample sizes. On the contrary, it was upward for $\hat{\beta}$ when the sample sizes were higher, usually for those greater than 150. Notice that all biases were negligibly small and approached zero as the sample size increased.

Table 4. Mean, bias, MSE, LCL, and UCL for Set-IV.

Sample Size	Parameter	Estimate	Bias	MSE	LCL	UCL
$n = 25$	α	0.4173	−0.0217	0.0024	0.4134	0.4212
	β	1.5168	0.0023	0.0037	1.5120	1.5215
$n = 50$	α	0.4251	−0.0138	0.0013	0.4237	0.4264
	β	1.5166	0.0021	0.0027	1.5146	1.5186
$n = 150$	α	0.4285	−0.0105	0.0007	0.4281	0.4288
	β	1.5205	0.0060	0.0015	1.5200	1.5210
$n = 350$	α	0.4314	−0.0076	0.0004	0.4313	0.4315
	β	1.5236	0.0091	0.0009	1.5234	1.5238
$n = 500$	α	0.4332	−0.0058	0.0003	0.4332	0.4333
	β	1.5203	0.0058	0.0009	1.5202	1.5203

Similarly, Table 4 shows a downward bias for $\hat{\alpha}$ and an upward bias for $\hat{\beta}$, but all biases were negigibly small and approached zero as the sample size increasd, and the same is true for the MSE. In summary, the above results show that the MLE is a suitable estimation method for realistic forecasting.

4. Model Compatibility and Its Application to Real-World Data

Here, the possibility of applying the UED model in terms of modeling empirical distributions of some real-world processes is discussed in more detail. To that end, by using several typical statistical indicators, the quality of fitting with the UED was also checked. The obtained results were also compared with the results of fitting using some of the previously known unit interval probability distributions, which additionally checked the possibility of applying the UED.

4.1. *Measures of Goodness-of-Fit*

In order to test the null hypothesis $H_0 : F_n(x) = F_0(x)$, where $F_n(x)$ is the empirical CDF and $F_0(x)$ is the CDF of some specified (theoretical) distribution, usually some well-known statistical tests are used. In order to test the hypothesis that some real-world data are taken from the UED (i.e., from some other stochastic distribution), the following statistical tests are used here:

- The Kolmogorov–Smirnov (KS) test, whose test-statistics are defined by

$$\mathrm{KS} = \max_{1 \le i \le k} \left\{ \frac{i}{k} - z_i, z_i - \frac{i-1}{k} \right\},$$

where k denotes the number of classes and z_i represents the values of the theoretical CDF.
- The Anderson–Darling (AD_0^*) test, which usually attaches more mass to the distributions tails and whose test-statistics are

$$A_0^* = \left(\frac{2.25}{k^2} + \frac{0.75}{k} + 1 \right) \left\{ -k - \frac{1}{k} \sum_{i=1}^{k} (2i-1) \ln(z_i(1 - z_{k-i+1})) \right\}.$$

- The Cramér–von Mises (CVM_0^*)-test is a derived version of the KS test, with test-statistics defined by

$$W_0^* = \sum_{i=1}^{K} \left(z_i - \frac{2i-1}{2k} \right)^2 + \frac{1}{12k}.$$

Additionally, in order to check the quality of fitting certain real-world data using the UED (i.e., some other distribution), the following indicators were used:

- The Akaike information criterion (AIC), defined as

$$\mathrm{AIC} = 2m - 2\ell(\hat{\Theta}),$$

where m denotes the number of parameters.
- The corrected Akaike information criterion (AICc), expressed as

$$\mathrm{AICc} = \mathrm{AIC} + \frac{2m(m+1)}{n-m-1}.$$

- The Bayesian information criterion (BIC), which is defined as

$$\mathrm{BIC} = m \ln(n) - 2\ell(\hat{\Theta}).$$

- The Hannan–Quinn information criterion (HQIC), expressed as

$$\mathrm{HQIC} = -2\ell(\hat{\Theta}) + 2m \ln(\ln(m)).$$

- The consistent Akaike information criterion (CAIC), given as

$$\mathrm{CAIC} = -2\ell(\hat{\Theta}) + m(\ln(n) + 1).$$

- The Vuong test was also used for model selection purposes.

For comprehensive details about these measures, readers may refer to Akaike [33], Hussain et al. [34], Murthy et al. [35], and Vuong [36], respectively.

4.2. Comparative Models

We also compared the proposed UED model with well-known unit interval models defined by the following PDFs:

- The beta distribution (BD) [4]:

$$f_\alpha^{\mathrm{BD}}(x) = \frac{1}{B(\alpha, \beta)} x^{\beta-1} (1-x)^{\alpha-1}, \qquad \alpha, \beta > 0, \quad 0 < x < 1,$$

- The Johnson S_B distribution (JSBD) [6]:

$$f_{\alpha,\beta}^{\text{JSBD}}(x) = \frac{\beta \exp\left[-\frac{1}{2}(\alpha + \beta \ln(\frac{x}{1-x}))^2 - \beta x\right]}{\sqrt{2\pi}x(1-x)}, \qquad \alpha, \beta > 0, \quad 0 < x < 1,$$

- The Kumaraswamy distribution (KwD) [8]:

$$f_{\alpha,\beta}^{\text{KwD}}(x) = \alpha\,\beta x^{\alpha-1}(1-x^{\alpha})^{\beta-1}, \qquad \alpha, \beta > 0, \quad 0 < x < 1,$$

- The unit Gompertz distribution (UGoMD) [15]:

$$f_{\alpha,\beta}^{\text{UGoMD}}(x) = \alpha\beta x^{-\alpha-1} e^{-\beta(x^{-\alpha}-1)}, \qquad \alpha, \beta > 0, \quad 0 < x < 1.$$

In order to compare the fitting results, we considered four different real-world datasets classified into two sections: (1) environmental and (2) engineering. The results obtained from the statistical analysis of these datasets are discussed below.

4.3. Environmental Datasets

Datasets I and II. The first two datasets were reported by Maiti [37], and they represent the following measured values:

- Soil moisture (Dataset I): 0.0179, 0.0798, 0.0959, 0.0444, 0.0938, 0.0443, 0.0917, 0.0882, 0.0439, 0.049, 0.0774, 0.0171, 0.0305, 0.0757, and 0.0468;
- Permanent wilting points (PWP) (Dataset II): 0.0821, 0.0561, 0.0202, 0.051, 0.0041, 0.0226, 0.0556, 0.0829, 0.0062, 0.0695, 0.0557, 0.0243, 0.0083, 0.0532, and 0.0118.

In this regard, we compiled both the descriptive and theoretical (UED) statistics, which are listed in Tables 5 and 6, respectively. Note that the descriptive statistics of all datasets include the sample size (SS), mean, median, standard deviation (SD), skewness (SK), and kurtosis (KU).

Table 5. Descriptive statistics for Datasets I and II.

Dataset	SS	Mean	Median	SD	SK	KU
I	15	0.0598	0.0490	0.0277	−0.1083	1.6247
II	15	0.0402	0.0510	0.0277	0.1083	1.6247

Table 6. Theoretical statistics from the UED.

Dataset	SS	Mean	Median	SD	SK	KU
I	15	0.0606	0.0621	0.0254	−0.2107	2.3825
II	15	0.0406	0.0384	0.0247	0.2942	2.3050

In addition, the total test time (TTT) plot, introduced in [38], is portrayed in Figure 4 for both datasets. Notice that, in particular, the TTT plot indicates the empirical HRF, portraying an IFR. Tables 5 and 6 also reveal that the theoretical UED statistics as well as the observed descriptive statistics showed remarkable closeness to each other, and it appears that both sets of data can be simulated by the proposed model. Furthermore, it is evident from Figure 5 that neither dataset contained any outliers.

Table 7 portrays that the model proposed by the UED is the best strategy for analyzing the observed dataset (Dataset I) in relation to all other distributions of unit intervals. Namely, although the p value of the KS statistics for the KwD was the highest, the other nonparametric tests, CVM_0^* and AD_0^*, indicate that for the UED, the minimum tested values were obtained. Also, based on the estimated values of the Vuong statistics, given in Table 8, the KwD and UED had an indecisive status. Thus, the UED is the best strategy, which is also confirmed by Figure 6. Similarly, Table 9 portrays that the proposed UED model is also one of the best strategies for the analysis of Dataset II in all aspects.Namely, the test statistics, including the KS test, CVM_0^*, and AD_0^*, had the lowest values compared with all the selected, previously known interval models. In addition, the Vuong statistic, which compares models based on the likelihood ratio phenomenon, openly supported the UED. Finally, Figure 6 also confirms our claim that the UED is the best strategy. Moreover, Tables 10 and 11 yield the lowest information criterion values for the UED compared with the competing models.

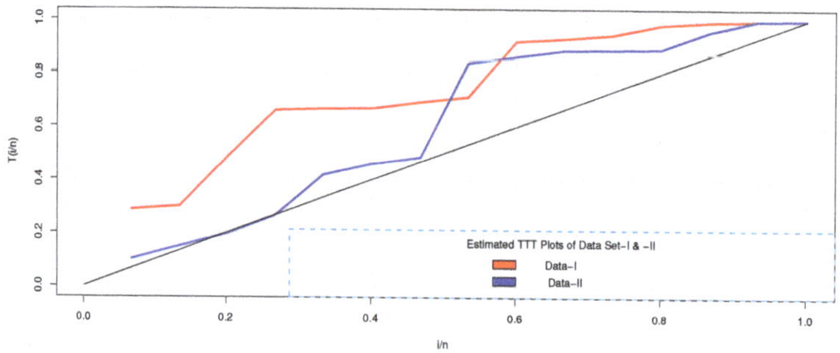

Figure 4. TTT plots of Datasets I and II.

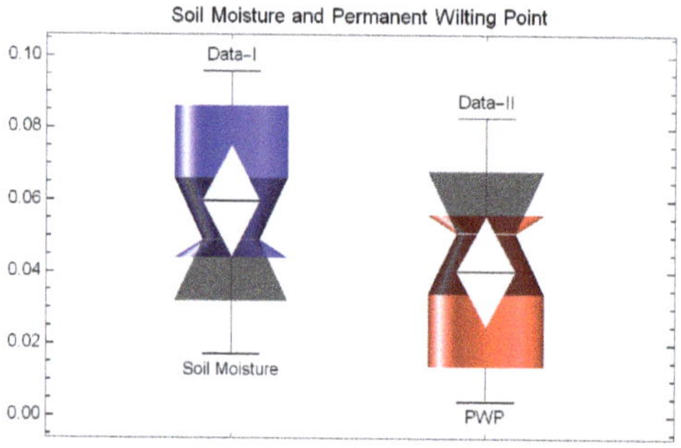

Figure 5. Box plots for datasets I and II.

Table 7. ML estimates and goodness-of-fit statistics for Dataset I.

Distribution	$\hat{\beta}$	$\hat{\alpha}$	CVM_0^*	AD_0^*	KS	p-Value
UED	18.4218	0.0773	**0.6239**	**0.1026**	0.2079	0.5361
BD	3.8233	60.2492	0.6858	0.1041	0.2099	0.5232
KwD	719.3842	2.4408	0.6887	0.1109	**0.2003**	**0.5844**
JSBD	4.9859	1.7279	0.7751	0.1117	0.2128	0.5056
UGoMD	1.6525	0.0048	1.0587	0.1613	0.2353	0.3769

Table 8. Vuong test statistics for Datasets I and II.

Models	Dataset I	Suitability	Dataset II	Suitability
UED-BD	1.4601	UED	2.5935	UED
UED-KwD	0.9738	Indecisive	3.4585	UED
UED-JSBD	1.5427	UED	1.6793	UED
UED-UGoMD	2.2142	UED	1.5955	UED

Table 9. MLE and goodness-of-fit statistics for Dataset II.

Distribution	$\hat{\beta}$	$\hat{\alpha}$	CVM_0^*	AD_0^*	KS	p-Value
UED	11.8676	0.4607	**0.6239**	**0.1096**	**0.1960**	**0.6118**
BD	1.5370	36.8071	0.6869	0.1199	0.2481	0.3142
KwD	78.9162	1.4011	0.7074	0.1224	0.2409	0.3487
JSBD	3.5837	1.0177	0.8112	0.1364	0.2619	0.2549
UGoMD	0.9497	0.0219	0.9011	0.1499	0.2386	0.3603

Table 10. Estimates of the maximum log-likelihood and information criteria for Dataset I.

Distribution	$-l$	AIC	AICC	BIC	HQIC	CAIC
UED	33.8617	−63.7233	−62.7233	−62.3072	−63.7384	−60.3072
BD	32.8026	−61.6052	−60.6052	−60.1891	−61.6203	−58.1891
KwD	33.3796	−62.7592	−61.7592	−61.3431	−62.7743	−59.3431
JSBD	32.0631	−60.1262	−59.1262	−58.7101	−60.1413	−56.7101
UGoMD	29.6463	−55.2925	−54.2925	−53.8764	−55.3076	−51.8764

Table 11. Estimates of the maximum log-likelihood and information criteria for Dataset II.

Distribution	$-l$	AIC	AICC	BIC	HQIC	CAIC
UED	35.2604	−66.5208	−65.5208	−65.1047	−66.5359	−63.1047
BD	34.1097	−64.2194	−63.2194	−62.8033	−64.2345	−60.8033
KwD	34.3392	−64.6784	−63.6784	−63.2623	−64.6935	−61.2623
JSBD	33.0448	−62.0896	−61.0896	−60.6735	−62.1047	−58.6735
UGoMD	31.1648	−58.3296	−57.3296	−56.9135	−58.3447	−54.9135

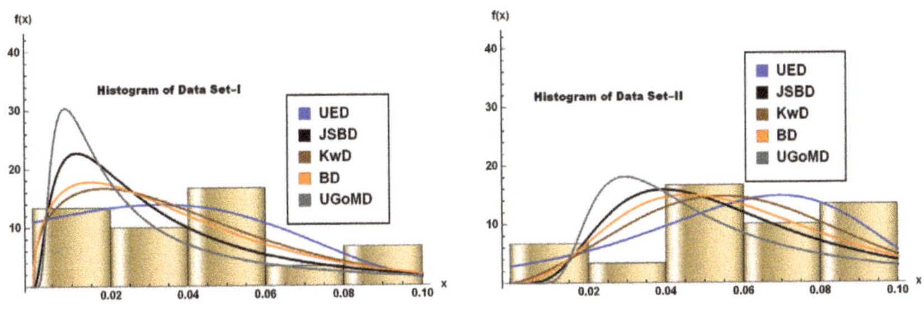

Figure 6. Datasets I and II (given by histograms) fitted via unit interval distributions (given by lines).

4.4. Engineering Datasets

Datasets III and IV. The third and fourth datasets were first introduced and studied in [39] for Burr measurements on iron sheets. For the third dataset of 50 observations of the Burr measurements (in the unit of millimeters), the hole diameter was 12 mm, and the sheet thickness was 3.15 mm. For the fourth dataset of 50 observations, the hole diameter and sheet thickness were 9 mm and 2 mm, respectively. Hole diameter readings were taken for jobs with respect to one hole and then selected and fixed as per a predetermined orientation. These two datasets refer to two different machines being compared, and one can see [39] for the technical details of measuring the datasets. Note that both datasets were also analyzed in [19,40–42].The descriptive statistics of these datasets, as well as the corresponding theoretical statistics for the UED, are presented in Tables 12 and 13, respectively. The TTT plot and box plots of the observed data are given in Figures 7 and 8, respectively. It can be observed that Datasets III and IV were positively skewed and platykurtic in nature, which is confirmed by Tables 12 and 13. In addition, from Figure 8, it is evident that the empirical and theoretical aspects of these datasets, in terms of the absence of outliers, are in close agreement and indicate that the proposed model can be used effectively. Such findings are also consolidated within Tables 14 and 15, which show that the UED exhibited minimal values in the almost all cases for the goodness-of-fit statistic, which ensures that the UED is one of the best strategies.

Table 12. Descriptive statistics for Datasets III and IV.

Dataset	SS	Mean	Median	SD	SK	KU
III	50	0.1632	0.1600	0.0810	0.0723	2.2166
IV	50	0.1520	0.1600	0.0785	0.0061	2.3012

Table 13. Theoretical statistics from the UED.

Dataset	SS	Mean	Median	SD	SK	KU
III	50	0.1633	0.1641	0.0809	0.0259	2.2511
IV	50	0.1519	0.1521	0.0777	0.0262	2.2521

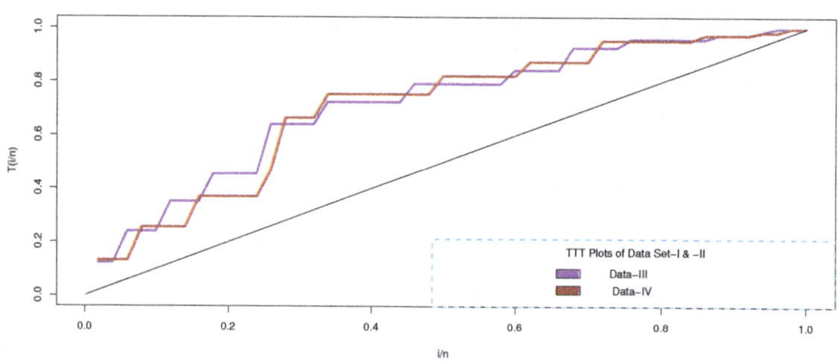

Figure 7. TTT plots of Datasets III and IV.

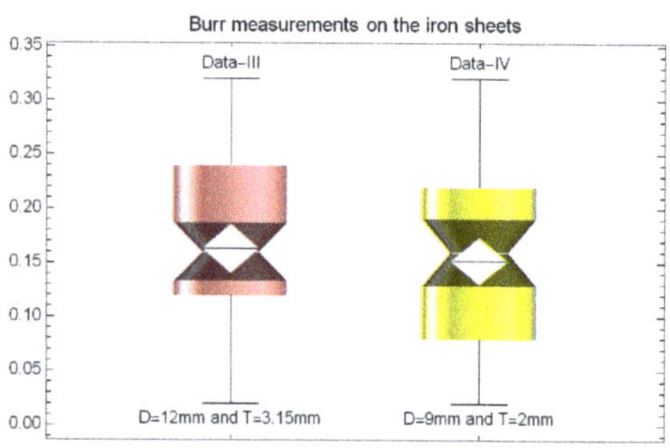

Figure 8. Box plots for Datasets III and IV.

Table 14. MLEs and goodness-of-fit statistics for Dataset III.

Distribution	$\hat{\beta}$	$\hat{\alpha}$	CVM_0^*	AD_0^*	KS	p-Value
UED	4.7879	0.1756	0.3274	**0.0419**	**0.1242**	**0.9881**
BD	2.6824	13.8640	**0.1538**	0.9120	0.1414	0.5555
KwD	1.0746	0.0925	12.2879	2.3943	0.7222	0.0000
JSBD	2.3767	1.3175	0.2495	1.4647	0.1740	0.0968
UGoMD	0.0924	1.0747	0.5213	3.0810	0.2046	0.0304

Table 15. MLEs and goodness-of-fit statistics for Dataset IV.

Distribution	$\hat{\beta}$	$\hat{\alpha}$	CVM_0^*	AD_0^*	KS	p-Value
UED	4.8518	0.1996	0.3224	**0.0339**	**0.1239**	**0.9928**
BD	2.4003	13.5218	0.2871	1.5649	0.1981	0.7340
KwD	1.9606	31.3769	**0.2093**	1.2683	0.1691	0.8825
JSBD	2.3682	1.2374	0.4145	2.2458	0.2285	0.5579
UGoMD	0.0916	1.0250	0.6091	3.4278	0.2312	0.5426

However, the likelihood aspects and information criterion values also favor the proposed UED model, which can be seen in Tables 16 and 17, respectively. Furthermore, the shape of our proposed model, as shown in Figure 9, matched the data in a better way compared with the other competing models. Finally, the Vuong statistic, as depicted in Table 18, also shows the capability of the proposed model.

Table 16. Estimates of the maximum log-likelihood and information criteria for Dataset III.

Distribution	$-l$	AIC	AICC	BIC	HQIC	CAIC
UED	−57.0712	−110.142	−109.887	−106.318	−108.686	−104.318
BD	−54.6066	−105.213	−104.958	−101.389	−103.757	−99.3892
KwD	−56.0686	−108.137	−107.882	−104.313	−106.681	−102.313
JSBD	− 51.3231	−98.6462	−98.3909	−94.8222	−97.19	−92.8222
UGoMD	−40.672	−77.344	−77.0887	−73.52	−75.8878	−71.52

Table 17. Estimates of the maximum log-likelihood and information criteria for Dataset IV.

Distribution	$-l$	AIC	AICC	BIC	HQIC	CAIC
UED	−59.3536	−114.707	−114.452	−110.883	−113.251	−108.883
BD	−55.9312	−107.862	−107.607	−104.038	−106.406	−102.038
KwD	−57.5214	−111.043	−110.788	−107.219	−109.587	−105.219
JSBD	− 52.305	−100.61	−100.355	−96.786	−99.1538	−94.786
UGoMD	−42.6099	−81.2198	−80.9645	−77.3957	−79.7636	−75.3957

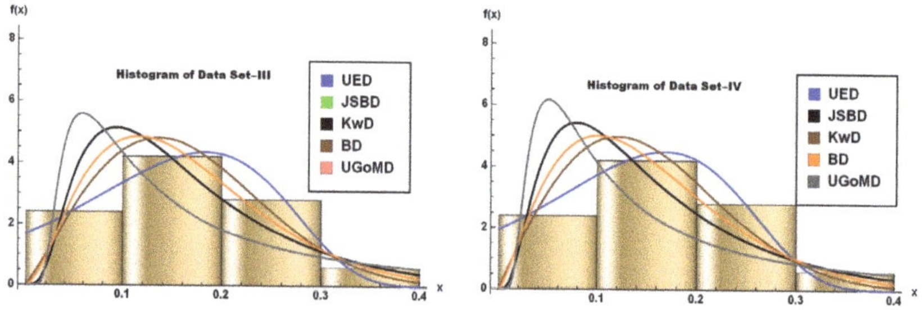

Figure 9. Datasets III and IV (given by histograms) fitted via unit interval distributions (given by lines).

Table 18. Vuong test statistic for Datasets III and IV.

Models	Dataset III	Suitability	Dataset IV	Suitability
UED-BD	0.4137	Indecisive	3.5339	UED
UED-KwD	−2.3203	KwD	3.9633	UED
UED-JSBD	2.1336	UED	3.4202	UED
UED-UGoMD	4.9679	UED	4.0306	UED

5. Concluding Remarks

We introduced a two-parameter bounded model called the unit exponential distribution (UED), which is appropriate for modeling skewed and IFR data. Some of its mathematical properties were studied, including the moments, quantiles, and other distributional behavior. A characterization of the UED via the HRF was made, which provided the identification requirements of the distribution and thus provided a reliable prediction compared with the well-known unit domain models. The model parameters were estimated with the MLE method. We also provided a guide line to choose the best model by using various goodness-of-fit statistics. Applications of the newly defined distribution showed that the proposed models have better modeling abilities than competitive models. For this purpose, we used four datasets in two different disciplines, namely environmental and engineering, and it was found that the proposed strategy was the best one in the unit interval domain. Moreover, in a further study, the proposed model could also be generalized over the interval $[0, s)$ by introducing the function

$$F(x) = 1 - \exp\left[\alpha\left(1 - \left(\frac{s+x}{s-x}\right)^{\beta s}\right)\right].$$

where, obviously, $F(x) = 0$ when $x = 0$ and $F(x) = 1$ when $x = s$.

Author Contributions: Conceptualization, H.S.B. and T.H.; methodology, H.S.B., M.T. and N.Q.; software, H.S.B. and T.H.; validation, H.S.B., M.T. and V.S.S.; formal analysis, H.S.B., T.H. and V.S.S.; data curation, H.S.B. and T.H.; writing—original draft preparation, H.S.B., T.H. and V.S.S.; writing—review and editing, M.T., V.S.S. and N.Q.; visualization, T.H. and M.T.; supervision, H.S.B. and V.S.S.; project administration, M.T. and N.Q. All authors have read and agreed to the published version of the manuscript.

Funding: This research received no external funding.

Acknowledgments: The authors gratefully acknowledge Princess Nourah bint Abdulrahman University Researchers Supporting Project number (PNURSP2023R376), Princess Nourah bint Abdulrahman University, Riyadh, Saudi Arabia for the financial support for this project.

Conflicts of Interest: The authors declare no conflict of interest.

References

1. Fleiss, J.L.; Levin, B.; Paik, M.C. *Statistical Methods for Rates and Proportions*, 3rd ed.; John Wiley & Sons Inc.: Hoboken, NJ, USA, 1993.
2. Gilchrist, W. *Statistical Modelling with Quantile Functions*; CRC Press: Abingdon, UK, 2000.
3. Seber, G.A.F. *Statistical Models for Proportions and Probabilities*; Springer: Berlin/Heidelberg, Germany, 2013.
4. Bayes, T. An Essay Towards Solving a Problem in the Doctrine of Chances. By the late Rev. Mr. Bayes, F.R.S. communicated by Mr. Price, in a letter to John Canton, A. M. F. R. S. *Philos. Trans. R. Soc.* **1763**, *53*, 370–418. [CrossRef]
5. Leipnik, R.B. Distribution of the Serial Correlation Coefficient in a Circularly Correlated Universe. *Ann. Math. Stat.* **1947**, *18*, 80–87. [CrossRef]
6. Johnson, N. Systems of Frequency Curves Derived From the First Law of Laplace. *Trabajos Estadistica* **1955**, *5*, 283–291. [CrossRef]
7. Jørgensen, B. Proper Dispersion Models. *Braz. J. Probab. Stat.* **1997**, *11*, 89–128.
8. Kumaraswamy, P. A Generalized Probability Density Function for Double-Bounded Random Processes. *J. Hydrol.* **1980**, *46*, 79–88. [CrossRef]
9. Topp, C.W.; Leone, F.C. A Family of J-Shaped Frequency Functions. *J. Am. Stat. Assoc.* **1955**, *50*, 209–219. [CrossRef]
10. Consul, P.C.; Jain, G.C. On the Log-Gamma Distribution and Its Properties. *Stat. Hefte* **1971**, *12*, 100–106. [CrossRef]
11. Smithson, M.; Shou, Y. CDF-Quantile. Distributions for Modelling RVs on the Unit Interval. *Br. J. Math. Stat. Psychol.* **2017**, *70*, 412–438. [CrossRef]
12. Nakamura, L.R.; Cerqueira, P.H.R.; Ramires, T.G.; Pescim, R.R.; Rigby, R.A.; Stasinopoulos, D.M. A New Continuous Distribution on the Unit Interval Applied to Modelling the Points Ratio of Football Teams. *J. Appl. Stat.* **2019**, *46*, 416–431. [CrossRef]
13. Ghitany, M.E.; Mazucheli, J.; Menezes, A.F.B.; Alqallaf, F. The Unit-Inverse Gaussian Distribution: A New Alternative to Two-Parameter Distributions on the Unit Interval. *Commun. Stat. Theory Methods* **2019**, *48*, 3423–3438. [CrossRef]
14. Altun, E.; Hamedani, G. The Log-Xgamma Distribution with Inference and Application. *J. Soc. Fr. Stat.* **2018**, *159*, 40–55.
15. Mazucheli, J.; Menezes, A.F.; Dey, S. Unit-Gompertz Distribution with Applications. *Statistica* **2019**, *79*, 25–43. [CrossRef]
16. Mazucheli, J.; Menezes, A.F.B.; Chakraborty, S. On the One Parameter Unit-Lindley Distribution and Its Associated Regression Model for Proportion Data. *J. Appl. Stat.* **2019**, *46*, 700–714. [CrossRef]
17. Mazucheli, J.; Menezes, A.F.B.; Fernandes, L.B.; de Oliveira, R.P.; Ghitany, M.E. The Unit-Weibull Distribution as an Alternative to the Kumaraswamy Distribution for the Modeling of Quantiles Conditional on Covariates. *J. Appl. Stat.* **2019**, *47*, 954–974. [CrossRef]
18. Altun, E. The Log-Weighted Exponential Regression Model: Alternative to the Beta Regression Model. *Commun. Stat. Theory Methods* **2020**, *50*, 2306–2321. [CrossRef]
19. Gündüz, S.; Mustafa, Ç.; Korkmaz, M.C. A New Unit Distribution Based on the Unbounded Johnson Distribution Rule: The Unit Johnson SU Distribution. *Pak. J. Stat. Oper. Res.* **2020**, *16*, 471–490. [CrossRef]
20. Korkmaz, M.Ç.; Korkmaz, Z.S. The Unit Log–log Distribution: A New Unit Distribution with Alternative Quantile Regression Modeling and Educational Measurements Applications. *J. Appl. Stat.* **2023**, *50*, 889–908. [CrossRef]
21. Afify, A.Z.; Nassar, M.; Kumar, D.; Cordeiro, G.M. A New Unit Distribution: Properties and Applications. *Electron. J. Appl. Stat.* **2022**, *15*, 460–484.
22. Fayomi, A.; Hassan, A.S.; Baaqeel, H.; Almetwally, E.M. Bayesian Inference and Data Analysis of the Unit–Power Burr X Distribution. *Axioms* **2023**, *12*, 297. [CrossRef]
23. Krishna, A.; Maya, R.; Chesneau, C.; Irshad, M.R. The Unit Teissier Distribution and Its Applications. *Math. Comput. Appl.* **2022**, *27*, 12. [CrossRef]
24. Biswas, A.; Chakraborty, S. A new method for constructing continuous distributions on the unit interval. *arXiv* **2021**, arXiv:2101.04661.
25. Dombi, J.; Jónás, T.; Tóth, Z.E. The Epsilon Probability Distribution and its Application in Reliability Theory. *Acta Polytech. Hung.* **2018**, *15*, 197–216.
26. Aslam, M.; Noor, F.; Ali, S. Shifted Exponential Distribution: Bayesian Estimation, Prediction and Expected Test Time Under Progressive Censoring. *J. Test. Eval.* **2020**, *48*, 1576–1593. [CrossRef]
27. Artzner, P.; Delbaen, F.; Eber, J.-M.; Heath, D. Coherent Measures of Risk. *Math. Financ.* **1999**, *9*, 203–228. [CrossRef]
28. Ahsanullah, M.; Shakil, M.; Kibria, B.M.G. Characterizations of Continuous Distributions by Truncated Moment. *J. Mod. Appl. Stat. Methods* **2016**, *15*, 316–331. [CrossRef]
29. Ahsanullah, M.; Ghitany, M.E.; Al-Mutairi, D.K. Characterization of Lindley Distribution by Truncated Moments. *Commun. Stat. Theory Methods* **2017**, *46*, 6222–6227. [CrossRef]
30. Hamedani, G.G. Characterizations of Univariate Continuous Distributions Based on Truncated Moments of Functions of Order Statistics. *Stud. Sci. Math. Hung.* **2010**, *47*, 462–468. [CrossRef]
31. Glänzel, W. A Characterization Theorem Based on Truncated Moments and Its Application to Some Distribution Families. In *Mathematical Statistics and Probability Vol. B*; Bauer, P., Konecny, F., Wertz, W., Eds.; D. Reidel Publishing Company: Dordrecht, The Netherlands, 1987; pp. 75–84.
32. Lindsay, B.G.; Li, B. On second-order optimality of the observed Fisher information. *Ann. Stat.* **1997**, *25*, 2172–2199. [CrossRef]
33. Akaike, H. A New Look at the Statistical Model Identification. *IEEE Trans. Autom. Control* **1974**, *9*, 716–723. [CrossRef]
34. Hussain, T.; Bakouch, H.S.; Chesneau, C. A New Probability Model with Application to Heavy-Tailed Hydrological Data. *Environ. Ecol. Stat.* **2019**, *26*, 127–151. [CrossRef]
35. Murthy, D.N.P.; Xie, M.; Jiang, R. *Weibull Models*; John Wiley and Sons: Hoboken, NJ, USA, 2004.
36. Vuong, Q.H. Likelihood Ratio Tests for Model Selection and Non-Nested Hypotheses. *Econometrica* **1989**, *57*, 307–333. [CrossRef]

37. Maity, R. *Statistical Methods in Hydrology and Hydroclimatology*; Springer Nature Singapore Pte Ltd.: Singapore, 2018.
38. Aarset, M.V. How to Identify a Bathtub Hazard Rate. *IEEE Trans. Reliab.* **1987**, *36*, 106–108. [CrossRef]
39. Dasgupta, R. On the Distribution of. Burr with Applications. *Sankhya B* **2011**, *73*, 1–19. [CrossRef]
40. Dey, S.; Mazucheli, J.; Anis, M. Estimation of Reliability of Multicomponent Stress–strength for a Kumaraswamy Distribution. *Commun. Stat. Theory Methods* **2017**, *46*, 1560–1572. [CrossRef]
41. Dey, S.; Mazucheli, J.; Nadarajah, S. Kumaraswamy Distribution: Different Methods of Estimation. *Comput. Appl. Math.* **2018**, *37*, 2094–2111. [CrossRef]
42. ZeinEldin, R.A.; Chesneau, C.; Jamal, F.; Elgarhy, M. Different Estimation Methods for Type I Half-Logistic Topp–Leone Distribution. *Mathematics* **2019**, *7*, 985. [CrossRef]

mathematics

MDPI

Article

Univariate Probability-G Classes for Scattered Samples under Different Forms of Hazard: Continuous and Discrete Version with Their Inferences Tests

Mohamed S. Eliwa [1,2], Muhammad H. Tahir [3], Muhammad A. Hussain [3], Bader Almohaimeed [4,*], Afrah Al-Bossly [5] and Mahmoud El-Morshedy [5,6]

1 Department of Statistics and Operation Research, College of Science, Qassim University, Buraydah 51482, Saudi Arabia
2 Department of Mathematics, Faculty of Science, Mansoura University, Mansoura 35516, Egypt
3 Department of Statistics, Faculty of Computing, The Islamia University of Bahawalpur, Bahawalpur 63100, Pakistan
4 Department of Mathematics, College of Science, Qassim University, Buraydah 51482, Saudi Arabia
5 Department of Mathematics, College of Science and Humanities in Al-Kharj, Prince Sattam bin Abdulaziz University, Al-Kharj 11942, Saudi Arabia
6 Department of Statistics and Computer Science, Faculty of Science, Mansoura University, Mansoura 35516, Egypt
* Correspondence: bsmhiemied@qu.edu.sa

Abstract: In this paper, we define a new generator to propose continuous as well as discrete families (or classes) of distributions. This generator is used for the DAL model (acronym of the last names of the authors, Dimitrakopoulou, Adamidis, and Loukas). This newly proposed family may be called the new odd DAL (NODAL) G-class or alternate odd DAL G-class of distributions. We developed both a continuous as well as discrete version of this new odd DAL G-class. Some mathematical and statistical properties of these new G-classes are listed. The estimation of the parameters is discussed. Some structural properties of two special models of these classes are described. The introduced generators can be effectively applied to discuss and analyze the different forms of failure rates including decreasing, increasing, bathtub, and J-shaped, among others. Moreover, the two generators can be used to discuss asymmetric and symmetric data under different forms of kurtosis. A Monte Carlo simulation study is reported to assess the performance of the maximum likelihood estimators of these new models. Some real-life data sets (air conditioning, flood discharges, kidney cysts) are analyzed to show that these newly proposed models perform better as compared to well-established competitive models.

Keywords: statistical model; odd G-class; discrete generators; failure analysis; dispersion phenomena; estimation; computer simulation; comparative study; statistics and numerical data

MSC: 60E05; 62E10; 62E15; 62F10

1. Introduction

There is an increasing trend in modern distribution theory by which new flexible models are being tested in different fields through modifications, extended versions, and, most preferably, through generalized classes (G-classes). Suppose that $W[G(\cdot)]$ is a mathematical function that helps in developing G-classes. In modern distribution theory, this function is described as a generator (i.e., a function which generates a G-class after fulfilling the desired criterion). Let T be a random variable (rv); then, the generator is basically a function of a baseline (or parent) cumulative distribution function (cdf) or survival function (sf) $\bar{G}(t) = 1 - G(t)$. $F(t)$ and $f(t)$ are the cdf and probability density function (pdf) of a new model or a G-class, and very few generators have been reported in the literature for developing new G-classes for an rv $T \in [(0,1),(0,\infty),(-\infty,\infty)]$. In the literature the following probability classes/generators have been listed so far for any rv T:

(i) $G(t)$ for range $T \in (0,1)$;
(ii) $-\log \bar{G}(t)$, $-\log G(t)$, $G(t)/\bar{G}(t)$ (odds) and $[-\log \bar{G}(t)]/\bar{G}(t)$ for range $T \in (0,\infty)$;
(iii) $\log[-\log \bar{G}(t)]$ and $\log\{G(t)/\bar{G}(t)\}$ (log-odds) for range $T \in (-\infty,\infty)]$.

The main objective of this article is to present a new G-class of distributions through some odds ratio (or function).

For a lifetime rv T, let $G(t)/\bar{G}(t)$ be the basic odds function criterion, which naturally turns into ratio $\lambda(t)/h(t)$ (reversed hazard rate function divided by the hazard rate function), as a useful measure for lifetime assessment of component(s) (or human organ(s)). Moreover, the probabilities of a uni-variate continuous rv spread over the range of the cdf and sf, that is, $G(t)+\bar{G}(t)=\int_{-\infty}^{\infty} g(t)\,dt = 1$. So, the ratio between these two alternatives ($G(t)$ and $\bar{G}(t)$) is very useful in investigating changes occurring within a model or a phenomenon. Furthermore, these two alternatives are also the key elements for the order statistics, entropies, and records (upper and lower) density functions. The other odds function measures can be chosen as the ratio of the identities in upper and lower records $[-\log \bar{G}(t)]/[-\log G(t)]$ (cumulative hazard rate function divided by the cumulative reversed hazard function), for instance:

(i) Ratio of Lehmann alternatives $(G^{\alpha}(t)/[1-\bar{G}^{\alpha}(t)])$, where $\alpha > 0$ is the power parameter (see Gupta et al. [1]);
(ii) Log odds function $(\log[G(t)/\bar{G}(t)])$ (see Al-Aqtash et al. [2]);
(iii) Logit function $[\log(t/(1-t)]$ (see Torabi and Montazeri [3] and Zubair et al. [4]).

Based on the difference of the two log-odds functions, a well-established tool in survival analysis is the proportional odds model, say $\log[G(t)/\bar{G}(t)] = h_0(t) + z_i'\beta$, where $h_0(t) = \log[G_0(t)/\bar{G}_0(t)]$ is the baseline log odds function and $G_0(t)$ is the probability of failure by time t for an individual with $z = 0$.

Furthermore, Cooray [5] pioneered the concept of the odd function while dealing with probability models, and then he established the odd Weibull model. Gleaton and Lynch [6], while modeling the "strength distribution of an inhomogeneous bundle of brittle elastic fibers under equal load sharing and for checking implementation of the maximum entropy principal (MEP)", proposed the generalized log-logistic transformation, which led to the odd log-logistic G-class. These two pioneering works motivated researchers and practitioners to develop odds-based G-classes, and to investigate special models from them. Some G-classes based on odd ratio $G(t)/\bar{G}(t)$, presented in the statistical literature, are included in Table 1. For more details about G-class, see Alzaatreh et al. [7].

Table 1. Odd ratio for G-classes of distributions.

No.	G-Class	Year	Authors
1	Odd log-logistic-G (OLL-G)	2006	Gleaton and Lynch [6]
2	Odd Gamma-G (OGa-G)	2012	Torabi and Montazeri [8]
3	Odd Weibull-G (OW-G)	2014	Bourguignon et al. [9]
4	Odd generalized-exponential-G (OGE-G)	2015	Tahir et al. [10]
5	Odd additive Weibull-G (OAddW-G)	2016	Hassan and Hemeda [11]
6	Odd Lindley-G (OLind-G)	2017	Gomes-Silva et al. [12]
7	Odd half-Cauchy-G (OHCa-G)	2017	Cordeiro et al. [13]
8	Odd half-Logistic-G (OHL-G)	2017	Affify et al. [14]
9	Odd Burr III-G (OBr3-G)	2017	Jamal et al. [15]
10	Odd Burr X-G (OBrX-G)	2017	Yousof et al. [16]
11	Odd Burr-XII-G (OBr-G)	2018	Cordeiro et al. [17]
12	Odd Frechét-G (OFr-G)	2018	Haq et al. [18]; Hassan and Nassr [19]
13	Odd power-Cauchy-G (OPCa-G)	2018	Alizadeh et al. [20]

Table 1. *Cont.*

No.	G-Class	Year	Authors
14	Odd Xgamma-G (OXGa-G)	2018	Maiti and Pramanik [21]
15	Odd power-Lindley-G (OPLind-G)	2019	Hassan and Nassr [22]; Korkmaz et al. [23]
16	Odd Lomax-G (OLx-G)	2019	Cordeiro et al. [24]
17	Odd Hyperbolic Cosine-G (OHC-G)	2019	Kharazmi et al. [25]
18	Odd flexible Weibull-H (OFW-H)	2019	El-Morshedy and Eliwa [26]
19	Odd inverse Pareto-G (OIPa-G)	2019	Aldahlan et al. [27]
20	Odd Nadarajah-Haghighi-G (ONH-G)	2019	Nascimento et al. [28]
21	Odd Chen-G (OChen-G)	2020	El-Morshedy et al. [29]; Anzagra et al. [30]
22	Odd DAL-G (ODAL-G)	2020	Ahmad et al. [31]
23	Odd Stacy's Gamma-G (OStGa-G)	2020	Nasir et al. [32]
24	Odd Maxwell-G (OMax-G)	2020	Ishaq and Abiodun [33]

2. Background

Several authors have suggested modifications and enhancements to both the exponential and Weibull models in the recent past, with the aim of enhancing their empirical performance and increasing their flexibility. The most peculiar ones are the Lomax exponentiated Weibull model (Ansari and Nofal [34]), extended exponential (ExtE) or generalized exponential(GE) (see Gupta and Kundu [35]), and Nadarajah–Haghighi (NH) (see, Nadarajah and Haghighi [36]). The cdfs of the GE and NH models are

$$F_{GE}(x) = (1 - \exp\{-\lambda\, x\})^{\alpha}, \quad x > 0 \tag{1}$$

and

$$F_{NH}(x) = 1 - \exp\{1 - (1 + \lambda\, x)^{\alpha}\}, \quad x > 0, \tag{2}$$

respectively, where $\lambda > 0$ is a scale parameter and $\alpha > 0$ is a power (or shape) parameter. Clearly, these two models reduce to the exponential model when $\alpha = 1$.

Dimitrakopoulou, Adamidis, and Loukas [37] presented an extension of the Weibull model, in the so-called DAL. The cdf and its corresponding pdf of the DAL distribution can be formulated as

$$F_{DAL}(x) = 1 - \exp\left\{1 - \left(1 + \lambda\, x^{\beta}\right)^{\alpha}\right\}, \quad x > 0 \tag{3}$$

and

$$f_{DAL}(x) = \lambda\alpha\beta\; x^{\beta-1}\left(1 + \lambda\, x^{\beta}\right)^{\alpha-1} \exp\left\{1 - \left(1 + \lambda\, x^{\beta}\right)^{\alpha}\right\}, \tag{4}$$

where the scale parameter is denoted by $\lambda > 0$, while the shape (or power) parameters are indicated by $\alpha > 0$ and $\beta > 0$. For $\alpha = 1$, the DAL model reduces to the Weibull, and for $\alpha = \beta = 1$, the DAL distribution becomes the exponential model. Nowadays, the DAL model has also been reported as the power generalized Weibull (PGW) distribution (Nikulin and Haghighi [38,39]). However, there is some difference in parametrization of the DAL and PGW models, which is apparent from the cdf of the PGW model, as follows:

$$F_{PGW}(x) = 1 - \exp\left\{1 - \left[1 + (x/\lambda)^{\beta}\right]^{1/\gamma}\right\}, \quad x > 0, \tag{5}$$

where $\lambda > 0$ is a scale parameter and $\alpha > 0$ and $\beta > 0$ are shape (or power) parameters. Some generalizations/modifications of the DAL model were derived and discussed in the literature. See, for example, exponentiated-DAL (Peña-Ramírez et al. [40]), half-logistic-DAL (Anwar and Bibi [41]), DAL-Logarithmic (Tafakori et al. [42]), MO-DAL (Afify et al. [43]), and transmuted-DAL (Khan [44]).

In the literature, some odd-based G-classes have been discussed as extensions of the exponential or Weibull models, for instance, Bourguignon et al. [9], Tahir et al. [10], Nascimento et al. [28], El-Morshedy et al. [26], El-Morshedy and Eliwa [29], and Ahmad et al. [31] proposed the OW-G, odd generalized Weibull-G (OGW-G), OGE-G, ONH-G, OFW-H, OChen-G, and ODAL-G classes of distributions.

Recently, Hussain et al. [45] defined two new generators (i) $H_1(x) = G(x)\exp\{\bar{G}(x)\}$ and (ii) $H_2(x) = \bar{G}(x)\exp\{G(x)\}$ for bounded unit interval $(0,1)$ and then introduced two new Kumaraswamy G-classes of distributions from them. In this paper, we develop a new generator $W[G(x)] = [1 - H_2(x)]/H_2(x)$ for $T \in [0,\infty)$, which seems less complicated in comparison to earlier published generators, but it performs better when compared with other models.

On the other hand, from the last two decades, discretizing continuous probability models has received wider attention in distribution theory. The phenomenon of discretization occurs when measuring the lifespan of a product or device becomes impractical or impossible on a continuous scale. In such cases, it may be necessary to record lifetimes on a discrete scale rather than a continuous one. This has led to the study of several discrete distributions in the literature. See, for example, Roy [46], Krishna and Pundir [47], Gómez-Déniz [48], Jazi et al. [49], Gómez-Déniz and Calderín-Ojeda [50], Hussain and Ahmad [51], Hussain et al. [52], Para and Jan [53,54], El-Morshedy et al. [55], Eliwa at al. [56], Eliwa and El-Morshedy [57], Eliwa et al. [58], among others. Despite the existence of several discrete probability models in the literature, there is still space for deriving new discretized probability distributions that are appropriate for various areas. To address this, our paper presents a flexible generator of discrete distributions, known as the discrete new odd DAL-G (DNODAL-G) family, which can cater to various conditions. Our proposal for introducing new G-classes is as follows:

- Generate probability models (ProM) with asymmetric "negatively-skewed, positively-skewed" or symmetric shapes;
- Define special ProM with all kinds of risk/failure rate functions;
- Propose ProM suitable for analyzing and discussing both over- and under-dispersed data;
- Develop ProM for modeling/analyzing both lifetime and counting data sets;
- Provide ProM that consistently produces a better fit than other ProM built using the same underlying model, in addition to other ProM known in the literature.

The article is organized as follows. A new odd G-class of distributions is introduced in Section 3. Some mathematical properties of a new G-class such as a linear representation for the density, moments, generating function, and estimation of the model parameters are addressed in Section 4. A new model (a special case of the newly proposed G-class for continuous rv) is studied in Section 5 along with a Monte Carlo simulation study. The new discrete odd G-class along with a sub-model is defined, and a Monte Carlo simulation study is investigated in Section 6. Empirical investigation of the proposed models is reported in Section 7 by means of real-life data sets. In Section 8, we conclude our paper with some remarks.

3. The New Odd DAL G-Class

Let T be an rv representing the lifetime of a stochastic system having a baseline $G(x)$ distribution. If the rv X represents the odd ratio, then the risk that a system will not be working at time x is given by $[1 - H_2(x)]/H_2(x)$. Therefore, the randomness of X can be modelled by the cdf

$$F(x;\lambda,\alpha,\beta,\xi) = Pr(X \leq x) = \Pi\left(\frac{1 - H_2(x;\xi)}{H_2(x;\xi)}\right), \tag{6}$$

where Π is the cdf of T, $H_2(x;\xi) = \bar{G}(x;\xi)\exp\{G(x;\xi)\}$ and then $W[G(x;\xi)] = [1 - H_2(x;\xi)]/H_2(x;\xi)$. The cdf of the odd DAL-G (NODALG) class is defined as

$$F(x;\lambda,\alpha,\beta,\xi) = \int_0^{[1-H_2(x)]/H_2(x)} \lambda\alpha\beta\, t^{\beta-1}\,(1+\lambda\, t^{\beta})^{\alpha-1}\exp\{1-(1+\lambda\, t^{\beta})^{\alpha}\}\,dt$$
$$= 1-\exp\left\{1-\left[1+\lambda\left(\frac{1-\bar{G}(x;\xi)\exp\{G(x;\xi)\}}{\bar{G}(x;\xi)\exp\{G(x;\xi)\}}\right)^{\beta}\right]^{\alpha}\right\}, \quad x>0, \quad (7)$$

where $\lambda > 0$ is a scale parameter, $\alpha > 0$ and $\beta > 0$ are shape parameters, and ξ is the vector of the baseline parameters. The pdf corresponding to Equation (7) can be expressed as

$$f(x;\lambda,\alpha,\beta,\xi) = \alpha\beta\lambda\, g(x;\xi)G(x;\xi)\exp\{G(x,\xi)\}[1-\bar{G}(x;\xi)\exp\{G(x;\xi)\}]^{\beta-1}$$
$$\times[\bar{G}(x;\xi)\exp\{G(x;\xi)\}]^{-\beta-1}\left[1+\lambda\left(\frac{1-\bar{G}(x;\xi)\exp\{G(x;\xi)\}}{\bar{G}(x;\xi)\exp\{G(x;\xi)\}}\right)^{\beta}\right]^{\alpha-1}$$
$$\times\exp\left\{1-\left[1+\lambda\left(\frac{1-\bar{G}(x;\xi)\exp\{G(x;\xi)\}}{\bar{G}(x;\xi)\exp\{G(x;\xi)\}}\right)^{\beta}\right]^{\alpha}\right\}. \quad (8)$$

Henceforth, the rv X with density (7) is denoted by $X \sim \text{NODALG}(\lambda,\alpha,\beta)$. The hazard rate function (hrf) $h(x)$ of X has the form

$$h(x) = \alpha\beta\lambda\, g(x;\xi)G(x;\xi)\exp\{G(x,\xi)\}[1-\bar{G}(x;\xi)\exp\{G(x;\xi)\}]^{\beta-1}$$
$$\times[\bar{G}(x;\xi)\exp\{G(x;\xi)\}]^{-\beta-1}\left[1+\lambda\left(\frac{1-\bar{G}(x;\xi)\exp\{G(x;\xi)\}}{\bar{G}(x;\xi)\exp\{G(x;\xi)\}}\right)^{\beta}\right]^{\alpha-1}.$$

Here, we let $G(x;\xi) = G(x)$, $\bar{G}(x;\xi) = \bar{G}(x)$ and $g(x;\xi) = g(x)$ to omit the dependence of the parameters.

Proposition. Following [37], if $X \sim \text{NODALG}(\lambda,\alpha,\beta)$, then the subsets of our proposed G-class are

(i) If $Y = G(x)$, then $F_Y(y) = 1 - e^{1-\left[1+\lambda\left(\frac{1-(1-y)\exp(y)}{(1-y)\exp(y)}\right)^{\beta}\right]^{\alpha}}$, for $0 < y < 1$;
(ii) If $Y = \log\left(\frac{G(x)}{1-G(x)}\right)$, then $X \sim \text{ODAL}(\lambda,\alpha,\beta)$;
(iii) If $Y = \log\left(\frac{G(x)}{1-G(x)}\right)^{\beta}$, then $X \sim \text{ONH}(\lambda,\alpha)$;
(iv) If $Y = \frac{1-\bar{G}(x)\exp[G(x)]}{\bar{G}(x)\exp[G(x)]}$, then $X \sim \text{DAL}(\lambda,\alpha,\beta)$;
(v) If $Y = \left(\frac{1-\bar{G}(x)\exp[G(x)]}{\bar{G}(x)\exp[G(x)]}\right)^{\beta}$, then $X \sim \text{NH}(\lambda,\alpha)$;
(vi) If $Y = \left[1+\left(\frac{1-\bar{G}(x)\exp[G(x)]}{\bar{G}(x)\exp[G(x)]}\right)\right]^{\alpha} - 1$, then $X \sim \text{Wei}(\lambda,\beta)$;
(vii) If $Y = \left[1+\left(\frac{1-\bar{G}(x)\exp[G(x)]}{\bar{G}(x)\exp[G(x)]}\right)^{\beta}\right]^{\alpha} - 1$, then $X \sim \text{Exp}(\lambda)$;
(viii) If $Y = \log\left[1+\left(\frac{1-\bar{G}(x)\exp[G(x)]}{\bar{G}(x)\exp[G(x)]}\right)^{\beta}\right]$, then $X \sim \text{Modified Extreme Value}(\alpha)$;
(ix) If $Y = \left\{\log\left[1+\left(\frac{1-\bar{G}(x)\exp[G(x)]}{\bar{G}(x)\exp[G(x)]}\right)^{\beta}\right]\right\}^{1/\beta}$, then $X \sim \text{Power exponential}(\alpha)$;

where Y is a random variable that can take different forms of probability generators.

4. Properties of the NKw-G Family

A G-class or a model is known from some important characteristics which they exhibit mathematically or graphically. In this segment, some mathematical and statistical features of the NKw-G class are derived, which will be useful for the readers.

4.1. Quantile Function

The quantile function (qf) is a useful statistical measure that is helpful in obtaining some useful properties, including simulation study. The qf of the NODAL-G class can be expressed as

$$Q(u) \quad = \quad G^{-1}\left[1+W\left(-e^{-1}\left[1+\left\{\frac{1}{\lambda}\left[\{1-\log(1-u)\}^{\frac{1}{\alpha}}-1\right]\right\}^{\frac{1}{\beta}}\right]^{-1}\right)\right],$$

where the u follows a uniform distribution over an interval $(0,1)$, G^{-1} is the inverse function of base line cdf, and the Lambert-W function is the inverse function of $F(w) = w\,e^{w}$. The power series expansion for $F(z) = ProductLog[z]$ using the software Mathematica 12 yields the principal solution for w in $F(w) = w\,e^{w} = z$

$$W(z) = z - z^2 + \frac{3z^3}{2} - \frac{8z^4}{3} + \frac{125z^5}{24} - \frac{54z^6}{5} + \frac{16807z^7}{720} - \frac{16384z^8}{315} + \frac{531441z^9}{4480} - \frac{156250z^{10}}{567},$$

where $ProductLog[z]$ is used as Lambert-W function in the software Mathematica.

4.2. Linear Representation

Here, a useful expansion for Equation (8) is derived. By utilizing the exponential power series in Equation (7), we can write

$$F(x) = 1 - e\sum_{i=0}^{\infty}\frac{(-1)^i}{i!}\left\{1+\lambda\left[\frac{1-\bar{G}(x;\xi)\exp[G(x;\xi)]}{\bar{G}(x;\xi)\exp[G(x;\xi)]}\right]^{\beta}\right\}^{\alpha i}. \tag{9}$$

For a real non-integer, the generalized binomial expansion holds $(1+z)^a = \sum_{j=0}^{\infty}\binom{a}{j}z^j$, and then applying in Equation (9) gives

$$F(x) = e\sum_{i=0}^{\infty}\sum_{j=1}^{\infty}\frac{\lambda^j(-1)^{i+1}}{i!}\binom{\alpha i}{j}[\bar{G}(x;\xi)\exp\{G(x;\xi)\}]^{-\beta j}[1-\bar{G}(x;\xi)\exp\{G(x;\xi)\}]^{\beta j}.$$

Using the previous expansion and the exponential power series, we obtain after some algebra

$$F(x) = \sum_{p=0}^{\infty}\sum_{r=0}^{\infty}V_{p,r}\,G(x;\xi)^{p+r}, \tag{10}$$

where

$$V_{p,r} = \sum_{i,m=0}^{\infty}\sum_{j=1}^{\infty}\frac{e\lambda^j(-1)^{i+m+p+r+1}}{i!p!}\binom{\alpha i}{j}\binom{\beta j}{m}\binom{-\beta j+m}{r}.$$

By differentiating Equation (10), the G-class density follows as

$$f(x) = \sum_{p=0}^{\infty}\sum_{r=0}^{\infty}V_{p,r}\,(p+r)\,g(x;\xi)\,G(x;\xi)^{p+r-1}. \tag{11}$$

Equation (11) reveals that the NODAL-G family density is a linear combination of exponentiated-G (exp-G) densities. Then, some statistical properties of X can be obtained from Equation (11) and well-established properties of the exp-G distributions.

4.3. Moments

In this segment, the ordinary moment (om), lower incomplete moment (lincm), and moment generating function (mgf) are derived. Let $Y_{p,r}$ be an rv having the exp-G family with power parameter $(p+r)$. First, the sth om of X, say $\mathbb{E}(X^s) = \int_{-\infty}^{\infty} x^s f(x)\, dx$, can be expressed from Equation (11) as

$$\mathbb{E}(X^s) = \sum_{p,r=0}^{\infty} V_{p,r}\, \mathbb{E}(Y_{p,r}^s) = \sum_{p,r=0}^{\infty} (p+r)\, V_{p,r}\, \tau_{s,p+r}, \tag{12}$$

where $\tau_{s,p+r} = \int_{-\infty}^{\infty} x^s\, G(x;\xi)^{p+r-1}\, g(x;\xi)\, dx = \int_0^1 Q_G(u;\xi)^s\, u^{p+r} du$, and $Q_G(u;\xi)$ is qf of baseline G. The well-known relationships can be used to derive the central moments and cumulants of X from Equation (12). Second, the sth lincm of X, say $m_s(y) = \int_{-\infty}^{y} x^s f(x)\, dx$, is

$$m_s(y) = \sum_{p,r=0}^{\infty} V_{p,r} \int_{-\infty}^{y} x^s\, h_{p+r}(x)\, dx = \sum_{p,r=0}^{\infty} (p+r)\, V_{p,r} \int_0^{G(y;\xi))} Q_G(u;\xi)^s\, u^{p+r} du. \tag{13}$$

For most G distributions, it is possible to numerically evaluate the last two integrals in the equation. The first lincm, $m_1(y)$, is useful in constructing popular measures such as Bonferroni and Lorenz curves in various fields such as demography, economics, reliability, medicine, and insurance. In addition, it can also be applied to determine the sum of the deviations from the mean and median of X. Furthermore, the mgf $M_X(t) = \mathbb{E}(e^{t,X})$ of X can be derived from (11).

$$M_X(t) = \sum_{p,r=0}^{\infty} V_{p,r}\, M_{p,r}(t) = \sum_{p,r=0}^{\infty} (p+r)\; V_{p,r}\, \rho_{p,r}(t), \tag{14}$$

where $M_{p,r}(t)$ is the mgf of $Y_{p,r}$ and $\rho_{p,r}(t) = \int_0^1 \exp[t\, Q_G(u;\xi)]\, u^{p+r} du$. Therefore, we can derive the mgfs of several particular NODAL-G models directly from Equation (14) and exp-G generating functions.

4.4. Maximum Likelihood Estimation

Uncensored maximum likelihood estimation, in which all of the data are observed without any censoring, is a technique for estimating the parameters of a probability distribution based on a sample of data. This segment deals with the estimation of the unknown NODAL-G class parameters via the maximum likelihood (ML) approach. The ML estimation refers to a method of estimating unknown parameters by selecting values that maximize the likelihood of observing a given set of data. This technique is often used in various types of statistical modeling, such as regression and classification. It is a popular approach due to its simplicity and the fact that it is easy to implement. At its core, ML estimation is a mathematical approach for finding the probability distribution of a unknown variable based on a given sample of data. This is achieved by finding the maximum value of the likelihood function, which is based on the probability distribution of the given data. The likelihood function is computed by taking the product of the probability of the observations in the data set. Max likelihood estimation is used in many areas of study, including economics, biology, engineering, and computer science. As an example, in economics, it is used to make predictions about the probability of future events based on past observations. In biology, it is used to estimate gene frequencies and relationships between genes. For more details about the ML approach and its statistical properties, see Casella and Berger [59]. The log-likelihood function $\ell(\Theta)$ for the parameter vector $\Theta = (\lambda, \alpha, \beta, \xi)'$ can be derived from n observations/notes $x_1, \ldots, x_n$.

$$\begin{aligned}\ell_n &= n\log\alpha + n\log\beta + n\log\lambda + \sum_{i=1}^{n}\log g(x_i;\xi) + (\beta-1)\sum_{i=1}^{n}\log[1-\bar{G}(x_i;\xi)\exp\{G(x_i;\xi)\}] \\ &\quad + \sum_{i=1}^{n}\log[G(x_i;\xi)\exp\{G(x_i,\xi)\}] + (\alpha-1)\sum_{i=1}^{n}\log\left[1+\lambda\left(\frac{1-\bar{G}(x_i;\xi)\exp\{G(x_i;\xi)\}}{\bar{G}(x_i;\xi)\exp\{G(x_i;\xi)\}}\right)^{\beta}\right] \\ &\quad -(\beta+1)\sum_{i=1}^{n}\log[\bar{G}(x_i;\xi)\exp\{G(x_i;\xi)\}] + \sum_{i=1}^{n}\left\{1-\left[1+\lambda\left(\frac{1-\bar{G}(x_i;\xi)\exp\{G(x_i;\xi)\}}{\bar{G}(x_i;\xi)\exp\{G(x_i;\xi)\}}\right)^{\beta}\right]^{\alpha}\right\}.\end{aligned}$$

One way to find the maximum likelihood estimate (MLE) $\widehat{\Theta}$ of Θ is to maximize the likelihood function $\ell(\Theta)$. There are several numerical optimization routines available in different programming languages such as `R`, `SAS`, and `Ox` that can be used to maximize $\ell(\Theta)$. For instance, the `optim` function in `R`, the `PROC NLMIXED` in `SAS`, and the (sub-routine `MaxBFGS`) `Ox` can be used for this purpose.

5. The NODAL-Weibull Distribution

In this Section, we consider a special model of the NODAL-G class, the NODAL-Weibull (NODALW) distribution, by taking the Weibull as a baseline model. The cdf and pdf of Weibull distributions are $G(x) = 1 - e^{-k\,x^c}$ and $g(x) = c\,k\,x^{c-1}\,e^{-k\,x^c}$, respectively, where $k > 0$ is a scale parameter and $c > 0$ is a shape parameter. By setting $\lambda = 1$, the cdf of the NODALW distribution reduces to

$$F(x) = 1 - \exp\left\{1 - \left[1 + \left(\frac{1-e^{-kx^c}\exp\left(1-e^{-kx^c}\right)}{e^{-kx^c}\exp(1-e^{-kx^c})}\right)^{\beta}\right]^{\alpha}\right\}. \tag{15}$$

The pdf corresponding to Equation (15) is

$$\begin{aligned} f(x) &= \alpha\beta c k x^{c-1} e^{-kx^c}\left[1-e^{-kx^c}\exp\left(1-e^{-kx^c}\right)\right]\left[1-e^{-kx^c}\exp\left(1-e^{-kx^c}\right)\right]^{\beta-1} \\ &\quad \times\left[e^{-kx^c}\exp\left(1-e^{-kx^c}\right)\right]^{-\beta-1}\left[1+\left(\frac{1-e^{-kx^c}\exp\left(1-e^{-kx^c}\right)}{e^{-kx^c}\exp(1-e^{-kx^c})}\right)^{\beta}\right]^{\alpha-1} \\ &\quad \times\exp\left\{1-\left[1+\left(\frac{1-e^{-kx^c}\exp\left(1-e^{-kx^c}\right)}{e^{-kx^c}\exp(1-e^{-kx^c})}\right)^{\beta}\right]^{\alpha}\right\}. \end{aligned} \tag{16}$$

Henceforth, let $X \sim \text{NODALW}(\alpha, \beta, k, c)$ be the rv with density (16). The hrf of X is

$$\begin{aligned} h(x) &= \alpha\beta c k x^{c-1} e^{-kx^c}\left[1-e^{-kx^c}\exp\left(1-e^{-kx^c}\right)\right]\left[1-e^{-kx^c}\exp\left(1-e^{-kx^c}\right)\right]^{\beta-1} \\ &\quad \times\left[e^{-kx^c}\exp\left(1-e^{-kx^c}\right)\right]^{-\beta-1}\left[1+\left(\frac{1-e^{-kx^c}\exp\left(1-e^{-kx^c}\right)}{e^{-kx^c}\exp(1-e^{-kx^c})}\right)^{\beta}\right]^{\alpha-1}. \end{aligned}$$

The sketches of the density and failure rate of X are plotted in Figure 1 for some parameter values. Figure 1a displays the uni-modal (right-skewed and left-skewed) and reversed-J shapes of the density of X. Figure 1b exhibits the failure rate shapes of X such as increasing, decreasing, and bathtub.

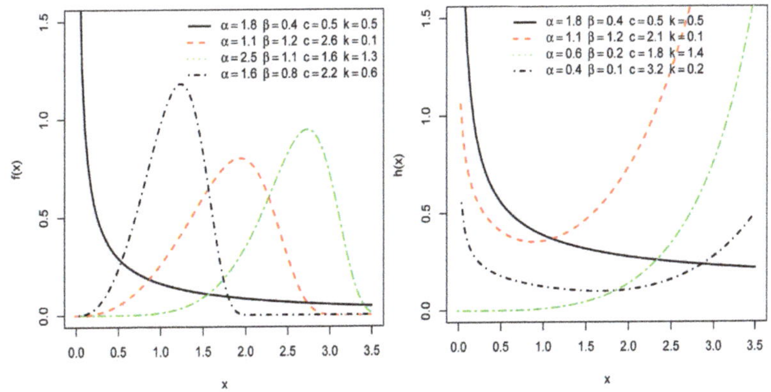

(a) (b)

Figure 1. Sketches of (**a**) the densities, and (**b**) the hrf of the NODALW model.

5.1. Linear Representation of NODALW Model

The NODALW density follows from Equation (11) as

$$f(x) = \sum_{p=0}^{\infty} \sum_{r=0}^{\infty} V_{p,r}\, k\,(p+r)\, c\, x^{c-1} \mathrm{e}^{-k x^c} \left(1 - \mathrm{e}^{-k x^c}\right)^{p+r-1}. \tag{17}$$

Using the generalized binomial expansion in Equation (17), we obtain

$$f(x) = \sum_{\tau=0}^{\infty} \omega_\tau\, k(\tau+1)\, c\, x^{c-1}\, \mathrm{e}^{-k(\tau+1)\, x^c}, \tag{18}$$

where $\omega_\tau = \frac{(-1)^\tau}{\tau+1}\binom{p+r-1}{\tau} \sum_{p,r=0}^{\infty} (p+r)\, V_{p,r}$. Equation (18) reveals that the NODALW density has a linear representation in terms of Weibull densities. So, several of its structural properties can be obtained from the Weibull density. The qf of the NODALW distribution is

$$Q(u) \;=\; \left\{ -\frac{1}{k} \log\left[-W\left(-\mathrm{e}^{-1}\left[1 + \left\{ [1 - \log(1-u)]^{\frac{1}{\alpha}} - 1 \right\}^{\frac{1}{\beta}} \right]^{-1} \right) \right] \right\}^{\frac{1}{c}}, \quad 0 < u < 1. \tag{19}$$

5.2. Properties of NODALW Model

Let Z_p be an rv with Weibull density $\pi(x; p, c)$. Then, some quantities of X can follow from those of Z_p. First, the sth om of X can be expressed as

$$\mu_s' = \Gamma\left(\frac{s}{c} + 1\right) \sum_{\tau=0}^{\infty} \frac{\omega_\tau}{[k(\tau+1)]^{s/c}}, \tag{20}$$

where $\Gamma(a) = \int_0^\infty t^{a-1} \mathrm{e}^{-t} dt$. Using Equation (20), we can recursively calculate the cumulants (κ_s) of X. Specifically, the sth cumulant is determined by subtracting the sum of products of previous cumulants (κ_k) and raw moments (μ_{s-k}'), where the products are taken over all k from 1 to $s-1$, inclusive. The formula is expressed as

$$\kappa_s = \mu' s - \sum k = 1^{s-1} \binom{s-1}{k-1}, \kappa_k, \mu_{s-k}'$$

The first cumulant, κ_1, is equal to the first raw moment, μ_1'. The skewness, γ_1, and kurtosis, γ_2, of X can be obtained by dividing the third and fourth standardized cumulants by the square of the second standardized cumulant, respectively. Some plots of skewness (sk) and kurtosis (ku) for X are presented in Figure 2. It can be seen that the proposed class can be used to discuss the different forms of kurtosis.

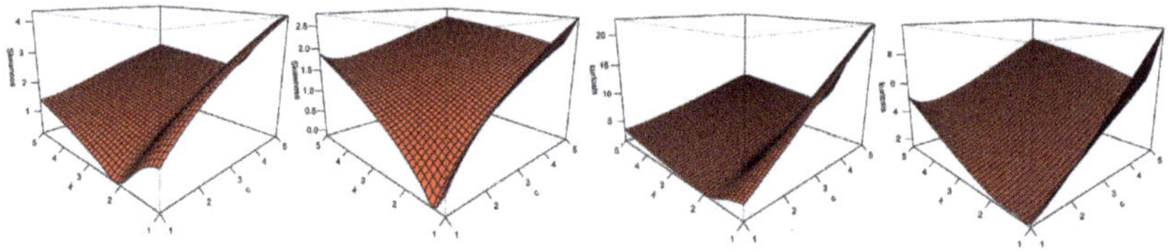

(a) (b)

Figure 2. Plots of the (**a**) sk and (**b**) ku of the NODALW model.

The sth incomplete moment of X, denoted by $m_s(y) = E(X^s \mid X \leq y) = \int_0^y x^s f(x)dx$, is easily obtained by changing variables from the lower incomplete gamma function $\gamma(s,x) = \int_0^\infty x^{s-1} e^{-x} dx$ when calculating the corresponding moment of Z_p. Then, we obtain

$$m_s(z) = \sum_{\tau=0}^{\infty} \omega_\tau \frac{\gamma(\frac{s}{c}+1, k(\tau+1)x^c)}{(k(\tau+1))^{s/c}}. \tag{21}$$

5.3. Simulation Study: NODALW Model

Simulation studies are a popular and effective method of testing estimator performance in a variety of scenarios. By running several simulations, it is possible to approximate real-world performance and gain insight into how well the estimator will function in the field. The first step of a simulation study is to establish the parameters of the experiment. This involves setting up criteria for the data to be sampled, including number of samples, sample size, and the sampling process. Once the parameters have been established, the next step is to generate a simulated dataset that matches the specified criteria. This dataset should have features that are as close as possible to the features of the real-world data. Once the dataset has been generated, the estimator can be applied to the data. Depending on the type of estimator, different metrics may be used to measure the performance of the estimator. These metrics may include root mean squared error, mean absolute error, and R-squared. In this Section, we conduct a Monte Carlo simulation study to assess the performance of the MLEs of the parameters α, β, c, and k. The random numbers of size 50, 100, 200, and 500 are generated by the inversion method and are repeated $N = 1000$ times for each sample size. The sample average biases (Bias), coverage probabilities (CPs), and mean-squared errors (MSEs) of the estimates are calculated. The following formulas are used:

$$Bias(\hat{\theta}) = \sum_{i=1}^{N} \frac{\hat{\theta}_i}{N} - \theta \text{ and } MSE(\hat{\theta}) = \sum_{i=1}^{N} \frac{(\hat{\theta}_i - \theta)^2}{N}$$

and

$$CP(\hat{\theta}) = \frac{1}{N} \sum_{i=1}^{N} I\left(\hat{\theta}_i - 1.9599 s_{\hat{\theta}_i} < \theta < \hat{\theta}_i + 1.9599 s_{\hat{\theta}_i}\right),$$

where $I(.)$ is the indicator function and $s_{\hat{\theta}_i} = \left(s_{\hat{\alpha}_i}, s_{\hat{\beta}_i}, s_{\hat{c}_i}, s_{\hat{k}_i}\right)$ are the standard errors of the MLEs. These quantities for some values of α, β, c, and k are reported in Tables 2–4. The figures in these tables reveal that the MLEs perform well for estimating the parameters of the NODALW distribution.

Table 2. Biases, MSEs, and CPs for $\alpha = 0.2$, $\beta = 0.5$, $c = 0.5$, and $k = 1$.

		$n = 50$			$n = 100$	
	Bias	**MSE**	**CP**	**Bias**	**MSE**	**CP**
α	0.246	0.134	0.98	0.227	0.104	0.95
β	0.078	0.245	0.93	0.222	0.106	0.97
c	0.072	0.040	0.99	0.054	0.021	0.99
k	−0.413	0.340	0.73	−0.405	0.296	0.76
		$n = 200$			$n = 500$	
α	0.144	0.053	0.98	0.075	0.016	0.99
β	0.007	0.008	0.96	0.004	0.003	0.98
c	0.026	0.006	0.99	0.008	0.001	0.98
k	−0.329	0.194	0.79	−0.216	0.097	0.86

Table 3. Biases, MSEs, and CPs for $\alpha = 0.2$, $\beta = 0.6$, $c = 1.8$, and $k = 1.5$.

		$n = 50$			$n = 100$	
	Bias	**MSE**	**CP**	**Bias**	**MSE**	**CP**
α	0.231	0.125	0.98	0.219	0.117	0.98
β	0.158	0.591	0.89	0.033	0.201	0.92
c	0.243	0.627	1.00	0.203	0.319	0.99
k	−0.563	0.633	0.80	−0.555	0.571	0.80
		$n = 200$			$n = 500$	
α	0.186	0.095	0.98	0.125	0.051	0.98
β	0.003	0.077	0.94	−0.007	0.005	0.95
c	0.118	0.138	0.99	0.056	0.036	0.98
k	−0.475	0.464	0.82	−0.372	0.314	0.82

Table 4. Biases, MSEs, and CPs for $\alpha = 0.4$, $\beta = 1.5$, $c = 0.9$, and $k = 1$.

		$n = 50$			$n = 100$	
	Bias	**MSE**	**CP**	**Bias**	**MSE**	**CP**
α	0.128	0.027	0.78	0.095	0.383	0.80
β	0.853	3.935	0.89	0.758	3.219	0.94
c	0.151	0.472	0.95	0.033	0.255	0.93
k	0.229	0.260	0.92	0.222	0.199	0.95
		$n = 200$			$n = 500$	
α	0.030	0.137	0.82	−0.007	0.050	0.84
β	0.524	1.745	0.96	0.349	1.203	0.91
c	0.022	0.163	0.91	0.017	0.107	0.93
k	0.218	0.152	0.97	0.157	0.070	0.98

6. Discrete NODAL-G Family

According to a survival discretization approach, the rv X is said to have the discrete NODAL-G (dNODAL-G) class if its cdf can be formulated as

$$V(x;\lambda,\alpha,\beta,\xi) = 1 - \exp\left\{1 - \left[1 + \lambda\left(\frac{1-\overline{G}(x+1;\xi)\exp\{G(x+1;\xi)\}}{\overline{G}(x+1;\xi)\exp\{G(x+1;\xi)\}}\right)^{\beta}\right]^{\alpha}\right\}, \quad x \in \mathbb{N}_0, \tag{22}$$

where $\lambda > 0$ is a scale parameter, $\alpha > 0$ and $\beta > 0$ are shape parameters, ξ is the vector of the baseline parameters, and $\mathbb{N}_0 = \{0, 1, 2, \ldots\}$. The probability mass function (pmf) and hrf corresponding to Equation (22) are

$$v(x;\lambda,\alpha,\beta,\xi) = \exp\left\{1-\left[1+\lambda\left(\frac{1-\overline{G}(x;\xi)\exp\{G(x;\xi)\}}{\overline{G}(x;\xi)\exp\{G(x;\xi)\}}\right)^{\beta}\right]^{\alpha}\right\} - \exp\left\{1-\left[1+\lambda\left(\frac{1-\overline{G}(x+1;\xi)\exp\{G(x+1;\xi)\}}{\overline{G}(x+1;\xi)\exp\{G(x+1;\xi)\}}\right)^{\beta}\right]^{\alpha}\right\}, \quad (23)$$

and $h(x;\lambda,\alpha,\beta,\xi) = \frac{v(x;\lambda,\alpha,\beta,\xi)}{1-V(x-1;\lambda,\alpha,\beta,\xi)}$, respectively, where $x \in \mathbb{N}_0$.

6.1. The DNODAL-Geometric (DNODALGeo) Distribution

Consider the cdf of the geometric (Geo) model. Then, the pmf of the DNODALGeo distribution is

$$V(x;\lambda,\alpha,\beta,p) = \exp\left\{1-\left[1+\lambda\left(\frac{1-p^{x+1}\exp\{1-p^{x+1}\}}{p^{x+1}\exp\{1-p^{x+1}\}}\right)^{\beta}\right]^{\alpha}\right\}, \quad x \in \mathbb{N}_0, \quad (24)$$

where $\lambda > 0, \alpha > 0, \beta > 0$, and $0 < p < 1$. For convenience, let $\lambda = 1$ in Equation (24). Figures 3 and 4 display the pmf and hrf of the DNODALGeo distribution for some parameter values.

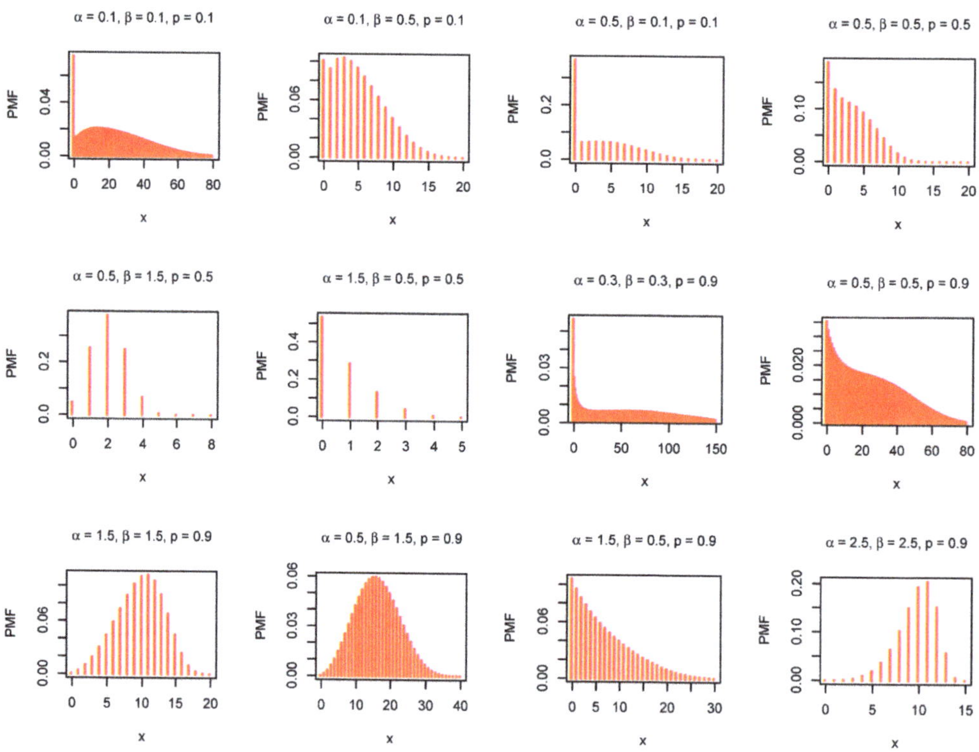

Figure 3. The pmf of the DNODALGeo model.

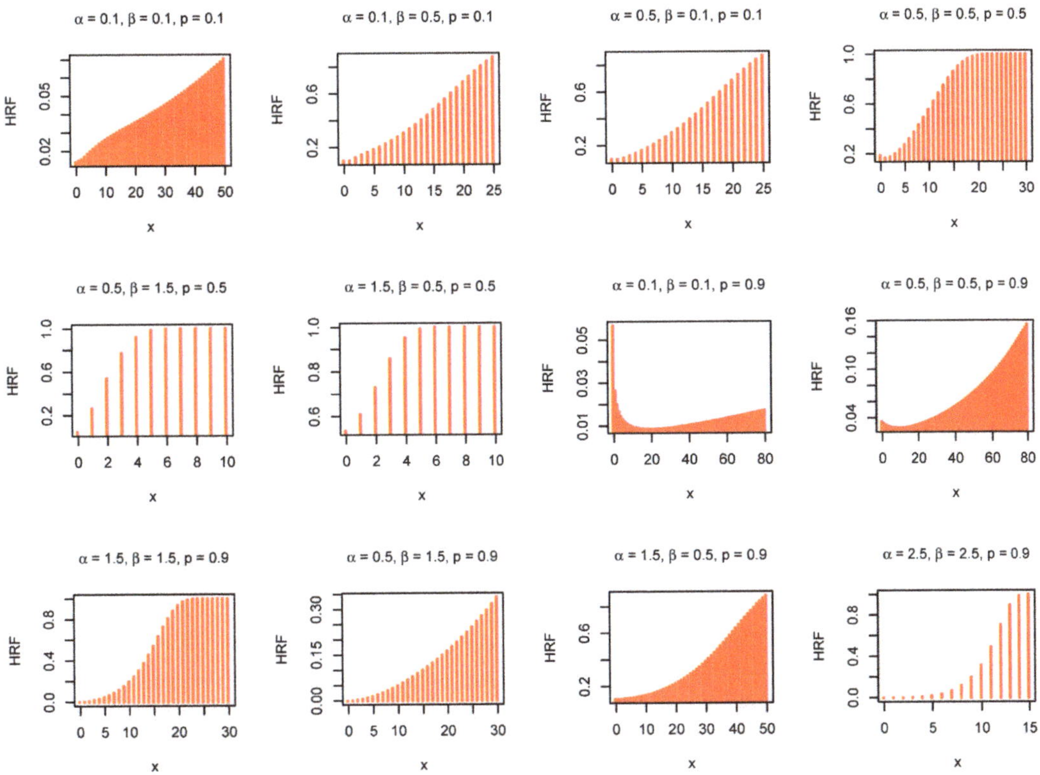

Figure 4. The hrf of the DNODALGeo model.

PMF can be either monomodal or bimodal and can be used to analyze different types of data (positively skewed, negatively skewed, as well as symmetric). Moreover, hrf can be either an increment, a fixed increment, a J-shape, or a bathtub.

6.2. Simulation

We generate a random variable X from the DNODALGeo distribution by generating the value Z from the continuous model and then discretize $X = [Z]$, which is the largest integer less than or equal to Z. We generate 1,000 samples of size $n = 20, 22, 24, \ldots, 150$ from the DNODALGeo$(0.5, 0.9, 0.8)$ and DNODALGeo$(1.5, 1.5, 0.5)$ models, respectively. The empirical results are given in Figures 5 and 6, respectively.

It is clear from Figures 5 and 6 that the biases and MSEs always tend to zero when n increases, which shows the consistency of the estimators.

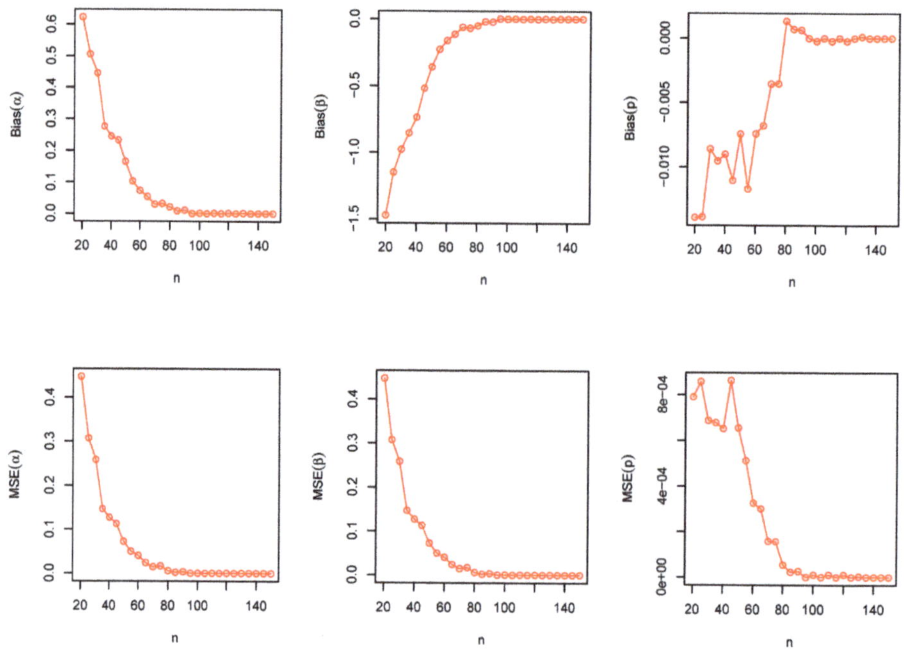

Figure 5. The biases and MSEs for the DNODALGeo(0.5, 0.9, 0.8) model.

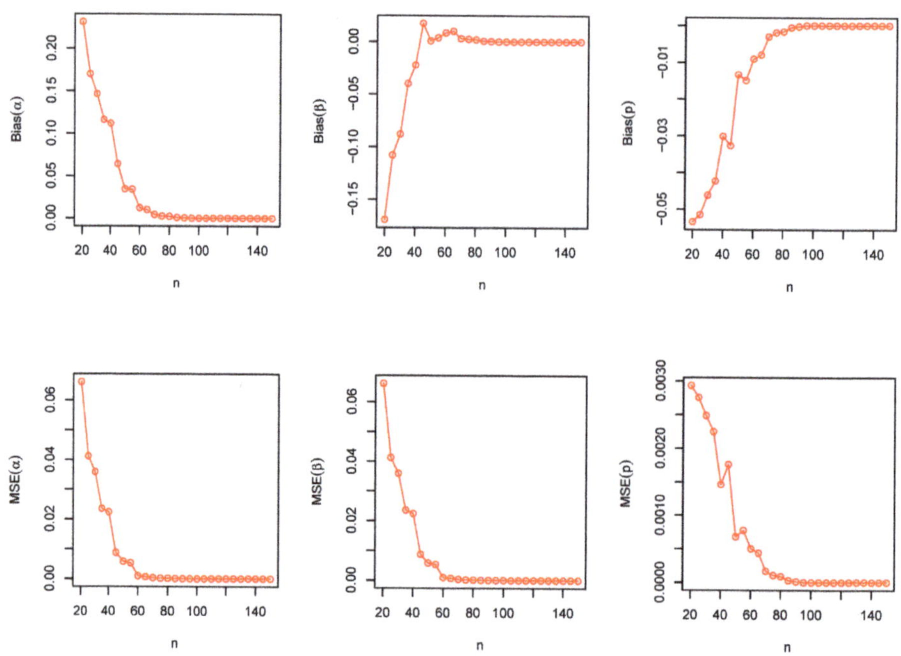

Figure 6. The biases and MSEs for the DNODALGeo(1.5, 1.5, 0.5) model.

7. Applications

In this Section, we illustrate the empirical importance of the NODALW and DNODALGeo models by means of three real-life data sets. First, two data sets are utilized to illustrate the flexibility of the NODALW distribution. Second, a third data set is used to test the usefulness of the DNODALGeo distribution.

7.1. Empirical Illustration of the NODAL-G Family

Here, we compare the NODALW distribution with some well-established competitive models: Kumaraswamy–Weibull (KwW) (see Cordeiro et al. [60]), beta-Weibull (BW) (see Lee et al. [61]), exponentiated-generalized Weibull (EGW) (see Oguntunde et al. [62]), McDonald-Weibull (McW) (see Cordeiro et al. [63]), gamma-Weibull (GaW) (see Cordeiro et al. [64]), and Weibull (W) to prove the flexibility of the new family. The cdf and pdf of NODALW distribution are, respectively, given as

$$F(x) = 1 - \exp\left\{1 - \left[1 + \left(\frac{1 - e^{-kx^c}\exp\left(1 - e^{-kx^c}\right)}{e^{-kx^c}\exp(1 - e^{-kx^c})}\right)^{\beta}\right]^{\alpha}\right\}.$$

and

$$\begin{aligned} f(x) &= \alpha\beta c k x^{c-1} e^{-kx^c}\left[1 - e^{-kx^c}\exp\left(1 - e^{-kx^c}\right)\right]\left[1 - e^{-kx^c}\exp\left(1 - e^{-kx^c}\right)\right]^{\beta-1} \\ &\quad \times\left[e^{-kx^c}\exp\left(1 - e^{-kx^c}\right)\right]^{-\beta-1}\left[1 + \left(\frac{1 - e^{-kx^c}\exp\left(1 - e^{-kx^c}\right)}{e^{-kx^c}\exp(1 - e^{-kx^c})}\right)^{\beta}\right]^{\alpha-1} \\ &\quad \times\exp\left\{1 - \left[1 + \left(\frac{1 - e^{-kx^c}\exp\left(1 - e^{-kx^c}\right)}{e^{-kx^c}\exp(1 - e^{-kx^c})}\right)^{\beta}\right]^{\alpha}\right\}. \end{aligned}$$

Data Set 1. Air Conditioning Data. The data are taken from Kus [65] representing the numbers of the successive failures for an air conditioning system. The shape of the data can be discussed through Figure 7. The data were found to be asymmetric and some extreme observations were reported.

Data Set 2. Precipitation Data. The data are taken from Katz et al. [66] and Asgharzadeh et al. [67] representing the maximum annual flood discharges (in units of 1000 cubic feet per second) of the North Saskachevan River at Edmonton, over a period of 48 years. The shape of the data can be displayed in Figure 8.

The NODALW model and other competitive models are fitted to these two data sets using the *AdequacyModel* package for the R statistical computing environment written by Marinho et al. [68].

The MLEs ($\hat{\ell}$) are used to evaluate the log-likelihood function, while various goodness-of-fit statistics ("GoFS"), such as Akaike-information-criterion ("AIC"), Bayesian-information-criterion ("BIC"), Hannan-Quinn-information criterion ("HQIC"), Anderson–Darling (AD), Cramér–von Mises (CvM), and Kolmogrov–Smirnov (KS), are employed to compare models. A good fit is indicated by lower values of these statistics and higher P-values of the KS statistic.

The values of the GoFS in Tables 5 and 7 show that the NODALW model gives small values for these statistics and then it provides the best fit as compared to other fitted distributions (KwW, BW, EGW, McW, GaW, and W) to the two data sets. Tables 6 and 8 report the MLEs and their standard errors (SEs) for the NODALW model and other competitive models. The plots in Figures 9 and 10 also support our claim. To establish the unique property of the maximum likelihood estimators, the profile log-maximum likelihood function (pllf) was plotted for each parameter for the first and second datasets. It can be noted that the values of the estimators gave the maximum likelihood function the largest value; see Figures 11 and 12. As can be seen, the form of the maximum likelihood function is unimodal for each parameter.

Table 5. Some statistics and p-value for the fitted models to data set 1.

Distribution	$\hat{\ell}$	AIC	BIC	HQIC	AD	CvM	KS	KS p-Value
NODALW	976.1618	1960.3240	1973.0730	1965.4940	0.1640	0.0196	0.0311	0.9951
KwW	978.2675	1964.5350	1977.2850	1969.7050	0.2925	0.0313	0.0388	0.9501
BW	977.0803	1962.1610	1974.9100	1967.3300	0.2001	0.0219	0.0391	0.9470
EGW	978.7362	1965.4720	1978.2220	1970.6420	0.5620	0.0878	0.0420	0.9100
McW	976.2409	1962.4820	1978.4190	1968.9440	0.1628	0.0202	0.0321	0.9928
GaW	979.8445	1965.6890	1975.2510	1969.5660	0.7633	0.1219	0.0504	0.753
W	981.1477	1966.2950	1972.6700	1968.8800	0.9755	0.1577	0.0567	0.6123

Table 6. MLEs and their SEs (in parentheses) for the fitted models to data set 1.

Distribution	α	β	c	k	θ
NODALW	0.1454	2.9036	0.4762	0.0914	–
	(0.0580)	(0.6640)	(0.0970)	(0.0151)	–
KwW	0.44370	0.64040	6.98780	0.13710	–
	(0.00330)	(0.00260)	(0.06740)	(0.01040)	–
BW	0.36620	0.65660	3.86960	0.14360	–
	(0.00470)	(0.00630)	(0.74020)	(0.01240)	–
EGW	0.01280	0.70890	1.36590	1.60630	–
	(0.01030)	(0.11060)	(0.83440)	(0.48390)	–
McW	0.04510	0.91630	0.18380	0.25040	9.685
	(0.03280)	(0.23770)	(0.1420)	(0.12550)	(4.51590)
GaW	0.01740	0.78540	1.28540	–	–
	(0.00820)	(0.12730)	(0.35230)	–	–
W	0.01180	0.90570	–	–	–
	(0.0010)	(0.05120)	–	–	–

Table 7. Some statistics and p-value for the fitted models to data set 2.

Distribution	$\hat{\ell}$	AIC	BIC	HQIC	AD	CvM	KS	KS p-Value
NODALW	215.1079	438.2157	445.7005	441.0442	0.2023	0.0286	0.0827	0.8981
KwW	215.5195	439.0389	446.5238	441.8675	0.2495	0.0347	0.0834	0.8924
BW	216.1573	440.3147	447.7995	443.1432	0.3387	0.0477	0.0973	0.7538
EGW	218.1801	444.3601	451.8449	447.1887	0.6147	0.0913	0.0973	0.7543
McW	215.7566	441.5132	450.8692	445.0489	0.2699	0.0374	0.0837	0.8895
GaW	219.4700	444.9401	450.5537	447.0615	0.8278	0.1250	0.1176	0.5203
W	225.7065	455.4131	459.1555	456.8273	1.7286	0.2765	0.1399	0.3048

Table 8. MLEs and their SEs (in parentheses) for the fitted models to data set 2.

Distribution	α	β	c	k	θ
NODALW	0.0686	16.0368	0.4969	0.0568	–
	(0.0379)	(9.1204)	(0.2109)	(0.0363)	–
KwW	0.16090	1.02520	54.78250	0.20410	–
	(0.01530)	(0.02760)	(0.13580)	(0.03820)	–
BW	0.13200	1.10800	23.06020	0.19400	–
	(0.00730)	(0.00680)	(8.79410)	(0.03240)	–
EGW	0.00900	0.77740	5.59660	10.54930	–
	(0.00410)	(0.13700)	(2.04580)	(5.68210)	–
McW	0.16080	1.00490	14.50780	0.22100	2.5180
	(0.03400)	(0.04660)	(9.82270)	(0.07570)	(0.08950)
GaW	4.61440	0.49830	14.72250	–	–
	(0.15180)	(0.02170)	(1.72390)	–	–
W	0.01710	1.77190	–	–	–
	(0.00150)	(0.17760)	–	–	–

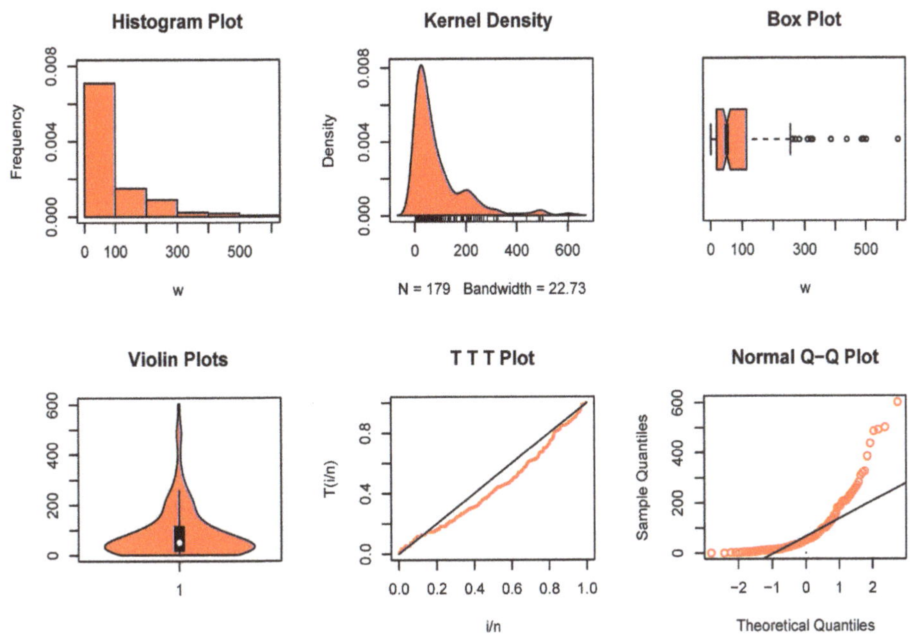

Figure 7. Non-parametric visualization plots for data set I.

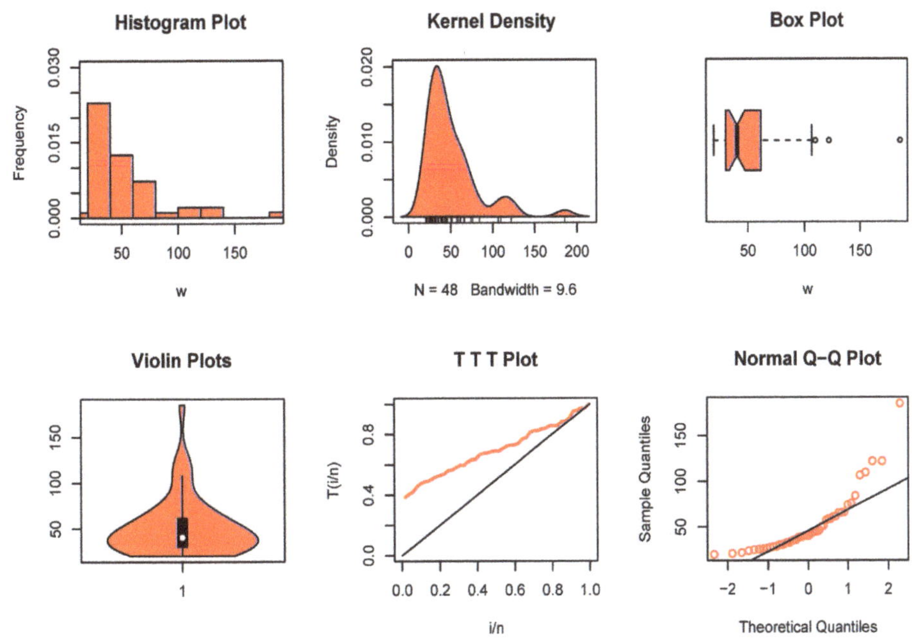

Figure 8. Non-parametric visualization plots for data set II.

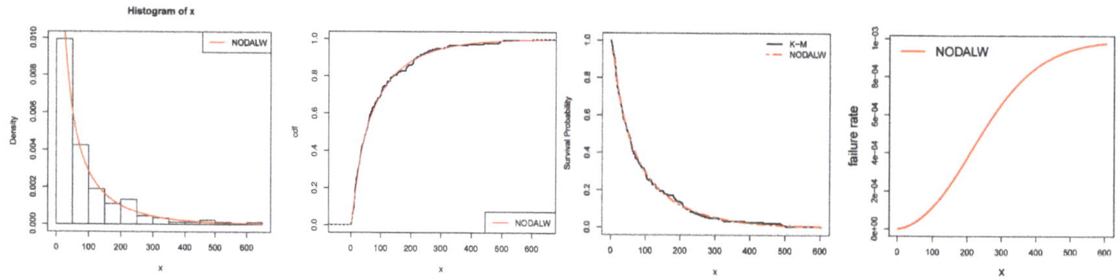

Figure 9. Plots of estimated density, cdf, Kaplan–Meier (K-M), and hrf plots for data set 1.

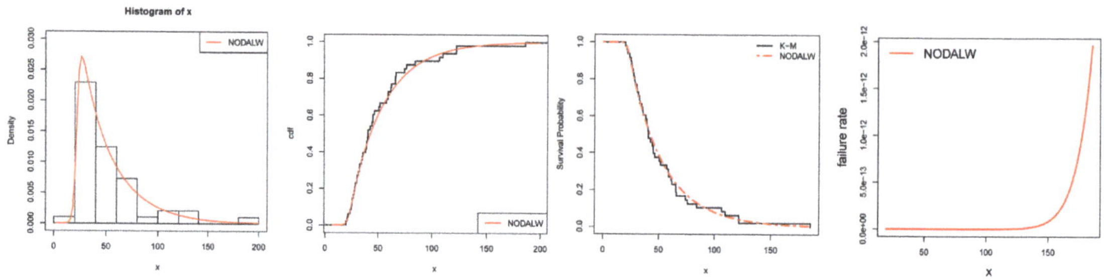

Figure 10. Plots of estimated density, cdf, Kaplan–Meier (K-M), and hrf plots for data set 2.

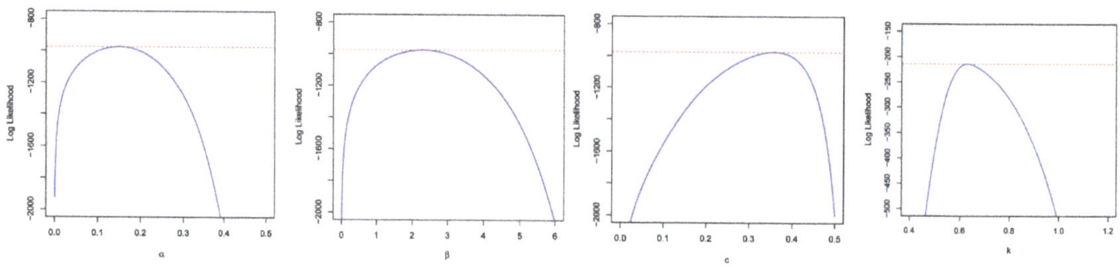

Figure 11. The pllf of data set 1.

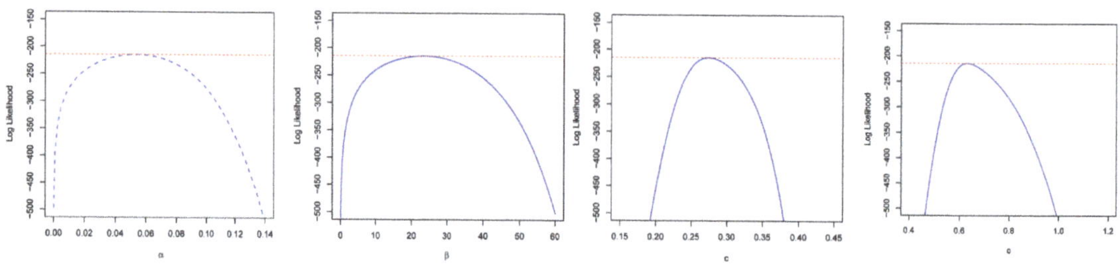

Figure 12. The pllf of data set 2.

7.2. Empirical Illustration of the DNODAL-G Family

Here, we illustrate the usefulness of the DNODALGeo model by means of an application to real count data. The data set represents the count of kidney cysts using steroids (see Chan et al. [69]). The shape of the data can be seen in Figure 13. The fitted distributions are compared using the AIC, CAIC, HQIC, and Chi-square (χ^2), having a degree of freedom (df) and its p-value. The competitive fitted models are reported in Table 9.

The MLEs and their corresponding SEs are listed in Table 10, whereas Tables 11 and 12 give the GoFS, expected frequencies (ExFr), and observed frequencies (ObFr), respectively.

Table 9. The competitive models.

No.	Distribution	Year	Author(s)
1	Geometric (Geo)	-	-
2	Generalized geometric (GGeo)	2010	Gómez-Déniz [48]
3	Discrete Rayleigh (DR)	2004	Roy [46]
4	Discrete inverse Rayleigh (DIR)	2014	Hussain and Ahmad [51]
5	Discrete inverse Weibull (DIW)	2010	Jazi et al. [49]
6	One parameter discrete Lindley (DLi-I)	2011	Gómez-Déniz and Calderín-Ojeda [50]
7	Two parameters discrete Lindley (DLi-II)	2016	Hussain et al. [52]
8	Three parameters discrete Lindley (DLi-III)	2020	Eliwa at al. [56]
9	Negative Binomial (NeBi)	-	-
10	Poisson (Poi)	1837	Poisson [70]
11	Discrete Pareto (DPa)	2009	Krishna and Pundir [47]
12	Discrete Burr type XII (DB-XII)	2016	Para and Jan [54]
13	Discrete log-logistic (DLogL)	2016	Para and Jan [53]
14	One parameter discrete flexible (DFx-I)	2020	Eliwa and El-Morshedy [57]
15	Discrete Lomax distribution (DLo)	2016	Para and Jan [54]

Table 10. The MLEs and their SEs for data set 3.

Parameter ⟶	p		α		β	
Model ↓	**MLE**	**SE**	**MLE**	**SE**	**MLE**	**SE**
DNODALGeo	0.711	0.130	1.587	0.392	0.240	0.034
Geo	–	–	–	–	0.582	0.030
DR	–	–	–	–	0.901	0.009
DIR	–	–	–	–	0.554	0.049
DLi-I	0.436	0.026	–	–	–	–
DFx-I	0.623	0.031	–	–	–	–
Poi	1.390	0.112	–	–	–	–
DPa	0.268	0.034	–	–	–	–
GGeo	–	–	0.188	0.089	0.800	0.064
DIW	–	–	1.049	0.146	0.581	0.048
DLo	0.152	0.098	1.830	0.952	–	–
DBX-II	0.278	0.045	1.053	0.167	–	–
NeBi	0.812	0.045	0.322	0.074	–	–
DLogL	0.780	0.136	1.208	0.159	–	–
DLi-II	0.581	0.045	0.001	0.058	–	–
DLi-III	0.582	0.005	358.728	11863.37	0.001	20.698

The DNODALGeo model performs better than all other tested models based on the numbers in Tables 11 and 12. Figure 14 supports the claims from these tables, and it is noted that data set 3 is explained by this model. Figure 15 shows the contour plot of log-Likelihood function of the DNODALGeo for the third data set.

Table 11. The GoFS for data set 3 "part I".

X	ObFr	ExFr							
		DNODALGeo	**Geo**	**DR**	**DIR**	**DLi-I**	**DFx-I**	**Poi**	**DPa**
0	65	64.97	45.98	10.89	60.89	40.29	45.26	27.39	65.84
1	14	14.69	26.76	26.62	33.99	29.83	29.09	38.08	18.27
2	10	8.46	15.58	29.45	8.12	18.36	16.51	26.47	8.16
3	6	5.73	9.06	22.29	3.00	10.34	8.89	12.26	4.51
4	4	4.19	5.28	12.63	1.42	5.52	4.70	4.26	2.82
5	2	3.18	3.07	5.54	0.78	2.85	2.49	1.19	1.91
6	2	2.44	1.79	1.91	0.47	1.44	1.34	0.27	1.37
7	2	1.87	1.04	0.53	0.31	0.71	0.73	0.05	1.02
8	1	1.41	0.61	0.12	0.21	0.35	0.41	0.01	0.79
9	1	1.04	0.35	0.02	0.15	0.17	0.23	0.01	0.63
10	1	0.74	0.21	0.00	0.11	0.08	0.14	0.01	0.51
11	2	1.28	0.27	0.00	0.55	0.06	0.21	0.00	4.17
Total	110	110	110	110	110	110	110	110	110
$-l$		166.48	178.77	277.78	186.55	189.11	182.29	246.21	171.19
AIC		338.96	359.537	557.56	375.09	380.22	366.58	494.42	344.38
HQIC		342.25	360.63	558.65	376.19	381.32	367.67	495.52	345.48
CAIC		339.19	359.577	557.59	375.13	380.26	366.61	494.46	344.42
χ^2		0.59	19.11	306.52	40.46	34.64	31.70	89.28	3.43
df		2	4	4	2	4	4	3	4
p-value		0.750	<0.001	<0.001	<0.001	<0.001	<0.001	<0.001	0.489

Table 12. The GoFS for data set 3 "part II".

X	ObFr	ExFr							
		DNODALGeo	**GGeo**	**DIW**	**DLo**	**DBX-II**	**NeBi**	**DLogL**	**DLi-II**	**DLi-III**
0	65	64.97	62.74	63.91	61.62	64.74	56.52	63.19	46.03	46.01
1	14	14.69	19.67	20.69	21.02	19.18	15.89	20.10	26.77	26.77
2	10	8.46	9.44	8.05	9.69	8.48	9.17	8.64	15.57	15.57
3	6	5.73	5.44	4.23	5.28	4.63	6.20	4.66	9.06	9.06
4	4	4.19	3.46	2.59	3.19	2.86	4.50	2.86	5.27	5.27
5	2	3.18	2.35	1.75	2.09	1.92	3.40	1.92	3.06	3.07
6	2	2.44	1.66	1.26	1.44	1.37	2.64	1.37	1.78	1.78
7	2	1.87	1.21	0.95	1.04	1.01	2.08	1.02	1.04	1.08
8	1	1.41	0.90	0.74	0.77	0.78	1.66	0.79	0.60	0.60
9	1	1.04	0.69	0.59	0.59	0.61	1.34	0.62	0.35	0.35
10	1	0.74	0.53	0.49	0.46	0.49	1.09	0.50	0.20	0.20
11	2	1.28	1.91	4.75	2.81	3.93	5.51	4.33	0.27	0.24
Total	110	110	110	110	110	110	110	110	110	110
$-l$		166.48	168.56	172.94	170.48	171.14	168.54	171.72	178.77	178.77
AIC		338.96	341.11	349.87	344.96	346.28	340.09	347.43	361.53	363.53
HQIC		342.25	343.30	352.06	347.15	348.47	343.28	349.62	363.72	366.82
CAIC		339.19	341.23	349.98	345.07	346.39	344.49	347.55	361.65	363.76
χ^2		0.59	2.44	6.45	3.24	2.59	4.29	4.033	19.09	19.09
df		2	3	3	3	2	4	3	3	2
p-value		0.750	0.485	0.092	0.356	0.274	0.369	0.258	0.0003	<0.0001

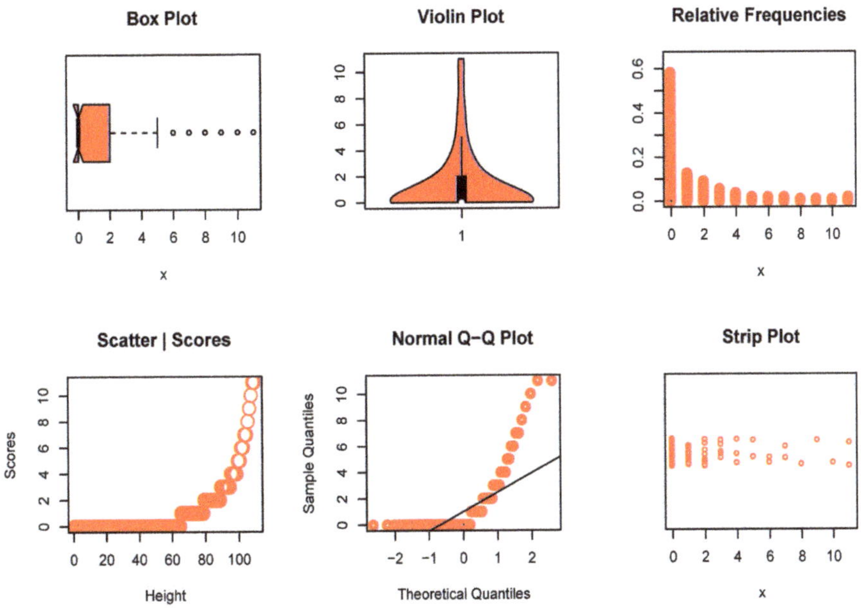

Figure 13. Non-parametric visualization plots for data set III.

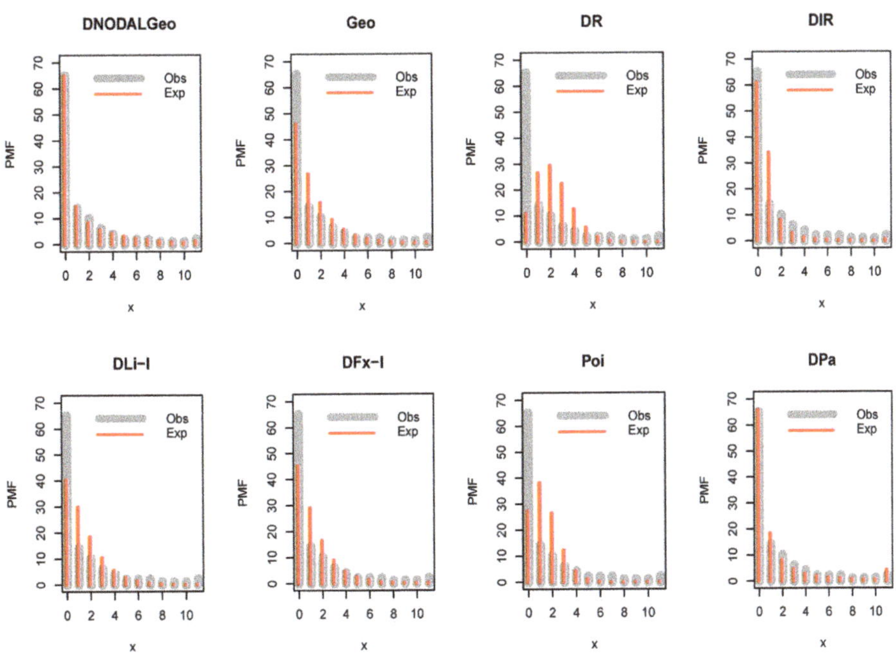

Figure 14. The fitted PMFs to data set 3.

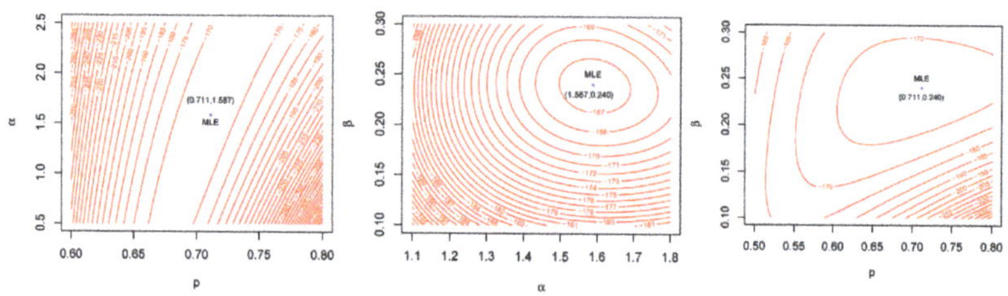

Figure 15. Contour plot of pllf for data set 3.

8. Concluding Remarks and Future Work

In this article, a new odd DAL-G family of models is presented from a new class/generator $W[G(x)] = (1 - \bar{G}(x;\xi)\exp\{G(x;\xi)\})/[\bar{G}(x;\xi)\exp\{G(x;\xi)\}]$ for $T \in (0,\infty)$. The new probability family $W[G(\cdot)]$ involves a different function of the cdf instead of existing generators. We obtain some structural properties of this new continuous and discussed discrete odd DAL-G family, and also studied some properties of the special models called the new odd DAL-Weibull (NODALW) and discrete new odd DAL-geometric (DNODALGeo) distributions. Both of two sub-models can be used to discuss asymmetric and symmetric data under different kinds of kurtosis. Furthermore, the two sub-models can be applied to discuss several shapes of risk/hazard rates. We compared the NODALW distribution with the well-known extended Weibull models (KwW, BW, EGW, McW, GaW, W) via six popular test statistics. Similarly, we compare the DNODALGeo distribution with the well-known extended models' (Geo, GGeo, DR, DIR, DIW, DLi-I, DLi-II, DLi-III, NeBi, Poi, DPa, DB-XII, DLogL, DFx-I, DLo) distributions using these test statistics. We found that the new generated distributions provide better estimates and minimum values of the test statistics. The new NODALW and DNODALGeo models outperform the above-described competitive models on the basis of numerical and graphical analysis. We foresee that the new family/class will be able to attract readers and applied statisticians. As a future work, the bivariate extension of the proposed generators with its applications will be discussed. Furthermore, some prediction models will be analyzed based on these generators.

Author Contributions: Conceptualization, M.S.E. and M.A.H.; Methodology, M.E.-M.; Software, M.A.H., B.A. and M.E.-M.; Validation, M.A.H. and M.E.-M.; Formal analysis, M.S.E., M.H.T. and A.A.-B.; Resources, B.A and M.E.-M.; Data curation, M.S.E., B.A. and A.A.-B.; Writing—original draft, M.H.T., M.S.E and M.A.H.; Writing—review & editing, M.S.E., M.A.H. and A.A.-B.; Visualization, B.A. and M.E.-M.; Supervision, M.H.T. All authors have read and agreed to the published version of the manuscript.

Funding: The paper did not receive any fund.

Data Availability Statement: The data sets are available in the paper.

Acknowledgments: The researchers would like to thank the Deanship of Scientific Research, Qassim University for funding publication of this project.

Conflicts of Interest: The authors declare no conflict of interests.

References

1. Gupta, R.C.; Gupta, P.L.; Gupta, R.D. Modeling failure time data by Lehman alternatives. *Commun. Stat. Theory Methods* **1998**, *27*, 887–904. [CrossRef]
2. Al-Aqtash, R.; Lee, C.; Famoye, F. Gumbel-Weibull distribution: Properties and applications. *J. Mod. Appl. Stat. Methods* **2014**, *13*, 201–225. [CrossRef]
3. Torabi, H.; Montazeri, N.H. The logistic-uniform distribution and its application. *Commun. Stat. Simul. Comput.* **2014**, *43*, 2551–2569. [CrossRef]
4. Zubair, M.; Pogany, T.K.; Cordeiro, G.M.; Tahir, M.H. The log-odd normal generalized family of distributions with application. *An. Acad. Bras. Ciênc.* **2019**, *91*, e20180207. [CrossRef] [PubMed]
5. Cooray, K. Generalization of the Weibull distribution: The odd Weibull family. *Stat. Methodol.* **2006**, *6*, 265–277. [CrossRef]

6. Gleaton, J.U.; Lynch, J.D. Properties of generalized log-logistic families of lifetime distributions. *J. Probab. Stat. Sci.* **2006**, *4*, 51–64.
7. Alzaatreh, A.; Famoye, F.; Lee, C. A new method for generating families of continuous distributions. *Metron* **2013**, *71*, 63–79. [CrossRef]
8. Torabi, H.; Montazeri, N.H. The gamma-uniform distribution and its application. *Kybernetika* **2012**, *48*, 16–30.
9. Bourguignon, M.; Silva, R.B.; Cordeiro, G.M. The Weibull-G family of probability distributions. *J. Data Sci.* **2014**, *12*, 53–68. [CrossRef]
10. Tahir, M.H.; Cordeiro, G.M.; Alizadeh, M.; Mansoor, M.; Zubair, M.; Hamedani, G.G. The odd generalized exponential family of distributions with applications. *J. Stat. Distrib. Appl.* **2015**, *2*, 1. [CrossRef]
11. Hassan, A.S.; Hemeda, S.E. A new family of additive Weibull-generated distributions. *Int. J. Math. Appl.* **2016**, *4*, 151–164.
12. Gomes-Silva, F.S.; Percontini, A.; de Brito, E.; Ramos, M.W.; Venancio, R.; Cordeiro, G.M. The odd Lindley-G family of distribution. *Austrian J. Stat.* **2017**, *46*, 65–87. [CrossRef]
13. Cordeiro, G.M.; Alizadeh, M.; Ramires, T.G.; Ortega, E.M.M. The generalized odd half-Cauchy family of distributions: Properties and applications. *Commun. Stat. Theory Methods* **2017**, *46*, 5685–5705. [CrossRef]
14. Afify, A.Z.; Altun, E.; Alizadeh, M.; Ozel, G.; Hamedani, G.G. The odd exponentiated half-logistic-G Family: Properties, characterizations and applications. *Chil. J. Stat.* **2017**, *8*, 65–91.
15. Jamal, F.; Nasir, M.A.; Tahir, M.H.; Montazeri, N.H. The odd Burr-III family of distributions. *J. Stat. Appl. Probab.* **2017**, *6*, 105–122. [CrossRef]
16. Yousof, H.M.; Afify, A.Z.; Hamedani, G.G. The Burr X generator of distributions for lifetime data. *J. Stat. Theory Appl.* **2017**, *16*, 288–305. [CrossRef]
17. Cordeiro, G.M.; Yousof, H.M.; Ramires, T.G.; Ortega, E.M.M. The Burr XII system of densities: Properties, regression model and applications. *J. Stat. Comput. Simul.* **2018**, *88*, 432–456. [CrossRef]
18. Haq, M.A.U.; Elgarhy, M. The odd Fréchet-G family of probability distributions. *J. Stat. Appl. Probab.* **2018**, *7*, 189–203. [CrossRef]
19. Hassan, A.S.; Nassr, S.G. The inverse Weibull generator of distributions: Properties and applications. *J. Data Sci.* **2018**, *16*, 723–742. [CrossRef]
20. Alizadeh, M.; Altun, E.; Cordeiro, G.M.; Rasekhi, M. The odd power-Cauchy family of distributions: Properties, regression models and applications. *J. Stat. Comput. Simul.* **2018**, *88*, 785–807. [CrossRef]
21. Maiti, S.S.; Pramanik, S. A generalized Xgamma generator family of distributions. *arXiv* **2018**, arXiv:1805.03892.
22. Hassan, A.S.; Nassr, S.G. Power Lindley-G family of distributions. *Ann. Data Sci.* **2019**, *6*, 189–210. [CrossRef]
23. Korkmaz, M.C.; Altun, E.; Yousof, H.M.; Hamedani, G.G. The odd power Lindley generator of probability distributions: Properties, characterizations and regression modeling. *Int. J. Stat. Probab.* **2019**, *8*, 70–89. [CrossRef]
24. Cordeiro, G.M.; Afify, A.Z.; Ortega, E.M.M.; Suzuki, A.K.; Mead, M.E. The odd Lomax generator of distributions: Properties, estimation and applications. *J. Comput. Appl. Math.* **2019**, *347*, 222–237. [CrossRef]
25. Kharazmi, O.; Saadatinik, A.; Alizadeh, M.; Hamedani, G.G. Odd hyperbolic cosine-FG family of lifetime distributions. *J. Stat. Theory Appl.* **2019**, *18*, 387–401. [CrossRef]
26. El-Morshedy, M.; Eliwa, M.S. The odd flexible Weibull-H family of distributions: Properties and estimation with applications to complete and upper record data. *Filomat* **2019**, *33*, 2635–2652. [CrossRef]
27. Aldahlan, M.A.; Afify, A.Z.; Ahmed, A.-H.N. The odd inverse Pareto-G class: Properties and applications. *J. Nonlinear Sci. Appl.* **2019**, *12*, 278–290. [CrossRef]
28. Nascimento, D.C.; Silva, K.F.; Cordeiro, G.M.; Alizadeh, M.; Yousof, H.M.; Hamedani, G.G. The odd Nadarajah-Haghighi family of distributions: Properties and applications. *Stud. Sci. Math. Hung.* **2019**, *56*, 185–210. [CrossRef]
29. El-Morshedy, M.; Eliwa, M.S.; Afify, A.Z. The odd Chen generator of distributions: Properties and estimation methods with applications in medicine and engineering. *J. Natl. Sci. Found. Sri Lanka* **2020**, *48*, 113–130.
30. Anzagra, L.; Sarpong, S.; Nasiru, S. Odd Chen-G family of distributions. *Ann. Data Sci.* **2020**, *9*, 369–391. [CrossRef]
31. Ahmad, Z.; Elgarhy, M.; Hamedani, G.G.; Butt, N.S. Odd generalized N-H generated family of distributions with application to exponential model. *Pak. J. Stat. Oper. Res.* **2020**, *16*, 53–71. [CrossRef]
32. Nasir, M.A.; Tahir, M.H.; Chesneau, C.; Jamal, F.; Shah, M.A.A. The odds generalized gamma-G family of distributions: Properties, regression and applications. *Statistica* **2020**, *80*, 3–38. [CrossRef]
33. Ishaq, A.I.; Abiodun, A.A. The Maxwell-Weibull distribution in modeling lifetime data sets. *Ann. Data Sci.* **2020**, *7*, 639–662. [CrossRef]
34. Ansari, S.I.; Nofal, Z.M. The Lomax exponentiated Weibull model. *Jpn. J. Stat. Data Sci.* **2021**, *4*, 21–39. [CrossRef]
35. Gupta, R.D.; Kundu, D. Generalized exponential distributions. *Aust. N. Z. J. Stat.* **1999**, *41*, 173–188. [CrossRef]
36. Nadarajah, S.; Haghighi, F. An extension of the exponential distribution. *Statistics* **2011**, *45*, 54–558. [CrossRef]
37. Dimitrakopoulou, T.; Adamidis, K.; Loukas, S. A lifetime distribution with an upside–down bathtub-shaped hazard function. *IEEE Trans. Reliab.* **2007**, *56*, 308–311. [CrossRef]
38. Nikulin, M.; Haghighi, F. A chi-squared test for the generalized power Weibull family for the head-and-neck cancer censored data. *J. Math. Sci.* **2006**, *133*, 1333–1341. [CrossRef]
39. Nikulin, M.; Haghighi, F. On the power generalized Weibull family: Model for cancer censored data. *Metron* **2009**, *67*, 75–86.
40. Peña-Ramírez, F.A.; Guerra, R.R.; Cordeiro, G.M.; Rinho, P.R.D. The exponentiated power generalized Weibull: Properties and applications. *An. Acad. Bras. Ciêc.* **2018**, *90*, 2553–2577. [CrossRef]

41. Anwar, M.; Bibi, A. The half-logistic generalized Weibull distribution. *J. Probab. Stat.* **2018**, *12*, 8767826. [CrossRef]
42. Tafakori, L.; Pourkhanali, A.; Nadarajah, S. A new lifetime model with different types of failure rate. *Commun. Stat. Theory Methods* **2018**, *47*, 4006–4020. [CrossRef]
43. Afify, A.Z.; Kumar, D.; Elbatal, I. Marshall-Olkin power generalized Weibull distribution with applications in engineering and medicine. *J. Stat. Theory Appl.* **2020**, *19*, 223–237. [CrossRef]
44. Khan, M.S. Transmuted generalized power Weibull distribution. *Thail. Stat.* **2018**, *16*, 156–172.
45. Hussain, M.A. Some New Generalized Kumaraswamy Families of Distributions. Ph.D. Thesis, The Islamia University of Bahawalpur, Bahawalpur, Pakistan, 2020.
46. Roy, D. Discrete Rayleigh distribution. *IEEE Trans. Reliab.* **2004**, *53*, 255–260. [CrossRef]
47. Krishna, H.; Pundir, P.S. Discrete Burr and discrete Pareto distributions. *Stat. Methodol.* **2009**, *6*, 177–188. [CrossRef]
48. Gómez-Déniz, E. Another generalization of the geometric distribution. *Test* **2010**, *19*, 399–415. [CrossRef]
49. Jazi, M.A.; Lai, C.D.; Alamatsaz, M.H. A discrete inverse Weibull distribution and estimation of its parameters. *Stat. Methodol.* **2010**, *7*, 121–132. [CrossRef]
50. Gómez-Déniz, E.; Calderín-Ojeda, E. The discrete Lindley distribution: Properties and applications. *J. Stat. Comput. Simul.* **2011**, *81*, 1405–1416. [CrossRef]
51. Hussain, T.; Ahmad, M. Discrete inverse Rayleigh distribution. *Pak. J. Stat.* **2014**, *30*, 203–222.
52. Hussain, T.; Aslam, M.; Ahmad, M. A two-parameter discrete Lindley distribution. *Rev. Colomb. Estad.* **2016**, *39*, 45–61. [CrossRef]
53. Para, B.A.; Jan T.R. Discrete version of log-logistic distribution and its applications in genetics. International *J. Mod. Math. Sci.* **2016**, *14*, 407–422.
54. Para, B.A.; Jan T.R. On discrete three parameter Burr type XII and discrete Lomax distributions and their applications to model count data from medical science. *Biom. Biostat. Int. J.* **2016**, *4*, 1–15.
55. El-Morshedy, M.; Eliwa, M.S.; Altun, E. Discrete Burr-Hatke distribution with properties, estimation methods and regression model. *IEEE Access* **2020**, *8*, 74359–74370. [CrossRef]
56. Eliwa, M.S.; Altun, E.; El-Dawoody, M.; El-Morshedy, M. A new three-parameter discrete distribution with associated INAR (1) process and applications. *IEEE* **2020**, *8*, 91150–91162.
57. Eliwa, M.S.; El-Morshedy, M. A one-parameter discrete distribution for over-dispersed data: Statistical and reliability properties with estimation approaches and applications. *J. Appl. Stat.* **2022**, *49*, 2467–2487 [CrossRef] [PubMed]
58. Eliwa, M.S.; Alhussain, Z.A.; El-Morshedy, M. Discrete Gompertz-G family of distributions for over-and under-dispersed data with properties, estimation, and applications. *Mathematics* **2020**, *8*, 358. [CrossRef]
59. Casella, G.; Berger, R.L. *Statistical Inference;* Cengage Learning: Boston, MA, USA, 2021.
60. Cordeiro, G.M.; Ortega, E.M.M.; Nadarajah, S. The Kumaraswamy Weibull distribution with application to failure data. *J. Frankl. Inst.* **2010**, *347*, 1399–1429. [CrossRef]
61. Lee, C.; Famoye, F.; Olumolade, O. Beta-Weibull distribution: Some properties and applications to censored data. *J. Mod. Appl. Stat. Methods* **2007**, *6*, 173–186. [CrossRef]
62. Oguntunde, P.E.; Odetunmibi, O.A.; Adejum, A.O. On the exponentiated generalized Weibull distribution: A generalization of the Weibull distribution. *Indian J. Sci. Technol.* **2015**, *8*, 1–7. [CrossRef]
63. Cordeiro, G.M.; Hashimoto, E.M.; Ortega, E.M.M. The McDonald Weibull model. *Statistics* **2012**, *48*, 256–278. [CrossRef]
64. Cordeiro, G.M.; Aristizábal, W.D.; Suárez, D.M.; Lozano, S. The gamma modified Weibull distribution. *Chil. J. Stat.* **2011**, *6*, 37–48.
65. Kus, C. A new lifetime distribution. *Comput. Stat. Data Anal.* **2007**, *51*, 4497–4509. [CrossRef]
66. Katz, R.W.; Parlange, M.B.; Naveau, P. Statistics of extremes in hydrology. *Adv. Water Resour.* **2002**, *25*, 1287–1304. [CrossRef]
67. Asgharzadeh, A.; Bakouch, H.S.; Habibi, M. A generalized binomial exponential 2 distribution: Modeling and applications to hydrologic events. *J. Appl. Stat.* **2017**, *44*, 2368–2387. [CrossRef]
68. Marinho, P.R.D.; Bourguignon, M.; Dias, C.R.B. Adequacy Model 1.0.8: Adequacy of Probabilistic Models and Generation of Pseudo-Random Numbers. 2015. Available online: http://cran.rproject.org/web/packages/AdequacyModel/AdequacyModel.pdf (accessed on 12 November 2015).
69. Chan, S.K.; Riley, P.R.; Price, K.L.; McEldu, F.; Winyard, P.J.; Welham, S.J.; Woolf, A.S.; Long, D.A. Corticosteroid-induced kidney dysmorphogenesis is associated with deregulated expression of known cystogenic molecules, as well as Indian hedgehog. *Am. J. Physiol.-Ren. Physiol.* **2010**, *298*, F346–F356. [CrossRef]
70. Poisson, S.D. *Probabilité des Jugements en Matié re Criminelle et en Matiére Civile, Précédées des Régles Génerales du Calcul des Probabilitiés;* Bachelier: Paris, France, 1837; pp. 206–207.

mathematics

Article

Unit Distributions: A General Framework, Some Special Cases, and the Regression Unit-Dagum Models

Francesca Condino * and Filippo Domma

Department of Economics, Statistics and Finance "Giovanni Anania", University of Calabria, Via P. Bucci, Cubo 0C, 87036 Rende, CS, Italy; filippo.domma@unical.it
* Correspondence: francesca.condino@unical.it

Abstract: In this work, we propose a general framework for models with support in the unit interval, which is obtained using the technique of random variable transformations. For this class, the general expressions of distribution and density functions are given, together with the principal characteristics, such as quantiles, moments, and hazard and reverse hazard functions. It is possible to verify that different proposals already present in the literature can be seen as particular cases of this general structure by choosing a suitable transformation. Moreover, we focus on the class of unit-Dagum distributions and, by specifying two different kinds of transformations, we propose the type I and type II unit-Dagum distributions. For these two models, we first consider the possibility of expressing the distribution in terms of indicators of interest, and then, through the regression approach, relate the indicators and covariates. Finally, some applications using data on the unit interval are reported.

Keywords: transformations; bounded support; flexible shape

MSC: 62J02

1. Introduction

In statistical literature, several authors have focused their attention on developing new and more flexible statistical distributions by using suitable transformation techniques (see, for example, [1–3]). Most of the obtained distributions deal with continuous random variables with unbounded support. Only in recent years has attention been devoted to filling the existing gap with respect to distributions with bounded support, in order to meet the need to describe empirical phenomena whose realizations cover limited ranges. Indeed, these kinds of data naturally arise in different contexts, such as rates, proportions, percentages, and so on, but just a few models, such as the widely used beta distribution model, the Kumaraswamy model [4], the Topp–Leone model [5], the arcsine model [6], the standard two-sided power model [7], and a few more (see [8,9]) were available in the past to describe them. Many others are very recent proposals. In particular, in the last decade, there have been many works in this field, for the most part, on models belonging to the class of so-called unit distributions. These models describe data with support in unit intervals and are often obtained by applying transformations to random variables. These include the unit-Burr III [10,11], unit-Lindley [12], unit-Gompertz [13], unit-Burr XII [14], unit inverse Gaussian [15], the arcsecant hyperbolic normal model [16], and logit slash [17], to name a few, as well as some new families of distributions [18,19].

The first aim of this work is to describe a general structure based on the random variable transformation technique, which includes most of the distributions for data on unit intervals already present in the literature. Moreover, other members of this class were obtained, considering different transformations. Particular attention is placed on building regression models, starting with unit distributions; this allows us to evaluate the impact of covariates on response variables with bounded support and consider alternative approaches to the most used regression models for unit data.

In a recent paper, [20] proposed a unified procedure to construct distribution functions in the (0,1) interval from the composition of two random variables with the same support, which turned out to be a special case of the $T-X$ family introduced by [21]. Our approach differs from the one just mentioned in that it does not require the knowledge of a second distribution function or a second quantile function. Furthermore, we envisaged a reparameterization and construction of the regression models on the indicators of interest.

The rest of the paper is organized as follows. In Section 2, we define the general class of distributions and derive the expressions for distribution and probability density functions. Quantiles, moments, and general expressions for the hazard and reverse hazard rate are given. A particular case of distributions belonging to the general class is described in Section 3, starting with the Dagum random variable and considering two particular kinds of transformations. The maximum likelihood estimation is discussed in Section 4. Section 5 is devoted to showing the possibility of employing the proposed models according to a regression perspective. Finally, in Section 6, two different examples of applications are shown.

2. General Framework

Many of the recently suggested distributions, proposed for modeling data belonging to the unit interval, can be described by resorting to a single probabilistic structure based on a simple technique of a random variable transformation.

To this end, let Y be a random variable (*rv*) with a distribution function (*pdf*) $F_Y(y;\boldsymbol{\theta})$ and probability density function (*df*) $F_Y(y;\boldsymbol{\theta})$, where $\boldsymbol{\theta}$ is the parameter vector and $y \in S_Y \subset \Re$, $S_Y = [\underline{S}_Y, \bar{S}_Y]$. Let $C : S_Y \longmapsto J_V$ be the application that identifies the transformation of Y *rv* in a new variable V, assuming values $V \in J_V = [\underline{J}_V, \bar{J}_V]$. In general, the distribution of V could also be characterized by a vector of parameters $\boldsymbol{a}$, i.e., $V := C(Y;\mathbf{a})$.

In the present paper, in order to simplify the discussion, we assume that the boundaries of the support of V are finite, i.e., $\lim_{y \to \underline{S}_Y} C(y;\mathbf{a}) = \underline{J}_V > -\infty$ and $\lim_{y \to \bar{S}_Y} C(y;\mathbf{a}) = \bar{J}_V < \infty$, and we assume that the function $C(y;\mathbf{a})$ is continuous, differentiable, and monotone over S_Y. Consequently, $C(y;\mathbf{a})$ is invertible and its inverse $C^{-1}(\cdot)$ is differentiable on J_V:

$$\left(C^{-1}(v;\mathbf{a})\right)' = \frac{1}{C'(C^{-1}(v;\mathbf{a}))}. \tag{1}$$

Knowing the distribution function of Y and considering the transformation $C(\cdot)$, it is easy to obtain the distribution function of V and its characteristics, such as quantiles and moments. Moreover, it is typical in the literature to study the behavior of the hazard function $h_Y(y;\boldsymbol{\theta})$ (*hf*) and the reverse hazard function (*rhf*) $rh_Y(y;\boldsymbol{\theta})$, with the aim of evaluating the flexibility of a distribution. Therefore, in the following, we obtain some general expressions of characteristics and properties for distributions belonging to this class. In doing this, we distinguish two cases, depending on whether $C(\cdot)$ is an increasing or a decreasing monotonic function.

(1) $C(\cdot)$ is an increasing monotonic function:

the df of V is given by:

$$F_V(v;\boldsymbol{\theta},\mathbf{a}) = P(V \le v) = P\left(Y \le C^{-1}(v;\mathbf{a})\right) = F_Y\left(C^{-1}(v;\mathbf{a});\boldsymbol{\theta}\right) \tag{2}$$

and, by (1), we can obtain the pdf of V as

$$f_V(v;\boldsymbol{\theta},\mathbf{a}) = \frac{\partial F_Y(C^{-1}(v;\mathbf{a});\boldsymbol{\theta})}{\partial C^{-1}(v;\mathbf{a})} \times \frac{\partial C^{-1}(v;\mathbf{a})}{\partial v} = \frac{f_Y(C^{-1}(v;\mathbf{a});\boldsymbol{\theta})}{C'(C^{-1}(v;\mathbf{a}))}. \tag{3}$$

Moreover, let $y(p) = F_Y^{-1}(y; \boldsymbol{\theta})$ be the *p-th* quantile of Y, with $p \in (0,1)$. It is easy to verify that, from (2), the *q-th* quantile of V is as follows:

$$v(q; \boldsymbol{\theta}, \mathbf{a}) = C(y(q; \boldsymbol{\theta}); \mathbf{a}), \tag{4}$$

with $q \in (0,1)$.
The general expressions for *hr* and *rhr* functions are, respectively, given by:

$$h_V(v; \boldsymbol{\theta}, \mathbf{a}) = \frac{f_V(v; \boldsymbol{\theta}, \mathbf{a})}{1 - F_V(v; \boldsymbol{\theta}, \mathbf{a})} = \frac{h_Y(C^{-1}(v; \mathbf{a}); \boldsymbol{\theta})}{C'(C^{-1}(v; \mathbf{a}))} \tag{5}$$

$$rh_V(v; \boldsymbol{\theta}, \mathbf{a}) = \frac{f_V(v; \boldsymbol{\theta}, \mathbf{a})}{F_V(v; \boldsymbol{\theta}, \mathbf{a})} = \frac{rh_Y(C^{-1}(v; \mathbf{a}); \boldsymbol{\theta})}{C'(C^{-1}(v; \mathbf{a}))}. \tag{6}$$

(2) $C(.)$ is a decreasing monotonic function.
In this case, with little algebra, we can determine the quantities previously considered. In particular, the *df* and *pdf* of V, respectively, are as follows:

$$F_V(v; \boldsymbol{\theta}, \mathbf{a}) = 1 - F_Y\Big(C^{-1}(v; \mathbf{a}); \boldsymbol{\theta}\Big),$$

$$f_V(v; \boldsymbol{\theta}, \mathbf{a}) = -\frac{f_Y(C^{-1}(v; \mathbf{a}); \boldsymbol{\theta})}{C'(C^{-1}(v; \mathbf{a}))}$$

and the quantile of order q is as follows:

$$v(q; \boldsymbol{\theta}, \mathbf{a}) = C(y(1 - q; \boldsymbol{\theta}); \mathbf{a}).$$

The *hf* and *rhf* are calculated accordingly.

We can use different methods, known in the literature, to determine the moment of order r.

We should note that most of the proposals in the literature can be thought of as particular cases of the comprehensive framework described earlier. For example, the most used transformations in the cases of positive *rvs* are as follows: $V = \frac{Y}{1+Y}$ and $V = e^{-Y}$. On the other hand, the most common transformation, when Y assumes a real value, is $V = \frac{1}{1+e^{-Y}}$, as in the case of the logit slash model. Moreover, $V = \frac{2}{e^{-Y}+e^{Y}}$ was used in the context of non-monotonic *rv* transformations to obtain the arcsecant hyperbolic normal model, which, strictly speaking, does not belong to the general framework proposed here, but it can be used in every case with small mathematical expedients. We should note that, in general, any distribution function $G(\cdot)$ can be used to transform Y *rv* in a new variable $V = G(Y)$. Table 1 summarizes a classification of some unit distributions proposed in the literature, according to the used transformation.

Table 1. Unit distributions proposed in the literature according to the used transformation.

Distribution, Reference	$C(Y;a)$	$f_V(v;\theta;a)$	Parameter Space
Unit-Burr III, [10]	$Y/(1+Y)$	$\theta_1\theta_2\left[1+\left(\frac{1}{v}-1\right)^{\theta_2}\right]^{-\theta_1-1}\left(\frac{1}{v}-1\right)^{\theta_2-1}\frac{1}{v^2}$	$\theta_1,\theta_2>0$
Unit-Half-Normal, [22]	$Y/(1+Y)$	$\frac{2}{\theta(1-v)^2}\phi\left(\frac{v}{\theta(1-v)}\right)$	$\theta>0$
Unit-modified Burr III, [23]	$Y/(1+Y)$	$\theta_1\theta_2 v^{-2}\left(\frac{1-v}{v}\right)^{\theta_2-1}\left[1+\theta_3\left(\frac{1-v}{v}\right)^{\theta_2}\right]^{-\frac{\theta_1}{\theta_3}-1}$	$\theta_1,\theta_2,\theta_3>0$
Unit-Lindley, [12]	$Y/(1+Y)$	$\frac{\theta^2}{1+\theta}(1-v)^{-3}\exp\left(-\frac{\theta v}{1-v}\right)$	$\theta>0$
Unit-Gompertz, [13]	$\exp\{-Y\}$	$\theta_1\theta_2 v^{-(\theta_2+1)}\exp\left[-\theta_1(v^{-\theta_2}-1)\right]$	$\theta_1,\theta_2>0$
Unit-Birnbaum-Saunders, [24,25]	$\exp\{-Y\}$	$\frac{1}{2v\theta_1\theta_2\sqrt{2\pi}}\left[\left(-\frac{\theta_2}{\log v}\right)^{1/2}+\left(-\frac{\theta_2}{\log v}\right)^{3/2}\right]\exp\left[\frac{1}{2\theta_1^2}\left(\frac{\log v}{\theta_2}+\frac{\theta_2}{\log v}+2\right)\right]$	$\theta_1,\theta_2>0$
Bounded Odd inv. Pareto exp., [26]	$\exp\{-Y\}$	$\frac{\theta_1\theta_2\theta_3 v^{\theta_3-1}(1-v^{\theta_3})^{\theta_1-1}}{(1-(1-\theta_2)v^{\theta_3})^{\theta_1+1}}$	$\theta_1,\theta_2,\theta_3>0$
Unit-Burr XII, [14]	$\exp\{-Y\}$	$\theta_1\theta_2 v^{-1}(-\log v)^{\theta_2-1}\left(1+(-\log v)^{\theta_2}\right)^{-\theta_1-1}$	$\theta_1,\theta_2>0$
Log-Bilal, [27]	$\exp\{-Y\}$	$\frac{6}{\theta}v^{2/\theta-1}\left(1-v^{1/\theta}\right)$	$\theta>0$
Unit-inverse Gaussian, [15]	$\exp\{-Y\}$	$\sqrt{\frac{\theta_1}{2\pi}}\frac{1}{v(-\log v)^{3/2}}\exp\left[-\frac{\theta_1}{2(\theta_2)^2\log v}(\log v+\theta_2)^2\right]$	$\theta_1,\theta_2>0$
Unit-Burr III, [11]	$\exp\{-Y\}$	$\theta_1\theta_2\frac{(log(1/v))^{-\theta_2-1}}{v(1+(log(1/v))^{-\theta_2})^{\theta_1+1}}$	$\theta_1,\theta_2>0$
Logit slash, [17]	$1/[1+\exp\{-Y\}]$	$\frac{\theta_1}{v(1-v)\theta_3}\int_0^1 t^{\theta_1}\phi\left(t\left[\frac{log(\frac{v}{1-v})-\theta_2}{\theta 3}\right]\right)dt$	$\theta_1,\theta_3>0;-\infty<\theta_2<\infty$

In many application contexts, researchers often focus on specific aspects when characterizing a distribution, such as quantiles, location measures (mode, median, mean), variability indicators, etc. For this reason, when possible, it is useful to express the distribution as a function of such characteristics. The utility derives from the fact that, with appropriate methodological tools, it is possible to construct regressive models on the characteristics of interest with the aim of inspecting the possible determinants of the phenomenon under investigation (see [28,29]). Each characteristic and/or indicator is, in general, a function of the vector of the distribution parameters, let us say $I = I(\boldsymbol{\theta})$, with reference to the unit's distribution function (2). If $\boldsymbol{\theta}$ is a vector of dimension p and the system

$$I_j = I_j(\theta_1, \theta_2, ..., \theta_p) \qquad for\ \ j = 1, ..., p$$

has a unique finite solution, say,

$$\theta_j = \theta_j(I_1, I_2, ..., I_p) \qquad for\ \ j = 1, ..., p$$

then the unit-distribution function

$$F_V(v; I_1, I_2, ..., I_p) = F_V(v; \theta_1(I_1, I_2, ..., I_p), \theta_2(I_1, I_2, ..., I_p), ..., \theta_p(I_1, I_2, ..., I_p))$$

represents a reparameterization in terms of indicators and/or characteristics of interest of the distribution in (2).

3. Two Kinds of Unit-Dagum Distributions

In this section, two different transformations of the widely used Dagum *rv* [30,31] will be described. Given the ability of the Dagum model in fitting real data, the resulting new models may potentially be more flexible than unit distributions that have already appeared in the literature.

The *df* and *pdf* of Dagum *rv* Y are given, respectively, by:

$$F_{Da}(y; \beta, \lambda, \delta) = \left(1 + \lambda y^{-\delta}\right)^{-\beta}, \tag{7}$$

and

$$f_{Da}(y; \beta, \lambda, \delta) = \beta\lambda\delta y^{-\delta-1}\left(1 + \lambda y^{-\delta}\right)^{-\beta-1}, \tag{8}$$

with $y > 0$ and $\beta,\ \lambda,\ \delta > 0$. In particular, the vector of parameters of Dagum distribution (hereafter, $Da(\beta, \delta, \lambda)$) is $\boldsymbol{\theta} = (\beta, \lambda, \delta)$, where λ represents a scale parameter and β and δ are shape parameters.

The Dagum model is positively skewed and it can be unimodal or zero-modal, depending on $\beta\delta > 1$ or $\beta\delta \leq 1$. In particular, the mode is given by

$$y_m = \lambda^{\frac{1}{\delta}}\left(\frac{\beta\delta - 1}{\delta + 1}\right)^{\frac{1}{\delta}}. \tag{9}$$

It is easy to verify that the *q-th* quantile is

$$y(q) = F_{Da}^{-1}(q; \beta, \lambda, \delta) = \lambda^{\frac{1}{\delta}}(q^{-\frac{1}{\beta}} - 1)^{-\frac{1}{\delta}}, \tag{10}$$

therefore, the expression of the median is explicit:

$$me = \lambda^{\frac{1}{\delta}}(2^{\frac{1}{\beta}} - 1)^{-\frac{1}{\delta}}. \tag{11}$$

It is also possible to obtain the expression of the *r-th* moment, as follows

$$\mu_{Da}^{r} = E(Y^r; \beta, \lambda, \delta) = \beta\lambda^{\frac{r}{\delta}} B\left(\beta + \frac{r}{\delta}, 1 - \frac{r}{\delta}\right), \tag{12}$$

which exists for $\delta > r$. Here, $B(\cdot,\cdot)$ indicates the complete beta function.

3.1. *The First Kind of Unit-Dagum Distribution*

In this section, we consider the hyperbolic secant transformation:

$$V := C(Y) = \frac{2e^Y}{1+e^{2Y}}.$$

In particular, it is simple to verify that, for $Y > 0$, it is a monotonic decreasing function with $\lim_{y\to 0^+} C(y) = 1$, $\lim_{y\to +\infty} C(y) = 0$ and $C'(y) = \frac{2e^y(1-e^{2y})}{(1+e^{2y})^2} < 0$. Furthermore, it is known that the inverse hyperbolic secant is given by $y = C^{-1}(v) = \log \frac{1+\sqrt{1-v^2}}{v}$.

Taking into account the characteristics of the proposed transformation, the distribution function of the new *rv* V is given by

$$\begin{aligned} F_{I-UDa}(v;\beta,\lambda,\delta) &= 1 - F_{Da}(\log\frac{1+\sqrt{1-v^2}}{v};\beta,\lambda,\delta) \\ &= 1 - \left\{1+\lambda\left[\log\frac{1+\sqrt{1-v^2}}{v}\right]^{-\delta}\right\}^{-\beta} \end{aligned} \tag{13}$$

with $v \in (0,1)$ and $\beta,\lambda,\delta > 0$ (hereafter, $I - UDa(\beta,\delta,\lambda)$). From (1), after simple algebra, we obtain the first derivative of the inverse of $C(y;\boldsymbol{a})$:

$$\left(C^{-1}(v;\mathbf{a})\right)' = \frac{-1}{v\sqrt{1-v^2}}$$

and, consequently, the *pdf* of $I - UDa(\beta,\delta,\lambda)$ *rv*:

$$f_{I-UDa}(v;\beta,\lambda,\delta) = \frac{\beta\lambda\delta}{v\sqrt{1-v^2}}[\log(v^*)]^{-\delta-1}\left\{1+\lambda[\log(v^*)]^{-\delta}\right\}^{-\beta-1} \tag{14}$$

where $v^* = \frac{1+\sqrt{1-v^2}}{v}$.

Figure 1 shows various behaviors of the *pdf* for the type I unit-Dagum model, according to different values of parameters.

The *q-th* quantile of the $I - UDa(\beta,\delta,\lambda)$ distribution, by (10), is

$$v(q;\beta,\lambda,\delta) = \frac{2e^{\lambda^{\frac{1}{\delta}}\left((1-q)^{-\frac{1}{\beta}}-1\right)^{-\frac{1}{\delta}}}}{1+e^{2\lambda^{\frac{1}{\delta}}\left((1-q)^{-\frac{1}{\beta}}-1\right)^{-\frac{1}{\delta}}}}. \tag{15}$$

In the following proposition, we show that the *r-th* moment of the type I unit-Dagum distribution can be expressed in terms of moments of the Dagum distribution.

Proposition 1. *The r-th moment of* $V \sim I - UDa(\beta,\delta,\lambda)$ *has the following expression:*

$$E[V^r] = \beta 2^r \sum_{j=0}^{+\infty}\binom{-r}{j}\sum_{s=0}^{+\infty}\frac{(-1)^s}{s!}(2j+r)^s\lambda^s B\left(\beta+\frac{s}{\delta},1-\frac{s}{\delta}\right). \tag{16}$$

Proof. See Appendix A.1. □

The *hf* and *rhz* are given, respectively, by

$$hf_{I-UDa}(v;\beta,\lambda,\delta) = \frac{\beta\lambda\delta}{v\sqrt{1-v^2}[\log(v^*)]\left\{\lambda+[\log(v^*)]^{\delta}\right\}} \tag{17}$$

and

$$rhf_{I-UDa}(v;\beta,\lambda,\delta) = \frac{\beta\lambda\delta[\log(v^*)]^{-\delta-1}\left\{1+\lambda[\log(v^*)]^{-\delta}\right\}^{-\beta-1}}{v\sqrt{1-v^2}\left[1-\left\{1+\lambda\left[\log\frac{1+\sqrt{1-v^2}}{v}\right]^{-\delta}\right\}^{-\beta}\right]} \tag{18}$$

The hazard rate function of the type I unit-Dagum model for some values of parameters is shown in Figure 2.

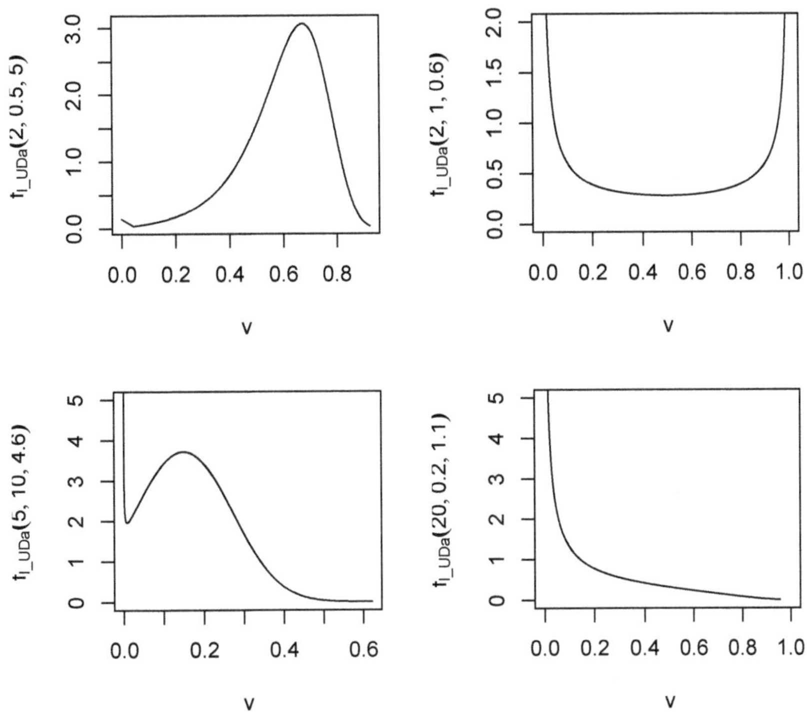

Figure 1. Pdf of the type I unit-Dagum model for different values of parameters.

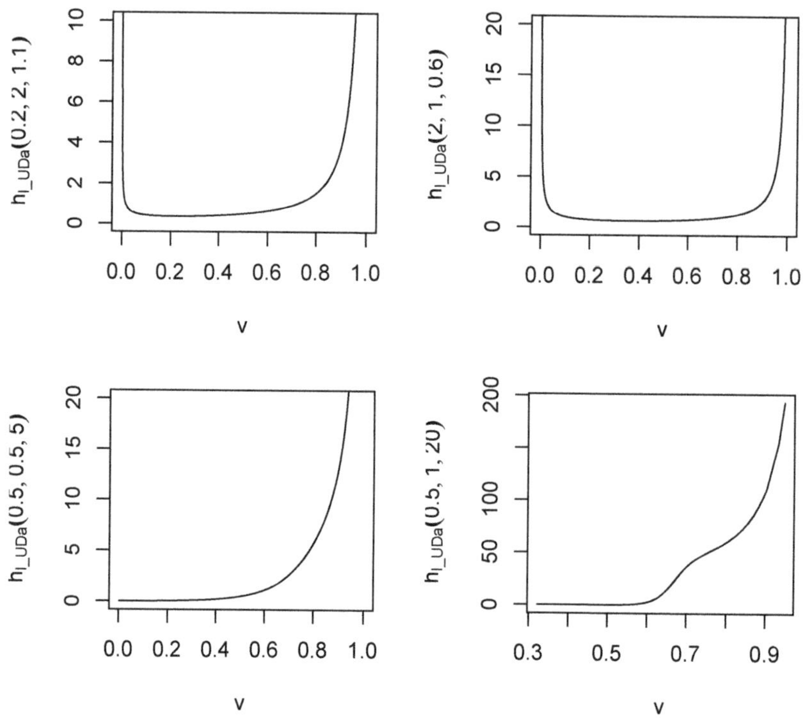

Figure 2. Hazard rate of the type I unit-Dagum model for different values of parameters.

We propose a possible reparametrization of the type I unit-Dagum distribution in terms of the median and the $q-th$ quantile. It is possible to verify that the system

$$\begin{cases} \beta_1 = \dfrac{1}{\beta} \\ me = \dfrac{2e^{\lambda^{\frac{1}{\delta}}\left[0.5^{-\frac{1}{\beta}}-1\right]^{-\frac{1}{\delta}}}}{1+e^{2\lambda^{\frac{1}{\delta}}\left[0.5^{-\frac{1}{\beta}}-1\right]^{-\frac{1}{\delta}}}} \\ v(q) = \dfrac{2e^{\lambda^{\frac{1}{\delta}}\left[(1-q)^{-\frac{1}{\beta}}-1\right]^{-\frac{1}{\delta}}}}{1+e^{2\lambda^{\frac{1}{\delta}}\left[(1-q)^{-\frac{1}{\beta}}-1\right]^{-\frac{1}{\delta}}}} \end{cases} \tag{19}$$

presents the following unique solution:

$$\begin{cases} \beta = \dfrac{1}{\beta_1} \\ \lambda = \left[0.5^{-\beta_1}-1\right]\left[\log\left(\frac{1+\sqrt{1-me^2}}{me}\right)\right]^{\delta^*} = \lambda^* \\ \delta = \dfrac{\log\left[0.5^{-\beta_1}-1\right]-\log\left[(1-q)^{-\beta_1}-1\right]}{\log\left[\log\left(\frac{1+\sqrt{1-v(q)^2}}{v(q)}\right)\right]-\log\left[\log\left(\frac{1+\sqrt{1-me^2}}{me}\right)\right]} = \delta^* \end{cases} \tag{20}$$

The corresponding distribution function is

$$F_{R-I-UDa}(v;\beta_1,me,v(q)) = 1 - \left\{1+\lambda^*\left[\log\frac{1+\sqrt{1-v^2}}{v}\right]^{-\delta^*}\right\}^{-\frac{1}{\beta_1}} \tag{21}$$

with $\beta_1 > 0$, $me \in (0,1)$ and $v(q) \in (0,1)$ for $q \in (0,1)$.

3.2. A Second Kind of Unit-Dagum Distribution

In this section, we consider the monotonic decreasing transformation $V := C(Y) = e^{-Y}$, with $\lim_{y\to 0^+} C(y) = 1$, $\lim_{y\to +\infty} C(y) = 0$ and $C'(y) = -e^{-y} < 0, \forall y$. The inverse is given by $y = C^{-1}(v) = -\log(v)$.

The distribution function of V is given by

$$\begin{aligned} F_{II-UDa}(v;\beta,\lambda,\delta) &= 1 - F_{Da}(-\log v;\beta,\lambda,\delta) \\ &= 1 - \left\{1+\lambda[-\log(v)]^{-\delta}\right\}^{-\beta} \end{aligned} \tag{22}$$

with $v \in (0,1)$ and $\beta, \lambda > 0, \delta > 0$ (hereafter, $II - UDa(\beta,\delta,\lambda)$). From (1), after simple algebra, we obtain the first derivative of the inverse of $C(y;\boldsymbol{a})$:

$$\left(C^{-1}(v;\mathbf{a})\right)' = -\frac{1}{v}$$

and, consequently, the *pdf* of $II - UDa(\beta,\lambda,\delta)$ *rv*:

$$f_{II-UDa}(v;\beta,\lambda,\delta) = \frac{\beta\lambda\delta}{v}[-\log(v)]^{-\delta-1}\left\{1+\lambda[-\log(v)]^{-\delta}\right\}^{-\beta-1}. \tag{23}$$

It is worth noting that the distribution in (23) can be viewed as an extension of the unit-Burr III obtained by [11], using the same transformation. Indeed, the Dagum model has one more parameter than Burr III, that is a scale parameter, thus, by putting $\lambda = 1$, the unit-Burr III is obtained. Although the unit-Burr III is already studied in the literature, for the purposes of this work, as will be seen later, the λ parameter is essential for carrying out the reparameterization and building the regression model; therefore, here, we consider the type II unit-Dagum distribution, also considering the scale parameter.

Figure 3 shows various behaviors of the *pdf* for the type II unit-Dagum model according to different parameter values.

The *q-th* quantile of the $II - UDa(\beta,\delta,\lambda)$ distribution, by (10), is

$$v(q;\beta,\lambda,\delta) = e^{-\lambda^{1/\delta}\left[(1-q)^{-1\beta}-1\right]^{-1/\delta}}. \tag{24}$$

It can be readily verified that the *r-th* moment of the type II unit-Dagum distribution coincides with the Laplace transform of the Dagum distribution and it can be expressed in terms of moments of the Dagum distribution.

Proposition 2. *The r-th moment of* $V \sim II - UDa(\beta,\delta,\lambda)$ *has the following expression:*

$$E[V^r] = \beta\sum_{s=0}^{+\infty}\frac{(-r)^s}{s!}\lambda^{\frac{s}{\delta}}B\left(\beta+\frac{s}{\delta},1-\frac{s}{\delta}\right). \tag{25}$$

Proof. See Appendix A.2. □

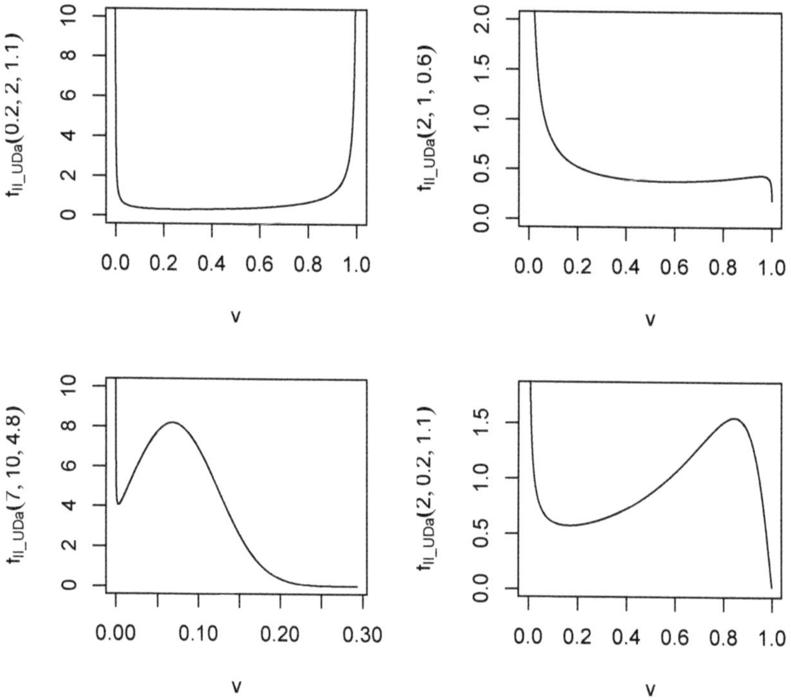

Figure 3. Pdf of II-UDa for different values of parameters.

The *hf* and *rhf* are given, respectively, by

$$h_{II-UDa}(v;\boldsymbol{\theta},\mathbf{a}) = \frac{\beta\lambda\delta[-\log(v)]^{-\delta-1}}{v\{1+\lambda[-\log(v)]^{-\delta}\}} \tag{26}$$

and

$$rhf_{II-UDa}(v;\beta,\lambda,\delta) = \frac{\beta\lambda\delta[-\log(v)]^{-\delta-1}\{1+\lambda[-\log(v)]^{-\delta}\}^{-\beta-1}}{v[1-\{1+\lambda[-\log(v)]^{-\delta}\}^{-\beta}]} \tag{27}$$

The hazard rate function of the type II unit-Dagum model for some values of parameters is shown in Figure 4.

It is easy to verify that a possible reparametrization of the type II unit-Dagum distribution in terms of the median and the $q-th$ quantile can be obtained as a solution of the following system:

$$\begin{cases} \beta_1 = \frac{1}{\beta} \\ me = e^{-\left[\frac{0.5^{-1/\beta}-1}{\lambda}\right]^{-1/\delta}} \\ v(q) = e^{-\left[\dfrac{(1-q)^{-1/\beta}-1}{\lambda}\right]^{-1/\delta}} \end{cases} \tag{28}$$

that presents the following unique solution

$$\begin{cases} \beta = \dfrac{1}{\beta_1} \\ \lambda = \left[0.5^{-\beta_1} - 1\right] \cdot [-\log(me)]^{\bar{\delta}} = \bar{\lambda} \\ \delta = \dfrac{\log\left[(1-q)^{-\beta_1} - 1\right] - \log\left[0.5^{-\beta_1} - 1\right]}{\log[\log(me)/\log(v(q))]} = \bar{\delta} \end{cases} \tag{29}$$

The corresponding distribution function is as follows:

$$F_{R-II-UDa}(v; \beta_1, me, v(q)) = 1 - \left\{1 + \bar{\lambda}[-\log(v)]^{-\bar{\delta}}\right\}^{-\frac{1}{\beta_1}} \tag{30}$$

with $\beta_1 > 0$, $me \in (0,1)$ and $v(q) \in (0,1)$ for $q \in (0,1)$.

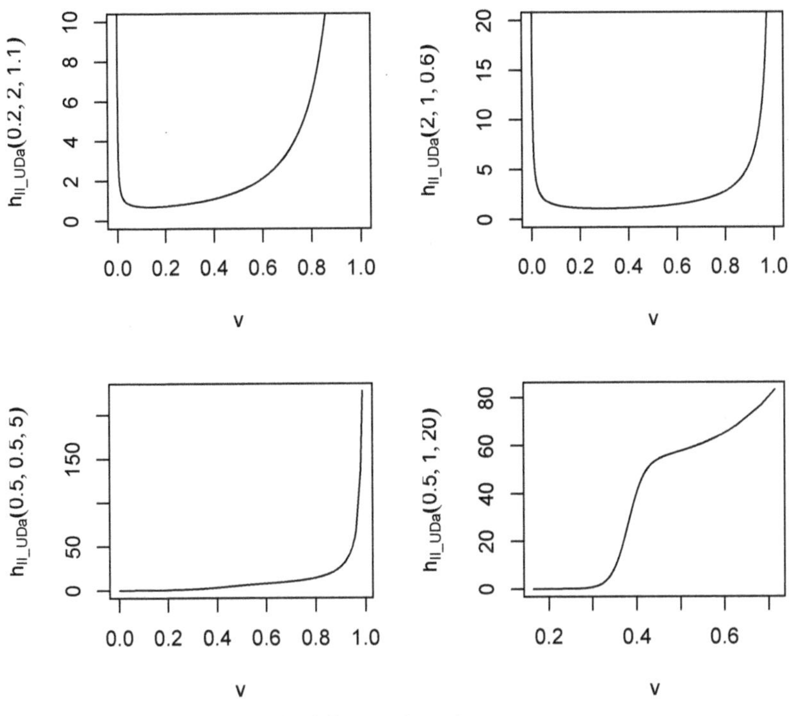

Figure 4. Hazard rate of II-UDa for different values of parameters.

4. Inference

In this section, we use the maximum likelihood (*ML*) method to estimate the parameters of type I and type II unit-Dagum distributions under the hypothesis of homogeneity of the statistical units, i.e., assuming that there are no systematic factors (covariates), which make the observations heterogeneous. To this end, we first rewrite the probability density functions (14) and (23), in a single expression as follows

$$f_{I-II-UDa}(v; \beta, \lambda, \delta) = \\ \beta\lambda\delta\left[C^{-1}(v)\right]^{-\delta-1}\left\{1 + \lambda\left[C^{-1}(v)\right]^{-\delta}\right\}^{-\beta-1}\left\{-\frac{\partial C^{-1}(v)}{\partial v}\right\} \tag{31}$$

where $C^{-1}(v) = \log \frac{1+\sqrt{1-v^2}}{v}$ in the case of the type I unit-Dagum distribution or $C^{-1}(v) = -\log v$ in the case of the type II unit-Dagum distribution. Let $\mathbf{v} = (v_1, ..., v_n)$ be a random sample of size n from (31), the log-likelihood function for $\boldsymbol{\theta} = (\beta, \lambda, \delta)$ is as follows:

$$\begin{aligned} \ell_{I-II-UDa}(\boldsymbol{\theta}; \mathbf{v}) \quad &\propto \quad n \log(\beta\lambda\delta) - (\delta+1) \sum_{i=1}^{n} \log C^{-1}(v_i) \\ &- \quad (\beta+1) \sum_{i=1}^{n} \log\left\{1 + \lambda\left[C^{-1}(v_i)\right]^{-\delta}\right\} \end{aligned} \tag{32}$$

Differentiating $\ell_{I-II-UDa}(\boldsymbol{\theta}; \mathbf{v})$ with respect to β, λ, and δ, respectively, we obtain the components of vector score $U(\boldsymbol{\theta}) = (U_\beta(\boldsymbol{\theta}), U_\lambda(\boldsymbol{\theta}), U_\delta(\boldsymbol{\theta}))$, where

$$U_\beta(\boldsymbol{\theta}) = \frac{\partial \ell_{I-II-UDa}(\boldsymbol{\theta}; \mathbf{v})}{\partial \beta} = \frac{n}{\beta} - \sum_{i=1}^{n} \log\left\{1 + \lambda\left[C^{-1}(v_i)\right]^{-\delta}\right\} \tag{33}$$

$$U_\lambda(\boldsymbol{\theta}) = \frac{\partial \ell_{I-II-UDa}(\boldsymbol{\theta}; \mathbf{v})}{\partial \lambda} = \frac{n}{\lambda} - (\beta+1) \sum_{i=1}^{n} \frac{\left[C^{-1}(v_i)\right]^{-\delta}}{1 + \lambda\left[C^{-1}(v_i)\right]^{-\delta}} \tag{34}$$

$$\begin{aligned} U_\delta(\boldsymbol{\theta}) \quad &= \quad \frac{\partial \ell_{I-II-UDa}(\boldsymbol{\theta}; \mathbf{v})}{\partial \delta} = \frac{n}{\delta} - \sum_{i=1}^{n} \log C^{-1}(v_i) \\ &+ \quad (\beta+1) \frac{\lambda[C(v_i)]^{-\delta} \log\left[C^{-1}(v_i)\right]}{1 + \lambda\left[C^{-1}(v_i)\right]^{-\delta}} \end{aligned} \tag{35}$$

and setting the components of the score vector equal to zero, we obtain the system of likelihood equations, whose solution gives the *ML* estimates $\hat{\boldsymbol{\theta}} = (\hat{\beta}, \hat{\lambda}, \hat{\delta})$ of the parameter vector $\boldsymbol{\theta} = (\beta, \lambda, \delta)$. The system does not admit any explicit solution; therefore, the *ML* estimates $\hat{\boldsymbol{\theta}}$ can only be obtained by means of numerical procedures.

Confidence intervals and hypothesis tests for $\boldsymbol{\theta}$ can be constructed using the usual asymptotic properties of the maximum likelihood estimators. In particular, we highlight that the expected Fisher information matrix of the parameter vector $\boldsymbol{\theta}$ coincides with the expected Fisher information matrix of $\boldsymbol{\theta}$ of the Dagum distribution (see Appendix A.3). This means that when constructing confidence intervals and hypothesis tests for the parameters of type I and II models of the unit-Dagum distribution, we can use the asymptotic variance and covariance matrix calculated in [32,33].

5. Unit-Dagum Regression Models

An important aspect to investigate is how heterogeneity among statistical units impacts possible measures of interest, such as median and extreme quantiles, simultaneously and directly. Given the particular nature of the dependent variable, this leads us to consider a regression approach where the response variable is defined on the unit interval.

The literature on this theme is wide and often deals with two different possibilities: properly transforming data to map the (0,1) interval to the real line and then using a common regression analysis, or choosing a suitable distribution and defining the relations among distribution parameters and covariates. Regarding the first kind of approach, various transformations are possible, and the logit is the most popular, but as [34] underlines, transformations can be inappropriate since the heteroscedasticity and skewness in data are not properly handled; moreover, the interpretation of results is possible only on the transformed scale. On the other hand, the second approach is nowadays preferred and widely explored, with different existing proposals based on various distributions and response variables. For example, when the attention is focused on the mean, the most popular distribution is the beta [35], but other possibilities are represented by simplex [36], log-Bilal [27], log-Lindley [37], log-weighted exponential [38], and unit gamma [39], to cite a few. When the focus is on the median or, in general, on the distribution quantiles, regression models can be based on Kumaraswamy [40], Johnson-t [41], log-extended exponential-geometric [42], L-logistic [43], or unit-type distributions (see, for example, [14,22,44]). Our proposal fits into the latter approach.

Specifically, given a sample of n observations, for each statistical unit i ($i = 1, \dots, n$), we observe the individual dependent variable value v_i and the sets of individual covariates supposedly related to indicators and summarized in the vectors, $\boldsymbol{x}_{j,i}$, for $j = 1, 2, 3$. The three sets of covariates $\boldsymbol{x}_{1,i}$, $\boldsymbol{x}_{2,i}$, and $\boldsymbol{x}_{3,i}$ are not necessarily the same, and, even if equal, their impact on the corresponding indicator may be different.

The vectors $\boldsymbol{x}_{ji} = (x_{ji1}, x_{ji2}, \dots, x_{jip_j})$ for $i = 1, \dots, n$, $j = 1, 2, 3$, define the rows of three block $n \times p_j$ matrices $\mathbf{X}_j$ of $\mathbf{X}$. Each one refers to the p_j covariates affecting the $j - th$ indicator I_j.

Each indicator, analogous to generalized linear models, is then related to the covariates, through an appropriate link function $h_j(\cdot)$, as follows:

$$I_{j,i} = h_j(\boldsymbol{x}_{j,i}, \gamma_j). \tag{36}$$

The link functions are chosen to guarantee suitable restrictions on the parameter space, considering if $I_{j,i}$ is positive or varies on $(0,1)$. The elements of the vector $\gamma_j = (\gamma_{j,1}, \gamma_{j,2}, \dots, \gamma_{j,p_j})'$ are the unknown regression coefficients related to the p_j individual characteristics to be estimated, applying the maximum likelihood method. By using the reformulation of unit-Dagum models in terms of indicators of interest, as shown in expressions (20) and (29), it is possible to relate the new parameters, such as the median and q-th quantile, to individual characteristics. In particular, observing that the solutions given in (20) and (29) are functions of the indicators of interest, i.e., $\lambda^* = \lambda^*(\beta_1, me, v(q))$, $\delta^* = \delta^*(\beta_1, me, v(q))$ for the type I unit-Dagum distribution and $\bar{\lambda} = \bar{\lambda}(\beta_1, me, v(q))$, $\bar{\delta} = \bar{\delta}(\beta_1, me, v(q))$ for the type II unit-Dagum distribution, and specifying the indicators of interest as functions of the covariates $\beta_{1,i} = h_1(\boldsymbol{x}_{1,i}, \gamma_1)$, $me_i = h_2(\boldsymbol{x}_{2,i}, \gamma_2)$ and $v(q)_i = h_3(\boldsymbol{x}_{3,i}, \gamma_3)$, from (21) and (30), for the *i-th* observation, we can rewrite the *pdfs* as functions of the regression coefficients γ_1, γ_2, and γ_3. Similar to what was done previously, we use a single structure to represent type I and type II unit-Dagum distributions, simultaneously, as follows:

$$\begin{aligned} f_{R-I-II-UDa}(v_i; \gamma_1, \gamma_2, \gamma_3) &= \frac{\tilde{\lambda}_i \tilde{\delta}_i}{\tilde{\beta}_{1,i}} \left[C^{-1}(v)\right]^{-\tilde{\delta}_i - 1} \left\{1 + \tilde{\lambda}_i \left[C^{-1}(v)\right]^{-\tilde{\delta}_i}\right\}^{-\frac{1}{\tilde{\beta}_{1,i}} - 1} \\ &\times \left\{-\frac{\partial C^{-1}(v)}{\partial v_i}\right\} \end{aligned} \tag{37}$$

where $\tilde{\lambda}_i = \lambda_i^*$, $\tilde{\delta}_i = \delta_i^*$ in the case of the type I unit-Dagum, and $\tilde{\lambda}_i = \bar{\lambda}_i$, $\tilde{\delta}_i = \bar{\delta}_i$ in the type II unit-Dagum distribution. Putting $\gamma = (\gamma_1^{'}, \gamma_2^{'}, \gamma_3^{'})^{'}$, by (37), the *i-th* element of the log-likelihood function is

$$\begin{aligned} \ell(\gamma; \mathbf{v}, \mathbf{X}) &\propto \log(\tilde{\lambda}_i) + \log(\tilde{\delta}_i) - \log(\tilde{\beta}_{1,i}) - (\tilde{\delta}_i + 1) \log\left[C^{-1}(v_i)\right] \\ &- \left(\frac{1}{\tilde{\beta}_{1,i}} + 1\right) \log\left(1 + \tilde{\lambda}_i \left[C^{-1}(v_i)\right]^{-\tilde{\delta}_i}\right). \end{aligned} \tag{38}$$

Remembering that the parameters $\tilde{\beta}_{1,i}$, $\tilde{\lambda}_i$, and $\tilde{\delta}_i$ are functions of the vector γ of the dimension $p = p_1 + p_2 + p_3$, the $jr_j - th$ equation of the likelihood system is given by

$$\begin{aligned}\frac{\partial \ell(\gamma; \mathbf{v}, \mathbf{X})}{\partial \gamma_{j,r_j}} &= \frac{1}{\tilde{\lambda}_i}\left(\frac{\partial \tilde{\lambda}_i}{\partial \gamma_{j,r_j}}\right) + \frac{1}{\tilde{\delta}_i}\left(\frac{\partial \tilde{\delta}_i}{\partial \gamma_{j,r_j}}\right) - \frac{1}{\tilde{\beta}_{1,i}}\left(\frac{\partial \tilde{\beta}_{1,i}}{\partial \gamma_{j,r_j}}\right) \\ &- \log\left[C^{-1}(v_i)\right]\left(\frac{\partial \tilde{\delta}_i}{\partial \gamma_{j,r_j}}\right) + \frac{1}{(\tilde{\beta}_{1,i})^2}\left(\frac{\partial \tilde{\beta}_{1,i}}{\partial \gamma_{j,r_j}}\right)\log\left(1 + \tilde{\lambda}_i\left[C^{-1}(v_i)\right]^{-\tilde{\delta}_i}\right) \\ &- \left(\frac{1}{\tilde{\beta}_{1,i}} + 1\right)\frac{\left(\frac{\partial \tilde{\lambda}_i}{\partial \gamma_{j,r_j}}\right) - \tilde{\lambda}_i\left(\frac{\partial \tilde{\delta}_i}{\partial \gamma_{j,r_j}}\right)\log\left[C^{-1}(v_i)\right]}{\left[C^{-1}(v_i)\right]^{\tilde{\delta}_i} + \tilde{\lambda}_i} = 0 \end{aligned} \tag{39}$$

for $j = 1,2,3$ and $r_j = 1,2,..,p_j$. The partial derivatives in system (39) are given in Appendix A.4.

The system of the likelihood equations does not admit any explicit solution; therefore, the ML estimates $\hat{\gamma}_{j,r_j}$ for $j = 1,2,3$ and $r_j = 1,2,...p_j$ can only be obtained by means of numerical procedures. Under the usual regularity conditions, the known asymptotic properties of the maximum likelihood method ensure that $\sqrt(n)(\hat{\gamma}_n - \gamma) \xrightarrow{d} N(\mathbf{0}, \mathbf{\Sigma}_\gamma)$, where $\mathbf{\Sigma}_\gamma = [\lim_{n\to\infty} \boldsymbol{I}(\gamma)/n]^{-1}$ is the $(p_1 + p_2 + p_3) \times (p_1 + p_2 + p_3)$ asymptotic variance–covariance matrix and $\boldsymbol{I}(\gamma)$ is the Fisher information matrix, given by $\boldsymbol{I}(\gamma) = -E(\mathbf{H})$, where $\mathbf{H}$ is the Hessian matrix of the second partial derivatives of the log-likelihood function, *i.e.*, $\frac{\partial^2 \ell(\gamma; v, \mathbf{X})}{\partial \gamma_{j,r_j} \gamma_{h,r_h}}$. Elements of the $\boldsymbol{I}(\gamma)$ matrix are not reported here for space purposes, but are available upon request.

6. Applications

In order to show the potentiality of the proposed models, we consider two famous and widely used datasets, referred to data that fall into the unit interval and contained in the R package, `betareg`, namely *household food expenditures* and *reading skills*. In particular, the household food expenditure data regard the proportion of income spent on food for 38 households living in a large U.S. city and contain information on the perceived income and the number of persons living in the household. The reading skills dataset refers to the scores obtained in a test on reading accuracy involving 44 Australian children, including 19 dyslexic subjects and 25 non-dyslexic subjects. Moreover, the status of each child, and information regarding the nonverbal intelligent quotient (iq), are available.

These datasets were used by [34] to describe the implementation of the beta regression in the `R` system and to underline the advantage of this kind of regression with respect to the linear one when data belong to the unit interval. Therefore, as a further aim of this section, we will compare the performance of the unit-Dagum regression models with that of the widely used beta regression. Indeed, both methodologies give us the possibility to evaluate, among other aspects, the impact of some covariates on measures of central tendency, namely the mean in the case of the beta regression, and the median in the case of the unit-Dagum regression. It is worth noting that when data exhibit skewness, the median should be preferred as the centrality measure. Therefore, the proposed regression could be more appropriate in some cases.

6.1. Modeling Food/Income and Accuracy Data

In this section, we consider the proportion of income spent on food and the scores regarding reading accuracy. The corresponding empirical distributions are shown in Figure 5. To evaluate the adequacy of the proposed models in describing the considered data, the maximum likelihood estimates (MLEs) of the parameters for the I-UDa and II-Da densities reported in (14) and (23) are obtained, along with the corresponding standard errors and the values for the Akaike information criterion (AIC). Moreover, we compare the obtained results with the analogs for the beta and Kumuraswamy (KW) models, which are likely the most used models for data on bounded support. Table 2 presents the obtained results. Both the AIC values and the inspection of Figure 5 suggest that the proposed models better describe the considered data if compared with the beta and KW distributions. In particular, the lower value of the AIC for food expenditure data is obtained in correspondence with the type II unit-Dagum model, while, for reading skills data, the type I unit-Dagum reaches the lower result, far from the beta and KW ones. We should note that the chosen data are very different from each other in terms of the distribution shape, so these examples give us the possibility of testing the flexibilities of our models and their ability to properly reproduce different characteristics of the phenomena, such as unimodality, increasing density, presence of asymmetry, fat tails, and so on.

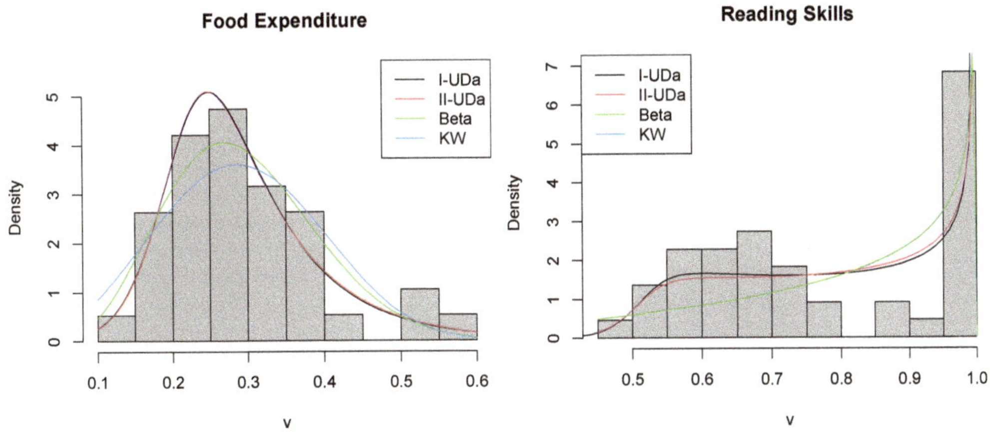

Figure 5. Empirical and fitted distributions for I-Da, II-Da, beta, and KW models.

Table 2. MLEs, corresponding standard errors (in brackets), and AIC values for I-Da, II-Da, beta, and KW models in food expenditure and reading skills data.

	I-UDa	II-UDa	Beta	KW
		Food Expenditures		
β	0.484 (1.618)	0.410 (1.631)	6.070 (1.358)	2.954 (0.309)
λ	30,279.37 (34.380)	62.520 (6.985)	14.819 (3.398)	26.964 (8.700)
δ	13.457 (1.326)	10.056 (1.360)		
AIC	−67.337	−67.400	−66.693	−62.978
		Reading Skills		
β	0.044 (1.661)	0.038 (1.670)	2.514 (0.578)	2.694 (0.589)
λ	529.384 (29.316)	0.004 (15.152)	0.675 (0.123)	0.665 (0.121)
δ	24.287 (1.604)	14.917 (1.617)		
AIC	−65.366	−64.134	−48.841	−49.218

6.2. Considering the Covariates: The Regression Models

In this section, we consider both type I and type II unit-Dagum distributions according to a regressive perspective and we compare their performances with results from the well-known beta regression.

To this end, we also take into account data regarding covariates and results reported in [34], corresponding with the best beta regression model for each dataset. We should note that, as can be viewed from Figure 5, both the income/food proportions and the reading accuracy scores show an asymmetric distribution; therefore, attention is placed on the median rather than the mean of the distribution, and it could be more appropriate to analyze the central tendency.

Food expenditure data

For the first dataset, information on household income and the number of people living in the household are available. Starting with the reparameterization data reported in (19) and (28), we consider the effect of these covariates on the median and 90th quantile, according to the regression models described in Section 5. Since both the indicators assume values in the unit interval, a logit-link function is used to relate the median and 90th quantiles to the covariates. Moreover, we consider an intercept term related to the β_1 indicator through a log-link function, which is suitable for positive indicators. The ML estimates of the coefficients, their standard errors, and results from the Wald test are reported in Table 3. In both models, we find that the median and 90th quantiles of the proportions spent on food decrease as income increases, while the number of persons living in a household shows a positive significant effect on the 90th quantile, ceteris paribus. Moreover, both models outperformed the beta regression in terms of AIC (-88.37 for beta regression), with the best results obtained for II-UDa regression. A comparison between empirical and fitted curves reported in Figure 6 confirms these results. In particular, here, two different curves are shown for each model. Indeed, through the regression approach and the resulting estimates, it is possible to consider the behaviors of density functions for different covariate values. The depicted curves refer to the median and $v(0.9)$ indicators for the I-Da and II-Da model, and to the mean and dispersion parameters for the beta model, when income and the number of persons are equal to the average level observed for $v \leq 0.5$ and $v > 0.5$, respectively ($\mu_{inc} = 60.65$; $\mu_{pers} = 3.37$ vs. $\mu_{inc} = 32.65$; $\mu_{pers} = 6$). This allows us to evaluate the ability of the models to describe the right distribution tail, as well as the central tendency.

Reading skills data

In the reading skills dataset, in addition to information regarding the presence of dyslexia, *z* scores for the nonverbal intelligent quotient (iq) test are available. Therefore, we can consider the effects of these characteristics on the median and 90th quantiles of reading accuracy scores, by specifying a logit-link function to relate indicators and covariates. In particular, as suggested by [34], we consider an interaction term between iq and dyslexia. Once again, we relate an intercept term to β_1, using a log-link function. Similar to that obtained by [34] for regression on the mean indicator, we find a significant main and interaction effect on the median for dyslexia and iq, for both I-Da and II-Da models. Specifically, results reported in Table 4 confirm the positive effect of iq and the negative effect for dyslexia and the interaction term. Moreover, we also find a significant negative effect of dyslexia on the 90th quantile.

In this case, the model with the best performance in terms of AIC is the I-Da one, but both of the proposed models show lower values than the beta regression (AIC = -117.8). Figure 7 shows the comparisons among empirical and fitted distributions for dyslexic and non-dyslexic subjects, considering an average iq level that is equal to -0.653 for dyslexic subjects and 0.4966 for control subjects.

Table 3. MLEs, corresponding standard errors, and Wald test results for the I-Da and II-Da regression models for food expenditure data.

	Estimate	SE	z	*p*-Value
		I-UDa		
		$I_1 = \beta_1$ (log-link)		
Intercept	−0.333	0.506	−0.659	0.51
		$I_2 = me$ (logit-link)		
Intercept	−0.544	0.016	−33.974	<0.001
income	−0.009	0.001	−16.758	<0.001
		$I_3 = v(0.9)$ (logit-link)		
Intercept	−0.727	0.022	−33.362	<0.001
income	−0.008	0.000	−21.604	<0.001
persons	0.167	0.022	7.425	<0.001
		AIC = −92.29		
		II-UDa		
	Estimate	**SE**	**z**	***p*-Value**
		$I_1 = \beta_1$ (log-link)		
Intercept	−3.672	4.586	−0.801	0.423
		$I_2 = me$ (logit-link)		
Intercept	−0.552	0.015	−36.371	<0.001
income	−0.009	0.000	−18.971	<0.001
		$I_3 = v(0.9)$ (logit-link)		
Intercept	−0.724	0.014	−50.203	<0.001
income	−0.008	0.000	−25.635	<0.001
persons	0.160	0.015	10.351	<0.001
		AIC = −97.25		

Table 4. MLEs, corresponding standard errors, and Wald test results for the I-Da and II-Da regression models for reading skills data.

	Estimate	SE	z	*p*-Value
		I-UDa		
		$I_1 = \beta_1$ (log-link)		
Intercept	−0.9626	0.9008	−1.069	0.285
		$I_2 = me$ (logit-link)		
Intercept	1.593	0.175	9.107	<0.001
dyslexia	−1.119	0.167	−6.707	<0.001
iq	0.504	0.093	5.389	<0.001
dyslexia × iq	−0.512	0.094	−5.451	<0.001
		$I_3 = v(0.9)$ (logit-link)		
Intercept	2.69045	0.03643	73.85	<0.001
Dyslexia	−1.914	0.03643	−52.544	<0.001
		AIC = −139.32		
		II-UDa		
	Estimate	**SE**	**z**	***p*-Value**
		$I_1 = \beta_1$ (log-link)		
Intercept	−0.7247	0.80705	−0.898	0.369
		$I_2 = me$ (logit-link)		
Intercept	1.60156	0.18082	8.857	<0.001
dyslexia	−1.1376	0.17224	−6.605	<0.001
iq	0.49774	0.09663	5.151	<0.001
dyslexia × iq	−0.5047	0.09701	−5.202	<0.001
		$I_3 = v(0.9)$ (logit-link)		
Intercept	2.69356	0.03759	71.648	<0.001
dyslexia	−1.9168	0.03768	−50.873	<0.001
		AIC = −137.41		

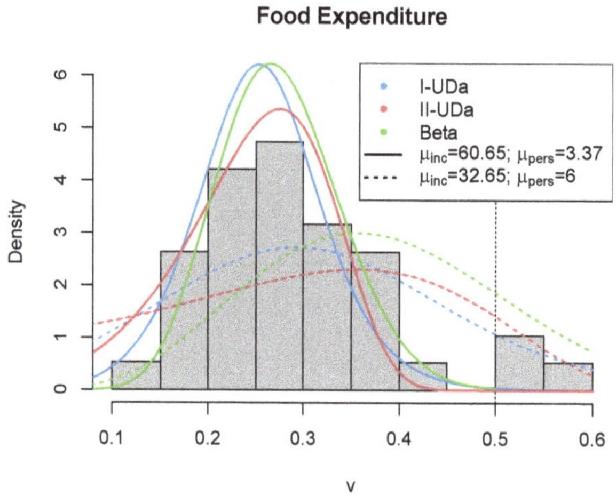

Figure 6. Empirical and fitted distributions for I-Da, II-Da, and beta models. The solid lines and the dotted lines refer to the average values of covariates obtained, respectively, for $v \leq 0.5$ and $v > 0.5$.

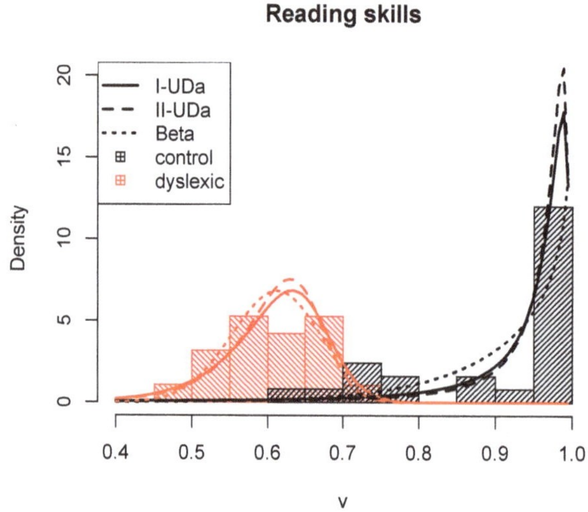

Figure 7. Empirical and fitted distributions for I-Da, II-Da, and beta models. Different curves refer to dyslexic and non-dyslexic subjects, considering the average iq level for each group.

7. Concluding Remarks

In this paper, we show that many of the existing proposals on probability distributions for data in the unit interval can be viewed as particular cases of a general class of models, obtained using the techniques of *rv* transformations. In the present paper, expressions on the distribution and density functions of the class are given and the principal characteristics are furnished. Through the proper transformation choice, it is possible to obtain new distribution functions on bounded support, whose characteristics are easy to derive. Indeed, two new distributions are proposed, starting with the Dagum model, and considering two different transformations. The resulting models are particularly flexible, as is evident by choosing different sets of parameter values and by looking at the behavior of their densities and hazard functions.

We also considered the possibility of reparameterizing the distributions in order to express them in terms of the indicators of interest. In particular, we obtained models that depend on the median and quantile; this gave us the opportunity to relate these quantities to covariates, according to a regressive perspective. Given the particular nature of the involved variables, this led us to consider the regression approach, where the response variable was defined on the unit interval. Therefore, the proposed methodology can be considered as an alternative to other approaches that are often employed when the response variable represents proportions, rates, or percentages. Furthermore, considering regression on the median could be more appropriate in the presence of asymmetry. The applications on two different datasets allowed us to evaluate the behaviors of the suggested models and compare their performances with the most widely used approach in this context, namely the beta regression. The obtained findings are encouraging since both models seem to be very competitive.

Author Contributions: Conceptualization, F.D.; Methodology, F.C. and F.D.; Software, F.C.; Formal analysis, F.C. and F.D.; Data curation, F.C.; Writing—review & editing, F.C. and F.D. All authors have read and agreed to the published version of the manuscript.

Funding: The authors gratefully acknowledge research grant 'Fondo sostegno aree socio-umanistiche-Cda del 26.03.2021-quota DESF' from the University of Calabria.

Conflicts of Interest: The authors declare no conflict of interest.

Appendix A

Appendix A.1. Proof of Proposition 1

First, in the following expression

$$\begin{aligned} E[V^r] \;=\; & \int_0^1 v^r \frac{\beta\lambda\delta}{v\sqrt{1-v^2}} \left[\log\left(\frac{1+\sqrt{1-v^2}}{v}\right)\right]^{-\delta-1} \\ & \left\{1+\lambda\left[\log\left(\frac{1+\sqrt{1-v^2}}{v}\right)\right]^{-\delta}\right\}^{-\beta-1} dv \end{aligned}$$

putting $z=\left\{1+\lambda\left[\log\left(\frac{1+\sqrt{1-v^2}}{v}\right)\right]^{-\delta}\right\}^{-1}$, with $dv = -\frac{v\sqrt{1-v^2}}{\lambda\delta}\left[\log\left(\frac{1+\sqrt{1-v^2}}{v}\right)\right]^{\delta+1}\left\{1+\lambda\left[\log\left(\frac{1+\sqrt{1-v^2}}{v}\right)\right]^{-\delta}\right\}^{2} dz$, after algebra, we obtain

$$E[V^r] = \beta\int_0^1 \left(2e^{\lambda^{\frac{1}{\delta}}\left(\frac{z}{1-z}\right)^{\frac{1}{\delta}}}\right)^r \left(1+e^{2\lambda^{\frac{1}{\delta}}\left(\frac{z}{1-z}\right)^{\frac{1}{\delta}}}\right)^{-r} z^{\beta-1}dz.$$

Now, using Newton's Binomial theorem, we can write

$$\left(\frac{2e^{\lambda^{\frac{1}{\delta}}\left(\frac{z}{1-z}\right)^{\frac{1}{\delta}}}}{1+e^{2\lambda^{\frac{1}{\delta}}\left(\frac{z}{1-z}\right)^{\frac{1}{\delta}}}}\right)^r = 2^r\frac{e^{-r\lambda^{\frac{1}{\delta}}\left(\frac{z}{1-z}\right)^{\frac{1}{\delta}}}}{\left(1+e^{-2\lambda^{\frac{1}{\delta}}\left(\frac{z}{1-z}\right)^{\frac{1}{\delta}}}\right)^r} = 2^r\sum_{j=0}^{+\infty}\binom{-r}{j}e^{-(2j+r)\lambda^{\frac{1}{\delta}}\left(\frac{z}{1-z}\right)^{\frac{1}{\delta}}}$$

substituting this last result in the *rth* moment, we obtain

$$E[V^r] = \beta 2^r\sum_{j=0}^{+\infty}\binom{-r}{j}\int_0^1 e^{-(2j+r)\lambda^{\frac{1}{\delta}}\left(\frac{z}{1-z}\right)^{\frac{1}{\delta}}} z^{\beta-1}dz$$

Putting $y = (2j+r)\lambda^{\frac{1}{\delta}}\left(\frac{z}{1-z}\right)^{\frac{1}{\delta}}$, with $y \in (0,\infty)$ and $dz = \delta(2j+r)^{\frac{1}{\delta}}\lambda y^{\delta-1}[(2j+r)^{\frac{1}{\delta}}\lambda + y^{\delta}]^{-2}dy$, after algebra, we obtain

$$\begin{aligned}
E[V^r] &= \beta 2^r \sum_{j=0}^{+\infty}\binom{-r}{j}\frac{1}{\beta}\int_0^{+\infty} e^{-y}\beta\delta(2j+r)^{\frac{1}{\delta}}\lambda y{-}\delta-1\left(1+(2j+r)^{\frac{1}{\delta}}\lambda y^{-\delta}\right)^{-\beta-1}dy \\
&= 2^r \sum_{j=0}^{+\infty}\binom{-r}{j} E\left[e^{-Y};\beta,\delta,\lambda(2j+r)^{\frac{1}{\delta}}\right] \\
&= \beta 2^r \sum_{j=0}^{+\infty}\binom{-r}{j}\sum_{s=0}^{+\infty}\frac{(-1)^s}{s!}\lambda^{\frac{s}{\delta}}(2j+r)^s B\left(\beta+\frac{s}{\delta},1-\frac{s}{\delta}\right).
\end{aligned}$$

Appendix A.2. Proof of Proposition 2

Given the considered transformation $V := C(Y) = e^{-Y}$, it is evident that the *r-th* moment of the type II unit-Dagum distribution coincides with the Laplace transform of the Dagum distribution, i.e.,

$$\begin{aligned}
E[V^r] &= E\left[e^{-rY}\right] \\
&= \beta\lambda\delta\int_0^{+\infty} e^{-rt}t^{-\delta-1}(1+\lambda t^{-\delta})^{-\beta-1}dt
\end{aligned}$$

and putting $e^{-rt} = \sum_{s=0}^{+\infty}\frac{(-rt)^s}{s!}$, we obtain:

$$\begin{aligned}
E[V^r] &= \sum_{s=0}^{+\infty}\frac{(-r)^s}{s!}\int_0^{+\infty} t^s\beta\lambda\delta t^{-\delta-1}(1+\lambda t^{-\delta})^{-\beta-1}dt \\
&= \sum_{s=0}^{+\infty}\frac{(-r)^s}{s!}\mu_{Da}^s.
\end{aligned}$$

Substituting expression (12) into the *s-th* moment of the Dagum distribution in the previous equation, we obtain the expression for the *r-th* moment of the type II unit-Dagum distribution.

Appendix A.3. Fisher Information Matrix

In order to compute the expected Fisher information matrix, we consider the following elements of the Hessian matrix:

$$\frac{\partial^2\ell_{I-II-UDa}(\boldsymbol{\theta};\mathbf{v})}{\partial\beta^2} = -\frac{n}{\beta^2} \tag{A1}$$

$$\frac{\partial^2\ell_{I-II-UDa}(\boldsymbol{\theta};\mathbf{v})}{\partial\beta\lambda} = -\sum_{i=1}^{n}\frac{[C^{-1}(v_i)]^{-\delta}}{1+\lambda[C^{-1}(v_i)]^{-\delta}} \tag{A2}$$

$$\frac{\partial^2\ell_{I-II-UDa}(\boldsymbol{\theta};\mathbf{v})}{\partial\beta\delta} = \sum_{i=1}^{n}\frac{\lambda[C^{-1}(v_i)]^{-\delta}\ln[C^{-1}(v_i)]}{1+\lambda[C^{-1}(v_i)]^{-\delta}} \tag{A3}$$

$$\frac{\partial^2\ell_{I-II-UDa}(\boldsymbol{\theta};\mathbf{v})}{\partial\lambda^2} = -\frac{n}{\lambda^2}+(\beta+1)\sum_{i=1}^{n}\frac{[C^{-1}(v_i)]^{-2\delta}}{\left\{1+\lambda[C^{-1}(v_i)]^{-\delta}\right\}^2} \tag{A4}$$

$$\frac{\partial^2 \ell_{I-II-UDa}(\boldsymbol{\theta};\mathbf{v})}{\partial\lambda\delta} = (\beta+1)\sum_{i=1}^{n}\frac{\left[C^{-1}(v_i)\right]^{-\delta}\ln\left[C^{-1}(v_i)\right]}{\left\{1+\lambda[C^{-1}(v_i)]^{-\delta}\right\}^2} \tag{A5}$$

$$\frac{\partial^2 \ell_{I-II-UDa}(\boldsymbol{\theta};\mathbf{v})}{\partial\delta^2} = -\frac{n}{\delta^2} - \lambda(\beta+1)\sum_{i=1}^{n}\frac{\left[C^{-1}(v_i)\right]^{-\delta}\left\{\ln\left[C^{-1}(v_i)\right]\right\}^2}{\left\{1+\lambda[C^{-1}(v_i)]^{-\delta}\right\}^2}. \tag{A6}$$

The elements of the expected Fisher information matrix are functions of the following expectation, with respect to the density function of the *rv* V

$$E_{j_1,j_2,j_3} = E_V\left\{\frac{\left[C^{-1}(V)\right]^{-j_1\delta}\left(\ln\left[C^{-1}(V)\right]\right)^{j_2}}{\left(1+\lambda[C^{-1}(V)]^{-\delta}\right)^{j_3}}\right\} \tag{A7}$$

We now observe that for a generic function $h(.)$ of $C^{-1}(V)$, by a simple transformation of the variable, we can write

$$\begin{aligned} E_V\left\{h\left[C^{-1}(V)\right]\right\} &= \int_0^1 h\left[C^{-1}(v)\right]f_V(v;\boldsymbol{\theta})dv = \\ &= \int_0^1 h\left[C^{-1}(v)\right]\beta\lambda\delta[C^{-1}(v)]^{-\delta-1}\left\{1+\lambda[C^{-1}(v)]^{-\delta}\right\}^{-\beta-1}\left[-\frac{\partial C^{-1}(v)}{\partial v}\right]dv = \\ &= \int_0^\infty h[y]\beta\lambda\delta[y]^{-\delta-1}\left\{1+\lambda[y]^{-\delta}\right\}^{-\beta-1}dy = E_Y[h(Y)] \end{aligned}$$

where $Y \sim Da(\beta,\lambda,\delta)$. Using this last observation, Equation (A7) can be rewritten as

$$\begin{aligned} E_{j_1,j_2,j_3} &= E_Y\left\{\frac{[Y]^{-j_1\delta}(\ln[Y])^{j_2}}{\left(1+\lambda[Y]^{-\delta}\right)^{j_3}}\right\} \\ &= \int_0^\infty \frac{y^{-j_1\delta}(\ln(y))^{j_2}}{(1+\lambda y^{-\delta})^{j_3}}\beta\lambda\delta y^{-\delta-1}\left(1+\lambda y^{-\delta}\right)^{-\beta-1}dy \\ &= \frac{\beta}{\lambda^{j_1}\delta^{j_2}}\int_0^1 y^{\beta-j_1+j_3-1}(1-y)^{\frac{2}{\delta}+j_1}[\ln(\lambda)+\ln(y)-\ln(1-y)]^{j_2}dy \end{aligned} \tag{A8}$$

Using the successive derivatives of the beta function, the expectations for determining the elements of the Fisher information matrix are

$$E_{1,0,1} = \frac{\beta}{\lambda}B(\beta,2+\frac{2}{\delta}) \tag{A9}$$

$$E_{2,0,2} = \frac{\beta}{\lambda^2}B(\beta,3+\frac{2}{\delta}) \tag{A10}$$

$$E_{1,1,1} = \frac{\beta}{\lambda\delta}\left\{\ln(\lambda)B(\beta,2+\frac{2}{\delta}) + A_1(\beta,2+\frac{2}{\lambda\delta}) + A_2(\beta+1,2+\frac{2}{\delta})\right\} \tag{A11}$$

$$E_{1,1,2} = \frac{\beta}{\lambda\delta}\left\{\ln(\lambda)B(\beta+1,2+\frac{2}{\delta}) + A_1(\beta,3+\frac{2}{\lambda\delta}) + A_2(\beta+1,2+\frac{2}{\delta})\right\} \tag{A12}$$

$$\begin{aligned} E_{1,2,2} &= \frac{\beta}{\lambda\delta^2}\Big\{[\ln(\lambda)]^2 B(\beta+1,2+\frac{2}{\delta}) + 2\ln(\lambda)A_1(\beta+1,2+\frac{2}{\lambda\delta}) - 2\ln(\lambda)A_2(\beta+1,2+\frac{2}{\delta}) \\ &+ A_3(\beta+1,2+\frac{2}{\delta}) - 2A_5(\beta+1,2+\frac{2}{\delta}) + A_4(\beta+1,2+\frac{2}{\delta})\Big\} \end{aligned} \tag{A13}$$

where

$$A_1(p,q) = B(p,q)\{\psi(p) - \psi(p+q)\}$$

$$A_2(p,q) = B(p,q)\{\psi(q) - \psi(p+q)\}$$

$$A_3(p,q) = B(p,q)\Big\{[\psi(p) - \psi(p+q)]^2 + [\psi'(p) - \psi'(p+q)]\Big\}$$

$$A_4(p,q) = B(p,q)\Big\{[\psi(q) - \psi(p+q)]^2 + [\psi'(q) - \psi'(p+q)]\Big\}$$

$$A_5(p,q) = B(p,q)\Big\{[\psi(q) - \psi(p+q)][\psi(p) - \psi(p+q)] + [\psi'(p) - \psi'(p+q)]\Big\}$$

with $\psi(.)$ and $\psi'(.)$ being digamma and trigamma functions, respectively.

In order to compute the expected Fisher information matrix, we compute the elements of the Hessian matrix, which, after some algebraic manipulation, for $j,s = 1,2,3$ and $r_j = 1,2,\ldots,p_j$ and $r_s = 1,2,\ldots,p_s$, turn out to be

$$\begin{aligned} \frac{\partial^2 \ell(\gamma;\mathbf{v},\mathbf{X})}{\partial\gamma_{j,r_j}\partial\gamma_{s,r_s}} &= k_1 + k_2 - k_3 + k_4 \ln\left(1+\tilde{\lambda}_i\left[C^{-1}(v_i)\right]^{-\tilde{\delta}_i}\right) + k_6\frac{\left[C^{-1}(v_i)\right]^{-\tilde{\delta}_i}}{1+\tilde{\lambda}_i[C^{-1}(v_i)]^{-\tilde{\delta}_i}} \\ &+ k_7\frac{\left[C^{-1}(v_i)\right]^{-\tilde{\delta}_i}\ln\left[C^{-1}(v_i)\right]}{1+\tilde{\lambda}_i[C^{-1}(v_i)]^{-\tilde{\delta}_i}} + \left(\frac{1}{\tilde{\beta}_{1,i}}+1\right) \\ &\times \left\{\left(\frac{\partial\tilde{\lambda}_i}{\partial\gamma_{j,r_j}}\right)\left(\frac{\partial\tilde{\delta}_i}{\partial\gamma_{s,r_s}}\right)\frac{\left[C^{-1}(v_i)\right]^{-\tilde{\delta}_i}(\ln\left[C^{-1}(v_i)\right])}{\left(1+\tilde{\lambda}_i[C^{-1}(v_i)]^{-\tilde{\delta}_i}\right)^2}\right. \\ &+ \left(\frac{\partial\tilde{\lambda}_i}{\partial\gamma_{j,r_j}}\right)\left(\frac{\partial\tilde{\lambda}_i}{\partial\gamma_{s,r_s}}\right)\frac{\left[C^{-1}(v_i)\right]^{-2\tilde{\delta}_i}}{\left(1+\tilde{\lambda}_i[C^{-1}(v_i)]^{-\tilde{\delta}_i}\right)^2} \\ &- \tilde{\lambda}_i\left(\frac{\partial\tilde{\delta}_i}{\partial\gamma_{j,r_j}}\right)\left(\frac{\partial\tilde{\delta}_i}{\partial\gamma_{s,r_s}}\right)\frac{\left[C^{-1}(v_i)\right]^{-\tilde{\delta}_i}(\ln\left[C^{-1}(v_i)\right])^2}{\left(1+\tilde{\lambda}_i[C^{-1}(v_i)]^{-\tilde{\delta}_i}\right)^2} \\ &- \left.\tilde{\lambda}_i\left(\frac{\partial\tilde{\delta}_i}{\partial\gamma_{j,r_j}}\right)\left(\frac{\partial\tilde{\lambda}_i}{\partial\gamma_{s,r_s}}\right)\frac{\left[C^{-1}(v_i)\right]^{-2\tilde{\delta}_i}(\ln\left[C^{-1}(v_i)\right])}{\left(1+\tilde{\lambda}_i[C^{-1}(v_i)]^{-\tilde{\delta}_i}\right)^2}\right\} \end{aligned} \tag{A14}$$

where

$$k_1 = \frac{1}{\tilde{\lambda}_i}\left[-\frac{1}{\tilde{\lambda}_i}\left(\frac{\partial\tilde{\lambda}_i}{\partial\gamma_{s,r_s}}\right)\left(\frac{\partial\tilde{\lambda}_i}{\partial\gamma_{j,r_j}}\right) + \left(\frac{\partial^2\tilde{\lambda}_i}{\partial\gamma_{j,r_j}\partial\gamma_{s,r_s}}\right)\right],$$

$$k_2 = \frac{1}{\tilde{\delta}_i}\left[-\frac{1}{\tilde{\delta}_i}\left(\frac{\partial\tilde{\delta}_i}{\partial\gamma_{s,r_s}}\right)\left(\frac{\partial\tilde{\delta}_i}{\partial\gamma_{j,r_j}}\right) + \left(\frac{\partial^2\tilde{\delta}_i}{\partial\gamma_{j,r_j}\partial\gamma_{s,r_s}}\right)\right],$$

$$k_3 = \frac{1}{\tilde{\beta}_{1,i}}\left[-\frac{1}{\tilde{\beta}_{1,i}}\left(\frac{\partial\tilde{\beta}_{1,i}}{\partial\gamma_{s,r_s}}\right)\left(\frac{\partial\tilde{\beta}_{1,i}}{\partial\gamma_{j,r_j}}\right)+\left(\frac{\partial^2\tilde{\beta}_{1,i}}{\partial\gamma_{j,r_j}\partial\gamma_{s,r_s}}\right)\right],$$
$$k_4 = \frac{1}{\tilde{\beta}_{1,i}^2}\left[-\frac{2}{\tilde{\beta}_{1,i}}\left(\frac{\partial\tilde{\beta}_{1,i}}{\partial\gamma_{s,r_s}}\right)\left(\frac{\partial\tilde{\beta}_{1,i}}{\partial\gamma_{j,r_j}}\right)+\left(\frac{\partial^2\tilde{\beta}_{1,i}}{\partial\gamma_{j,r_j}\partial\gamma_{s,r_s}}\right)\right],$$
$$k_5 = \left(\frac{\partial\tilde{\lambda}_i}{\partial\gamma_{s,r_s}}\right)\left(\frac{\partial\tilde{\lambda}_i}{\partial\gamma_{j,r_j}}\right)+\tilde{\lambda}_i\left(\frac{\partial^2\tilde{\delta}_i}{\partial\gamma_{j,r_j}\partial\gamma_{s,r_s}}\right),$$
$$k_6 = \frac{1}{\tilde{\beta}_{1,i}^2}\left(\frac{\partial\tilde{\beta}_{1,i}}{\partial\gamma_{j,r_j}}\right)\left(\frac{\partial\tilde{\lambda}_i}{\partial\gamma_{s,r_s}}\right)-\left(\frac{1}{\tilde{\beta}_{1,i}}+1\right)\left(\frac{\partial^2\tilde{\lambda}_i}{\partial\gamma_{j,r_j}\partial\gamma_{s,r_s}}\right)$$

and

$$k_7 = k_5\left(\frac{1}{\tilde{\beta}_{1,i}}+1\right)-\frac{\tilde{\lambda}_i}{\tilde{\beta}_{1,i}}\left(\frac{\partial\tilde{\beta}_{1,i}}{\partial\gamma_{j,r_j}}\right)\left(\frac{\partial\tilde{\delta}_i}{\partial\gamma_{s,r_s}}\right).$$

The elements of the expected Fisher information matrix are functions of the following expectations:

$$E\left\{\frac{[C^{-1}(V)]^{-\tilde{\delta}_i}}{\left(1+\tilde{\lambda}_i[C^{-1}(V)]^{-\tilde{\delta}_i}\right)}\right\}=E_{1,0,1}\ ;\quad E\left\{\frac{[C^{-1}(V)]^{-\tilde{\delta}_i}\ln[C^{-1}(V)]}{\left(1+\tilde{\lambda}_i[C^{-1}(V)]^{-\tilde{\delta}_i}\right)}\right\}=E_{1,1,1} \tag{A15}$$

$$E\left\{\frac{[C^{-1}(V)]^{-\tilde{\delta}_i}\ln[C^{-1}(V)]}{\left(1+\tilde{\lambda}_i[C^{-1}(V)]^{-\tilde{\delta}_i}\right)^2}\right\}=E_{1,1,2}\ ;\quad E\left\{\frac{[C^{-1}(V)]^{-2\tilde{\delta}_i}}{\left(1+\tilde{\lambda}_i[C^{-1}(V)]^{-\tilde{\delta}_i}\right)^2}\right\}=E_{2,0,2} \tag{A16}$$

$$E\left\{\frac{[C^{-1}(V)]^{-\tilde{\delta}_i}\left(\ln[C^{-1}(V)]\right)^2}{\left(1+\tilde{\lambda}_i[C^{-1}(V)]^{-\tilde{\delta}_i}\right)^2}\right\}=E_{1,2,2} \tag{A17}$$

$$\begin{aligned} E_{2,1,2} &= E\left\{\frac{[C^{-1}(V)]^{-2\tilde{\delta}_i}\ln[C^{-1}(V)]}{\left(1+\tilde{\lambda}_i[C^{-1}(V)]^{-\tilde{\delta}_i}\right)^2}\right\}=E_Y\left\{\frac{Y^{-2\tilde{\delta}_i}\ln(Y)}{\left(1+\tilde{\lambda}_iY^{-\tilde{\delta}_i}\right)^2}\right\} \\ &= \frac{1}{\tilde{\beta}_{1,i}\tilde{\delta}_i\tilde{\lambda}_i^2}\left\{\ln(\tilde{\lambda}_i)B(\frac{1}{\tilde{\beta}_{1,i}},5+\frac{2}{\tilde{\delta}_i})+A_1(\frac{1}{\tilde{\beta}_{1,i}},5+\frac{2}{\tilde{\delta}_i})-A_2(\frac{1}{\tilde{\beta}_{1,i}},5+\frac{2}{\tilde{\delta}_i})\right\} \end{aligned} \tag{A18}$$

and finally

$$\begin{aligned} E_V\left\{\ln\left(1+\tilde{\lambda}_i\left[C^{-1}(V)\right]^{-\tilde{\delta}_i}\right)\right\} &= E_Y\left\{\ln\left[\left(1+\tilde{\lambda}_iY^{-\tilde{\delta}_i}\right)\right]\right\} \\ &= -\frac{1}{\tilde{\beta}_{1,i}}A_1(\frac{1}{\tilde{\beta}_{1,i}},3+\frac{2}{\tilde{\delta}_i}). \end{aligned} \tag{A19}$$

Appendix A.4. Partial Derivatives Of System (39)

Evidently, in system (39), the partial derivatives are given by

$$\frac{\partial\tilde{\beta}_{1,i}}{\partial\gamma_{1,r_1}}=\frac{\partial h_1(x_{1,i},\gamma_1)}{\partial\gamma_{1,r_1}}\qquad \text{for}\quad r_1=1,\dots,p_1$$

$$\frac{\partial\tilde{\lambda}_i}{\partial\gamma_{1,r_1}}=\frac{\partial\tilde{\lambda}(\beta_{1,i},me_i,v(q)_i)}{\partial\gamma_{1,r_1}}=\frac{\partial\tilde{\lambda}(\beta_{1,i},me_i,v(q)_i)}{\partial\beta_{1,i}}\left(\frac{\partial\beta_{1,i}}{\partial\gamma_{1,r_1}}\right)\quad \text{for}\ \ r_1=1,\dots,p_1$$

$$\frac{\partial \tilde{\lambda}_i}{\partial \gamma_{2,r_2}} = \frac{\partial \tilde{\lambda}(\beta_{1,i}, me_i, v(q)_i)}{\partial \gamma_{2,r_2}} = \frac{\partial \tilde{\lambda}(\beta_{1,i}, me_i, v(q)_i)}{\partial me_i}\left(\frac{\partial me_i}{\partial \gamma_{2,r_2}}\right) \text{ for } r_2 = 1, \ldots, p_2$$

$$\frac{\partial \tilde{\lambda}_i}{\partial \gamma_{3,r_3}} = \frac{\partial \tilde{\lambda}(\beta_{1,i}, me_i, v(q)_i)}{\partial \gamma_{3,r_3}} = \frac{\partial \tilde{\lambda}(\beta_{1,i}, me_i, v(q)_i)}{\partial v(q)_i}\left(\frac{\partial v(q)_i}{\partial \gamma_{3,r_3}}\right) \text{ for } r_3 = 1, \ldots, p_3$$

$$\frac{\partial \tilde{\delta}_i}{\partial \gamma_{1,r_1}} = \frac{\partial \tilde{\delta}(\beta_{1,i}, me_i, v(q)_i)}{\partial \gamma_{1,r_1}} = \frac{\partial \tilde{\delta}(\beta_{1,i}, me_i, v(q)_i)}{\partial \beta_{1,i}}\left(\frac{\partial \beta_{1,i}}{\partial \gamma_{1,r_1}}\right) \text{ for } r_1 = 1, \ldots, p_1$$

$$\frac{\partial \tilde{\delta}_i}{\partial \gamma_{2,r_2}} = \frac{\partial \tilde{\delta}(\beta_{1,i}, me_i, v(q)_i)}{\partial \gamma_{2,r_2}} = \frac{\partial \tilde{\delta}(\beta_{1,i}, me_i, v(q)_i)}{\partial me_i}\left(\frac{\partial me_i}{\partial \gamma_{2,r_2}}\right) \text{ for } r_2 = 1, \ldots, p_2$$

$$\frac{\partial \tilde{\delta}_i}{\partial \gamma_{3,r_3}} = \frac{\partial \tilde{\delta}(\beta_{1,i}, me_i, v(q)_i)}{\partial \gamma_{3,r_3}} = \frac{\partial \tilde{\delta}(\beta_{1,i}, me_i, v(q)_i)}{\partial v(q)_i}\left(\frac{\partial v(q)_i}{\partial \gamma_{3,r_3}}\right) \text{ for } r_3 = 1, \ldots, p_3$$

Moreover, by specifying the appropriate link functions of indicators of interest

$$\tilde{\beta}_{1,i} = e^{\mathbf{x}'_{1,i}\gamma_1}, \quad me_i = \frac{e^{\mathbf{x}'_{2,i}\gamma_2}}{1 + e^{\mathbf{x}'_{2,i}\gamma_2}}, \quad v(q)_i = \frac{e^{\mathbf{x}'_{3,i}\gamma_3}}{1 + e^{\mathbf{x}'_{3,i}\gamma_3}},$$

we have

$$\frac{\partial \beta_{1,i}}{\partial \gamma_{1,r_1}} = e^{\mathbf{x}'_{1,i}\gamma_1} x_{1,r_1,i}, \quad \frac{\partial me_i}{\partial \gamma_{2,r_2}} = \frac{e^{\mathbf{x}'_{2,i}\gamma_2}}{\left(1 + e^{\mathbf{x}'_{2,i}\gamma_2}\right)^2} x_{2,r_2,i} \text{ and } \frac{\partial v(q)_i}{\partial \gamma_{3,r_3}} = \frac{e^{\mathbf{x}'_{3,i}\gamma_3}}{\left(1 + e^{\mathbf{x}'_{3,i}\gamma_3}\right)^2} x_{3,r_3,i}.$$

References

1. Alzaatreh, A.; Famoye, F.; Lee, C. A New Method for Generating Families of Continuous Distributions. *Metron* **2013**, *71*, 63–79. [CrossRef]
2. Eugene, N.; Lee, C.; Famoye, F. Beta-normal distribution and its application. *Commun. Stat. Theory Methods* **2002**, *31*, 497–512. [CrossRef]
3. Jones, M. Families of distributions arising from the distributions of order statistics. *Test* **2004**, *13*, 1–43. [CrossRef]
4. Kumaraswamy, P. A generalized probability density function for double-bounded random processes. *J. Hydrol.* **1980**, *46*, 79–88. [CrossRef]
5. Topp, C.; Leone, F. A family of J-shaped frequency functions. *J. Am. Stat. Assoc.* **1955**, *50*, 209–219. [CrossRef]
6. Arnold, B.; Groeneveld, R. Some properties of the arcsine distribution. *J. Am. Stat. Assoc.* **1980**, *75*, 173–175. [CrossRef]
7. Van Dorp, R.; Kotz, S. The standard two-sided power distribution and its properties. *Am. Stat.* **2002**, *56*, 90–99. [CrossRef]
8. Kotz, S.; Van Dorp, J.R. *Beyond Beta: Other Continuous Families of Distributions with Bounded Support and Applications*; World Scientific Publishing Co.: Singapore, 2004.
9. Marshall, A.W.; Olkin, I. *Life Distributions*; Springer: New York, NY, USA, 2007.
10. Modi, K.; Gill, V. Unit Burr III distribution with application. *J. Stat. Manag. Syst.* **2019**, *23*, 579–592. [CrossRef]
11. Singh, D.P.; Jha, M.; Tripathi, Y.; Wang, L. Reliability estimation in a multicomponent stress-strength model for unit Burr III distribution under progressive censoring. *Qual. Technol. Quant. Manag.* **2022**, *19*, 605–632. [CrossRef]
12. Mazucheli, J.; Menezes, A.; Chakraborty, S. On the one parameter unit-Lindley distribution and its associated regression model for proportion data. *J. Appl. Stat.* **2019**, *46*, 700–714. [CrossRef]
13. Mazucheli, J.; Menezes, A.; Dey, S. Unit-Gompertz distribution with applications. *Statistica* **2019**, *79*, 26–43.
14. Korkmaz, M.; Chesneau, C. On the unit Burr-XII distribution with the quantile regression modeling and applications. *Comput. Appl. Math.* **2021**, *40*, 29. [CrossRef]
15. Ghitany, M.; Mazucheli, J.; Menezes, A.; Alqallaf, F. The unit-inverse Gaussian distribution: A new alternative to two-parameter distributions on the unit interval. *Commun. Stat. Theory Methods* **2018**, *48*, 3423–3438. [CrossRef]
16. Korkmaz, M.; Chesneau, C.; Korkmaz, Z. On the arcsecant hyperbolic normal distribution. Properties, quantile regression modeling and applications. *Symmetry* **2021**, *13*, 117. [CrossRef]
17. Korkmaz, M. A new heavy-tailed distribution defined on the bounded interval: The logit slash distribution and its applications. *J. Appl. Stat.* **2019**, *473*, 2097–2119. [CrossRef]

18. Arslan, T. A new family of unit-distributions: Definition, properties and applications. *Twms J. Appl. Eng. Math.* **2023**, *13*, 782–791.
19. Ferreira, A.; Mazucheli, J. The zero-inflated, one and zero-and-one-inflated new unit-Lindley distributions. *Braz. J. Biom.* **2022**, *40*, 291–326. [CrossRef]
20. Rodrigues, J.; Bazán, J.; Suzuki, A.K. A flexible procedure for formulating probability distributions on the unit interval with applications. *Commun. Stat. Theory Methods* **2020**, *49*, 738–754. [CrossRef]
21. Aljarrah, M.; Lee, C.; Famoye, F. On generating $T-X$ family of distributions using quantile functions. *J. Stat. Distrib. Appl.* **2014**, *1*, 2. [CrossRef]
22. Bakouch, H.; Nik, A.; Asgharzadeh, A.; Salinas, H. A flexible probability model for proportion data: Unit-half-normal distribution. *Commun. Stat. Case Stud. Data Anal. Appl.* **2021**, *7*, 271–288. [CrossRef]
23. Haq, M.; Hashmi, S.; Aidi, K.; Ramos, P.F.L. Unit Modified Burr-III Distribution: Estimation, Characterizations and Validation Test. *Ann. Data Sci.* **2023**, *10*, 415–449. [CrossRef]
24. Mazucheli, J.; Leiva, V.; Alves, B.; Menezes, A. A New Quantile Regression for Modeling Bounded Data under a Unit Birnbaum–Saunders Distribution with Applications in Medicine and Politics. *Symmetry* **2021**, *13*, 682. [CrossRef]
25. Mazucheli, J.; Menezes, A.; Dey, S. The unit Birnbaum-Saunders distribution with applications. *Chil. J. Stat.* **2018**, *9*, 47–57.
26. Nasiru, S.; Abubakari, A.; Angbing, I. Bounded Odd Inverse Pareto Exponential Distribution: Properties, Estimation, and Regression. *Int. J. Math. Math. Sci.* **2021**, *2021*, 9955657. [CrossRef]
27. Altun, E.; El-Morshedy, M.; Eliwa, M. A new regression model for bounded response variable: An alternative to the beta and unit Lindley regression models. *PLoS ONE* **2021**, *16*, e0245627. [CrossRef] [PubMed]
28. Domma, F.; Condino, F.; Giordano, S. A New Formulation of the Dagum Distribution in terms of Income Inequality and Poverty Measures. *Physica A Stat. Mech. Its Appl.* **2018**, *511*, 104–126. [CrossRef]
29. Domma, F.; Condino, F.; Franceschi, S.; De Luca, D.; Biondi, D. On the extreme hydrologic events determinants by means of Beta-Singh-Maddala reparameterization. *Sci. Rep.* **2022**, *12*, 15537. [CrossRef]
30. Dagum, C. *A New Model of Personal Distribution: Specification and Estimation*; Springer: New York, NY, USA, 1977; pp. 413–437.
31. Dagum, C. The Generation and Distribution of Income, the Lorenz Curve and the Gini Ratio. 1980. Available online: https://pascal-francis.inist.fr/vibad/index.php?action=getRecordDetail&idt=PASCAL8130438924 (accessed on 23 June 2023).
32. Latorre, G. Proprieta' campionarie del modello di Dagum per la distribuzione dei redditi. *Statistica* **1988**, *48*, 15–27.
33. Kleiber, C.; Kotz, S. *Statistical Size Distributions in Economics and Actuarial Science*; Wiley Series in Probability and Statistics; Wiley Interscience, John Wiley and Sons Inc.: Hoboken, NJ, USA, 2003.
34. Cribari-Neto, F.; Zeileis, A. Beta Regression in R. *J. Stat. Softw.* **2020**, *34*, 1–24.
35. Ferrari, S.; Cribari Neto, F. Beta regression for modelling rates and proportions. *J. Appl. Stat.* **2004**, *31*, 799–815. [CrossRef]
36. Song, P.; Tan, M. Marginal models for longitudinal continuous proportional data. *Biometrics* **2000**, *56*, 496–502. [CrossRef] [PubMed]
37. Gómez-Déniz, E.; Sordo, M.; Calderín-Ojeda, E. The log-Lindley distribution as an alternative to the beta regression model with applications in insurance. *Insur. Math. Econ.* **2014**, *54*, 49–57. [CrossRef]
38. Altun, E. The log-weighted exponential regression model: Alternative to the beta regression model. *Commun. Stat. Theory Methods* **2021**, *50*, 2306–2321. [CrossRef]
39. Mousa, A.; El-Sheikh, A.; Abdel-Fattah, M. A gamma regression for bounded continuous variables. *Adv. Appl. Stat.* **2016**, *49*, 305–326. [CrossRef]
40. Mitnik, P.; Baek, S. The Kumaraswamy distribution: Median-dispersion re-parameterizations for regression modeling and simulation-based estimation. *Stat. Pap.* **2013**, *54*, 177–192. [CrossRef]
41. Lemonte, A.; Moreno-Arenas, G. On a heavy-tailed parametric quantile regression model for limited range response variables. *Comput. Stat.* **2020**, *35*, 379–398. [CrossRef]
42. Jodrá, P.; Jiménez-Gamero, M. A quantile regression model for bounded responses based on the exponential-geometric distribution. *Revstat* **2020**, *4*, 415–436.
43. Paz, R.; Balakrishnan, N.; Bazán, J. L-logistic regression models: Prior sensitivity analysis, robustness to outliers and applications. *Braz. J. Probab. Stat.* **2019**, *33*, 455–479.
44. Mazucheli, J.; Menezes, A.; Fernandes, L.; de Oliveira, R.; Ghitany, M. The unit Weibull distribution as an alternative to the Kumaraswamy distribution for the modeling of quantiles conditional on covariates. *J. Appl. Stat.* **2020**, *47*, 954–974. [CrossRef]

mathematics

MDPI

Article

Zero-Dependent Bivariate Poisson Distribution with Applications

Najla Qarmalah [1,*] and Abdulhamid A. Alzaid [2]

[1] Department of Mathematical Sciences, Princess Nourah bint Abdulrahman University, Riyadh 84428, Saudi Arabia
[2] Department of Statistics and Operations Research, King Saud University, Riyadh 145111, Saudi Arabia
* Correspondence: nmbinqurmalah@pnu.edu.sa; Tel.: +966-118236238

Abstract: The bivariate Poisson model is the most widely used model for bivariate counts, and in recent years, several bivariate Poisson regression models have been developed in order to analyse two response variables that are possibly correlated. In this paper, a particular class of bivariate Poisson model, developed from the bivariate Bernoulli model, will be presented and investigated. The proposed bivariate Poisson models use dependence parameters that can model positively and negatively correlated data, whereas more well-known models, such as Holgate's bivariate Poisson model, can only be used for positively correlated data. As a result, the proposed model contributes to improving the properties of the more common bivariate Poisson regression models. Furthermore, some of the properties of the new bivariate Poisson model are outlined. The method of maximum likelihood and moment method were used to estimate the parameters of the proposed model. Additionally, real data from the healthcare utilization sector were used. As in the case of healthcare utilization, dependence between the two variables may be positive or negative in order to assess the performance of the proposed model, in comparison to traditional bivariate count models. All computations and graphs shown in this paper were produced using R programming language.

Keywords: Poisson; Bernoulli; count data; maximum likelihood; moment method; regression; bivariate models

MSC: 60E05; 62H10; 62H12; 62E10

1. Introduction

Bivariate count models have received increasing scholarly attention in recent years, mainly because they offer flexibility for fitting across a wide variety of random phenomena. For instance, applications based on discrete bivariate models are often used in the fields of health sciences, traffic accidents, economics, actuarial science, social sciences, environmental studies, and so forth [1]. For more information about bivariate count models, the reader is directed to [2–8]. The most widely used model for bivariate counts is the bivariate Poisson model, which was developed by [9]. The bivariate Poisson model, which was developed by [9], is considered the limit of a bivariate contingency table model. The literature outlines the main contributions and applications of bivariate Poisson models. For instance, the bivariate Poisson model can be used in modelling data in sports [10,11], health [12–14], econometrics and insurance [15,16], and so forth. Furthermore, the use of the bivariate Poisson model is not unique in its different methodological applications. One of the methods is the trivariate reduction, which was studied by [17] and developed by [18]. Bivariate Poisson models have been developed based on the method of trivariate reduction using convolutions of independent Poisson random variables. These models allow for only non-negative correlation between variables. For a comprehensive review of the bivariate Poisson model and its applications, the reader is directed to references [4,19–21].

More recently, researchers have developed bivariate Poisson regression models. These models analyse two response variables that are possibly correlated, and they allow the two response variables to be affected by different predictive factors. This means that bivariate Poisson regression models can be used for inference and prediction purposes. Early studies of the use of bivariate count regression models to analyse correlated count events include those by [3], who use a bivariate Poisson regression in a labour mobility study. Furthermore, using a bivariate Poisson regression model, [22] study the relationship between types of health insurance and various responses that measure the demand for health care. Only recently have bivariate regression models been compared and their application in different fields analysed in depth. A study by [13] examines bivariate and zero-inflated bivariate Poisson regression models using the conditional method, as compared with the standard method, using a joint probability distribution (j.p.d). Therefore, bivariate Poisson regression models play a vital role in modeling, analyzing, and improving the fit results when two dependent variables in a data set are highly correlated [1,12,23].

Although the bivariate Poisson regression model offers useful properties for modeling paired count data that exhibits correlations, some models have major drawbacks. One drawback is that some models can only model data with positive correlations [24]. For instance, a bivariate Poisson model based on the trivariate reduction method studied by [17] lacks generality, because it shows a positive correlation only. A few previous studies have explored and developed bivariate Poisson regression models that allow for negative correlations, including bivariate Poisson distribution as a product of Poisson marginals with a multiplicative factor [5]. In addition, [25] have proposed a bivariate Poisson distribution that allows for negative correlations by using conditional probabilities. This current paper will consider a class of bivariate Poisson models generated from the bivariate Bernoulli model, which can model positively and negatively correlated data. This is a progression on from other bivariate Poisson models already proposed in previous research, including the well-known Holgate [17] bivariate Poisson model. One of the merits of the proposed model is that its structure is relatively simple. The proposed models seek to contribute to improving the properties of commonly used bivariate Poisson models. In this paper, the statistical properties of the new model are studied, and the parameters of the proposed model are estimated using the maximum likelihood and moment methods. In this respect, a simulation study was carried out to investigate the performance of the parameter estimation ability of the proposed model using the maximum likelihood and moment method. Finally, applications of the proposed model will be presented in the healthcare sector, and the model's performance will be compared against well-known bivariate Poisson models.

This paper is organized into sections as follows: Section 2 will detail the proposed bivariate Poisson model and the relevant estimation methods used. Section 3 will present relevant application of this model, using data drawn from different fields and will compare the results with well-known models. Finally, a conclusion will be presented in Section 4.

2. Zero-Dependent Bivariate Poisson Model (ZDBP)

Different methods have been used to construct bivariate Poisson distributions, with specified marginal distributions. Most of the well-known bivariate Poisson models use the popular reduction method [4]. However, this method has two main drawbacks. Firstly, it does not support negative correlation values and secondly, it does not cover the entire range of feasible correlations. In the current study, the construction of a developed bivariate Poisson model is presented, without the aforementioned drawbacks as follows:

If we consider that $(B_1,\ B_2)$ has Bernoulli marginals, then it has only four possible values $(1,\ 1)$, $(1,\ 0)$, $(0,\ 1)$, and $(0,\ 0)$ with the probabilities p_{11}, p_{10}, p_{01}, and p_{00}, which are $p_{ij} = P(B_1 = i,\ B_2 = j),\ i, j = 0, 1$. If the marginal probability discrete random variables are independent of (B_1, B_2), and have a probability mass function of zero-truncated Poisson distribution with the parameters θ_1 and θ_2, respectively, then the probability mass function can be defined as follows:

$$P(X_i = j) = \frac{e^{-\theta_i}}{1 - e^{-\theta_i}} \frac{\theta_i{}^j}{j!},\ j = 1,2,\ldots,\ i = 1,2$$

.

Here, set $Y_i = B_i X_i$, $i = 1,2$, where $p_i = 1 - e^{-\theta_i}$, $i = 1,2$. Then, Y_i has a Poisson distribution with the parameter θ_i. The j.d.f of the two random variables, Y_1 and Y_2, can be expressed as follows:

$$P(Y_1 = y_1,\ Y_2 = y_2) = \sum_{i,j=0}^{1} P(Y_1 = y_1,\ Y_2 = y_2 | B_1 = i,\ B_2 = j) p_{ij}$$

Then:

$$\begin{aligned} &P(Y_1 = y_1,\ Y_2 = y_2) \\ &= \frac{\theta_1{}^{y_1}}{y_1!}\frac{\theta_2{}^{y_2}}{y_2!}\left(\frac{1-p_1}{p_1}\right)^{1-\delta(y_1)}\left(\frac{1-p_2}{p_2}\right)^{1-\delta(y_2)} p_{00}{}^{\delta(y_1)\delta(y_2)} p_{10}{}^{(1-\delta(y_1))\delta(y_2)} p_{01}{}^{\delta(y_1)(1-\delta(y_2))} p_{11}{}^{(1-\delta(y_1))(1-\delta(y_2))} \end{aligned} \quad (1)$$

for $y_1, y_2 = 0,1,\ldots$ where $\delta(x) = 1$ if $x = 0$ and 0 is otherwise.

Generally, Y_1 and Y_2 are dependent and therefore (1) defines a new bivariate Poisson distribution, which will be called the zero-dependent Bivariate Poisson Model (ZDBP) model. Since bivariate Bernoulli distribution is completely determined by the three parameters p_1, p_2, and p_{11}, then, the above shows that the ZDBP model is completely determined by the three parameters θ_1, θ_2, and p_{11}. Therefore, the ZDBP $(\theta_1, \theta_2,\ p_{11})$ model can be used whenever the parameters matter and as a result, (1) can be rewritten as follows:

$$\begin{aligned} &P(Y_1 = y_1,\ Y_2 = y_2) \\ &= \frac{\theta_1{}^{y_1}}{y_1!}\frac{\theta_2{}^{y_2}}{y_2!}\left(\frac{e^{-\theta_1}}{1-e^{-\theta_1}}\right)^{1-\delta(y_1)}\left(\frac{e^{-\theta_2}}{1-e^{-\theta_2}}\right)^{1-\delta(y_2)} \left(e^{-\theta_1} + e^{-\theta_2} + p_{11} - 1\right)^{\delta(y_1)\delta(y_2)} (1 - e^{-\theta_1} \\ &- p_{11})^{\delta(y_2)(1-\delta(y_1))} \left(1 - e^{-\theta_2} - p_{11}\right)^{\delta(y_1)(1-\delta(y_2))} p_{11}{}^{(1-\delta(y_1))(1-\delta(y_2))} \end{aligned} \quad (2)$$

To visualize the j.p.d for the ZDBP model in (2), the representative j.p.d plots for different parameter choices are shown in Figures 1–3, where negative dependence is apparent in Figures 1 and 3. The package "plot3D" in R is needed to represent the plots in Figures 1–3.

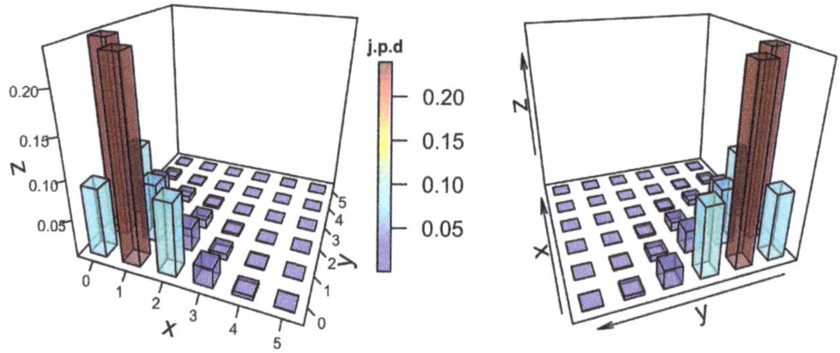

Figure 1. The j.p.d of the ZDBP model for $\theta_1 = 0.79, \theta_2 = 0.79$ and $p_{11} = 0.19$ with $cor = -0.3$.

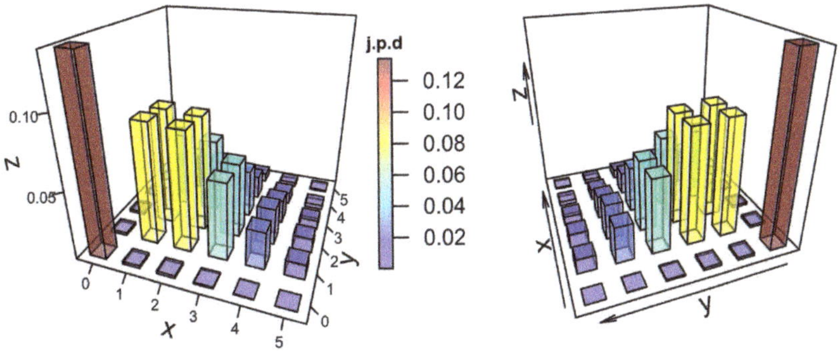

Figure 2. The j.p.d of the ZDBP model for $\theta_1 = 1.96, \theta_2 = 1.96$ and $p_{11} = 0.85$ with $cor = 0.3$.

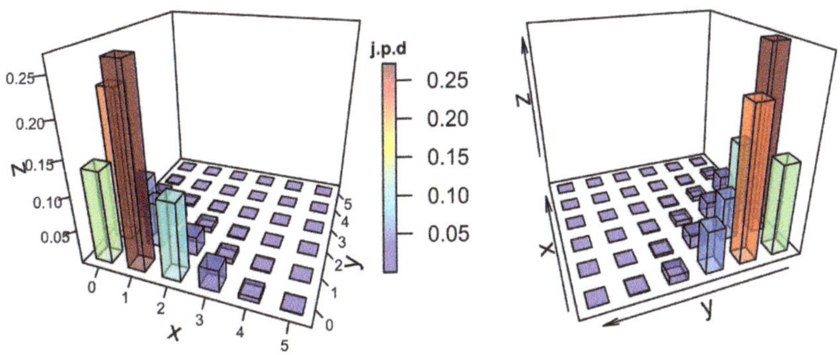

Figure 3. The j.p.d of the ZDBP model for $\theta_1 = 0.84, \theta_2 = 0.58$ and $p_{11} = 0.15$ with $cor = -0.3$.

2.1. Statistical Properties

The ZDBP model has statistical properties that can be easily proven. These properties are shown as follows:

Theorem 1. *The conditional probability function of Y_1 given Y_2 is*

$$P(Y_1 = y_1 | \, Y_2 = y_2) = \begin{cases} P_0(y_2) \; y_1 = 0 \\ (1 - P_0(y_2)) \frac{\theta_1^{y_1}}{y_1!} \left(\frac{e^{-\theta_1}}{1 - e^{-\theta_1}} \right) \; y_1 = 1, 2, \ldots \end{cases},$$

where,

$$P_0(y_2) = e^{\theta_2} \left(\frac{e^{-\theta_2}}{1 - e^{-\theta_2}} \right)^{1 - \delta(y_2)} \left(e^{-\theta_1} + e^{-\theta_2} + p_{11} - 1 \right)^{\delta(y_2)} \left(1 - e^{-\theta_2} - p_{11} \right)^{(1 - \delta(y_2))}$$

Proof . Dividing (2) by $\frac{\theta_2^{y_2}}{y_2!} e^{-\theta_2}$ one gets

$$P(Y_1 = y_1 | \, Y_2 = y_2) = e^{\theta_2} \frac{\theta_1^{y_1}}{y_1!} \left(\frac{e^{-\theta_1}}{1 - e^{-\theta_1}} \right)^{1 - \delta(y_1)} \left(\frac{e^{-\theta_2}}{1 - e^{-\theta_2}} \right)^{1 - \delta(y_2)} \left(e^{-\theta_1} + e^{-\theta_2} + p_{11} - 1 \right)^{\delta(y_1)\delta(y_2)}$$

$$\left(1 - e^{-\theta_1} - p_{11} \right)^{\delta(y_2)(1 - \delta(y_1))} \left(1 - e^{-\theta_2} - p_{11} \right)^{\delta(y_1)(1 - \delta(y_2))} p_{11}^{(1 - \delta(y_1))(1 - \delta(y_2))}.$$

Therefore, for $y_1 = 0$, we have

$$P(Y_1 = 0 | \, Y_2 = y_2) = e^{\theta_2} \left(\frac{e^{-\theta_2}}{1 - e^{-\theta_2}} \right)^{1 - \delta(y_2)} \left(e^{-\theta_1} + e^{-\theta_2} + p_{11} - 1 \right)^{\delta(y_2)} \left(1 - e^{-\theta_2} - p_{11} \right)^{(1 - \delta(y_2))} = P_0(y_2).$$

In addition, for $y_1 \neq 0$, we have

$$P(Y_1 = y_1 | \, Y_2 = y_2) = e^{\theta_2} \frac{{\theta_1}^{y_1}}{y_1!} \left(\frac{e^{-\theta_1}}{1 - e^{-\theta_1}} \right) \left(\frac{e^{-\theta_2}}{1 - e^{-\theta_2}} \right)^{1-\delta(y_2)} \left(1 - e^{-\theta_1} - p_{11} \right)^{\delta(y_2)} {p_{11}}^{(1-\delta(y_2))}$$

From the two cases $y_2 = 0$ and $y_2 \neq 0$, we conclude that

$$e^{\theta_2} \left(\frac{e^{-\theta_2}}{1 - e^{-\theta_2}} \right)^{1-\delta(y_2)} \left[\left(e^{-\theta_1} + e^{-\theta_2} + p_{11} - 1 \right)^{\delta(y_2)} \left(1 - e^{-\theta_2} - p_{11} \right)^{(1-\delta(y_2))} + e^{\theta_2} \frac{{\theta_1}^{y_1}}{y_1!} \left(1 - e^{-\theta_1} - p_{11} \right)^{\delta(y_2)} {p_{11}}^{(1-\delta(y_2))} \right] = 1,$$

As a result, we get

$$e^{\theta_2} \left(\frac{e^{-\theta_2}}{1 - e^{-\theta_2}} \right)^{1-\delta(y_2)} \left(1 - e^{-\theta_1} - p_{11} \right)^{\delta(y_2)} {p_{11}}^{(1-\delta(y_2))} = 1 - P_0(y_2).$$

This completes the proof. □

From the above, it is clear that Theorem 1 implies that the conditional distribution of Y_1 given Y_2 is mixture of degenerated distribution at zero and zero-truncated Poisson distribution with mixing probabilities dependent on the value of y_2. In other words, we can write $Y_1 \big| Y_2 =^d I(Y_2)R,$ where $I(Y_2)$ is the Bernoulli random variable with failure probability as $P_0(Y_2)$ independent of the zero-truncated Poisson random variable R. Therefore, we have the following corollary.

Corollary 1.

$$E[Y_1|Y_2 = y_2] = \frac{\theta_1}{1 - e^{-\theta_1}} [1 - P_0(y_2)] = \frac{\theta_1}{1 - e^{-\theta_1}} \begin{cases} e^{\theta_2}(1 - e^{-\theta_1} - p_{11}), \; y_2 = 0 \\ \frac{p_{11}}{1 - e^{-\theta_2}}, \; y_2 \neq 0 \end{cases}$$

Theorem 2. *The covariance of Y_1 and Y_2 is $cov(Y_1, Y_2) = \frac{\theta_1\theta_2}{p_1p_2}(p_{11} - p_1p_2)$*

Proof. The covariance of Y_1 and Y_2 according to the assumption $Y_i = B_iX_i, \; i = 1,2$ can be defined as follows:

$$cov(Y_1, Y_2) = cov(B_1X_1, B_2X_2) = E(B_1X_1B_2X_2) - E(B_1X_1)E(B_2X_2)$$

Since X_1 and X_2 are independent of (B_1, B_2), then

$$\begin{aligned} cov(Y_1, Y_2) = E(X_1)E(X_2)E(B_1B_2) - E(X_1)E(X_2)E(B_1)E(B_2) &= E(X_1)E(X_2)[E(B_1B_2) - E(B_1)E(B_2)] \\ &= \frac{\theta_1\theta_2}{(1 - e^{-\theta_1})(1 - e^{-\theta_2})} cov(B_1, B_2) \end{aligned}$$

Since $cov(B_1, B_2) = p_{11} - p_1p_2$ and $p_i = 1 - e^{-\theta_i}$, therefore we get the result

$$cov(Y_1, Y_2) = \frac{\theta_1\theta_2}{p_1p_2}(p_{11} - p_1p_2)$$

□

From Corollary 1, it is clear that Y_1 and Y_2 will be independent variables when $p_{11} = p_1p_2$.

Corollary 2. *The correlation of Y_1 and Y_2 is $cor(Y_1, Y_2) = \sqrt{\frac{\theta_1\theta_2(1-p_1)(1-p_2)}{p_1p_2}} cor(B_1, B_2)$.*

Proof . The correlation of Y_1 and Y_2 according to the assumption $Y_i = B_i X_i,\ i = 1,2$ is defined as follows:

$$cor(Y_1, Y_2) = cor(B_1 X_1, B_2 X_2) = \frac{cov(Y_1, Y_2)}{\sigma(Y_1)\sigma(Y_2)}$$

From Corollary 1 and since $Y_i \sim Poisson(\theta_i),\ i = 1,2$, then

$$cor(Y_1, Y_2) = \frac{\sqrt{\theta_1\theta_2}}{p_1 p_2}(p_{11} - p_1 p_2)$$

Since $cor(B_1, B_2) = \frac{p_{11} - p_1 p_2}{\sqrt{p_1(1-p_1)p_2(1-p_2)}}$, then the equation above can be written as

$$cor(Y_1, Y_2) = \sqrt{\frac{\theta_1\theta_2(1-p_1)(1-p_2)}{p_1 p_2}}\, cor(B_1, B_2)$$

□

From Corollary 2, we can conclude that the correlation of Y_1 and Y_2 allows the ZDBP model to be positively or negatively correlated since it depends on $cor(B_1, B_2)$, which can be a negative or a positive correlation.

2.2. Parameter Estimation

An estimation of the ZDBP model parameters was obtained using the maximum likelihood estimation (ML) and moment methods (MM). The ZDBP model has six parameters that can be estimated based on three parameters, which are θ_1, θ_2, and p_{11}. If we consider n as the independent vectors (y_{i1}, y_{i2}), where the i-th vector is the ZDBP model shown in (2), then the estimators can be expressed as follows:

2.2.1. Maximum Likelihood Estimation (ML)

The likelihood function of (2) is shown below as

$$\begin{aligned} L(\theta_1, \theta_2, p_{11}, p_{00}, \quad & p_{10}, p_{01}, p_{11}; y_{1i}, y_{2i}) \\ & = \prod_{i=1}^{n} \frac{\theta_1^{y_{1i}}}{y_{1i}!}\frac{\theta_2^{y_{2i}}}{y_{2i}!}\left(\frac{e^{-\theta_1}}{1-e^{-\theta_1}}\right)^{1-\delta(y_{1i})}\left(\frac{e^{-\theta_2}}{1-e^{-\theta_2}}\right)^{1-\delta(y_{2i})}(e^{-\theta_1} + e^{-\theta_2} + p_{11} - 1)^{\delta(y_{1i})\delta(y_{2i})}(1 - e^{-\theta_1} \\ & p_{11})^{\delta(y_{2i})(1-\delta(y_{1i}))}(1 - e^{-\theta_2} - p_{11})^{\delta(y_{1i})(1-\delta(y_{2i}))} p_{11}^{(1-\delta(y_{1i}))(1-\delta(y_{2i}))} \end{aligned}$$

It is worth mentioning that θ_1, θ_2, and p_{11} are sufficient to be used with ML method in order to estimate the other parameters. This is because of the dependent relationship between the parameters. The corresponding log likelihood can be given as follows:

$$\begin{aligned} \ell = logL(\theta_1, \theta_2, \quad & p_{11}; y_{1i}, y_{2i}) \\ & = \sum_{i=1}^{n} [y_{1i}\log(\theta_1) - \log(y_{1i}!) + y_{2i}\log(\theta_2) - \log(y_{2i}!) - (1 - \delta(y_{1i}))(\theta_1 + \log(1 - e^{-\theta_1})) \\ & -(1 - \delta(y_{2i}))(\theta_2 + \log(1 - e^{-\theta_2})) + \delta(y_{1i})\delta(y_{2i})\log(e^{-\theta_1} + e^{-\theta_2} + p_{11} - 1) \\ & +\delta(y_{2i})(1 - \delta(y_{1i}))log(1 - e^{-\theta_1} - p_{11}) + \delta(y_{1i})(1 - \delta(y_{2i}))log(1 - e^{-\theta_2} - p_{11}) \\ & +(1 - \delta(y_{1i}))(1 - \delta(y_{2i}))\log(p_{11})] \end{aligned}$$

Furthermore, the corresponding likelihood equations are shown below:

$$\frac{\partial \ell}{\partial \hat{\theta}_1} = 0, \frac{\partial \ell}{\partial \hat{\theta}_2} = 0 \text{ and } \frac{\partial \ell}{\partial \hat{p}_{11}} = 0 \qquad (3)$$

These equations can be solved numerically to estimate the parameters θ_1, θ_2, and p_{11}. Following on from this, other parameters were estimated using the following equations:

$$\left.\begin{aligned} \hat{p}_1 &= 1 - e^{-\hat{\theta}_1} \\ \hat{p}_2 &= 1 - e^{-\hat{\theta}_2} \\ \hat{p}_{10} &= 1 - e^{-\hat{\theta}_1} - \hat{p}_{11} \\ \hat{p}_{01} &= 1 - e^{-\hat{\theta}_2} - \hat{p}_{11} \\ \hat{p}_{00} &= e^{-\hat{\theta}_1} + e^{-\hat{\theta}_2} + \hat{p}_{11} - 1 \end{aligned}\right\} \quad (4)$$

2.2.2. Moment Method Estimation (MM)

Using the MM, the following equations were considered in order to estimate the parameters θ_1, θ_2, and p_{11} as follows:

$$\left.\begin{aligned} \overline{y}_1 &= \hat{\theta}_1 \\ \overline{y}_2 &= \hat{\theta}_2 \\ \hat{p}_{11} &= \left(1 - e^{-\hat{\theta}_1}\right)\left(1 - e^{-\hat{\theta}_2}\right)\left[\frac{\hat{\gamma}}{\hat{\theta}_1\hat{\theta}_2} + 1\right] \end{aligned}\right\}$$

Following on from this, other parameters were estimated using (4).

2.2.3. Simulation Study

A simulation study was conducted to assess the performance of the ML method and MM used for the estimation of ZDBP's parameters. The simulation was executed according to the steps outlined below:

1. A total of 1000 data sets with sizes of 20, 50, 200, and 1000, relating to each data set, were generated from the ZDBP model using four different theoretical parameters values, with varying positive and negative correlations as follows:
   (a) Case 1: Model ZDBP $(0.30, 1.57,\ 0.05)$ with $cor = -0.5$;
   (b) Case 2: Model ZDBP $(0.54, 0.89,\ 0.07)$ with $cor = -0.5$;
   (c) Case 3: Model ZDBP $(0.44, 0.37,\ 0.19)$ with $cor = 0.3$;
   (d) Case 4: Model ZDBP $(0.17, 0.19,\ 0.13)$ with $cor = 0.7$.
2. Calculating the ML estimates of θ_1, θ_2, and p_{11} and considering that $1 - e^{-\hat{\theta}_1} - e^{-\hat{\theta}_2} \leq \hat{p}_{11} \leq \min\left\{1 - e^{-\hat{\theta}_1},\ 1 - e^{-\hat{\theta}_2}\right\}$, the obtained estimates by step 1 were ignored.
3. The bias and mean square error (MSE) were calculated for all considered models.

In Step 1, packages "mipfp", "VGAM", and "actuar" in R were used in order to generate data from the ZDBP model. In addition, in Step 2, Equation (3) is solved numerically using the function "optim" in R. The method "BFGS", a quasi-Newton method, was chosen for the optimization problem among other methods in optim function because it is relatively quick. Tables 1–4 below show the performance of the ML method and the MM used for estimation of the ZDBP' parameters, taking into account the MSE and bias relating to the cases shown in Step 1 of the simulation study. In general, the results revealed the superiority of the ML method for the estimation of positive and negative correlations in comparison with the MM, taking into account the MSE. In addition, the ML results of θ_1, θ_2, and p_{11} were better than the MM results of these parameters based on the MSE for n = 20, except for the ML results of θ_1, θ_2, when $\theta_1 > \theta_2$, as shown in Table 1.

It can be seen that the performance using the ML method for the estimation of the parameters θ_1, θ_2, and p_{11} is similar to that generated by the MM for 1000, especially for positive correlations. See Table 3.

The MSE of ML for θ_1 and θ_2 are the same as the MSE of MM estimates of these parameters when n = 50 for θ_2 only, and when n = 200 for both parameters. Moreover, Table 4 shows that the MSE of ML for θ_1 and p_{11} are the same as the MSE of MM estimates of these parameters when n = 200. For n = 1000, the performance of ML in general is the same as MM for the estimation of θ_1, θ_2, and p_{11}, according to the MSE when either the correlation is positive or negative. As a result, it can be concluded that the ML estimates of the ZDBP model's parameters are useful for estimation, in comparison with the MM estimates, especially for small samples and for when $\theta_1, \theta_2 < 1$.

Figure 4 shows the MSE results using the ML of θ_1, θ_2, where *cor* related to the cases is shown in Step 1 of the simulation study. It is clear from Figure 4a–d that using the MLE, as the sample size increases, the MSE for θ_1, θ_2 and *cor* decreases simultaneously. Using the ML method, the MSE for θ_1 and θ_2 is less than the MSE for *cor* in relation to the positive correlation, as shown in Figure 4c,d. On the other hand, using the ML method, the MSE for *cor*, as shown in Figure 4a,b, is less than the MSE for θ_1 and θ_2 for the large sample sizes and for the negative correlation.

Table 1. MSE and bias between parentheses for the different simulated data sizes: n = 20, 50, 200, 1000 for the ZDBP (0.30, 1.57, 0.05) model with cor = −0.5.

n		20		50		200		1000	
Method		ML	MM	ML	MM	ML	MM	ML	MM
$\hat{\theta}_1$	MSE	0.0038	0.0022	0.0101	0.0014	0.0002	0.0017	0.0002	0.0004
	bias	0.0467	0.0468	0.2867	0.0368	0.0092	0.0393	0.0087	0.0138
$\hat{\theta}_2$	MSE	0.1937	0.1092	0.0002	0.0271	0.0090	0.0096	0.0007	0.0004
	bias	−0.4347	−0.2630	−0.0138	0.1570	0.0948	0.0970	−0.0254	−0.0205
$\hat{p}_{11}$	MSE	0.0027	0.0047	0.0001	0.0001	0.0005	0.0006	0.0001	0.0001
	bias	−0.0329	−0.0600	0.0075	0.0010	0.0213	0.0204	0.0010	−0.0031
$\hat{cor}$	MSE	0.0165	0.0682	0.0004	0.0088	0.0016	0.0010	0.0001	0.0007
	bias	−0.1118	−0.2447	0.0145	−0.0809	0.0397	−0.0034	−0.0032	−0.0257

Table 2. MSE and bias between parentheses for the different simulated data sizes: n = 20, 50, 200, 1000 for the ZDBP (0.54, 0.89, 0.07) model with cor = −0.5.

n		20		50		200		1000	
Method		ML	MM	ML	MM	ML	MM	ML	MM
$\hat{\theta}_1$	MSE	0.0227	0.0251	0.0082	0.0097	0.0022	0.0027	0.0004	0.0005
	bias	−0.0048	0.0192	0.0026	0.0135	−0.0047	−0.0037	0.0001	0.0002
$\hat{\theta}_2$	MSE	0.0390	0.0415	0.0149	0.0162	0.0040	0.0043	0.0008	0.0009
	bias	−0.0061	0.0132	0.0012	0.0090	0.0006	0.0009	0.0005	0.0011
$\hat{p}_{11}$	MSE	0.0021	0.0040	0.0010	0.0017	0.0003	0.0005	0.0001	0.0001
	bias	−0.0155	−0.0163	0.0017	0.0018	−0.0003	0.0006	0.0005	0.0006
$\hat{cor}$	MSE	0.0123	0.0290	0.0045	0.0100	0.0012	0.0027	0.0002	0.0005
	bias	−0.0600	−0.0900	−0.0048	−0.0164	0.0006	0.0021	0.0008	0.0007

Table 3. MSE and bias between parentheses for the different simulated data sizes: n = 20, 50, 200, 1000 for the ZDBP (0.44, 0.37, 0.19) model with cor = 0.3.

n		20		50		200		1000	
Method		ML	MM	ML	MM	ML	MM	ML	MM
$\hat{\theta}_1$	MSE	0.0194	0.0200	0.0091	0.0093	0.0023	0.0023	0.0004	0.0004
	bias	0.0161	0.0125	−0.0026	−0.0036	−0.0013	−0.0016	−0.0001	−0.0003
$\hat{\theta}_2$	MSE	0.0175	0.0181	0.0073	0.0073	0.0019	0.0019	0.0004	0.0004
	bias	−0.0068	−0.0108	0.0020	0.0002	−0.0016	−0.0018	−0.0004	−0.0003
$\hat{p}_{11}$	MSE	0.0060	0.0070	0.0027	0.0032	0.00070	0.0008	0.0001	0.0001
	bias	0.0157	0.0178	0.0024	0.0006	−0.0007	−0.0008	0.0003	0.0003
$\hat{cor}$	MSE	0.0275	0.0415	0.0131	0.0209	0.0031	0.0054	0.0007	0.0011
	bias	0.0375	0.0524	0.0010	−0.0031	−0.0012	−0.0015	0.0011	0.0012

Table 4. MSE and bias between parentheses for the different simulated data sizes: n = 20, 50, 200, 1000 from the ZDBP (0.17, 0.19, 0.13) model with cor = 0.7.

n		20		50		200		1000	
Method		**MLE**	**MM**	**MLE**	**MM**	**MLE**	**MM**	**MLE**	**MM**
$\hat{\theta}_1$	MSE bias	0.0070 −0.0356	0.0081 −0.0403	0.0029 −0.0069	0.0033 −0.0100	0.0007 −0.0002	0.0007 −0.0007	0.0002 0.0001	0.0002 0.0001
$\hat{\theta}_2$	MSE bias	0.0072 −0.0219	0.0079 −0.0264	0.0035 0.0014	0.0037 −0.0006	0.0008 0.0010	0.0009 0.0005	0.0002 0.0001	0.0002 −0.0001
$\hat{p}_{11}$	MSE bias	0.0034 0.0119	0.0035 0.0099	0.0019 0.0075	0.0020 0.0070	0.0005 0.0012	0.0005 0.0008	0.0001 0.00003	0.0001 −0.00002
$c\hat{o}r$	MSE bias	0.0599 0.2130	0.0662 0.2143	0.0153 0.0664	0.0191 0.0736	0.0030 0.0051	0.0047 0.0048	0.0006 −0.0006	0.0010 −0.0008

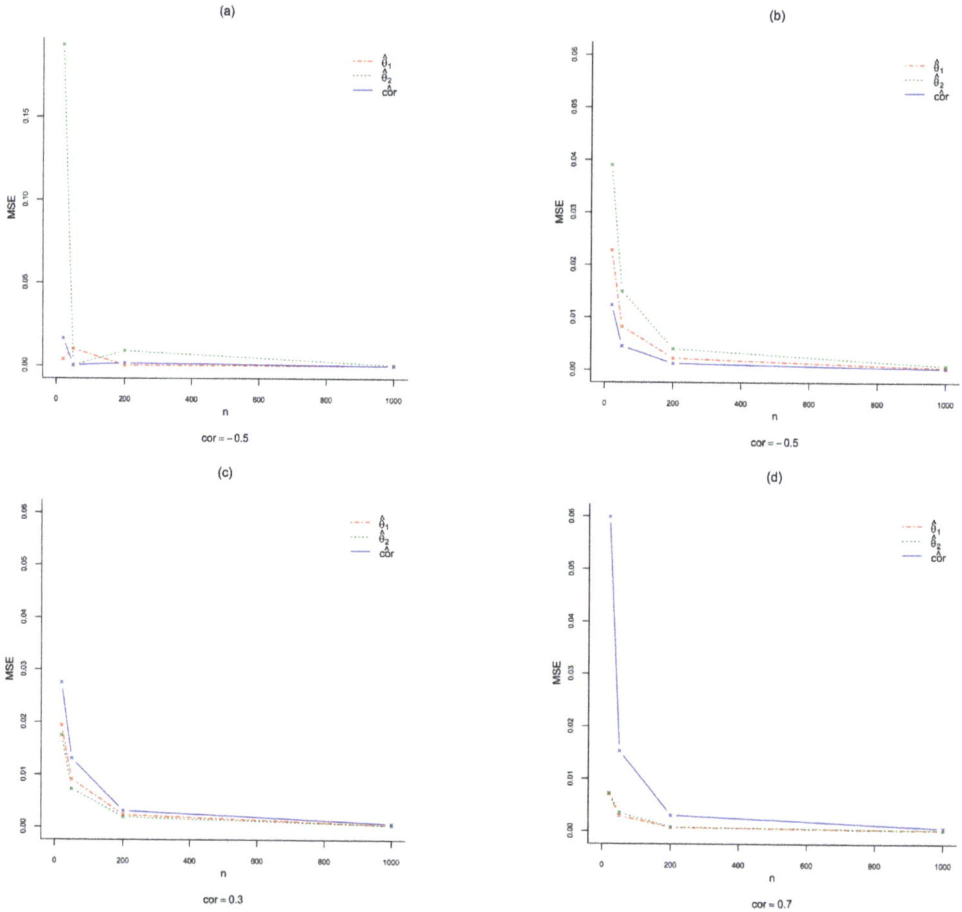

Figure 4. Summary of the results provided by lines of MSE of the estimates $\hat{\theta}_1$, $\hat{\theta}_2$, and $c\hat{o}r$ for the different simulated data sizes n = 20, 50, 200, 1000 relating to the models (**a**) ZDBP (0.30, 1.57, 0.05), (**b**) ZDBP (0.54, 0.89, 0.07), (**c**) ZDBP (0.44, 0.37, 0.19), and (**d**) ZDBP (0.17, 0.19, 0.13).

2.2.4. Applications

Real data examples were studied to investigate the performance of the ZDBP model for fitting positively and negatively correlated bivariate data compared to other models.

Health and Retirement Study (HRS) Data

The first data set used to illustrate the application of the ZDBP model was drawn from the tenth wave of the Health and Retirement Study (HRS). A summary of the descriptive statistics of dependent variables for this data are provided by Islam and Chowdhury [26]. In the same study, bivariate Poisson-Poisson (BP-P) and bivariate right-truncated Poisson-Poisson (BRTP-P) models are fitted to the data from the Health and Retirement Study. The variables comprise the number of conditions a patient has ever had, as noted by doctors, X_1, and the utilization of healthcare services, where the services derive from hospitals, nursing homes, doctors, and home care assistants, X_2. The sample size is 5567 and the correlation between X_1 and X_2 is 0.06.

For the current study, the proposed ZDBP model was fitted to the same data and compared with the models in [26]. Table 5 summarises results for the fittings for the ZDBP model, the bivariate Poisson model with independent marginals (BP), and the BP-PR and the BRTP-P models. These results are shown in terms of the number of parameters used, and according to the Akaike Information Criteria (AIC), Bayesian Information Criteria (BIC), and loglikelihood estimate (ℓ). The results show the superiority of the ZDBP model for fitting the Health and Retirement Study (HRS) data in comparison with the other models, based on AIC and BIC, show the ability of the ZDBP model to fit positively correlated data. An analysis of the ML estimates derived for the ZDBP model is presented in Table 6.

Table 5. Comparison between models from the Health and Retirement Study data.

Model	AIC	BIC	ℓ
ZDBP	31,727.26	31,747.14	−15,860.63
BP	32,707.61	32,720.86	−16,351.81
BP-P	33,419.33	33,432.58	−16,707.66
BRTP-P	33,196.42	33,209.67	−16,596.21

Table 6. Fitting Results for the ZDBP model from the Health and Retirement Study data.

Model	Parameter	Estimate	SE
Parameter	p_{11}	0.582	0.006
	θ_1	2.768	0.023
	θ_2	0.545	0.013
	cor	0.588	

Australian Health Data (1977–1978)

The data discussed in this example comes from the Journal of Applied Econometrics 1997 Data Archive [27]. The data covers 5190 single-person households, and provides healthcare service utilization information from the 1977–1978 Australian Health Survey. A study by [28] uses this data in their analysis of various measures of health-care utilisation. A detailed summary of the statistics for the dependent and explanatory variables of this data is provided in [28]. We consider the number of consultations with doctors during the two-week period prior to the survey (Y_1) and the number of prescribed medicines used in the past 2 days (Y_2). The mean and the standard deviation of Y_1 are 0.302 and 0.798, respectively. The corresponding values for Y_2 are 0.863 and 1.415 and the correlation between Y_1 and Y_2 is 0.31.

The ZDBP model was fitted to the data and compared with the BP model. Table 7 presents a summary of results for the ZDBP and BP models, in terms of the number of parameters, AIC, BIC, and ℓ. The results show the superiority of the ZDBP model compared with the BP model for fitting the Australian Health data, based on AIC and BIC. An analysis of the ML parameter estimates derived for the ZDBP model is shown in Table 8. In addition, we consider the dependent variables, Y_2, and the number of non-prescribed medications used in past two days, Y_3. The mean and the standard deviation of Y_2 are 0.863 and 1.42, the corresponding values for Y_3 are 0.356 and 0.71, and the correlation between Y_2 and Y_3 is −0.04. Table 9 presents a summary of the results for the ZDBP and BP models, in terms of the number of parameters, AIC, BIC, and ℓ. The results show that the ZDBP model appears to be competitive with the BP model for fitting the Australian Health data in comparison with the other models, based on AIC and BIC. Therefore, this example emphasises the ability of the ZDBP model to fit positively and negatively correlated data. An analysis of the ML estimates derived for the ZDBP model is provided in Table 10.

Table 7. Comparison between the ZDBP and BP models from the Australian Health data.

Model	AIC	BIC	ℓ
ZDBP	22,498.39	22,518.05	−11,246.19
BP	23,176.13	23,189.24	−11,586.07

Table 8. Fitting results for the ZDBP model from the Australian Health data.

Model	Parameter	Estimate	SE
Parameter	p_{11}	0.261	0.006
	θ_1	0.367	0.009
	θ_2	0.891	0.013
	cor	0.252	

Table 9. Comparison between ZDBP and BP models from the Australian Health data.

Model	AIC	BIC	ℓ
ZDBP	23,543.50	23,563.16	−11,768.75
BP	23,541.73	23,554.84	−11,768.86

Table 10. Fitting results for the ZDBP model from the Australian Health data.

Model	Parameter	Estimate	SE
Parameter	p_{11}	0.172	0.006
	θ_1	0.862	0.013
	θ_2	0.354	0.009
	cor	−0.01	

3. Zero-Dependent Bivariate Poisson Regression Model (ZDBPR)

In this section, the Bivariate Bernoulli Poisson Regression Model will be considered. In this context, $\alpha_k = z_i^T \beta_{kl}$, $k = 1, 2,$ and 3 is where z_i denotes a vector of explanatory variables of length l for the i-th observation related to the k-th parameter. This means that β_{kl} is the corresponding vector of regression coefficients. In this respect, the ZDBPR model can take the following form:

$$\left. \begin{array}{c} (Y_{1i}, Y_{2i}) \sim \text{ZDBPR}(\theta_{1i}, \theta_{2i}, p_{11i}) \\ p_{11i} = \frac{e^{\alpha_{1i}}}{D},\ p_{10i} = \frac{e^{\alpha_{2i}}}{D}, p_{01i} = \frac{e^{\alpha_{3i}}}{D}, p_{00i} = \frac{1}{D} \end{array} \right\} \quad (5)$$

where $D = 1 + e^{\alpha_{1i}} + e^{\alpha_{2i}} + e^{\alpha_{3i}}$, $P(B_j = 0) = p_{01i} + p_{00i} = e^{-\theta_{ji}}$, $j = 1, 2,$ and $i = 1, 2, \cdots, n$ and n denotes the observation number.

The ZDBPR model uses two response variables that are positively and negatively correlated. In addition, this model can be compared with other models to show that it has identical AIC, BIC, and parameter estimates.

3.1. Applications

3.1.1. Health and Retirement Study (HRS) Data

In this example, the same dependent variables used by [26] were considered, as outlined in "Health and Retirement Study (HRS) Data" Section. A study by [26] fit this data using bivariate right-truncated Poisson-Poisson regression (BRTP-PR), and bivariate Poisson-Poisson regression (BP-PR) models. They found that the BRTP-PR model appears to be significantly better than the BP-PR model for fitting the data.

For the purpose of this research, the ZDBPR model was used to fit the data, and was compared with the model used by [26]. Furthermore, the ZDBPR model was compared with the joint bivariate Poisson regression (JBPR) model used by [13], in which the covariates are gender (1 male, 0 female), age (in years), race (1 Hispanic, 0 others), and veteran status (1 yes, 0 no). Table 11 shows the results for the ZDBPR, JBPR, BPR, BP-PR, and BRTP-PR models in terms of the number of parameters, i.e., AIC, BIC, and ℓ. The results show the superiority of the ZDBPR model for fitting the Health and Retirement Study data in comparison with the other models, based on AIC and BIC. This suggests that the ZDBPR model is able to fit positively correlated data. An analysis of the ML estimates derived for this model is provided in Table 12.

Table 11. Comparison between models for the Health and Retirement Study data.

	Number of Parameters	AIC	BIC	ℓ
ZDBPR	15	31,982.88	32,082.25	−15,976.44
JBPR	15	32,524.53	32,623.90	−16,247.26
BPR	15	32,514.53	32,580.77	−16,247.26
BP-PR	15	33,192.13	33,258.38	−16,586.07
BRTP-PR	15	33,021.41	33,087.66	−16,500.71

Table 12. Fitting results for the ZDBPR model from the Health and Retirement Study data.

Parameter	Covariate	Coefficient	SE
α_1	constant	−0.471	0.591
	gender	0.014	0.063
	age	3.265	0.804
	Hispanic	−0.107	0.090
	Veteran	0.209	0.072
α_2	constant	−2.295	0.655
	gender	−0.528	0.072
	age	5.716	0.889
	Hispanic	0.201	0.093
	Veteran	−0.011	0.088
α_3	constant	−15.164	135.930
	gender	−2.239	706.157
	age	2.519	19.098
	Hispanic	−0.166	417.107
	Veteran	−1.296	1572.270

3.1.2. Australian Health Data (1977–1978)

In this example, the same dependent variables as used by [13] are used, namely Y_1 and Y_2. The covariates used are gender (1 female, 0 male), age in years divided by 100 (measured as midpoints of age groups), and the annual income in Australian dollars divided by 1000 (measured as midpoint of coded ranges). In the study by [13], model (A) was fitted as a JBPR model, where the covariates were gender, age, income, and age multiplied by gender, with gender as a covariate on the covariance scale. In addition, model (B) was fitted as a JBPR model, where the covariates were gender, age, and income, with a constant covariance term. A study by [13] concludes that the JBPR model performs better than the other models examined in their study. For the purposes of this current research, Model A and B have been fitted for the ZDBPR model. Table 13 shows the results for the ZDBPR and JBPR models, relating to the number of parameters, AIC, BIC, and ℓ. These results show the superiority of the ZDBPR model for fitting the Health Care Australia data in comparison with the JBPR model, based on AIC and BIC. This suggests that the ZDBPR model can positively fit the correlated data. An analysis of the ML estimates derived for this model is provided in Table 14.

Table 13. Comparison between ZDBPR and JBPR models from the Health Care Australia data.

	Model	Number of Parameters	AIC	BIC	ℓ
ZDBPR	A	15	19,856.41	19,954.73	−9913.21
JBPR		12	19,912.90	19,991.55	−9944.45
ZDBPR	B	12	19,910.80	19,989.45	−9943.40
JBPR		11	19,942.16	20,014.26	−9960.08

Table 14. Fitting results for the ZDBPR model from the Health Care Australia data using Model A.1 and B.1.

Model		**A**		**B**	
Parameter	**Covariate**	**Coefficient**	**SE**	**Coefficient**	**SE**
	constant	−3.161	0.170	−2.670	0.127
	gender	5.980	0.298	4.780	0.177
	age	1.621	0.184	0.762	0.073
	income	−0.531	0.110	−0.509	0.106
	Age∗gender	−1.963	0.361		
	constant	−2.302	0.212	−2.202	0.188
	gender	0.894	0.491	0.430	0.324
α_2	age	0.547	0.263	0.254	0.123
	income	−0.133	0.167	−0.105	0.167
	Age∗gender	−0.974	0.657		
	constant	−3.371	0.158	−2.798	0.116
	gender	6.031	0.286	4.589	0.162
α_3	age	2.065	0.167	1.139	0.069
	income	−0.101	0.089	−0.076	0.091
	Age∗gender	−2.196	0.341		

This current study also considered the same dependent variables used by Zamani et.al. [29], which are Y_2 and Y_3. Furthermore, [29] fit their data using a bivariate Poisson regression model, whereby the j.p.d is proposed by [5]. The bivariate Poisson model developed by [5] is defined from the product of two Poisson marginals with a multiplicative factor parameter. For ease of notation, the current study will refer to the Zamani et al. model as BPR [29]. Table 15 shows that the ZDBPR model performs better than the BPR [29] model in terms of AIC and BIC. This suggests that the ZDBPR model can fit negatively correlated data. Table 16 provides an analysis of the ML estimates derived for this model.

Table 15. Comparison between ZDBPR and BPR [29] models from the Health Care Australia data.

	Number of Parameters	AIC	BIC	ℓ
ZDBPR	39	19,025.4	19,281.03	−9473.70
BPR [29]	26	19,097.2	19,267.60	−9522.59

Table 16. Results from fitting the ZDBPR model to the Health Care Australia data.

Parameter	Covariate	Coefficient	SE
α_1	constant	−5.791	0.349
	gender	1.383	0.110
	age	6.083	1.785
	agesq	−4.448	1.970
	income	0.323	0.152
	levyplus	0.442	0.126
	freepoor	−0.036	0.293
	freerepa	0.243	0.173
	illness	0.695	0.032
	actdays	0.097	0.014
	hscore	0.080	0.020
	chcond1	1.217	0.118
	chcond2	1.569	0.155
α_2	constant	−3.278	0.251
	gender	0.949	0.071
	age	1.737	1.343
	agesq	1.674	1.481
	income	0.052	0.110
	levyplus	0.225	0.089
	freepoor	−0.165	0.205
	freerepa	0.277	0.122
	illness	0.463	0.032
	actdays	0.077	0.014
	hscore	0.056	0.017
	chcond1	1.098	0.077
	chcond2	1.541	0.114
α_3	constant	−2.422	0.283
	gender	0.348	0.084
	age	5.403	1.671
	agesq	−6.079	1.946
	income	0.083	0.122
	levyplus	−0.145	0.089
	freepoor	−0.083	0.179
	freerepa	−0.449	0.167
	illness	0.344	0.032
	actdays	−0.010	0.020
	hscore	0.054	0.020
	chcond1	0.312	0.089
	chcond2	0.067	0.164

4. Conclusions

This paper has presented new bivariate Poisson models that can be fitted to bivariate and correlated count data with and without covariates. The main advantage of the ZDBP model and the ZDBPR model is their ability to fit positively and negatively correlated count data. This advantage is valuable for fitting different kinds of data in the healthcare field, as in the case of healthcare data, dependence between the two variables may be positive or negative. The statistical properties of the ZDBP model were discussed, and some properties of this model were proven, which shows that the pair of ZDBP variables can be positively or negatively correlated. Estimation for the ZDBP model was achieved using the ML and the MM methods, with different parameters, and with positive and negative correlations. In the simulation, the ML method showed good performance for estimation in comparison with the MM. Real data were used to examine the performance of the ZDBP model and the ZDBPR model for fitting positive and negative correlated count data, in comparison with other models. The applications for both models show the superiorities of these models in comparison with other models. This suggests that the ZDBP model and the ZDBPR model can allow the correlation structure to be positive or negative. Finally, although the proposed model was applied in two healthcare data sets, the model can be generalized and utilized in the other areas of research as well.

Author Contributions: Conceptualization, A.A.A.; methodology, A.A.A.; software, N.Q.; validation, A.A.A. and N.Q.; formal analysis, A.A.A. and N.Q.; investigation, A.A.A. and N.Q.; resources, A.A.A. and N.Q.; data curation, A.A.A. and N.Q.; writing—original draft preparation, A.A.A. and N.Q.; writing—review and editing, A.A.A. and N.Q.; visualization, N.Q.; supervision, A.A.A.; project administration, A.A.A.; funding acquisition, N.Q. All authors have read and agreed to the published version of the manuscript.

Funding: This research project was funded by the Deanship of Scientific Research, Princess Nourah bint Abdulrahman University, through the Program of Research Project Funding After Publication, grant No (PRFA-P-43-1).

Institutional Review Board Statement: Not applicable.

Informed Consent Statement: Not applicable.

Data Availability Statement: We make use of publicly available data. Health and Retirement Study (HRS) data can be downloaded from R package 'bpglm' and Australian Health data can be downloaded from Reference [27].

Acknowledgments: The authors gratefully acknowledge Princess Nourah bint Abdulrahman University, represented by the Deanship of Scientific Research, for the financial support for this research under the number (PRFA-P-43-1).

Conflicts of Interest: The funders had no role in the design of the study; in the collection, analyses, or interpretation of data; in the writing of the manuscript; or in the decision to publish the results.

References

1. Islam, M.A.; Chowdhury, R.I. Models for bivariate count data: Bivariate poisson distribution. In *Analysis of Repeated Measures Data*; Springer: Berlin/Heidelberg, Germany, 2017; pp. 97–124.
2. Ghosh, I.; Marques, F.; Chakraborty, S. A new bivariate poisson distribution via conditional specification: Properties and applications. *J. Appl. Stat.* **2021**, *48*, 3025–3047. [CrossRef] [PubMed]
3. Jung, R.C.; Winkelmann, R. Two aspects of labor mobility: A bivariate poisson regression approach. *Empir. Econ.* **1993**, *18*, 543–556. [CrossRef]
4. Kocherlakota, S.; Kocherlakota, K. *Bivariate Discrete Distributions*; CRC Press: Boca Raton, FL, USA, 2017.
5. Lakshminarayana, J.; Pandit, S.N.; Srinivasa Rao, K. On a bivariate poisson distribution. *Commun. Stat.-Theory Methods* **1999**, *28*, 267–276. [CrossRef]
6. Marshall, A.W.; Olkin, I. A family of bivariate distributions generated by the bivariate bernoulli distribution. *J. Am. Stat. Assoc.* **1985**, *80*, 332–338. [CrossRef]
7. Ma, Z.; Hanson, T.E.; Ho, Y.Y. Flexible bivariate correlated count data regression. *Stat. Med.* **2020**, *39*, 3476–3490. [CrossRef]
8. Lee, H.; Cha, J.H.; Pulcini, G. Modeling discrete bivariate data with applications to failure and count data. *Qual. Reliab. Eng. Int.* **2017**, *33*, 1455–1473. [CrossRef]

9. Campbell, J. The poisson correlation function. *Proc. Edinb. Math. Soc.* **1934**, *4*, 18–26. [CrossRef]
10. Benz, L.S.; Lopez, M.J. Estimating the change in soccer's home advantage during the COVID-19 pandemic using bivariate poisson regression. *Adv. Stat. Anal.* **2021**, 1–28. [CrossRef]
11. Koopman, S.J.; Lit, R. A dynamic bivariate poisson model for analysing and forecasting match results in the english premier league. *J. R. Stat. Soc. Ser. A* **2015**, *178*, 167–186. [CrossRef]
12. Chou, N.-T.; Steenhard, D. Bivariate count data regression models—A sas®macro program. *Stat. Data Anal. Pap.* **2011**, *355*, 1–10.
13. AlMuhayfith, F.E.; Alzaid, A.A.; Omair, M.A. On bivariate poisson regression models. *J. King Saud Univ.-Sci.* **2016**, *28*, 178–189. [CrossRef]
14. Su, P.-F.; Mau, Y.-L.; Guo, Y.; Li, C.-I.; Liu, Q.; Boice, J.D.; Shyr, Y. Bivariate poisson models with varying offsets: An application to the paired mitochondrial DNA dataset. *Stat. Appl. Genet. Mol. Biol.* **2017**, *16*, 47–58. [CrossRef]
15. Bermúdez, L.; Karlis, D. A posteriori ratemaking using bivariate poisson models. *Scand. Actuar. J.* **2015**, *2017*, 148–158. [CrossRef]
16. I Morata, L.B. A priori ratemaking using bivariate poisson regression models. *Insur. Math. Econ.* **2009**, *44*, 135–141. [CrossRef]
17. Holgate, P. Estimation for the bivariate poisson distribution. *Biometrika* **1964**, *51*, 241–287. [CrossRef]
18. Mardia, K.V. *Families of Bivariate Distributions*; Lubrecht & Cramer Limited: Port Jervis, NY, USA, 1970.
19. Johnson, N.L.; Kotz, S.; Balakrishnan, N. *Discrete Multivariate Distributions*; Wiley: New York, NY, USA, 1997.
20. Inouye, D.I.; Yang, E.; Allen, G.I.; Ravikumar, P. A review of multivariate distributions for count data derived from the poisson distribution. *Wiley Interdiscip. Rev. Comput. Stat.* **2017**, *9*, e1398. [CrossRef]
21. Weems, K.S.; Sellers, K.F.; Li, T. A flexible bivariate distribution for count data expressing data dispersion. *Commun. Stat.-Theory Methods* **2021**, 1–27. [CrossRef]
22. Cameron, A.C.; Trivedi, P.K. *Regression Analysis of Count Data*; Cambridge University Press: Cambridge, UK, 2013.
23. Hofer, V.; Leitner, J. A bivariate sarmanov regression model for count data with generalised poisson marginals. *J. Appl. Stat.* **2012**, *39*, 2599–2617. [CrossRef]
24. Famoye, F.; Consul, P. Bivariate generalized poisson distribution with some applications. *Metrika* **1995**, *42*, 127–138. [CrossRef]
25. Berkhout, P.; Plug, E. A bivariate poisson count data model using conditional probabilities. *Stat. Neerl.* **2004**, *58*, 349–364. [CrossRef]
26. Islam, M.A.; Chowdhury, R.I. A generalized right truncated bivariate poisson regression model with applications to health data. *PLoS ONE* **2017**, *12*, e0178153. [CrossRef] [PubMed]
27. Australian Bureau of Statistics. *Australian Health Survey 1977–78: Outline of Concepta*; Methodology and Procedures Used (Cat. No. 4323.0); Australian Bureau of Statistics: Sydney, Australia, 1982.
28. Cameron, A.C.; Trivedi, P.K.; Milne, F.; Piggott, J. A microeconometric model of the demand for health care and health insurance in Australia. *Rev. Econ. Stud.* **1988**, *55*, 85–106. [CrossRef]
29. Zamani, H.; Faroughi, P.; Ismail, N. Bivariate generalized poisson regression model: Applications on health care data. *Empir. Econ.* **2016**, *51*, 1607–1621. [CrossRef]

mathematics

MDPI

Article

Statistical Inference on a Finite Mixture of Exponentiated Kumaraswamy-G Distributions with Progressive Type II Censoring Using Bladder Cancer Data

Refah Alotaibi [1], Lamya A. Baharith [2], Ehab M. Almetwally [3,4,5], Mervat Khalifa [6], Indranil Ghosh [7,*] and Hoda Rezk [6]

1 Department of Mathematical Sciences, College of Science, Princess Nourah Bint Abdulrahman University, Riyadh 11671, Saudi Arabia
2 Department of Statistics, King Abdulaziz University, Jeddah 21589, Saudi Arabia
3 Department of Statistical, Faculty of Business Administration, Delta University for Science and Technology, Gamasa 11152, Egypt
4 Department of Mathematical Statistical, Faculty of Graduate Studies for Statistical Research, Cairo University, Cairo 12613, Egypt
5 The Scientific Association for Studies and Applied Research, Al Manzalah 35646, Egypt
6 Department of Statistics, Al-Azhar University, Cairo 11751, Egypt
7 Department of Mathematics and Statistics, University of North Carolina, Wilmington, NC 27599, USA
* Correspondence: ghoshi@uncw.edu

Abstract: A new family of distributions called the mixture of the exponentiated Kumaraswamy-G (henceforth, in short, ExpKum-G) class is developed. We consider Weibull distribution as the baseline (G) distribution to propose and study this special sub-model, which we call the exponentiated Kumaraswamy Weibull distribution. Several useful statistical properties of the proposed ExpKum-G distribution are derived. Under the classical paradigm, we consider the maximum likelihood estimation under progressive type II censoring to estimate the model parameters. Under the Bayesian paradigm, independent gamma priors are proposed to estimate the model parameters under progressive type II censored samples, assuming several loss functions. A simulation study is carried out to illustrate the efficiency of the proposed estimation strategies under both classical and Bayesian paradigms, based on progressively type II censoring models. For illustrative purposes, a real data set is considered that exhibits that the proposed model in the new class provides a better fit than other types of finite mixtures of exponentiated Kumaraswamy-type models.

Keywords: Kumaraswamy-G distribution; Bayesian approach; finite mixture; exponentiated Kumaraswamy Weibull distribution; loss function; progressive type II censoring

MSC: 65C20; 60E05; 62P30; 62L15

1. Introduction

The utility of mixture distributions during the last decade or so have provided a mathematical-based strategy to model a wide range of random phenomena effectively. Statistically speaking, the mixture distributions are a useful tool and have greater flexibility to analyze and interpret the probabilistic alias random events in a possibly heterogenous population. In modeling real-life data, it is quite normal to observe that the data have come from a mixture population involving of two or more distributions. One may find ample evidence(s) in terms of applications of finite mixture models not limited to but including in medicine, economics, psychology, survival data analysis, censored data analysis and reliability, among others. In this article, we are going to explore such a finite mixture model based on bounded (on (0,1)) univariate continuous distribution mixing with another baseline (G) continuous distribution and will study its structural properties with some applications. Next, we provide some useful references related to finite mixture models that are pertinent in this context. Ref. [1] introduced the classical and Bayesian inference on the finite mixture of exponentiated Kumaraswamy Gompertz and exponentiated Kumaraswamy Fréchet (MEKGEKF) distributions under progressively type II censoring with applications and it appears that this MEKGEKF distribution might be useful in analyzing certain dataset(s), for which either or both of its component distributions will be inadequate to completely explain the data. Consequently, this also serves as one of the main purposes for the current work.

In recent years, there has been a lot of interest in the art of parameter(s) induction to a baseline distribution. The addition of one or more extra shape parameter(s) to the baseline distribution makes it more versatile, particularly for examining the tail features. This parameter(s) induction also improved the goodness-of-fit of the proposed generalized family of distributions, despite the computational difficulty in some cases. Over two decades, there have been numerous generalized G families of continuous univariate distributions that have been derived and explored to model various types of data adequately. The exponentiated family, Marshall–Olkin extended family, beta-generated family, McDonald-generalized family, Kumaraswamy-generalized family, and exponentiated generalized family are among the well-known and widely recognized G families of distributions that are addressed in [2]. Some Marshall–Olkin extended variants and the Kumaraswamy-generalized family of distributions are proposed. For the exponentiated Kumaraswamy distribution and its log-transform, one can refer to [3]. Refs. [4,5] defined the probability density function (pdf) of exponentiated Kumaraswamy G (henceforth, in short, EKG) distributions, which is as follows:

$$f(x) = abcg(x)G^{a-1}(x)[1 - G^a(x)]^{b-1}\left\{1 - [1 - G^a(x)]^b\right\}^{c-1} \tag{1}$$

where a, b, c are all positive parameters and $x > 0$.

The associated cumulative distribution function (cdf) is given by

$$F(x) = \left\{1 - [1 - G^a(x)]^b\right\}^c, \; x > 0.$$

If $u \in (0, 1)$, the associated quantile function is given by

$$x(u) = G^{-1}\left\{1 - \left[1 - u^{\frac{1}{c}}\right]^{\frac{1}{b}}\right\}^{\frac{1}{a}} \tag{2}$$

In this paper, we consider a finite mixture of two independent EKW distributions with mixing weights and consider an absolute continuous probability model, namely the two-parameter Weibull, as a baseline model.

The rest of this article is organized as follows. In Section 2, we provide the mathematical description of the proposed model. In Section 3, some useful structural properties of the proposed model are discussed. The maximum likelihood function of the mixture exponentiated Kumaraswamy-G distribution based on progressively type II censoring is given in Section 4. Section 5 deals with the specific distribution of the mixture of exponentiated Kumaraswamy-G distribution when the baseline (G) is a two parameter Weibull, henceforth known as EKW distribution. In Section 6, we provide a general framework for the Bayes estimation of the vector of the parameters and the posterior risk under different loss functions of the exponentiated Kumaraswamy-G distribution. In Section 7, we consider the estimation of the EKW distribution under both the classical and Bayesian paradigms via a simulation study and under various censoring schemes. For illustrative purposes, an application of the EKW distribution is shown by applying the model to bladder cancer data in Section 8. Finally, some concluding remarks are presented in Section 9.

2. Model Description

A density function of the mixture of two components' densities with mixing proportions $p \in [0,1]$ and $q = 1 - p$ of EKG distributions is given as follows:

$$f(x) = pf_1(x) + qf_2(x),$$

where

$$f_j(x) = a_j b_j c_j g(x) G^{a_j - 1}(x)[1 - G^{a_j}(x)]^{b_j - 1}\left\{1 - [1 - G^{a_j}(x)]^{b_j}\right\}^{c_j - 1}$$

for $x > 0$, with $a_j b_j c_j > 0$, and $j = 1,2$, the j-th component and the pdf of the mixture of the two EKG distributions is given by

$$\begin{aligned} f(x) &= pa_1b_1c_1 g(x)G^{a_1-1}(x)[1 - G^{a_1}(x)]^{b_1-1}\left\{1 - [1 - G^{a_1}(x)]^{b_1}\right\}^{c_1-1} + qa_2b_2c_2 g(x)G^{a_2-1}(x) \\ &[1 - G^{a_2}(x)]^{b_2-1}\left\{1 - [1 - G^{a_2}(x)]^{b_2}\right\}^{c_2-1} I(0 < x < \infty), \end{aligned} \tag{3}$$

meaning the associated cdf of the distribution is

$$\begin{aligned} &F(x) = pF_1(x) + qF_2(x) \\ &i.e., F(x) = p\left\{1 - [1 - G^{a_1}(x)]^{b_1}\right\}^{c_1} + q\left\{1 - [1 - G^{a_2}(x)]^{b_2}\right\}^{c_2},\ x > 0. \end{aligned} \tag{4}$$

The component wise cdf can be obtained as

$$F_j(x) = \left\{1 - [1 - G^{a_j}(x)]^{b_j}\right\}^{c_j},\ x > 0.$$

For the density in Equation (3), (a_1, b_1), (a_2, b_2), are all playing the role of shape parameters. Consequently, for the varying choices of a_1, b_1, a_2 and b_2 one may obtain various possible shapes of the pdf, as well as for the hrf function.

3. Structural Properties

We begin this section by discussing the asymptotes and shapes of the proposed mixture model in Equation (3).

- **Result 1: Shapes.** The cdf in Equation (3) can be obtained analytically. The critical points of the pdf are the roots of the following equation:

$$\begin{aligned} \frac{\partial}{\partial x}\Big[pa_1b_1c_1 g(x)G^{a_1-1}(x)[1 - G^{a_1}(x)]^{b_1-1}\left\{1 - [1 - G^{a_1}(x)]^{b_1}\right\}^{c_1-1} + qa_2b_2c_2 g(x)G^{a_2-1}(x)[1 - G^{a_2}(x)]^{b_2-1}\left\{1 - [1 - G^{a_2}(x)]^{b_2}\right\}^{c_2-1}\Big] &= 0, \\ = pa_1b_1c_1[A_1(x)] + (1-p)a_2b_2c_2[A_2(x)] &= 0, \end{aligned} \tag{5}$$

where

$$\begin{aligned} A_1(x) &= \acute{g}(x)G^{a_1-1}(x)[1 - G^{a_1}(x)]^{b_1-1}\left\{1 - [1 - G^{a_1}(x)]^{b_1}\right\}^{c_1-1} + g(x)(a_1 - 1)G^{a_1-2}(x)g(x)[1 - G^{a_1}(x)]^{b_1-1}\left\{1 - [1 - G^{a_1}(x)]^{b_1}\right\}^{c_1-1}, \\ &= a_1(b_1 - 1)g(x)G^{a_1-1}(x)[1 - G^{a_1}(x)]^{b_1-2} g(x)\left\{1 - [1 - G^{a_1}(x)]^{b_1}\right\}^{c_1-1} \\ &+ g(x)G^{a_1-1}(x)g(x)[1 - G^{a_1}(x)]^{b_1-1}(c_1 - 1)\left\{1 - [1 - G^{a_1}(x)]^{b_1}\right\}^{c_1-2}\left\{b_1[1 - G^{a_1}(x)]^{b_1-1}\right\}a_1 \\ &g(x)G^{a_1}(x), \\ &= G^{a_1-1}(x)[1 - G^{a_1}(x)]^{b_1-1} g(x)\left\{1 - [1 - G^{a_1}(x)]^{b_1}\right\}^{c_1-1} \\ &\left\{(a_1 - 1)\frac{g^2(x)}{G(x)} - \frac{a_1(b_1-1)g^2(x)G^{a_1-1}(x)}{[1 - G^{a_1}(x)]} + \frac{a_1b_1(c_1-1)g^2(x)G^{a_1-1}(x)[1 - G^{a_1}(x)]^{b_1-1}}{1 - [1 - G^{a_1}(x)]^{b_1}}\right\}, \end{aligned}$$

Similarly,

$$\begin{aligned} A_2(x) &= G^{a_2-1}(x)[1 - G^{a_2}(x)]^{b_2-1}\left\{1 - [1 - G^{a_2}(x)]^{b_2}\right\}^{c_2-1} \\ &\left\{(a_2 - 1)\frac{g^2(x)}{G(x)} - \frac{a_2(b_2-1)g^2(x)G^{a_2-1}(x)}{[1-G^{a_2}(x)]} + \frac{a_2b_2(c_2-1)g^2(x)G^{a_2-1}(x)[1-G^{a_2}(x)]^{b_2-1}}{1-[1-G^{a_2}(x)]^{b_2}}\right\}, \end{aligned}$$

There may be more than one root to the Equation (5). If $x = x^*$ is the root of the equation, it corresponds to a local maximum, or a local minimum or a point of inflexion depending on $\xi(x^*) < 0,\ \xi(x^*) = 0,\ or\ \xi(x^*) > 0$, where $\xi(x^*) = \frac{\partial^2}{\partial x^2}[f(x)]|x = x^*$.

- **Result 2: Mixture Representation**

A random variable is said to have the exponentiated-G distribution with parameter $a > 0$ if $y \sim Exp - G(a)$ and if its pdf and cdf is given by $f(y) = a\, g(x)G^a(x)$ and $F(y) = G^a(x)$, as shown in [6,7].

If one considers the following, we have the following equations:

$$f_1(x) = a_1 b_1 c_1 g(x) G^{a_1-1}(x)[1 - G^{a_1}(x)]^{b_1-1}\left\{1 - [1 - G^{a_1}(x)]^{b_1}\right\}^{c_1-1}$$
$$= a_1 b_1 c_1 g(x) G^{a_1-1}(x)[1 - G^{a_1}(x)]^{b_1-1} \sum_{j_1=0}^{\infty} (-1)^{j_1} \binom{c_1-1}{j_1} [1 - G^{a_1}(x)]^{j_1 b_1}$$
$$= a_1 b_1 c_1 \sum_{j_1=0}^{\infty} (-1)^{j_1} \sum_{j_2=0}^{\infty} (-1)^{j_2} \binom{c_1-1}{j_1} \binom{b_1(j_1+1)-1}{j_2} g(x) G^{a_1-1}(x) G^{a_1 j_2}(x),$$
$$= a_1 b_1 c_1 \sum_{j_1=0}^{\infty} \sum_{j_2=0}^{\infty} (-1)^{j_1+j_2} \frac{\binom{c_1-1}{j_1}\binom{b_1(j_1+1)-1}{j_2}}{a_1(j_2+1)} G^{a_1(j_2+1)}(x).$$

Likewise,

$$f_2(x) = a_2 b_2 c_2 \sum_{j_1=0}^{\infty} \sum_{j_2=0}^{\infty} (-1)^{j_1+j_2} \frac{\binom{c_2-1}{j_1}\binom{b_2(j_2+1)-1}{j_2}}{a_2(j_2+1)} G^{a_2(j_2+1)}(x).$$

Therefore,

$$f(x) = p(a_2 b_2 c_2)^{-1} \sum_{j_1=0}^{\infty} \sum_{j_2=0}^{\infty} \Psi_1(j_1, j_2, b_1, c_1) G^{a_1(j_2+1)}(x) + q(a_2 b_2 c_2)^{-1} \sum_{j_1=0}^{\infty} \sum_{j_2=0}^{\infty} \Psi_2(j_1, j_2, b_2, c_2) G^{a_2(j_2+1)}(x)$$

where $\Psi_1(j_1, j_2, b_1, c_1) = \frac{(-1)^{j_1+j_2}}{a_1(j_2+1)} \binom{c_1-1}{j_1}\binom{b_1(j_1+1)-1}{j_2}$ and $\Psi_2(j_1, j_2, b_2, c_2) = \frac{(-1)^{j_1+j_2}}{a_2(j_2+1)} \binom{c_2-1}{j_1}\binom{b_2(j_2+1)-1}{j_2}$.

Note that if b_1, c_1, b_2, c_2 are integers, then the repective sums will stop at b_1, c_1, b_2 and c_2.

The above expression shows the fact that the pdf of the finite mixture of EKG can be represented as the finite mixture of infinite exponentiated-G distribution with parameters $a_1(j_2+1)$ and $a_2(j_2+1)$, respectively.

Therefore, structural properties, such as moments, entropy, etc., of this model can be obtained from the knowledge of the exponentiated-G distribution and one can refer to [8] for some pertinent details.

- **Result 3: Simulation Strategy**

Method 1. Direct cdf inversion method

Step 1: Generate $U \sim Uniform\ (0,1)$.

Step 2: Then, set $X_i = p_i \left\{1 - \left[1 - U_i^{\frac{1}{c_i}}\right]^{\frac{1}{b_i}}\right\}^{\frac{1}{a_i}}$, $\Sigma_{i=1}^{2} p_i = 1, for(a_i, b_i, c_i) > 0$ $\forall\, i = 1,2$.

Method 2. Via acceptance-rejection sampling plan

This will work if $a \geq 1,\ b \geq 1,\ c \geq 1$.

One must define $D_1 = \dfrac{a_1^{b_1 c_1} b_1 (a_1-1)^{1-\frac{1}{a_1}} (b_1-1)^{b_1-1} (c_1-1)^{c_1-1}}{(a_1 b_1 c_1 - 1)^{c_1 - \frac{1}{a_1 b_1}}}$

and $D_2 = \dfrac{a_2^{b_2c_2} b_2 (a_2-1)^{1-\frac{1}{a_2}} (b_2-1)^{b_2-1} (c_2-1)^{c_2-1}}{(a_2b_2c_2-1)^{c_2-\frac{1}{a_2b_2}}}$.

$M = max\{D_1, D_2\}$. Then, the following scheme will work:

(i) Simulate $X = x$ from the pdf in Equation (3).
(ii) Simulate $Y = UMg(x)$, where $U \sim Uniform\ (0,1)$.
(iii) Accept $X = x$ as a sample from the target density if $y < f(x)$. If $y \geq f(x)$, one must go to step (ii).

One may obtain an expression of the reliability function of mixture EKG, which takes the following form:

$$R(x) = pR_1(x) + qR_2(x)$$

where the component-wise reliability function of the mixture model is given by

$$R_j(x) = 1 - \left\{1 - [1 - G^{a_j}(x)]^{b_j}\right\}^{c_j},\ x > 0.$$

The density in Equation (1) is flexible in the sense that one can obtain different shapes of hazard rate function (hrf) of the mixture model, which is given by

$$h_j(x) = \frac{a_jb_jc_jg(x)[1 - G^{a_j}(x)]^{b_j-1}\left\{1 - [1 - G^{a_j}(x)]^{b_j}\right\}^{c_j-1}}{1 - \left\{1 - [1 - G^{a_j}(x)]^{b_j}\right\}^{c_j}}.$$

The quantile function of the mixture model is given by

$$q(x) = pG^{-1}\left\{1 - \left[1 - U^{\frac{1}{c_1}}(x)\right]^{\frac{1}{b_1}}\right\}^{\frac{1}{a_1}} + qG^{-1}\left\{1 - \left[1 - U^{\frac{1}{c_2}}(x)\right]^{\frac{1}{b_2}}\right\}^{\frac{1}{a_2}}.$$

For example, the median, x_m, of $f(x)$ for $U = 0.5$ will be

$$x_m = pG^{-1}\left\{1 - \left[1 - 0.5^{\frac{1}{c_1}}(x)\right]^{\frac{1}{b_1}}\right\}^{\frac{1}{a_1}} + qG^{-1}\left\{1 - \left[1 - 0.5^{\frac{1}{c_2}}(x)\right]^{\frac{1}{b_2}}\right\}^{\frac{1}{a_2}},$$

The various shapes of the pdf and the hrf when the baseline distribution (G) is Weibull is provided in Figure 1. In the next section, we discuss the maximum likelihood estimation strategy for the finite mixture of exponentiated Kumaraswamy-G (EKG) distribution under the progressive type-II censoring scheme. For more details, one can refer to [9]. The necessary and sufficient conditions for identifiability and identifiability properties are discussed in the Appendix A.

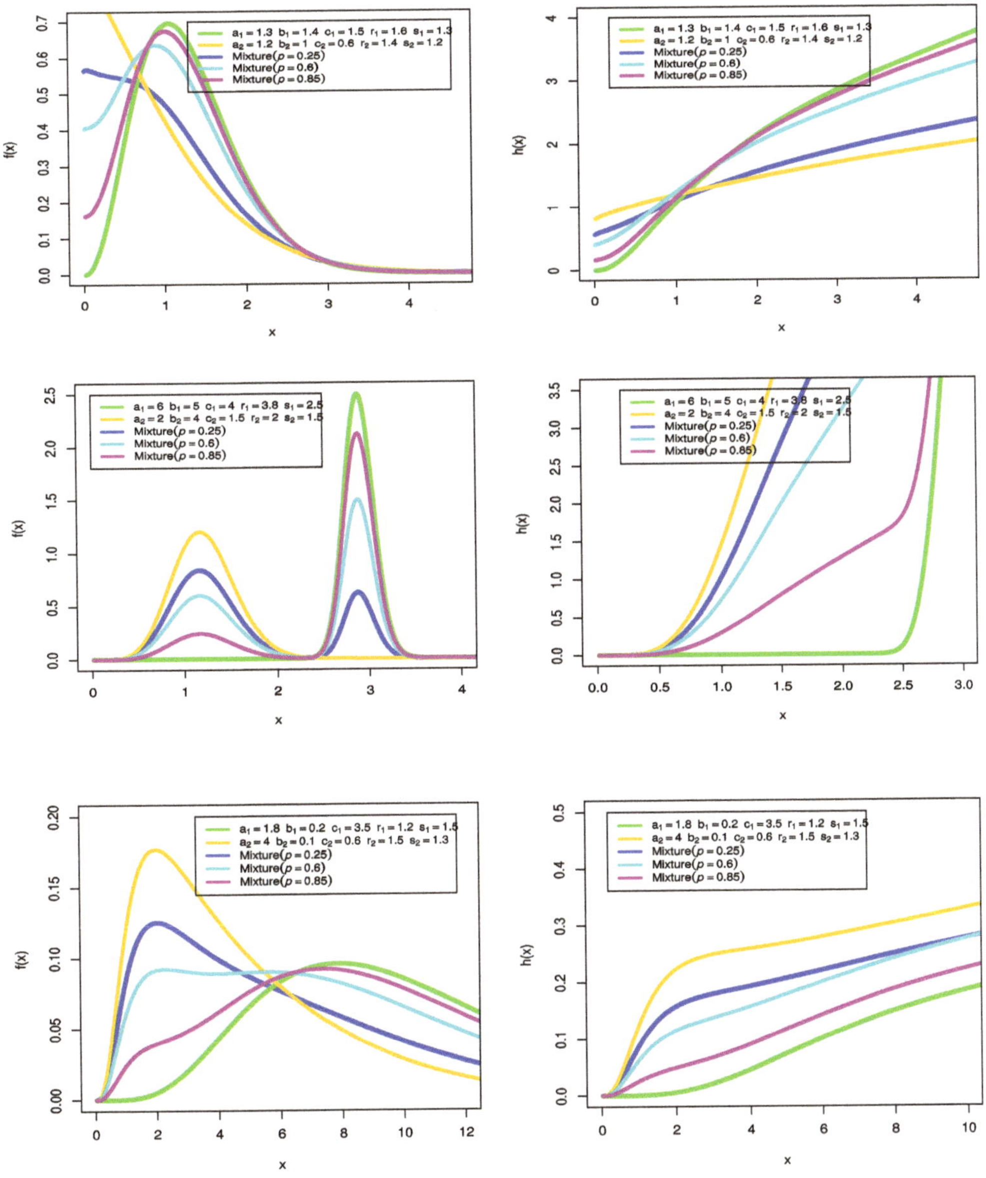

Figure 1. The pdf and hrf of the MEKW model for different values of its parameters.

4. Maximum Likelihood Estimation of EKG Distribution under Progressive Type-II Censoring

One must suppose that n units are put on life test at time zero and the experimenter decides beforehand the quantity m, the number of failures to be observed. At the time of first failure, R_1 units are randomly removed from the remaining n-1 surviving units. At the second failure, R_2 units from the remaining $n-2-R_1$ units are randomly removed. The test continues until the mth failure. At this time, all remaining $R_m = n - m - R_1 - R_2 - \ldots - R_{m-1}$ units are removed. In this censoring scheme, R_i and m are prefixed. The resulting m is ordered. Values, which are obtained as a consequence of this type of censoring, are appropriately referred to as progressive type II censored ordered statistics. One must note that if $R_1 = R_2 = \ldots = R_{m-1} = 0$, so that $R_m = n - m$, this scheme reduces to a conventional type II on the stage right censoring scheme.

One must also note that if $R_1 = R_2 = \ldots = R_m = 0$, so that m = n, the progressively type II censoring scheme reduces to the case of a complete sample (the case of no censoring).

One must allow $(X_{1:m:n}, X_{2:m:n}, \ldots, X_{m:m:n})$ to be a progressively type II censored sample, with $(R_1, R_2, \ldots, R_m)$ being the progressive censoring scheme. The likelihood function based on the progressive censored sample of EKG distributions is given by

$$L(\underline{x}\,|a_j, b_j, c_j, s_j, r_j, p, q) = K\prod_{i=1}^{m} g(X_{i:m:n})[1 - G(X_{i:m:n})]^{R_i}$$

where $k = n(n-1-R_1)(n-1-R_2)\ldots(n-m+1-R_1\ldots - R_m)$, $g(x)$ and $G(x)$ are given in Equations (3) and (4) and we obtain the log likelihood function without the constant term, which is is given by

$$L(\underline{x}\,|a_j, b_j, c_j, s_j, r_j, p, q) \propto \prod_{i=1}^{m} g_j(X_{i:m:n})\left[1 - G_j(X_{i:m:n})\right]^{R_i}$$

To simplify, we take the logarithm of the likelihood function, $\imath$, and for illustration purposes, let $g_j(X_{i:m:n}) = f_j(X_{i:m:n})$ and $G_j(X_{i:m:n}) = F_j(X_{i:m:n})$ as follows:

$$\imath \propto \sum_{i=1}^{m} log\left[f_j(X_{i:m:n})\right] + R_i log\left[1 - F_j(X_{i:m:n})\right]$$

Next, for illustrative purposes, we consider the baseline (G) distribution to be a two parameter Weibull distribution on the EKG distribution and discuss its estimation under both the classical and Bayesian set up.

5. Finite Mixture of Exponentiated Kumaraswamy Weibull Distribution

Exponentiated Kumaraswamy Weibull (EKW) distribution is a special case that can be generated from exponentiated Kumaraswamy -G distributions. The EKW distribution is found by taking $G(x)$ of the Weibull distribution in Equation (1). One of the most important advantages of the EKW distribution is its capacity to fit data sets with a variety of shapes, as well as for censored data, compared to the component distributions. One must let G be the Weibull distribution with the pdf and the cdf are given by

$$g(x) = \frac{r}{s}\left(\frac{x}{s}\right)^{r-1} exp\left[-\left(\frac{x}{s}\right)^{r}\right], x > 0,$$

and

$$G(x) = \left(1 - exp\left[-\left(\frac{x}{s}\right)^{r}\right]\right).$$

The inverse of the cdf is given by

$$s(-ln(1 - G(u)))^{\frac{1}{r}} = Q(u)$$

The pdf of a mixture of two component densities with mixing proportions, $(p_j,\ j = 1, 2)$ for $q = 1 - p$ of the exponentiated Kumaraswamy Weibull distribution (henceforth, in short is MKEW) is given by

$$\begin{aligned} f(x) = {} & p\frac{a_1 b_1 c_1 r_1}{s_1}\left(\frac{x}{s_1}\right)^{r_1-1} exp\left[-\left(\frac{x}{s_1}\right)^{r_1}\right]\left[1 - exp\left(-\left(\frac{x}{s_1}\right)^{r_1}\right)\right]^{a_1-1}\left[1 - \left[1 - exp\left(-\left(\frac{x}{s_1}\right)^{r_1}\right)\right]^{a_1}\right]^{b_1-1} \\ & \left[1 - \left[1 - \left[1 - exp\left(-\left(\frac{x}{s_1}\right)^{r_1}\right)\right]^{a_1}\right]^{b_1}\right]^{c_1-1} + q\frac{a_2 b_2 c_2 r_2}{s_2}\left(\frac{x}{s_2}\right)^{r_2-1} exp\left[-\left(\frac{x}{s_2}\right)^{r_2}\right]\left[1 - exp\left(-\left(\frac{x}{s_2}\right)^{r_2}\right)\right]^{a_2-1} \\ & \left[1 - \left[1 - exp\left(-\left(\frac{x}{s_2}\right)^{r_2}\right)\right]^{a_2}\right]^{b_2-1}\left[1 - \left[1 - \left[1 - exp\left(-\left(\frac{x}{s_2}\right)^{r_2}\right)\right]^{a_2}\right]^{b_2}\right]^{c_2-1}, x > 0 \end{aligned} \quad (6)$$

For the pdf in Equation (6), the following is noted:

(i) s_1 and s_2 are the scale parameters and r_1 and r_2 are the shape parameters for the Weibull component.

(ii) a_1, a_2, b_1 and b_2 are the shape parameters arising from the finite mixture pdf in Equation (4);

(iii) p, and q are the mixing proportions , where $p + q = 1$.

Depending on the different values of the parameters, different shapes of the pdf and the hrf of the MEKW distribution are shown in Figure 1. From Figure 1 (left panel), it appears that the MEKW pdf can include symmetric, asymmetric, right-skewed, and decreasing shapes, depending on the values of parameters. From Figure 1 (right panel), one can observe that the hrf may assume shapes with constants and that are down-upward and increasing.

The associated cdf is given by

$$F(x) = p\left[1-\left[1-\left[1-exp\left(-\left(\frac{x}{s_1}\right)^{r_1}\right)\right]^{a_1}\right]^{b_1}\right]^{c_1} + q\left[1-\left[1-\left[1-exp\left(-\left(\frac{x}{s_2}\right)^{r_2}\right)\right]^{a_2}\right]^{b_2}\right]^{c_2}$$

The hazard rate function of MEKW, $hr(x)$, model is flexible, as it allows for different shapes, which is given by

$$hr(x) = \frac{f(x)}{S(x)} = \frac{pf_1(x) + qf_2(x)}{pS_1(x) + qS_2(x)}.$$

The quantile function is given by

$$Q_j(u) = pG^{-1}\left\{1-\left[1-u^{\frac{1}{c_1}}\right]^{\frac{1}{b_1}}\right\}^{\frac{1}{a_1}} + qG^{-1}\left\{1-\left[1-u^{\frac{1}{c2}}\right]^{\frac{1}{b_2}}\right\}^{\frac{1}{a_2}}. \tag{7}$$

In the next section, by using a quantile function-based formula for skewness and kurtosis, we plot the coefficients of skewness and kurtosis for the MEKW distribution for different values of the parameters, as shown in Figure 2. From Figure 2, one can observe that the distribution can be positively skewed, negatively skewed, and could also assume platykurtic and mesokurtic shapes.

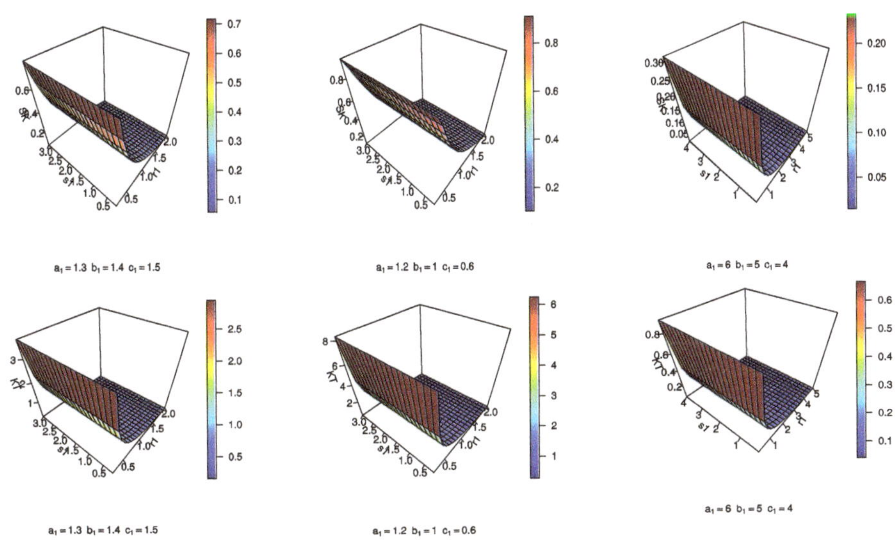

Figure 2. Coefficients of skewness and kurtosis for EKW distribution.

In the next section, we discuss a strategy of estimating parameters for the EKG model under the Bayesian paradigm using independent gamma priors.

5.1. Bayesian Estimation Using Gamma Priors for the Finite Mixture of Exponentiated Kumaraswamy-G Family

In this section, we consider the Bayes estimates of the model parameters that are obtained under the assumption that the component random variables for the random vector $\Phi = [a_j, b_j, c_j, s_j, r_j, p, q,], \; for \; j = 1,\ 2,$ have independent gamma priors with hyper parameters a_k and $\varnothing_k$, $k = 1,2,3,4,5,6,7$, which is given by

$$f(\Phi; a, \varnothing) = \frac{{\varnothing_k}^{a_k}}{\Gamma a_k} \Phi^{a_k - 1} e^{-\varnothing_k \Phi}, \Phi > 0, \tag{8}$$

By multiplying Equation (6) with the joint posterior density of the vector Φ, given the data, we can obtain the following:

$$\begin{aligned} \pi(\Phi|\underline{x}) &\propto L(\mathrm{x}|\Phi) f(\Phi; a_k, \varnothing_k) \\ &\propto \prod_{i=1}^{m} [a_1 b_1 c_1 p g(X_{i:m:n}) G^{a_1 - 1}(X_{i:m:n}) \\ &[1 - G^{a_1-1}(X_{i:m:n})]^{b_1 - 1} \left\{ [1 - G^{a_1-1}(X_{i:m:n})]^{b_1 - 1} \right\}^{c_1 - 1} \left[1 - \left[[1 - G^{a_1-1}(X_{i:m:n})]^{b_1 - 1} \right] \right\}^{c_1} \Big]^{R_i} \\ &+ q a_2 b_2 c_2 p g(X_{i:m:n}) G^{a_2-1}(X_{i:m:n}) [1 - G^{a_2-1}(X_{i:m:n})]^{b_2-1} \left[[1 - G^{a_2-1}(X_{i:m:n})]^{b_2-1} \right]^{c_2 - 1} \\ &\left[1 - \left[[1 - G^{a_2-1}(X_{i:m:n})]^{b_2-1} \right]^{c_2} \right]^{R_i} \Bigg] \frac{{\varnothing_k}^{a_k}}{\Gamma a_k} \Phi^{a_k - 1} e^{-\varnothing_k \Phi},\ \mathrm{I}(\Phi > 0). \end{aligned} \tag{9}$$

Marginal posterior distributions of Φ can be obtained by integrating out the nuisance parameters. Next, we consider the loss function that will be used to derive the estimators from the marginal posterior distributions.

5.2. Bayes Estimation of the Vector of Parameters and Evaluation of Posterior Risk under Different Loss Functions

This section spotlights the derivation of the Bayes estimator (BE) under different loss functions and their respective posterior risks (PR). For a detailed study on different loss error functions, one can refer to [10]. The Bayes estimators are evaluated using the squared error loss function (SELF), weighted squared error loss function (WSELF), precautionary loss function (PLF), modified (quadratic) squared error loss function (M/Q SELF), logarithmic loss function (LLF), entropy loss function (ELF), and K-Loss function. The K-loss function proposed by [11] is well fitted for a measure of inaccuracy for an estimator of a scale parameter of a distribution defined by $R^+ = (0, \infty)$; this loss function is called the K-loss function (KLF). Table 1 shows the Bayes estimators and the associated posterior risks under each specific loss functions considered in this paper.

Next, we derive the Bayes estimators of the model parameters under different loss functions. They were originally used in estimation problems when the unbiased estimator of Φ was being considered. Another reason for its popularity is due to its relationship to the least squares theory. The *SEL* function makes the computations simpler. Under the *SEL*, *WSEL*, $\frac{Q}{M}$*SEL*, *PL*, *LL*, *EL* and *KL* functions in Table 1, the Bayesian estimation for the random vector $\Phi = (a_j, b_j, c_j, s_j, r_j, p, q)$, for $j = 1, 2$, and under various loss functions, it can be obtained as follows.

$$\widehat{\Phi}_{SEL} = E(\Phi|\underline{x}) = \int_{\Phi} \left(\Phi - \widehat{\Phi}\right)^2 \pi(\Phi|\underline{x}) d\Phi.$$

$$\widehat{\Phi}_{WSEL} = E(\Phi|\underline{x}) = \int\limits_{\Phi} \frac{\left(\Phi - \widehat{\Phi}\right)^2}{\Phi} \pi(\Phi|\underline{x}) d\Phi.$$

$$\hat{\Phi}_{\frac{Q}{M}SEL} = E(\Phi|\underline{x}) = \int_{\Phi}\left(1-\frac{\hat{\Phi}}{\Phi}\right)^2 \pi(\Phi|\underline{x})d\Phi.$$

$$\hat{\Phi}_{PL} = E(\Phi|\underline{x}) = \int_{\Phi}\frac{\left(\Phi-\hat{\Phi}\right)^2}{\hat{\Phi}}\pi(\Phi|\underline{x})d\Phi.$$

$$\hat{\Phi}_{LL} = E(\Phi|\underline{x}) = \int_{\Phi}\left(log\Phi - log\hat{\Phi}\right)^2 \pi(\Phi|\underline{x})d\Phi.$$

$$\hat{\Phi}_{KL} = E(\Phi|\underline{x}) = \int_{\Phi}\left(\sqrt{\frac{\hat{\Phi}}{\Phi}}-\sqrt{\frac{\Phi}{\hat{\Phi}}}\right)^2 \pi(\Phi|\underline{x})d\Phi. \tag{10}$$

It is evident that each of the integrals in the above section have no closed form for the resulting joint posterior distribution as given in Equation (9). Therefore, they need to be solved analytically. Consequently, the MCMC technique is proposed to generate samples from the posterior distributions and then the Bayes estimates of the parameter vector Φ are computed under progressively type II censored samples. Next, we provide the general form of the Bayesian credible intervals.

Table 1. Bayes estimator and posterior risk under different loss functions.

Loss Function	Bayes Estimator (BE)	Posterior Risk (PR)
$L_1 = SEL = \left(\Phi-\hat{\Phi}\right)^2$	$E(\Phi\|X)$	$V(\Phi\|X)$
$L_2 = WSEL = \frac{\left(\Phi-\hat{\Phi}\right)^2}{\Phi}$	$\left[E\left(\Phi^{-1}\|X\right)\right]^{-1}$	$E(\Phi\|X) - \left[E\left(\Phi^{-1}\|X\right)\right]^{-1}$
$L_3 = \frac{Q}{M}SEL = \left(1-\frac{\hat{\Phi}}{\Phi}\right)^2$	$\frac{E(\Phi^{-1}\|X)}{E(\Phi^{-2}\|X)}$	$1-\frac{E(\Phi^{-1}\|X)^2}{E(\Phi^{-2}\|X)}$
$L_4 = PL = \frac{\left(\Phi-\hat{\Phi}\right)^2}{\hat{\Phi}}$	$\sqrt{E\left(\Phi^2\|X\right)}$	$2\left[\sqrt{E\left(\Phi^2\|X\right)} - E(\Phi\|X)\right]$
$L_5 = LL = \left(log\Phi - log\hat{\Phi}\right)^2$	$exp[E(log\Phi\|X)]$	$V(log\Phi\|X)$
$L_6 = EL = \left(\frac{\hat{\Phi}}{\Phi} - log\frac{\hat{\Phi}}{\Phi} - 1\right)$	$\left[E\left(\Phi^{-1}\|X\right)\right]^{-1}$	$E(log\Phi\|X) - logE\left(\Phi^{-1}\|X\right)$
$L_7 = KL = \left(\sqrt{\frac{\hat{\Phi}}{\Phi}}-\sqrt{\frac{\Phi}{\hat{\Phi}}}\right)^2$	$\sqrt{\frac{E(\Phi\|X)}{E(\Phi^{-1}\|X)}}$	$2\left[E(\Phi\|X)E\left(\Phi^{-1}\|X\right)-1\right]$

5.3. Credible Intervals

In this subsection, asymmetric $100(1-\tau)\%$ two-sided Bayes probability interval estimates of the parameter vector Φ, denoted by $[L_\Phi, U_\Phi]$, are obtained by solving the following expression:

$$p[L(\underline{t}) < \Phi < U(\underline{t})] = \int_{L(\underline{t})}^{U(\underline{t})} \pi(\theta,\beta,\lambda|\underline{t})d\Phi = 1-\tau. \tag{11}$$

Since it is difficult to find the interval L_Φ and U_Φ analytically, we apply suitable numerical techniques to solve Equation (11).

6. Bayesian Estimation of the Exponentiated Kumaraswamy Weibull Distribution

G is assumed to be the Weibull distribution with pdf and cdf, which are given by

$$g(x) = \frac{r}{s}\left(\frac{x}{s}\right)^{r-1} exp\left[-\left(\frac{x}{s}\right)^r\right],$$

where r is the shape parameter $(r > 0)$, and s is the scale parameter $(s > 0)$ and

$$G(x) = \left(1 - exp\left[-\left(\frac{x}{s}\right)^{r}\right]\right), x > 0.$$

The joint posterior density for the parameter vector Φ, given the data, becomes the following:

$$\begin{aligned}
\pi(\Phi|\underline{x}) &\propto L(x|\Phi) f(\Phi; a_k, \varnothing_k) \\
&\propto \prod_{i=1}^{m}\Bigg[a_1 b_1 c_1 p \frac{r_1}{s_1}\left(\frac{x}{s_1}\right)^{r_1-1} exp\left[-\left(\frac{x}{s_1}\right)^{r_1}\right]\left[1 - exp\left[-\left(\frac{x}{s_1}\right)^{r_1}\right]\right]^{a_1-1} \\
&\left[1 - \left[1 - exp\left[-\left(\frac{x}{s_1}\right)^{r_1}\right]\right]^{a_1-1}\right]^{b_1-1}\left\{\left[1 - \left[1 - exp\left[-\left(\frac{x}{s_1}\right)^{r_1}\right]\right]^{a_1-1}\right]^{b_1-1}\right\}^{c_1-1} \\
&\left[1 - \left[\left[1 - \left[1 - exp\left[-\left(\frac{x}{s_1}\right)^{r_1}\right]\right]^{a_1-1}\right]^{b_1-1}\right]^{c_1}\right]^{R_i} \\
&+ q a_2 b_2 c_2 \frac{r_2}{s_2}\left(\frac{x}{s_2}\right)^{r_2-1} exp\left[-\left(\frac{x}{s_2}\right)^{r_2}\right]\left[1 - exp\left[-\left(\frac{x}{s_2}\right)^{r_2}\right]\right]^{a_2-1} \\
&\left[1 - \left[1 - exp\left[-\left(\frac{x}{s_2}\right)^{r_2}\right]\right]^{a_2-1}\right]^{b_2-1}\left[\left[1 - \left[1 - exp\left[-\left(\frac{x}{s_2}\right)^{r_2}\right]\right]^{a_2-1}\right]^{b_2-1}\right]^{c_2-1} \\
&\left[1 - \left[\left[1 - \left[1 - exp\left[-\left(\frac{x}{s_2}\right)^{r_2}\right]\right]^{a_2-1}\right]^{b_2-1}\right]^{c_2}\right]^{R_i} \frac{{\varnothing_k}^{a_k}}{\Gamma a_k} \Phi^{a_k-1} e^{-\varnothing_k \Phi},\ I(\Phi > 0)
\end{aligned} \quad (12)$$

Marginal distributions of the parameter vector Φ can be obtained by integrating the nuisance parameters. Next, we consider the loss function that will be used to derive the estimators from the marginal posterior distributions.

7. Simulation Study

In this section, we evaluate the performance of the maximum likelihood and the Bayesian estimation methods to estimate the parameters using Monte Carlo simulations. We conduct the simulations using the (Maxlik) package in R software, as shown in [12]. The values of the biases, and the relative mean square errors (RMSEs) in the results indicate that the maximum likelihood and the Bayesian estimation methods performs quite well to estimate the model parameters.

Simulation Study for MEKW

In this subsection, we evaluate the performance of the maximum likelihood method and Bayesian estimation method to estimate the parameters for the MEKW model using Monte Carlo simulations. Based on progressively type II censored samples selected from the MEKW pdf in Equation (3), a total of eight parameter combinations, and assuming the sample sizes n = 25, 50, censored at 60% and 80% of the sample size, are considered. The process is repeated 1000 times and the biases (estimate–actual), RMSEs and length of confidence intervals (CI) of the estimates are reported in Tables 2–7. In computing the length of CI, we obtain length asymptotic CI (LACI) for the likelihood estimators, and also obtain the length credible CI (LCCI) for the Bayesian estimators. In addition, we compared the performance of the estimation by considering the following schemes.

Scheme 1. $R_{k\imath} = 0,\ \imath = 1, \ldots, n_k - m_k$

Scheme 2. $R_{k\imath} = \begin{cases} n_k - m_k,\ \imath = 1 \\ 0,\ \imath = 2, \ldots, m_k \end{cases}$

Scheme 3. $R_{k\imath} = \begin{cases} n_k - m_k,\ \imath = m_k \\ 0,\ \imath = 1, \ldots, m_{k-1} \end{cases}$

MLE, average bias Abs(Bias) and the RMSE for the MLE of the parameters are presented for different sample sizes and different sampling schemes

For Case 1, the selected initial values are as follows: a1 = 1.4, b1 = 1.5, c1 = 1.35, r1 = 1.7, s1 = 1.2, a2 = 1.4, b2 = 1.5, c2 = 1.35, r2 = 1.5, s2 = 1.3; $p = 0.7$.

For Case 2, the initial values are a1 = 1.8, b1 = 0.2, c1 = 3.5, r1 = 1.2, s1 = 1.5, a2 = 4, b2 = 0.1, c2 = 0.65, r2 = 1.5, s2 = 1.3, $p = 0.6$.

Table 2. Bias, RMSE and length of CI for the MLE and Bayesian estimates of the parameters are presented for different sample sizes: Scheme 1 (complete sample), Case 1.

		MLE			Bayesian		
n		Bias	RMSE	LACI	Bias	RMSE	LCCI
25	a1	0.1363	0.7467	2.8809	0.0743	0.2569	0.9628
	b1	−0.2161	0.7758	2.9236	0.1091	0.2275	0.7848
	c1	0.1374	0.9482	3.6814	0.0941	0.2920	0.9927
	r1	0.6883	1.2519	4.1030	0.1441	0.2783	0.8962
	s1	−0.1083	0.3819	1.4369	0.0243	0.1426	0.5350
	a2	0.2119	0.8836	3.3659	0.1080	0.2499	0.8166
	b2	−0.2985	0.8408	3.0842	0.1432	0.3119	1.0558
	c2	0.2908	1.0364	3.9034	0.0380	0.2224	0.8259
	r2	0.7734	1.4002	4.5801	0.1438	0.2855	0.9685
	s2	−0.2023	0.5034	1.8088	0.0052	0.0335	0.1289
	p	−0.0112	0.0952	0.3710	−0.0342	0.0885	0.3028
50	a1	0.0325	0.6253	2.4502	0.0364	0.1648	0.6325
	b1	−0.1865	0.6440	2.4185	0.0602	0.1333	0.4764
	c1	0.0006	0.7457	2.9259	0.0262	0.1634	0.6277
	r1	0.5867	0.9923	3.1401	0.1102	0.1835	0.5522
	s1	−0.0360	0.3025	1.1784	0.0103	0.0898	0.3480
	a2	0.1064	0.7523	2.9225	0.0364	0.1389	0.5130
	b2	−0.1927	0.6604	2.4784	0.1101	0.2216	0.7209
	c2	0.1501	0.8913	3.4475	0.0396	0.1470	0.5468
	r2	0.6011	1.0677	3.4625	0.0978	0.1756	0.5552
	s2	−0.1098	0.4171	1.5790	0.0000	0.0219	0.0854
	p	−0.0012	0.0648	0.2540	−0.0146	0.0622	0.2353
100	a1	−0.0776	0.5013	1.9434	0.0156	0.1205	0.4462
	b1	−0.1608	0.5400	2.0228	0.0506	0.1193	0.4208
	c1	−0.1454	0.5745	2.1809	0.0136	0.1412	0.5552
	r1	0.6321	0.9161	2.6022	0.1030	0.1609	0.4740
	s1	0.0369	0.2611	1.0143	−0.0010	0.0701	0.2702
	a2	0.0565	0.6470	2.5289	0.0162	0.1004	0.3790
	b2	−0.1245	0.6024	2.3128	0.0673	0.1583	0.5709
	c2	0.0053	0.7704	3.0230	0.0203	0.1138	0.4199
	r2	0.5095	0.9132	2.9741	0.0713	0.1396	0.4697
	s2	−0.0214	0.3687	1.4443	−0.0005	0.0179	0.0671
	p	0.0019	0.0521	0.2043	−0.0050	0.0497	0.1896

Table 3. Bias, RMSE and length of CI for the MLE and Bayesian estimates of the parameters are presented for different schemes: Case 1 and n = 25.

			MLE			Bayesian		
Scheme	**n, m**		**Bias**	**RMSE**	**LACI**	**Bias**	**RMSE**	**LCCI**
2	25, 15	a1	0.2086	0.6935	2.5950	0.1157	0.2775	0.9395
		b1	−0.3516	0.7858	2.7576	0.0911	0.2282	0.7983
		c1	0.1511	0.7569	2.9101	0.0765	0.2676	0.9211
		r1	0.5921	1.1801	4.0056	0.1478	0.3511	1.1950
		s1	−0.2418	0.4328	1.4085	0.0366	0.2240	0.8323
		a2	0.3463	0.9475	3.4605	0.0217	0.2295	0.8224
		b2	−0.4146	0.9381	3.3021	0.2170	0.4221	1.4613
		c2	0.2505	0.8901	3.3515	0.0471	0.2519	0.9327
		r2	1.1189	1.5792	4.3727	0.1465	0.2942	0.9666
		s2	−0.4516	0.6420	1.7906	−0.0091	0.0436	0.1606
		p	0.0232	0.2115	0.8248	−0.0054	0.1803	0.5545
	25, 20	a1	0.1707	0.6897	2.5622	0.0455	0.1439	0.5135
		b1	−0.3438	0.7705	2.7060	0.0500	0.1341	0.4665
		c1	0.0316	0.7494	2.9038	0.0436	0.1566	0.5762
		r1	0.6538	1.0314	3.3474	0.0571	0.2067	0.7663
		s1	−0.1799	0.4067	1.3144	0.0404	0.1491	0.5154
		a2	0.2747	0.8731	3.2521	0.0371	0.1507	0.5460
		b2	−0.3155	0.8002	2.8854	0.1040	0.2557	0.8661
		c2	0.2094	0.8093	3.0556	0.0354	0.1428	0.5314
		r2	0.9609	1.2634	3.0120	0.0999	0.1988	0.6814
		s2	−0.2952	0.5144	1.6531	−0.0030	0.0250	0.0908
		p	0.0099	0.1339	0.5238	−0.0169	0.1143	0.4068
3	25, 15	a1	0.1161	0.7157	2.7713	0.0909	0.2582	0.9175
		b1	−0.3936	0.7869	2.6737	0.0994	0.2208	0.7204
		c1	0.1617	0.8577	3.3051	0.0683	0.2632	0.9451
		r1	0.6209	1.2826	4.4038	0.1023	0.2885	0.9627
		s1	−0.1745	0.4339	1.5587	0.0754	0.1732	0.6193
		a2	0.2977	0.8905	3.2933	0.0859	0.2325	0.8070
		b2	−0.3494	0.8102	2.8682	0.1131	0.3168	1.0870
		c2	0.3593	0.9570	3.4806	0.0930	0.2529	0.8532
		r2	0.7486	1.2881	4.1132	0.1310	0.2876	0.9885
		s2	−0.2523	0.5078	1.7293	0.0091	0.0347	0.1240
		p	−0.0110	0.2158	0.8458	−0.0355	0.1884	0.5606
	25, 20	a1	0.1607	0.7128	2.7250	0.0563	0.1489	0.5512
		b1	−0.2165	0.7084	2.5194	0.0502	0.1247	0.4392
		c1	0.1249	0.8100	3.0788	0.0470	0.1634	0.6065
		r1	0.5943	1.0322	3.6334	0.0650	0.1916	0.6970
		s1	−0.1554	0.4023	1.4562	0.0235	0.1069	0.4019
		a2	0.1888	0.8684	3.2622	0.0552	0.1365	0.4698
		b2	−0.2937	0.8115	2.6968	0.0614	0.1984	0.6992
		c2	0.2993	0.8063	3.0035	0.0473	0.1400	0.5285
		r2	0.5807	1.0457	4.0757	0.0732	0.1829	0.6418
		s2	−0.1663	0.5084	1.4885	0.0048	0.0200	0.0761
		p	−0.0107	0.1419	0.5554	−0.0354	0.1267	0.4211

Table 4. Bias, RMSE and length of CI for the MLE and Bayesian estimates of the parameters are presented for different schemes: Case 1 and n = 50.

			MLE			Bayesian		
Scheme	**n, m**		**Bias**	**RMSE**	**LACI**	**Bias**	**RMSE**	**LCCI**
2	50, 30	a1	0.1740	0.6464	2.4428	0.0985	0.2686	0.9424
		b1	−0.2839	0.6850	2.4461	0.1049	0.2627	0.9051
		c1	0.0535	0.6684	2.6143	0.0815	0.2862	0.9613
		r1	0.4536	1.0329	3.6413	0.1323	0.3722	1.2898
		s1	−0.1768	0.3914	1.3701	0.0462	0.2367	0.8292
		a2	0.1538	0.7803	3.0018	−0.0047	0.2490	0.9586
		b2	−0.3140	0.7485	2.6661	0.3206	0.5488	1.6380
		c2	0.0664	0.7585	2.9649	0.0245	0.2544	0.9684
		r2	1.1236	1.6130	4.5412	0.2103	0.3669	1.1379
		s2	−0.3536	0.5499	1.6526	−0.0264	0.0637	0.2052
		p	0.0273	0.1937	0.7527	0.0109	0.1774	0.5251
	50, 40	a1	0.1385	0.6058	2.3526	0.0378	0.1515	0.5607
		b1	−0.3216	0.6863	2.3792	0.0357	0.1402	0.5168
		c1	0.0496	0.5807	2.5146	0.0318	0.1757	0.6541
		r1	0.4528	0.9119	3.5998	0.0671	0.2231	0.7929
		s1	−0.1435	0.3782	1.3732	0.0488	0.1514	0.5324
		a2	0.1669	0.7759	2.9731	0.0134	0.1514	0.5693
		b2	−0.1764	0.7496	2.5859	0.1789	0.3302	0.9973
		c2	−0.0199	0.7398	2.9020	0.0129	0.1412	0.5300
		r2	1.0421	1.5571	4.5399	0.1420	0.2564	0.8151
		s2	−0.2003	0.4252	1.4718	−0.0121	0.0342	0.1166
		p	0.0261	0.1170	0.4475	0.0095	0.1047	0.3537
3	50, 30	a1	0.1031	0.6498	2.5174	0.0779	0.2654	0.9538
		b1	−0.2174	0.6665	2.4724	0.0968	0.2433	0.8425
		c1	0.1599	0.7887	3.0306	0.0804	0.3027	1.0356
		r1	0.3891	0.9908	3.5757	0.0807	0.2552	0.9065
		s1	−0.1131	0.3722	1.3915	0.0546	0.1587	0.5932
		a2	0.2047	0.7134	2.6817	0.0921	0.2352	0.7769
		b2	−0.1824	0.6974	2.6414	0.0814	0.2837	0.9804
		c2	0.2089	0.8528	3.2443	0.0572	0.2373	0.8509
		r2	0.4022	0.9146	3.2231	0.1108	0.2715	0.9205
		s2	−0.1485	0.4358	1.6076	0.0124	0.0368	0.1380
		p	−0.0058	0.2060	0.8079	−0.0190	0.1904	0.5459
	50, 40	a1	0.1919	0.6064	2.4934	0.0457	0.1469	0.5373
		b1	−0.1360	0.6266	2.4002	0.0501	0.1353	0.4797
		c1	0.2024	0.6306	2.9215	0.0371	0.1646	0.6183
		r1	0.2577	0.8736	3.2753	0.0444	0.1767	0.6505
		s1	−0.1101	0.3609	1.3485	0.0333	0.0997	0.3671
		a2	0.1838	0.7048	2.5844	0.0389	0.1382	0.5167
		b2	−0.1898	0.6913	2.6081	0.0503	0.1826	0.6657
		c2	0.2209	0.8492	3.1514	0.0355	0.1405	0.5139
		r2	0.4817	0.9032	3.1583	0.0666	0.1764	0.6511
		s2	−0.1363	0.4060	1.5724	0.0040	0.0233	0.0878
		p	−0.0106	0.1194	0.4667	−0.0238	0.1120	0.3631

Table 5. Bias, RMSE and length of CI for the MLE and Bayesian estimates of the parameters are presented for different sample sizes: Scheme 1 (complete sample), Case 2.

		MLE			Bayesian		
n		Bias	RMSE	LACI	Bias	RMSE	LCCI
25	a1	0.4950	1.2585	5.9078	0.1046	0.2725	0.9632
	b1	0.0025	0.0974	0.3819	0.0691	0.0811	0.3175
	c1	0.3392	1.2556	4.7436	0.0663	0.1757	0.6258
	r1	0.1166	0.2492	0.8640	−0.0189	0.1458	0.5568
	s1	0.1338	0.4568	1.7138	0.1819	0.2823	0.8286
	a2	0.0850	1.9085	7.4814	0.0398	0.1079	0.3711
	b2	0.0461	0.1245	0.4540	0.0312	0.0675	0.2063
	c2	0.2599	0.5643	1.9656	0.0475	0.2313	0.7513
	r2	0.0984	0.3444	1.2950	−0.0534	0.1993	0.7545
	s2	−0.0048	0.3695	1.4497	0.0216	0.0382	0.1283
	p	−0.0035	0.0920	0.3607	−0.0116	0.0816	0.3071
50	a1	0.2532	1.0781	4.9156	0.0615	0.1727	0.6082
	b1	0.0039	0.0774	0.3032	0.0425	0.0778	0.2230
	c1	0.3267	1.0900	4.0806	0.0339	0.1189	0.4407
	r1	0.0774	0.1588	0.5440	−0.0128	0.1009	0.3987
	s1	0.1067	0.4314	1.6401	0.0985	0.1755	0.5609
	a2	−0.1625	1.4809	5.7759	0.0299	0.0781	0.2910
	b2	0.0457	0.1183	0.4281	0.0296	0.0515	0.1509
	c2	0.2415	0.4634	1.8299	0.0410	0.1641	0.5968
	r2	0.0369	0.2309	0.8944	−0.0655	0.1306	0.4482
	s2	0.0314	0.3073	1.4569	0.0157	0.0265	0.0823
	p	−0.0036	0.0692	0.2712	−0.0094	0.0648	0.2451
100	a1	0.1000	0.9519	3.7145	0.0397	0.1558	0.5863
	b1	0.0054	0.0522	0.2037	0.0249	0.0539	0.1661
	c1	0.2833	0.7983	2.9286	0.0349	0.1158	0.4385
	r1	0.0534	0.1129	0.3903	0.0063	0.0776	0.3142
	s1	0.0688	0.3142	1.2030	0.0658	0.1410	0.4920
	a2	−0.1731	1.1550	4.4811	0.0199	0.0732	0.2684
	b2	0.0396	0.0985	0.3541	0.0233	0.0381	0.1088
	c2	0.1359	0.3042	1.0677	0.0174	0.1019	0.3844
	r2	0.0006	0.1304	0.5117	−0.0566	0.0978	0.3237
	s2	0.0363	0.2320	1.2465	0.0114	0.0254	0.0740
	p	−0.0014	0.0485	0.1903	−0.0031	0.0472	0.1834

Table 6. Bias, RMSE and length of CI for the MLE and Bayesian estimates of the parameters are presented for different schemes: Case 2 and n = 25.

			MLE			Bayesian		
Scheme	n, m		Bias	RMSE	LACI	Bias	RMSE	LCCI
2	25, 15	a1	0.3219	1.5006	5.7511	0.0890	0.2609	0.9529
		b1	−0.0140	0.1061	0.4125	0.0409	0.1046	0.3430
		c1	0.2475	1.3018	5.0149	0.0303	0.1680	0.6187
		r1	0.3045	0.6054	2.0533	0.1003	0.2511	0.8449
		s1	0.1760	0.5871	2.1980	0.1423	0.2544	0.7830
		a2	−0.1057	2.0364	7.9800	0.0373	0.1059	0.3868
		b2	0.0533	0.2103	0.7982	0.0260	0.0679	0.2227
		c2	0.2514	0.6190	2.2198	0.0491	0.2189	0.7067
		r2	0.2421	0.5800	2.0680	−0.0026	0.2304	0.9165
		s2	0.1230	0.5706	2.1865	0.0203	0.0362	0.1182
		p	−0.0230	0.1544	0.5992	−0.0320	0.1371	0.5096
	25, 20	a1	0.4450	1.2772	4.7292	0.0502	0.1432	0.5073
		b1	−0.0071	0.1040	0.4072	0.0391	0.0990	0.3048
		c1	0.2764	1.2067	4.6092	0.0235	0.1010	0.3778
		r1	0.1954	0.4030	1.3830	0.0309	0.1768	0.6555
		s1	0.1461	0.5049	1.8965	0.0819	0.1589	0.5218
		a2	0.1944	2.0450	7.9880	0.0235	0.0627	0.2217
		b2	0.0341	0.1379	0.5242	0.0239	0.0581	0.1891
		c2	0.2256	0.6054	2.2044	0.0551	0.2044	0.7016
		r2	0.1582	0.4093	1.4811	−0.0506	0.1708	0.6461
		s2	0.0712	0.4372	1.6925	0.0127	0.0223	0.0712
		p	−0.0200	0.1178	0.4557	−0.0314	0.1056	0.3854
3	25, 15	a1	0.3756	1.5466	5.8871	0.0977	0.2491	0.8675
		b1	0.0086	0.1149	0.4497	0.0728	0.1016	0.3220
		c1	0.2402	1.1652	4.4740	0.0407	0.1576	0.6094
		r1	0.1513	0.2897	0.9695	−0.0267	0.1492	0.5809
		s1	0.2196	0.5639	2.0382	0.1517	0.2645	0.8215
		a2	0.0220	1.8220	7.1490	0.0473	0.1138	0.3973
		b2	0.0456	0.1589	0.5971	0.0289	0.0658	0.2128
		c2	0.2686	0.6084	2.1420	0.0957	0.2510	0.8332
		r2	0.2490	0.4789	1.6053	−0.0177	0.2134	0.8030
		s2	0.1015	0.4697	1.7995	0.0246	0.0406	0.1244
		p	−0.1750	0.2005	0.3840	−0.1599	0.1814	0.3204
	25, 20	a1	0.3345	1.4388	5.4909	0.0556	0.1509	0.5303
		b1	0.0026	0.1035	0.4058	0.0504	0.0942	0.2754
		c1	0.3566	1.0276	4.2807	0.0291	0.1015	0.3685
		r1	0.1413	0.2619	0.8653	−0.0160	0.1250	0.4882
		s1	0.1898	0.5521	2.0346	0.0960	0.1626	0.5275
		a2	0.2065	1.7882	5.3390	0.0242	0.0622	0.2171
		b2	0.0523	0.1422	0.5190	0.0218	0.0566	0.1773
		c2	0.3228	0.5461	2.0235	0.0667	0.2028	0.7112
		r2	0.1509	0.4165	1.5231	−0.0344	0.1565	0.5786
		s2	0.0576	0.4180	1.6247	0.0128	0.0232	0.0730
		p	−0.0859	0.1294	0.3797	−0.0773	0.1171	0.3043

Table 7. Bias, RMSE and length of CI for the MLE and Bayesian estimates of the parameters are presented for different schemes: Case 2 and n = 50.

			MLE			Bayesian		
Scheme	**n, m**		**Bias**	**RMSE**	**LACI**	**Bias**	**RMSE**	**LCCI**
I	50, 30	a1	0.1607	1.1624	4.5175	0.0950	0.2756	0.9877
		b1	−0.0156	0.0926	0.3583	0.0425	0.1156	0.3975
		c1	0.1410	0.9550	3.7064	0.0340	0.1804	0.7061
		r1	0.3582	0.6997	2.3586	0.1390	0.3104	1.0253
		s1	0.1687	0.6128	2.3115	0.1347	0.2730	0.8936
		a2	−0.3925	1.4224	5.3648	0.0466	0.1148	0.4057
		b2	0.0444	0.1538	0.5779	0.0233	0.0643	0.2126
		c2	0.1707	0.4040	1.4368	0.0621	0.2132	0.7099
		r2	0.2614	0.6599	2.3776	0.0353	0.2589	0.9918
		s2	0.1804	0.6739	2.5479	0.0192	0.0394	0.1334
		p	−0.0440	0.2016	0.7719	−0.0479	0.1859	0.5668
	50, 40	a1	0.1322	1.0365	4.2045	0.0616	0.1823	0.6517
		b1	−0.0061	0.0903	0.3536	0.0218	0.0800	0.2685
		c1	0.1406	0.9028	3.6985	0.0214	0.1105	0.4222
		r1	0.1619	0.3606	1.2642	0.0606	0.1810	0.6664
		s1	0.1229	0.4318	1.6243	0.0673	0.1532	0.5163
		a2	−0.2044	1.3552	4.5038	0.0219	0.0698	0.2580
		b2	0.0286	0.1166	0.4435	0.0224	0.0498	0.1704
		c2	0.1682	0.3741	1.4034	0.0500	0.1703	0.5965
		r2	0.1231	0.3405	1.2457	−0.0294	0.1568	0.6370
		s2	0.0647	0.4849	1.8859	0.0107	0.0238	0.0771
		p	−0.0117	0.1050	0.4094	−0.0171	0.0996	0.3911
II	50, 30	a1	0.3428	1.2479	4.7083	0.1173	0.3037	1.1006
		b1	0.0019	0.0856	0.3357	0.0651	0.1078	0.2946
		c1	0.2610	1.0548	4.0104	0.0631	0.1839	0.6537
		r1	0.1252	0.2271	0.7435	−0.0133	0.1284	0.5061
		s1	0.1625	0.4028	1.4461	0.1708	0.2807	0.7910
		a2	−0.0189	1.2375	4.8553	0.0595	0.1238	0.4057
		b2	0.0300	0.0986	0.3684	0.0344	0.0626	0.1887
		c2	0.1687	0.3744	1.3115	0.1112	0.2300	0.7343
		r2	0.1328	0.3041	1.0733	−0.0624	0.1694	0.5980
		s2	0.0893	0.3474	1.3174	0.0302	0.0480	0.1460
		p	−0.2414	0.2501	0.2563	−0.2261	0.2345	0.2025
	50, 40	a1	0.1323	0.9504	4.6244	0.0602	0.1719	0.6060
		b1	0.0084	0.0855	0.3337	0.0488	0.0886	0.2672
		c1	0.2795	0.8144	3.8352	0.0355	0.1176	0.4267
		r1	0.0950	0.1849	0.6223	−0.0175	0.1077	0.4235
		s1	0.1539	0.3912	1.4114	0.0958	0.1742	0.5624
		a2	−0.1510	0.9435	4.5993	0.0280	0.0748	0.2571
		b2	0.0406	0.0914	0.3440	0.0239	0.0483	0.1573
		c2	0.1276	0.3428	1.2532	0.0524	0.1699	0.6015
		r2	0.1008	0.2956	1.0090	−0.0475	0.1378	0.4887
		s2	0.0880	0.3042	1.2462	0.0133	0.0258	0.0864
		p	−0.1212	0.1366	0.2472	−0.1148	0.1298	0.1923

8. Application on Bladder Cancer Data

In this section, we provide a real data analysis to illustrate some practical applications of the proposed distributions. The data are from [13], which correspond to the remission times (in months) of a random sample of n = 128 bladder cancer patients. These data are given as follows:

0.08, 2.09, 3.48, 4.87, 6.94, 8.66, 13.11, 23.63, 0.20, 2.23, 3.52, 4.98, 6.97, 9.02, 13.29, 0.40, 2.26, 3.57, 5.06, 7.09, 9.22, 13.80, 25.74, 0.50, 2.46, 3.64, 5.09, 7.26, 9.47, 14.24, 25.82, 0.51, 2.54, 3.70, 5.17, 7.28, 9.74, 14.76, 26.31, 0.81, 2.62, 3.82, 5.32, 7.32, 10.06, 14.77, 32.15, 2.64, 3.88, 5.32, 7.39, 10.34, 14.83, 34.26, 0.90, 2.69, 4.18, 5.34, 7.59, 10.66, 15.96, 36.66, 1.05, 2.69, 4.23, 5.41, 7.62, 10.75, 16.62, 43.01, 1.19, 2.75, 4.26, 5.41, 7.63, 17.12, 46.12, 1.26, 2.83, 4.33, 5.49, 7.66, 11.25, 17.14, 79.05, 1.35, 2.87, 5.62, 7.87, 11.64, 17.36, 1.40, 3.02, 4.34, 5.71, 7.93, 11.79, 18.10, 1.46, 4.40, 5.85, 8.26, 11.98, 19.13, 1.76, 3.25, 4.50, 6.25, 8.37, 12.02, 2.02, 3.31, 4.51, 6.54, 8.53, 12.03, 20.28, 2.02, 3.36, 6.76, 12.07, 21.73, 2.07, 3.36, 6.93, 8.65, 12.63, 22.69.

Before proceeding further, we fitted the mixture EKW distribution to the complete data set. Table 8 reports the ML and Bayesian estimates for the parameters for the complete bladder cancer data. Figure 3 represents the overall fit of EKW for these data.

Table 8. ML estimates of the EKW parameters with the corresponding bladder data.

	a	b	c	r	s	KSD	PVKS	CVM	AD
Estimates	3.6537	3.1179	1.1311	0.4578	5.2873	0.0443	0.9629	0.0408	0.2700

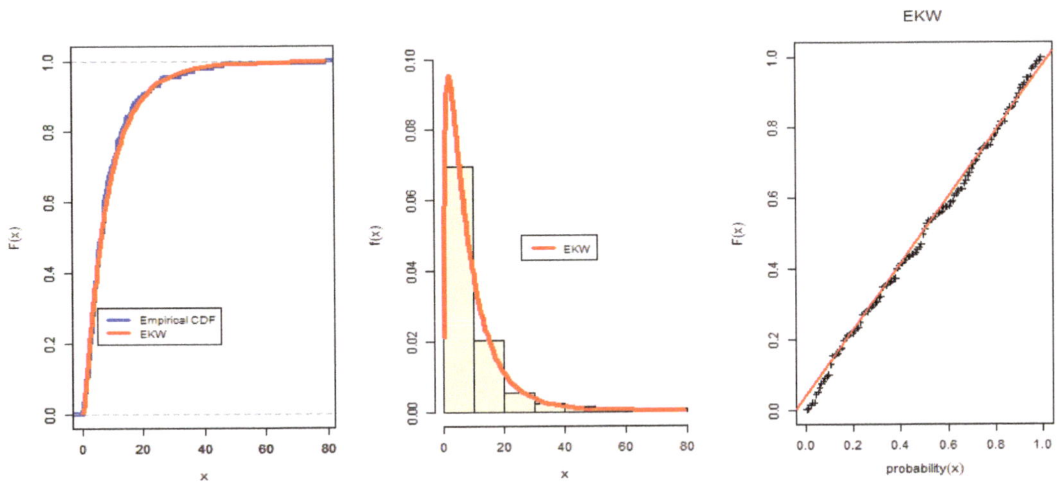

Figure 3. ML estimates of the EKW parameters for the complete bladder cancer data.

The validity of the fitted model is assessed by computing the Kolmogorov–Smirnov distance (KSD) statistics with *p*-Value KS (PVKS) in Table 8. In addition, we plotted the fitted cdf and the empirical cdf, as shown in Figure 3. This was conducted by replacing the parameters with their ML (in red) estimates, as shown in Figure 3. The KSD statistics for ML are 0.0443 and the corresponding *p*-value is 0.9629. Therefore, the KS test, along with Figure 3, indicate that the EKW distribution provides the best fit for this data set.

Next, we fitted the MEKW distribution to the complete data set. Table 9 reports the ML and Bayesian estimates for the parameters for the complete bladder cancer data.

Table 9. ML estimates of the MEKW parameters for the complete sample of the bladder data.

	MLE				Bayesian			
	Estimates	**SE**	**Lower**	**Upper**	**Estimates**	**SE**	**Lower**	**Upper**
a1	8.2459	0.0171	8.2125	8.2794	8.3297	0.0075	8.2310	8.2601
b1	0.1491	0.0123	0.1250	0.1733	0.1866	0.0008	0.1477	0.1506
c1	27.6825	7.5314	12.9208	42.4441	27.2578	0.1975	27.5327	27.8240
r1	1.1925	0.0015	1.1896	1.1954	1.1456	0.0015	1.1800	1.1984
s1	4.4770	0.0014	4.4742	4.4798	4.3029	0.0003	4.4620	4.4911
a2	12.2492	0.0079	12.2337	12.2648	12.2200	0.0075	12.2343	12.2634
b2	0.1526	0.0126	0.1279	0.1773	0.2207	0.0008	0.1511	0.1540
c2	22.6763	5.8063	11.2960	34.0567	22.6720	0.0754	22.5266	22.8179
r2	1.2810	0.0024	1.2763	1.2858	0.3040	0.0014	1.2661	1.2952
s2	5.6261	0.0026	5.6210	5.6313	0.1922	0.0025	5.6115	5.6406
p	0.5004	0.0347	0.4325	0.5684	0.6039	0.0075	0.4858	0.5149

In Figures 4 and 5, we provide the trace plots of the MCMC results, showing the MCMC procedure converges. Figures 6 and 7 show the MCMC density and HDI intervals for the results of the Bayesian estimation of the MEKW model for the complete sample. Therefore, we will use the estimate for the mixing parameter $\hat{p} = 0.5004$ in computing the ML and Bayesian estimates for other parameters when using complete samples.

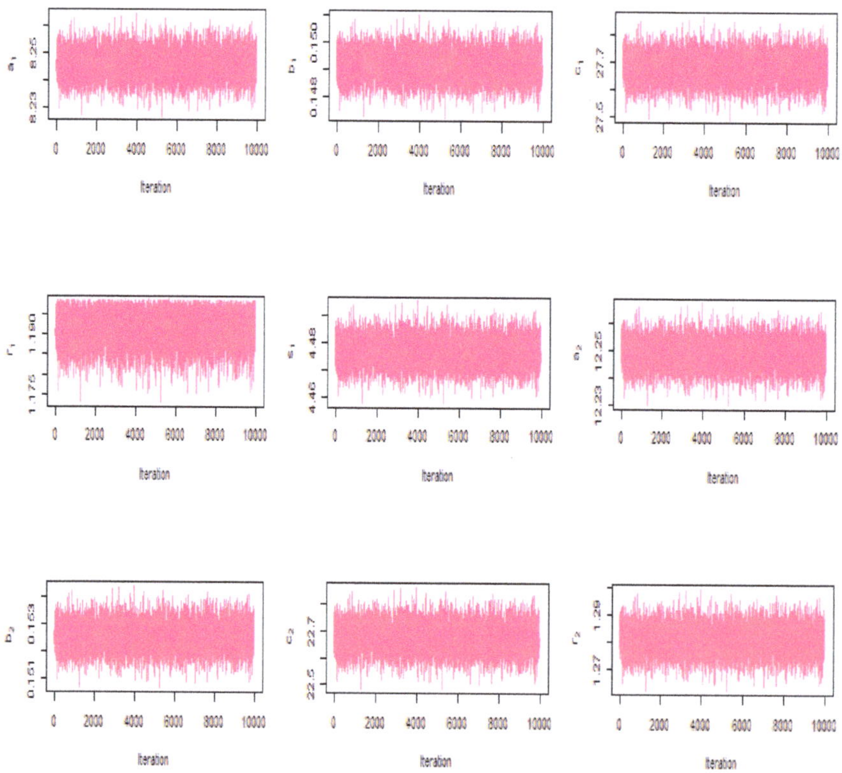

Figure 4. MCMC trace for results of Bayesian estimation of model for complete Bladder data for first 9 parameters.

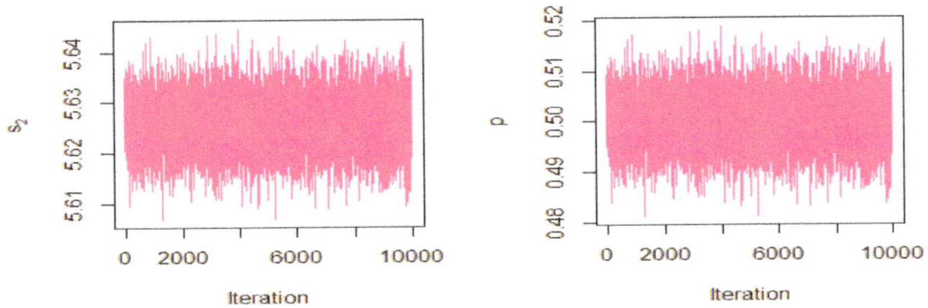

Figure 5. MCMC trace for results of Bayesian estimation of model for complete Bladder data for the last two parameters.

Two different sampling schemes are used to generate the progressively censored samples from the bladder cancer data with m = 100, which are as follows:

Strategy 1: (99*0,28); $R_{k\imath} = \begin{cases} n_k - m_k, & \imath = 1 \\ 0, & \imath = 2, \ldots, m_k \end{cases}$ (type II censoring scheme).

Strategy 2: (28,99*0); $R_{k\imath} = \begin{cases} n_k - m_k, & \imath = m_k \\ 0, & \imath = 1, \ldots, m_{k-1} \end{cases}$.

In both cases, we have considered the optimization algorithm to compute the ML estimates. Table 10 shows the ML estimates for these two schemes.

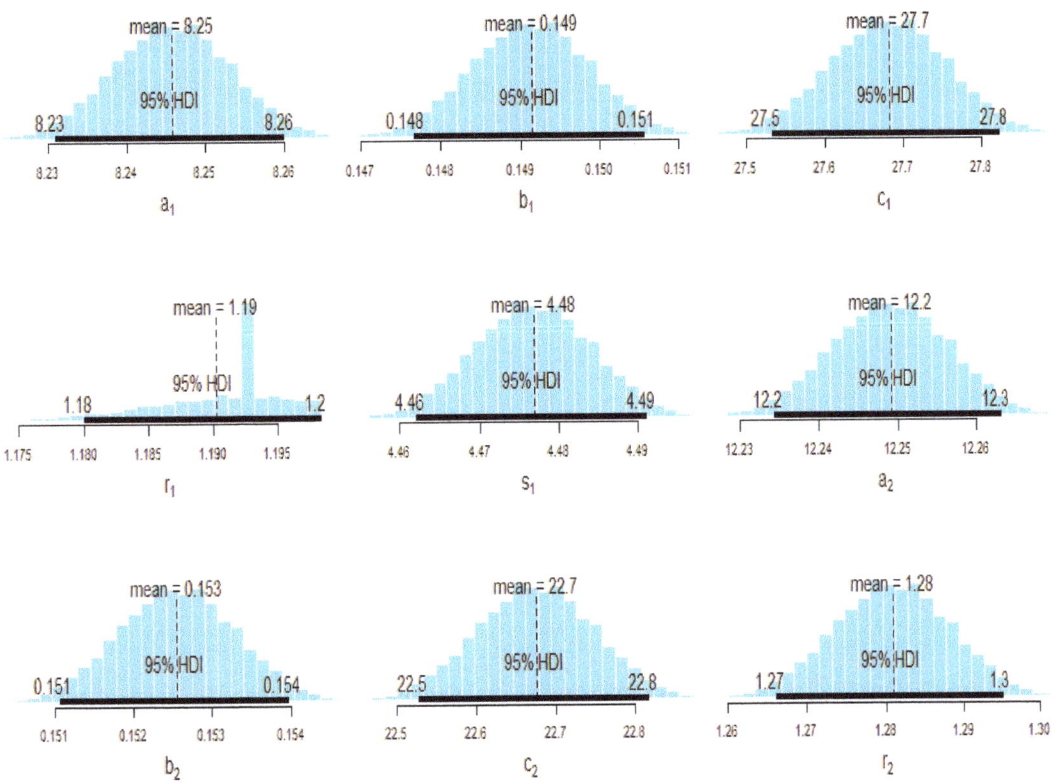

Figure 6. MCMC density and HDI intervals for results of Bayesian estimation of model for complete Bladder data for 9 parameters.

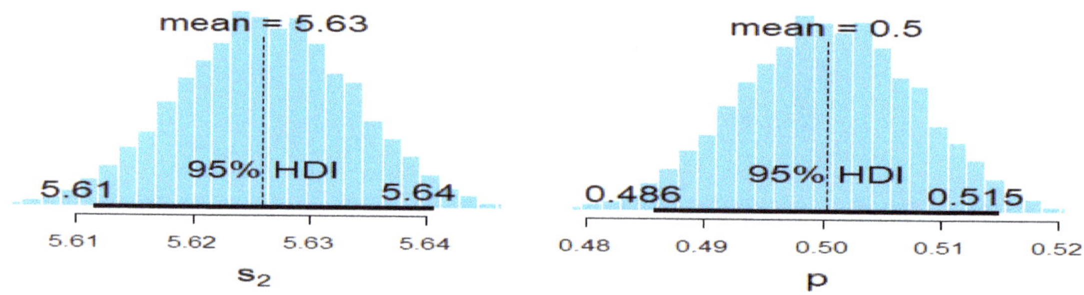

Figure 7. MCMC density and HDI intervals for the Bayesian estimation of model for complete Bladder data for the last two parameters.

Table 10. ML estimates of the MEKW parameters for different censoring schemes of the bladder data.

			MLE		Bayesian			
m			Estimates	SE	Estimates	SE	Lower	Upper
100	I	1	0.7798	0.6666	2.3379	0.1443	2.0831	2.5781
		2	0.3701	0.2945	1.4005	0.1141	1.1089	1.5987
		3	1.5890	1.5642	1.0217	0.0929	0.8747	1.2007
		4	1.0476	0.3145	0.6716	0.0607	0.5607	0.8075
		5	2.5998	1.4655	6.1628	0.1388	5.9327	6.4243
		6	0.3585	0.4015	0.4015	0.0689	0.2564	0.5199
		7	0.0910	0.1559	0.3354	0.0565	0.2526	0.4543
		8	2.2788	1.9297	4.1502	0.1257	3.9216	4.3922
		9	0.8801	0.2630	0.6598	0.0461	0.5720	0.7408
		10	0.3263	0.4107	0.7023	0.1030	0.4812	0.8705
		11	0.4996	0.0312	0.4978	0.0307	0.4320	0.5622
	II	1	3.1095	1.2115	2.9865	0.8578	1.3865	4.5300
		2	5.4366	1.2115	5.5720	0.5985	4.7450	7.8209
		3	1.6154	1.5705	2.0721	0.9825	0.4263	3.9153
		4	0.3895	0.5488	0.3989	0.0817	0.2433	0.5639
		5	9.4701	3.0546	10.1271	2.1945	5.8077	14.0496
		6	3.1391	0.2030	3.2203	0.1536	2.1766	3.9201
		7	5.3816	4.7374	6.0417	2.5953	1.8477	11.4996
		8	1.6035	1.5762	1.8511	1.1209	0.4448	4.2545
		9	0.3891	0.3544	0.4127	0.1405	0.1992	0.7092
		10	9.2241	5.6376	11.1351	4.8638	3.1418	19.6341
		11	0.5000	0.0312	0.5031	0.0245	0.4146	0.5892

For Case 1, where m = 100 and under the Scheme 1, the following can be noted: 0.08 0.20 0.40 0.50 0.51 0.81 0.90 1.05 1.19 1.26 1.35 1.40 1.46 1.76 2.02 2.02 2.07 2.09 2.23 2.26 2.46 2.54 2.62 2.64 2.69 2.69 2.75 2.83 2.87 3.02 3.25 3.31 3.36 3.36 3.48 3.52 3.57 3.64 3.70 3.82 3.88 4.18 4.23 4.26 4.33 4.34 4.40 4.50 4.51 4.87 4.98 5.06 5.09 5.17 5.32 5.32 5.34 5.41 5.41 5.49 5.62 5.71 5.85 6.25 6.54 6.76 6.93 6.94 6.97 7.09 7.26 7.28 7.32 7.39 7.59 7.62 7.63 7.66 7.87 7.93 8.26 8.37 8.53 8.65 8.66 9.02 9.22 9.47 9.74 10.06 10.34 10.66 10.75 11.25 11.64 11.79 11.98 12.02 12.03 12.07.

For Case 2, where m = 100 and under the Scheme 2, the following can be noted: 0.08 0.20 0.40 0.50 0.90 1.05 1.19 1.35 1.40 1.46 1.76 2.02 2.09 2.23 2.26 2.46 2.64 2.69 2.69 2.75 2.83 3.02 3.25 3.31 3.36 3.36 3.48 3.52 3.57 3.64 3.82 4.18 4.23 4.26 4.33 4.34 4.40 4.50 4.51 4.87 4.98 5.06 5.09 5.17 5.32 5.32 5.41 5.41 5.49 5.62 5.71 6.25 6.54 6.76 6.93 6.94 6.97 7.09 7.28 7.32 7.39 7.59 7.62 7.63 7.66 8.37 8.53 8.65 9.02 9.47 9.74 10.06 10.66 10.75 11.25 11.64 11.79 11.98 12.02 12.07 12.63 13.29 14.24 14.77 16.62 17.12 17.36 18.10 19.13 20.28 22.69 23.63 25.74 25.82 26.31 34.26 36.66 43.01 46.12 79.05.

In addition, Bayesian credible interval estimates of the parameters are obtained numerically using Markov chain Monte Carlo (MCMC) techniques. That is, samples are simulated from the joint posterior distribution in Equation (12) using the Metropolis–Hasting algorithm to obtain the posterior mean values of the estimates of the parameters by MCMC. Table 10 reports the estimates of the MEKW parameters with the corresponding SE and credible confidence intervals using the HDI algorithm of the Bayesian estimators.

9. Concluding Remarks

Finite mixture models under both the continuous and the discrete domain have received considerable attention over the last decade or so due to its flexibility of modeling an observed phenomenon when each component cannot adequately explain the entire nature of the data. In this paper, we have developed and studied a finite mixture of exponentiated Kumaraswamy-G distribution under a progressively type II censored sampling scheme, when the baseline distribution (G) is a two parameter Weibull. The efficacy of the proposed model has been established through applying it to model data from the healthcare domain. From the simulation study as well as from the application, it has been observed that, depending on the censoring scheme, either of the two estimation methods (i.e., maximum likelihood and the Bayesian estimation under independent gamma priors) could be useful. Among the various loss functions assumed for the Bayesian estimation, the results based on the small simulation study are inconclusive as to which loss function will be the most suitable for this type of finite mixture models. Most likely, a full-scale simulation study with varying parameter choices and a wide range of censoring schemes would give us an idea. Currently, we are working on this and it will be published when it is ready for submission.

Author Contributions: Conceptualization, R.A., L.A.B., E.M.A., M.K., I.G. and H.R.; Data curation, R.A.; Formal analysis, R.A., L.A.B., E.M.A., M.K. and H.R.; Funding acquisition, R.A.; Investigation, I.G.; Methodology, R.A., L.A.B., E.M.A., M.K., I.G. and H.R.; Resources, R.A.; Software, L.A.B., M.K. and H.R.; Supervision, L.A.B. and E.M.A.; Validation, L.A.B., E.M.A., I.G. and H.R.; Visualization, R.A., M.K., I.G. and H.R.; Writing—original draft, R.A., L.A.B., E.M.A., M.K., I.G. and H.R.; Writing—review & editing, I.G. All authors have read and agreed to the published version of the manuscript.

Funding: This research was funded by Princess Nourah bint Abdulrahman University Researchers Supporting Project number (PNURSP2022R50), Princess Nourah bint Abdulrahman University, Riyadh, Saudi Arabia.

Institutional Review Board Statement: Not applicable.

Informed Consent Statement: Not applicable.

Data Availability Statement: The data used to support the findings of this study are included within the article.

Acknowledgments: Princess Nourah bint Abdulrahman University Researchers Supporting Project number (PNURSP2022R50), Princess Nourah bint Abdulrahman University, Riyadh, Saudi Arabia).

Conflicts of Interest: The authors declare no conflict of interest.

Appendix A

A parameter point ε^0 in A is said to be identifiable if there is no other ε in A, which is observed to be equivalent, as shown in [14].

Appendix A.1. Necessary and Sufficient Conditions for Identifiability

(i) **Assumption 1**: The structural parameters space A is an open set in $\mathbb{R}^m$; $\mathbb{R} = (-\infty, +\infty)$. This true in our case, as for Equation (3), the mixture model density. The associated parameter vector, $\vec{\Delta} = (a_1, b_1, c_1, a_2, b_2, c_2, r_1, r_2, s_1, s_2, p, q\ )$, with the parameter space $\vec{\Psi} = \{(a_1, a_2) \geq 1; (b_i, c_i) \in (0, 1]\,\forall i = 1, 2,\ (r_i, s_i) \in \mathbb{R}^+; (p, q) \in (0, 1]\ \}$ and the associated support parameters space show that $\vec{\Psi}$ is an open set in $\mathbb{R}^{12}$. Then, the function f is a proper density.

(ii) **Assumption 2**: Functions for every $\vec{\Psi}$. In particular, f is non-negative and the equation $\int f\left(y; \vec{\Delta}\right) dy = 1$, holds for all $\vec{\Delta}$ in $\vec{\Psi}$. This is true for the density in Equation (3).

(iii) **Assumption 3**: The sample space of y, say B, for which f is strictly positive, is the same for all $\vec{\Delta}$ in the parameter space $\vec{\Psi}$. This is also true and immeditely holds for the density in Equation (3).

(iv) **Assumption 4**: For all $\vec{\Delta}$ in a convex set containing $\vec{\Psi}$ and for all y in the sample space B, the functions $f\left(y; \vec{\Delta}\right)$ and $log_e\left[f\left(y; \vec{\Delta}\right)\right]$ are continuously differentiable, with respect to each element in $\vec{\Delta}$. This is also true for the density in Equation (3).

(v) **Assumption 5**: The elements of the information matrix (FIM) (in this case, the observed Fisher information matrix), $R\left(\vec{\Delta}\right) = \left[\frac{\partial logf}{\partial \vec{\Delta}_i}, \frac{\partial logf}{\partial \vec{\Delta}_j}\right]$, exists and are continuous functions of $\vec{\Delta}$ everywhere in $\vec{\Psi}$ for the density in Equation (3); the associated log-likelihood function will be (for a single observation)

$$
\begin{aligned}
log\left[f\left(x; \vec{\Delta}\right)\right] = {} & log\left[p\frac{a_1 b_1 c_1 r_1}{s_1}\left(\frac{x}{s_1}\right)^{r_1-1} exp\left[-\left(\frac{x}{s_1}\right)^{r_1}\right]\left[1 - exp\left(-\left(\frac{x}{s_1}\right)^{r_1}\right)\right]^{a_1-1}\right] \\
& \left[1 - \left[1 - exp\left(-\left(\frac{x}{s_1}\right)^{r_1}\right)\right]^{a_1}\right]^{b_1-1}\left[1 - \left[1 - \left[1 - exp\left(-\left(\frac{x}{s_1}\right)^{r_1}\right)\right]^{a_1}\right]^{b_1}\right]^{c_1-1} \\
& +q\frac{a_2 b_2 c_2 r_2}{s_2}\left(\frac{x}{s_2}\right)^{r_2-1} exp\left[-\left(\frac{x}{s_2}\right)^{r_2}\right]\left[1 - exp\left(-\left(\frac{x}{s_2}\right)^{r_2}\right)\right]^{a_2-1} \\
& \left[1 - \left[1 - exp\left(-\left(\frac{x}{s_2}\right)^{r_2}\right)\right]^{a_2}\right]^{b_2-1}\left[1 - \left[1 - \left[1 - exp\left(-\left(\frac{x}{s_2}\right)^{r_2}\right)\right]^{a_2}\right]^{b_2}\right]^{c_2-1}\Bigg]
\end{aligned}
$$

For illustrative purposes, we will discuss one element from the observed FIM of dimension 12 × 12. The proof of existence of the remaining elements and continuity can be similarly established. For brevity, the complete details are avoided. It is available upon request to the authors. Next, one must consider

$$\frac{\partial^2 logf}{\partial a_1 \partial a_2} = \frac{-D_1}{D_2} \tag{A1}$$

where

$$D_1 = \Bigg[b_1 b_2 c_1 c_2 exp\left[\left(\frac{x}{s_1}\right)^{r_1} + \left(\frac{x}{s_2}\right)^{r_2}\right]\left[1-exp\left(-\left(\frac{x}{s_1}\right)^{r_1}\right)\right]^{a_1}\left[1-exp\left(-\left(\frac{x}{s_2}\right)^{r_2}\right)\right]^{a_2}\left[1-\left[1-exp\left(-\left(\frac{x}{s_1}\right)^{r_1}\right)\right]^{a_1}\right]^{b_1-2}$$
$$\left[1-\left[1-exp\left(-\left(\frac{x}{s_2}\right)^{r_2}\right)\right]^{a_2}\right]^{b_2-2}\left[1-\left[1-\left[1-exp\left(-\left(\frac{x}{s_1}\right)^{r_1}\right)\right]^{a_1}\right]^{b_1}\right]^{c_1-1}$$
$$\left[1-\left[1-\left[1-exp\left(-\left(\frac{x}{s_2}\right)^{r_2}\right)\right]^{a_2}\right]^{b_2}\right]^{c_2-2} pqr_1r_2\left(\frac{x}{s_1}\right)^{r_1}\left(\frac{x}{s_2}\right)^{r_2}$$
$$\left(-1+\left[1-exp\left(-\left(\frac{x}{s_1}\right)^{r_1}\right)\right]^{a_1}\right)\left(-1+\left[1-\left[1-exp\left(-\left(\frac{x}{s_1}\right)^{r_1}\right)\right]^{a_1}\right]^{b_1}\right)$$
$$+a_1\left(1-\left[1-\left[1-exp\left(-\left(\frac{x}{s_1}\right)^{r_1}\right)\right]^{a_1}\right]^{b_1}\right)$$
$$+b_1\left[1-exp\left(-\left(\frac{x}{s_1}\right)^{r_1}\right)\right]^{a_1}$$
$$\left(-1+c_1\left[1-\left[1-exp\left(-\left(\frac{x}{s_1}\right)^{r_1}\right)\right]^{a_1}\right]^{b_1}\right)log\left[1-exp\left(-\left(\frac{x}{s_1}\right)^{r_1}\right)\right]$$
$$\left(-1+\left[1-exp\left(-\left(\frac{x}{s_2}\right)^{r_2}\right)\right]^{a_2}\right)\left(-1+\left[1-\left[1-exp\left(-\left(\frac{x}{s_2}\right)^{r_2}\right)\right]^{a_2}\right]^{b_2}\right)a_2b_2$$
$$\left(1-\left[1-\left[1-exp\left(-\left(\frac{x}{s_2}\right)^{r_2}\right)\right]^{a_2}\right]^{b_2}\right)$$
$$+log\left[1-exp\left(-\left(\frac{x}{s_2}\right)^{r_2}\right)\right]\left(-1+c_2\left[1-\left[1-exp\left(-\left(\frac{x}{s_2}\right)^{r_2}\right)\right]^{a_2}\right]^{b_2}\right)\Bigg],$$

$$D_2 = \left(-1+exp\left(-\left(\frac{x}{s_1}\right)^{r_1}\right)\right)$$
$$\left(-1+exp\left(-\left(\frac{x}{s_2}\right)^{r_2}\right)\right)\Bigg[pr_1a_1b_1c_1\left[1-exp\left(-\left(\frac{x}{s_1}\right)^{r_1}\right)\right]^{a_1-1}$$
$$\left[1-\left[1-exp\left(-\left(\frac{x}{s_1}\right)^{r_1}\right)\right]^{a_1}\right]^{b_1-1}\left[1-\left[1-\left[1-exp\left(-\left(\frac{x}{s_1}\right)^{r_1}\right)\right]^{a_1}\right]^{b_1}\right]^{c_1-1}\left(\frac{x}{s_1}\right)^{r_1}$$
$$+qr_2a_2b_2c_2\left[1-exp\left(-\left(\frac{x}{s_2}\right)^{r_2}\right)\right]^{a_2-1}$$
$$\left[1-\left[1-exp\left(-\left(\frac{x}{s_2}\right)^{r_2}\right)\right]^{a_2}\right]^{b_2-1}$$
$$\left[1-\left[1-\left[1-exp\left(-\left(\frac{x}{s_2}\right)^{r_2}\right)\right]^{a_2}\right]^{b_2}\right]^{c_2-1}\left(\frac{x}{s_2}\right)^{r_2}\Bigg]^2$$

From Equation (A1), it is obvious that these derivatives exist for all possible choices of the parameter vector $\vec{\Delta}$ and for the parameter space $\vec{\Psi}$, as well as for all possible values of $x \in (0, \infty)$. This derivative function is also continuous. The proof is simple, and thus excluded.

- **Identifiability of the MEKW Model**

Before considering the aspect of estimation and associated inference and classification of random variables, which are based on observations from a mixture, it is necessary to address the subject of identifiability of the mixture(s) and possibly its components. We suggest our readers to refer to the following pertinent reference: [14] for more information on the identifiability of mixture distributions. The identification of a mixture for two EK (with the same baseline G's as given in (2)) components will now be explored.

We begin with the combination of two survival functions. One must consider a linear combination of two separate distributions, one of which is EKW$(a_1, b_1, c_1, s_1, r_1)$ distribution, and the other distribution is EKW$(a_2, b_2, c_2, s_2, r_2)$, as shown below.

$$\sum_{i=0}^{2} p_i S_i(x) = 0,$$

where $S_1(x) = 1 - \left[1 - \left[1 - \left[1 - exp\left(-\left(\frac{x}{s_1}\right)^{r_1}\right)\right]^{a_1}\right]^{b_1}\right]^{c_1}$, $0 < x < \infty,\ a_1, b_1, c_1, s_1, r_1 > 0$,

$S_2(x) = 1 - \left\{1 - \left[1 - \left(1 - exp\left[-\left(\frac{x}{s_2}\right)^{-r_2}\right]\right)^{a_2}\right]^{b_2}\right\}^{c_2}$, $0 < x < \infty,\ a_2, b_2, c_2, s_2, r_2 > 0$,

and p_1 and p_2 are the mixing weights, such that $p_1 + p_2 = 1$ and $0 < p_i < 1\ \forall\ i = 1,2$. The finite mixture of EKW $(a_1, b_1, c_1, s_1, r_1)$, and EKW $(a_2, b_2, c_2, s_2, r_2)$ distributions are identifiable, if $S_1(x)$, $S_2(x)$ are linearly independent. This means, if $(a_1, b_1, c_1, s_1, r_1) \neq (a_2, b_2, c_2, s_2, r_2)$, this implies $p_1 = p_2 = 0$.

If $x = 0$, then $S_1(0) = S_2(0) = 1 \rightarrow\ p_1 + p_2 = 0 \rightarrow p_1 = -p_2$.

Then,

$$1 - \left[1 - \left[1 - \left[1 - exp\left(-\left(\frac{x}{s_1}\right)^{r_1}\right)\right]^{a_1}\right]^{b_1}\right]^{c_1} = 1 - \left\{1 - \left[1 - \left(1 - exp\left[-\left(\frac{x}{s_2}\right)^{-r_2}\right]\right)^{a_2}\right]^{b_2}\right\}^{c_2},$$

$$\left[1 - \left[1 - \left[1 - exp\left(-\left(\frac{x}{s_1}\right)^{r_1}\right)\right]^{a_1}\right]^{b_1}\right]^{c_1} = \left\{1 - \left[1 - \left(1 - exp\left[-\left(\frac{x}{s_2}\right)^{-r_2}\right]\right)^{a_2}\right]^{b_2}\right\}^{c_2},$$

$$\sum_{i_1=0}^{\infty} \binom{c_1}{i_1} (-1)^{i_1} \left(1 - \left(1 - exp\left(-\left(\frac{x}{s_1}\right)^{r_1}\right)\right)^{a_1}\right)^{b_1 i_1} = \sum_{i_2=0}^{\infty} \binom{c_2}{i_1} (-1)^{i_1} \left(1 - \left(1 - exp\left(-\left(\frac{x}{s_2}\right)^{r_2}\right)\right)^{a_2}\right)^{b_2 i_1},$$

$$\sum_{i_1=0}^{\infty} \binom{c_1}{i_1} \sum_{i_2=0}^{\infty} \binom{b_1 i_1}{i_2} (-1)^{i_1+i_2} \left(1 - exp\left(-\left(\frac{x}{s_1}\right)^{r_1}\right)\right)^{a_1 i_2} = \sum_{i_1=0}^{\infty} \binom{c_2}{i_1} \sum_{i_2=0}^{\infty} \binom{b_2 i_1}{i_2} (-1)^{i_1+i_2} \left[exp\left(-\left(\frac{x}{s_2}\right)^{-r_2}\right)\right]^{a_2 i_2},$$

$$\sum_{i_1=0}^{\infty} \binom{c_1}{i_1} \sum_{i_2=0}^{\infty} \binom{b_1 i_1}{i_2} (-1)^{i_1+i_2} \sum_{i_3=0}^{\infty} \binom{a_1 i_2}{i_3} (-1)^{i_1+i_2+i_3} \left(exp\left(-\left(\frac{x}{s_1}\right)^{r_1}\right)\right) = \sum_{i_1=0}^{\infty} \binom{c_2}{i_1} \sum_{i_2=0}^{\infty} \binom{b_2 i_1}{i_2} (-1)^{i_1+i_2} \sum_{i_3=0}^{\infty} \binom{a_2 i_2}{i_3} (-1)^{i_1+i_2+i_3} \left(exp\left(-\left(\frac{x}{s_2}\right)^{r_2}\right)\right),$$

$$\sum_{i_1=0}^{\infty} \binom{c_1}{i_1} \sum_{i_2=0}^{\infty} \binom{b_1 i_1}{i_2} (-1)^{i_1+i_2} \sum_{i_3=0}^{\infty} \binom{a_1 i_2}{i_3} (-1)^{i_1+i_2+i_3} \left(\frac{x}{s_1}\right)^{r_1} = \sum_{i_1=0}^{\infty} \binom{c_2}{i_1} \sum_{i_2=0}^{\infty} \binom{b_2 i_1}{i_2} (-1)^{i_1+i_2} \sum_{i_3=0}^{\infty} \binom{a_2 i_2}{i_3} (-1)^{i_1+i_2+i_3} \left(\frac{x}{s_2}\right)^{r_2}$$

where $i_1! = i_1(i_1 - 1)(i_1 - 2) \ldots .3.2.1$, $i_1 = i_2 = i_3$, and the coefficients of x on both sides are compared and it is discovered that $a_1 = a_2,\ b_1 = b_2,\ c_1 = c_2,\ s_1 = s_2\ ,\ r_1 = r_2$, and $p_1 = p_2 = 0$.

$S_1(x)$ and $S_2(x)$ are, thus, linearly independent. As a result, the EKW$(a_1, b_1, c_1, s_1, r_1)$ and EKW $(a_2, b_2, c_2, s_2, r_2)$ distributions can be identified as a finite mixture.

References

1. Al Alotaibi, R.; Almetwally, E.M.; Ghosh, I.; Rezk, H. Classical and Bayesian inference on finite mixture of exponentiated Kumaraswamy Gompertz and exponentiated Kumaraswamy Frechet distributions under progressive Type II censoring with applications. *Mathematics* **2022**, *10*, 1496. [CrossRef]
2. Tahir, M.H.; Nadarajah, S. Parameter induction in continuous univariate distributions: Well-established G families. *Ann. Braz. Acad. Sci.* **2015**, *87*, 539–568. [CrossRef] [PubMed]
3. Lemonte, J.A.; Barreto-Souza, W.; Cordeiro, M.G. The exponentiated Kumaraswamy distribution and its log-transform. *Braz. J. Probab. Stat.* **2003**, *27*, 31–53. [CrossRef]
4. Alzghal, A.; Felix, F.; Carl, L. Exponentiated T-X family of distributions with some applications. *Int. J. Stat. Probab.* **2013**, *2*, 31–49. [CrossRef]
5. Nadarajah, S.; Rocha, R. Newdistns: An R Package for new families of distributions. *J. Stat. Softw.* **2016**, *69*, 1–32. [CrossRef]
6. Mudholkar, G.S.; Srivastava, D.K.; Kollia, G.D. A generalization of the Weibull distribution with application to the analysis of survival data. *J. Am. Stat. Assoc.* **1996**, *91*, 1575–1583. [CrossRef]

7. Gupta, R.C.; Gupta, P.L.; Gupta, R.D. Modeling failure time data by Lehman alternatives. *Comm. Statist. Theory Methods* **1998**, *27*, 887–904. [CrossRef]
8. Nadarajah, S.; Bakouch, H.S.; Tahmabi, R. Ageneralized Lindley distribution. *Sankhya B* **2011**, *73*, 331–359. [CrossRef]
9. Blanchet, J.H.; Sigman, K. On exact sampling of stochastic perpetuilies. *J. Appl. Probab.* **2011**, *48A*, 165–182. [CrossRef]
10. Ali, S.; Aslam, M.; Mohsin, S.; Kazmi, A. A study of the effect of the loss function on Bayes estimate, posterior risk and hazard function for Lindley distribution. *Appl. Math. Model.* **2013**, *23*, 6068–6078. [CrossRef]
11. Wasan, M.T. *Parametric Estimation*; Mcgraw-Hill: New York, NY, USA, 1970.
12. R Core Team. *R: A Language and Environment for Statistical Computing*; R Foundation for Statistical Computing: Vienna, Austria, 2019. Available online: https://www.R-project.org/ (accessed on 12 July 2022).
13. Lee, E.T.; Wang, J. *Statistical Methods for Survival Data Analysis*; John Wiley & Sons: New York, NY, USA, 2003; 476p.
14. Rothenberg, T.J. Identification in Parametric Models. *Econometrica* **1971**, *39*, 577–591. [CrossRef]

MDPI AG
Grosspeteranlage 5
4052 Basel
Switzerland
Tel.: +41 61 683 77 34

Mathematics Editorial Office
E-mail: mathematics@mdpi.com
www.mdpi.com/journal/mathematics

www.ingramcontent.com/pod-product-compliance
Lightning Source LLC
Chambersburg PA
CBHW061821210926
51850CB00006B/769
* 9 7 8 3 7 2 5 8 4 9 8 3 3 *